THE FOOD PROFESSIONAL'S GUIDE

THE JAMES BEARD FOUNDATION

Directory of People, Products and Services

THE FOOD PROFESSIONAL'S GUIDE

THE JAMES BEARD FOUNDATION

Directory of People, Products and Services

Compiled by Irena Chalmers

Co-publishers

AMERICAN SHOWCASE

AMERICAN SHOWCASE, INC.   NEW YORK

WILEY

JOHN WILEY AND SONS, INC.   NEW YORK

Co-published with:
John Wiley & Sons, Inc.
605 Third Avenue
New York NY 10158
Wiley ISBN 0-471-52460-3

Prepared and produced by:
American Showcase, Inc.
724 Fifth Avenue, 10th Floor
New York NY 10019
212-245-0981

Please send us information about products and purveyors you feel should be included in future editions.

Designed by:
Ross Culbert Holland & Lavery, Inc. NYC

Printed and bound in Hong Kong by
Everbest Printing Co. Ltd: First Printing

ISBN 0-931144-62-0
ISSN 1046-2414

Contents

From Julia Child's Kitchen vii
About The James Beard Foundation viii
Introduction ix
Acknowledgments x

Section 1	**THE WHO'S WHO OF COOKING IN AMERICA**	**1**

Section 2	**SPECIALTY FOOD RESOURCES**	**17**
	Wholesale Produce Markets	19
	Specialty Food Wholesalers	22
	Specialty Food Retailers	40
	Direct Mail Order Catalogs	48
	Organic and Health Food Suppliers	53
	Kosher Food Suppliers	61

Section 3	**THE BIG BUSINESS OF FOOD**	**67**
	The Top 100 Food Companies	69
	Major Supermarket Chains	73
	Foodservice Companies	76

Section 4	**RESTAURANT OPERATIONS**	**93**
	Restaurant Designers and Design Firms	95
	Chefs and Chef/Restaurant Owners	100
	The James Beard Foundation's Awards Programs	111
	Spas and Spa Chains	112
	Caterers	114

Section 5	**ALCOHOLIC BEVERAGES**	**129**
	100 Fine Wineries	131
	Breweries	135
	Wines and Spirits Importers	138

Section 6	**SCHOOLS**	**141**
	Cooking Schools	143
	Professional	143
	Professional & Avocational	144
	Avocational	145
	University Home Economics Departments	151
	University Restaurant and Hotel Management Schools	155

Section 7	**HOME AND PROFESSIONAL KITCHENS**	**157**
	Kitchen Designers	159
	Major Kitchen Appliances	162
	Small Electric Appliances	164
	Cookware and Cooking Accessories	167

Section 8	**FOOD PROMOTION**	**177**
	Food Associations and Institutes	179
	Product Promotion Associations	183
	Public Relations and Advertising	188
	TV and Radio Networks	192

Section 9	**FOOD GRAPHICS**	**197**
	Food Photographers	199
	Food Stylists	204
	Food Illustrators	210
	Graphic Designers	218
	Food Videos	221

Section 10	**FOOD PUBLICATIONS**	**225**
	Cookbook and Food Book Publishers	227
	Literary Agents	228
	Specialized Cookbook Stores and Dealers	231
	Specialized Libraries and Sources of Information on Food	232
	Consumer Food Magazines	234
	Food Trade Magazines	235
	Professional Food Journals	238
	Food Newsletters	240
	Food Authors	243
	Food Journalists	248
	Newspaper & Wire Service Editors	248
	Writers & Columnists	259

Section 11	**SCIENTIFIC AND GOVERNMENT INFORMATION SOURCES**	**261**
	Scientific Research Centers	263
	Nutrition Study Centers, Associations and Action Groups	265
	Federal Government Agencies	267
	State Government Agencies	270
	Chambers of Commerce	273
	Consumer Advocacy and Environmental Resource Groups	276
	Registered Food Lobbyists	278

Section 12	**FOOD FAIRS AND FESTIVALS**	**283**
	State Fairs	285
	Food Festivals	288
	Cook-Offs and Competitions	291

Appendix	**FOOD CONVENTIONS: A CALENDAR**	**295**

	Members of The James Beard Foundation	299
	Additional Food Professionals Who Are Members of The James Beard Foundation	304
	Index	308

From Julia Child's Kitchen

The James Beard Foundation exists in Jim Beard's own house in New York, where he lived, and taught, and entertained his friends. The Foundation and the Beard House serve all those who love good food and wine, both from the enthusiast's point of view and the professional's. The Beard House is conceived as a meeting ground as well as a gastronomic information center for all of us, whether we live in and around the Big Apple or come there on friendly or business visits. We need such a place in New York, where we can meet and commune and dine and celebrate—and where we can honor our generous patron saint, James A. Beard.

Jim was a prime source of information on everyone and everything in the food and wine world, and if he didn't know the answer he knew where to find it. Always generous with his knowledge, he loved nothing better than to give out with names, places, ingredients, people—and gossip, too. He seemed to know everything that went on in the business, and he thoroughly enjoyed sharing.

It is particularly fitting, then, that this first official publication of The James Beard Foundation be a wide-ranging directory of people and things and institutions serving the food and wine professions. Here in one place are all the names that we used to have to find by hunting through a dozen different directories. You no longer have to spend hours on your own tracing down a fact, a service or a person; the editors of this directory have done the work for you.

Here is the first edition; updated editions will be in the works in future years, because this directory must remain a reliable and current source of facts for the entire food and wine community.

A better living tribute to the memory of James Andrew Beard, that legendary fount of information, can hardly be imagined. In fact, I can't imagine how we have all lived without it.

Julia Child

About The James Beard Foundation

James Beard, known as the father of American gastronomy, was born in Portland, Oregon, on May 5, 1903. When he died in New York City, on January 22, 1985, his name had become synonymous with American food.

This country's first nationally recognized food personality, James Beard wrote more than 20 cookbooks and published thousands of weekly syndicated newspaper columns on food, in addition to numerous magazine articles, principally for *Gourmet* and *House & Garden.* He had one of the first television cooking shows, was a familiar voice on the radio and gave classes all over the country. Always, he preached a doctrine of rational simplicity, good native ingredients—and, above all, direct pleasure from food without too much fuss.

He would have been delighted at the publication of this directory, which provides accurate information and expert help in so many of his areas of knowledge.

The idea of saving Jim's home in Greenwich Village was conceived by Julia Child as an element in establishing gastronomy as a recognized and valued American art. Today the Beard House, home of the Beard Foundation, is North America's first and only culinary center, where dinners, classes and all kinds of special events are held almost nightly.

The idea of showcasing the talents of young rising stars, as well as the great chefs of the world, has developed rapidly. Scholarships for deserving culinary students and apprenticeships for cooking school graduates, enabling them to work with the great chefs, will be awarded this year.

Our monthly newsletter, which goes to our more than 1,600 members, has blossomed with articles on upcoming events, profiles of visiting chefs, cookbook reviews, recipes and unexpected tidbits such as "The Nitty-Gritty on Grits."

We sponsor educational programs, including lectures, exhibits and workshops but there is still much to do to develop a fuller program of continuing education for those in the world of fine food.

The James Beard Foundation welcomes new members from across the country. We invite all fine food professionals and other supporters of gastronomy to become members and join us in our ongoing work.

Peter Kump
President
The James Beard Foundation
167 West 12th Street
New York NY 10011
April, 1990

We have broken new ground with this first directory of food professionals. It is, though, only a beginning. The business of food is so immense that it would take a volume the size of the Manhattan telephone book to include the names of everyone who labors in this vast field.

We have not attempted to undertake such a daunting task. Instead, we have identified more than 50 different categories and compiled representative listings within each area. Each list has been very carefully considered and we have tried our best to arrange it in the way that you will find most useful.

Frequently, we have drawn on several sources in order to develop a genuinely comprehensive reference. In each case, the criteria we used are described in the introduction that precedes the list; we have also supplied directions for obtaining more extensive directories.

The book is as accurate as we could make it. Countless hours were spent calling to verify the correct spellings of names and to confirm addresses and telephone numbers. We readily concede that there will have been changes within hours of our having closed the directory. Nevertheless, we hope that even if a representative of a company has changed position, a call to the number we have supplied will get you pointed in the right direction.

We foresee that *The Food Professional's Guide* will be useful in very many ways, and to a wide range of people. Restaurant owners and chefs will use it to find sources for new products and equipment. Cottage industries of all kinds will use it to find distributors. With its aid, food packagers can be in touch with photographers and stylists, health food suppliers can locate specialty food stores, manufacturers of kitchen equipment can identify foodservice organizations who will want to know about their newest machinery, and journalists can find sources for obtaining stories and verifying facts.

Amateurs, too, will use this book to find a reliable caterer or a good cooking school in their area, while everyone will benefit from its listings of the organizations and associations that research and supply information about the food business and of the vast range of publications serving every aspect of the industry.

But the greatest benefit of all will surely be the advantage and convenience of having colleagues' and business associates' names gathered in one place, instead of having to hunt through several sources to find them.

Irena Chalmers

Acknowledgments

Throughout the preparation of *The Food Professional's Guide* we have received encouragement and support from the literally thousands of people we have contacted. We are also greatly indebted to the consultants to whom we turned for guidance and advice and to the many companies who gave us their help in compiling the lists.

One of the greatest joys of working in the food and hospitality business is the number of friends that we make in many different fields of expertise. I have worked as a specialty food retailer, wholesaler, importer, cooking school teacher, writer and publisher and have had my life enriched by chefs, writers, winemakers, manufacturers, photographers, designers and illustrators. I shamelessly called on them all, and now is the time to thank each one, and especially...

Reynaldo Alejandro
Michael Bartlett
Joe Baum
Barry Benepe
Peter Berlinsky
Phillip S. Cooke
Marilyn Einhorn
Lisa Ekus
Edith Friedland
Margaret Gale
Alice Gautsch
Rozanne Gold
Mary Goodbody
Jeffrey Joseph
Wayne Karjala
Monica Kass
Matthew Klein
Phyllis Koegel
Lee Kraft

Peter Kump
Beth Lorenzini
Lothian Lynas
Fritz Maytag
Stephen Michaelides
Jessica Miller
Leonard Pickell
Warren Picower
Justin Rashid
Michael Roman
Lorna Sass
Scott Schulke
Howard Solganik
Maggie Waldron
Nach Waxman
Karl Weddle
Elaine Yannuzzi
L. Andrew Zausner

The Who's Who

OF COOKING
IN AMERICA

Taryn
212 533-0613

The Who's Who of Cooking in America

Cook's Magazine founded the Who's Who awards in 1984. There are now over 100 top American professionals who have won this coveted award. They are the trailblazers, innovators and chroniclers of the revolution in American food and wine, who have been voted by their peers as worthy of recognition. The current inductees were honored at a ceremony and celebration of American foods held in New York City in October 1989.

Len Allison
chef/part owner, Hubert's, New York NY (1984)

Len Allison and his wife, Karen, first opened Hubert's (Karen's maiden name) in a converted old tavern-house in Brooklyn. Word spread about Hubert's Thursday night guest chef series where soon-to-be-famous chefs and writers tried their hand in the kitchen. Hubert's moved to Manhattan's Gramercy Park area in 1981, where it featured new American cuisine. The Allisons' fondness for the Far East inspired a Japanese chef exchange program and ultimately, in 1988, a new menu inspired by the Orient. Hubert's moved to its current location on East 63rd Street in 1988.

Colman Andrews
freelance writer, cookbook author, Santa Monica CA (1984)

Colman Andrews has become widely recognized for his knowledge of the foods of Spain's Catalonia region. In 1988 he published *Catalan Cuisine* and he has authored several articles on Catalan cooking for leading food and wine publications. Andrews has been reviewing restaurants in the Los Angeles area and writing on food and wine since 1972. In addition to his ongoing weekly restaurant reviews for the *Los Angeles Times*, Andrews is a contributing editor to *Metropolitan Home* and has a monthly wine column in *Los Angeles Magazine*.

Richard L. Arrowood
executive vice president/winemaster, Chateau St. Jean, Kenwood CA (1984)

While remaining executive vice president and winemaster at Chateau St. Jean, Richard Arrowood and his wife, Alis Demers Arrowood, built Arrowood Winery in 1987. Their first wines were Chardonnays from the 1986 and 1987 vintages and a 1985 Sonoma County Cabernet Sauvignon.

Arrowood holds a degree in chemistry from California State University, Sacramento, and completed his graduate work in oenology at California State University, Fresno. Before joining Chateau St. Jean in 1974, he worked for Korbel Champagne Cellars, United Vintners and Sonoma Vineyards.

Gerald Asher
wine writer, San Francisco CA (1986)

Robert Mondavi says, "Gerald Asher writes about wine the way I like to make it—elegant, enjoyable, brilliant, civilized and yet down to earth." Asher writes for *Gourmet* magazine, and for the *San Francisco Chronicle*.

Educated in England and trained in the wine trade in France, Spain and Germany, Asher came to the United States in 1970. He served as vice president and national sales manager of Imported Wines at Austin, Nichols & Company in New York and later, until 1985, as president of the Mosswood Wine Company in New York and San Francisco.

Joseph Baum
restaurant consultant, The Joseph Baum Company, Inc., New York NY (1985)

As one of the country's most influential restaurant consultants, Joseph Baum has to his credit the creation and opening of some of New York City's most innovative restaurants. These include the Rainbow Room at Rockefeller Center, The Four Seasons, Aurora and Windows on the World. According to Baum, the secret to the success of a great restaurant is its ability to change to meet the needs of its patrons. "A successful restaurant conjures up taste memories," he says. "It excites the senses and the mind and encourages the sharing of experience. You don't go there just because you are hungry."

James Beard
"Dean of American Cooking" (1984)

Beard entered the food world professionally by opening Hors d'Oeuvres, Inc., in New York, a very successful catering house that led to the publication of his first book, *Hors d'Oeuvres and Canapes*. He followed it with 21 additional books, the last of which was published shortly before his death in 1985.

Beard's writings include articles in most of the country's major magazines and a nationally syndicated column on cooking. He was featured in the first televised food program in the United States, "Elsie Presents." In the 1960s, he had his own television series in Canada and, for five years, his own daily radio program. Beard worked as a consultant for Restaurant Associates, Pillsbury, Green Giant, and Nestle.

Simone Beck
cooking instructor, Chateauneuf de Grasse, France (1986)

Simone ("Simca") Beck is, according to Julia Child, the "grande dame" of cooking. Trained by Cordon Bleu chef and author Henri-Paul Pellaprat in the 1930s, Simca began a partnership with Julia Child in the early 1950s by opening L'Ecole des Trois Gourmandes cooking school in Paris. The two collaborated on *Mastering the Art of French Cooking, Volumes I and II*. Simca later authored two more cookbooks and is writing an autobiography that will include 200 new recipes. She continues to teach cooking from her home in the south of France. "You must never stop learning," she says, "because every day I discover something new—even in my old age."

Paul Bertolli
chef, Chez Panisse, Berkeley CA (1985)

Paul Bertolli's life changed keys—from music to menus—after he had traveled extensively throughout Italy. He worked at three restaurants in Florence, Italy, and later served as chef at the Fourth Street Grill in Berkeley, California, before moving to Chez Panisse in 1982. The restaurant has been widely acclaimed for its commitment to cooking with the highest quality and the freshest seasonal ingredients, both of which are reflected in Bertolli's dishes. He is co-author with Alice Waters of the *Chez Panisse Cookbook*.

Alexis Bespaloff
wine writer, New York NY (1989)

Bespaloff is the wine columnist for *New York* magazine and, in addition, has written about wine for *Connoisseur*, *Travel & Leisure* and *House Beautiful*. His *New Signet Book of Wine* has become the best-selling wine book in America, and Bespaloff is recognized as one of the country's foremost wine writers.

Anthony Dias Blue
food and wine journalist, San Francisco CA (1988)

Blue's food and wine criticisms on CBS Radio, New York, have been broadcast for 11 years, and elicit a flood of mail. Since 1981, Blue has been wine and spirits editor for *Bon Appetit*. He writes regularly for the *Los Angeles Daily News*, *Arizona Republic*, *Sacramento Bee*, *San Francisco Magazine*, *Wine Spectator* and a number of other periodicals. Blue is an active lecturer and judge for numerous wine and food competitions and is chairman of the California Wine Perspective.

Dick and Ella Brennan
co-owners, Commander's Palace, New Orleans LA (1984)

In New Orleans, one name, Brennan, has inspired the spirit and tradition of haute Creole cooking at its finest. In 1946, the Brennan family bought Commander's Palace; in 1974, brother/sister team Dick and Ella Brennan took over supervision of the restaurant, which continues to this day to be one of the

highlights of many a visitor's trip to the city and an inspiration for chefs nationwide. Says Ella, "The restaurant business has never been as exciting and challenging. It is bursting with talented people."

Ellen Brown
writer, food consultant, Washington DC (1985)

Brown planned the 1987 PBS television series, "Great Chefs of the West" and, in 1988, founded Gourmet Gazelle, the country's first nutritionally controlled carry-out restaurant. A graduate of Mt. Holyoke College, she worked for both the *Cincinnati Post* and *Cincinnati Enquirer* before becoming founding food editor of *USA Today*. She has her own consulting and writing business and has appeared in numerous newspapers and national magazines.

Giuliano Bugialli
cooking instructor and cookbook author, New York NY and Florence, Italy (1986)

Bugialli grew up in Florence and started his professional life as a teacher of Italian history and language. He has become an internationally recognized cooking teacher, with cooking schools in Italy and the United States. He has been recognized with numerous awards of excellence for his outstanding contribution to Italian cuisine. Two of his cookbooks have earned Tastemaker awards.

Marian Burros
food columnist, The New York Times, New York NY (1985)

Burros is influential with restaurateurs and food executives who watch health and food safety trends across the country. The author of many cookbooks, she was food editor of the *Washington Daily News*, *Washington Star*, and *Washington Post* before joining *The New York Times*, where she has been a food writer/restaurant critic, and is now food columnist.

Frieda Caplan
chairman, Frieda's Finest/Produce Specialties, Los Angeles CA (1985)

Many of the exotic fruits and vegetables that have become household names today got their marketing start with the expertise of Frieda Caplan. She is best known for mass marketing specialty produce items. She works with

growers around the world, year-round, to search out, develop and merchandise exotic and unusual produce items. The highlight of her career was popularizing the kiwifruit in the United States and the rest of the world. Recent exotic "discoveries" include purple potatoes, coquitos (miniature baby coconuts), and the Frieda Fajita.

Irena Chalmers
founder/president and publisher of Irena Chalmers Books, Inc., New York NY (1988)

Before founding her own publishing and book-producing company in 1980, Chalmers wrote more than 100 cookbooks and a series of international cookbooks with sales exceeding 18 million copies. Her books have received nine Tastemaker awards. She has been extensively interviewed on television and radio. A former president of Les Dames d'Escoffier, she is currently serving her second term on the board of directors of the Society for American Cuisine. She is secretary/treasurer of the International Association of Cooking Professionals and a member of the Culinary Institute of America.

Donn Chappellet
president, Chappellet Vineyards, St. Helena, CA (1985)

Donn Chappellet has been in the wine business ever since he turned his hobby into a profession and started Chappellet Vineyards in the late 1960s. A small, specialized operation in St. Helena, Chappellet has been producing excellent Chardonnays and other wines for more than 15 years. A graduate of Pomona College with a degree in economics, Donn Chappellet worked in industrial foodservice and vending before seeking greener vineyards. He avows that California has turned out "top-quality wines that can compete with any other wine, from anywhere else in the world."

Laura Chenel
owner/cheesemaker, Laura Chenel's Chevre, Santa Rosa CA (1984)

Since 1984, cheesemaker Laura Chenel has created three new cheeses and is now working on a fourth. She developed her expertise as a cheesemaker over several years, following a three-month apprenticeship in France.

Chenel comments, "Three significant

developments have contributed to the evolution of the domestic specialty cheese industry: the influx of French cheese companies into the United States and the devaluation of the dollar; the continued increase of small-scale specialty cheese producers in this country; and increased consumer awareness of sodium, fat and cholesterol in the American diet."

Julia Child
author and teacher, Cambridge MA and Santa Barbara CA (1984)

Julia Child started her culinary career in 1949 at the Cordon Bleu and later opened L'Ecole des Trois Gourmandes in Paris, with Simone Beck and Louisette Bertholle. Their jointly authored book, *Mastering the Art of French Cooking*, published in 1961, made culinary history; so did Child's PBS television series "The French Chef," which first aired in 1963. After some 200 programs she starred in several other TV series, wrote more books and in 1984 made six videos titled *The Way to Cook*. She has just published *The Way to Cook* in book form.

Tom Haruya Chino
farmer, Chino Nojo, Inc., Del Mar CA (1985)

"The most integral part of our operation is that everything is picked fresh and sold the same day," says Chino. He runs the ranch along with three of his brothers and sisters, their mother and father. Shoppers drive as long as two hours and line up to buy Chino's produce. Only Alice Waters of Chez Panisse has the produce shipped to her restaurant; buyers from all other restaurants, including Wolfgang Puck's Spago, must queue up with everyone else. A graduate of the University of California, Berkeley, Chino has done research at the Salk Institute and the Scripps Clinic and Research Foundation.

Craig Claiborne
food editor/author, East Hampton NY (1984)

In 1988 Claiborne retired from *The New York Times*, after 30 years as its food editor. He received his degree in journalism from the University of Missouri in 1942 and is a graduate of L'Ecole Hoteliere de la Societe Suisse de Hoteliers in Switzerland. Among his perennially popular cookbooks are *The New York Times Cookbook* and *Craig Claiborne's Gourmet Diet*.

Darrell Corti
wine buyer, Corti Brothers, Sacramento CA (1989)

Corti is an internationally known wine expert and a force in the development and growth of the California wine industry. In 1964 he entered the family grocery business, Corti Brothers, located in Sacramento. Since then he has been in charge of its wine department. In the late 1960s and early 1970s, he was a catalyst in the re-evaluation and renaissance of Zinfandels grown in Amador County, California. He has served as a member of several prestigious wine societies and sits on tasting panels for regional, national and foreign competitions.

Marion Cunningham
writer/teacher, Walnut Creek CA (1984)

A culinary teacher for almost two decades, Cunningham is author of several cookbooks, the most recent being *The Breakfast Book*, recipient of *Cook's* Magazine's 1988 Platinum Plate Award for Best American Cookbook.

She studied with the late James Beard and worked as his assistant. A contributor to numerous national publications, including *Bon Appetit* and *The New York Times*, Cunningham is currently working on her third revision of *The Fanny Farmer Cookbook*. She is also a restaurant consultant.

Jack L. Davies
managing director/owner, Schramsberg Vineyards, Calistoga CA (1985)

Winemaking is both an art and a craft, according to Davies. He acquired the vineyard in 1965 and has restored it as a producer of premium champagnes. In 1990 Schramsberg will celebrate its 25th vintage of sparkling wines.

Davies views the dramatic growth in consumption of domestic and imported premium wines and champagnes as the most significant development in the wine industry today. "I am proud of leading the renaissance in quality U.S. methode champenoise wines," he says. "Now, more than seven French producers have come here and there are more than 40 new American brands. Northern California will one day be world center for the finest sparkling wines."

Robert Del Grande
co-owner/chef, Cafe Annie and Cafe Express, Houston TX (1987)

Del Grande has helped Texas reach new culinary peaks with his sophisticated interpretations of Southwest specialties. He has served as co-owner and chef at Cafe Annie since 1981, and at Cafe Express since 1984. This year, he opened a second Cafe Express, also in Houston. He views the continuing development of local growers who consider quality an essential part of their operations as one of the most significant features of the culinary arena today.

Marcel Desaulniers
executive chef/co-owner, The Trellis Cafe, Restaurant & Grill, Williamsburg VA (1984)

Visitors to Colonial Williamsburg can enjoy a taste of contemporary American cooking prepared by Marcel Desaulniers at The Trellis. After graduating from the Culinary Institute of America in 1965, Desaulniers worked in New York City at the Irving Trust Company dining room and the Colony Club, and served as saucier at the Hotel Pierre. He opened The Trellis with Tom Power and John Curtis in 1980 and authored *The Trellis Cookbook— Contemporary American Cooking in Williamsburg, Virginia* in 1988. Consumers' growing preference for healthy eating is one development that has greatly influenced Desaulniers' menu.

Paul Draper
chairman/winemaker, Ridge Vineyards, Cupertino CA (1984)

Paul Draper spent six years studying winemaking with vintners in Italy and France. He also worked and studied agricultural development in South America, including setting up a vineyard in Chile. He joined Ridge Vineyards in 1969 as a winemaker and later became a full partner. Of late, he has been busy producing the 1984 to 1987 Monte Bello Cabernets, which he says are "probably the finest consecutive vintages in the 26-year history of Ridge Monte Bellos." With interest in French winemaking and viticulture at a peak in California today, one hears the question, "Are Californians trying to imitate Bordeaux?" For fine producers like Draper, the answer is an unequivocal "No."

Dafne and Mats Engstrom

food producers/distributors, California Sunshine Fine Foods, Inc., San Francisco CA (1984)

Husband-and-wife team Dafne and Mats Engstrom founded California Sunshine Fine Foods in 1975. Since becoming Who's Who members, they have been busy marketing their Sturgeon Farms products and working with a large indoor well-water recycler to produce a cleaner flavored fish. They observe, "Sturgeon are the fastest growing farmed fish." The recycled water plant is new to America and it is hoped that it will work wonders, especially with pollution problems. The Engstroms took 10 quality-control people to China's Amur River in order to process and buy 10 tons of caviar to market worldwide.

Florence Fabricant

columnist, The New York Times, New York NY (1989)

As the "Food Notes" columnist at *The New York Times* for the past five years, Fabricant is particularly well known for the breadth of the topics that she covers, as well as the fine palate she brings to the New York food scene. In addition to her regular column, she also writes about food and wine for the Living, Travel, Weekend and regional weekly sections of the *Times*. "One aspect of being a food writer that I find truly invigorating is that it is a constant learning process," she says. "There is always something new happening."

Dean Fearing

chef, Mansion on Turtle Creek, and corporate chef, Rosewood Hotels, Dallas TX (1987)

Fearing is achieving national acclaim for his development of American Southwest cuisine. Relying on classic techniques, he uses seasonal and indigenous products in unconventional combinations. A graduate of the Culinary Institute of America, he came to Dallas as saucier at the Pyramid Room in the Fairmont Hotel and from there joined the Mansion on Turtle Creek. He left to become chef in Agnew's Restaurant and served as executive chef at the Verandah Club at Loew's Anatole Hotel. His awards include *Food & Wine*'s "Up and Coming Young Chef of America" and the 1989 Ivy award from *Restaurants & Institutions*.

Susan Feniger and Mary Sue Milliken

co-owners/chefs, City Restaurant and Border Grill, Los Angeles CA (1985)

Collecting recipes from Mexico and Asia, Feniger and Milliken combine ethnic specialties with their extensive French and American training to produce an unusual and diverse array of dishes at their two Los Angeles restaurants. Both have received numerous awards and are the only women to receive the California Restaurant Writers Association's Chef of the Year award (1987-88). They currently teach cooking classes around the country and have consulted on two major restaurant projects.

M. F. K. Fisher

writer, Glen Ellen CA (1985)

Mary Frances Kennedy Fisher might well be considered the first lady of American food writing. Her books have inspired writers and cooks ever since her first volume, *Serve It Forth*, published in 1937 and reissued in 1989. At age 80, she is still writing, most recently *Dubious Honors*, published in 1988, and is working on a new book. She has also annotated and translated from Jean-Anthelme Brillat-Savarin's *The Physiology of Taste*.

Michael Foley

chef/proprietor, Printer's Row and Foley's, Chicago (1984)

As a government history major at Georgetown University, Foley hardly seemed destined to become one of America's most innovative and acclaimed chefs. A third-generation member of a restaurant family, he is co-owner/operator with his father, Bob, of Printer's Row restaurant, opened in 1981, and Foley's, opened in 1986. Michael Foley has received numerous awards and is a member of several professional associations. He writes a food column for the *Chicago Sun-Times* and is currently working with the National Heart Association to develop a sophisticated menu that concerns itself with calories and nutrition.

Larry Forgione

chef/owner, An American Place, New York NY (1984)

A 1974 graduate of the Culinary Institute of America, Forgione worked as chef/saucier at the Connaught Hotel in London from 1975 to 1977. He later worked as chef at Regine's until 1979, then became executive chef at the River Cafe, both in New York City. In 1983 Forgione opened An American Place, where critics and patrons alike have enjoyed the restaurant's approach to new American cuisine.

Forgione is co-founder of American Spoon Foods, Inc., in Michigan. He is currently working on an in-depth book of American food and is planning another restaurant, American Place Cookery, in Ramapo, New York.

Pierre Franey

food writer, East Hampton NY (1986)

Franey is renowned for his many cookbooks and his "60-Minute Gourmet" columns in *The New York Times*. Born in France, he became a restaurant apprentice there at age 13. He originally came to this country to work in the French Pavilion at the 1939 World's Fair and after serving in World War II, he returned to America to live. He has served as chef at Le Pavillon, vice president for Howard Johnson's and food writer for *The New York Times*.

Jerry Goldstein

vice president, marketing, Los Angeles Brewing Company, Inc., Los Angeles CA (1985)

In 1979 Goldstein joined a friend in starting Acacia Winery. His success can be measured by the consistently high quality of Acacia's Pinot Noir. In 1986, upon the sale of Acacia Winery to Chalone, Inc., Goldstein began a second venture, the Los Angeles Brewing Company, Inc., with Wolfgang Puck. He hopes to produce a high-quality Bavarian-style lager beer to be named Eureka. "With the proliferation of regional breweries, America is beginning to focus on foods that match and pair with beer, much as we explored foods that match wines over the past several years," he notes.

Joyce Goldstein

chef/owner, Square One Restaurant, San Francisco CA (1985)

For Goldstein, opening her own restaurant in 1984 has been the highlight of an illustrious career that began in the art field. In the interim, she served as founder and director of San Francisco's acclaimed California Street

Cooking School, food writer for *Rolling Stone*, food reporter for KQED, food stylist, restaurant and kitchen design consultant, and chef at Chez Panisse. In addition to her continued success with Square One, Goldstein writes a food column, "California Cuisine," for the San Francisco Chronicle and has just published a cookbook, *The Mediterranean Kitchen*.

Richard Graff

chairman and chief operating officer, Chalone Vineyards, Inc., San Francisco CA (1984)

Graff is considered a pioneer in the U.S. wine industry. After studying all aspects of winemaking at the University of California, Davis, Graff began producing wine at Chalone in 1966 and has been in charge of operations ever since. From 1967 to 1974, he developed and ran an importing company, which was the first to bring French cooperage (barrels) to the United States. In 1969 he began consulting for Mt. Eden Vineyards in Saratoga and in 1972 launched the wine production there. Graff now oversees three additional wineries: Edna Valley Vineyard Winery, Carmenet and Acacia.

In 1981 he co-founded, with Julia Child and Robert Mondavi, the American Institute of Wine and Food. He now serves on the national board.

Randall Grahm

winemaker, Bonny Doon Vineyard, Santa Cruz CA (1989)

Grahm discovered the joys of French wine while working as a floor sweeper in a Beverly Hills wine shop. He has since earned a reputation as one of America's most talented, innovative and daring winemakers. In 1981 he and his family started the Bonny Doon Vineyard. Here, he embarked on a search for the "Great American Pinot Noir." Although he describes this goal as "systematically elusive," he has firmly established his French-style Pinots. His 1986 release of the 1984 vintage of Cigare Volant, "our rendition of Chateauneuf-du-Pape," stimulated a wave of interest in Rhonelike varieties made in California.

Bert Greene

cooking instructor, writer and critic, New York NY (1984)

Playwright turned chef, artist, entrepreneur and television chef, Greene wrote numerous feature stories,

cookbooks, magazine and newspaper columns, as well as plays and screenplays. The Store, in Amagansett, New York, the nation's first fancy take-out shop, was co-founded by Greene. Before his death in 1988, he was president-elect of the International Association of Cooking Professionals.

Marcella Hazan

cooking instructor, New York NY and Venice, Italy (1986)

Hazan has earned doctorates in the natural sciences and biology at the University of Ferrara in Italy. In the mid-1960s, she took a Chinese cooking class as a break from a laboratory job in New York. "The students asked me what I was cooking at home, and I told them 'Italian food.' They asked if I liked to teach, and I said 'Yes,' because I was thinking of my science field. But they meant Italian cooking." Soon, Hazan was teaching cooking classes from her New York home. She later opened a school in Bologna, Italy, and more recently has been teaching in Venice.

Maida Heatter

cookbook author, Miami Beach FL (1988)

Heatter, America's grande dame of desserts, has developed a loyal following through her five books on the subject. Her devotion to the last course began when her husband, Ralph Daniels, started what was planned as a coffee shop. By the time it opened, it had become a full-scale restaurant, with Heatter making the desserts at home. They made the news in 1968, when during the Republican convention, their restaurant featured omelettes made with canned elephant meat. Craig Claiborne came to visit, tasted the desserts and told Heatter she should write a cookbook. Five best-sellers followed.

Jeff Hvid

collector of wild foods, San Anselmo CA (1984)

Hvid learned much about wild mushrooms from Larry Stickney, past president of the San Francisco Mycological Society. The Oakville Grocery in San Francisco promoted a range of specialty foods and was interested in increasing the diversity and quality of their offerings. The grocery found in Hvid a local, knowledgeable and consistent collector of at least 10 different species. "It was the right time and the right

place. I tried to provide them with the cream of the crop, gathered no more than two days earlier," says Hvid. He also credits Alice Waters and Larry Forgione as influential buyers who have helped shape his career.

Evan Jones

freelance journalist, New York NY and East Hardwick VT (1984)

Minnesota-born Evan Jones wrote for his family's newspaper business for 35 years; he became interested in frontier American history and began food writing. His interest in writing about food was inspired while he was stationed in Paris during World War II, where he started a magazine called *Weekend*. Jones is currently a contributor to *Travel & Leisure* and *Gourmet*, and is working on the biography of James Beard.

Judith Jones

senior editor, vice president, Alfred A. Knopf, New York NY (1985)

In her 30-year-plus career as a book editor at Knopf, and before that at Doubleday, Judith Jones has helped bring numerous books into the world. Having always been attracted to American cooking, Jones has published various cookbooks by American authors, including Marian Morash and Edna Lewis. She developed an avid interest in French cooking during a three-and-a-half-year stint in Paris, but lamented that the plethora of recipe books included no comprehensive work that really taught people how to cook. When the manuscript for *Mastering the Art of French Cooking* crossed her desk, she eagerly championed it.

Barbara Kafka

president, Barbara Kafka Associates, New York NY (1984)

Kafka has served as a consultant to a number of nationally known restaurants and has helped to develop prototypes for major fast food chains. In addition to her various writing assignments, she has taught cooking classes, both alone and in collaboration with the late James Beard, and consulted for various food concerns. Most recently food editor for *Vogue* magazine, she writes food columns for *Family Circle*, *Gourmet* and *The New York Times*. Her books include *Microwave Gourmet* and *Microwave Gourmet Healthstyle Cookbook*.

7

Madeleine Kamman
director of the School for American Chefs,
Beringer Vineyards, St. Helena CA (1986)

Teaching people to cook has been Kamman's main concern since 1962. She apprenticed in a family-owned Michelin-starred restaurant and had schools in Philadelphia, Boston and in France. She was educated at the Cordon Bleu and L'Ecole des Trois Gourmandes in Paris and at the Lausanne Hotel School. Kamman has been owner and executive chef of two restaurants, a restaurant consultant, and host of several television series on PBS. Her articles have appeared in numerous magazines and she has authored several cookbooks.

Diana Southwood Kennedy
writer, Zitacuaro, Michoacan, Mexico
(1985)

"People are going wild, quite understandably, about chilies," says Kennedy. "The fact is every chile is different, and with every chile you get a different flavor. It is important to understand this because not all flavors go together; not all aromas go together." Chilies and other Southwestern and Mexican ingredients have long been staples for author Kennedy. She has spent 32 years living, working or traveling in Mexico, interspersed with periods of teaching in the United States.

Paul Keyser
owner/operator, Keyser Chicken Farm,
Warwick NY (1984)

Keyser has held jobs as diverse as police recorder, welder's apprentice and truck driver. He has a master's degree and a doctorate in microbiology. His education helps him analyze the various feed formulations that are available and also permits him to create his own. He is interested in how microorganisms decay complex chemicals, which resist decomposition and accumulate in the biosphere or food web, presenting health hazards. He has also become interested in chicken ethology (behavior). There are striking differences between the various European and American varieties.

Paul Kovi and Tom Margittai
co-owners, The Four Seasons, New York NY
(1985)

The Four Seasons, under ownership of Kovi and Margittai since 1973, has served as one of New York City's landmark restaurants and has been at the forefront of American cooking. Both men were born in Europe. After coming to the United States, they worked at New York's Waldorf-Astoria and Sherry Netherlands hotels and at Restaurant Associates. The two are the originators of the Four Seasons Foursome Dinners and the Annual California Vintners' Barrel-Tasting Dinners. In 1986 each was honored with New York City's Award of Liberty for his outstanding gastronomic and culinary contributions to America.

Sibella Kraus
produce marketing consultant and agricul-
tural writer, San Francisco CA (1985)

Kraus began her professional career as a cook at Chez Panisse. In 1983 she organized the first annual Tasting of Summer Produce, to bring together farmers, restaurateurs, produce buyers and other food professionals with a common interest in local high-quality produce. The tasting has evolved into a nationally acclaimed event for catalyzing the regional agricultural marketplace.

Currently Kraus works as a produce marketing consultant and as a produce reporter and agricultural writer. "In the last few years, consumers have become increasingly concerned about safety and the healthfulness of their food and have become adamant about improving the quality of their produce, especially the flavor," she says.

Peter Kump
certified culinary professional and founder of
Peter Kump's New York Cooking School,
New York NY (1988)

In 1974 Kump started a school in his own kitchen. Today, his Manhattan cooking school is one of the best in the country. He writes a syndicated cooking column and has won a Tastemaker Award for his book *Quiche & Pate*. He is a founder and past president of the New York Association of Cooking Teachers, a former president of the International Association of Cooking Professionals, and president of The James Beard Foundation. He currently appears on CNBC.

Emeril Lagasse
chef, Commander's Palace, New Orleans LA
(1989)

At the age of 26, Lagasse became executive chef at Commander's Palace in New Orleans, a position he has held for the past five years. While there, Lagasse has been refining and modernizing traditional Creole recipes. His goal is to make the dishes fit the preferences of today's diner, yet retain their intensity of taste. He has also been very active in reviving the cottage food industries in the New Orleans area and in making the Commander's Palace kitchen almost completely self-sufficient.

George Lang
senior advisor, The George Lang Corporation,
and owner, Cafe des Artistes, New York NY
(1986)

Hungarian-born Lang came to the United States in 1946 as a professional violinist, but decided against a career in music. He worked as a busboy, waiter, chef and restaurant manager, eventually joining Restaurant Associates in the 1960s. In 1970 he founded the George Lang Corporation, an international food consulting service. He has developed major restaurants and other food operations and has been involved with more than 400 hotels and restaurants throughout the world. He contributes to a number of magazines, among them *Esquire, Food & Wine, Travel & Leisure* and *Connoisseur*.

David Lett
winemaker, Eyrie Vineyards, Dundee OR
(1987)

With his Eyrie Vineyards, Lett has put Oregon's Willamette Valley on the world's map of important wine regions. The valley is one of the few areas on earth where Pinot Noir grapes flourish, maturing slowly and late because of the area's exceptionally long growing and cool season. Lett planted Oregon's first Pinot Noir grapes in 1966. In the Gault-Millau Olympiades of Wines of the World in 1980, Eyrie Vineyards' 1975 "South Block" was judged second-place winner by 0.2 points, while first place went to a 1959 Chambolle-Musigny. Since then, Eyrie Vineyards has set the standard for Oregon Pinot Noirs.

Edna Lewis
chef, Orange County VA and New York NY
(1984)

A legendary Southern food connoisseur, Lewis has graced restaurants from the Carolinas to New York, where she began her career in 1947 as a chef at Cafe Nicholson. She later worked as a chef in

New York and Chapel Hill, North Carolina, which included a chef residency at South Carolina's historic Middleton Place Plantation from 1984 to 1987. Lewis returned to New York in 1987 as food consultant to Uncle Sam's restaurant and is currently the chef at Gage & Tollner in Brooklyn. She is author of several cookbooks and has contributed to *Cook's, Connoisseur, Southern Homes, House Beautiful* and *McCall's*, among other publications.

Leon Lianides
owner, The Coach House, New York NY (1988)

Since opening his restaurant in 1949, Lianides has been a champion and connoisseur of American cooking. His Coach House menu has played a major role in achieving international recognition for American cuisine.

Born in Corfu, Greece, Lianides came to the United States as a teenager. After years of experience in the kitchens of restaurants, hotels and resorts, working in every position from busboy to saucier to chef, he trained with Julia Child and Simone Beck at L'Ecole des Trois Gourmandes in Paris. Today, if a key staff member is absent, Lianides steps in to perform any task required for the presentation of Coach House meals.

Sirio Maccioni
owner/manager, Le Cirque, New York NY (1987)

Maccioni has spent 40 years working in the restaurant field and, among other achievements, introduced New York to the joys of pasta primavera, now a standard on so many menus. As owner and manager of New York's Le Cirque since 1974, Maccioni has kept its classic food and service miraculously new—an enduring classic in a city where trendy restaurants come and go. He has established the meticulous standards and refined atmosphere that make CEOs and celebrities comfortable. Le Cirque now has an 18 - 20 rating with Gault-Millau.

John Mariani
writer, New York NY (1985)

In 1977 Mariani drove across America with his wife in search of the perfect pie pastry and the best barbecue. The result was *A Dictionary of American Food & Drink*, the first of several books that have made him an authority in this field. Mariani, who holds a doctorate in English literature from Columbia University, is food and travel correspondent for *Esquire*, food critic for IBM's Prodigy database system, a food writer for *USA Today* and host of a new PBS show, "Crazy for Food."

Tony May
restaurateur, Tony May Group, New York NY (1989)

May arrived in New York City from Italy in 1963 and was hired by the Rainbow Room in Rockefeller Center. Twelve years later he signed a long-term lease to operate the restaurant. In 1986 he opened Palio, which attracted critical acclaim throughout the world. In 1988 he opened San Domenico, which was voted Best New Restaurant in the United States by *Esquire* magazine.

Currently, May owns La Camelia and Sandro's, which, together with San Domenico, constitute the Tony May Group. He is chairman of Gruppo Ristoratori Italiani and serves on the boards of the National Restaurant Assocation, the New York Convention and Visitors Bureau and the Culinary Institute of America.

Fritz Maytag
owner, York Creek Vineyards, St. Helena CA, chairman of the board, Maytag Dairy Farms, Inc., Newton IA, and president/brewmaster, Anchor Brewing Company, San Francisco CA (1989)

In 1965 Maytag acquired the Anchor Brewing Company of San Francisco, the last "steam" brewery left in America. In the years since then, he has not only saved steam beer, but has also made Anchor Steam into a national brand without compromising its high standards. In addition to serving as the firm's president and brewmaster, Maytag is a director of the Beer Institute. He is also chairman of the board of the Maytag Dairy Farms in Newton, Iowa, owns the York Creek Vineyards in St. Helena, California, and serves on several civic and educational boards, including that of Grinnell College in Grinnell, Iowa.

Michael McCarty
chef/proprietor, Michael's Restaurant, Santa Monica CA (1984)

Since starting Michael's in Santa Monica, McCarty has expanded his successes to other cities across the country, opening the Adirondacks restaurants in Denver, Colorado, in 1985 and in Washington DC in 1989, and Michael's in New York in 1989. He also operates the Santa Monica Beach Hotel.

His extensive culinary education includes the Ecole Hoteliere de Paris, the Cordon Bleu and the Academie du Vin. He ran a small restaurant in France, attended the Cornell University School of Hotel Administration, taught at the University of Colorado and earned a degree there in the business and art of gastronomy. Before opening Michael's he taught food and wine seminars in Los Angeles. He has begun producing wine and also works extensively with the American Institute of Wine and Food.

Moncef Meddeb
chef/owner, L'Espalier, Boston MA (1985)

When Meddeb opened L'Espalier restaurant, the adventurous daily specials became so popular with the customers that he ultimately scrapped the conventional menu altogether. Meddeb has no formal training in cooking but fondly remembers the food his Tunisian family cooked when he was growing up in France: fresh fruits, vegetables, rabbits and chickens raised in the yard. Working in restaurants was to be only temporary employment until he could get his career on course after graduation from Harvard, but he ended up as chef/owner of his own restaurant instead.

Richard Melman
president/co-founder, Lettuce Entertain You Enterprises, Inc., Chicago IL (1989)

When you talk about a restaurateur who has a finger on the pulse of America, the name has to be that of Richard Melman. No individual has more accurately gauged the moods, desires and tastes of the modern American diner. Melman's own statement says it all: "We have been lucky enough to give people what they want, before they know they want it."

As president of Lettuce Entertain You Enterprises, Inc., Melman has created more than 25 different concepts that embody his personal artistic flair and imagination. With every one of them a unifying principle is observed: "People feel good when they are in our restaurants," he says.

Ferdinand Metz
president, Culinary Institute of America, Hyde Park NY (1985)

Metz oversees the operations of the two-year school for foodservice professionals at the "CIA." Apprenticed in pastry and baking at the Cafe Feld-errnhalle and in cooking at the Hotel Deutscher Kaiser, both in Munich, Germany, Metz came to the United States in 1962 and began working at Le Pavillon in New York City. Chairman and past president of the American Culinary Federation, Metz was elected Chef of the Year in 1968 by the ACF, and again in 1975 by the CIA. In 1982 he attained the rank of certified master chef, after completing the ACF program. He has received numerous awards.

Mark Miller
chef/proprietor, Coyote Cafe, Santa Fe NM (1984)

For Miller, cooking is a practical application of his anthropological interests and studies. Born and raised in Boston but drawn to the West, he studied Chinese art history and anthropology at the University of California, Berkeley.

In 1979 Miller opened the Fourth Street Bar and Grill in Berkeley, and began using one of the first mesquite grills. It was at Fourth Street that he was finally able to merge cooking and anthropology by focusing on the ethnic foods of different countries he had traveled to. Miller opened his second Berkeley restaurant, the Santa Fe Bar and Grill, in 1980. Eventually, he moved to Santa Fe, New Mexico, where in 1987 he opened his new restaurant, Coyote Cafe.

Robert Mondavi
chairman of the board, Robert Mondavi Winery, Oakville CA (1984)

Mondavi has been in the wine business since 1936, when his Italian father became a partner at Sunnyhill Winery in St. Helena, California. In 1945 his family bought Charles Krug Winery, where he served as general manager. He was the first Napa Valley vintner to utilize cold fermentation extensively in the winemaking process and was responsible for popularizing new styles of wine, such as Chenin Blanc and Fume Blanc, at the Robert Mondavi Winery, opened in 1986. With his wife, Margrit Biever, Mondavi sponsors numerous activities to further the

appreciation of fine food and wine, including the Great Chefs at Robert Mondavi Winery school. He is also founding co-chairman with Julia Child of the American Institute of Wine and Food.

Marian Morash
writer/chef, Lexington MA (1984)

Culinary curator on the national PBS television series "The Victory Garden" since 1979, "Chef Marian" is a self-taught cook who has authored *The Victory Garden Cookbook* as well as a home video-book derived from the programs. She served as executive chef on Julia Child's last two PBS series and also on Child's six-volume video-book series, "The Way to Cook."

Co-founder and former executive chef of the Straight Wharf Restaurant in Nantucket, Massachusetts, Morash continues to write food columns and give cooking demonstrations.

James A. Nassikas
hotelier, Deer Valley UT (1984)

The renowned reputation of San Francisco's Stanford Court Hotel is the result of the stewardship of Nassikas, its creator. A graduate of the University of New Hampshire with a degree in hotel administration, he studied at L'Ecole Hoteliere de la Societe Suisse des Hoteliers in Lausanne, Switzerland. He was food and beverage director for the Mayflower Hotel in Washington DC and the Plaza in New York, then vice president and general manager of New Orleans' Royal Orleans Hotel before forming the Stanford Court Hotel Management Company in 1969. In 1986 *Hotels & Restaurants International* magazine named him "Independent Hotelier of the World."

Stanford Court was sold in the spring of 1989. After the sale, Nassikas focused his attention on the Deer Valley Resort in Utah, a venture in which he has participated since 1978.

Patrick O'Connell
chef/owner, The Inn at Little Washington, Washington VA (1984)

In 1972 O'Connell and his partner Reinhard Lynch began a catering enterprise that ultimately evolved into the remarkable Inn at Little Washington. A member of the Paris-based Relais & Chateaux Association, the Inn became

the first and only establishment in America to achieve five stars from the Mobil Travel Guide, five diamonds from the American Automobile Association and the top national rating from the Zagat Hotel Survey, with the first "perfect" score for its cuisine in the history of the Zagat rating system. Most recently, O'Connell's hotel earned the distinction of being designated the only Relais Gourmand kitchen in North America.

Bradley Ogden
chef, San Francisco CA (1984)

From 1983 to 1989, Ogden was responsible for overseeing the kitchen of Campton Place, one of San Francisco's top-rated restaurants. He graduated from the Culinary Institute of America, with honors, and was selected "Most Likely to Succeed." He worked at a number of hotels and resorts before overseeing the American Restaurant, in Kansas City. He was named one of 1983's Great American Chefs by the International Food and Wine Society.

Ogden plans to open the Lark Creek Inn in Larkspur, California, with Michael Diller.

Richard Olney
writer and painter, Sollies-Pont, France (1986)

Olney's writing has had far-reaching impact—the 27-volume *Good Cook* series he edited for Time-Life Books between 1977 and 1982 has been translated into several languages, and cooks around the world rely on it for information on just about every cooking topic. He is highly respected in the food community.

Born in Iowa and trained as a painter at the University of Iowa and the Brooklyn Museum Art School, Olney moved to France in 1951—and has lived there ever since.

Jean-Louis Palladin
chef/owner, Jean-Louis at Watergate, Washington DC (1987)

The Americanization of French cuisine—combining classic techniques with New World ingredients—is Palladin's favorite pastime as well as his claim to culinary fame. Ten years ago, his enthusiasm for America as a "new culinary frontier" lured him here from France, where he had been that nation's youngest two-star chef. His intimate restaurant (14 tables) is recognized as serving the finest French food in Washington and was ranked among the top 10 restaurants in the United States by the 1987 *Playboy* poll of food writers. French critic Henri Gault has acclaimed Palladin as the best chef outside France.

Alex Patout
chef/owner, Alex Patout's, New Orleans LA and Houston TX (1987)

Patout earned his degree in accounting from the University of Southwestern Louisiana. His first restaurant, Patout's, in New Iberia, Louisiana, was opened in 1978 by Patout and his sister, Gigi. The restaurant led to a food booth at the 1984 New Orleans World's Fair and eventually to Patout's Cajun Festival at the Jackson Brewery riverfront complex. The restaurant eventually closed, as a result of the downturn in Louisiana's oil-based economy. Since then Patout married Marcia Burns of Houston and they opened two Alex Patout's Louisiana Restaurants in the French Quarter of New Orleans and another in Houston.

Cindy Pawlcyn
executive chef/restaurateur, Mustards Grill and Tra Vigne in the Napa Valley, and of Fog City Diner, Bix and the Bistro Roti, San Francisco CA (1988)

Pawlcyn earned an associate's degree from the Chef Program at Hennepin Technical Institute and graduated with honors and a B.S. in hotel and restaurant administration from the University of Wisconsin, Stout. She also studied at the Cordon Bleu and La Varenne in Paris and the Ken Hom School in Hong Kong and was a member of the Shanghai/San Francisco Culinary Exchange program. After working for other restaurateurs, she opened her first restaurant, Mustards Grill, in 1983. Following its success, Pawlcyn opened Fog City Diner and Bix, both in San Francisco. She is co-owner of the Tra Vigne restaurant in Napa Valley.

Jacques Pepin
master chef, cookbook author and cooking instructor, Madison CT (1986)

Pepin's first exposure to cooking was working as an apprentice in his parents' restaurant, Le Pelican, at age 13. He moved on to Paris, where he served as personal chef to three French presidents, and then came to the United States in 1959. He worked at New York's Le Pavillon and later at the Howard Johnson Company. He helped develop the concept of La Potagerie, a successful soup restaurant in New York. In addition to producing best-selling books, he writes for a number of newspapers and magazines and is a frequent radio and television guest.

Richard Perry
chef/owner, Richard Perry Restaurant, St. Louis MO (1984)

Perry studied history at the University of Illinois and worked for McGraw-Hill in New York and Chicago. He went into the restaurant business as an amateur in 1972, when he purchased the Jefferson Avenue Boarding House in St. Louis. In 1982, he changed the name of the restaurant to Richard Perry Restaurant. In March 1988, after five years of preparation, Perry relocated his restaurant to the small, luxurious Hotel Majestic in downtown St. Louis. Says Perry, "The quality of food and its innovative preparation are only a part of the total restaurant experience. It is now time to develop an American service on a par with American cuisine."

Joseph Phelps
president, Joseph Phelps Vineyards, St. Helena, and owner of Oakville Grocery stores, Oakville and San Francisco CA (1985)

With a degree in engineering from Colorado State University, Phelps spent a number of years in the construction business, accumulating capital to support his lifelong interest in wine and food, which he pursued in 1972 with the establishment of Joseph Phelps Vineyards. The winery has garnered him much esteem, and his late-harvest Rieslings are exceptional. "Being a vintner was a second career for me," says Phelps. "I had intended it to be a retirement career, but it is too exciting for me to retire." Phelps later bought the Oakville Grocery Company in Oakville, California, and converted the 100-year-old general store into a specialty foods store.

Alfred Portale
chef, Gotham Bar and Grill, New York NY (1989)

A jewelry designer before becoming a chef, Portale has retained his concern with design, craftsmanship and value and now applies it to his customers' dining experiences. To create the compelling dining experience that is the Gotham Bar and Grill, Portale combined his love for all things American with his three years of training in France under the tutelage of Michel Guerard and the Troigros brothers. In the years that he has managed the Gotham kitchen he has catapulted his restaurant to the three-star status it now enjoys.

Steve Poses
founder/president, Frog & Co., Inc., Philadelphia PA (1984)

Poses' Frog & Co. is a premium foodservice company that operates five restaurants, a catering business and a retail food store in the center of Philadelphia. Operations include the Frog/Commissary Catering, The Commissary, 16th Street Bar & Grill, the USA Cafe, The Market of the Commissary and, at the Franklin Institute Science Museum, Ben's and the Omni Cafe (1990). Poses employs approximately 400 people and serves an average of 4,000 meals each day.

Paul Prudhomme
chef/proprietor, K-Paul's Louisiana Kitchen, New Orleans LA (1984)

Prudhomme, the youngest of 13 children, began cooking with his mother at age 7. He spent 12 years traveling throughout the country to work with chefs, after which he returned to Louisiana. From 1975 to 1980 Prudhomme served as corporate chef for the Brennan family. He and his wife, K Hinrichs Prudhomme, opened K-Paul's Louisiana Kitchen in 1979, where he specializes in Cajun and Creole cooking. The reputation of the restaurant quickly spread, and it has been featured in morning and evening national news and television programs, along with virtually every daily newspaper in the nation. Prudhomme has received numerous awards.

Wolfgang Puck
chef/owner, Spago, Los Angeles CA and Tokyo, Japan, and of Chinois on Main, Santa Monica, and Postrio, San Francisco CA (1984)

Austrian-born Puck began his formal training at age 14. He apprenticed in France and came to the United States in 1973. Within a short time he was the star attraction at Ma Maison in Los Angeles. After publishing his first cookbook, Puck left French cooking and opened Spago on Sunset Boulevard in

1982, where his trademark gourmet pizzas and the restaurant's chic interior (designed by his wife, Barbara Lazaroff) have continually attracted a glamorous Hollywood crowd. In 1986 he created a line of frozen versions of his gourmet pizzas and desserts.

Stephan Pyles
chef/co-owner, Routh Street Cafe and Baby Routh, Dallas TX, and of Goodfellow's and Telas, Minneapolis MN (1985)

Pyles has been instrumental in sparking a new regional revolution in the American Southwest. Largely self-taught, he worked for two years as chef's assistant to Michel Guerard, the Troigros brothers and Georges Blanc at the Great Chefs Cooking School at the Robert Mondavi Winery. In 1982 he started a successful catering business in Dallas which introduced him to his current partner, John Dayton. The two opened Routh Street Cafe in 1983, and both restaurant and chef have been acclaimed by critics nationwide. Pyles's specialties can be enjoyed in Minneapolis, at Telas, featuring Southwestern dishes, and Goodfellow's, which resembles Routh Street Cafe in concept.

Justin Rashid
president and co-founder, American Spoon Foods, Petoskey MI (1984)

Rashid is the son of a first-generation Lebanese-American who owned a grocery store in Detroit. He joined his father on buying trips to the Great Lakes fisheries, fruit terminals and farms. After several robbery attempts on their store, his family purchased a farm, which is where Rashid learned about foraging in the wild for edible growing things. After a brief time in New York City, he returned to Michigan, where he co-founded American Spoon Foods, which sells wild and cultivated berries, mushrooms and nuts to gourmet specialty shops, fine restaurants and mail-order customers all over the United States.

Ruth Reichl
restaurant editor, Los Angeles Times, Los Angeles CA (1984)

The explosion of new American cooking and the proliferation of new restaurants has kept Reichl busy. She expanded the restaurant coverage in the *Los Angeles Times* and now reviews restaurants in all regional editions on Fridays and includes a large section of profiles and trend pieces on Sundays.

Reichl, who spent much of her childhood in France, has a master's degree in art history. She opened a small restaurant, The Swallow, in Berkeley, California, in 1973. In addition to being a book author, she is a contributor to *Metropolitan Home* and other magazines.

Leslee Reis
chef/owner, Cafe Provencal, Evanston IL (1987)

Praised for creating a refined style of American cooking, Reis is not only a restaurateur, she's a pacesetter—serving tapas when most of Chicago barely knew the word. The Zagat Guide lists her Cafe Provencal just outside Chicago as the fifth best restaurant in the country. In addition to being nominated to the *Cook's* Who's Who, she received the 1988 Hall of Fame award for Cafe Provencal from *Nation's Restaurant News*. She also cooks for charity events from coast to coast.

Seppi Renggli
executive chef, The Four Seasons, New York NY (1984)

Born in Switzerland, Renggli has worked in Amsterdam, the Grand Hotel in Stockholm, the Hotel de la Paix in Lucerne, and the Carlton Elite in Zurich. He became chef at the Hermitage in the Channel Islands and later joined the Holland America Lines. He held the position of chef at various Caribbean hotels and was an executive chef at Restaurant Associates from 1966 to 1973. He then joined The Four Seasons, where his creativity and high standards have received international recogition ever since.

William Rice
food and wine columnist, Chicago Tribune, Chicago IL (1984; Platinum Plate Award for Best Food Journalism, 1988)

William Rice holds degrees from the University of Virginia and Columbia University Graduate School of Journalism, as well as the Cordon Bleu in Paris. He has been executive food editor of *The Washington Post* and editor-in-chief of *Food & Wine* before moving to the *Tribune*.

Rice notes that the "decline in the value of the dollar is forcing up prices of imported products and the cost of European travel. This has given American products and restaurants an opportunity to gain wider exposure and to be seen as relative bargains."

Phyllis Richman
food critic, The Washington Post, and syndicated columnist, Washington DC (1985)

Richman enjoys "the excitement of discovering a new dish, a new chef, a new restaurant, and exploring what's new and what's happening." She has been in training, "feeding new American children for over 20 years." Her background is in sociology and urban planning, but her fantasy was always to be a food writer. She is author of four editions of *Best Restaurants & Others: Washington DC* and writes a syndicated column, "Richman's Table," for the Washington Post Writers Group. She has been a contributor to numerous magazines around the country and to the Gault-Millau Guides.

Michael Roberts
chef, Trumps, Los Angeles CA (1984)

Roberts, a former New Yorker, was well on his way to a career in music when he decided he would rather cook. He earned the Certificat d'Aptitude Professionel after study at L'Ecole Jean-Ferrandi in Paris and worked in restaurants in Paris, Brittany and New York before coming to Los Angeles. His specialties at Trumps include fried cornmeal cake with chicken and clams, potato pancakes with goat cheese and sauteed apples, and plantains with caviar, sour cream, onions and refried beans.

Judy Rodgers
chef, Zuni Cafe, San Francisco CA (1984)

At 16, Rodgers went to France as an exchange student and lived with the Troisgros family. She learned to cook by watching and tasting. She worked at Chez Panisse and was chef at the Union Hotel before becoming the chef at Zuni Cafe in San Francisco. Rodgers is "excited about the increasing accessibility of wonderful produce. I hope the future is moving toward greater simplicity, frankness and food everyone can understand."

Anne Rosenzweig
chef/co-owner, Arcadia, and president/chief operating officer, The "21" Club, New York NY (1987)

Rosenzweig's interest in food and culinary culture began in the late 1980s when she was pursuing an initial career as an anthropologist, researching in Africa. On her return to New York in 1980 she embarked on a chef-apprenticeship and eventually became the chef of Vanessa. In 1984 she opened Arcadia. Two years ago, she helped to rejuvenate the menu and style of The "21" Club, a New York landmark. She is a member of the board of the New York chapter of the American Institute of Wine and Food and a founder of the Entropy Trust, whose primary purpose is to fund small food charities and develop nutritional programs for New York City schools.

Jon Rowley
owner, Fish Works!, Seattle WA (1987)

Rowley attended Reed College in Portland and L'Institut d'Etudes Europeennes in Paris. Pursuing a childhood dream, he became a commercial fisherman in Alaska, skippering his own vessel for eight years. A lifelong scholar of the seafood industry, he has traveled widely throughout the United States and Europe, gaining hands-on experience in every level of the business. He has also studied the culinary applications of fish and shellfish in different cultures. His company, Fish Works!, provides consulting services.

Shirley Sarvis
food and wine writer and consultant, San Francisco CA (1987)

Matching wine with food is a centuries-old preoccupation. To Sarvis it is both instinct and science. She is unique in that she expounds a pioneering "let your palate be your guide" outlook that flouts many conventional wine experts' reams of rules. She feels the best way to find good combinations of wine and food is to taste. And trust your taste. "I suggest you don't think too much," she says. She is author and editor of more than a dozen books; a food and wine consultant; designs and conducts tasting entertainments for companies, clubs, especially gathered groups; and writes on food and wine for magazines, newspapers and books.

Jimmy Schmidt
owner/executive chef, The Rattlesnake Club, Detroit MI (1984)

A native Midwesterner, Schmidt received a French classic and provincial culinary arts diploma from Luberon College in Avignon, France, and the Institut Technique du Vin diploma from the Maison du Vin in Avignon in 1974. In 1976 he received his professional chef's diploma, magna cum laude, graduating first in his class from Modern Gourmet, Inc., Newton Center, Massachusetts, under the direction of Madeleine Kamman. In 1985 Schmidt, along with partner Michael McCarty, opened The Rattlesnake Club in Denver, Colorado. They opened The Rattlesnake Club in Detroit in June 1988 and Adirondacks, in Washington DC, in January 1989.

John Sedlar
chef/co-owner, Saint Estephe, Los Angeles CA (1984)

Sedlar's earliest memories of good eating were in his family's adobe home outside Santa Fe. He began his professional cooking career in Santa Fe in 1971, working at a restaurant featuring a combination French-Southwest menu. He moved to Los Angeles in 1973 and worked at several restaurants. In 1976-77 he apprenticed with Jean Bertanou of L'Ermitage. In 1980 he opened Saint Estephe with Steve Garcia. Originally specializing in nouvelle-style French cooking, Sedlar began incorporating more and more native Southwestern dishes as popularity for this regional cooking grew.

Piero Selvaggio
owner/restaurateur, Valentino's, Santa Monica, and of Primi, West Los Angeles CA (1988)

Born in Sicily, Selvaggio came to the United States to attend college in the 1960s, working in Los Angeles eateries for extra money. In 1972 he opened his own Italian restaurant, Valentino's, even though he feels that "to be a restaurateur is insane—the long hours, the pressure, the demands, the high risk, the competition, and yet every lawyer I know dreams

of owning his own restaurant." In addition to anticipating the current vogue for all things Italian, Selvaggio has earned his place in American cookery by importing Italian foods and classic combinations and then preparing them L.A. style.

Mimi Sheraton
food critic, New York NY (1986)

Mimi Sheraton has been known to wear a disguise to preserve her anonymity when reviewing a restaurant. She is *Time* magazine's food critic and has reviewed hundreds of restaurants for *The New York Times*. She recently introduced the restaurant review newsletter, "Mimi Sheraton's Taste." She also is a contributing food columnist to *Conde Nast Traveler* and the author of many successful books about food.

Lydia Shire
owner, Biba, Boston MA (1984)

Shire trained in London at the Cordon Bleu Cookery School. She then became chef of Bonhomme Richard in Boston. She moved from there to become chef at Harvest Restaurant in Cambridge and Cafe Plaza in Boston, and then became dining room chef of Parker's Restaurant. In 1982 she went to work as sous chef for the Seasons Restaurant, where she was promoted to executive chef. Her dishes focused on seasonal and local specialties and were much admired. In 1986 she opened the Four Seasons Hotel in Beverly Hills as executive chef. She returned to Boston in 1989 to open her own restaurant, Biba.

Gordon Sinclair
owner, Gordon, Chicago IL, and operator of Sinclair's Grill and Dune Dog Cafe, Jupiter FL (1984)

Sinclair has a degree in economics from Michigan State University and did graduate study at the University of Paris. He has been in the restaurant business since 1976, when he opened Gordon restaurant in Chicago. Today, he operates three restaurants in Illinois and Florida and has opened a restaurant consulting business, Sinclair and Associates, Inc. He founded and is chairman of the Chicago chapter of the American Institute of Wine and Food. He also runs a catering business. Sinclair notes, "The blending of the world's food with American cookery has moved this country's cuisine into a leadership role in culinary invention."

Andre Soltner
chef/owner, Lutece, New York NY (1986)

Soltner *is* Lutece. His devotion to his art has made his restaurant a revered American institution, whose patrons invariably remark on the congeniality of the chef as well as the excellence of his cuisine. Born in France, Soltner cooked in kitchens in France and Switzerland before coming to the United States in 1961 to open Lutece with Andre Surmain. In 1972 he became the restaurant's sole proprietor. Soltner has received numerous awards of distinction for his mastery since 1951 from culinary organizations around the world, including, in 1986, Chef of the Year from the Culinary Institute of America and the Medaille d'Honneur de Vermeil from the Maitres-Cuisiniers de France.

Andre Tchelistcheff
consulting oenologist, Napa CA (1984)

Moscow-born Tchelistcheff studied in Czechoslovakia at the Institute of National Agronomy and in Paris at the Institut Pasteur and the Trade Arboriculture School at Versailles. He worked at Beaulieu Vineyards for 35 years, starting as oenologist-viticulturist and later serving as technical director and vice president. He pioneered frost protection techniques as well as the so-called cold fermentation process widely used in the production of white and rose wines. After his retirement in 1973, he became a consultant to wineries around the country. He has received numerous awards and honors and, at age 87, is still working full time, consulting for some 15 wineries.

Jeremiah Tower
owner/executive chef, Stars, Stars Cafe, Starfish and 690, San Francisco CA (1984)

Tower graduated from Harvard College with a degree in architecture. His passion for great wine and food and his creative genius in the kitchen eventually led him into the restaurant arena. He first distinguished himself at Chez Panisse in Berkeley, California, when he turned a small neighborhood country French restaurant into a showplace of regional American cooking, of which he is rightly recog-

nized as the "father." He went on to develop his definitive and widely imitated style at Ventana Inn in Big Sur, Santa Fe Bar & Grill in Berkeley and the Balboa Cafe in San Francisco. His recent endeavors include Starfish, Stars Cafe and 690.

Jovan Trboyevic
owner, Les Nomades, Chicago IL (1987)

Iconoclast and autocrat, Trboyevic has dominated the Chicago restaurant scene for more than 20 years. His first restaurant, Jovan, opened in 1967, introducing Chicago to simple, not gussied-up French food. When Jovan opened Le Perroquet, a year before Gault and Millau posted the tenets of nouvelle cuisine, he was already serving light, beautiful, innovative food—to a somewhat bemused, hitherto steak-and-potatoes Chicago audience. His current endeavor, Les Nomades, is a private club where Jovan welcomes guests with flawless service and exquisite food. There, he has led the way back to the basics by reverting to comfortable, substantial dishes like cassoulet. His fingers are on the country's culinary pulse, before its heart even beats.

Calvin Trillin
writer, New York NY (1986)

Food has not been the cornerstone of Trillin's career, and yet his writing on the subject has struck a responsive chord in the food world. Staff writer for the *New Yorker* since 1963, Trillin has written about food, among other topics, as a way of writing about the United States. He found that humorous pieces about food provided a welcome change of pace from the community controversies about which he often wrote. Besides serving as comic relief, the food pieces reflected Trillin's belief that the country holds a bounty of good, local specialties, of which many Americans have only just become aware.

Barbara Tropp
chef/owner, China Moon Cafe, San Francisco CA (1989)

A Princeton-trained China scholar turned Chinese cook, Tropp is chef/owner of China Moon Cafe, an internationally reviewed restaurant. She is known for the lightness, complex flavors and impeccable freshness of her California-Chinese cuisine. Prior to opening China Moon in 1986, she

taught Chinese cooking nationwide and authored articles about both Chinese food and her experiences during the years she lived in Taiwan. She was also featured in the PBS series "Great Chefs of San Francisco."

Bill Tuttle
owner/manager, Glen Echo Farms, Wendell NJ (1984)

Tuttle was a New York tugboat captain for 20 years and has been a livestock producer and supplier for more than 12 years. He has worked to improve sheep and lamb grading systems, supplying restaurants with baby (20 to 24 pounds) as well as full-size (up to 60 pounds) lambs. Tuttle's favorite food: "Baby lamb, most any way."

Patricia Unterman
chef/owner, Hayes Street Grill and Vicolo Pizzeria, and restaurant critic, San Francisco Chronicle, San Francisco CA (1984)

After studying cooking with Josephine Araldo in San Francisco, Unterman opened Beggar's Banquet in Berkeley and worked as a chef there for six years. In 1979 she opened Hayes Street Grill. She has been restaurant critic for the *San Francisco Chronicle* for 10 years. She has opened several Vicolo Pizzerias—a self-service pizzeria that also specializes in salads. She finds "there's always a tension in restaurants between production and quality. I think quality is most often found in smaller, independent houses with chef/owners."

James Villas
writer and food and wine editor, Town & Country, New York NY (1985)

Villas is food and wine editor of *Town & Country* magazine and has shared his love for rustic cooking in several books. He thinks things are getting better and better for food in America, but his crusade is for a comeback of gutsy chilies, long-simmering stews, old-fashioned country breads and traditional New England bean recipes. "There's a wealth of food out there to be rediscovered and redefined; only an *n*th degree of what is American has been uncovered," says Villas.

Maggie Waldron
senior vice president, Ketchum Communications, San Francisco CA (1989)

Waldron grew up in the hotel and restaurant business, graduated from Cornell University, attended La Varenne in Paris, and then studied cooking in Italy, Asia and throughout America. Following periods as food editor at *McCall's*, television producer, author and independent food marketing consultant, she joined Ketchum Communications in 1973 and now directs Ketchum's Food Centers in San Francisco and New York City. Her pioneering promotional efforts on behalf of American farmers have been widely recognized. A national leader in food marketing, recipe development and public relations, she is a major creative force in the food industry.

Brendan Walsh
chef, New York NY (1987)

Walsh graduated from the Culinary Institute of America in 1980. As chef at Arizona 206, he introduced the best of the Southwest to Manhattan's East Side. He worked his magic by combining classic techniques with ideas he gleaned from travels in Europe and from experience working with chef Jeremiah Tower. Walsh's international reputation for his creative American-Southwestern cuisine was also achieved at the Arizona Cafe, which opened in 1987. He recently left Arizona 206, and has plans to open a new restaurant in Manhattan. He was chosen as one of the 10 top chefs in the country for the American Chefs' Tribute to James Beard in 1987.

Alice Waters
chef/owner, Chez Panisse Cafe and Cafe Fanny, Berkeley CA (1984)

Alice Waters received a degree in French cultural studies from the University of California, Berkeley. She traveled throughout France in 1964 and became captivated by French country cooking. In 1971 she opened Chez Panisse, serving a single, prix-fixe, French-inspired, five-course menu, and also developed a network of special food sources. Chez Panisse Cafe opened in 1980, with an a la carte menu, open kitchen and wood pizza oven, while Cafe Fanny, serving cafe au lait, finger sandwiches and wine by the glass, opened in 1984.

Waters is currently involved with issues relating to sustainable agriculture and is working on a children's cookbook.

Jonathan Waxman
chef, New York NY (1984)

A native of California, Waxman studied politics and music at the University of Nevada and University of California. He studied at the Tante Marie Cooking School in San Francisco and at L'Ecole de Cuisine La Varenne in France. Waxman worked at a restaurant in France for a summer before returning to California to work at Domaine Chandon in Napa Valley. In 1978 he became chef at Chez Panisse in Berkeley and later was chef at Michael's in Santa Monica. He moved to New York City in 1983 and opened Jams in 1984. Bud's, his second restaurant, opened in 1985 (and was sold in 1987) and Hulot's opened in 1986. Waxman opened a second Jams, in London, in 1987.

Jasper White
chef/owner, Jasper's, Boston MA (1984)

A 1973 graduate of the Culinary Institute of America, White worked as executive sous chef at the Copley Plaza Hotel, executive chef at Seasons, and general manager of the Harvard Bookstore Cafe, all in Boston. He also worked for three years as consulting executive chef for Dunfey Hotels across the country. White opened Restaurant Jasper in 1983. Today, the restaurant—officially renamed Jasper's—is firmly established among Boston's (and New England's) top eateries.

Anne Willan
president/founder, L'Ecole de Cuisine La Varenne, Paris, and Burgundy, France; president-elect, International Association of Cooking Professionals, 1990-91 (1986)

Willan was born in England, holds a master's degree in economics from Cambridge, a diploma from the London Cordon Bleu, and the Grand Diplome from Cordon Bleu in Paris. She came to the United States in 1965 to work with *Gourmet* magazine and later as food editor of the *Washington Star*. She has just published a major encyclopedia of cooking techniques, *La Varenne Pratique*.

Barry Wine
chef/owner, The Quilted Giraffe and Casual Quilted Giraffe, New York NY (1984)

Wine grew up in Wisconsin and learned to cook for his family because both his parents worked. He became a New York attorney, but eventually left the legal profession. Wine opened the popular Quilted Giraffe and Casual Quilted Giraffe in 1986. He has helped "pioneer the service charge system" in America, hoping to influence the restaurant industry to adopt the service charge and eliminate tipping. "Waiters will gain self-esteem and professionalism, restaurants will be better managed, and the whole aura of greed and the demeaning aspects of working for handouts will disappear from the restaurant dining room," he believes.

Paula Wolfert
writer and cooking instructor, New York NY (1986; Platinum Plate Award for Best Cookbook, 1989)

Wolfert's award-winning books, based on her years of living and traveling in the parts of the world she writes about, are solidly authentic. Her pages bring to life the cuisines of southwest France, Morocco and other Mediterranean regions. She travels extensively each year to teach cooking, and applauds the proliferation of new and better produce in America.

Kevin Zraly
wine director, Inhilco, New York NY (1988)

Zraly took a leave of absence from college to study winemaking, later used a six-month rail pass to tour vineyards throughout Europe. On returning home he secured a sales job with a wine distributor. A sales call to Windows on the World resulted in his appointment as cellarmaster at the age of 25. He set out to assemble a collection of more than 60,000 bottles to back up a list that is 700-plus wines strong. Twelve years later, Windows on the World sells 12,000 bottles per month, more than most large retail wine stores. Today, Zraly is wine director of Inhilco, the company that manages the complex of restaurants in the World Trade Center; he also directs the Windows on the World wine school.

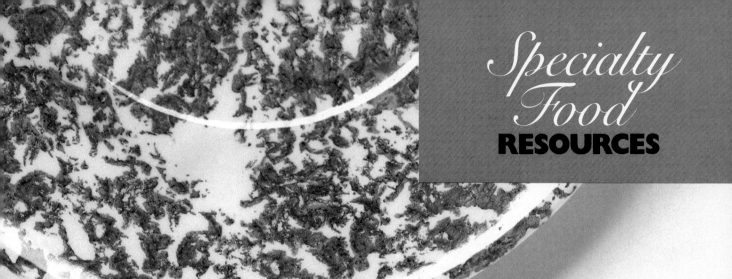

Specialty Food RESOURCES

19
Wholesale Produce Markets

22
Specialty Food Wholesalers

Beverages & Syrups; Bread, Baked Goods, Cookies, & Mixes; Condiments & Relishes; Confections, Chocolates & Hard Candy; Cheese; Coffee & Tea; Crackers, Crisps & Biscuits; Ethnic Foods; Fish & Caviar; Food Gifts & Food Decoratives; Gift Food Packaging; Grains, Rice & Pasta; Herbs, Spices, Seasonings & Flavorings; Jams, Jellies, Preserves, Honey & Syrups; Meats, Poultry & Pates; Nuts, Dried Fruits & Snack Foods; Oils, Vinegars, Salad Dressings & Marinades; Sauces & Soups

40
Specialty Food Retailers

48
Direct Mail Order Catalogs

Cheese; Chocolates & Candy; Coffee & Tea; Fish, Caviar & Seafood; Fruit & Nuts; Health Foods; Herbs & Spices; Meat & Poultry; Pastry & Baked Goods; Specialty Foods & Food Gifts; Cooks' Tools & Kitchen Accessories

53
Organic and Health Food Suppliers

Farm Products; Free Range

61
Kosher Food Suppliers

Wholesale Produce Markets

This listing of the nation's major produce markets is organized regionally, then alphabetically within each state. Some markets are wholesale only, others combine wholesale and retail. Markets may be privately owned by individuals or cooperative groups or organized as shipping points by regional or public authorities.

The list is derived from the *Green Book* Produce Market Information Directory, published annually by the National Association of Produce Market Manufacturers in association with the U.S. Department of Agriculture, which gives complete details of each market. For information about the directory or joining the association, contact the Editor, 1354 Rutherford Road, Greenville SC 29609.

There is no nationwide "umbrella" organization for the retail farmers' market operations sponsored by various regional and local authorities, and the best way to find them is through each area's chamber of commerce. The largest is the Greenmarket Farmers' Market sponsored by New York City's Council on the Environment. It operates 23 retail markets in 16 city locations and has served as a model for other groups. For information, contact Barry Benepe, Director, Greenmarket Farmers' Market, 130 East 16th Street, New York, NY 10003.

NORTHEAST

CONNECTICUT

Connecticut Regional Market
101 Reserve Road
Hartford CT 06115
203-527-5047
Contact:
Robert A. Badal, Market Manager

New Haven Food Terminal, Inc.
301 Food Terminal Plaza
New Haven CT 06511
203-562-7268
Contact:
James Lamberti, Market Manager

MASSACHUSETTS

New England Produce Center, Inc.
90 New England Produce Center
Chelsea MA 02150
617-889-2700
Contact:
Roger Pevear, Market Manager

NEW JERSEY

Newark Farmers' Market
41 Joseph Street
Newark NJ 07105
201-589-4823
Contact:
John Francavilla, Market Manager

Swedesboro Auction, Inc.
Anderson & Leahy Avenues
Swedesboro NJ 08085
609-467-0313
Contact:
John Womack, Market Manager

NEW YORK

Capital District Cooperative, Inc. (Menands Market)
Broadway (Menands Village)
Albany NY 12204
518-465-1023
Contact:
Ralph Miller, Market Manager

Hunts Point Terminal Produce Cooperative Market
Halleck and Spoffords Streets
Bronx NY 10474
212-542-2944
Contact:
Joseph P. Cvetas, Market Manager

Niagara Frontier Growers' Cooperative Market
Clinton Street & Bailey Avenue
Buffalo NY 14206
716-822-2466
Contact:
Les Schummer, Market Manager

Niagara Frontier Food Terminal
Clinton Street & Bailey Avenue
Buffalo NY 14206
716-826-4844
Contact:
Jay H. Wattles, President

Genesee Valley Regional Market Authority
900 Jefferson Road
Rochester NY 14623
716-424-4600
Contact:
William Mulligan, Administrator

Rochester Public Market
280 North Union Street
Rochester NY 14607
716-428-6907
Contact:
Lewis Panzarella, Market Manager

Central New York Regional Market Authority
2100 Park Street
Syracuse NY 13208
315-422-8647
Contact:
Larry S. Cimino, Market Manager

PENNSYLVANIA

Philadelphia Fresh Food Terminal Corporation
3301 South Galloway Street
256 Produce Building
Philadelphia PA 19148
215-336-3003
Contact:
Ray Farber, Market Manager

Wholesale Produce Market of Pittsburgh
1903 Penn Avenue
Pittsburgh PA 15222
412-391-8711
Contact:
Earle Guyer, Secretary

Providence Produce Market
22 Harris Avenue
Providence RI 02903
401-331-2955
Contact:
Charles Loring, Market Manager

SOUTH

ALABAMA

Jefferson County Truck Growers' Association—Farmers' Market
414 Finley Avenue
Birmingham AL 35204
205-251-8737
Contact:
Bert Swann, Market Manager

Montgomery State Farmers' Market
1655 Federal Drive
Montgomery AL 36107
205-261-5350
Contact:
Ben B. Hitch Jr., Manager

FLORIDA

Florida City/State Farmers' Market
Florida City FL 33034
305-247-1727
Contact:
Joe Mitchell, Market Manager

Fort Pierce State Farmers' Market
P.O. Box 866
Fort Pierce FL 33050
305-468-3917
Contact:
Peter Serra, Market Manager

Immokalee State Farmers' Market
424 New Market Road
Immokalee FL 33934
813-657-3112
Contact:
Jim Warner Jr., Market Manager

Jacksonville Farmers' Market
1780 West Beaver Street
Jacksonville FL 32209
904-354-2821
Contact:
Jean Bowman, Market Manager

The Miami Produce Center
2141 13th Avenue NW
Miami FL 33142
305-325-8975
Contact:
John Ballard, Market Manager

Plant City, State Farmers' Market
P.O. Box 637
Plant City FL 33566
813-752-7446
Contact:
Ed Musser, Market Manager

Pompano State Farmers' Market
Administration Building, Suite 4
Pompano Beach FL 33060
305-946-6570
Contact:
Max D. Goza, Market Manager

Gadsden County State Farmers' Market
P.O. Box 384
Quincy FL 32351
904-627-6484
Contact:
Ron Rentz, Market Manager

Sanford State Farmers' Market
P.O. Box 908
Sanford FL 32271
305-322-1293
Contact:
Sam Brashear, Market Manager

Tampa Wholesale Produce Market, Inc.
P.O. Box 11027
Tampa FL 33630
813-237-3314
Contact:
Tony Ippolito, General Manager

GEORGIA

Atlanta State Farmers' Market
16 Forest Parkway
Forest Park GA 30050
404-366-6910
Contact:
Mike Bonner, Market Manager

Augusta State Farmers' Market
1150 Fifth Street
Augusta GA 30901
404-721-3004
Contact:
Dane Stanford, Market Manager

Cairo State Farmers' Market
Pelham Highway
Cairo GA 31728
912-377-4504

Columbus State Farmers' Market
318 Tenth Avenue
Columbus GA 31901
404-828-3004
Contact:
Taylor Lee, Market Manager

Cordele State Farmers' Market
U.S. 41 North
P.O. Box 896
Cordele GA 31015
912-273-2161

Macon State Farmers' Market
2055 Eisenhower Parkway
Macon GA 31206
912-742-8403
Contact:
Connie Mathis, Market Manager

Moultrie State Farmers' Market
Quitman Highway 33 South
Moultrie GA 31768
912-985-3602
Contact:
Rex C. Gay, Market Manager

Savannnah State Farmers' Market
701 U.S. Highway 80 West
Savannah GA 31408
912-964-6351
Contact:
John Parsons, Market Manager

Thomasville State Farmer's Market
502 Smith Avenue
Thomasville GA 31792
912-226-3988
Contact:
Don Butler, Market Manager

KENTUCKY

Louisville Produce Terminal
4601 Jennings Lane
Louisville KY 40218
502-454-3740
Contact:
Vernon B. Austin, Market Manager

MARYLAND

Maryland Wholesale Produce Market
7460 Conowingo Avenue
Jessup MD 20794
301-799-3880
Contact:
George Maroulis, Market Manager

MISSISSIPPI

Mississippi Farmers' Central Market
P.O. Box 4357
Jackson MS 39205
601-354-6573
Contact:
Marion Ueltschey, Market Manager

NORTH CAROLINA

Western North Carolina Farmers' Market
570 Brevard Road
Asheville NC 28806
704-253-1691
Contact:
Clayton Davis, Market Manager

State Farmers' Market
1401 Hodges Street
Raleigh NC 27604
919-733-7417
Contact:
Charles Edwards, Market Manager

SOUTH CAROLINA

Columbia State Farmers' Market
P.O. Box 13504
Columbia SC 29202
803-253-4041
Contact:
Lee Sowell, Market Manager

Greenville State Farmers' Market
1354 Rutherford Road
Greenville SC 29609
803-244-4023
Contact:
Jack Watson, Market Manager

TENNESSEE

Farmers' Market/Shelby County Growers' Association, Inc.
814 Scott Street
Memphis TN 38112
901-327-8828
Contact:
Bill Brown, Market Manager

WEST VIRGINIA

Charleston Farmers' Market
P.O. Box 3441
Charleston WV 25334
304-348-0185
Contact:
Henry Bender, Market Manager

MIDWEST

ILLINOIS

South Water Market
108 South Water Market
Chicago IL 60608
312-421-1176
Contact:
Roger Murphy, Market Master
President

INDIANA

Producer Realty Corporation
Indianapolis Produce
Terminal Market
4101 Massachusetts Avenue
Indianapolis IN 46204
317-547-3501
Contact:
Cosma Mascari, President

MICHIGAN

Benton Harbor Fruit Market, Inc.
P.O. Box 127
Benton Harbor MI 48022
616-925-0681
Contact:
Martin Bass, Market Manager

Detroit Produce Terminal
7201 West Fort Street
Detroit MI 48209
313-841-8700
Contact:
Arthur McHardy, Market Manager

City Market
Cedar & Schiawassee Streets
Lansing MI 48933
517-483-4300
Contact:
Patrick Miller, Market Manager

MINNESOTA

Kasota Fruit Terminal
754 Kasota Avenue
Minneapolis MN 55414
612-378-1234
Contact:
Ray Bergin Jr., Manager

MISSOURI

Kansas City, Missouri, Terminal Market
Retail Market Building
20 East Fifth Street
Kansas City MO 64106
Contact:
Charles Donnici, Market Manager

St. Louis Produce Market, Inc.
45 Produce Row
St.Louis MO 63102
314-621-4383
Contact:
Joseph Chapo, Market Manager

OHIO

The Plum Street Market
Plum Street (bounded by
Second Street and Ohio River)
Cincinnati OH 45202

Northern Ohio Food Terminal, Inc.
3800 Orange Avenue
Cleveland OH 44115
216-881-5100
Contact:
Robert Gwinner, Market Manager

SOUTHWEST

TEXAS

Dallas Market
South Pearl & South Central
Expressway
Dallas TX 75201
214-670-5879
Contact:
Ted Lanford, Administrator
Arnold Garza, Market Manager

Houston Produce Center
3144 Produce Row
Houston TX 77023
713-928-2481
Contact:
George Minton, Market Manager

San Antonio Produce Terminal Market
1500 South Zarzamora Street
San Antonio TX 78207
Contact:
Ivan Grabhorn, Market Manager

WEST

CALIFORNIA

City Market of Los Angeles (Ninth Street)
1057 South San Pedro Street
Los Angeles CA 90015
213-746-0646
Contact:
Peter M. Fleming, Market Manager

Los Angeles Union Terminal, Inc. (Seventh Street)
746 South Central Avenue,
Suite 250
Los Angeles CA 90021
213-627-9767
Contact:
John Armenta, Vice President and
General Manager

Los Angeles Wholesale Produce Market
1601 East Olympic Boulevard
Los Angeles CA 90021
213-629-2132
Contact:
Warren Sinclair, Market Manager

San Francisco Produce Terminal
2095 Jerrold Avenue
San Francisco CA 94124
415-826-7133
Contact:
George Constant, Market Manager

Golden Gate Produce Terminal
131 Terminal Court
South San Francisco CA 94080
415-583-4887
Contact:
Primo R. Repetto, Market Manager

Specialty Food Wholesalers

Specialty foods are usually the more unusual foods that represent new, ground-breaking trends, such as bagel crisps, for example, which later move on to win general acceptance. This selection of major wholesalers in the field has been made by Elaine Yannuzzi, founder of Expression unltd., to achieve as wide a variety as possible within a broad geographic spread. The companies are classified under the specialty that best describes them, but this does not imply that they are limited to that particular specialty, and many firms listed under one classification often stock or manufacture other products as well.

The industry is represented by the Wholesale Division of the National Association for the Specialty Food Trade, Inc., 215 Park Avenue South, New York NY 10003, from whom more information is obtainable.

A food producer would contact a wholesaler to arrange to distribute a particular food being manufactured; a retailer would contact a wholesaler to purchase foods to sell on the retail market. The manufacturer of a product sets a quantity price; the product is stocked by a wholesaler, who adds a markup for selling and distributing it to the retailers; retail markups vary with store type and location. Most wholesalers will accept orders with a quantity discount from any legitimate food business with good credit.

BEVERAGES & SYRUPS

Evian Waters of France, Inc.
600 West Putnam Avenue
Greenwich CT 06830
203-629-3642
Contact:
David Daniel

First American Marketing Group, Ltd.
P.O. Box 347
East Rochester NY 14445
716-385-1184
Contact:
Kenneth Gauntlett

International Beverages, Inc.
P.O. Box 1598
Ogden UT 84402
801-627-1813
Contact:
Jack Elwoods

The John C. Meier Grape Juice Company
6955 Plainfield Pike
Cincinnati OH 45236
513-891-2900
Contact:
Glouster F. Strouse

Old Tyme Soft Drinks, Inc.
933 Route 23
Pompton Plains NJ 07444
201-839-5454
Contact:
Robert W. Tuckman

BREAD, BAKED GOODS, COOKIES & MIXES

Bahlsen, Inc.
1 Quality Lane
Cary NC 27512
919-469-0647
Contact:
Henry E. Witte

Byrd Cookie Company, Inc.
2233 Norwood Avenue
P.O. Box 13086
Savannah GA 31406
912-355-1716
Contact:
Stephanie Curl

Cafe Beaujolais Bakery
P.O. Box 730
Mendocino CA 95460
707-964-0292
Contact:
Margaret S. Fox

The Cake Stylists, Inc.
56-64 58th Place
Maspeth NY 11378
718-894-3494
Contact:
Glenn R. Goodman

The CPG/Goldrush Sourdough Mix, Victorian Pantry/Polly Jean's
4561 Mission Gorge Place, Suite K
San Diego CA 92120
619-283-5429
Contact:
Michele Vasilescu

Cookie Man Company
787 Susquehanna Avenue
P.O. Box 144
Franklin Lakes NJ 07417
201-891-8070
Contact:
Robert Kurschner

Country Epicure, Inc.
525 Executive Boulevard
Elmsford NY 10523
914-347-3737
Contact:
Ray Petrino

Desserts by David Glass, Inc.
140-150 Huyshope Avenue
Hartford CT 06106
203-525-0345
Contact:
David Glass

Di Camillo Baking Company, Inc.
811 Linwood Avenue
Niagara Falls NY 14305
716-282-2341
Contact:
Michael J. Di Camillo

Dinkel's Bakery, Inc.
3329 North Lincoln Avenue
Chicago IL 60657
312-281-7300
Contact:
Norman J. Dinkel Jr.

Downey's Products, Inc.
510 Thornall Street
Edison NJ 08837
201-549-5666
Contact:
Steven Weiss

Dufour Pastry Kitchens, Inc.
808 Washington Street
New York NY 10014
212-929-2800
Contact:
Judith Arnold

Dufour Pastry Kitchens produces "elegant savory pastries" and is "one of the best sources for top-quality puff pastry," according to *The New York Times*. The finest chefs seek out the individualized and creative foods we develop in our kitchens. We make puff-pastry dough sheets; finely prepared hors d'oeuvres, appetizers and meals; unfilled tart shells; vol-au-vents. Our products are frozen ready-to-bake, available in both institutional and retail packaging.

The Famous Pacific Dessert Company
420 East Denny Way
Seattle WA 98122
206-328-1950
Contact:
Margot Narver
Michael Mooney

Food of Our Own Design
1988 Springfield Avenue
Maplewood NJ 07040
201-762-0985
Contact:
Judith Arbaugh-Garbarini

French Meadow Bakery
2610 Lindale Avenue South
Minneapolis MN 55408
612-870-4740
Contact:
Lynn Gordon

Jake's Famous Products, Inc.
4910 North Basin
Portland OR 97217
503-226-1420
Contact:
Ross A. Hawkins

John Wm. Macy's CheeseSticks
410 East 13th Street
New York NY 10009
212-260-7667
Contact:
John Macy

Unlike extruded, homogeneous breadsticks, John Wm. Macy's Cheese-Sticks are prepared from a laminated dough which is layered and folded repeatedly and then hand rolled to preserve the sumptuous striation of cheeses, cayenne butter and sourdough. The result is a crispy twice-baked morsel of exceptional flavor which has become a favorite of patrons of some of New York's finest hotels, restaurants and specialty food shops.

La Piccolina & Company, Inc.
2834 Franklin Street
Avondale GA 30002
404-296-1624
Contact:
Olympia F. Manning

La Tempesta
425 Littlefield Avenue
South San Francisco CA 94080
415-873-8944
Contact:
Bonnie Tempesta

Love & Quiches, Ltd.
178 Hanse Avenue
Freeport NY 11520
516-623-8800
Contact:
Susan Axelrod

Ms. Desserts, Inc.
4103 Amos Avenue
Baltimore MD 21215
301-358-9090
800-423-6703
Contact:
Jeffrey Peisach

Northwest Specialty Bakers, Ltd.
P.O. Box 25240
Portland OR 97225
503-643-2351
Contact:
Scott MacCaskill

Parco Foods, Inc.
2200 West 138th Street
Blue Island IL 60406
708-371-9200
800-323-5635
Contact:
Charles A. Hoch

Plaza Sweets Bakery
178 South Fulton Street
White Plains NY 10606
914-997-0220
Contact:
Jo-Anne Schoenfeld

Rubschlager Baking Corporation
3220 West Grand Avenue
Chicago IL 60651
312-826-1245
Contact:
Paul A. Rubschlager

Specialty breads from Rubschlager Baking Corporation: Cocktail loaves in rye and pumpernickel; eight varieties of European-style squares; three giant, 18-pound loaves; portion packs of individually wrapped bread slices. Bread shelf life: four weeks, room temperature; six weeks, refrigerated; minimum six months, frozen.

New from Rubschlager: Frozen dinner and sandwich rolls, bulk pack and individually wrapped. Zero cholesterol, high fiber, U pareve.

A quality product since 1913.

Stefano's Gourmet Products
5 Tulip Street
P.O. Box 250
Huntington NY 11743
516-754-0375
Contact:
Enrico Piraino

Turf Cheesecake Corporation
158 South 12th Avenue
Mt. Vernon NY 10550
212-654-1622
Contact:
Richard J. Hoffman

Vie de France Corporation
8201 Greensboro Drive,
Suite 1200
McLean VA 22102
703-442-9205
Contact:
Dyan Maiale

The Well-Bred Loaf, Inc.
200 Brenner Drive
Congers NY 10920
914-268-3500
Contact:
Steven Caccavo

Wolferman's
8900 Marshall Drive
Lenexa KS 66215
913-888-4499
Contact:
Peet Crissey

Yohay Baking Company, Inc.
75 Grand Avenue
Brooklyn NY 11205
718-857-4514
Contact:
Leonard Yohay

CONDIMENTS & RELISHES

Annie's Enterprises, Inc.
Foster Hill Road
North Calais VT 05650
802-456-8866
Contact:
Ann Christopher

Chalif, Inc.
P.O. Box 27220
Wyndmoor PA 19118
215-233-2023
Contact:
Nicholas B. Thomas

**Miss Scarlett,
Division of Rhett, Inc.**
P.O. Box 1488
Burlingame CA 94011
415-342-9234
415-340-9600
Contact:
Peggy E. Luper

Weathervane Foods, Inc.
15 Linscott Road
Woburn MA 01801
617-935-5458
Contact:
Harold G. Pratt

CONFECTIONS, CHOCOLATES & HARD CANDY

Acme Candy Company, Inc.
4839 Don Drive
Dallas TX 75247
214-634-2825
800-882-NUTS
Contact:
Malcolm S. Cohen

**Allied International Corporation/
European Chocolate Shops**
P.O. Box 898
Newington VA 22122
703-550-5507
Contact:
Chad Akhavan

Andre Prost, Inc.
P.O. Box AX
Old Saybrook CT 06475
203-388-0838
800-243-0897
Contact:
Charles Landrey

Callebaut
1 Northbrook Place
5 Revere Drive, Suite 200
Northbrook IL 60062
708-272-4460
Contact:
Richard Callebaut

The Candy Jar
2065 Oakdale Avenue
San Francisco CA 94124
415-550-8846
Contact:
Maria Stacho

Chipurnoi Incorporated
Main Street
Sharon CT 06069
203-364-0870
800-982-9002
Contact:
Judy Schmidt

Cocolat, Inc.
2547 Ninth Street
Berkeley CA 94710
415-843-1182
Contact:
Glen T. Ishikata

Dae-Julie, Inc.
4500 West Dickens Avenue
Chicago IL 60639
312-342-9100
Contact:
David E. Babiarz

Deer Park Baking Company
South Egg Harbor Road
P.O. Box 500
Hammonton NJ 08037
609-561-2900
Contact:
Harvey Green

Fabio Imports
P.O. Box 1009
Bonsall CA 92003
619-726-7040
Contact:
Rosa Marie Peraro

**George C. Brown's Biscuit
and Confections, Inc.**
1621 Eastchester Road
Bronx NY 10461
212-824-5610
Contact:
George C. Brown

Ghirardelli Chocolate Company
1111 139th Avenue
San Leandro CA 94578
415-483-6970
Contact:
Andrew G. Nestler

Godiva Chocolatier, Inc.
260 Madison Avenue
New York NY 10016
212-951-2883
Contact:
Robert J. Smith

Go-Lightly Candy Company
35 Hillside Avenue
Hillside NJ 07205
201-926-2300
800-524-1304
Contact:
Ted J. Cohen

Herman Goelitz, Inc.
2400 North Watney Way
Fairfield CA 94533
707-428-2800
Contact:
Peter F. Cain

Jacobs Suchard Brach, Inc.
4656 West Kinzie Street
Chicago IL 60644
312-626-1200
Contact:
Colleen McGrath

Jaret International, Inc.
2670 Stillwell Avenue
Brooklyn NY 11224
718-946-1810
Contact:
Wilhelm Kraus

Jerbeau Chocolate Classics
2697 Lavery Court, Suite 19
Newbury Park CA 91320
805-499-0071
Contact:
Katalin A. Christopher

Kencraft, Inc.
119 East 200 North
Alpine UT 84004
801-756-6916
Contact:
Marlene G. Matheson

**Kopper's Chocolate
Specialty Company, Inc.**
39 Clarkson Street
New York NY 10014
212-243-0220
800-325-0026
Contact:
Leslye Alexander

Kron Chocolatier, Inc.
241 Post Road
Milford CT 06460
203-877-6575
Contact:
John H. Schiering

Krum's Chocolatiers
4 Dexter Plaza
P.O. Box 1020
Pearl River NY 10965
914-735-5100
Contact:
Ron Krum

Le Chocolatier Manon
872 Madison Avenue
New York NY 10021
212-288-8088
Contact:
Gary Woods

Lynard Company, Inc.
15 Maple Tree Avenue
Stamford CT 06906
203-323-0231
Contact:
H. Flaster

Lindt & Sprungli (USA), Inc.
777 West Putnam Avenue
Greenwich CT 06830
203-531-5001
800-338-0839
Contact:
Richard Hiera

M-B Hard Candies, Inc.
1859 South 55th Avenue
Cicero IL 60650
708-242-4469
Contact:
Warren A. Miller

**Madelaine Chocolate
Novelties, Inc.**
96-03 Beach Channel Drive
Rockaway Beach NY 11693
718-945-1500
800-322-1505
Contact:
Joan L. Sweeting

Marich Confectionery Company
65 Hangar Way
Watsonville CA 95076
408-728-3381
800-624-7055
Contact:
Richard L. Shaffer

Moreau, Inc.
384 Oyster Point Boulevard,
Suite 3
South San Francisco CA 94080
415-588-5417
Contact:
Barbara Graves

The Multiflex Company
455 Braen Avenue
Wyckoff NJ 07481
201-447-3888
Contact:
Ralph Keller

Neuhaus (USA), Inc.
2 Secatoag Avenue
Port Washington NY 11050
516-883-7400
Contact:
Sandy Sthandier

**Perugina Chocolates
& Confections, Inc.**
450 Huyler Street
South Hackensack NJ 07606
201-641-3770
Contact:
Joseph Dattoli

**The San Francisco
Chocolate Company**
55 Rodgers Street
San Francisco CA 94103
415-558-9995
800-858-4888
Contact:
Rilla Ginsberg

Sheila Kaye Candies
P.O. Box 250107,
Lefferts Station
Brooklyn NY 11225
718-756-4515
Contact:
Sherry Edwab

Stichler Products, Inc.
522 Chestnut Street
P.O. Box 227
Reading PA 19603
215-374-2794
Contact:
Martin A. Deutschman

The Thompson Candy Company
80 South Vine Street
Meriden CT 06450
203-235-2541
Contact:
Jeffrey H. White

William A. Greca Company
371 Seventh Avenue, Suite 12-U
New York NY 10001
212-947-6150
212-947-6061
Contact:
William A. Greca

CHEESE

Anco Foods Corporation
149 New Dutch Lane
Fairfield NJ 07006
201-575-9120
Contact:
Terry De Amicis

Auricchio Cheese, Inc.
5810 Highway North
Denmark WI 54208
414-863-2123
Contact:
Errico Auricchio

Battaglia & Company, Inc.
140 Route 17 North
Paramus NJ 07652
201-265-4500
Contact:
Robert Quattrone

Bel Paese Sales Company, Inc.
445 Brick Boulevard, Suite 203
Bricktown NJ 08723
201-477-3700
Contact:
Angelo Dominioni

Besnier USA
180 Madison Avenue, 18th Floor
New York NY 10016
212-696-9090
Contact:
John D. Wissner Jr.

**Bongrain International
(American) Corporation**
1190 Route 22
P.O. Box 1161
Mountainside NJ 07092
201-654-8330
Contact:
Roland L. Schinbeckler

Bresse Bleu, Inc.
North 2002, Highway 26
Watertown WI 53094
414-261-3036
800-262-3886
Contact:
Bruno Bardet

Bridel USA
Paramus Plaza
12 Route 17 North, Suite 315
Paramus NJ 07652
201-587-9555
Contact:
Philippe Duleyrie

The Coach Farm
Mill Hill Road, R.R. 1
P.O. Box 445
Pine Plains NY 12567
518-398-5325
518-398-5326
Contact:
Miles Cahn

Continental Cheese Corporation
8 Harrison Street
New York NY 10013
212-966-2740
Contact:
Bruce Abramson

Crystal Food Import Corporation
245 Sumner Street
East Boston MA 02128
617-569-7500
Contact:
L. Dechet

Dorman-Roth Foods, Inc.
14 Empire Boulevard
Moonachie NJ 07074
201-440-3600
Contact:
Rick Boutillier

Emmental Cheese Corporation
175 Clearbrook Road
Elmsford NY 10523
914-592-3820
Contact:
H. J. Gasser

Epicure Foods Corporation
31 Evans Terminal
Hillside NJ 07205
201-527-8080
Contact:
Damir Drezga

Fleur de Lait Foods, Ltd.
254 South Custer Avenue
New Holland PA 17557
717-354-4411
Contact:
Joe Wodyka

Kaukauna Cheese
P.O. Box 1974
Kaukauna WI 54130
414-788-3524
Contact:
Robert P. Gilbert

**Long Island Cheese
Specialties, Inc.**
190 Adams Avenue
Hauppauge NY 11788
516-231-1050
Contact:
Joseph Gellert

Love At First Bite
1067 South Railroad Avenue
San Mateo CA 94402
415-571-1991
Contact:
Donald Weck

Mozzarella Company
2944 Elm Street
Dallas TX 75226
214-741-4072
Contact:
Paula S. Lambert

When Paula Lambert couldn't find the cheeses she had loved while living in Europe, she returned to Italy to study cheesemaking, then opened a cheese factory in Dallas. Since 1982 the Mozzarella Company has produced an array of specialty cheeses handmade from fresh milk (cow, goat and sheep), including: Italian cheeses (mozzarella, ricotta, mascarpone, scamorza, crescenza); fresh cheeses (cream and goat cheeses, fromage blanc, queso fresco,

T he Bridel family began to develop the art of cheesemaking back in 1848. Art, as the saying goes, is eternal.

Those who have inherited the cheesemaker's art from Monsieur Bridel are well aware that the same qualities can be found in America's Dairyland. It is this common bond that has brought the tradition-bound French producer to seek out Wisconsin's milk and cream for its products.

Bridel's newest product, **Père Brie**, is a top of the line 60-percent, double-creme soft-ripened cheese. It is available in three sizes and three flavors - plain, herb and peppercorn.

Bridel's Wisconsin facility also produces a traditional **camembert** but has added that continental touch to three all-American favorites: cheddar, jack and colby cheeses.

Bridel has also made it much simpler for chefs who want to top off their menus in the elegant European manner: it produces traditional **crème fraiche** in its Wisconsin plant.

The cheesemaker's art: eternal, indeed.

For more information about Bridel cheeses, call Philippe Duleyrie at (201) 587-9555.

Oaxacan string cheese); Southwestern flavored caciottas; and full-flavored aged taleggio, montasio and pecorino.

Pollio Dairy Products
120 Mineola Boulevard
Mineola NY 11501
516-741-8000
800-876-5596
Contact:
Kathleen Horton

The San Francisco International Cheese Imports
1908 Innes Street
San Francisco CA 94124
415-648-5252
Contact:
Phillip S. Quattrociocchi

Stauffer Cheese, Inc.
2819 Highway F South
Blue Mounds WI 53517
608-437-5598
Contact:
Albert P. Keller

Swissrose International, Inc.
650 New Country Road
Secaucus NJ 07094
201-330-0005
Contact:
William S. Hennings

Importer and distributor of fine cheeses from around the world, Swissrose offers over 50 years of experience in selection, storage, distribution and merchandising of specialty cheese. The product line consists of more than 350 items from 20 countries, including Italy, France, Holland, England, Denmark, Switzerland, Germany, Austria and the USA. Available through distributors and specialty stores nationwide or on a direct-order basis. Shipped via our trucks or common carriers.

Tholstrup Cheese USA, Inc.
P.O. Box 4194
Warren NJ 07060
201-756-6320
Contact:
Vince Staiger

Walker Foods, Inc.
66 Fadem Road
Springfield NJ 07081
201-467-9400
Contact:
Ben Moskowitz

COFFEE & TEA

Barrie House Gourmet Coffee
216 South 13th Avenue
P.O. Box 4444
Mt. Vernon NY 10550
914-664-3626
Contact:
Daniel Kopf

Barrows Tea Company
142 Arnold Street
New Bedford MA 02740
508-990-2745
Contact:
Samuel Barrows

Barrows Tea Company imports only the finest teas and packages them under the **Barrows** brand name. Currently available are: an FTGFOP.1 Single Estate/Unblended *Darjeeling* (highest grade), an *American Breakfast* (Assam and Ceylon blend), and a *Japanese Fine Grade Sencha*. Barrows tea products are sold in many of the leading specialty food stores in America, and in a few select hotels and restaurants.

Boston Tea Company
520 Secaucus Road
Secaucus NJ 07094
201-865-0200
800-631-3195
Contact:
Andrew Jacobs

Caravali Coffees
1301 First Avenue
Seattle WA 98101
206-447-0532
800-647-0647
Contact:
Bart Wilson

Coffee Bean International, Inc.
2181 Northwest Nicolai Street
Portland OR 97210
503-227-4490
Contact:
Gary Talboy

Community Kitchens
2151 Riverside North
Baton Rouge LA 70802
504-381-3900
Contact:
Roland R. Saurage

Eastern Shore Tea Company, Inc.
P.O. Box 84
Church Hill MD 21623
301-556-6676
Contact:
Janice W. Burns

Fairwinds Gourmet Coffee Company
Route 3A
P.O. 1294
Concord NH 03301
800-645-4515
Contact:
Peter Donovan

First Colony Coffee & Tea Company
218 West 22nd Street
P.O. Box 11005
Norfolk VA 23517
804-622-2224
800-4466-8555
Contact:
J. Gill Brockenbrough Jr.

Gillies Coffee Comapny
160 Bleecker Street
New York NY 10012
212-614-0900
Contact:
Donald N. Schoenholt

Grace Tea Company, Ltd.
50 West 17th Street
New York NY 10011
212-255-2935
Contact:
Richard G. Sanders

Grosvenor Marketing, Ltd.
East 210 Route 4
Paramus NJ 07652
201-843-1022
Contact:
P. M. Clode

Hena, Inc.
383 Third Avenue
Brooklyn NY 11215
718-596-7649
Contact:
Robert J. Shedlock

Jablum USA
Route 3A
P.O. Box 1294
Concord NH 03301
603-224-5381
Contact:
Michael J. Sullivan

Kona Kai Farms
1824 Fifth Street
Berkeley CA 94710
415-486-8334
800-222-KONA
Contact:
Michael Norton

McNulty's Specialty Coffee & Tea Company
109 Christopher Street
New York NY 10014
212-242-3320
Contact:
Victor Stein

Schapira's Coffee & Tea Company
Factory Lane
P.O. Box 327
Pine Plains NY 12567
518-398-7109
Contact:
Joel Schapira

Stash Tea Company
P.O. Box 910
Portland OR 97207
503-684-4482
Contact:
Steven Smith

Superior Coffee & Foods Company
990 Supreme Drive
Bensenville IL 60106
708-8601-1400
800-323-6179
Contact:
Charlie McBride

Trade Marcs Group, Inc.
55 Nassau Avenue
Brooklyn NY 11222
718-387-9696
Contact:
Marc G. Greenberg

Van Cortlandt Coffee Corporation
1127 North Halsted Street
Chicago IL 60622
312-280-7632
Contact:
Ellen Jordan-Reidy

White Coffee Corporation
18-35 38th Street
Long Island City NY 11105
718-204-7900
800-221-0140
Contact:
Angel Fontanez

CRACKERS, CRISPS & BISCUITS

Bremner Biscuit Company
4600 Joliet Street
Denver CO 80239
303-371-8180
Contact:
Edward G. Bremner

H.S.F. Enterprises
847 East 52nd Street
Brooklyn NY 11203
718-629-6502
Contact:
Herb Ferleger

Hye Quality Bakery
2222 Santa Clara
Fresno CA 93721
209-445-1511
Contact:
Sammy Ganimian

J. J. Bredflats, Inc.
1776 East Chester Road
Bronx NY 10461
212-518-2706
Contact:
John Curcio

Jacquet USA
46 Central Avenue
Farmingdale NY 11735
516-293-4030
Contact:
Francois Bogrand

Lavosh-Hawaii
134 Chapala Street
Santa Barbara CA 93101
805-965-2265
Contact:
Adrienne O'Donnell

Nejaime's of the Berkshires, Inc.
5 South Street
P.O. Box 497
Stockbridge MA 01262
413-298-4246
Contact:
Nabih Nejaime

The Original Trenton Cracker Company
54 North Union Street
P.O. Box 186
Lambertville NJ 08530
609-397-8060
800-851-0395
Contact:
Albert M. Van Wagenen

The Seckinger-Lee Company, Inc.
P.O. Box 14263
Atlanta GA 30324
404-231-4039
Contact:
Lee Bufford

ETHNIC FOOD

American Roland Food Corporation
71 West 23rd Street
New York NY 10010
212-741-8799
Contact:
Charles Scheidt

Atalanta Corporation
Atalanta Plaza
Elizabeth NJ 07206
201-351-8000
Contact:
Jim Marsh

Bel Canto Fancy Foods
555 Second Avenue
New York NY 10016
212-689-4433
Italian
Contact:
Angela Zambelli

Bel Canto Fancy Foods is an importer and distributor of domestic and imported specialty foods. The extensive line of products includes cheeses, fresh filled pastas, extra-virgin olive oils, olives, dried porcini mushrooms, confections, vinegars, sun-dried tomatoes and Arborio rice. Bel Canto imports many of these products under its Bel Aria brand label.

Bertolli USA, Inc.
1 Harmon Plaza
P.O. Box 2617
Secaucus NJ 07096
201-863-2088
Italian
Contact:
William C. Monroe

Bewley Irish Imports
606 Howard Road
West Chester PA 19380
215-696-2682
Irish
Contact:
Jo Bewley

Blue Corn Connection
3825 Academy Parkway South NE
Albuquerque NM 87109
505-344-9768
Tex-Mex
Contact:
Ross W. Edwards

Caltex Foods, Division of Caltex Trading, Inc.
9045 Eton Avenue, Suite A
Canoga Park CA 91304
818-700-8657
800-5-CALTEX
Israeli
Contact:
Mehrdad Pakravan

Casbah/Sahara Natural Foods, Inc.
2820 Eighth Street
Berkeley CA 94710
415-548-1868
Middle Eastern
Contact:
Dimitri Cados

Christopher Reeves Brookes Company
3006 29th Street SW, Suite F
Tumwater WA 98502
206-352-5051
English
Contact:
Sandra B. Worrell

Highest quality specialty foods. Taylors Teas, skillfully blended by master tea blenders from Chinese and Indian teas, then packaged beautifully. Ashbourne Bakery uses pure ingredients and recipes handed down for generations to make their Gingerbread, Shortbreads and Butter Cookies. Other outstanding products include Jon's Butter Fudge and Toffee, Devon Country Preserves and Marmalades, Cole's Plum Pudding, Kantolan Crackers and Fuller's Hard Candies. We ship daily. No minimum order. Color catalog and free tea sample.

Commerce Foods, Inc.
1133 Avenue of the Americas,
Suite 3718
New York NY 10036
212-398-0991
Contact:
Steve Roth

Cowan & Fransman, Division of Jaret International, Inc.
339 Buena Vista Road
New City NY 10956
914-634-4038
Contact:
Julian Cowan

Dana Import
P.O. Box 718
Pine Brook NJ 07058
201-575-6299
Scandinavian
Contact:
Erik Johansen

Dean & DeLuca Imports, Inc.
560 Broadway
New York NY 10012
212-431-1691
Contact:
Eugenio Pozzolini

De Choix Specialty Foods Company
58-25 52nd Avenue
Woodside NY 11377
718-507-8080
800-DE-CHOIX
Contact:
Gene Kaplan

Delftree Shiitake
234 Union Street
North Adams MA 01247
413-664-4907
Contact:
Bill Greenwald

Desert Rose Salsa Corporation
P.O. Box 5391
Tucson AZ 85703
602-743-0450
Mexican
Contact:
Patricia Swidler

Dolefam Corporation
2000 K Street NW, Suite 401
Washington DC 20006
202-775-9715
Contact:
Vincent Dole

EFCO Importers
P.O. Box 741
Jenkintown PA 19046
215-885-8597
Contact:
Edith Friedland

Elki Corporation
6306 215th Street SW
Mountlake Terrace WA 98043
206-774-6344
Danish
Contact:
Gunnar Lie

The El Paso Chili Company
100 Ruhlin Court
El Paso TX 79922
915-544-3434
Mexican
Contact:
W. Park Kerr

Estee Corporation
169 Lackawanna Avenue
Parsipanny NJ 07054
201-335-1000
Oriental
Contact:
Rick Krall

Europa Foods, Ltd.
170 Commerce Drive
Hauppauge NY 11788
516-273-0011
800-521-0141
Contact:
Leon Wechsler

European Imports, Ltd.
1334 West Fulton Street
Chicago IL 60607
312-226-8060
800-323-3464
Contact:
Seymour Binstein

Ferrero Specialty Food Division
410 Commerce Boulevard
Carlstadt NJ 07072
201-460-9266
Italian
Contact
Myrna Alperin

Finnfoods, Inc.
2355 Waukegan Road,
Building B, Suite S-250
Bannockburn IL 60015
708-940-7500
Finnish
Contact:
Terro Vahakayla

Foah Enterprises, Inc.
1300 Post Road, Suite 102
Fairfield CT 06430
203-254-7008
Italian
Contact:
Mario L. Foah

Frieda's Finest Produce Specialties
P.O. Box 58752
Los Angeles CA 90058
Contact:
Karen Caplan

Gerbeaud, Inc.
217 East 85th Street, Suite 348
New York NY 10028
212-628-2692
Contact:
Edward Weiss

The Gilway Company Limited
299 Forest Avenue
Paramus NJ 07652
201-262-6766
English
Contact:
Jim McGilloway

Gourmet America, Inc.
937 Main Street
South Weymouth MA 02190
617-337-3140
Contact:
Linda S. Luke

Haddon House Food Products, Inc.
P.O. Box 907
Medford NJ 08055
609-654-7901
Contact:
Joseph Kuder

Haram-Christensen Corporation
303 Veterans Boulevard
Carlstadt NJ 07072
201-507-8544
Contact:
Walter Seifert

Hawaiian Plantations
802 Lehua Avenue
Pearl City HI 96782
808-456-7078
Hawaiian
Contact:
Garleen Umetsu

Hope's Specialty Foods, Inc.
99 Steamwhistle Drive
Ivyland PA 18974
215-355-1229
Contact:
Hope Klayman

House of Tsang, Inc.
P.O. Box 294
Belmont CA 94002
415-243-9760
Oriental
Contact:
Bill Sher

International Marketing Services
200 West 57th Street, Suite 1402
New York NY 10019
212-333-5555
Contact:
Tim Metzger

Jardine's Texas Foods
P.O. Box 18868
Austin TX 78760
512-444-5001
Tex-Mex
Contact:
Dan Jardine

Joyva Corporation
53 Varick Avenue
Brooklyn NY 11237
718-497-0170
Middle Eastern
Contact:
Milton Radutzky

Kreiner Imports
3155 South Shields
Chicago IL 60616
312-225-5100
West German
Contact:
Johanna E. Karpus

Kuhn's Imports, Inc.
3118 McArthur Boulevard
Northbrook IL 60062
708-480-9698
West German
Contact:
Frank Wagner

LaPace Imports, Inc.
80 Cottage Place
Gillette NJ 07933
201-647-4408
Italian
Contact:
Peter Carolan

La Preferida Inc. of New York
945 Close Avenue
Bronx NY 10473
212-589-6800
Mexican
Contact:
Frederick J. Umbach

Liberty Richter, Inc.
400 Commerce Boulevard
Carlstadt NJ 07072
201-935-6850
Contact:
Bill Williams

Mandarin Soy Sauce, Inc.
419 North Street
Middletown NY 10940
914-343-1505
Oriental
Contact:
Michael Wu

Melba Food Specialties, Inc.
186 Huron Street
Brooklyn NY 11222
718-383-3142
Contact:
Marie Cook

Miguel's
Stowe-Away Lodge, R.R.1
P.O. Box 1360
Stowe VT 05672
802-253-7574
Mexican
Contact:
John M. Henzel

Pecos Valley Spice Company
500 East 77th Street, Suite 2324
New York NY 10162
212-628-5374
Tex-Mex
Contact:
Jane Butel de Calles

Peloponnese
2227 Poplar Street
Oakland CA 94607
415-839-8153
Greek
Contact:
Sotiris Kitrilakis

Products-From-Sweden, Inc.
5 Westchester Plaza
Elmsford NY 10523
914-592-3000
Swedish
Contact:
Bengt Liljestrand

Reese Finer Foods, Inc.
25 Lake Street
Paterson NJ 07501
201-345-1802
800-631-8578
Contact:
John A. Fressie

Steiner Foods, Inc.
302 Walnut Avenue
Bronx NY 10454
212-585-1122
Contact:
George Steiner

FISH & CAVIAR

California Sunshine Fine Foods
144 King Street
San Francisco CA 94107
415-543-3007
Contact:
Mats Engstrom

**Carolyn Collins Caviar
Company, Inc.**
P.O. Box 662
Crystal Lake IL 60014
815-459-6210
Contact:
Carolyn Collins

Cascade Seafoods
P.O. Box 5221
Bellingham WA 98227
206-733-9090
Contact:
Rick Ray

Caspian Star Caviar, Inc.
46 Washington Avenue
Brooklyn NY 11205
718-797-9090
Contact:
Alex Gaft

**Caviar Direct, Caspian
Imperial Caviar**
690 East 133rd Street
Bronx NY 10454
212-757-8990
Contact:
Abdi Nodjoumi

Epicurean International, Inc.
12351B Wilkins Avenue
Rockville MD 20852
301-231-0700
Contact:
Hossein Lolavar

Gold Star Smoked Fish, Inc.
570 Smith Street
Brooklyn NY 11231
718-522-1545
Contact:
Robert Pincow

Hansen Caviar Comapny, Inc.
391-A Grand Avenue
Englewood NJ 07631
201-568-9653
Contact:
Arnold H. Hansen-Sturm

Homarus, Inc.
76 Kisco Avenue
Mt. Kisco NY 10549
914-668-8992
Contact:
Karen Heineman Ransom

Iron Gate Products Company, Inc.
424 West 54th Street
New York NY 10019
212-757-2670
Contact:
Gerald M. Stein

Kasilof Fish Company
1222 Mukilteo Boulevard
Everett WA 98020
206-252-7552
Contact:
Russ Lamb

**Norton National Marketers' Group,
The H. G. Norton Company, Inc.**
P.O. Drawer 269
New Milford CT 06776
203-354-3966
Contact:
H. G. Norton

Pinneys USA, Inc.
200 West 57th Street, Suite 1402
New York NY 10019
212-333-5555
Contact:
Kim Bruhn

Port Chatham Packing Company
632 Northwest 46th Street
Seattle WA 98107
206-783-8200
Contact:
Bob Emel

Purepak Foods, Inc.
47-39 49th Street
Woodside NY 11377
718-784-3344
Contact:
George A. Hessol

Romanoff Foods, Inc.
1200 Milik Street
Carteret NJ 07008
201-969-1600
800-243-5293
Contact:
Hope Kalmanson

Seafood, Inc.
Route 5
P.O. Box 360
Henderson LA 70517
318-228-7506
Contact:
Charles Friedman

FOOD GIFTS & FOOD DECORATIVES

Brans Nut Company
581 Bonner Road
Wauconda IL 60084
708-526-0700
800-238-0400
Contact:
Bill Collins

California Hi-Lites, Inc.
6636 East 26th Street
Los Angeles CA 90040
213-888-1900
Contact:
Wilbur A. Lee

Crinklaw Farms—Gourmet Decoratives
P.O. Box 706
King City CA 93930
408-385-6658
800-842-7542
Contact:
Chris B. Crinklaw

Green County Foods, Inc.
1112 Seventh Avenue
Monroe WI 53566
608-328-8800
800-233-3564
Contact:
Wally Wagner

House of Webster, Inc.
U.S. 62B
P.O. Box 488
Rogers AR 72756
501-636-4640
Contact:
Dale Webster

Houston Foods
4245 Knox Avenue
Chicago IL 60641
312-777-2700
Contact:
Gary D. Musick

John Wagner & Sons, Inc.
900 Jacksonville Road
P.O. Box C 5013
Ivyland PA 18974
215-674-5000
Contact:
Ralph T. Starr

Luke's Almond Acres
11281 South Lac Jac
Reedley CA 93654
209-638-3483
Contact:
Lucas Nersesian

McFadden Farm
Potter Valley CA 95469
707-743-1122
Contact:
Guinness McFadden

Mille Lacs MP Company
P.O. Box 8919
Madison WI 53708
608-837-8535
Contact:
Arny Strom

Pacific Gold
4325 West Shaw Avenue
Fresno CA 93722
209-275-4999
Contact:
Patricia Locktov

Torn Ranch Wholesale
3095 Kerner Boulevard, Suite N
San Rafael CA 94901
415-459-1660
Contact:
Milton B. Torn

Vacaville Fruit Company, Inc.
P.O. Box 339
Vacaville CA 95696
707-448-5292
Contact:
Richard Nola

Wonder Bar Products, Inc.
1624 Stillwell Avenue
Bronx NY 10461
212-597-9600
Contact:
L. G. Schwartz

GIFT FOOD PACKAGING

Agri-Pack, Division of Liberty Carton Company
870 Louisiana Avenue South
Minneapolis MN 55426
612-540-9615
800-328-1784
Contact:
Carol Sylvester

Atlantic Bedford Paper Bag Company
7075 West 20th Avenue
Hialeah FL 33014
305-821-5901
Contact:
Susan Hernandez

Atlantic Can Company, Inc., Division of Centennial Industries, Inc.
101 Seventh Street
P.O. Box 119
Passaic NJ 07055
201-777-4500
Contact:
LeRoy H. Kersting

Bagcraft Corporation of America
3900 West 43rd Street
Chicago IL 60632
312-254-8000
Contact:
Alden M. Cohen

Charlotte Charles, Inc.
2501 North Elston Avenue
Chicago IL 60647
312-772-8310
Contact:
Stewart H. Reich

Dyna-Pak Corporation Retail Packaging
P.O. Box 627
Elmira NY 14902
607-734-2117
800-722-4887
Contact:
Helen Faulkner

Garry Packing, Inc.
P.O. Box 249
Del Rey CA 93616
209-888-2126
Contact:
James W. Garry

Gaylord Specialties Corporation
225 Fifth Avenue, Suite 4400
New York NY 10010
212-683-6182
800-831-3500
Contact:
Barbara Niad

Gift Basket Supplies, Inc.
65 North Main Street
P.O. Box 1684
Brockton MA 02401
508-583-5900
800-BASKET-1
Contact:
Robert B. Kresser

**The Gifted Line,
John Grossman, Inc.**
2656 Bridgeway
Sausalito CA 94965
800-5-GIFTED
800-3-GIFTED
Contact:
Kathy Riedesel

The Gifted Line is a leading supplier of high-quality designer gift packaging based on exquisite turn-of-the-century images. We offer a beautiful selection of full-color Gifted Boxes, Bags, Giftwrap, Stickers, Tags and Enclosure Cards—the perfect enhancement for gift baskets, candy, coffee beans, wine and a multitude of gourmet gifts. The Gifted Line is distributed throughout the United States, Canada, Japan, Australia and Europe.

Glerup-Revere Company, Inc.
P.O. Box 15770
Seattle WA 98115
206-523-4203
Contact:
Mark E. Revere

The House of Hasenfratz
662 Blue Hills Avenue
Hartford CT 06112
203-242-5515
Contact:
Luiz V. Carvalho

Keller-Charles of Philadelphia
2413-27 Federal Street
Philadelphia PA 19146
215-732-2614
Contact:
Sam Katz

Nowco International, Inc.
1 George Avenue
Wilkes-Barre PA 18705
215-277-2221
717-822-5255
800-233-8302
Contact:
Thomas W. Catanese Jr.

Spectrum Ascona, Inc.
1305 Fraser, Suite D-1
Bellingham WA 98226
206-647-0877
800-356-1473
Contact:
Bruce W. Maynard

U.S. Box Corporation
1296 McCarter Highway
Newark NJ 07104
718-387-1510
Contact:
Alan S. Kossoff

V.C.F. Packaging Films, Inc.
1100 Sutton Avenue
Howell MI 48843
517-546-2300
Contact:
William C. Plahta

Gift Basket Supplies, Inc.

65 North Main St., Brockton, MA 02401

Toll-Free National 1-800-BASKET-1
Toll-Free MASS Only 1-800-BASKET-2
(508) 583-5900

We did this for you! Fifteen years of dedication to this industry - we have brought to you many new and innovative products. We created the products, built the automatic machinery, and produced them in our own factory. This helps us control quality, price, and service. 80% of our sales are from products which we manufacture.

Write or call us for our full color catalog and help yourself into new and better ways of creative merchandising.

Use our extraordinary line of 26 matching colors of tissue, ribbon, and excelsior. Let your store make a statement about you.

GRAINS, RICE & PASTA

Al Dente, Inc.
9815 Main Street
Whitmore Lake MI 48189
313-449-8522
Contact:
Monique Deschaine

Arrowhead Mills, Inc.
P.O. Box 2059
Hereford TX 79045
806-364-0730
Contact:
Carla Smith

Arrowhead Mills's full line of certified organic whole grains, beans, seeds and nuts comes in packages and/or bulk for your convenience. Our whole grain, dietary and specialty flours include stone-ground whole wheat, whole-wheat pastry, cornmeal, amaranth, garbanzo, buckwheat, soy, teff, brown rice, barley, oat and millet. We carry a wide variety of whole grain cereals and packaged quick brown rices, as well as our famous Deaf Smith Peanut Butter. Educational/sales materials are available.

Deer Creek Wild Rice Company, Inc.
707 North George Washington
Yuba City CA 95991
916-673-8053
Contact:
Jack Boyan

Fini USA Corporation
110 Ridgedale Avenue
P.O. Box 2205
Morristown NJ 07960
201-267-3800
Contact:
Doon Wintz

Gaston Dupre, Inc.
7904 Hopi Place
Tampa FL 33634
813-885-9445
800-937-9445
Contact:
Emmannuel Roux

Putney Pasta Company, Inc.
Hickory Ridge Road
P.O. Box 599
Putney VT 05346
802-387-4848
Contact:
Jonathan H. Altman

Putney Pasta of Putney, Vermont, for the last six years has been a purveyor of some of the most outstanding pastas and sauces available today. From Tomato Tortelloni filled with sun-dried tomatoes, fresh basil and mozzarella to Agnolotti with aged Vermont cheddar and fresh broccoli, Putney Pasta has always been on the cutting edge of pasta products. All our pastas and sauces are available in retail and bulk sizes. Call for a complete listing.

Trio's Original Italian Pasta Products Company, Inc.
36 Auburn Street
Chelsea MA 02150
617-884-5211
Contact:
Paul Stevens

Voyageur Trading Company
P.O. Box 35121,
Normandale Branch
Minneapolis MN 55435
612-942-7766
Contact:
Richard C. Sampson

HERBS, SPICES, SEASONINGS & FLAVORINGS

Flavorchem Corporation
1525 Brook Drive
Downers Grove IL 60515
708-932-8100
Contact:
John P. Barba

Flavorbank Company, Inc.
4710 Eisenhower Boulevard,
Building E-8
Tampa FL 33614
813-885-1797
800-835-7603
Contact:
Warren Ansley

Pelican Bay, Ltd.
1260 West Bay Drive
Largo FL 34640
813-585-5338
800-826-8982
Contact:
Char Pfaelzer

Select Origins, Inc.
Suffolk County Airport,
Building 139
Westhampton Beach NY 11978
516-288-1381
800-822-2092
Contact:
Thomas H. Siplon

The Spice Hunter, Inc.
254 Granada Drive
San Luis Obispo CA 93401
805-544-4466
Contact:
Lucia M. McMillan

Spice Market, Inc.
664 Bergen Street
Brooklyn NY 11238
718-636-6300
Contact:
Joel Bahr

Vanns Spices, Inc.
1238 East Joppa Road
Baltimore MD 21204
301-583-1643
301-583-1653
Contact:
Ann Wilder

Victoria Packing Corporation
443 East 100th Street
Brooklyn NY 11236
718-649-1635
Contact:
Ben Aquilina

World of Spices, Inc.
328 Essex Street
Stirling NJ 07980
201-647-1218
Contact:
Charles Newman

JAMS, JELLIES, PRESERVES, HONEY & SYRUPS

A. M. Braswell Jr. Food Company, Inc.
P.O. Box 485
Statesboro GA 30458
912-764-6191
Contact:
Al Braswell III

American Spoon Foods
1668 Clarion Avenue
P.O. Box 566
Petoskey MI 49770
616-347-9030
Contact:
Justin Rashid

American Spoon Foods, a unique specialty food company founded by Chef Larry Forgione and Forager Justin Rashid, are makers of award-winning preserves of wild and cultivated Michigan fruits, no sugar added Spoon Fruits®, no-oil salad Dazzlers, and Larry Forgione's sauces and condiments. They also offer Dried Red Tart Cherries, dried berries, dried Morel mushrooms, native Midwestern nuts and Northern varietal honeys through specialty food stores and direct to restaurants and consumers, through wholesale and mail-order catalogs.

Berry Best Farm, Inc.
Coryell's Crossing
2 Mount Hope Street
P.O. Box 189
Lambertville NJ 08530
609-397-0748
Contact:
Gilles Carter

California Soleil Vineyards
1873 Yountville Cross Road
P.O. Box 3150
Napa Valley CA 94599
707-224-7989
800-225-8463
Contact:
Ray M. Mayeri

Clearbrook Farms
5514 Fair Lane
Fairfax OH 45227
513-271-2053
Contact:
Dan William Cohen

Crabtree & Evelyn
P.O. Box 167
Woodstock CT 06281
203-928-2766
Contact:
Mary Jane Tremblay

The Dickinson Family, Inc.
Strawberry Lane
Orrville OH 44667
216-682-0015
Contact:
Chuck Laine

Honey Acres, Inc.
Highway 67
Ashippun WI 53003
414-474-4411
800-558-7745
Contact:
Eugene Brueggeman

J. M. Specialties
126 Jefferson Street
P.O. Box 345
Ripon WI 54971
414-748-2858
800-535-5437
Contact:
Richard W. Long

Knott's Berry Farm Foods
200 Boysenberry Lane
Placentia CA 92670
714-579-2436
Contact:
Marty O'Connor

Kozlowski Farms' Sonoma County Classics
5566 Gravenstein Highway North
Forestville CA 95436
707-887-1587
Contact:
Carol Kozlowski Every

**Maple Grove Farms
of Vermont, Inc.**
167 Portland Street
St. Johnsbury VT 05819
802-748-5141
800-525-2540
Contact:
William F. Callahan III

Narsai's Specialty Foods
350 Berkeley Park Boulevard
Kensington CA 94707
415-527-7900
Contact:
Narsai M. David

Sarabeth's Kitchen, Inc.
169 West 78th Street
New York NY 10024
212-580-8335
Contact:
William J. Levine

Sarabeth produces her line of
award-winning preserves in the
kitchen of one of her two highly
acclaimed restaurants in New York
City. Her products are sold wholesale
to the finest gourmet shops, gift shops
and department stores in the United
States. They are also marketed directly
to the consumer by mail order and
over the counter in her restaurants. All
Sarabeth products are 100 percent
natural, containing no fillers, thicken-
ers or preservatives of any kind.

The Silver Palate, Inc.
274 Columbus Avenue
New York NY 10023
212-799-6340
800-847-4747
Contact:
Peter Harris

Thomson Berry Farms
525 Lake Avenue South
Duluth MN 55802
218-722-2529
Contact:
Robert B. Pokorney

Trappist Preserves
St. Joseph's Abbey
Spencer MA 01562
508-885-4773
Contact:
Bernard Matthews, O.C.S.O.

**Tropical Blossom
Honey Company, Inc.**
P.O. Box 8
Edgewater FL 32032
904-428-9027
Contact:
David K. McGinnis

Wilds of Idaho
1308 West Boone
Spokane WA 99201
509-326-0197
Contact:
Louise Marie Sevier

MEATS, POULTRY & PATES

Certified Prime, Inc.
4538 South Marshfield Avenue
Chicago IL 60609
312-376-7445
Contact:
Martin B. Bergerson

Charcuterie Tour Eiffel, Inc.
260 Lanes Mill Road
P.O Box 541
Howell NJ 07731
201-370-3440
Contact:
Clarence McDowell

Charles Hollenbach, Inc.
2653 West Ogden Avenue
Chicago IL 60608
312-521-2500
800-621-4629
Contact:
Guy K. Vanes

Cher-Make Sausage Company
2915 Calumet Avenue
P.O. Box 1267 (54221)
Manitowoc WI 54220
414-682-7719
800-242-7679
Contact:
Tom Chermak

Citterio USA Corporation
51-15 35th Street
Long Island City NY 11101
718-706-7390
Contact:
Tony Caraluzzi

D'Artagnan, Inc.
399 St. Paul Avenue
Jersey City NJ 07306
201-792-0748
Contact:
George Faison

Fiorucci Foods Corporation
1800 Ruffin Mill Road
P.O. Box 39
Colonial Heights VA 23834
804-520-7775
Contact:
Jim Mancuso

High Valley Farm, Inc.
14 Alsace Way
Colorado Springs CO 80906
719-634-2944
Contact:
Richard H. Ostien

Les Trois Petits Cochons Pate Company
453 Greenwich Street
New York NY 10013
212-219-1230
Contact:
Alain Sinturel

Marcel et Henri Charcuterie Francaise
415 Browning Way
South San Francisco CA 94080
415-871-4230
800-227-6436
Contact:
Joyce A. Smith

Henri Lapuyade, America's first and most renowned charcutier, introduced fresh pates to America in 1960. Beginning with a few recipes from his native France, he created pates in his small shop in San Francisco. Before long, thousands of Americans were enjoying their first taste of this great culinary tradition as Henri's charcuterie became nationally distributed. Marcel et Henri now offers more than 50 varieties of pates, galantines, boudins and sausages, still produced under Henri's personal supervision.

Menuchah Farms Smokehouse
Route 22
P.O. Box 39
Salem NY 12865
518-854-9423
Contact:
Sandy Dumas

Michel's Magnifique of NYC, Ltd.
34 North Moore Street
New York NY 10013
212-431-1070
Contact:
Kenneth Blanchette

Nueske Hillcrest Farm Meats
Rural Route 2
Wittenberg WI 54499
715-253-2226
Contact:
Jim Nueske

Old Wisconsin Sausage Company
11914 South Peoria Street
Chicago IL 60643
312-468-0900
800-621-0868
Contact:
Tim Dam

S. Wallace Edwards & Sons, Inc.
P.O. Box 25
Surry VA 23883
804-294-3121
800-222-4267
Contact:
Samuel W. Edwards III

Schaller & Weber, Inc.
22-35 46th Street
Long Island City NY 11105
718-721-5480
800-847-4115
Contact:
Frank J. Schaller

Sparrer Sausage Company, Inc.
4325 West Ogden Avenue
Chicago IL 60623
312-762-3334
800-66-MEATS
Contact:
Michael S. Hammersley

Stockmeyer (North America), Inc.
404 Clifton Avenue
Clifton NJ 07011
201-340-4464
Contact:
Lothar Bachem

NUTS, DRIED FRUITS & SNACK FOODS

A. L. Bazzini Company, Inc.
339 Greenwich Street
New York NY 10013
212-227-6241
800-288-0172
Contact:
George G. Pappas

California Treats, Inc.
820 East Colorado Street
Glendale CA 91205
818-241-2076
Contact:
Mary F. Ohms

DeSoto Confectionery & Nut Company
P.O. Box 72
DeSoto GA 31743
912-874-1200
800-237-8689
Contact:
Nancy Carlan

Dole Nut Company
P.O. Box 845
Orland CA 95963
916-865-5511
Contact:
F. L. Woods

Hershey Import Company, Inc.
700 East Lincoln Avenue
Rahway NJ 07065
201-388-9000
800-526-4349
Contact:
Mitchell Hershey

The Maui Chip, Inc.
263 Quigley Boulevard
New Castle DE 19720
302-322-5655
Contact:
Christopher Eld Markson

Nunes Farms Almonds
P.O. Box 146
San Anselmo CA 94960
415-459-7201
Contact:
Kathleen Nunes Civetz

Snack Factory, Inc.
P.O. Box 3562
Princeton NJ 08543
609-683-5400
Contact:
Warren Wilson

OILS, VINEGARS, SALAD DRESSINGS & MARINADES

Blanchard & Blanchard
P.O. Box 1080
Norwich VT 05055
802-295-9200
Contact:
Sharon Trainor Smith

Cook's Classics
2672 Bayshore Parkway, Suite 900
Mountain View CA 94043
415-968-8665
800-553-6044
Contact:
Sheila Cook

Cuisine Perel
P.O. Box 1064
Tiburon CA 94920
415-435-1282
Contact:
Leonardo Perel

De Medici Imports, Ltd.
1775 Broadway, Suite 2310
New York NY 10019
212-974-8101
Contact:
Paul L. Farber

Dugan's Ingredients
1365 Interior Street, Complex A
Eugene OR 97402
503-343-8697
Contact:
Robert Peak

Indian Summer, Inc.
1325 Evans Avenue
San Francisco CA 94124
415-285-5304
Contact:
Elaine Santo Thomas

Kendall-Brown Foods
86 Forest Lane
San Rafael CA 94903
415-499-1621
Contact:
Barbara Kendall

Le Steak Gourmet International, Ltd.
4088-B Howard Avenue
Kensington MD 20895
301-493-6301
Contact:
Jacques Finnell

Nicholas Gold, Inc.
2716 Ocean Park Boulevard, Suite 1050
Santa Monica CA 90405
213-396-1126
Contact:
Ray Romano

Pace Foods, Inc./La Martinique
P.O. Box 12636
San Antonio TX 78212
512-224-2211
Contact:
Thomas R. Clarke

Peter Christian's Specialty Food Company
P.O Box 1817
New London NH 03257
603-763-9858
800-346-8794
Contact:
Candice J. Blank

Rothschild Berry Farm
3143 East Route 36
P.O. Box 311
Urbana OH 43078
513-653-7397
800-356-8933
Contact:
Robert B. Rothschild

SAUCES & SOUPS

Casa DiLisio Products, Inc.
486 Lexington Avenue
Mt. Kisco NY 10549
914-666-5021
800-247-4199
Contact:
Louis J. DiLisio

"The Ultimate in Italian Sauces" has been the watchword of Casa DiLisio Products since 1973. We pride ourselves on the quality and range of our sauces, made from the freshest ingredients and flavored with flair. Pesto Alla Genovese or Walnut Pesto, Clam Sauce, Provencal Sauce, Puttanesca Tomato Sauce—each one tastes as if there were a real Italian Mama in the kitchen. For more information, call or write us at the address above.

Chalet Suzanne Foods, Inc.
P.O. Box A.C.
Lake Wales FL 33859
813-676-6011
Contact:
Carl F. Hinshaw

Ci'Bella
30801 Pacific Coast Highway,
Suite 64
Laguna Beach CA 92651
714-499-1477
Contact:
Connie Vlasis

Dominique Gourmet Foods, Inc.
10302 Southard Drive
Beltsville MD 20705
202-223-0662
202-223-0663
Contact:
George D. Hardy

Firehouse Bar-B-Que
2097 Market Street, Suite A
San Francisco CA 94114
415-864-2693
Contact:
Peter van der Pol

Helen's Tropical-Exotics, Inc.
3519 Church Street
Clarkston GA 30021
404-296-6100
800-544-JERK
Contact:
Helen Willinsky

Judyth's Mountain, Inc.
1737 Lorenzen Drive
San Jose CA 95124
408-264-3330
Contact:
Mona Palmer Onstead

Lusco's Sauces
722 Carrolton Avenue
P.O. Box 79
601-453-5365
Contact:
Andy Pinkston

Mayacamas Fine Foods, Inc.
1206 East MacArthur Street
Sonoma CA 95476
707-996-0955
Contact:
Ross W. Webber

Papa Leone Food Enterprises, Inc.
449 South Beverly Drive,
Suite 211
213-277-1272
Contact:
Edmond Negari

Wisconsin Wilderness Food Products, Inc.
7841 North 47th Street
Milwaukee WI 53223
414-355-0001
Contact:
Donna Willmert

Specialty Food Retailers

The specialty food industry is a field that, by definition, is constantly changing as new foods are introduced and become popular. This listing was selected by Elaine Yannuzzi, founder of Expression unltd., both to give an idea of the variety of specialties available and to achieve as wide a geographic range as possible. Divided into seven regions, it is alphabetized within states by the name under which the company does business. Complete information about the industry is available from the Retail Division of the National Association for the Specialty Food Trade, Inc., 215 Park Avenue South, New York NY 10003. Much detailed information on specialty foods appears in the *Thomas Grocery Register*, available from Thomas Publishing Company, 1 Penn Plaza, New York NY 10119.

Many specialty food retailers stock a variety of foods, which may range from cheeses or oils to such esoteric items as reindeer meatballs. In most cases, the contact named owns or manages the store and decides which items will be carried.

Almost all specialty food retailers are independent and obtain their supplies from wholesalers, distributors and manufacturers. Someone interested in developing a line of foods might want to select a store to test-market one or two items, then set up distribution services through a specialty food wholesaler for items that sell well.

NORTHEAST

CONNECTICUT

Cheese Shop International, Inc.
255 Greenwich Avenue
Greenwich CT 06830
203-869-2540
Contact:
Cornelius Hearn

The Depot Market
East Brook Mall
Willimantic CT 06226
203-429-3663
Contact:
Mary Murtha
Susan Murtha-Smith

The Litchfield Food Company, Inc.
Box 150
Litchfield CT 06759
203-567-3113
Contact:
Dale Puckett

Walter Stewart's Market
229 Elm Street
P.O. Box 268
New Canaan CT 06840
203-966-4848
Contact:
R. B. Stewart

MASSACHUSETTS

Bruni Farm
24 Essex Road
Ipswich MA 01938
508-356-4877
Contact:
Jan Marcaurelle

Gourmet Take-Away
93 High Ridge Road
Boxford MA 01921
508-882-6383
Contact:
Mansour Boustani

La Patisserie
30 Church Street
Winchester MA 01890
617-729-9441
Contact:
Stephen Pazyra

NEW HAMPSHIRE

Maggie's
14 Main Street
Peterborough NH 03458
603-924-7671
Contact:
Janet Quinn

NEW JERSEY

C'est Bon
1260 Springfield Avenue
New Providence NJ 07974
201-464-3815
Contact:
Elsa Schwarz

Carson/Smith Fine Foods
172B Woodport Road
Sparta NJ 07871
201-729-1233
Contact:
Andrea Carson

Dearborn Farms, Inc.
2170 Highway 35
Holmdel NJ 07733
201-264-0256
Contact:
Dominick Luccarelli

Expression unltd.
165 Washington Valley Road
Warren NJ 07060
201-469-6969
Contact:
Martin Orlowsky

Kings Super Markets, Inc.
2 Dedrick Place
West Caldwell NJ 07006
201-575-3320
Contact:
Bob Schwartz

NEW YORK

B. J. Carey Provisions
444 Atlantic Avenue
Brooklyn NY 11217
718-624-5331
Contact:
Sandra Diamond

Balducci's
424 Sixth Avenue
New York NY 10011
718-361-2055
Contact:
Andrew Balducci

**Barney Greengrass
"The Sturgeon King"**
541 Amsterdam Avenue
New York NY 10024
212-724-4707
Contact:
Gary Greengrass

Since 1908, Barney Greengrass has been a leading New York purveyor of appetizing specialties. Besides running a successful local and restaurant business, the Greengrass family ship their famous Sturgeon, Nova Scotia Salmon, Caviar, Whitefish, Pickled Herring, Vegetable and Scallion Cream Cheese, New York Bagels and Bialys all over the United States. The delicacies are packed in synthetic dry ice and delivered overnight via UPS Next Day Air. Everything arrives fresh, never frozen. Mail-order brochures available.

Bell's Suprecentre
4050 North Buffalo Road
Orchard Park NY 14127
716-662-7856
Contact:
Ray Fabiniak

Braden's Inc.
9920 Main Street
Clarence NY 14031
716-759-2942
Contact:
David Thomas

Crumpets
15 Birch Hill Road
Locust Valley NY 11560
516-759-1152
Contact:
A. Meyer

Dean & DeLuca
560 Broadway
New York NY 10012
212-431-1691
Contact:
Giorgio DeLuca
Joel Dean

Eagle Provisions Company, Inc.
628 Fifth Avenue
Brooklyn NY 11215
718-499-0226
Contact:
John Zawisny

Empire Market
14-26 College Point Boulevard
College Point NY 11356
718-359-0209
Contact:
Michael L. Tine

Ideal Cheese Shop
1205 Second Avenue
New York NY 10021
212-688-7579
Contact:
Edward Jack Edelman

Grace's Marketplace
1237 Third Avenue
New York NY 10021
212-737-0600
Contact:
Grace Balducci

**Michael's Fine Cheese
& Gourmet Foods**
6 Harwood Court
Scarsdale NY 10583
914-723-3024
Contact:
R. Michael Cairo

Todaro Brothers
555 Second Avenue
New York NY 10016
212-532-0633
Contact:
Luciano Todaro

Todaro Brothers has been offering the finest in imported and domestic foods for more than 60 years. The selection includes over 200 varieties of cheese (including homemade mozzarella), fresh pasta, home-baked sweets, prepared foods, coffee beans, fresh breads and meats (including homemade sausages). In addition, a catering staff is on hand for private or office functions. We create customized gift baskets for all occasions. Mail-order service and gift certificates are also available.

Toscani & Sons
119 Main Street
New Paltz NY 12561
914-255-6770
Contact:
Rachel Toscani

William Groceries & Meat Fair
628 South Main Street
North Syracuse NY 13212
315-458-3890
Contact:
Ann William

William Poll, Inc.
1051 Lexington Avenue
New York NY 10021
212-288-0501
Contact:
Stanley Poll

Zabar's
2245 Broadway
New York NY 10024
212-787-2002
Contact:
Melen Ham

PENNSYLVANIA

Food Stuffs
533 North 22nd Street
Philadelphia PA 19130
215-665-8410
Contact:
Joel Marycheck

McGinnis Sisters
284 Joseph Street
Pittsburgh PA 15227
412-884-2323
Contact:
Bonnie Vello

Shammo's Fancy Foods
4701 East Trindle Road
Mechanicsburg PA 17055
717-761-5570
Contact:
Donald W. Schultz

RHODE ISLAND

Grandma's Pantry
34 Narragansett Avenue
Jamestown RI 02835
401-423-1124
Contact:
Linda Martino

J. D. Mercantile
21 West Main Street
Wickford RI 02852
401-295-8190
Contact:
Joseph Dube

VERMONT

Mother Myrick's Confectionery
Box 1142, Route 7A
Manchester Center VT 05255
802-362-1560
Contact:
Jacqueline Baker

Vermont Country Kitchen
3 Park Street
Middlebury VT 05753
802-388-8646
Contact:
Cathy Nief

SOUTH

ALABAMA

Andree's Wine, Cheese & Things
403 Fairhope Avenue
Fairhope AL 36532
205-928-8863
Contact:
Andree Burton

Contri Brothers' Gift Basket
6911 First Avenue North
Birmingham AL 35206
205-836-7236
Contact:
Raymond Contri

Grate Things
105-6 Westgate Parkway
Dothan AL 36303
205-793-2038
Contact:
June Groover

ARKANSAS

Diane's
10700 Rodney Parham
Little Rock AR 72212
501-224-2639
Contact:
Diane Knight

Fudge 'n' Such Gourmet Shoppe
3515 John F. Kennedy Boulevard
North Little Rock AR 72116
501-771-0736
Contact:
Ken Armbrust

DELAWARE

Chateau Specialties
2008 South Woodmill Drive
Wilmington DE 19808
302-995-1300
Contact:
Jeff Sidell

McCabe's Gourmet Market
U.S. Route 1
York Beach Mall
South Bethany DE 19930
302-539-8550
Contact:
Richard Mais
Rebecca Mais

DISTRICT OF COLUMBIA

Federal Market
1215 23rd Street NW
Washington DC 20037
202-333-6630
Contact:
Ronald Hailey

Sutton Place Gourmet
3201 New Mexico Avenue NW
Washington DC 20016
202-363-5800
Contact:
Susan Derecksky

FLORIDA

A Place for Cooks
1447 South Fort Harrison
Clearwater FL 34616
813-446-5506
Contact:
Thomas Di Nicola
Diane Di Nicola

Bay Window Deli
911 Gulf Breeze Parkway
Gulf Breeze FL 32561
904-932-0817
Contact:
Connie Simmons

Crayton Cove Gourmet, Inc.
800 12th Avenue South
Naples FL 33940
813-262-4362
Contact:
Nancy Burkhalter

Rosella's, Inc.
630 Northeast Eighth Street
Delray Beach FL 33483
407-276-6847
Contact:
Janice Federspiel

Scotty's Grocery
3117 Bird Avenue
Miami FL 33133
305-443-5257
Contact:
Scott McDaniel

GEORGIA

**East 48th Street Market/
Italian Food Specialties**
2462 Jett Ferry Road
Atlanta GA 30338
404-392-1499
Contact:
Charles Augello

Happy Herman's
204 Johnson Ferry Road
Atlanta GA 30328
404-256-3354
Contact:
Ann Marie Moraitakis

Helms Foods
1815 Garrard Street
Columbus GA 31901
404-323-3865
Contact:
Vicki Helms

KENTUCKY

A Taste of Kentucky
510 Production Court
Louisville KY 40299
502-491-0771
Contact:
Sharon Hassmann

Enjoy A Taste of Kentucky—the best foods and crafts of the bluegrass state. Our baskets are filled with jellies, barbecue sauce, Derby pie, bourbon candies, cookbooks, mint julep mix, country hams, cheese and official Derby products from T-shirts to party goods.

Say "Thank You" to a friend or a corporate client or enjoy the products yourself. Call collect for more information and a catalog. We ship worldwide and accept all major credit cards.

Burger's Market
1927 Alfresco Place
Louisville KY 40205
502-454-0462
Contact:
John Burger

The Cheddar Box
3909 Chenoweth Square
Louisville KY 40207
502-893-2324
Contact:
Nancy Tarrant

Dial-A-Gift
215 Broadway
Paducah KY 42001
502-443-4060
Contact:
Tina Terrell

Randall's
344 Romany Road
Lexington KY 40502
606-266-0471
Contact:
Walt Barbour

LOUISIANA

Acadiane Piggly Wiggly
3655 Perkins Road
Baton Rouge LA 70808
504-343-2788
Contact:
Al Porche

The Pickle Barrel
1827 Avenue of America
Monroe LA 71201
318-325-5996
Contact:
Stewart Bashner

MARYLAND

Kaufman's Fancy Fruits & Vegetables
The Market House, City Dock
Annapolis MD 21401
301-269-0941
Contact:
Alvin Kaufman

Mary Ann's Place
3200 Fait Avenue
Baltimore MD 21224
301-563-4213
Contact:
Angela Matthews

Village Food Store
90 Village Square
Baltimore MD 21210
301-323-8330
Contact:
Alan Tossman

MISSISSIPPI

Olde Tyme Delicatessen
P.O. Box 16505
Jackson MS 39236
601-362-2565
Contact:
Irving Feldman

NORTH CAROLINA

A Southern Season
Eastgate
Chapel Hill NC 27514
919-929-7133
Contact:
Michael Barefoot

Fowler's Food Store of Durham
P.O. Box 336
Durham NC 27702
919-683-2555
Contact:
Bob Fowler

Grogan's
349 West King's Highway
Eden NC 27288
919-627-4365
Contact:
Suzon Carter

SOUTH CAROLINA

The Gourmet Shop, Inc.
724 Saluda Avenue
Columbia SC 29205
803-799-3705
Contact:
Linda Messier

In Good Taste
1124 Sam Rittenberg Boulevard
Charleston SC 29417
803-763-5597
Contact:
J. Boyd

Nell's Harbour Shop
P.O. Box 3071
Hilton Head Island SC 29928
803-671-2133
Contact:
Nell Smith

TENNESSEE

Conte Philips
73 White Bridge Road
Nashville TN 37205
615-352-5837
Contact:
Andrea Conte

Gourmet's Market, Inc.
5120 Kingston Pike
Knoxville TN 37919
615-584-8739
Contact:
Barbara Strehlow

VIRGINIA

The Butlery, Ltd.
1710 Altamont Avenue
Richmond VA 23230
804-359-2644
Contact:
Donald Bleau

The Cheese Shop of Virginia
424 Prince George Street
Williamsburg VA 23185
804-220-1234
Contact:
Thomas Power

Edwards' Virginia Ham Shoppe
P.O. Box 25
Surry VA 23883
804-294-3688
Contact:
Sam Edwards

The Farm Basket
2008 Langhorne Road
Lynchburg VA 24501
804-528-1107
Contact:
Sarah Youell

Foods of All Nations
2121 Ivy Road
Charlottesville VA 22903
804-296-6131
Contact:
Keith King

In business more than 30 years as a specialty foods retailer. We stock an incredible selection of the world's most exciting new products and epicurean

staples. Unique **free** monthly catalog/
newsletter for gourmets and professional
chefs; high response rate—write or call
to get on our list. We buy from over 200
suppliers to provide a selection un-
matched and too numerous to describe.
We specialize in hard-to-find items.

Taste Unlimited
213 36th Street
Virginia Beach VA 23451
804-425-3011
Contact:
Peter Coe

WEST VIRGINIA

The Greenbrier
Station A
White Sulphur Springs WV 24986
304-536-1118
Contact:
Stephen Baldwin

Mansour's Food Market Company
1049 12th Street
Huntington WV 25701
304-529-6225
Contact:
Michael Mansour

MIDWEST

ILLINOIS

Art Mart & Art Mart Foods
127 Lincoln Square
Urbana IL 61801
217-344-7979
Contact:
Carol Ann Hurt

Bockwinkel's Incorporated
5075 Shoreline Road
Barrington IL 60010
708-382-8787
Contact:
Jerry Bockwinkel

Brightwaters
234 East Golf Road
Arlington Heights IL 60005
708-952-0101
Contact:
Laurie Keenan

Don's Finest Foods
850 Western Avenue
Lake Forest IL 60045
708-234-2700
Contact:
Don Ruffolo

40 Village Place Gourmet
40 Village Place
Hinsdale IL 60521
708-323-0149
Contact:
Pat Hildebrand

The General Store
1309 North Avenue
Crystal Lake IL 60014
815-459-8105
Contact:
Carolyn Collins

Zambrana's
The Food Emporium
2346 North Clark Street
Chicago IL 60614
312-935-0200
Contact:
Manuel Zambrana

INDIANA

The Big Cheese
925 Promenade
Richmond IN 47374
317-962-3036
Contact:
Rose Melody

D'oeuvres by Dottie
24 North Washington Road
Valparaiso IN 46383
219-462-1416
Contact:
Dottie Harms

The Eight Mice
Market Square
Lafayette IN 47904
317-447-5255
Contact:
Joanne Force

Loaf 'n' Ladle
814 South Calhoun Street
Fort Wayne IN 46802
219-422-6003
Contact:
Clarita Whelchel

KANSAS

Cero's
2919 East Kellogg Drive
Wichita KS 67211
316-683-5561
Contact:
Ed Cero

Confection Connection
2103 Fairlawn Plaza Drive
Topeka KS 66614
913-272-8016
Contact:
Barbara Schwartz

Wolferman's
8900 Marshall Drive
Lenexa KS 66215
913-888-4499
Contact:
Robin Copas

MICHIGAN

Koeze Specialty Foods, Inc.
2880 East Paris SE
Kentwood MI 49512
616-957-2420
Contact:
Ruth Koeze

Merchant of Vino
254 West Maple
Birmingham MI 48011
313-354-6506
Contact:
Edward Jonas

Zingerman's Delicatessen
422 Detroit Street
Ann Arbor MI 48104
313-663-3354
Contact:
Ari Weinzweig

MISSOURI

The Deli Gourmet Food & Wine
2316 North Belt
St. Joseph MO 64506
816-279-3354
Contact:
Dick Rosenthal

Lafayette Gourmet
1915 Park Avenue
St. Louis MO 63104
314-436-7177
Contact:
Charlotte Charles
Dave Lyon

OHIO

**Busy Bee Gourmet Food
and Wine, Inc.**
2707 Erie Avenue
Cincinnati OH 45208
513-871-2898
Contact:
Julia Vanover

The Culinary Emporium
11279 Cornell Park Drive
Cincinnati OH 45242
513-530-5426
Contact:
Robert Badura

Darci's
7328 Kenwood Road
Cincinnati OH 45236
513-793-2020
Contact:
William Beattie

DiSalvo's Deli & Italian Store
1383 East Stroop Road
Kettering OH 45429
513-298-5053
Contact:
Rinaldo DiSalvo

Dorothy Lane Market
2710 Far Hills Avenue
Dayton OH 45419
513-299-3561
Contact:
Norman Mayne

The West Point Market
1711 West Market Street
Akron OH 44313
216-864-2151
Contact:
Russell Vernon

OKLAHOMA

Nayphe's International Foods
7519 North May Avenue
Oklahoma City OK 73116
405-848-2002
Contact:
Violet Nayphe

Nayphe's International Foods, Oklahoma City, specializes in fine foods from around the world. Included are chocolate bars and chocolate for baking, eating and molding, biscottes, bulk and packaged rice, pastas, herbs and spices. Also available are extracts and flavorings, coffee and tea and accessories, olives, oils and vinegars, pickles, mustards and cheeses. Cookbooks, decorative handicrafts, gifts and housewares are also specialties. For further information, call or write.

Petty's Fine Foods
1964 Utica Square
Tulsa OK 74114
918-747-8616
Contact:
Bradley Petty

WISCONSIN

Buon Appetito
8751 North Port Washington Road
Fox Point WI 53217
414-224-0895
Contact:
Randy Nelson

The Country Cupboard
126 Jefferson Street
P.O. Box 345
Ripon WI 54971
414-748-7190
Contact:
Don Jorgensen

Krane & Rush
159 East Silver Spring Drive
Whitefish Bay WI 53217
414-321-8568
Contact:
Karen Krajniak

Larry's Brown Deer Market
8737 North Deerwood Drive
Brown Deer WI 53209
414-355-9650
Contact:
Lawrence Ehlers

Manz Specialty Foods, Inc.
Country Walk
Sister Bay WI 54234
414-854-5040
Contact:
Lawrence Manz

SOUTHWEST

ARIZONA

C. Steele & Company
4110 North 70th Street,
Suite 205-A
Scottsdale AZ 85251
602-994-0755
Contact:
Catt Steele

Cheese House
15450 North 99th Avenue
Sun City AZ 85351
602-974-0843
Contact:
Roland Schlueter

Duck & Decanter
1651 East Camelback
Phoenix AZ 85016
602-274-5429
Contact:
Earl Mettler

The Euro Market
5017 North Central Avenue
Phoenix AZ 85012
602-252-3876
Contact:
Rory Drwinga

Gourmet Emporium
4744 East Sunrise Drive
Tucson AZ 85718
602-299-5576
Contact:
Michael Galkin

NEVADA

Unique Delicatessen
551 East Moana Lane
Reno NV 89502
702-825-1661
Contact:
Jody Coli
Debbie Codding

NEW MEXICO

Old Town Gourmet
206 1/2 North Felipe
Old Town
Albuquerque NM 87104
505-842-5643
Contact:
Beverly Peterson

TEXAS

Ambrosia
1721 Harold Street
Houston TX 77098
713-465-1212
Contact:
Edward Ambrose

Cheese Shop International, Inc.
5301 Belt Line Road, Suite 2032
Dallas TX 75240
214-233-9964
Contact:
James Stevens

Leibman's Wine & Fine Foods
14010A Memorial Drive
Houston TX 77079
713-497-6116
Contact:
Ettienne Leibman

Mary of Puddin Hill, Inc.
P.O. Box 241
Greenville TX 75401
214-455-2651
Contact:
Pud Kearns

Minyard Food Stores, Inc.
Freeport Parkway
P.O. Box 518-777
Coppell TX 75019
214-462-8700
Contact:
Nita Tucker

MOUNTAIN STATES

COLORADO

Charcuterie & Cheese Market
520 East Durant Street
Aspen CO 81611
303-925-8010
Contact:
Robert Deutsch

The Cheese Shop of Vail
P.O. Box 778
Vail CO 81658
303-476-1482
Contact:
Ginny Williams

FBC Foods International
900 East 11th Avenue
Denver CO 80218
303-832-6800
Contact:
Emery Dorsey III

UTAH

The Cheese Haus
1316 Foothill Drive
Salt Lake City UT 84108
801-582-7758
Contact:
G. R. Garlick

WEST COAST

CALIFORNIA

Al Dente
11092 Los Alamitos Boulevard
Los Alamitos CA 90720
213-598-1124
Contact:
Sydney Silvi

Bel Air Marketplace
640 North Sepulveda Boulevard
Los Angeles CA 90049
213-471-6858
Contact:
Susan Fine

Bwarie's Emporium
5211 Kester Avenue
Van Nuys CA 91411
818-981-8222
Contact:
Tom Bwarie

The Courtyard
1349 Parks Street
Alameda CA 94501
415-521-1521
Contact:
Peggy Williams

Fike's Finer Foods
2100 19th Street
Bakersfield CA 93301
805-325-5012
Contact:
Bob Vibe

Vivande
2125 Fillmore Street
San Francisco CA 94115
415-346-4430
Contact:
Elizabeth Middione

Vivande embodies Old World culinary values in a European-style food business, making exclusively prepared dishes fresh from scratch daily. Eating in its small Cafe is said to be "like having lunch in the fantasy kitchen of a three-star restaurant." The Retail Deli sells wine, pantry items and cookbooks as well as fresh foods. Catering of all types rounds out Vivande's active multi-dimensional business. Chef-owner is Carlo Middione, well-known vocational cooking instructor and food writer.

OREGON

Cook's Nook
2807 Oak Street
Eugene OR 97405
503-484-5725
Contact:
Ann Gruber

Fare with Flair
831 Northeast Seventh
Grants Pass OR 97526
503-474-0182
Contact:
Emily Renaud

Fare with Flair is found in an older, remodeled home. Its interior is quaint country style, complete with hand-painted tables. We offer gourmet lunches Monday through Saturday from an ever-changing menu. We sell specialty food items, gift baskets, picnic baskets, specialty desserts and candy. We also cater for all occasions and manufacture Peach-Ginger Spread, Peach Butter and Curried Dipping Sauce for shipment throughout the United States.

Sally's Marketbasket International
110 Hansen Avenue South
Salem OR 97302
503-399-1657
Contact:
Sally Edmiston

WASHINGTON

Chanterelle Specialty Foods, Inc.
9311 Olympic View Drive
Edmonds WA 98020
206-774-0650
Contact:
Deborah Bettag
Jochen Bettag

DeLaurenti Specialty Food Market
1435 First Avenue
Seattle WA 98101
206-622-0141
Contact:
Kurt Chambers

Truffles, Inc.
3701 Northeast 45th
Seattle WA 98105
206-522-3016
Contact:
Roberta Smythe
Joan Wright

ALASKA & HAWAII

The Deli
P.O. Box 871540
Wasilla AK 99687
907-376-2914
Contact:
Marian Worrell

The Gift Company
13 Ahipuu Street
Honolulu HI 96817
808-625-2229
Contact:
Sharon Ishii

Direct Mail Order Catalogs

The major direct mail order catalogs serving the food industry span an amazing range of ethnic and specialty foods and all kinds of kitchen needs. This listing has been compiled to include as many varieties of American foods as possible.

For convenience, the various catalogs are listed alphabetically under the category that represents the largest proportion of their offerings. Those that specifically offer a wide range of foods are listed under Specialty Foods & Food Gifts; more general kitchen catalogs appear under Cooks' Tools & Kitchen Accessories.

CHEESE

Crowley Cheese
Healdsville VT 05147
802-259-2340
Free

Hickory Farms
P.O. Box 75
Maumee OH 43537
419-893-6446
Free

Ideal Cheese
1205 Second Avenue
New York NY 10021
212-688-7579
Free

Kolb-Lena Cheese Company
3990 North Sunnyside Road
Lena IL 61048
815-369-4577
Free

Maytag Dairy Farms
Box 806
Newton IA 50208
515-792-1133
Free

**New England Cheesemaking
Supply Company**
Box 8555
Ashfield MA 01330
413-628-3808
Free

Sonoma Cheese Factory
2 Spain Street
Sonoma CA 95476
800-535-2855
Free

**Tillamook County Creamery
Association**
P.O. Box 313
Tillamook OR 97141
503-842-4481
Free

CHOCOLATES & CANDY

Bissinger's Sweet Tooth
1020 Saratoga Street
Newport KY 41071
606-581-4663
Free

**The Brigittine Monks
Gourmet Confections**
23300 Walker Lane
Amity OR 97101
503-835-8080
Free

The Chocolate Catalogue
3983 Gratiot Street
St. Louis MO 63110
314-534-2401
800-325-8881
Free

Estee Candy Company
169 Lackawanna Avenue
Parsippany NJ 07054
201-335-1000
Free

Godiva Chocolatier
260 Madison Avenue
New York NY 10016
212-951-2888
Free

Hershey's Chocolate World
Park Boulevard
P.O. Box 800
Hershey PA 17033
800-544-1347
Free

Kron Chocolatier
241 Boston Post Road
Milford CT 06460
203-877-6575
$1.00

Li-Lac Chocolates, Inc.
120 Christopher Street
New York NY 10014
212-242-7374
Free

Perugina of Italy
636 Lexington Avenue
New York NY 10022
212-688-2490
Free

COFFEE & TEA

**Community Coffee Kitchen
The Art of Food**
P.O. Box 3778
Baton Rouge LA 70821
504-381-3900
800-535-9901
$2.00; refundable

Empire Coffee & Tea Company
592 Ninth Avenue
New York NY 10036
212-586-1717
Free

**Georgetown Coffee, Tea and
Spice**
1330 Wisconsin Avenue NW
Washington DC 20007
202-338-3801
Free

Mauna Kea Coffee Company
P.O. Box 829
Captain Cook HI 96704
808-328-2511
Free

McNulty's Tea and Coffee Company
109 Christopher Street
New York NY 10014
212-242-5351
Free

Schapira Coffee Company
117 West Tenth Street
New York NY 10011
212-675-3733
Free

Thomas J. Lipton, Inc.
800 Sylvan Avenue
Englewood Cliffs NJ 07632
201-567-8000
Free

FISH, CAVIAR & SEAFOOD

Caviarteria
29 East 60th Street
New York NY 10022
212-759-7410
800-4CA-VIAR
Free

Iron Gate Products Company
520 Barretto Street
Bronx NY 10474
212-757-2670
Free

Legal Sea Foods
33 Everett Street
Boston MA 02134
617-254-7000
800-343-5804
Free

Nelson Crab
Box 520
Tokeland WA 98590
206-267-2911
Free

FRUIT & NUTS

Ace Pecan Company
P.O. Box 65
Cordele GA 31015
912-273-1072
Free

Bowlby Candy Company
P.O. Box 312
Waupaca WI 54981
715-258-3711
Free

Colvada Date Company
P.O. Box 908
Coachella CA 92236
619-398-3551
Free

DeSoto Confectionery & Nut Company
P.O. Box 72
DeSoto GA 31743
912-874-1200
Free

Gourmet Nut Center
1430 Railroad Avenue
Orland CA 95963
916-865-5511
Free

Hale Indian River Groves
Indian River Plaza
Wabasso FL 32970
407-589-4334
800-289-4253
Free

Harry & David
2518 South Pacific Highway
Medford OR 97501
503-776-2121
Free

Hawaii Holiday Macadamia Nut Company, Inc.
P.O. Box 707
Honokaa HI 96727
808-775-7255
Free

Orange Blossom Groves
5800 Seminole Boulevard
Seminole FL 34642
813-391-2313
Free

Sternberg Pecan Company
P.O. Box 193
Jackson MS 39205
601-366-6310
Free

Young's Pecan Sales Corporation
P.O. Drawer 5779
Florence SC 29502
803-662-2452
Free

HEALTH FOODS

Barth-Spencer
865 Merrick Avenue
Westbury NY 11590
516-683-0900
Free

Better Foods Foundation
200 North Washington
Greencastle PA 17225
717-597-3105
Free

Brownville Mills
Brownville NE 68321
402-825-4131
Free

Fearn International, Inc.
9353 West Belmont Avenue
Franklin Park IL 60131
708-678-1241
Free

Natural Food Distributors, Inc.
3040 Hill Avenue
Toledo OH 43607
419-537-1713
Free

Nature Food Centres
1 Nature's Way
Wilmington MA 01887
508-657-5000
Free

Northern Natural Foods
13 South Fourth Street
Moorhead MN 56560
218-236-5999
Free

Walnut Acres
Penns Creek PA 17862
717-837-0601
Free

Westbrae Natural Foods
5701 South Eastern Avenue, Suite 330
Commerce CA 90040
213-722-1692
Free

HERBS & SPICES

Aphrodisia Products
282 Bleecker Street
New York NY 10014
212-989-6440
$2.00

Ram Island Farm Herbs
Cape Elizabeth ME 04107
207-767-5700
Free

San Francisco Herb Company
250 14th Street
San Francisco CA 94103
415-861-7174
800-227-4530
Free

The Spice Market
664 Bergen Street
Brooklyn NY 11238
718-636-6300
Free

Well-Sweep Herb Farm
317 Mt. Bethel Road
Port Murray NJ 07865
201-852-5390
$1.00

MEAT & POULTRY

Broadbent's B & B Products
6321 Hopkinsville Road
Cadiz KY 42211
502-235-5294
Free

Cavanaugh Lakeview Farms
821 Lowery Road
P.O. Box 580
Chelsea MI 48118
313-475-9391
Free

Dakin Farm
Route 7
Ferrisburg VT 05456
802-425-3971
Free

Day & Young
P.O. Box 6947
San Jose CA 95150
408-297-2127
Free

Gaspar's Sausage Company
Faunce Corner Road
P.O. Box 436
North Dartmouth MA 02747
508-998-2012
800-542-2038
Free

Harrington's
Main Street
Richmond VT 05477
802-434-3411
Free

High Valley Farm
14 Alsace Way
Colorado Springs CO 80906
719-634-2944
Free

Jordan Virginia Ham Company
P.O. Box 447
Smithfield VA 23430
804-357-4321
Free

Lawrence's Smoke House
Route 30
Townshend VT 05353
802-365-7372
Free

New Braunfels Smokehouse
P.O. Box 311159
New Braunfels TX 78131
512-625-3721
Free

Nodine's Smokehouse
65 Fowler Avenue
P.O. Box 1787
Torrington CT 06790
203-489-3213
Free

Omaha Steaks International
P.O. Box 3300
Omaha NE 68103
402-391-3660
800-228-9055
Free

Oscar's Hickory House, Inc.
205 Main Street
Warrensburg NY 12885
518-623-3431
Free

Ozark Mountain Smoke House
P.O. Box 37
Farmington AR 72730
501-267-3339
Free

Pfaelzer Brothers
281 West 83rd Street
Burr Ridge IL 60521
708-325-9700
800-621-0226
Free

Schaller and Weber
22-35 46th Street
Long Island City NY 11105
212-879-3047
Free

Smithfield Collection
Highway 10,
Industrial Section
Smithfield VA 23430
804-357-2121
800-628-2242
Free

Smithfield Packing Company
P.O. Box 447
Smithfield VA 23430
804-357-4321
Free

Fred Usinger, Inc.
1030 North Old World Third Street
Milwaukee WI 53203
414-276-9100
Free

PASTRY & BAKED GOODS

Baldwin Hill Bakery
Baldwin Hill Road
Phillipston MA 01331
508-249-4691
Free

Bocock-Stroud Company
P.O. Box 3198
Winston-Salem NC 27012
919-724-2421
Free

Cafe Beaujolais Bakery
P.O. Box 730
Mendocino CA 95460
707-964-0292
Free

C'est Croissant
22138 South Vermont Avenue,
Suite F
Torrance CA 90502
800-633-2767
Free

DiCamillo Baking Company
811 Linwood Avenue
Niagara Falls NY 14305
716-282-2341
800-634-4363
Free

Fantasia Confections
3465 California Street
San Francisco CA 94118
415-752-0825
Free

Mail Order Muffins
910 Orange Street
Wilmington DE 19801
302-656-6500
Free

Mary of Puddin Hill
P.O. Box 241
Greenville TX 75401
214-455-2651
Free

Miss Grace Lemon Cake Company
422 North Canon Drive
Beverly Hills CA 90210
213-274-2879
Free

Mrs. Fields Cookies, Inc.
P.O. Box 400
Park City UT 84060
801-649-2404
800-444-CHIP
Free

Santa Fe Cookie Company
110 West San Francisco Street
Santa Fe NM 87501
505-983-7707
800-243-0353
Free

**Wolferman's Original
English Muffin Company**
8900 Marshall Drive
Lenexa KS 66215
913-888-4499
Free

SPECIALTY FOODS & FOOD GIFTS

American Spoon Foods
P.O. Box 566
Petoskey MI 49770
616-347-9030
800-222-5886
Free

Bainbridge's Festive Foods
P.O. Box 587
White Bluff TN 37187
615-383-5157
Free

Balducci's
424 Sixth Avenue
New York NY 10011
212-673-2600
Free

Bremen House
218 East 86th Street
New York NY 10028
212-288-5500
Free

Chalet Suzanne Foods
1 West Starr Avenue
P.O. Box AC
Lake Wales FL 33859
813-676-6011
Free

Charles & Company
340 Madison Avenue
New York NY 10017
212-682-8900
Free

Crabtree & Evelyn, Ltd.
Peake Brook Road
P.O. Box 167
Woodstock CT 06281
203-928-2766
$3.50

Dean & DeLuca
560 Broadway
New York NY 10012
212-431-1691
Free

E.A.T.
1064 Madison Avenue
New York NY 10028
212-772-0022
Free

The Epicures' Club
107-F Corporate Boulevard
P.O. Box 271
South Plainfield NJ 07080
201-753-1220
Free

Ferrara Foods & Confections
195 Grand Street
New York NY 10013
212-226-6150
Free

Figi's
3200 South Maple Avenue
Marshfield WI 54449
715-387-1771
Free

Fraser-Morris Fine Foods
931 Madison Avenue
New York NY 10021
212-288-2727
Free

Gazin's, Inc.
P.O. Box 19221
New Orleans LA 70179
504-482-0302
$1.00; refundable

Gump's Mail Order
P.O. Box 890910
Dallas TX 75389
800-284-8677
Free

Jurgensen's Grocery Company
842 East California Boulevard
Pasadena CA 91109
818-792-3121
Free

Jurgensen's gift baskets come in all shapes and sizes—from traditional hampers packed for a gourmet picnic to silver bowls of caviar and champagne, baskets of fine wine to bushels of imported beer. We've been crafting creative gifts with fine foods and wines since 1935. Call us toll-free at 800-344-4313 for a catalog bursting with mouth watering ideas.

Jurgensen's: Gourmet food with thought.

Konriko Company Store
P.O. Box 10640
New Iberia LA 90562
318-367-6163
800-551-3245
Free

Kozlowski Farms
5566 Gravenstein Highway
Forestville CA 95436
707-887-2104
Free

Knott's Berry Farm
8039 Beach Boulevard
Buena Park CA 90620
714-827-1776
Free

Maison Glass
111 East 58th Street
New York NY 10022
212-755-3316
$5.00

Manganaro Foods
488 Ninth Avenue
New York NY 10018
212-563-5331
Free

Narsai's Market
350 Berkeley Park Boulevard
Kensington CA 94707
415-527-7900
Free

New England Country Fare
378 Washington Street
Westwood MA 02090
617-329-4874
800-274-FARE
$2.00; refundable

**Old Covered Bridge Farm
Gift Shop**
Route 7
Ferrisburg VT 05456
802-877-2576
Free

**Oriental Food Market &
Cooking School**
2801 West Howard Street
Chicago IL 60645
312-274-2826
Free

Paprikas Weiss Importer
1546 Second Avenue
New York NY 10028
212-288-6117
Free

Pepper Patch, Inc.
1250 Old Hillsboro Road
Franklin TN 37064
615-790-1012
Free

**Pepperidge Farm
Mail Order Company**
P.O. Box 119
Clinton CT 06413
203-669-4131
800-243-9314
Free

S. E. Rykoff & Company
P.O. Box 21467
Market Street Station
Los Angeles CA 90021
800-421-9873
Free

The Silver Palate Kitchens
274 Columbus Avenue
New York NY 10023
212-799-6340
Free

Sugar's Kitchen
P.O. Box 41886
Tucson AZ 85717
602-299-6027
Free

The Swiss Colony
1112 Seventh Avenue
Monroe WI 53566
608-324-4000
Free

Timber Crest Farms
4791 Dry Creek Road
Healdsburg CA 95448
707-433-8251
Free

Todaro Brothers
555 Second Avenue
New York NY 10016
212-679-7766
Free

Paul A. Urbani Truffles
P.O. Box 2054
Trenton NJ 08607
609-394-5851
Free

**Wilds of Idaho-Gourmet Huckle-
berry Products**
1308 West Boone
Spokane WA 99201
509-326-0197
Free

William Poll Gourmet Shop
1051 Lexington Avenue
New York NY 10021
212-288-0501
Free

The Wisconsin Cheeseman
P.O. Box 1
Madison WI 53701
608-837-5166
Free

Zabar's
2245 Broadway
New York NY 10024
212-787-2000
Free

COOKS' TOOLS & KITCHEN ACCESSORIES

Chantry
P.O. Box 3039
Clearwater FL 34530
800-242-6879
Free

The Crate and Barrel
P.O. Box 3057
Northbrook IL 60065
800-323-5461
Free

European Home Products
236 East Avenue
Norwalk CT 06855
203-866-9683
800-225-0760
$1.00; refundable

Hammacher Schlemmer
212 West Superior Street
Chicago IL 60610
312-664-8170
800-543-3366
$2.00

**Jessica's Biscuit
Cookbook Catalog**
P.O. Box 301
Newtonville MA 02160
800-225-4264
Free

John H. Murcott, Inc.
200 Cabot Street
West Babylon NY 11704
516-845-5555
$5.00

Williams-Sonoma
P.O. Box 7456
San Francisco CA 94120
415-421-4242
Free

The Wooden Spoon
P.O. Box 931
Clinton CT 06413
800-431-2207
Free

The popularity of organic foods is increasing enormously. Health foods have left the fringe and become a preoccupation manifest in everyone's vocabulary and lifestyle.

The two major sources of detailed information in this area are the comprehensive list of mail-order suppliers of organic foods compiled by Americans for Safe Food, a project of the Center for Science in the Public Interest, and *Organic Gardening* magazine's annually updated listing of organic food producers and associations.

In this selected listing, made by Elaine Yannuzzi of Expression unltd., suppliers are listed by region under three headings: Farm Products, Free Range and Baked Goods, with contact names from whom more detailed information can be obtained.

"Organic" generally indicates food grown and processed without the use of synthetic pesticides, fertilizers or growth stimulants in an ecologically sound environment; definitions for certification vary from state to state. As many growers are very regional, they should be contacted individually for information on specific products and sales structure. An annual listing of distributors nationwide, *The Organic Wholesalers Directory and Yearbook*, is obtainable from California Action Network, P.O. Box 464, Davis CA 95617.

FARM PRODUCTS

NORTHEAST

MAINE

Johnny's Selected Seeds
Foss Hill Road
Albion ME 04910
207-437-9294
Contact:
Rob Johnston

Hidden Valley Farm
Hollywood Boulevard
Alna ME 04535
207-586-5837
Contact:
Bambi Jones and David Moskovitz

Maine Organic Farmers' and Gardeners' Association
Box 2176
283 Water Street
Augusta ME 04338
Contact:
Nancy Ross

Fiddler's Green Farm
R.R. 1, Box 656
Belfast ME 04915
207-338-3568
Contact:
Nancy Galland

Horsepower Farm
R.F.D. 1, Box 63
Blue Hill ME 04614
207-347-5038
Contact:
Mollie and Paul Birdsall

King Hill Farm/Hay's Farm Stand
P.O. Box 92
Blue Hill ME 04614
207-374-2822
Contact:
Dennis King and Jean Hay

Wood Prairie Farm
R.F.D. 1, Box 164
Bridgewater ME 04735
207-429-9765
Contact:
Jim and Megan Gerritsen

Patchwork Organic Gardens
R.F.D. 5, Box 5577
Brunswick ME 04011
207-442-8195
Contact:
George and Susan Sergeant

Red Maple Farm
R.F.D. 1, Box 2000
Cambridge ME 04923
207-848-5714
Contact:
William and Carol Ewell

Hillside Farm
P.O. Box 399
Camden ME 04843
207-236-2029
Contact:
Tony and Mary Bok

Sand Hill Farm
R.D. 2, Box 1886
Coopers Mills ME 04341
207-549-7802
Contact:
Mark and Bonnie Miller

Pleasant Valley Farm
547 Pleasant Valley Road
Cumberland Center ME 04021
207-829-5588
Contact:
Elizabeth Weir

Peacemeal Farm
North Road, Box 1010
Dixmont ME 04932
207-257-3943
Contact:
Benjamin and Ariel Wilcox,
Tom Roberts

Happy Town Farm
R.R. 2, Box 3760
East Holden ME 04429
207-667-9212
Contact:
Paul and Karen Volckhausen

Maine Coast Sea Vegetables
Shore Road
Franklin ME 04634
207-565-2907
Contact:
Carl Karush

Blueberry Ledge Farm
R.F.D. 2, Box 374
Gardiner ME 04345
207-737-8522
Contact:
Rudd and Elizabeth Douglass

Crossroad Farm
P.O. Box 71A
Jonesport ME 04649
207-497-2641
Contact:
Arnold and Bonnie Pearlman

Fulford Brothers Nursery
R.R. 1, Box 3000
Monroe ME 04951
207-525-7761
Contact:
Mark B. Fulford

Beech Hill Farm
H.C.R. 62, Box 307
Mount Desert ME 04660
207-288-4348
Contact:
Kevin Ernst

F & A Farm
Route 1, Box 725
Palermo ME 04354
207-993-2755
Contact:
Jamie Greager and Martie Crone

New Leaf Farm
470 Davis Road
Pownal ME 04069
207-353-5263
Contact:
David Colson

Willow Pond Farm
R.F.D. 2, Box 4105, Route 9
Sabattus ME 04280
207-375-6662
Contact:
Jill and Charlie Agnew

Rocky Hills Farm
90 York Woods Road
South Berwick ME 03908
207-384-2582
Contact:
Rae and William Avery

MASSACHUSETTS

Organic Food Production Association of North America
P.O. Box 31
Belchertown MA 01007
413-323-6821
Contact:
Judith Fuller Gillan

White Oak Farm
c/o New England Small Farm Institute
Jepson House
169 Jackson Street
Belchertown MA 01007
413-323-4531
Contact:
Judith Gillan

Stearns Organic Farm
859 Edmands Road
Framingham MA 01701
508-877-3882
Contact:
Penelope Turton

Lightlife Foods, Inc.
P.O. Box 870
Greenfield MA 01302
413-774-6001
Contact:
Chia Collins

Lightlife is one of the nation's leading manufacturers of soy foods, specializing in tofu-based "meatless meats" and tempeh products. Makers of TofuPups®, Fakur Bacon®, Foney Baloney,™ American Grill™ and Lemon Grill.™ Retail, foodservice and ingredient packs. All items are all-natural, cholesterol-free and low-fat. Contract manufacturing is available.

Bread & Circus
1163 Walnut Street
Newton Highlands MA 02161
617-332-2400
Contact:
Chris Kilham

Natural Organic Farmers' Association of Massachusetts
21 Great Plain Avenue
Wellesley MA 02181
617-235-1447
Contact:
Stacy Miller

NEW HAMPSHIRE

Water Wheel Sugar House
Route 2
Jefferson NH 03583
Contact:
Barbara Clukay

Apple Jacks Cider Mill
24 Francestown Road
New Boston NH 03070
603-487-5522
Contact:
Robert Belanger

NEW JERSEY

Black Cloud Farm
R.D. 5, Box 560,
Joe Ent. Road
Flemington NJ 08822
201-788-4955
Contact:
Mary Ann Cornelissen

Lee's Turkey Farm
Hickory Corner Road
Hightstown NJ 08520
609-448-0629
Contact:
Ruth Lee

Organicly Yours
P.O. Box 186
Riverside NJ 08075
609-786-2777
Contact:
Paul Keiser and Nancy Jones

NEW YORK

Deer Valley Farm
R.D. 1
Guilford NY 13780
607-764-8556
Contact:
Robert Carsten

Natural Organic Farmers' Association
P.O. Box 454
Ithaca NY 14851
607-648-5557
Contact:
Pat Kane

Earth's Harvest
700 Columbus Avenue
New York NY 10025
212-864-1376
Contact:
Christy Rockhold

Prana Foods
125 First Avenue
New York NY 10003
212-982-7306
Contact:
Bruce Raddock

Community Mill and Bean
R.D. 1, Route 89
Savannah NY 13146
315-365-2664
Contact:
Catherine Fallon

Rich Lynn Forest Farm
R.D. 1, Box 433
Savona NY 14879
607-583-7345
Contact:
Lynn Lynds

PENNSYLVANIA

Better Foods Foundation, Inc.
200 North Washington Street
Greencastle PA 17225
717-597-3105
Contact:
John Eshleman

Krystal Wharf Farms
R.D. 2, Box 191-A
Mansfield PA 16933
717-549-8194
Contact:
Burt Israel

Rising Sun Distributors
P.O. Box 627
Milesburg PA 16853
814-355-9850
Contact:
Hope Woodring

Garden Spot Distributors
438 White Oak Road
New Holland PA 17557
717-354-4936
Contact:
Kathy Clough

Walnut Acres
Penn's Creek PA 17862
717-837-0601
Contact:
Emma Mattern

Organic Crop Improvement Association
R.D. 2, Box 116-A
Volant PA 16156
412-530-7220
Contact:
Ron Gargasz

RHODE ISLAND

Meadowbrook Herb Gardens
Wyoming RI 02898
401-539-7603
Contact:
Margie Fortier

VERMONT

Gourmet Produce Company
R.R. 2, Box 348
Chester VT 05143
802-875-3820
Contact:
Richard Rommer

Louis Pulver
R.R. 1, Box 2345
East Hardwick VT 05836
802-533-7175
Contact:
Louis Pulver

Elmore Roots Nursery
P.O. Box 171
Lake Elmore VT 05657
802-888-3305
Contact:
David Fried

Littlewood Farm
R.F.D. 1, Box 1400
Plainfield VT 05667
802-454-8466
Contact:
Joey Klein

Hill and Dale Farms
West Hill-Daniel Davis Road
Route 2, Box 1260
Putney VT 05346
802-387-5817
Contact:
Esther Poneck

Carpenter Farms
R.R. 1, Box 130
Randolph Center VT 05061
802-728-3782
Contact:
David Carpenter

Tinmouth Channel Farm
Town Highway 19, Box 428-B
Tinmouth VT 05773
802-446-2812
Contact:
Carolyn Fuhrer

S O U T H

ALABAMA

Hillcrest Farms
30497 Hixon Road
Elberta AL 36530
205-962-2500
Contact:
Laurel Hixon

Yuchi Pines
Route 1, Box 423
Seale AL 36875
205-855-3804
Contact:
Carl Malcolm

ARKANSAS

Eagle Agricultural Products
407 Church Avenue
Huntsville AR 72740
501-738-2203
Contact:
Kathy Turner

FLORIDA

Bellevue Gardens Organic Farm
625 Bellevue Lane
Archer FL 32618
904-495-2348
Contact:
Tommy Simmons

Rus Organic Farm
7359 Hypoluxo Farms Road
Lake Worth FL 33463
Contact:
Raymond Rus

Starr Organic Produce, Inc.
P.O. Box 561502
Miami FL 33256
305-262-1242
Contact:
David Weingast

GEORGIA

Harry's Market
Alpharetta GA 30201
404-664-6300
Contact:
Harry Blazer

Georgia Organic Growers' Association
P.O. Box 567661
Atlanta GA 30356
404-621-4661
Contact:
Honey Rubin

Michael's Mountain Honey
Route 4, Box 826
Blairsville GA 30512
404-745-4170
Contact:
Michael Surles

DeKalb Farmers' Market
3000 East Ponce De Leon
Decatur GA 30030
404-377-6400
Contact:
Robert Blazer

Rainbow Grocery
2118 North Decatur Road
Decatur GA 30033
404-636-5533
Contact:
Kirk Evan

MARYLAND

Organic Foods Express
11003 Emack Road
Beltsville MD 20705
301-937-8608
Contact:
Scott Nash

MISSISSIPPI

Owen McCullar
6203 Goodman Road
Olive Branch MS 38654
601-895-3143
Contact:
Owen McCullar

TENNESSEE

Jim Joyner
Route 1
Liberty TN 37095
615-563-2353
Contact:
Jim Joyner

Homegrown Produce Company
59 The Farm
Summertown TN 38483
615-964-2435
Contact:
Martin Holsinger

VIRGINIA

Kennedy's Natural Foods
1051 West Broad Street
Falls Church VA 22046
703-533-8484
Contact:
Mary Kennedy

Virginia Association of Biological Farmers
Box 252
Flint Hill VA 22627
Contact:
Diana Bird

Golden Acres Orchard
Route 2, Box 2450
Front Royal VA 22630
703-636-9611
Contact:
A. P. Thomson

Golden Acres Apiary
P.O. Box 2
Singers Glen VA 22850
Contact:
Dennis Whetzel

WEST VIRGINIA

Hardscrabble Enterprises, Inc.
Route 6, Box 42
Cherry Grove WV 26804
304-567-2727
Contact:
Paul Goland

MIDWEST

ILLINOIS

The Green Earth
2545 Prairie Avenue
Evanston IL 60201
708-864-8949
800-322-3662
Contact:
Karin Dittmar, Kyra Walsh

Golden Key Farm
R.R. 2, Box 416
Grant Park IL 60940
708-946-6686
Contact:
Frank Pilotte

INDIANA

Lone Pine Farm
P.O. Box 38
Inglefield IN 47618
812-867-3149
Contact:
W. Marvin Lundy

IOWA

Rolling Acres Farm
R.R. 2, Box 79
Atlantic IA 50022
712-243-3264
Contact:
Larry Harris, Denise O'Brien

Iowa State Natural Food Associates
R.R. 1, Box 153
Epworth IA 52045
319-744-3157
Contact:
Ron and Val Lucas

Clarence Van Sant
1501 Sixth Avenue
Grinnell IA 50208
515-236-4437
Contact:
Clarence Van Sant

Old Man's Creek Organics
R.R. 3, Box 216
Iowa City IA 52240
319-683-2727
Contact:
Jim Walters

Paul's Grains
2475-B 340 Street
Laurel IA 50141
515-476-3373
Contact:
Wayne Paul

KANSAS

Loyd Fight
Route 3, Box 493
Leavenworth KS 66048
913-727-6037
Contact:
Loyd Fight

MICHIGAN

Eden Foods, Inc.
701 Tecumseh Road
Clinton MI 49236
313-973-9400
Contact:
Martha Johnson

Richards Natural Food Farm
15213 Hinman Road
Eagle MI 48822
517-627-7965
Contact:
Richard and Janet Osterbeck

Saintz Farm
2225 63rd Street
Fennville MI 49408
616-561-2761
Contact:
Eugene and Joan Saintz

Sunshower
48548 60th Avenue
Lawrence MI 49064
616-674-3103
Contact:
Paul Schultz

Organic Growers of Michigan
c/o Paw Paw Food Co-op
243 East Michigan Avenue
Paw Paw MI 49079
616-657-5934
Contact:
Mark Thomas

American Spoon Foods
P.O. Box 566
Petoskey MI 49770
616-347-9030
800-327-7984
Contact:
Justin Rashid

Country Life Natural Foods
109th Avenue
Pullman MI 49450
616-236-5011
Contact:
Berwyn Rogers

Tom Vreeland
5861 Geddes Road
Ypsilanti MI 48198
313-483-0803
Contact:
Tom Vreeland

MINNESOTA

Organic Growers' and Buyers' Association
1405 Silver Lake Road
New Brighton MN 55112
612-636-7933
Contact:
Yvonne Buckley

Diamond K. Enterprises
R.R. 1, Box 30-A
St. Charles MN 55972
507-932-4308
Contact:
Jack Kranz

NEBRASKA

M & M Distributing
R.R. 2, Box 61-A
Oshkosh NE 69154
308-772-3664
Contact:
Mark Jones

NORTH DAKOTA

David Podoll
Route 1, Box 33
Fullerton ND 58441
701-883-4429
Contact:
David Podoll

OHIO

Millstream Natural Health Supplies
1310-A East Tallmadge Avenue
Akron OH 44310
216-630-2700
Contact:
Jonathon Miller

Organic Crop Improvement Association
3185 Road 179
Bellefontaine OH 43311
513-592-4983
Contact:
Betty Kananen

Clearview Farm
11015 Mill Street SW
Pataskala OH 43062
614-927-8268
Contact:
The Hohmann Family

OKLAHOMA

Earth Natural Foods
309 South Flood
Norman OK 73069
405-364-3551
Contact:
Tempie Nichols

Earth Natural Foods Deli
1101 Northwest 49th Street
Oklahoma City OK 73118
405-840-0502
Contact:
Tempie Nichols

SOUTH DAKOTA

Virgil Van Der Boom
Box 45
Newell SD 57760
605-456-2819
Contact:
Virgil Van Der Boom

WISCONSIN

Lubbert's Organic Products
5585 Fork Road, R.R. 2
Hartford WI 53027
414-629-9371
Contact:
Raymond Lubbert

Dennis Bries
P.O. Box 334
Johnson Creek WI 53038
414-699-3767
Contact:
Dennis Bries

SOUTHWEST

ARIZONA

Arjoy Acres
H.C.R. Box 1410
Payson AZ 85541
602-474-1224
Contact:
Arne Koch

Wind Spirit
2444 Dripping Springs Road
Winkelman AZ 85292
213-280-9992
Contact:
John Cohen

NEW MEXICO

New Mexico Organic Growers' Association
1312 Lobo Place NE
Albuquerque NM 87106
505-268-5504
Contact:
Sarah McDonald

TEXAS

J. Francis Company
Route 2, Box 54
Atlanta TX 75551
214-796-5364
Contact:
Joe Francis

Whole Foods Market and Restaurant
2218 Greenville Avenue
Dallas TX 75206
214-824-1744
Contact:
David Matthis

Arrowhead Mills
P.O. Box 2059
Hereford TX 79045
806-364-0730
Contact:
Pete Holcombe

Hawkins Creek Farm
P.O. Box 6552
Longview TX 75608
214-759-8820
Contact:
Jim Collins

South Tex Organics
6 Betty Drive
Mission TX 78572
512-581-1040
Contact:
Dennis Holbrook

MOUNTAIN STATES

IDAHO

David Ronniger
Star Route
Moyie Springs ID 83845
208-267-7938
208-267-5743
Contact:
David Ronniger

Mountain Star Honey Company
P.O. Box 179
Peck ID 83545
208-486-6821
Contact:
Kent and Sharon Wenkheimer

WEST COAST

CALIFORNIA

Wiggin Farms
6590 Hillgate Road
Arbuckle CA 95912
916-476-2288
Contact:
Sharon Wiggin

Knudsen Company
P.O. Box 369
Chico CA 95927
916-891-1517
Contact:
Pete Crawford

Weiss' Kiwifruit
595 Paseo Companeros
Chico CA 95928
916-343-2354
Contact:
Gary Weiss

Great Date in the Morning
P.O. Box 31
Coachella CA 92236
619-398-6171
Contact:
Jim Dunn

Lee Anderson's Covalda Date Company
P.O. Box 908
Coachella CA 92236
619-398-3441
Contact:
Charlotte Stocks

Paul A. Buxman
Sweet Home Ranch
Dinuba CA 93618
209-591-4424
Contact:
Jim Stewart (WesPak Sales)

Santa Cruz Orchards
Box 1510
Freedom CA 95019
408-728-0414
Contact:
John Battenbieri

G. Grell
P.O. Box 7092
Halcyon CA 93420
805-489-2227
Contact:
G. Grell

Timber Crest Farms
4791 Dry Creek Road
Healdsburg CA 95448
707-433-8251
Contact:
Linda Waltenspiel

West Valley Produce Company
726 South Mateo Street
Los Angeles CA 90021
213-627-4131
Contact:
Murray Cherness

Your Land, Our Land
P.O. Box 485
Los Altos CA 94022
415-821-6732
Contact:
Kevin Martin

Ahler's Organic Date Garden
P.O. Box 1726
Mecca CA 92254
619-396-2337
Contact:
Fred Wendler

Dach Ranch
P.O. Box 44
Philo CA 95466
707-895-3173
Contact:
John Dach

Lundberg Family Farm
P.O. Box 369
Richvale CA 95974
916-882-4551
Contact:
Peter Milbury

Blue Heron Farm
P.O. Box 68
Rumsey CA 95679
916-796-3799
Contact:
John Ceteras

Gold Mine Natural Food Company
1947 30th Street
San Diego CA 92102
800-647-2929
Contact:
Carlos A. Richardson III

California Certified Organic Farmers
P.O. Box 8136
Santa Cruz CA 95061
Contact:
Robert Scowcroft

The Worm Concern
580 Erbes Road
Thousand Oaks CA 91362
805-496-2872
Contact:
Richard Morhar

Sun Mountain Medicine Ways
35751 Oak Springs Drive
Tollhouse CA 93667
209-855-3710
Contact:
George Ballis

Jaffe Brothers
P.O. Box 636
Valley Center CA 92082
619-749-1133
Contact:
Allen Jaffe

OREGON

Herb Pharm
P.O. Box 116
Williams OR 97544
503-849-7178
Contact:
Ed Smith

WASHINGTON

Cascadian Farm
311 Dillard
P.O. Box 568
Concrete WA 98237
206-853-8175
Contact:
Jim Watkins

Farmers' Wholesale Cooperative
P.O. Box 7446
Olympia WA 98507
206-754-8989
Contact:
Susan Kravit

Sweet Wind Gardens
Route 2, Box 540
Twisp WA 98856
509-997-4891
Contact:
Richard Murray

Russell Elliott Organic Gardens
P.O. Box 183
Wapato WA 98951
509-877-3159
Contact:
Russell Elliott

ALASKA & HAWAII

ALASKA

Alaska Honey Farm
1812 Central Avenue
Fairbanks AK 99709
907-456-7202
Contact:
Harold Livingstone

Diamond Ridge Farms
H.C. 31, Box 5113
Wasilla AK 99687
907-376-5679
Contact:
Leroy Heaven

FREE RANGE

NORTHEAST

MAINE

Hidden Valley Farm
Hollywood Boulevard
Alna ME 04535
207-586-5837
Contact:
Bambi Jones and David Moskovitz

King Hill Farm/Hay's Farm Stand
P.O. Box 92
Blue Hill ME 04614
207-374-2822
Contact:
Dennis King and Jean Hay

Wood Prairie Farm
R.F.D. 1, Box 164
Bridgewater ME 04735
207-429-9765
Contact:
Jim and Megan Gerritsen

Sand Hill Farm
R.D. 2, Box 1886
Coopers Mills ME 04341
207-549-7802
Contact:
Mark and Bonnie Miller

Pleasant Valley Farm
547 Pleasant Valley Road
Cumberland Center ME 04021
207-829-5588
Contact:
Elizabeth Weir

Happy Town Farm
R.R. 2, Box 3760
East Holden ME 04429
207-667-9212
Contact:
Paul and Karen Volckhausen

Wolfe's Neck Farm
R.R. 1, Box 71
Freeport ME 04032
207-865-4469
Contact:
Charles De Grandpre

NEW YORK

Hawthorne Valley Farm
R.D. 2, Box 225-A
Ghent NY 12075
518-672-7500
Contact:
Gary Lamb

Deer Valley Farm
R.D. 1
Guilford NY 13780
607-764-8556
Contact:
Robert Carsten

VERMONT

Pine Meadow Farm
East Hill
Brookfield VT 05036
Contact:
Steve and Gina Paradise

SOUTH

FLORIDA

Maverick Ranch Beef
402 North Pine Meadow Drive
DeBary FL 32713
407-668-6361
Contact:
David Feldman

GEORGIA

Bricker's Organic Farm, Inc.
824 Sandbar Ferry Road
Augusta GA 30901
404-722-0661
Contact:
Bill Bricker

VIRGINIA

Summerfield Farm
Star Route 4, Box 195-A
Brightwood VA 22715
703-948-3100
Contact:
Jamie Nicholl

Red Gate Farm
Brownsburg VA 24415
703-348-5439
Contact:
Reid T. Putney

Natural Beef Farms Food Distribution Company
4399-A Henninger Court
Chantilly VA 22021
703-631-0881
Contact:
Susan and Stephan Donner

Blue Ridge Food Service
Route 3, Box 304
Edinburg VA 28824
703-459-3376
Contact:
Bob Peer

WEST VIRGINIA

Brier Run Farm
Route 1, Box 73
Birch River WV 26610
304-649-2975
Contact:
Gregory Sava

MIDWEST

INDIANA

John McMahan
Box 111
Clifford IN 47226
812-372-4368
Contact:
John McMahan

IOWA

Rolling Acres Farm
R.R. 2, Box 79
Atlantic IA 50022
712-343-3264
Contact:
Larry Harris, Denise O'Brien

Paul's Grains
2475-B 340 Street
Laurel IA 50141
515-476-3373
Contact:
Wayne Paul

MICHIGAN

Roseland Farms
27427 M-60 West
Cassopolis MI 49031
616-445-8987
Contact:
Merrill Clark

Richards Natural Food Farm
15213 Hinman Road
Eagle MI 48822
517-627-7965
Contact:
Richard and Janet Osterbeck

MISSOURI

Morningland Dairy
Route 1, Box 188-B
Mountain View MO 65548
417-469-3817
Contact:
Jim Reiners

OHIO

Clearview Farm
11015 Mill Street SW
Pataskala OH 43062
614-927-8268
Contact:
The Hohmann Family

SOUTH DAKOTA

Virgil Van Der Boom
Box 45
Newell SD 57760
605-456-2819
Contact:
Virgil Van Der Boom

Dennis W. Schaefer
R.R. 2, Box 56
Tripp SD 57376
605-935-6582
Contact:
Dennis Schaefer

MOUNTAIN STATES

UTAH

Aquaculture Marketing Service
356 West Redview Drive
Monroe UT 84754
801-527-4528
Contact:
Jeanette Young

BAKED GOODS

NORTHEAST

MASSACHUSETTS

Baldwin Hill Bakery
Baldwin Hill Road
Phillipston MA 01331
508-249-4691
Contact:
Phil Leger

NEW YORK

Bread Alone
Route 28
Boiceville NY 12412
914-657-3328
Contact:
Lynne Gilson

Hawthorne Valley Farm
R.D. 2, Box 225-A
Ghent NY 12075
518-672-7500
Contact:
Gary Lamb

Deer Valley Farm
R.D. 1
Guilford NY 13780
607-764-8556
Contact:
Robert Carsten

MIDWEST

MINNESOTA

Mill City Sourdough Bakery
1566 Randolph Avenue
St. Paul MN 55105
612-698-4705
Contact:
Mark Jozwik

Kosher Food Suppliers

This listing of kosher food suppliers has been compiled by Elaine Yannuzzi, founder of Expression unltd. It includes all the food companies that exhibited at the 1989 New York Kosherfest, the first trade show ever to be devoted exclusively to kosher food products.

The list is organized by state, then alphabetically by each company's name, with contact names and an indication of each firm's specialties.

Kosher means food sanctioned as ritually fit for use according to Jewish law. More than 6 million consumers currently use kosher food products. Many of them are not doing so for religious reasons, but because they believe it is healthier and of better quality.

Today there are more than 17,000 kosher food products on the market and almost every type of food product that can be provided in kosher form is being or is about to be produced. Suppliers include supermarkets (who are starting to offer some private-label products as kosher), independent retailers, caterers, restaurants, institutions and wholesalers.

CALIFORNIA

Pepper House International
1321-J Virginia Avenue
Baldwin Park CA 91706
818-960-4733
Contact:
Jimmy Tani
Peeled garlic, shallots

SinBad Sweets, Inc.
324 North Minnewawa
Clovis CA 93612
209-298-3700
Contact:
Edwina Muhawi
Baklava, strudel

DISTRICT OF COLUMBIA

Creative Cookie Company
3900 16th Street NW, Suite 338
Washington DC 20011
202-722-1048
800-451-4005
Contact:
Emily Warwick
Fortune cookies

FLORIDA

Carolyn Candies
Florida Citrus Tower
U.S. Highway 27
Clermont FL 34711
904-394-8555
800-248-7871
Contact:
Diane James

Creative Kosher Foods, Inc.
14811 Hadleigh Way
Tampa FL 33624
813-251-2038
Contact:
Dan Stein
Pizza wraps

ILLINOIS

Eli's Chicago's Finest, Inc.
6510 West Dakin Street
Chicago IL 60634
312-736-3417
Contact:
Charlene Myer
Cheesecakes

Rubschlager Baking Corporation
3220 West Grand Avenue
Chicago IL 60651
312-826-1245
Contact:
Joan Rubschlager
Variety breads

Vita Food Products
222 West Lake Street
Chicago IL 60612
312-738-4500
Herring, smoked salmon

MAINE

Maine Coast Smokehouse
1 Cumberland Wharf
Box 308 DTS
Portland ME 04101
207-775-7114
Contact:
John Cardano

Mr. Zablotsky's
1 Main Street
Bangor ME 04401
207-947-1654
Contact:
Richard Zabot
Pizza pot pie, Oriental pot pie

MARYLAND

Tivall, USA
9633 East Bexhill Drive
Kensington MD 20895
301-946-8855
Contact:
Arthur Burns
Vegetarian frozen entrees, health foods, institutional

MASSACHUSETTS

Lightlife Foods, Inc.
74 Fairview Street
Greenfield MA 01302
413-774-6001
Contact:
Chia Collins
Tempeh (soy-based) products, tofu pups

New England Food Company, Inc.
370 Commercial Street
Malden MA 02148
617-324-7500
Contact:
Eli Cohen
Pita breads

MINNESOTA

Natural Way Mills, Inc.
Route 2, Box 37
Middle River MN 56737
218-222-3677
Contact:
Ray Juhl

NEW JERSEY

Camerican International
480 Alfred Avenue
Teaneck NJ 07666
201-833-2000
Contact:
Mari Chiriff
Chilled citrus segments

Carmel Kosher Food Products
Boumar Place
Elmwood Park NJ 07407
201-797-2824
Contact:
Shulem Einhorn
Soup bases, potato pancake mix, matzo ball mix, pudding mix, gravies

Drake Bakeries
75 Demarest Drive
Wayne NJ 07470
201-696-5010
Contact:
Joel Sherman

Dream Confectioners, Ltd.
467 Warwick Avenue
Teaneck NJ 07666
212-655-5200
Contact:
Joseph L. Podolski

Globe Products
(Holly Farms Corporation)
750 Bloomfield Avenue
Clifton NJ 07015
201-773-1800
800-524-0868
Contact:
Jeff Biev
Retail & foodservice products for baking & foodservice industries

Golden Fluff Popcorn Company
55 Park Avenue
Lakewood NJ 08701
201-367-5448
Contact:
Ephraim Schwinder

Go Lightly Candy Company
35 Hillside Avenue
Hillside NJ 07205
201-926-2300
Contact:
Ted Cohen

Goldman's Dairy
520 Main Avenue
Wallington NJ 07057
800-631-7739
Contact:
Ira Ginsberg

Intermili, Inc.
185 Linden Street
Hackensack NJ 07601
201-488-4242
Contact:
Israel Fromer
Precooked poultry products

Legume, Inc.
116 Fairfield Road
Fairfield NJ 07006
201-882-9190
Contact:
Gary Barat

Mama's Old-Fashioned Food Products
(Gili/G'Dam Kosher Cheese Company)
2 Webster Place
Ridgefield Park NJ 07660
201-440-3300
Contact:
Howard Teamkin

Oehme Pie Company/Rewco
110 Ridgedale Avenue
Morristown NJ 07960
201-267-3800
800-631-8041
Contact:
David A. Humm

The Old-Fashioned Kitchen, Inc.
1045 Towbin Avenue
Lakewood NJ 08701
201-364-4100
Contact:
Tom McGongle
Blintzes, pierogis

Sandy's Kitchen
(Clearview Baking)
47 East Madison Avenue
Dumont NJ 07628
201-387-7780
Contact:
Heidi Weiner
Cookies

Shmulka Bernstein Kosher Meats
105 William Street
Middlesex NJ 08846
201-560-1919
Contact:
Bernard Bernstein

Shofar Kosher Foods
124 Malvern Street
P.O. Box 5609
Newark NJ 07105
201-242-2434
800-3-HOTDOG
Contact:
Michelle Posnock
Salami, bologna, frankfurters, corned beef,
pastrami

Tofutti
1098 Randolph
Rahway NJ 07065
201-499-8500
Contact:
David Mintz

Tabatchnick Soups
2951 Vauxhall Road
Vauxhall NJ 07088
201-687-6447
Contact:
Ben Tabatchnick

NEW YORK

Abel & Schafer, Inc.
20 Alexander Court
Ronkonkoma NY 11779
516-737-2220
800-443-1260
Contact:
Harald Netzel
Bread mixes, cake mixes, cremes,
fillings, glazes

Abeles & Heymann
3498 Third Avenue
Bronx NY 10456
212-589-0100
Contact:
Michael Goldfarb
Salami, bologna, frankfurters, knockwurst,
corned beef briskets, tongue, beef fry, pastrami,
cerelat, liverwurst

Best Quality Breadsticks
641 62nd Street
P.O. Box 200154
Brooklyn NY 11220
718-439-6800
Contact:
Bill Antico
Breadsticks

Bloom's Kosher Candy
121 31st Street
Brooklyn NY 11232
718-768-1919
Contact:
M. J. Elias

Blue Ridge Farms, Inc.
3301 Atlantic Avenue
Brooklyn NY 11208
718-827-9000
Contact:
Mandel Portoy
Chopped liver, knishes, puddings,
kasha varnishkes

Chocolate Photos
637 West 27th Street
New York NY 10001
212-714-1880
Contact:
Victor Syrmis

Dagorim Tahorim
1679 54th Street
Brooklyn NY 11204
718-851-1832
Contact:
Isaac Stephansky
Fish

Drink Tyme Vending
770 East 94th Street
Brooklyn NY 11236
718-342-8102
Contact:
Richard Scher

Glenn Foods, Inc.
999 Central Avenue, Suite 300
Woodmere NY 11598
516-374-0135
Contact:
Jerry Schwartz
Natural snacks & candy

Gold Pure Food Products
Company, Inc.
895 McDonald Avenue
Brooklyn NY 11218
718-435-1910
800-422-4681
Contact:
Neil Gold

Golden Glow Cookie Company
18-44 Givan Avenue
Bronx NY 10469
212-379-6223
Contact:
Mike Florio

Golden Simcha Poultry, Inc.
1602 Troy Avenue
Brooklyn NY 11234
718-253-7733
800-825-5725
Contact:
Samuel H. Gross

Green & Ackerman Baking
Company
216 Ross Street
Brooklyn NY 11211
718-625-0289
Contact:
Shmuel Green

GSO, Inc.
666 Third Avenue
New York NY 10016
212-818-9620
Contact:
Shaya Berzel

H. R. Bordeaux, Ltd., Cheese
250 Clearbrook Road
P.O. Box 504
Elmsford NY 10523
914-592-9000
Contact:
Steven Klotzman

Hebrew National Kosher
Foods, Inc.
600 Food Center Drive
Bronx NY 10474
212-842-5000
Contact:
Walt Stugis
Meats, poultry, pickle products

Kemach Food Products
Corporation
778 Rockaway Parkway
Brooklyn NY 11236
718-385-1544
Contact:
Solomon Salzman

Kineret Foods Corporation
24 Jericho Turnpike
Jericho NY 11753
516-333-2626
Contact:
Jerry Krupncik
Poultry products

King David Knishes
67-07 Main Street
Flushing NY 11367
718-268-1734
Contact:
Aryeh Klein

Kopper's Chocolate Specialty
Company
30 Clarkson Street
New York NY 10014
212-243-0220
Contact:
Leslye Alexander

**Kojel Food Company
(V.I.P. Foods)**
137 Gardner Avenue
Brooklyn NY 11237
718-821-5330
Contact:
Esther Freund
Jello pudding, food bases

Krum's Chocolatiers
4 Dexter Plaza
Pearl River NY 10965
914-735-5100
800-ME-CANDY
Contact:
Ronald Krum

Lieber's Kosher Food Specialties
142 44th Street
Brooklyn NY 11232
718-499-0888
Contact:
Hesh Beigel

Margareten Enterprises
2900 Review Avenue
Long Island City NY 11101
718-729-5420
Contact:
Lucille Margareten
Cookies, cheese products

Meal Mart/Schreiber
56-20 59th Street
Maspeth NY 11378
718-894-2000
800-245-5620
Contact:
Sy Goren
Frozen meals, specialty products

Mendel's Haymish Brand
33-01 Atlantic Avenue
Brooklyn NY 11208
718-827-9000
Contact:
Alan Kaplinsky
Imitation shellfish

Morris Erde, Inc.
170 Wythe Avenue
Brooklyn NY 11211
718-387-5816
Contact:
Michael Polsunas
Rye bread, corn bread, challah, pumpernickel

Mrs. Adler's Food, Inc.
902 Essex Street
Brooklyn NY 11208
718-649-9121
800-252-4448
Contact:
Lance Friedman
Gefilte fish, matzo ball soup, borscht, tube soups

Mrs. Weinberg's Food Products
F3 Hunts Point Market
Bronx NY 10474
212-328-8336
Contact:
Sidney Weinberger
Chopped liver, stuffed derma

M. Y. Quality Trading
3917 14th Avenue
Brooklyn NY 11218
718-854-8714
Contact:
Moshe Geller
Nuts, dried fruit, seeds, spices

Naturally Good Foods
440 Forest Home Drive
Ithaca NY 14850
607-277-0983
Contact:
David Sayada
Frozen falafel patties

Noam Gourmet
392 Classon Avenue
Brooklyn NY 11238
718-230-3371
Contact:
Eli Gertner
Herring, fish & vegetable salads, deli cuts, horseradish

**Paradise International
Trading, Ltd.**
9 Meadowbrook Lane
Monsey NY 10952
914-425-1255
Contact:
Asher Devere Gershberg

Parve Frozen Delights, Inc.
15-20 Central Avenue
Far Rockaway NY 11691
718-327-1098
Contact:
Isaac Levin

Paskesz Candy Company, Inc.
125 51st Street
Brooklyn NY 11232
718-439-6222
Contact:
Henry Schmidt

**Paleta Frozfruit
International Corporation**
38 Hall Street
Brooklyn NY 11205
718-858-7827
Contact:
Harold Lefkowitz

**Post Cereals
(General Foods)**
250 North Street
White Plains NY 10625
914-335-2500
Contact:
Yosi Heber

Sabra Food Products Corporation
79 Bridgewater Street
Brooklyn NY 11222
718-387-3547
Contact:
Norman Zohar
Middle Eastern & European salads

Sara's Ravioli
75 Remsen Avenue
Monsey NY 10952
914-353-5472
Contact:
Jonathan Yunger

Schreiber/Meal Mart
56-20 59th Street
Maspeth NY 11378
718-894-2000
800-245-5620
Contact:
Sy Goren
Frozen meals, specialty products

Setton International Foods
150 Dupont Street
Plainview NY 11803
516-349-8090
800-227-4397
Contact:
Morris Setton
Dried fruits, cashews, chocolate-covered raisins, yogurt-covered peanuts

Taam Tov Foods, Inc.
188 28th Street
Brooklyn NY 11232
718-965-1840
Contact:
Dov Rapps
Cheeses, Swiss chocolates

Taim Salad
1685 McDonald Avenue
Brooklyn NY 11229
718-375-8890
Contact:
Barry Barak

Tami Great Food Corporation
40 20th Street
Brooklyn NY 11232
718-788-4200
Contact:
Renee or Martin Rosenberg

Track Marketing
111 West 57th Street, Suite 1120
New York NY 10019
212-245-4580
Contact:
Yvette Perry
*Naturally flavored regular & diet
sodas*

Wilton Foods
710 South Main Street
Spring Valley NY 10971
914-352-4800
Contact:
Don Peikes
*Preplated meals, hors d'oeuvres,
bulk entrees*

Yoni's Kosher Pasta
15 Drake Avenue
New Rochelle NY 10805
914-576-7030
Contact:
Henry Guarnero

Zetov, Inc.
1515 60th Street
Brooklyn NY 11204
718-972-0808
Contact:
Norman Nadler
Snacks, breadsticks, wafers

NORTH CAROLINA

Bahlsen, Inc.
1 Quality Lane
Cary NC 27512
919-677-3200
Cookies, crackers

Charles F. Cates & Sons, Inc.
P.O. Box 158
Faison NC 28341
919-267-4711
Pickles, relishes

Harvest Time Foods
P.O. Box 3215
Greenville NC 27836
919-746-6675
Contact:
Bryan Grimes Jr.
Frozen dumplings

Murray Bakery Products
P.O. Box 900
Charlotte NC 28299
704-334-7611
Contact:
Steve Keller

PENNSYLVANIA

Empire Kosher Poultry, Inc.
P.O. Box 165
Mifflintown PA 17059
717-436-2131
Poultry

Herr Foods, Inc.
Routes 131 & 272, Box 300
Nottingham PA 19362
800-523-5030
Contact:
Ben Fenninger
Snack foods

H. J. Heinz
1062 Progress Street
Pittsburgh PA 15212
412-237-5917
Contact:
Debby Rudoy

Knouse Foods, Inc.
800 Peach Glen-Idaville Road
Peach Glen PA 17306
717-677-8181
Applesauce, apple juice, pie fillings

Trappey's Fine Foods, Inc.
202 Dutt's Mill East
Dutt's Mill
West Chester PA 19382
215-436-4230
*Red Devil hotsauce, Chef Magic sauces,
jalapeno peppers, hot cherry peppers,
mild pickle okra*
Contact:
James S. Ceribelli

OREGON

Taste 1, Inc.
410 South Dell Road
Troutdale OR 97060
503-254-5309
Contact:
Lynda Nestelle
Wine cookies

TEXAS

Feste Foods, Inc.
3355 West Alabama, Suite 160
Houston TX 77098
713-622-1498
Contact:
Greg Feste
Mexicana dips

Lawler Foods, Inc.
1219 Carpenter Road
Humble TX 77396
713-446-0059
Contact:
Carol Lawler
Cheesecake, key lime pie

VERMONT

Janeric Products of Vermont, Inc.
Overhill Road, Box 386
Johnson VT 05656
802-635-7470
Contact:
Eric P. Lande
Maple products

The
BIG BUSINESS OF FOOD

69
The Top 100 Food Companies
73
Major Supermarket Chains
76
**Foodservice Companies
and Catering**
*Multiservice Companies; Contract Foodservice
Companies; Hotel & Resort Chains; Restau-
rant Chains; Cafeteria Suppliers; Fast Food
Chains; Health Care Suppliers; Airline
Suppliers*

The Top 100 Food Companies

These companies are arranged in order of their ranking in *Food Processing* magazine's December 1988 listing of the TOP 100® Food Companies. This annual comprehensive survey ranks companies on the basis of each one's food sales in dollars for its most recently concluded fiscal year, and reprints can be obtained from the Putnam Publishing Company, 301 East Erie Street, Chicago IL 60611.

This list, checked with *Dun & Bradstreet's Million-Dollar Directory*, includes each firm's current media contact. No list adds up to 100 for long in the food industry, with its billion-dollar mergers—and this one is no exception.

Philip Morris Companies, Inc.
120 Park Avenue
New York NY 10017
212-880-5000
Contact:
George L. Knox,
Staff Vice President,
Public Affairs

Kraft, Inc.
Kraft Court
Glenview IL 60025
708-998-2000
Contact:
J. Bruce Harrold,
Senior Vice President,
Chief Information Officer

RJR Nabisco, Inc.
300 Galleria Parkway NW
Atlanta GA 30339
404-852-3000
Contact:
Marshall B. Bass,
Senior Vice President,
Public Affairs

Anheuser-Busch Companies, Inc.
1 Busch Place
St. Louis MO 63118
314-577-2000
Contact:
Stan Wessel,
Communications Services

Coca-Cola USA
P.O. Drawer 1734
Atlanta GA 30301
404-676-2121
Contact:
Ron Coleman, Public Relations

PepsiCo, Inc.
Anderson Hill Road
Purchase NY 10577
914-253-2000
Contact:
Elaine Franklin, Manager,
Corporate Information

IBP, Inc.
IBP Avenue
P.O. Box 515
Dakota City NE 68731
402-494-2061
Contact:
Gary Mickelson,
Communications Specialist
Mike Cummings,
Communications Specialist

ConAgra, Inc.
1 Central Park Plaza
Omaha NE 68102
402-978-4000
Contact:
Martin G. Calladay, Vice President,
Public Affairs

Archer Daniels Midland Company
466 Faries Parkway
Decatur IL 62525
217-424-5200
Contact:
Richard Burket, Vice President,
Media & Advertising

Nestle Foods Corporation
100 Manhattanville Road
Purchase NY 10577
914-251-3000
Contact:
Barbara Campbell, Director,
   Public Relations
Bonnie Carlson,
   Promotional Services

Sara Lee Corporation
3 First National Plaza
Chicago IL 60602
312-726-2600
Contact:
Anne McCarthy, Manager,
Public Relations

H. J. Heinz Company
600 Grant Street
Pittsburgh PA 15219
412-456-5700
Contact:
D. Edward I. Smythe, Director,
   Corporate Affairs
Debora S. Foster, General Manager,
   Corporate Communications

CPC International, Inc.
International Plaza,
Suite B 3035
P.O. Box 8000 (07631)
Englewood Cliffs NJ 07633
201-894-4000
Contact:
Steve Williams, Director,
Communications

Campbell Soup Company
Campbell Place
Camden NJ 08103
609-342-4800
Contact:
David Hackney, Manager,
Public Relations

The Quaker Oats Company
Quaker Tower
321 North Clark
P.O. Box 9001
Chicago IL 60604
312-222-7111
Contact:
Kathi Boylan,
Consumer Communications

Borden, Inc.
277 Park Avenue
New York NY 10172
212-573-4000
Contact:
James T. McCrory, Vice President,
Public Affairs

Ralston Purina Company
Checkerboard Square
St. Louis MO 63164
314-982-3231
Contact:
Elmer Richars,
Vice President, Director,
Public Relations

Beatrice Company
2 North La Salle Street
Chicago IL 60602
312-782-3820
Contact:
Lizabeth Sode, Vice President,
Corporate Relations

Kellogg Company
1 Kellogg Square
Battle Creek MI 49016
616-961-2000
Contact:
Joseph M. Stewart, Vice President,
Public Affairs

General Mills, Inc.
1 General Mills Boulevard
P.O. Box 1113
Minneapolis MN 55440
612-540-2311
Contact:
Austin P. Sullivan Jr.,
Vice President, Public Affairs

The Pillsbury Company
Pillsbury Center
200 South 6th Street
Minneapolis MN 55402
612-330-4718
Contact:
Johnny W. Thompson,
Vice President, Public Relations

Monfort, Inc.
1930 AA Street
Greeley CO 80631
303-353-2311
Contact:
Gene Meakins, Vice President,
Industrial & Public Relations

United Brands Company
1 East 4th Street
Cincinnati OH 45202
513-784-8000
Contact:
Sandra Heimann,
Vice President, Public Relations

A. E. Staley Manufacturing Company
2200 East Eldorado Street
Decatur IL 62521
217-423-4411
Contact:
Irene Leishner

The Procter & Gamble Company
2 Procter & Gamble Plaza
Cincinnati OH 45202
513-562-1100
Contact:
Don Tassone, Public Relations

The Kroger Company
1014 Vine Street
Cincinnati OH 45201
513-762-4000
Contact:
Paul Bernish, Director,
    Public Relations
Dick Owens, Vice President,
    Advertising

Associated Milk Products, Inc.
6609 Blanco Road
San Antonio TX 78216
512-340-9100
Contact:
Jim Eskin,
Communications Coordinator

Castle & Cooke, Inc.
10900 Wilshire Boulevard
Los Angeles CA 90024
213-824-1500
Contact:
Robert Fisher, President
Linda Simmons,
    Director of Advertising

George A. Hormel & Company
501 16th Avenue NE
P.O. Box 800
Austin MN 55912
507-437-5611
Contact:
Allen Crejci, Director,
Public Relations

Joseph E. Seagram & Sons, Inc.
375 Park Avenue
New York NY 10152
212-572-7000
Contact:
Carol M. Connell, Director,
Public Relations

Whitman Corporation
111 East Wacker Drive
Chicago IL 60601
312-565-3000
Contact:
Charles H. Connolly,
Vice President, Corporate
Communications

Hershey Foods Corporation
100 Mansion Road East
Hershey PA 17033
717-534-4000
Contact:
Carla Andrews, Manager,
Public Information

Central Soya Company, Inc.
1300 Ft. Wayne National Bank
Building
P.O. Box 1400 (46801)
Ft. Wayne IN 46802
Contact:
Barry G. Collinsworth, Manager,
Corporate Communications

Tyson Foods, Inc.
2210 West Oaklawn Drive
P.O. Drawer E (72765)
Springdale AR 72764
501-756-4000
Contact:
Kristin Ferguson, Vice President,
    Food Service Marketing
Jack Dunn, Vice President,
    Retail Marketing

Holly Farms Corporation
1755-D Lynnfield Road, Suite 149
Memphis TN 38187
901-761-3610
Contact:
Ted Bailey, Vice President

Dean Foods Company
3600 North River Road
Franklin Park IL 60131
708-625-6200
Contact:
Dave Rotunno, Administrative
Manager

Mid-America Dairymen, Inc.
3253 East Chestnut Expressway
Springfield MO 65802
417-865-7100
Contact;
Forest Bradley,
    Director of Communications
Bill Bakeslee,
    Corporate Vice President,
    Marketing & Planning

Land O'Lakes, Inc.
P.O. Box 116
Minneapolis, MN 55440
612-481-2222
Contact:
Terry Nagel, Director of
Communications

Thomas J. Lipton, Inc.
800 Sylvan Avenue
Englewood Cliffs NJ 07632
201-567-8000
Contact:
Pamela Stetson, Manager,
Product Communications

Wilson Foods Corporation
4545 North Lincoln Boulevard
P.O. Box 26724 (73126)
Oklahoma City OK 73105
405-525-4545
Contact:
David Smoak, President-CEO
John Hanes,
    Executive Vice President,
    Sales & Marketing

Adolph Coors Company
311 10th Street
Golden CO 80401
303-279-6565
Contact:
Anita K. Russell, Director,
Corporate Communications

Keebler Company
1 Hollow Tree Lane
Elmhurst IL 60126
708-833-2900
Contact:
Stuart Greenblatt, Manager,
    Corporate Communications
Roger Kalinowski, Vice President,
    Marketing

**International Multifoods
Corporation**
Multifoods Tower
P.O. Box 2942
Minneapolis MN 55402
612-340-3300
Contact:
Linda Berg, Director,
Communications

McCormick & Company, Inc.
11350 McCormick Road
Hunt Valley MD 21031
301-771-6000
Contact:
Mac Barrett, Manager,
    Press Relations
Norm Maged,
    Senior Brand Manager

G. Heileman Brewing Company, Inc.
100 Harborview Plaza
LaCrosse WI 54601
608-785-1000
Contact:
Bill Eiler, Communications
Ian Crichton,
    Senior Vice President,
    Marketing & Sales

Dairymen, Inc.
10140 Linn Station Road
Louisville KY 40223
502-426-6455
Contact;
Jeff Durden, Marketing
James Sumner, Director,
    Corporate Communications

Idle Wild Foods, Inc.
256 Franklin Street
Worcester MA 01615
508-757-7761
Contact:
Lois Brownell, Corporate
Accounting Officer

Smithfield Foods, Inc.
501 North Church Street
Smithfield VA 23430
202-223-4224
Contact:
Aaron Trub, Vice President

Interstate Bakeries Corporation
12 East Armour Boulevard
Kansas City MO 64111
816-561-6600
Contact:
Mark Dirks, Vice President,
Corporate Marketing

Sunkist Growers, Inc.
14130 Riverside Drive
P.O. Box 7888
Van Nuys CA 91409
818-986-4800
Contact:
Barbara Robison, Manager,
    Consumer Affairs
Gee Winands, Manager,
    Domestic Advertising

Savannah Foods & Industries, Inc.
2 East Bryan Street
P.O. Box 339 (31402)
Savannah GA 31401
Contact:
Nancy Barbee, Manager,
    Consumer Communications
Edward Hill, Director,
    Marketing & Advertising

MorningStar Foods
5956 Sherry Lane, Suite 1100
Dallas TX 75225
214-360-4700
Contact:
Nancy Thorn, Manager
    Marketing Services
Wesley Gross, Manager,
    Marketing

Gold Kist, Inc.
244 Parameter Center Parkway NE
Atlanta GA 30346
404-393-5000
Contact:
Paul Brower, Vice President,
Communications

Agway, Inc.
333 Butternut Drive
De Witt NY 13214
315-449-7061
Contact:
Ted J. Nakowski, Vice President,
Food Group

Ocean Spray Cranberries, Inc.
1 Ocean Spray Drive
Lakeville MA 02349
508-946-1000
Contact:
Herbert Colcord, Manager,
    Consumer Affairs
Tom Bullock, National Advertising

Wm. Wrigley Jr. Company
410 North Michigan Avenue
Chicago IL 60611
312-644-2121
Contact:
Joan Weber, Consumer Affairs
Advertising

Warner-Lambert Company
201 Tabor Road
Morris Plains NJ 07950
201-540-2000
Contact:
Ronald E. Zier, Vice President,
Public Affairs

Flowers Industries, Inc.
U.S. Highway 19 South
P.O. Box 1338
Thomasville GA 31799
912-226-9110
Contact:
Marta Jones, Manager,
Communications

Brown-Forman Corporation
P.O. Box 1080
Louisville KY 40201
502-585-1100
Contact:
Lois Musselman,
Senior Vice President

Universal Foods Corporation
433 East Michigan Street
Milwaukee WI 53202
414-271-6755
Contact:
Paul Norton, Director,
Corporate Communications

Rich Products Corporation
1150 Niagara Street
P.O. Box 245
Buffalo NY 14240
716-878-8000
Contact:
Gabrielle P. DeRose, Director,
Corporate Communications & Public
Relations

Tri/Valley Growers, Inc.
1255 Battery Street
San Francisco CA 94111
415-445-1600
Contact:
Susanne Norton Coffey,
Public Relations Manager

FDL Foods, Inc.
2040 Kerper Boulevard
Dubuque IA 52001
319-588-5400
Contact:
Clyde Maddux, Marketing

General Cinema Corporation
27 Boylston Street
Newton MA 02167
617-232-8200
Contact:
Philip Nardone, Director,
Corporate Communications

Curtice-Burns, Inc.
90 Linden Place
Rochester NY 14625
716-383-1850
Contact:
Ted Holmgren,
    Senior Vice President
Joan Miller, Executive
    Administrator to CEO

Cadbury Schweppes, Inc.
High Ridge Park
Stamford CT 06905
203-329-0911
Contact:
Brian Walker, Director,
Corporate Communications

Imperial Holly Corporation
1 Imperial Square, Suite 200
P.O. Box 9
Sugar Land TX 77487
713-491-9181
Contact:
Robert Guffey, Sales Manager

Riceland Foods, Inc.
2120 Park Avenue
P.O. Box 927
Stuttgart AR 72160
501-673-5521
Contact:
Bill Reed,
    Assistant Vice President,
    Corporate Development
Beverly Harlan,
    Director, Communication

Sun-Diamond Growers of California
P.O. Box 9024
Pleasanton CA 94566
415-463-8200
Contact:
Noreen Griffee, Director,
Consumer Services

**California & Hawaiian Sugar
Company**
1390 Willow Pass Road
Concord CA 94520
415-356-6000
Contact:
Fred Sammis, Director,
Marketing

Farmland Industries, Inc.
3315 North Oak Trafficway
Kansas City MO 64116
816-459-6000
Contact:
David Cox, Vice President, Sales

Thorn Apple Valley, Inc.
18700 West Ten Mile Road
Southfield MI 48075
313-552-0700
Contact:
Joseph McCloskey,
Vice President, Marketing

**American Home Products
Corporation**
685 Third Avenue
New York NY 10017
212-878-5000
Contact:
Carol G. Emeriling,
    Corporate Secretary
Richard Feldheim, Advertising

Hudson Foods, Inc.
13th Street at Highway 102
P.O. Box 777 (72757)
Rogers AR 72756
501-636-1100
Contact:
Annette Lechler, Public Relations
Sherry Hunter, Manager,
    Marketing Services

Ragu Foods, Inc.
75 Merritt Boulevard
P.O. Box 7013
Trumbull CT 06611
800-444-7248
Contact:
Louise Milano, Manager,
Advertising Services

American Crystal Sugar Company
101 North 3rd Street
Moorhead MN 56560
218-236-4400
Contact:
Marc Dillon, Manager,
Public Relations

Wisconsin Dairies Cooperative
P.O. Box 111
Baraboo WI 53913
608-356-8316
Contact:
Pamela J. Karg,
    Communications Coordinator
Joan Behr,
    Public Relations Coordinator

Prairie Farms Dairy, Inc.
1100 North Broadway
P.O. Box 499
Carlinville IL 62626
217-854-2547
Contact:
Donald Kullman, Marketing
Specialist

Gerber Products Company
445 State Street
Fremont MI 49412
616-928-2000
Contact:
Jane Lovejoy, Director,
    Corporate Communications
Robert Erber, Vice President,
    Marketing

Blue Diamond Growers
P.O. Box 1768
Sacramento CA 75812
916-442-0771
Contact:
Susan Brauner, Director,
    Communications
Al Greenlee, Manager,
    Advertising

Moyer Packing Company
249 Allentown Road
P.O. Box 395 (18965)
Souderton PA 18964
215-723-5555
Contact:
Director of Public Relations

Metz Baking Company
1014 Nebraska Street
Sioux City IA 51105
712-255-7611
Contact:
Mike Downing, Director, Marketing

Lance, Inc.
8600 South Boulevard
P.O. Box 32368 (28232)
Charlotte NC 28210
704-554-1421
Contact:
Jack Moore, Vice President, Sales

Leaf, Inc.
2355 Waukegan Road, Suite 250
Bannockburn IL 60015
708-940-7500
Contact:
Chuck Trado, Senior Vice President,
    Marketing Director
Tom Giglio, Director,
    Advertising & Promotion

Hyplains Dressed Beef, Inc.
P.O. Box 539
Dodge City KS 67801
316-227-7135
Contact:
Tod Schoonover, Controller

Lucky Stores, Inc.
P.O. Box BB
Dublin CA 94568
415-833-6000
Contact:
Judith Decker, Communications
Coordinator

Fresh Mark, Inc.
1888 Southway Street SE
Massillon OH 44648
216-832-7491
Contact:
Jack Painter, Director, Marketing

J. M. Smucker Company
Strawberry Lane
Orrville OH 44667
216-682-0015
Contact:
Vickie Limbach, Manager,
    Communications
John Carpenter, Director,
    Advertising & Marketing Services

Welch Foods, Inc.
100 Main Street
Concord MA 01742
508-371-1000
Contact:
Daniel Dillon, Vice President,
Marketing

Riviana Foods, Inc.
2777 Allen Parkway
Houston TX 77252
713-529-3251
Contact:
Wayne Rutherford, Director,
Operations

Citrus World, Inc.
P.O. Box 1111
Lake Wales FL 33859
813-676-1411
Contact:
Walt Lincer, Director, Marketing

American Maize-Processing Company
1100 Indianapolis Boulevard
Hammond IN 46320
203-356-9000
Contact:
Lynn Lundeberg, Marketing
Manager of Foods

Major Supermarket Chains

The names of the companies that follow were included in *Supermarket News*'s list of the nation's top 50 retail chains as of January 1989. They are listed in the order of their ranking, which was based on total sales volume for the latest fiscal year.

The information has been checked with *Dun & Bradstreet's Million-Dollar Directory* and expanded to include the territory each company serves and the name of an appropriate contact.

For a comprehensive account of this constantly changing field, consult the 1989 edition of *Distribution Study of Grocery Store Sales*, published by Fairchild Publications Book Division, 825 Seventh Avenue, New York NY 10019.

Another valuable source of information is *Thomas Grocery Register*, published by Thomas Publishing Company, 1 Penn Plaza, New York NY 10119.

American Stores
5201 Amelia Earhart Drive
Salt Lake City UT 84116
801-539-0112
Territory:
National
Contact:
Troy D'Ambrosio, Director
of Public Relations

Kroger Company
1014 Vine Street
Cincinnati OH 45201
513-762-4000
Territory:
National, primarily Midwest, South
and Southwest
Contact:
Jack Partridge, Director
of Public Affairs

Safeway Stores
Oakland CA 94667
415-891-3000
Territory:
United States and Canada
Contact:
Robert E. Bradford, Senior
Vice President of Public Affairs

A & P
2 Paragon Drive
Montvale NJ 07645
201-573-9700
Territory:
Primarily East Coast and Canada
Contact:
Michael Rourke, Vice President,
Communications and Corporate Affairs

Winn-Dixie Stores
P.O. Box B
Jacksonville FL 32203
904-783-5000
Territory:
Thirteen Sunbelt states
Contact:
G. E. Clerc, Director of
Public Relations

Albertson's
250 Parkcenter Boulevard
Boise ID 83706
208-385-6200
Territory
Seventeen Western
and Southern states
Contact:
Gary Michaels, Vice Chairman
and CFO

Supermarkets General
200 Milik Street
Carteret NJ 07008
201-499-3000
Territory:
East Coast
Contact:
Robert Wunderle, Vice President
of Public Affairs

Publix Super Markets
1936 George Jenkins Boulevard
Lakeland FL 33802
813-688-1188
Territory:
Florida
Contact:
Bill Shroeter, Vice President,
Public Relations

Vons Companies
10150 Lower Azusa Road
El Monte CA 91731
818-579-1400
Territory:
Nevada and Southern California
Contact:
Mary McAboy, Director
of Public Relations

Food Lion
P.O. Box 1330
Salisbury, NC 28145
704-633-8250
Territory:
Nine states in the Southeast
Contact:
Mike Mozingo, Manager
of Corporate Communications

Grand Union
201 Willowbrook Boulevard
Wayne NJ 07470
201-890-6000
Territory:
East Coast
Contact:
Don Baillancourt,
Vice President, Public Relations

Giant Food, Inc.
6300 Sheriff Road
Landover MD 20785
301-341-4100
Territory:
Maryland, Virginia and
District of Columbia
Contact:
Barry F. Scher, Vice President,
Public Affairs

Stop & Shop Companies
P.O. Box 369
Boston MA 02101
617-770-8000
Territory:
Connecticut, Massachusetts,
Maine, New Hampshire, New Jersey
and New York
Contact:
Aileen Gorman, Vice President,
Public Affairs

Ralph's Grocery Company
P.O. Box 54143
Los Angeles CA 90054
213-637-1101
Territory:
Southern California
Contact:
Gene Brown, Senior Vice President
of Human Resources and
Public Relations

H. E. Butt Grocery Company
646 South Main Avenue
San Antonio TX 78204
512-270-8000
Territory:
Texas
Contact:
Mike De La Garza, Director,
Public Affairs

Smith's Management
1550 South Redwood Road
Salt Lake City UT 84104
801-974-1400
Territory:
Southwest
Contact:
Jeff Smith, Chairman and CEO

Bruno's
P.O. Box 2486
Birmingham AL 35201
205-940-9400
Territory:
Southeast
Contact:
Beth Dunaway, Consumer
Affairs Director

Dominick's Finer Foods
505 Railroad Avenue
Northlake IL 60164
708-379-5200
Territory:
Chicago area
Contact:
Larry Nauman, Vice President,
Public Relations and Advertising

Fred Meyer, Inc.
3800 Southeast 22nd Avenue
Portland OR 97202
503-232-8844
Territory:
Oregon, Alaska, Washington, Idaho,
Montana, Utah and California
Contact:
Sherill Perrin, Vice President,
Public Affairs

Giant Eagle
RIDC Industrial Park
Pittsburgh PA 15238
412-963-6200
Territory:
Ohio, Pennsylvania
and West Virginia
Contact:
James Dorsey, Director
of Advertising

Hy-Vee Food Stores
1801 Oscada Avenue
Chariton IA 50049
515-774-2121
Territory:
Midwest
Contact:
John Rhodes, Director
of Information

First National Supermarkets
Eastern Division
500 North Street
Windsor Locks CT 06096
203-627-0241
Territory:
Eastern United States

First National Supermarkets
Ohio Division
1700 Rockside Road
Maple Heights OH 44137
216-587-7100
Territory:
Ohio
Contact:
Susan Alcorn, Public Relations

Shaw's Supermarkets, Inc.
P.O. Box 3566
Portland ME 04104
207-773-0211
Territory:
New England
Contact:
Margaret McEwan, Director,
Consumer Affairs

National Supermarkets
6050 North Lindbergh
Hazlewood MO 63042
314-731-5511
Territory:
Illinois and Missouri
Contact:
Patrick Maginn, Vice President,
Advertising and Public Relations

Furr's
1708 Avenue G
Lubbock TX 79401
806-763-1931
Territory:
Texas and New Mexico
Contact:
Bob Hurmence, Vice President,
Public Affairs

Hannaford Brothers
145 Pleasant Hill Road
Scarborough ME 04074
207-883-2911
Territory:
New England
Contact:
Helen Chase, Manager
of Communications

Weis Markets
1000 South 2nd Street
Sunbury PA 17801
717-286-4571
Territory:
Northeast
Contact:
Carol Ernst, Consumer Relations

Borman's
P.O. Box 33446
Detroit MI 48232
313-270-1000
Territory:
Michigan
Contact:
Gilbert Borman, Director,
Public Relations and Advertising

Cullum Companies
14303 Inwood Road
Dallas TX 75244
214-661-9700
Territory:
Dallas
Contact:
Cherie Stowe, Director,
Public Relations

Stater Brothers Markets
P.O. Box 150
Colton CA 92324
714-783-0515
Territory:
Southern California
Contact:
Debbie Brown, Director,
Public Relations

Wegman's
1500 Brooks Avenue
Rochester NY 14624
716-328-2550
Territory:
Upper New York State
Contact:
Fred Kopp, Director, Advertising

Riser Foods
5300 Richmond Road
Bedford Heights OH 44146
216-292-7000
Territory:
Northern Ohio
Contact:
Anthony Rego, Chief Executive
Officer

Raley's
500 West Capitol Avenue
West Sacramento CA 95605
916-373-3333
Territory:
Northern California
and Northern Nevada
Contact:
Dick Schrudder, Director,
Advertising

Big Bear Stores
770 West Goodale Boulevard
Columbus OH 43212
614-464-6500
Territory:
Central and Southern Ohio,
West Virginia
Contact:
Pete Kooiker, Director,
Advertising

DeMoulas/Market Basket
875 East Street
Tewksbury MA 01876
508-851-7381
Territory:
Northern Massachusetts
and New Hampshire
Contact:
Bill Marsden, Vice President,
Store Operations

Tops Markets

60 Dingens Street
Buffalo NY 14206
716-823-3712
Territory:
Upstate New York
Contact:
Tom Zarbo, Director,
Corporate Communications

Price Chopper

501 Duanesburg Road
Schenectady NY 12306
518-355-5000
Territory:
New York, Massachusetts,
Vermont and Pennsylvania
Contact:
David Henry, Vice President,
Advertising

Hughes Market

2716 San Fernando Road
Los Angeles CA 90065
213-227-8211
Territory:
Southern California
Contact:
Jack Ackroyd, Director,
Advertising

Randall's Food Market

3663 Briarpark Drive
Houston TX 77042
713-268-3500
Territory:
Greater Houston area
Contact:
Rebecca Linkous, Director,
Public Affairs & Communications

Red Food Stores

5901 Shallowford Road
Chattanooga TN 37422
615-892-8029
Territory:
Middle & Eastern Tennessee,
Northern Georgia
Contact:
Jesse A. Lewis, Executive
Vice President, Store Operations
& Merchandising

Farm Fresh

P.O. Box 1289
Norfolk VA 23501
804-480-6700
Territory:
Virginia and North Carolina
Contact:
Susan Mayo, Vice President,
Consumer Affairs & Public Relations

Smitty's Super Valu

262 South 7th Street
Phoenix AZ 85034
602-262-1000
Territory:
Greater Phoenix area
Contact:
Michael E. Gant, Vice President,
Human Resources

King Kullen

1194 Prospect Avenue
Westbury NY 11590
516-333-7100
Territory:
Long Island, New York
Contact:
Thomas Cullen, Vice President,
Government & Industry Relations

Foodservice Companies

Foodservice is the largest single private employer in the United States, with a projected 11.4 million jobs available by the year 2000. This thriving industry specializes in the design and supply of finished foods in quantity to restaurants and caterers and to institutional groups such as airlines, hospitals, prisons, schools, colleges and universities.

Phillip S. Cooke, founder and president of Foodservice Associates, selected this listing to indicate the major players in each of eight categories: Multiservice Companies, Contract Foodservice Companies, Hotel and Resort chains, Restaurant Chains, Cafeteria Suppliers, Fast Food Chains, Health Care Suppliers and Airline Suppliers. The list was compiled from the "400" Executive Directory prepared by *Restaurants & Institutions*. This annual listing is available at $125.00 per copy to foodservice professionals by contacting the magazine at

1350 East Touhy Avenue, Des Plaines IL 60018.

Each firm is listed alphabetically, followed by the names of those subsidiaries reachable through the main company address; those companies operated from another address are listed separately with ownership shown in parentheses. In most cases, the contact is the food and beverage director or person responsible for placing and receiving orders.

MULTISERVICE COMPANIES

ARA Services, Inc.
ARA Tower
1101 Market Street
Philadelphia PA 19107
215-238-3000
Contact:
Robert F. Dick

Associated Hosts, Inc.
8447 Wilshire Boulevard
Beverly Hills CA 90211
213-653-6010
Contact:
Paul Sandbloom

Atlanta Family Restaurants, Inc.
4901 South Royal Atlantic Drive
Tucker GA 30084
404-493-3999
Shoney's (franchisee)
Pizza Inn (franchisee)
Contact:
Prescott Bowden

Baskin-Robbins Ice Cream Company
31 Baskin-Robbins Place
Glendale CA 91201
818-956-0031
Contact:
Norm Klipfel

Bobby McGee's USA, Inc.
2701 East Camelback Road,
Suite 500
Phoenix AZ 85016
602-956-7660
Contact:
Arthur Ozols

Bob Evans Farms, Inc.
3776 South High Street
Columbus OH 43207
614-491-2225
Contact:
L. Merl Beery

Braum Ice Cream and Dairy Stores Company
3000 Northeast 63rd Street
Oklahoma City OK 73121
405-478-1656
Contact:
Larry McMillon

Buffets, Inc.
10260 Viking Drive, Suite 100
Eden Prairie MN 55344
612-942-9760
Contact:
Jean Rostollan

Carson Pirie Scott & Company
36 South Wabash Street
Chicago IL 60603
312-641-8000
Contact:
Patricia Pastelli

Carvel Corporation
201 Saw Mill River Road
Yonkers NY 10701
914-969-7200
Contact:
Patricia Lobb

The C&C Organization
8653 Madrone Avenue
Rancho Cucamonga CA 91730
714-981-5771
Contact:
Duayne Bliss

CHE, Inc.
115 South Acacia
Solana Beach CA 92075
619-755-8281
Paradise Bakery
Contact:
Tim Perreira

The Circle K Corporation
1601 North 7th Street
Phoenix AZ 85006
602-253-9600
Contact:
Edward Doyle

Club Corporation of America
P.O. Box 819012
Dallas TX 75381
214-243-6191
Contact:
Marty Monnat

Collins Foods International, Inc.
12655 West Jefferson Boulevard
Los Angeles CA 90066
213-827-2300
Contact:
Nydia Casas

The Continental Companies
3250 Mary Street
Miami FL 33133
305-445-2493
Contact:
Ron Sampiero

Convenient Food Marts
9701 West Higgins Road,
Suite 850
Rosemont IL 60018
708-692-9150
Contact:
Martin Benturini

Corporate Food Services, Inc.
25 East 21st Street
New York NY 10010
212-475-5959
Contact:
Anthony Seddo

Country Hospitality, Inc.
7800 Metro Parkway
Minneapolis MN 55420
612-854-6333
Contact:
Allan L. Post

Cracker Barrel Old Country Store, Inc.
Hartmann Drive
Lebanon TN 37088
615-444-5533
Contact:
Mark Tanzer

David's Specialty Foods
406 East 50th Street
New York NY 10022
212-644-3930
Contact:
David Liederman

**Dayton Hudson Department
Store Company**
700 Nicollet Mall
Minneapolis MN 55402
612-375-2200
Contact:
Ed Silver

Del E. Webb Corporation
2231 East Camelback Road
Phoenix AZ 85016
602-468-6800
Contact:
Ken Plonski

Dobbs International
See Greyhound Food Management, Inc.

**Faber Enterprises
(Greyhound Food Management, Inc.)**
55 East Monroe Street,
Suite 3530
Chicago IL 60603
312-558-8900
Contact:
Craig Papadourakis

Fosters Freeze International
P.O. Box 266
Arroyo Grande CA 93420
805-481-9577
Contact:
Linda Mroczkowski

GFM Public Service Division
See Greyhound Food Management, Inc.

Greyhound Food Management, Inc.
4040 North Central
Phoenix AZ 85012
602-248-6070
Restaura Dining Services
GFM Public Service Division
Dobbs International
Contact:
Bruce Pauzus

**Haagen-Dazs Company, Inc.
(The Pillsbury Company
Restaurant Group)**
Glen Pointe Center East
Teaneck NJ 07666
201-907-6816
Contact:
Cliff Stecker

HRI-Purchase Connection
201 North Figueroa Street, 4th Floor
Los Angeles CA 90012
213-250-5600
Contact:
Lisa Cooper

K Mart Corporation
3100 West Big Beaver Road
Troy MI 48084
313-643-1000
Contact:
Gary Prosser

La Petite Boulangerie
See Mrs. Field's Cookies

Marriott Corporation
1 Marriott Drive
Washington DC 20058
301-897-7770
Contact:
Robert T. Pras

May Department Stores
611 Olive Street
St. Louis MO 63101
314-342-6300
Contact:
Donald Denhard

Mrs. Field's Cookies
P.O. Box 4000
Park City UT 84060
801-649-1304
La Petite Boulangerie
Contact:
Wayne Selph

C. A. Muer Corporation
1548 Porter Street
Detroit MI 48216
313-965-5555
Contact:
Tony Adams

Nestle Enterprises, Inc.
5757 Harper Road
Solon OH 44139
216-349-5757
Contact:
B. Richard Atkinson

North Central Food Systems, Inc.
3001 Metro Drive, Suite 234
Minneapolis MN 55425
612-854-7944
Contact:
William G. Boosalis

**Original Great American Chocolate
Chip Cookie Company**
4685 Frederick Drive
Atlanta GA 30336
404-696-1700
Contact:
Richard Gully

Paradise Bakery
See CHE, Inc.

PepsiCo Foodservice Division
700 Anderson Hill Road
Purchase NY 10577
914-253-2000
Contact:
Stephan Bishop

**The Pillsbury Company
Restaurant Group**
Glen Pointe Center East
Teaneck NJ 07666
201-907-6816
Contact:
Cliff Stecker

Pizza Inn Franchise
See Atlanta Family Restaurants, Inc.

Restaura Dining Services
See Greyhound Food Management, Inc.

The Riese Organization
162 West 34th Street
New York NY 10001
212-563-7440
Contact:
Michael Lerner

Roma Corporation
10000 North Central Expressway,
Suite 900
Dallas TX 75231
214-891-7600
Contact:
Dennis Ziolkowski

RTM, Inc.
2130 La Vista Executive Park
Tucker GA 30084
404-939-6582
Contact:
Sharron Barton

Servico Management Corporation
1601 Belvedere Road South,
Suite 501
West Palm Beach FL 33406
407-689-9970
Contact:
Tony Aboushama

Shoney's Franchise
See Atlanta Family Restaurants, Inc.

The Southland Corporation
2828 North Haskell Avenue
Dallas TX 75204
214-828-7011
Contact:
Gene Hoggard

Universal Services, Inc.
International
417 Second Avenue West
Seattle WA 98119
206-340-9200
Contact:
Ed Wilson

Walt Disney Company
1313 Harbor Boulevard
Anaheim CA 92803
714-999-4000
Contact:
Bob Bowman

CONTRACT FOODSERVICE COMPANIES

ARA Services
ARA Tower
1101 Market Street
Philadelphia PA 19107
215-238-3590
Contact:
Michael Cronk

Bon Appetit Management Company
548 7th Street
San Francisco CA 94103
415-621-4481
Contact:
Fedele Bauccio

Canteen Company
(TW Services, Inc.)
222 North LaSalle Street
Chicago IL 60601
312-701-2047
Contact:
Harold Ritchie

Corporate Food Services, Inc.
25 East 21st Street
New York NY 10010
212-475-5959
Contact:
Jack Gallione

FLIK International Corporation
910 East Boston Post Road
Mamaroneck NY 10543
914-381-4400
Contact:
Julieann Flik

Food Dimensions, Inc.
2749 Hyde Street
San Francisco CA 94109
415-928-4900
Contact:
Norman F. Simon

Guckenheimer Enterprises, Inc.
1450 Oddstav Drive
Redwood City CA 94063
415-365-5303
Contact:
C. Stewart Ritchie III

Marriott Corporation
1 Marriott Drive
Washington DC 20058
301-897-7652
Contact:
Daniel P. Howells

Morrison's Custom Management
4721 Morrison Drive
Mobile AL 36625
205-344-3000
Contact:
Joe Byrum

Professional Foodservice
Management, Inc.
1458 Portsmouth Court
Northbrook IL 60062
708-272-0544
Contact:
Martin Gehres

Restaura Dining Services
(Greyhound Food Management, Inc.)
3131 Greyhound Tower
Phoenix AZ 85077
602-248-6079
Contact:
Edward Sirhall

Sands & Company, Inc.
1633 Sands Place
Marietta GA 30067
404-955-5887
Contact:
Charles Harper-Smith

The Seiler Corporation
153 Second Avenue
Waltham MA 02254
617-890-6200
Contact:
Philip Lyseth

Service America Corporation
88 Gatehouse Road
Stamford CT 06904
203-351-8929
Contact:
Tighe Merkert

Southern Foodservice
Management, Inc.
200 Office Park Drive
Birmingham AL 35223
205-871-8000
Contact:
Don Lutomski

Harry M. Stevens, Inc.
521 Fifth Avenue
New York NY 10175
212-661-0400
Contact:
Jerry Barlow

Total Foodservice Direction, Inc.
6401 Southwest 87th Avenue
Miami FL 33173
305-596-1500
Contact:
Gus Gregory

The Wood Company
6081 Hamilton Boulevard
Allentown PA 18106
215-395-3800
Contact:
Don Brannan

HOTEL & RESORT CHAINS

AIRCOA
9250 East Costilla Avenue,
Suite 300
Englewood CO 80112
303-779-1219
Contact:
Jim McClernon

Bally's Grand (Las Vegas)
See Bally Manufacturing Corporation

Bally's Grand (Reno)
See Bally Manufacturing Corporation

Bally Manufacturing Corporation
8700 West Bryn Mawr Avenue
Chicago IL 60631
312-399-1300
Bally's Grand (Reno)
Bally's Grand (Las Vegas)
Bally's Park Place
Golden Nugget
Contact:
Chris Trunda

Bally's Park Place
See Bally Manufacturing Corporation

Caesar's World, Inc.
1801 Century Park East,
Suite 2600
Los Angeles CA 90067
213-552-2711
Contact:
Jack Leone

Carlson Companies, Inc.
12755 State Highway 55
Minneapolis MN 55441
612-540-5000
Contact:
Juergen Bartels

**Colony Resorts, Inc.
(Carlson Companies, Inc.)**
15250 Ventura Boulevard,
2nd Floor
Sherman Oaks CA 91403
818-988-0530
Contact:
Judy Keys

**Crowne Plaza
(Holiday Corporation)**
3796 Lamar Avenue
Memphis TN 38195
901-362-4858
Contact:
Julie Craig

daka
5 Lakeside Office Park
Wakefield MA 01880
617-246-2525
Contact:
Richard M. Cochrane

Days Inns of America, Inc.
2751 Buford Highway NE
Atlanta GA 30324
404-325-4000
Contact:
Roger Treadaway

Doubletree, Inc.
410 North 44th Street,
Suite 700
Phoenix AZ 85008
602-220-6666
Contact:
Scott Pollack

**Embassy Suites
(Holiday Corporation)**
Xerox Center, Suite 1700
222 Los Colinas Boulevard
Irving TX 75039
214-556-1133
Contact:
Doren Chisholm

Fairmont Hotel Company
950 Mason Street
San Francisco CA 94106
415-772-5000
Contact:
Andrew Szilagyi

Forte Hotels International
1973 Friendship Drive
El Cajon CA 92020
619-448-1884
Contact:
John Hulton

Golden Nugget
See Bally Manufacturing Corporation

Guest Services, Inc.
3055 Prosperity Avenue
Fairfax VA 22031
703-849-9300
Contact:
John Hughes

**Harrah's Hotels and Casinos
(Holiday Corporation)**
P.O. Box 10
Reno NV 89520
702-788-2605
Contact:
Bernard Viola

Helmsley Hotels
455 Madison Avenue
New York NY 10022
212-888-7000
Contact:
Jean Hermans

Hilton Hotels Corporation
9336 Civic Center Drive
Beverly Hills CA 90210
213-278-4321
Contact:
Peter Kleiser

Holiday Corporation
1023 Cherry Road
Memphis TN 38117
901-362-4001
Contact:
W. C. Sweely

**Holiday Inn Hotel Group
(Holiday Corporation)**
3796 Lamar Avenue
Memphis TN 38195
901-362-4858
Contact:
Julie Craig

Hospitality International, Inc.
152 Spring Street, Suite A
Atlanta GA 30309
404-873-5926
Master Host Inns
Red Carpet Inns
Scottish Inns
Contact:
Barbara Reid

Host International
See Marriott Corporation

Hyatt Hotels Corporation
200 West Madison Plaza
Chicago IL 60606
312-750-1234
Contact:
Allan Studzinski

**Integra Hotel and Restaurant
Company**
4441 West Airport Freeway
Irving TX 75062
214-258-8500
Monterey House, Inc.
Contact:
Mike Irwin

**Inter-Continental Hotels
Corporation**
100 Paragon Drive
Montvale NJ 07645
201-307-3300
Contact:
Lester Pinkow

Interstate Hotels Corporation
Foster Plaza 10
680 Andersen Drive
Pittsburgh PA 15220
412-937-0600
Contact:
C. Norman Hull

Jolly Porpoise
See daka

Loews Hotels
1 Park Avenue
New York NY 10016
212-545-2000
Contact:
John Van Ingen

Manor Care, Inc.
10750 Columbia Pike
Silver Spring MD 20901
301-593-5600
Quality Inns, Inc.
Quality Inns International
Contact:
James Hoffmaster

The Mariner Hotel Corporation
15770 Dallas Parkway, Suite 300
Dallas TX 75248
214-980-2700
Contact:
Sue Clark

Marriott Corporation
1 Marriott Drive
Washington DC 20058
301-897-7770
Host International
Residence Inns
Contact:
Robert T. Pras

Master Host Inns
See Hospitality International, Inc.

Monterey House, Inc.
See Integra Hotel and Restaurant Company

Oliver's
See daka

Omni Hotels Corporation
500 Lafayette Road
Hampton NH 03842
603-926-8911
Contact:
Sara Diosi

Plaza Club
See daka

Pointe Resorts
7500 North Dreamy Draw Drive,
Suite 215
Phoenix AZ 85020
602-997-7777
Contact:
Rick Greenberg

Prime Motor Inns
700 Route 46 East
Fairfield NJ 07007
201-882-1010
Contact:
Richard Bennett

Princess Hotels International
805 Third Avenue
New York NY 10022
212-715-7000
Contact:
Nancy Krsulic

Quality Inns, Inc.
See Manor Care, Inc.

Quality Inns International
See Manor Care, Inc.

Radisson Hotel Corporation
12805 State Highway 55
Minneapolis MN 55441
612-540-5526
Contact:
Andrew Weingartner

Ramada Inns, Inc.
P.O. Box 29004
Phoenix AZ 85038
602-273-4000
Contact:
Robert Lansdell

Red Carpet Inns
See Hospitality International, Inc.

The Registry Hotel Corporation
16250 Dallas North Parkway, Suite 105
Dallas TX 75248
214-248-4300
Contact:
Peter Ambros

Residence Inns
See Marriott Corporation

Resorts International, Inc.
915 Northeast 125th Street
North Miami FL 33161
305-891-2500
Contact:
Jim Keenan

Rodeway Inns International, Inc.
3838 East Van Buren
Phoenix AZ 85008
602-273-4550
Contact:
Thomas Bogart

Scottish Inns
See Hospitality International, Inc.

The Sheraton Corporation
60 State Street
Boston MA 02109
617-367-3600
Contact:
Robert Brumfield

Six Flags Corporation
611 Ryan Plaza Drive, Suite 1200
Arlington TX 76011
817-274-5800
Contact:
Larry Wittenberg

Stouffer Hotel Company
29800 Bainbridge Road
Solon OH 44139
216-248-3600
Contact:
Giulio Comacchio

Trusthouse Forte Hotels, Inc.
1973 Friendship Drive
El Cajon CA 92020
619-448-1884
Contact:
Mel Schneider

RESTAURANT CHAINS

**Acapulco
(Restaurant Associates
Industries, Inc.)**
40001 Via Oro, Suite 200
Long Beach CA 90810
213-513-7500
Contact:
John McCubbin

American Festival Cafe
See Restaurant Associates Industries, Inc.

American Restaurant Group, Inc.
450 Newport Center Drive,
Suite 600
Newport Beach CA 92660
714-721-8000
Stuart Anderson's
Spectrum Foods
Contact:
Jim Campbell

Antonio's Pizza
See Levy Restaurants, Inc.

Astor Restaurant Group, Inc.
740 Broadway, Suite 602
New York NY 10003
212-673-5900
Blimpie
The Border Cafe
Contact:
Patrick Pompeo

**Bakers Square Restaurants
(VICORP Restaurants, Inc.)**
4343 Lincoln Highway, Suite 201
Matteson IL 60443
708-747-8640
Contact:
Gerald Clark

Bay Street
See S&A Restaurant Corporation

Benihana of Tokyo, Inc.
8685 Northwest 53rd Terrace
Miami FL 33166
305-593-0770
Contact:
Glen Simoes

Bennigan's
See S&A Restaurant Corporation

Big Wheel
See Consolidated Specialty Restaurants, Inc.

Bill Knapp's Michigan, Inc.
110 Knapp Drive
Battle Creek MI 49015
616-968-1121
Contact:
Patrick Mulhern

Blackeyed Pea Restaurant
See Unigate Restaurants, Inc.

Blimpie
See Astor Restaurant Group, Inc.

Bonanza Family Restaurants
See USA Cafes

The Border Cafe
See Astor Restaurant Group, Inc.

Borel's
See Stouffer Restaurant Company

Brasserie
See Restaurant Associates Industries, Inc.

Bristol
See Restaurant Enterprises Group, Inc.

Brook-Hill Restaurants
See The Happy Steak, Inc.

Brown Derby, Inc.
7850 Northfield Road
Cleveland OH 44146
216-439-8200
Contact:
Don Zorich

Burger King
See U.S. Restaurants, Inc.

Cactus Restaurants and Clubs
See El Chico Corporation

**Canteen Company
(TW Services, Inc.)**
222 North La Salle Street
Chicago IL 60601
312-701-2000
Gulliver's
Contact:
Ken Davidson

Cantina Laredo
See El Chico Corporation

Captain D's
See Shoney's, Inc.

Carlos Sweeney's
See Consolidated Specialty Restaurants, Inc.

Casa Bonita
See Unigate Restaurants, Inc.

Casa Gallardo
See Restaurant Enterprises Group, Inc.

Casa Rosa Restaurantes
See El Chico Corporation

**Charlie Brown's
(Restaurant Associates
Industries, Inc.)**
2700 U.S. Highway 22 East
Union NJ 07083
201-688-8000
Contact:
Tim O'Brien

Charley Brown's
See Restaurant Enterprises Group, Inc.

Chi-Chi's, Inc.
10200 Linn Station Road
Louisville KY 40223
502-426-3900
Contact:
Tony Canale

Chili's, Inc.
6820 LBJ Freeway, Suite 200
Dallas TX 75240
214-980-9917
Flyer's Island Express
Contact:
Lynn Clark

**Cinnabon World-Famous
Cinnamon Rolls**
See Restaurants Unlimited, Inc.

Coco's
See Restaurant Enterprises Group, Inc.

Consolidated Products, Inc.
500 Century Building
36 South Pennsylvania Street
Indianapolis IN 46204
317-633-4100
Steak 'n Shake
Contact:
William Hart

**Consolidated Specialty
Restaurants, Inc.**
500 Century Building
36 South Pennsylvania Street
Indianapolis IN 46204
317-633-4160
Big Wheel
Carlos Sweeney's
Charley Horse
Gold Rush
Jeremiah Sweeney's
Santini's Italian Cafe
Snak's Park Avenue
Contact:
Robert Foulks

Consul Restaurant Corporation
4815 West 77th Street, Suite 105
Minneapolis MN 55435
612-893-0230
Contact:
Keith Streitenberger

Crystal's Pizza & Spaghetti
See Unigate Restaurants, Inc.

Dalts
See TGI Friday's, Inc.

D. B. Kaplan's Deli
See Levy Restaurants, Inc.

Devon
See Restaurant Enterprises Group, Inc.

Dixie House
See Unigate Restaurants, Inc.

Eat'N Park Restaurants, Inc.
100 Park Manor Drive
Pittsburgh PA 15205
412-923-1000
Contact:
Ronald J. Champe

El Chico Corporation
12200 Stemmons Freeway
Dallas TX 75234
214-241-5500
Cactus Restaurants and Clubs
Cantina Laredo
Casa Rosa Restaurantes
Contact:
John Anderson

Elias Brothers Restaurants, Inc.
4199 Marcy
Warren MI 48091
313-759-6000
Contact:
Joseph Michaels

El Torito
See Restaurant Enterprises Group, Inc.

Entertainment One
1900 Yorktown
Houston TX 77056
713-871-0212
Ocean Club
R&R
Studebaker's
Contact:
Chuck Badrick

Famous Fish
See Famous Restaurants, Inc.

Famous Restaurants, Inc.
4725 North Scottsdale, Suite 350
Scottsdale AZ 85251
602-990-1123
Famous Fish
Garcia's of Scottsdale, Inc.
Contact:
Reid Pope

Fifth Quarter Steak House
See Shoney's, Inc.

First Ranch
See The Happy Steak, Inc.

Florenz
See Jerrico, Inc.

Flyer's Island Express
See Chili's, Inc.

French Bakery & Cafe
See Vie de France Restaurant Corporation

Garcia's of Scottsdale, Inc.
See Famous Restaurants, Inc.

**General Mills Restaurant
Group, Inc.**
6770 Lake Ellenor Drive
Orlando FL 32802
407-422-7711
The Olive Garden
Red Lobster USA
York Steakhouses
Contact:
Anne Powell

Gold Rush
See Consolidated Specialty Restaurants, Inc.

Golden Corral Corporation
See Investors' Management Corporation

Grandy's
See Restaurant Management Company

Gratzi
See Jerrico, Inc.

The Ground Round, Inc.
541 Main Street
South Weymouth MA 02190
617-331-7005
Contact:
Warren C. Hutchins

Gulliver's
See Canteen Company

The Happy Steak, Inc.
2246 East Date Avenue
Fresno CA 93706
209-485-8520
Brook-Hill Restaurants
First Ranch
Happy Steak Restaurants
Perko's Koffee Kup
Contact:
Gordon Sloan

Happy Steak Restaurants
See The Happy Steak, Inc.

Hillary's
See Levy Restaurants, Inc.

Houlihan's
See Restaurant Enterprises Group, Inc.

Houston's Restaurants
8 Piedmont Center, Suite 720
Atlanta GA 30305
404-231-0161
Contact:
Bob Lynn

Hungry's
See The Jan Companies

IHOP Corporation
6837 Lankershim Boulevard
North Hollywood CA 91605
818-982-2620
Contact:
Miriam Blake

International King's Table, Inc.
1500 Valley River Drive,
Suite 300
Eugene OR 97401
503-686-8030
Contact:
Matthew Loughney

**Investors' Management
Corporation**
5151 Glenwood Avenue
Raleigh NC 27626
919-781-9310
Golden Corral Corporation
Nicho's
Oh! Brian
Contact:
Larry Dial

Jamco, Ltd./Mr. Steak
2329 West Main Street
P.O. Box 9006
Littleton CO 80120
303-794-2166
Contact:
Bob Michalscheck

James Taverns
See Stouffer Restaurant Company

The Jan Companies
35 Sockanosset Cross Road
Cranston RI 02920
401-946-4000
Hungry's
Contact:
Les Rich

J. B. Winberie's
See Stouffer Restaurant Company

J.B.'s Restaurants, Inc.
1010 West 2610 South
Salt Lake City UT 84119
801-974-4300
Contact:
Larry A. Vest

Jeremiah Sweeney's
See Consolidated Specialty Restaurants, Inc.

Jerrico, Inc.
101 Jerrico Drive
Lexington KY 40511
606-263-6000
Florenz
Gratzi
Jerry's Restaurants
Long John Silver's
Contact:
Ron W. Cegnar

Jerry's Restaurants
See Jerrico, Inc.

Jojo's
See Restaurant Enterprises Group, Inc.

Jolly Roger
See Trans/Pacific Restaurants, Inc.

K-Bob's Steak Houses, Inc.
5307 East Mockingbird, Suite 710
Dallas TX 75206
214-824-9898
Contact:
Layne Walker

Kettle Restaurants, Inc.
P.O. Box 2964
Houston TX 77252
713-621-5246
Contact:
Bill Craven

Key West Grill
See S&A Restaurant Corporation

**La Villa Taxco
Restaurant Associates
Industries, Inc.)**
40001 Via Oro, Suite 200
Long Beach CA 90810
213-513-7500
Contact:
John McCubbin

L&N Seafood Grill
See Morrison's, Inc.

Lee's Famous Recipe Chicken
See Shoney's, Inc.

Legal Sea Foods, Inc.
33 Everett Street
Boston MA 02134
617-783-8084
Contact:
David Revah

Lettuce Entertain You
5419 North Sheridan Road
Chicago IL 60640
312-878-7340
Contact:
Bob Wattel

Levy Restaurants, Inc.
980 North Michigan Avenue,
Suite 400
Chicago IL 60611
312-664-8200
Antonio's Pizza
D. B. Kaplan's Deli
Hillary's
Spiaggia
Contact:
Lisa Howard

Long John Silver's
See Jerrico, Inc.

Lifestyle Restaurants, Inc.
11 East 26th Street,
8th Floor
New York NY 10010
212-696-7700
Nathan's Detroit
Contact:
Scott Kriger

Long John Silver
See Restaurant Management Company

Lyon's Restaurants, Inc.
1165 Triton Drive
Foster City CA 94404
415-349-5966
Contact:
Frank D. Dunkel

Magic Pan
50 Francisco Street, Suite 400
San Francisco CA 94133
415-421-9750
Contact:
Robert Gray

Mama Leone's
See Restaurant Associates Industries, Inc.

Michelle's Bakery & Cafe
See Vie de France Restaurant Corporation

Monterey Bay Canners
See Trans/Pacific Restaurants, Inc.

Morrison's, Inc.
4721 Morrison Drive
Mobile AL 36625
205-344-3000
L&N Seafood Grill
Ruby Tuesday
Silver Spoon
Contact:
Robert McClenagan

Nathan's Detroit
See Lifestyle Restaurants, Inc.

Nestle Enterprises, Inc.
5757 Harper Road
Solon OH 44139
216-349-5757
Contact:
B. Richard Atkinson

Nicho's
See Investors' Management Corporation

94th Aero Squadron Restaurants
See Specialty Restaurants Corporation

Ocean Club
See Entertainment One

Oh! Brian
See Investors' Management Corporation

The Olive Garden
See General Mills Restaurant Group, Inc.

Palm Restaurants
837 Second Avenue
New York NY 10017
212-687-7698
Contact:
Bruno Molinari

Pango's
See Shoney's, Inc.

Papa Gino's of America, Inc.
600 Providence Highway
Dedham MA 02026
617-461-1200
Contact:
Steve Feyman

Paragon Restaurant Group, Inc.
6610 Convoy Court
San Diego CA 92111
619-292-8050
Casual Dining Division
Rusty Pelican Restaurants, Inc.
Steak House
Contact:
Bill Seckinger

Parkers' Lighthouse
See Stouffer Restaurant Company

Perkins Family Restaurants L.P.
6075 Poplar, Suite 800
Memphis TN 38119
901-766-6400
Contact:
Paul Freeman

Perko's Koffee Kup
See The Happy Steak, Inc.

Phillips Seafood Restaurants
2004 Philadelphia Avenue
Ocean City MD 21842
301-289-6821
Contact:
Paul Wall

The Pillsbury Company Restaurant Group
200 South 6th Street
Minneapolis MN 55402
612-330-4966
Contact:
Mary Carroll

Pizza Hut
See Restaurant Management Company

Pizzeria Uno
See Uno Restaurants Corporation

Ponderosa
See U.S. Restaurants, Inc.

Prufrock
See Unigate Restaurants, Inc.

Quincy's Family Steakhouse
See TW Services, Inc.

Rally's
See Restaurant Management Company

Red Lion
4001 Main Street
Vancouver WA 98663
206-696-0001
Contact:
Herman Haastrup

Red Robin International
9 Executive Circle, Suite 190
Irvine CA 92714
714-756-2121
Contact:
George Cudhea

R&R
See Entertainment One

Red Lobster USA
See General Mills Restaurant Group, Inc.

Restaurant Associates Industries, Inc.
36 West 44th Street
New York NY 10036
212-642-1500
American Festival Cafe
Brasserie
Mama Leone's
Sea Grill
Contact:
Dick Cattani

Restaurant Enterprises Group, Inc.
2701 Alton Avenue
Irvine CA 92714
714-863-6300
Bristol
Casa Gallardo
Charley Brown's
Coco's
Devon
El Torito
Houlihan's
Jojo's
Reuben's
Contact:
Bob Craig

Restaurant Management Company
555 North Woodlawn, Suite 3102
Wichita KS 67208
316-684-5119
Grandy's
Long John Silver
Pizza Hut
Rally's
Contact:
Wes Frye

Restaurants Unlimited, Inc.
1818 North Northlake Way
Seattle WA 98103
206-634-0550
Cinnabon World-Famous Cinnamon Rolls
Contact:
David Johnson

Reuben's
See Restaurant Enterprises Group, Inc.

Ribby's
See USA Cafes

Ruby Tuesday
See Morrison's, Inc.

Rusty Pelican Restaurants, Inc.
See Paragon Restaurant Group, Inc.

Rusty Scupper
See Stouffer Restaurant Company

Ryan's Family Steak Houses, Inc.
405 Lancaster Avenue
Green SC 29651
803-879-1000
Contact:
Edward McCranie

S&A Restaurant Corporation (The Pillsbury Company Restaurant Group)
12404 Park Central Drive
Dallas TX 75251
214-404-5000
Bay Street
Bennigan's
Key West Grill
Steak and Ale
Contact:
Charles Lonsignont

Sailmaker
See Shoney's, Inc.

Santini's Italian Cafe
See Consolidated Specialty Restaurants, Inc.

Sbarro Licensing Corporation
763 Larkfield Road
Commack NY 11725
516-864-0200
Contact:
Joe Sbarro

Seafood Broiler Restaurants
5150 Candlewood Street, Suite 4
P.O. Box 850
Lakewood CA 90714
213-925-7451
Contact:
Monica Gaudlitz

Sea Grill
See Restaurant Associates Industries, Inc.

Shoney's, Inc.
1727 Elm Hill Pike
Nashville TN 37202
615-391-5201
Captain D's
Fifth Quarter Steak House
Lee's Famous Recipe Chicken
Pango's
Sailmaker
Shoney's Restaurants
Contact:
David Dobbs

Shoney's Restaurants
See Shoney's, Inc.

Silver Spoon
See Morrison's, Inc.

Snak's Park Avenue
See Consolidated Specialty Restaurants, Inc.

**Spartan Food Systems
(TW Services, Inc.)**
P.O. Box 3168
Spartanburg SC 29304
803-579-1220
Quincy's Family Steakhouse
Contact:
Jody Traywick

Specialty Restaurants Corporation
2099 South State College Boulevard,
Suite 300
Anaheim CA 92806
714-634-0300
94th Aero Squadron Restaurants
Contact:
Robert P. Wahlstrom

Spectrum Foods
See American Restaurant Group, Inc.

Spiaggia
See Levy Restaurants, Inc.

Steak and Ale
See S&A Restaurant Corporation

Steak House
See Paragon Restaurant Group, Inc.

Steak'n Shake
See Consolidated Products, Inc.

**Stouffer Restaurant Company
(Nestle Enterprises, Inc.)**
Corporate Circle
30050 Chagrin Boulevard
Pepper Pike OH 44124
216-464-6606
Borel's
James Taverns
Parkers' Lighthouse
Rusty Scupper
Top Restaurants
J. B. Winberie's
Contact:
David Jablonski

Stuart Anderson's
See American Restaurant Group, Inc.

Studebaker's
See Entertainment One

Swensen's Ice Cream Company
200 Andover Business Park Drive,
Suite 1000
River Road
Andover MA 01810
617-975-1283
Contact:
Jeffrey Fadok

Taco Bueno
See Unigate Restaurants, Inc.

TGI Friday's, Inc.
14665 Midway Road
Dallas TX 75244
214-450-5400
Dalts
Contact:
John Acupine

Top Restaurants
See Stouffer Restaurant Company

Trans/Pacific Restaurants, Inc.
17042 Gillette
Irvine CA 92714
714-250-0331
Jolly Roger
Monterey Bay Canners
Contact:
Clinton Goo

TW Services, Inc.
P.O. Box 3168
Spartanburg SC 29304
803-579-1220
Quincy's Family Steak House
Hardee's (franchisee)
Contact:
Jody Traywick

Unigate Restaurants, Inc.
8115 Preston Road
Dallas TX 75225
214-363-9513
Blackeyed Pea Restaurant
Casa Bonita
Crystal's Pizza & Spaghetti
Dixie House
Prufrock
Taco Bueno
Contact:
David Fry

Uno Restaurants Corporation
100 Charles Park Road
West Roxbury MA 02132
617-323-9200
Pizzeria Uno
Contact:
Brian Whicher

USACafes
8080 North Central Expressway,
Suite 500
Dallas TX 75206
214-891-8400
Bonanza Family Restaurants
Ribby's
Contact:
Dennis Violkowski

VICORP Restaurants, Inc.
400 West 48th Avenue
P.O. Box 16601
Denver CO 80216
303-296-2121
Village Inn Family Restaurants
Contact:
Timothy R. Kanaly

**Vie de France Restaurant
Corporation
(VICORP Restaurants, Inc.)**
8201 Greensboro Drive
McLean VA 22102
703-442-9205
French Bakery & Cafe
Michelle's Bakery & Cafe
Contact:
Matt Spielman
Vie de France Bakery Corporation
Contact:
Paul Hoftyzer

Village Inn Family Restaurants
See VICORP Restaurants, Inc.

Western Steer–Mom'n'Pop's, Inc.
P.O. Box 399
Claremont NC 28610
704-459-7626
Contact:
Jack Busic

Wheel Works
See Consolidated Specialty Restaurants, Inc.

York Steakhouses
See General Mills Restaurant Group, Inc.

CAFETERIA SUPPLIERS

**Bishop Buffets, Inc.
(Furr's/Bishop's Cafeterias L.P.)**
385 Collins Road NE
Cedar Rapids IA 52402
319-393-6830
Contact:
Jacob Hitt

Davis Brothers Cafeterias
2631 Buford Highway NE
Atlanta GA 30324
404-320-1800
Contact:
Philip Yochum

Furr's/Bishop's Cafeterias L.P.
P.O. Box 6747
Lubbock TX 79493
806-792-7151
Contact:
Sara Stalcup

Laughner Brothers, Inc.
4004 South East Street
Indianapolis IN 46227
317-783-2907
Contact:
Mike Fiddler

Luby's Cafeterias, Inc.
P.O. Box 33069
San Antonio TX 78265
512-654-9000
Contact:
Bill Robson

MCL Cafeterias, Inc.
2730 East 62nd Street
Indianapolis IN 46220
317-257-5425
Contact:
Mark Lawrance

Morrison's Family Dining, Inc.
4721 Morrison Drive
Mobile AL 36625
205-344-3000
Contact:
Larry Davis

Piccadilly Cafeterias, Inc.
3232 Sherwood Forest Boulevard
Baton Rouge LA 70816
504-293-9440
Contact:
William B. Schwarting

S&S Cafeterias
See Smith and Sons Foods, Inc.

Smith and Sons Foods, Inc.
2124 Riverside Drive
Macon GA 31204
912-745-4759
S&S Cafeterias
Contact:
T. E. Perryman

Wyatt Cafeterias, Inc.
10726 Plano Road
P.O. Box 38388
Dallas TX 75238
214-349-0060
Contact:
Stan Hammack

FAST FOOD CHAINS

American Restaurant Group, Inc.
450 Newport Center Drive,
Suite 600
Newport Beach CA 92660
714-721-8000
Contact:
Wilfred Partridge

A&W Restaurants, Inc.
17197 North Laurel Park Drive,
Suite 500
Livonia MI 48152
313-462-0029
Contact:
Mary Smith

Arby's, Inc.
3495 Piedmont Road NE,
Building 10, Suite 700
Atlanta GA 30305
404-262-2729
Contact:
Betty Marshall

Big Boy
See Marriott Corporation

BK Root Beer Drive Inns, Inc.
See DeNovo Corporation

Boddie-Noell Enterprises, Inc.
1021 Noell Lane
Rocky Mount NC 27802
919-937-2000
Contact:
Richard Jenkins

Bojangle's Chicken & Biscuits
See The Horn & Hardart Company

Brown & Portillo, Inc.
3777 East Butterfield Road
Lombard IL 60148
708-960-5200
Brown's Chicken
Contact:
Greg Burn

Brown's Chicken
See Brown & Portillo, Inc.

Burger Chef
See Hardee's Food Systems, Inc.

**Burger King Corporation
(ownership in transition)**
P.O. Box 520783 CMF
Miami FL 33152
305-378-7011
Contact:
Don Manson

Carl's Jr.
See Carl Karcher Enterprises, Inc.

Carl Karcher Enterprises, Inc.
1200 North Harbor Boulevard
P.O. Box 4349
Anaheim CA 92801
714-774-5796
Carl's Jr.
Contact:
David Parsley

Carrols Corporation
968 James Street
Syracuse NY 13203
315-424-0513
Contact:
Steven A. F. Cox

Chi-Chi's
See Foodmaker, Inc.

Chick-fil-A, Inc.
5200 Buffington Road
Atlanta GA 30349
404-765-8000
Contact:
Steve Hester

Concept Development, Inc.
See Pantera's Corporation

Copeland's
See A. Copeland Enterprises, Inc.

A. Copeland Enterprises, Inc.
1333 South Clearview Parkway
Jefferson LA 70121
504-733-4300
Copeland's
Church's Fried Chicken
Popeyes Chicken & Biscuits
Contact:
Cathy Marsh

Dairy Isle
See DeNovo Corporation

Del Taco, Inc.
(American Restaurant Group, Inc.)
345 Baker Street
Costa Mesa CA 92626
714-540-8914
Contact:
Wilfred Partridge

Denny's, Inc.
16700 Valley View Avenue
La Mirada CA 90637
714-739-8100
Contact:
Sue Henderson

DeNovo Corporation
8345 Hall Road
Utica MI 48087
313-739-5520
BK Root Beer Drive Inns, Inc.
Dairy Isle
Dog n Suds, Inc.
Tastee Freez International, Inc.
Contact:
Jim Brasier

Dog n Suds, Inc.
See DeNovo Corporation

Dobbs Houses, Inc.
Dobbs International Services, Inc.
(Greyhound Food Management, Inc.)
5100 Poplar Avenue
Memphis TN 38137
901-766-3600
Contact:
Ken Miller

Domino's Pizza, Inc.
30 Frank Lloyd Wright Drive
Ann Arbor MI 48106
313-668-4000
Contact:
Don Volcek

Dunkin' Donuts, Inc.
14 Pacella Drive
Randolph MA 02368
617-961-4000
Contact:
Steven Pinard

Druther's International, Inc.
2440 Grinstead Drive
P.O. Box 4999
Louisville KY 40204
502-458-0040
Contact:
David Newman

El Pollo Loco
P.O. Box 37201
La Mirada CA 90637
714-670-5440
Contact:
Margaret Jenkins

Foodmaker, Inc.
9330 Balboa Avenue
San Diego CA 92123
619-571-2121
Jack In The Box
Chi-Chi's
Contact:
Bruce Bowers

Galardi Group
4440 Von Karman
Newport Beach CA 92660
714-752-5800
Original Hamburger Stands
Weldons
Wienerschnitzel
Contact:
Wayne Lam

Godfather's Pizza, Inc.
(The Pillsbury Company
Restaurant Group)
9140 West Dodge Road
Omaha NE 68144
402-391-1452
Contact:
Jim Lewis

Golden Skillet
See International Dairy Queen, Inc.

Greyhound Food Management, Inc.
4040 North Central
Phoenix AZ 85012
602-248-6070
Contact:
Bruce Pauzus

Hamburger Hamlets, Inc.
14156 Magnolia Boulevard
Sherman Oaks CA 91423
818-995-7333
Contact:
David Fox

Hardee's Food Systems, Inc.
1233 Hardees Boulevard
Rocky Mount NC 27802
919-977-2000
Burger Chef
Hardee's
Contact:
John Kimber

The Horn & Hardart Company
730 Fifth Avenue
New York NY 10019
212-398-9000
Bojangle's Chicken & Biscuits
Contact:
Carlos Garcia

Integra Hotel & Restaurant
Company
4441 West Airport Freeway
Irving TX 75062
214-258-8500
Showbiz Pizza Time, Inc.
Contact:
Terry Spaight

International Dairy Queen, Inc.
5701 Green Valley Drive
Minneapolis MN 55437
612-830-0200
Golden Skillet
Karmelkorn
Contact:
Michael Leary

Jack In The Box
See Foodmaker, Inc.

Karmelkorn
See International Dairy Queen, Inc.

KFC Corporation
(PepsiCo Foodservice Division)
1441 Gardiner Lane
Louisville KY 40213
502-456-8300
Contact:
Edward Dudley

The Krystal Company
Union Square
Chattanooga TN 37402
615-757-1560
Contact:
Michael Bass

Little Caesar Enterprises, Inc.
24210 Haggarty
Farmington Hills MI 48024
313-478-6200
Contact:
Dave Deal

Marriott Corporation
1 Marriott Drive
Washington DC 20058
301-897-7770
Big Boy
Roy Rogers
Contact:
Robert T. Pras

Mazzio's Corporation
4441 South 72nd East Avenue
Tulsa OK 74145
918-663-8880
Contact:
Archie Dixon

McDonald's
McDonald's Plaza
Oak Brook IL 60521
708-575-3000
Contact:
Lynal Root

Metromedia Company, Inc.
1 Harmon Plaza
Secaucus NJ 07096
Contact:
Arnold Wadler

Mister Donut of America
P.O. Box 2942
Minneapolis MN 55402
612-340-3300
Contact:
Joseph Ban Bourgondien

Mr. Gatti's, Inc.
220 Foremost Drive
Austin TX 78745
512-282-5580
Contact:
Gilbert McCoy

National Pizza Company
720 West 20th Street
Pittsburg KS 66762
316-231-3390
Contact:
Marilyn McIver

Original Hamburger Stands
See Galardi Group

Pantera's Corporation
2930 Stemmons Freeway
Dallas TX 75247
214-638-7250
Concept Development, Inc.
Pizza Inn
Contact:
Gary Lomax

PepsiCo Foodservice Division
700 Anderson Hill Road
Purchase NY 10577
914-253-2000
Contact:
Edward Dudley

The Pillsbury Company
Restaurant Group
200 South 6th Street
Minneapolis MN 55402
612-330-4966
Contact:
Edward C. Stringer

Pizza Hut, Inc.
(PepsiCo Foodservice Division)
9111 East Douglas
P.O. Box 428
Wichita KS 67201
316-681-9000
Contact:
Bob Carney

Pizza Inn
See Pantera's Corporation

Pizza Management, Inc.
6903 Sunbelt Drive South
P.O. Drawer 65100
San Antonio TX 78265
512-829-4111
Contact:
Jerry J. Hopp

Po Folks, Inc.
P.O. Box 17406
Nashville TN 37217
615-366-0900
Contact:
Al Lyczkowski

Ponderosa, Inc.
(Metromedia Company, Inc.)
P.O. Box 578
Dayton OH 45401
513-454-2400
Contact:
Richard Haydes

Popeyes Chicken & Biscuits
See A. Copeland Enterprises, Inc.

Quik Wok, Inc.
(The Pillsbury Company
Restaurant Group)
511 East Carpenter Freeway,
Suite 600
Irving TX 75062
214-506-0700
Contact:
Joe Kregler

Rax Restaurants, Inc.
1266 Dublin Road
Columbus OH 43215
614-486-3669
Contact:
Mike Link

Rib-It
See U.S. Restaurants, Inc.

Rocky Rococo
340 West Washington Avenue
Madison WI 53703
608-256-0603
Contact:
Ralph Skordas

Round Table Franchise Corporation
655 Montgomery Street, Suite 700
San Francisco CA 94111
415-392-7500
Contact:
Jeane Boyer

Roy Rogers
See Marriott Corporation

RPM Pizza, Inc.
Highway 49 and 5th Street
Gulfport MS 39503
601-832-4000
Contact:
Tom Holliday

Sea Galley Stores, Inc.
6920 220th SW
Mountlake Terrace WA 98043
206-775-0411
Contact:
Paula Lacy

Shakey's, Inc.
1320 Greenway Drive, Suite 600
Irving TX 75038
214-580-0388
Contact:
Georgette Harris

Showbiz Pizza Time, Inc.
See Integra Hotel & Restaurant Company

Skipper's, Inc.
14450 Northeast 29th Place
Bellevue WA 98007
206-885-2116
Contact:
John Torza

Sonic Industries, Inc.
The Sonic Center
120 Robert S. Kerr
Oklahoma City OK 73102
405-232-4334
Contact:
Gary Johnson

Sonny's Real Pit Bar-B-Q, Inc.
3631 Southwest Archer Road
Gainesville FL 32608
904-376-9721
Contact:
Ted Hires

Taco Bell, Inc.
(PepsiCo Foodservice Division)
17901 Von Karman
Irvine CA 92630
714-863-4500
Contact:
Ken Sovey

Taco John's International
808 West 20th Street
Cheyenne WY 82003
307-635-0101
Contact:
Brent Murray

Taco Time International, Inc.
3880 West 11th Street
P.O. Box 2056
Eugene OR 97402
503-687-8222
Contact:
Doug Furlong

Tastee Freez International, Inc.
See DeNovo Corporation

TCBY Enterprises, Inc.
425 West Capitol Avenue,
Suite 1100
Little Rock AR 72201
501-688-8229
Contact:
Herald Walden

U.S. Restaurants, Inc.
1780 Swede Road
Blue Bell PA 19422
215-277-4200
Burger King (franchisee)
Ponderosa (franchisee)
Rib-It
Contact:
Steven Lewis

Waffle House, Inc.
5986 Financial Drive
Norcross GA 30071
404-447-4488
Contact:
T. G. Franks

Weldons
See Galardi Group

Wendy's International, Inc.
4288 West Dublin-Granville Road
P.O. Box 256
Dublin OH 43017
614-764-3100
Contact:
Dennis Campbell

Whataburger, Inc.
4600 Parkdale Drive
Corpus Christi TX 78411
512-851-0650
Contact:
Haydon Rabon

White Castle System, Inc.
555 West Goodale Street
P.O. Box 1498
Columbus OH 43216
614-228-5781
Contact:
Robert D. Gioux

Wienerschnitzel
See Galardi Group

Winchell's Donut House
16424 Valley View Street
La Mirada CA 90638
714-739-2774
Contact:
Dawn Stuyvenberg

HEALTH CARE SUPPLIERS

Beverly Enterprises
99 South Oakland Avenue
Pasadena CA 91101
818-577-6111
Contact:
Ken Cooper

Hospital Corporation of America
1 Park Plaza
P.O. Box 550
Nashville TN 37202
615-327-9551
Contact:
John O. Colton

Hospital Purchasing Services
491 Arlington Street
Middleville MI 49333
616-795-3308
Contact:
Jerry L. Welsh

Humana, Inc.
500 West Main Street
P.O. Box 1438
Louisville KY 40201
502-561-2000
Contact:
Paul B. Powell

Manor Care, Inc.
10770 Columbia Pike
Silver Spring MD 20901
301-681-9400
Manor HealthCare
Contact:
Gene Zeiser

Manor HealthCare
See Manor Care, Inc.

Metropolitan Chicago Healthcare Council
222 South Riverside Plaza,
17th Floor
Chicago IL 60606
312-906-6000
Contact:
Charles Tortorello

Morrison's Custom Management
4721 Morrison Drive
Mobile AL 36625
205-344-3000
Contact:
Joe Byrum

Unicare Health Facilities, Inc.
105 West Michigan Street
Milwaukee WI 53203
414-271-9696
Contact:
Wayne Goldman

AIRLINE SUPPLIERS

American Airlines
P.O. Box 619616
Dallas TX 75261
817-355-2475
Contact:
J. G. Katz

Braniff, Inc.
Airside Commerce Park
9413 Tradeport Drive
Orlando FL 32827
407-856-8540
Contact:
Jeff Snodgrass

Continental Airlines
2929 Allen Parkway
Houston TX 77019
713-284-5643
Contact:
Greg Hatcher

Delaware North Companies, Inc.
700 Delaware Avenue
Buffalo NY 14209
716-881-6500
Contact:
Gary C. Fraker

Delta Airlines, Inc.
Hartsfield International Airport
P.O. Box 20531
Atlanta GA 30320
404-765-2811
Contact:
S. J. Cavallaro

Dobbs International Services, Inc.
5100 Poplar Avenue
Memphis TN 38137
901-766-3789
Contact:
George Alvord

Eastern Airlines
Miami International Airport
Miami FL 33148
305-873-6132
Contact:
Lynda Zane

Jerry's Caterers
P.O. Box 24618
West Palm Beach FL 33416
407-683-2569
Contact:
Jerry Pendergast

Marriott In-Flite Services
1 Marriott Drive
Washington DC 20058
301-380-1850
Contact:
Carl Dunaway

Northwest Airlines, Inc.
Minneapolis/St. Paul International
Airport
St. Paul MN 55111
612-726-2111
Contact:
Gilbert Peters

Ogden Allied Services Corporation
Air La Carte
2 Penn Plaza
New York NY 10121
212-868-6000
Contact:
Kent Belvin

Sky Chefs, Inc.
P.O. Box 619777
Dallas/Ft. Worth Airport TX 75261
817-792-2389
Contact:
William Temple

Trans World Airlines, Inc.
605 Third Avenue
New York NY 10158
212-692-3000
Contact:
Mark Mulvany

United Airlines
P.O. Box 66919,
P.O. Box 66100
Chicago IL 60666
312-952-4000
Contact:
Patrick O'Brien

USAir Inc.
Greater Pittsburgh International Airport
Pittsburgh PA 15232
412-747-5870
Contact:
Peter Wetli

95
**Restaurant Designers
and Design Firms**

100
**Chefs and Chef/Restaurant
Owners**

111
**The James Beard Foundation's
Awards Programs:**

Great American Chefs at The Beard House;

Great American Cooks at The Beard House;

Great Regional Chefs at The Beard House;

*Rising Stars of American Cuisine at
The Beard House*

112
Spas and Spa Chains

Spas; Vegetarian Spas

114
Caterers

SAMUEL BOTERO ASSOCIATES, INC.

Phillip Ennis

ORSINI'S

CAFE JAPONAIS

PRIMA DONNA

LE CLUB
The Party Room

SIGN OF THE DOVE
The Music Room

150 East 58 Street, 23 Floor, New York, N.Y. 10155
Tel: 212·935·5155   Fax: 212·832·0714

Restaurant Designers and Design Firms

This listing is based on the annual design awards listing assembled from information published by *Restaurants & Institutions* magazine and compiled by Beth Lorenzini and Monica Kass. It lists the major designers in the field alphabetically by city or town within regions.

The design of a restaurant is comparable to that of a theatrical set, creating the mood and the "feel" that the owners envisage by achieving just the right combinations of color, decoration and tabletop accessories that are essential to success.

Restaurant designers frequently work hand in hand with architects, lighting experts and other specialists who concern themselves with traffic flow and seating arrangements.

NORTHEAST

MASSACHUSETTS

Kenneth E. Hurd & Associates
205 Portland Street
Boston MA 02114
617-523-7334

Cole and Goyette, Architects and Planners, Inc.
540 Franklin Street
Cambridge MA 02139
617-491-5662

Stubbins Associates
1033 Massachusetts Avenue
Cambridge MA 02138
617-491-6450

Graham-Solano, Ltd.
282 Montvale Avenue
Woburn MA 01801
617-935-3444

NEW JERSEY

BDG, Inc.
5217 Wellington Avenue
Ventnor NJ 08406
609-487-0077

Q5, Inc.
50 Galesi Drive
Wayne NJ 07470
201-256-7900

NEW YORK

Walter M. Ballard, Ltd. SPGA Group, Inc.
65 Bleecker Street
New York NY 10012
212-505-6300

Bonsignore, Brignati & Mazzotta, P.C.
275 Seventh Avenue
New York NY 10001
212-633-1400

Samuel Botero Associates, Inc.
150 East 58th Street, 23rd Floor
New York NY 10022
212-935-5155

Nicholas A. Calder Interiors, Ltd.
1365 York Avenue, Suite 3K
New York NY 10021
212-861-9055

Croxton Collaborative
1122 Madison Avenue
New York NY 10028
212-794-2285

Al DiOrio Design
45 West 81st Street
New York NY 10024
212-362-6435

Donghia Associates
315 East 62nd Street
New York NY 10021
212-486-1100

Dorf Associates
106 East 19th Street
New York NY 10003
212-473-9667

Dorothy Draper & Company, Inc.
60 East 56th Street
New York NY 10022
212-758-2810

Forbes-Ergas Design Associates
138 Ninth Avenue
New York NY 10011
212-727-1110

Grandesign Architects
1841 Broadway, Suite 400
New York NY 10023
212-489-2255

Haverson/Rockwell Architects
18 West 27th Street
New York NY 10001
212-889-4182

As an award-winning, innovative design firm, our spectrum of services to the hospitality industry includes architectural and interior design, lighting design, graphics and kitchen design. Our completed projects range in size from a series of small gourmet food shops to many well-known and successful restaurants and several large banqueting facilities. Every project receives the personal attention of the firm's principals, with emphasis on creating a distinctive, meaningful environment that fits the client's needs.

Hochheiser-Elias Design Group
322 East 86th Street
New York NY 10028
212-535-7437

Interior Design Force, Inc.
42 Greene Street
New York NY 10013
212-431-0999

Interior Design International
40 East 12th Street
New York NY 10003
212-777-6007

Tom Lee, Ltd.
136 East 57th Street
New York NY 10022
212-421-4433

Sam Lopata, Inc.
27 West 20th Street, Suite 501
New York NY 10011
212-691-7924

Ellen L. McCluskey Associates, Inc.
139 East 57th Street
New York NY 10022
212-838-6850

MacDonald Design Group
515 Madison Avenue, Suite 910
New York NY 10022
212-888-9786

Charles Morris Mount
Mount & Company
104 West 27th Street, 9th Floor
New York NY 10001
212-807-0800

Mount & Company create award-winning interior designs with a proven formula for success. They also offer menu consultation and graphic design. Their food-related projects range from fine dining restaurants and fast-food facilities to catering kitchens, gourmet food markets and retail bakeries.

Great design sells. Mount & Company work with clients to develop an image and integrate the entire design concept. Charles Morris Mount celebrates 20 years of creating unique and exciting projects internationally. Illustrated brochure available.

Orsini Design Associates, Inc.
358 East 57th Street
New York NY 10022
212-371-8400

Gwathmey Siegel & Associates
475 Tenth Avenue
New York NY 10018
212-947-1240

Spitzer & Associates Architects
47 West 34th Street, Suite 608
New York NY 10001
212-563-6290

Judith Stockman & Associates
285 Lafayette Street
New York NY 10012
212-925-1130

Swanke Hayden Connell
4 Columbus Circle
New York NY 10019
212-977-9696

Charles Swerz Interior Design
41 Union Square West, Suite 1121
New York NY 10003
212-627-4222

Switzer Group
902 Broadway, 12th Floor
New York NY 10010
212-674-8700

Adam Tihany International
57 East 11th Street
New York NY 10003
212-505-2360

Xanadu Design, Ltd.
260 Fifth Avenue, 4th Floor
New York NY 10001
212-213-2340

B. Shervan & Son
2 Seaview Boulevard, Suite 100
Port Washington NY 11050
516-484-2200

PENNSYLVANIA

**George Conte Design
Consultants, Inc.**
619 East Pittsburgh Street
Greensburg PA 15601
412-832-7055

Bartley, Bronstein, Long & Mirenda
924 Cherry Street
Philadelphia PA 19107
215-625-2500

Daroff Design, Inc.
2300 Ionic Street
Philadelphia PA 19103
215-636-9900

Charles W. Letier
Wallace Building
642 North Broad Street
Philadelphia PA 19103
215-329-9951

Miraglia Contract International
518 South 3rd Street
Philadelphia PA 19147
215-592-7774

PHH Environments
2300 Chestnut Street
Philadelphia PA 19103
215-557-6800

RHODE ISLAND

Morris Nathanson Design, Inc.
163 Exchange Street
Pawtucket RI 02860
401-723-3800

DiLeonardo International, Inc.
2346 Post Road
Warwick RI 02886
401-732-2900
800-556-7408

SOUTH

ARKANSAS

Wellborn Henderson Associates
212 Center Street
Little Rock AR 72201
501-374-8254

DISTRICT OF COLUMBIA

Copeland Krieger Associates
2715 M Street NW
Washington DC 20007
202-337-0500

Daniels & Stine
3 Riggs Court NW
Washington DC 20036
202-483-6565

Hellmuth, Obata & Kassabaum
1110 Vermont Avenue NW,
Suite 300
Washington DC 20005
202-457-9400

FLORIDA

Jeffrey Howard & Associates
101 Aragon Avenue
Coral Gables FL 33134
305-446-5431

L. E. Seitz Associates, Inc.
395 Alhambra Circle
Coral Gables FL 33134
305-445-2200

Michelle Lessirard Designs, Inc.
4850 West Prospect
Ft. Lauderdale FL 33309
305-739-9484

Forum Architecture & Planning
202 Lookoutplace
Maitland FL 32751
407-539-0909

Carole Korn Interiors, Inc.
825 South Bayshore Drive, Penthouse
Miami FL 33137
305-375-8080

Servico
1601 Belvedere Road
West Palm Beach FL 33406
305-689-9970

GEORGIA

Design Continuum
1801 Peachtree, Suite 200
Atlanta GA 30309
404-350-2400

Design Solutions, Inc.
2727 Paces Ferry Road,
Suite 1230
Atlanta GA 30339
404-434-5400

Designers II, Inc.
3690 North Peachtree Road,
Suite 100
Atlanta GA 30341
404-458-9111

Image Design, Inc.
2500 Windy Ridge SE
Marietta GA 30067
404-952-7171

MARYLAND

Rita St. Clair & Associates
1009 North Charles Street
Baltimore MD 21201
301-752-1313

NORTH CAROLINA

One Design Center, Inc.
P.O. Box 29426
Greensboro NC 27429
919-288-0134

TENNESSEE

M²=Mitchell x Mitchell, Inc.
100 Cherokee Boulevard,
Suite 311
Chattanooga TN 37405
615-266-1067

Renovation & Design, Inc.
262 German Oak Drive
Cordova TN 38018
901-756-7600

VIRGINIA

Thomas Hamilton & Associates
11000 Staples Mill Road
Glen Allen VA 23060
804-798-4339

Edwards Design Group
8603 Westwood Center Drive,
Suite 201
Vienna VA 22182
703-847-9770

Hugh W. Dear & Associates, Inc.
1300 Garrison Drive
Williamsburg VA 23185
804-220-1300

MIDWEST

ILLINOIS

Banks/Eakin Architects
410 South Michigan Avenue,
Suite 908
Chicago IL 60605
312-922-2410

Norman DeHaan Associates, Inc.
355 North Canal Street
Chicago IL 60606
312-454-0004

Jerome Eastman, Inc.
3 East Ontario Street
Chicago IL 60611
312-642-2790

Ann Milligan Gray, Inc.
1416 North Astor Street
Chicago IL 60610
312-787-1416

Meisel Associates, Ltd.
800 North Clark Street
Chicago IL 60610
312-664-4814

Lynn Rosenberg Design
77 North Milwaukee Avenue
Chicago IL 60622
312-738-1970

Zakaspace Corporation
636 South Michigan Avenue
Chicago IL 60605
312-939-4060

Ascher, Inc.
1455 Golf Road
Des Plaines IL 60016
708-827-9490

Artifax Design International
1 South 072 Luther Avenue
Lombard IL 60148
708-953-1010

Aumiller Youngquist, P.C.
800 East Northwest Highway
Mt. Prospect IL 60056
708-253-3761

O'Donnell, Wicklund & Pigozzi
3239 Arnold Lane
Northbrook IL 60062
708-940-9600

Design Works, Inc.
815 Garfield
Oak Park IL 60304
708-386-3010

Equipment Planners, Inc.
3720 11th Street
Rock Island IL 61201
309-786-8010

INDIANA

CSO Interiors
9100 Keystone Crossing,
Suite 600
Indianapolis IN 46240
317-848-2800

Kasler & Associates, Inc.
1 American Square
Indianapolis IN 46282
317-636-8048

IOWA

Larkin, Inc.
3330 Southgate Court SW
P.O. Box 1808
Cedar Rapids IA 52404
319-366-7237

MINNESOTA

Albitz Design, Inc.
1800 Girard Avenue South
Minneapolis MN 55403
612-377-2165

MISSOURI

Spener Restaurant Design, Inc.
728 Hanley Industrial Court
Brentwood MO 63144
314-781-2200

GB Design, Inc.
712 Broadway, Suite 700
Kansas City MO 64105
816-842-2115

Professional Interiors, Ltd.
9467 Dielman Rock Island Drive
St. Louis MO 63132
314-432-1375

OHIO

Babcock & Schmid Associates, Inc.
Design Management
3689 Ira Road
Bath OH 44210
216-666-8826

Dimensional Interiors
23715 Mercantile Road
Beachwood OH 44122
216-831-5231

Space Design International
311 Elm Street, Suite 600
Cincinnati OH 45202
513-241-3000

SOUTHWEST

NEVADA

SLC Design
4050 South Industrial
Las Vegas NV 89103
702-791-5600

TEXAS

ABV & Associates
1605-C Stemmons Freeway
Dallas TX 75207
214-744-4040

Design & Associates, Inc.
5001 LBJ Freeway, Suite 700
Dallas TX 75224
214-386-6119

Carolyn Henry & Associates, Inc.
14850 Quorum Drive
Dallas TX 75240
214-788-0155

Sue Wade & Associates, Inc.
2911 Turtle Creek Boulevard
Dallas TX 75219
214-520-3390

Wilson & Associates
3811 Turtle Creek Boulevard,
15th Floor
Dallas TX 75219
214-521-6753

Joyce K. Wynn, Inc.
2404 Cedar Springs
Dallas TX 75201
214-953-0152

Index The Design Firm
5701 Woodway Drive, Suite 200
Houston TX 77057
713-977-2594

Mitchell, Carlson & Associates, Inc.
3221 West Alabama Street
Houston TX 77098
713-522-1054

3D/International
1900 West Loop South
Houston TX 77027
713-871-7000

Ziegler Cooper, Inc.
1331 Lamar, Suite 1450
Houston TX 77010
713-654-0000

MOUNTAIN STATES

COLORADO

VHA, Inc.
2675 South Abilene Street
Aurora CO 80014
303-751-7333

Aiello Associates
1441 Wazee Street
Denver CO 80202
303-892-7024

Design Services, Inc.
4600 South Ulster Street
Denver CO 80237
303-220-2299

J. Kattman Associates
1660 Wynkoop Street
Denver CO 80202
303-573-7447

Noble/Sysco
1101 West 48th Avenue
Denver CO 80221
303-458-4000

**William Hetherington
& Associates, Inc.**
5990 Greenwood Plaza Boulevard,
Suite 138
Englewood CO 80111
303-779-9979

WEST COAST

CALIFORNIA

Erickson Associates, Inc.
1112 South Garfield Avenue
Alhambra CA 91801
213-283-9461

International Design Concepts
400 South Beverly Hills Drive
Beverly Hills CA 90212
213-659-6283

Barbara Elliot Interiors, Inc.
1038-1 Shary Circle
Concord CA 94518
415-798-8550

Beckham/Eisenman
16811 Milliken Avenue
Irvine CA 92714
714-660-1260

Raygal Design
2719 White Road
Irvine CA 92714
714-474-1000

Barry Design Associates, Inc.
1333 Westwood Boulevard
Los Angeles CA 90024
213-478-6081

Design 1 Interiors
2049 Century Park East
Los Angeles CA 90067
213-553-5032

Intradesign, Inc.
910 North La Cienega Boulevard
Los Angeles CA 90069
213-652-6114

James Northcutt Associates
717 La Cienega Boulevard
Los Angeles CA 90069
213-659-8595

Richard Predroza Associates, Inc.
830 Traction Avenue, Suite 300
Los Angeles CA 90012
213-680-4567

Project Associates, Inc.
2029 Century Park East,
Suite 1100
Los Angeles CA 90067
213-277-0303

**S. E. Rykoff & Company,
Design Division**
761 Terminal Street
P.O. Box 21917
Los Angeles CA 90021
213-622-4131

Tamarind, Inc.
7961 West 3rd Street
Los Angeles CA 90048
213-938-5251

Yates-Silverman, Inc.
6330 San Vicente Boulevard
Los Angeles CA 90048
213-937-1503

James Adams & Associates, Inc.
206 Riverside Avenue, Suite B
Newport Beach CA 92663
714-645-1791

Braselle Design Company
423 31st Street
Newport Beach CA 92663
714-673-6522

Design Restaurant Systems
30 Hegenberger Loop
Oakland CA 94621
415-638-8373

JungDesigns, Inc.
3726 Grand Avenue
Oakland CA 94610
415-444-3500

Gruwell-Pheasant-Design
311 Forest Avenue
Pacific Grove CA 93950
408-372-1688

Design Interpretation, Inc.
6806 Vista Del Mar Lane
Playa Del Rey CA 90293
213-821-0369

J. M. Graven Company
777 Front Street
San Diego CA 92101
619-230-8666

Gensler & Associates
550 Kearney Street
San Francisco CA 94108
415-433-3700

Charles Pfister Associates
9 Maritime Plaza
San Francisco CA 94111
415-392-4455

**Blair Spangler Interior &
Graphic Design, Inc.**
60 Federal Street
San Francisco CA 94107
415-543-9355

Stone, Marraccini and Patterson
1 Market Plaza
Spear Street Tower
San Francisco CA 94105
415-227-0100

Don Wudke & Associates
945 Front Street, Suite 100
San Francisco CA 94111
415-398-0606

**Torin Knorr/Shari Pulcrano
Interior Design**
800 Miramonte Drive
Santa Barbara CA 93109
805-564-1410

Archisis Design Corporation
1920 Main Street
Santa Monica CA 90405
213-392-5755

Hirsch/Bedner and Associates
3216 Nebraska Avenue
Santa Monica CA 90404
213-829-9087

P F F/Contract
290 Easy Street, Suite 2
Simi Valley CA 93065
805-583-0722

Design Development
6047 Tampa Avenue, Suite 305
Tarzana CA 91356
818-881-8506

Kovacs and Associates, Inc.
4425 Riverside Drive, Suite 201
Toluca Lake CA 91505
818-846-7834

Edward Carson Beall & Associates
23727 Hawthorne Boulevard
Torrance CA 90505
213-378-1280

CHRO, Inc.
195 South C Street, Suite 200
P.O. Box 10066
Tustin CA 92681
714-832-1834

OREGON

ZGF Interiors
320 Southwest Oak Street
Portland OR 97204
503-224-3860

WASHINGTON

G. "Skip" Downing Architects
607 19th Avenue East
Seattle WA 98112
206-323-8500

Chefs and Chef/ Restaurant Owners

This listing of chefs and chef/restaurant owners nationwide has been selected by The James Beard Foundation and includes both chefs with established reputations and some of the new men and women who are rapidly becoming known for their fine cooking. The field of food is attracting some of the most diverse and imaginative talents in America—and we are all the beneficiaries.

Sergio Abramolf
Giovanni's
25550 Chagrin Boulevard
Beechwood OH 44122
216-831-8625

Catherine Alexandrou
Chez Catherine
431 North Avenue
Westfield NJ 07090
201-232-1680

Lynne Alpert
The New French Cafe
128 North 4th Street
Minneapolis MN 55401
612-338-3790

French bread, cafe-au-lait, seasonal menus, daily specials, wines and beers by the glass and bottle are all to be found in this busy downtown storefront restaurant that has been open since 1977. Breakfast, lunch and dinner are served every day in a dining room featuring an exposed kitchen and service bar. There is also a separate small bar down the hall offering soups, salads, pates, cheeses and desserts.

Len Allison
Hubert's
575 Park Avenue
New York NY 10021
212-826-5911

Anthony Ambrose
Julien Restaurant
Hotel Meridien
250 Franklin Street
Boston MA 02110
617-451-1900

Regarded by many as Boston's most beautiful dining room, the Julien Restaurant features the contemporary French cuisine of Olivier Roellinger, owner of "de Bricourt" in Brittany (two stars, *Guide Michelin*) and Anthony Ambrose, Julien chef. Seasonal menus emphasize local ingredients and unusually creative sauces, often flavored with spices from India and the Orient. The two chefs' passion for light sauces and exquisite presentations is evident on every plate. Service is black-tie and impeccable.

Tim Anderson
Goodfellow's
800 Nicollet Mall
Minneapolis MN 55402
612-332-4800

Francesco Antonucci
Remi
323 East 79th Street
New York NY 10021
212-744-4272

Enzo Arpaia
Lello Ristorante
65 East 54th Street
New York NY 10022
212-751-1555

Lello Arpaia
Scarlatti
34 East 52nd Street
New York NY 10022
212-753-2444

John Ash
John Ash & Company
4330 Barnes Road
Santa Rosa CA 95401
707-527-7687

Michel Attali
Petrossian
182 West 58th Street
New York NY 10019
212-245-2214

Gary Bachman
Odeon, Bistrot a Vin
114 South 12th Street
Philadelphia PA 19107
215-922-5875

Open for two years on Philadelphia's "Left Bank," Odeon offers an extensive menu of French regional specialties updated by chef Gary Bachman in an atmosphere inspired by the bistrots and restaurants surrounding the Theatre de l'Odeon in Paris. Odeon is both an elegant setting for lunch and dinner and a casual place to meet for a drink (with the city's largest selection of wines by the glass and single-malt whiskies).

Call 215-922-5875 for information and reservations.

Mark Baker
Aujourd'hui
200 Boylston Street
Boston MA 02114
617-338-4400

Ali Barker
150 Wooster
150 Wooster Street
New York NY 10012
212-995-1010

John H. Barnhill
Driver's Seat Restaurant
Box 990
Southampton NY 11968
516-283-7428

Lidia Bastianich
Felidia Ristorante
243 East 58th Street
New York NY 10022
212-758-1479

Rick Bayless
Frontera Grill
445 North Clark Street
Chicago IL 60610
312-661-1434

Dan Baylis
Jane's Bar and Grill
208 East 60th Street
New York NY 10021
212-935-3481

Karl Beckley
Green Lake Grill
7850 Green Lake Drive North
Seattle WA 98103
206-522-3490

Domenico Berardicurti
Tuscany
4150 East Mississippi Avenue
Denver CO 80222
303-782-9300

Paul Bertolli
Chez Panisse
1517 Shattuck Avenue
Berkeley CA 94709
415-548-5525

Christian Bertrand
Bertrand
253 Greenwich Avenue
Greenwich CT 06830
203-661-4459
Restaurant Bertrand: * * * (*The New York Times*, December 1987).
   "One of the best 10 new restaurants in the nation" (*Esquire* magazine)
   "Best restaurant in the state" (*Connecticut* magazine, 1989)
   Private room available.
   Christian Bertrand, *maitre cuisinier de France*, chef-proprietor.

Joe Bitici
Chelsea Trattoria
108 Eighth Avenue
New York NY 10011
212-924-7786

Michel Blanchet
L'Ermitage
730 North La Cienega Boulevard
West Los Angeles CA 90069
213-652-5840

Fritz Blank
Deux Cheminees
251 South Camac Street
Philadelphia PA 19107
215-383-0596

Michael Bomberg
The Fairmount Restaurant
The Fairmount Hotel
401 South Alamo Street
San Antonio TX 78205
512-224-8800

Daniel Bonnot
Le Restaurant de la Tour Eiffel
2040 St. Charles Avenue
New Orleans LA 79130
504-895-6304

Jean-Pierre Bosc
Fennel
1535 Ocean Avenue
Santa Monica CA 90401
213-394-2079

Parker Bosley
Parker's Restaurant
6802 St. Clair Avenue
Cleveland OH 44103
216-881-0700

   Parker Bosley makes use of the abundant, high-quality products grown in Northeast Ohio and prepares them in a style based on traditional French presentation. In addition to buying his produce from family farms, many of which are organic operations, Parker also grows many of his own vegetables and herbs in the restaurant garden. The care and attention of the kitchen staff are paralleled by the gracious and professional service in the dining room.

Claude Bougard
L'Etoile
1075 California Street
San Francisco CA 94108
415-771-1529

David Bouley
Bouley's
165 Duane Street
New York NY 10013
212-608-3852

Daniel Boulud
Le Cirque
58 East 65th Street
New York NY 10021
212-794-9292

Antoine Bouterin
Le Perigord
405 East 52nd Street
New York NY 10022
212-755-6244

Michael Braun
Lion's Rock
316 East 77th Street
New York NY 10021
212-988-3610

Terrance Brennan
The Polo
Westbury Hotel
15 East 69th Street
New York NY 10021
212-535-2000

Frank Brigtsen
Brigtsen's
723 Dante Street
New Orleans LA 70118
504-861-7610

Robert Brody
Sheraton Harbor Island Hotel
1380 Harbor Island Drive
San Diego CA 92101
619-291-2900

Ruth Adams Bronz
Miss Ruby's Cafe
135 Eighth Avenue
New York NY 10011
212-620-4055

Daniel Bruce
Rowes Wharf Restaurant
Boston Harbor Hotel
70 Rowes Wharf
Boston MA 02116
617-439-7000

Zachary Bruell

Z Contemporary Cuisine
20600 Chagrin Boulevard
Shaker Heights OH 44122
216-991-1580

Each week Chef Zachary Bruell offers a different menu of fresh grilled seafood and meats. Sauces are made from reductions and a blending of Southeast Asian, Japanese and French nouvelle flavors. The wine list features more than 200 selections from California and France.

Food is of primary importance in the 95-seat white restaurant designed in the Bauhaus style. Black leather and chrome chairs and modern artwork are the only accents.

Jeffrey Buben

Occidental
1475 Pennsylvania Avenue NW
Washington DC 20004
202-783-1475

Annie Burke

Pot au Feu
44 Custom House Street
Providence RI 02903
401-273-8953

David Burke

The River Cafe
1 Water Street
Brooklyn NY 11201
718-522-5200

Jim Burke

Allegro
313 Moody Street
Waltham MA 02154
617-891-5486

Carolyn Buster

The Cottage Restaurant
525 Torrance Avenue
Calumet City IL 60409
708-891-3900

Yannick Cam

Le Pavillon
1050 Connecticut Avenue
Washington DC 20036
202-833-3846

Scott Campbell

The Box Tree
250 East 49th Street
New York NY 10017
212-758-8320

Bill Cardwell

Cardwell's
8100 Maryland Avenue
Clayton MO 63105
314-726-5055

Kathy Pavletich Casey

(in transition)
206-367-6412

Steve Cavagnaro

Cavey's
45 East Center Street
Manchester CT 06040
203-643-2751

Luigi Chiesia

Barbetta
321 West 46th Street
New York NY 10036
212-246-9171

Opened in 1906 by Sebastiano Maioglio, and currently owned by his daughter, Laura Maioglio, Barbetta is the oldest restaurant in New York still owned by its founding family.

In a spectacular setting decorated with authentic 18th-century Italian furnishings, Barbetta serves the cuisine of Italy's northwestern region, Piedmonte. In summer its romantic, exuberantly flowering garden is one of the most sought-after dining sites in the city. Period 19th-century private rooms are available.

Milos Cihelka

The Golden Mushroom
18100 West 10 Mile Road
Southfield MI 48075
313-559-4230

Reid Ashton's Golden Mushroom Restaurant features cuisine created by Master Chef Milos, co-owner and first master chef certified in the United States. Specialties include wild game, wild mushroom and fresh fish dishes. An extensive wine list is also offered and off-premise catering is available. Open Monday through Saturday. Reservations recommended.

1988 Restaurant of the Year *(Detroit Monthly* magazine)

"Outstanding: * * * *" *(Detroit Free Press)*

"Among the very finest" *(DetroitNews)*

"One of America's Top 10 restaurants" *(Esquire* magazine)

John Clancy

John Clancy's
206 East 63rd Street
New York NY 10021
212-752-6666

John Clancy's
181 West 10th Street
New York NY 10011
212-242-7350

Milton G. Clarke

Green Parrot Restaurant
Magens Point Resort
St. Thomas, USVI 00802
809-775-7887

Patrick Clark

Metro
23 East 74th Street
New York NY 10021
212-249-3030

Jim Cohen

The Wildflower Inn
174 East Gore Creek Drive
Vail CO 81657
303-476-8111

Located in The Lodge at Vail, Vail's most prestigious hostelry, The Wildflower Inn offers a truly elegant dining experience. Tastefully decorated with masses of magnificent floral arrangements that accent the walls, upholstery and carpets, The Wildflower Inn provides a gracious evening out. The extensive wine list and excellent service complement the American cuisine prepared and served under the watchful eye of Chef Jim Cohen. This Travel/Holiday Award-winning restaurant is truly Vail's finest.

Patti Constantin

Constantin's
8402 Oak Street
New Orleans LA 80118
504-861-2111

Pascal Coudouy

Ambassador Grill
1 United Nations Plaza
44th Street and First Avenue
New York NY 10017
212-702-5014

Bruno Creglia and Joseph Scarpati

Giordano
409 West 39th Street
New York NY 100018
212-947-9811

Noel Cunningham
Strings
1700 Humboldt
Denver CO 80218
303-831-7310

Casual contemporary cuisine featuring pasta and fresh fish. Strings offers lunch and dinner Monday through Saturday; dinner only on Sunday.

Serving continuously, Monday-Thursday 11:00 a.m.-11:00 p.m. Friday and Saturday 11:00 a.m.-12:00 midnight. Sunday 5:00-10:00 p.m.

Private dining areas are available seating 10 to 50 people. Reservations are suggested.

Jack Czarnecki
Joe's Restaurant
7th and Laurel Streets
Reading PA 19602
215-373-9191

Andrew D'Amico
The Sign of the Dove
1110 Third Avenue
New York NY 10021
212-861-8080

Renowned for 27 years as one of the most beautiful dining settings in New York, The Sign of the Dove's French-influenced modern American cuisine makes the romantic decor only a backdrop for Chef Andrew D'Amico's wonderful food. Bryan Miller of *The New York Times* gave this multidimensional restaurant three stars and Gault-Millau rated it one of the top 15 restaurants in New York City.

Gary J. Danko
Chateau Souverain
400 Souverain Road
Geyserville CA 95441
707-433-3141

Sally Darr
La Tulipe
104 West 13th Street
New York NY 10011
212-691-8860

Robert Del Grande
Cafe Annie
1728 Post Oak Boulevard
Houston TX 77057
713-780-1522

Will De Pascale
Spencer's
1590 Harbor Island Drive
San Diego CA 92101
619-291-6400

Marcel Desaulniers
The Trellis
403 Duke of Gloucester Street
Williamsburg VA 23185
804-229-8610

Ivana Di Marco
Restaurant Osteria Romana
935 Ellsworth Street
Philadelphia PA 19147
215-271-9191

Jean-Michel Diot
Park Bistro
414 Park Avenue South
New York NY 10010
212-689-1360

Ralph Di Orio
Sammy's Restaurant
1400 West 10th Street
Cleveland OH 44113
216-523-5560

Sammy's enters its tenth year as Cleveland's premier fine dining restaurant. Noted for its "seafood" raw bar, live jazz, award-winning wine list, expert service and creative kitchen.

Number 1 People's Choice Award 1987-1989, Travel/Holiday Award 1988, Wine Spectator's Award of Excellence 1989.

Lunch: Monday-Saturday 11:30-2:30. Dinner Monday-Thursday 5:30-10:00; Friday and Saturday to 12:00 midnight. Valet parking, private dining rooms. Call 800-535-6375 or 216-523-5560 for information and reservations.

Andrew DiVincenzo
Billy Ogden's Lovejoy Grill
1834 William Street
Buffalo NY 14206
716-896-8018

Tom Douglas
Cafe Sport
2020 Western Avenue
Seattle WA 98121
206-443-6000

Clive DuVal III
Tila's Restaurant
Wisconsin and Western Avenues
Chevy Chase MD 20815
301-652-8452

Clive DuVal, Tila's owner-chef, samples one of today's entrees. "This is Mole Grilled Mako Shark with an exotic fruit relish—what do you think?" It's fantastic. And just as tantalizing is the rest of the menu: Coro-Lime Shrimp, Oriental Glaze Grilled Yellowfin Tuna; even Empanadas and Burritos have a delicious twist. The decor is every bit as interesting with a gigantic painting of a South American sky and a jungle mural with natives standing guard.

Terry Endow
Michela's
1 Athenaeum Street
East Cambridge MA 02142
617-225-3366

Todd English
Olive's
67 Main Street
Charlestown MA 02150
617-242-1999

Henri Eudes and Francois Kerohas
Auberge Argenteuil
42 Healy Avenue
Hartsdale NY 10530
914-948-0597

Keith Famie
Les Auteurs—An American Bistro
222 Sherman Drive
Royal Oak MI 48067
313-544-2887

Dean Fearing
The Mansion on Turtle Creek
2821 Turtle Creek Boulevard
Dallas TX 75219
214-559-2100

Susan Feniger and Mary Sue Milliken
Border Grill
7407 1/2 Melrose Avenue
Los Angeles 90046
213-938-2155
City Restaurant
180 South La Brea Avenue
Los Angeles CA 90036
213-658-7495

Barbara Figueroa
The Hunt Club
Sorrento Hotel
900 Madison Street
Seattle WA 98104
206-622-6400

Sandro Fioriti
Sandro's
420 East 59th Street
New York NY 10021
212-355-5150

Michel Fitoussi
(in transition)
c/o La Cote Basque
5 East 55th Street
New York NY 10022
212-688-6525

Michael Foley
Printer's Row
550 South Dearborn Street
Chicago IL 60605
312-461-0780

Susanna Foo
Susanna Foo
1512 Walnut Street
Philadelphia PA 19102
215-545-2666

Larry Forgione
An American Place
2 Park Avenue
New York NY 10016
212-684-2122

Ken Frank
Fenix
8171 Sunset Boulevard
Los Angeles CA 90046
213-656-7515

Bruce Frankel
Panache
798 Main Street
Cambridge MA 02139
617-492-9500

Mark Franz
Stars
150 Redwood Alley
San Francisco CA 94102
415-861-7827

Martin Gagne
Cafe 21
21 East Bellevue Place
Chicago IL 60611
312-266-2100

Andre Gaillard
La Reserve
4 West 49th Street
New York NY 10020
212-247-2993

Martin Garcia
Michael's
1147 3rd Street
Santa Monica CA 90403
213-451-0843

Jean-Louis Gerin
Restaurant Jean-Louis
61 Lewis Street
Greenwich CT 06830
203-622-8450

George Germon and Johanne Killeen
Al Forno/Lucky's
577 South Main Street
Providence RI 02903
401-272-7980

Victor Gielisse
Actuelle
2800 Routh Street, Suite 125
Dallas TX 75201
214-855-0440

Anne and David Gingrass
Postrio
545 Post Street
San Francisco CA 94102
415-776-7825

Joyce Goldstein
Square One Restaurant
190 Pacific Avenue at
Front Street
San Francisco CA 94111
415-788-1110

Jean-Pierre Goyenvalle
Le Lion D'Or
1150 Connecticut Avenue
Washington DC 20036
202-296-7972

Kevin Graham
The Grill Room
Windsor Court Hotel
300 Gravier Street
New Orleans LA 70130
504-522-1992

Gerald Granvay
Cafe Pierre
Pierre Hotel
Fifth Avenue and 61st Street
New York NY 10021
212-940-8185

Christopher Gross
Christopher's
Biltmore Financial Center
2398 East Camelback Road
Phoenix AZ 85016
602-957-3214

Recently named one of the country's top 10 chefs by *Food & Wine* magazine, Christopher Gross opened his namesake restaurant in the Biltmore Financial Center at 24th Street and Camelback in Phoenix.

Christopher's features an upscale dining room exclusively for dinner with limited seating, adjacent to a charming bistro offering lunch and dinner for up to 120 people, with patio seating.

Both feature the innovative cuisine, fine wines and intimate atmosphere for which Christopher Gross is known.

Vincent Guerithault
Vincent's on Camelback
3930 East Camelback Road
Phoenix AZ 85018
602-224-0225

Jean-Claude Guillossou
L'Auberge Bretonne
200 South Brentwood Boulevard
Clayton MO 63105
314-993-8890

Andre Guillou
Cafe des Artistes
1 West 67th Street
New York NY 10023
212-877-3500

Fernand Gutierrez
The Dining Room
Ritz Carlton Hotel
160 East Pearson Street
Chicago IL 60611
312-266-1000

Gordon Hamersley
Hamersley's Bistro
578 Tremont Street
Boston MA 02118
617-267-6068

Patrick Healy
Champagne
10506 Little Santa Monica Boulevard
Los Angeles CA 90025
213-470-8446

James Heywood
American Bounty
Culinary Institute of America
Route 9
Hyde Park NY 12538
914-452-4600

Josefina Howard
Rosa Mexicano
1063 First Avenue
New York NY 10022
212-753-7407

Jose Hurtado-Prud'homme
Cinco de Mayo
349 West Broadway
New York NY 10013
212-226-5255
Cinco de Mayo
153 East 53rd Street
New York NY 10022
212-755-5033

Our SoHo restaurant has served as a refuge for those seeking authentic Mexican cooking in a casual atmosphere. Now our award-winning chef Jose Hurtado-Prud'homme has brought this same concept to the midtown location in the Citicorp Center.

Cinco de Mayo features a fiesta feeling for those who are eager to become or who already are aficionados of the very best in Mexican food.

Michael Hutchings
Michael's Waterside
50 Los Patos Way
Santa Barbara CA 93108
805-969-0307

Diana Isaiou
Cafe Sport
2020 Western Avenue
Seattle WA 98121
206-443-6000

Cafe Sport, located at the north end of Seattle's Pike Place Farmers' Market, is open seven days a week for breakfast, lunch and dinner. Our location's association with local farmers enables us to acquire the finest locally produced foods available. Cafe Sport features Northwest seafood, meats and game with a Pacific Rim influence.

Jeff Jackson
La Tour
Park-Hyatt Hotel
800 North Michigan Avenue
Chicago IL 60611
312-280-2230

Ed Janos
Chez Raphael
27155 Sheraton Drive
Novi MI 48050
313-348-5555

Jean Joho
The Everest Room
The La Salle Club
440 South La Salle Street,
40th Floor
Chicago IL 60605
312-663-8920

Jean Joho, chef de cuisine, carefully orchestrates his culinary symphony at The Everest Room. Chef Joho's cuisine is refreshingly light and delicate, with a maximum of artistry on the plate.

Serving lunch Monday-Friday 11:30 a.m.-1:30 p.m.

Dinner Tuesday-Thursday 5:30-8:30 p.m., Friday and Saturday 5:30-9:30 p.m.

William R. Jones
Upper Montclair Country Club
177 Hepburn Road
Clifton NJ 07012
201-779-7505

David Kantrowitz
The Colony
384 Boylston Street
Boston MA 02116
617-536-8500

Stacy Karelis
Jimmy's Harborside Restaurant
242-266 Northern Avenue
Boston MA 02210
617-423-1000

Shiro Kashiba
Nikko
1306 South King Street
Seattle WA 98144
206-322-4905

Yoshi Katsumura
Yoshi's Cafe
3257 North Halsted Street
Chicago IL 60657
312-248-6160

Hubert Keller
Fleur de Lys
777 Sutter Street
San Francisco CA 94109
415-673-7779

Thomas Keller
Rakel Restaurant
231 Varick Street
New York NY 10014
212-929-1630

Francois Kerohas and Henri Eudes
Auberge Argenteuil
42 Healy Avenue
Hartsdale NY 10530
914-948-0597

Johanne Killeen and George Germon
Al Forno/Lucky's
577 South Main Street
Providence RI 02903
401-272-7980

Robert Kinkead
Twenty-One Federal
1736 L Street NW
Washington DC 20036
202-331-9771

Evan Kleiman
Angeli Caffe
7274 Melrose Avenue
Los Angeles CA 90046
213-936-9086

Heidi Insalata Khraling
Restaurant at Smith Ranch Homes
100 Deervalley Road
San Rafael CA 94903
415-491-4918

Christopher Kump
Cafe Beaujolais
961 Ukiah Street
Mendocino CA 95460
707-937-5614

Cafe Beaujolais, located in a Victorian house on the Mendocino coast, has been serving delicious meals for years with an affectionate regard for fine food and fine dining. Fresh local produce and meats (chemical-free whenever possible) are featured for breakfast, lunch and dinner. From our brick, wood-fired oven come crusty loaves of specialty breads with an emphasis on sourdough. In addition, crisp pizzas with imaginative toppings are available on premises and for take-out.

Gray Kuntz
Adrienne
700 Fifth Avenue
New York NY 10019
212-247-2200

Jean-Marie La Croix
The Fountain Restaurant
The Four Seasons Hotel
Logan Square
Philadelphia PA 19103
215-963-1500

Emeril Lagasse
Commander's Palace
1403 Washington Avenue
New Orleans LA 70130
504-899-8221

Stephen Langlois
Prairie
Omni Morton Hotel
500 South Dearborn
Chicago IL 60605
312-663-1143

The Midwest's finest foods and ingredients are celebrated at Prairie Restaurant in the landmark Omni Morton Hotel. Award-winning Executive Chef Stephen Langlois creates seasonal menus based upon the heartland's culinary traditions.

Inspired by the genius of Frank Lloyd Wright, the intimate, 125-seat restaurant is decorated in subdued colors and rich honey oak. The bilevel restaurant is dominated by an open kitchen.

Prairie is open seven days a week for breakfast, lunch and dinner.

Christer Larsson
Aquavit
13 West 54th Street
New York NY 10019
212-307-7311

Gilbert LeCoze
Le Bernardin
Equitable Center
155 West 51st Street
New York NY 10019
212-489-1515

Larry LeRuth
Le Ruth's
636 Franklin Street
Gretna LA 77053
504-362-4914

Edna Lewis
Gage & Tollner
372 Fulton Street
Brooklyn NY 11201
718-875-5181

Leon Lianides
The Coach House Restaurant
110 Waverly Place
New York NY 10011
212-777-0303

Roland Liccioni
Le Francais
269 South Milwaukee Avenue
Wheeling IL 60090
708-541-7470

Bruce Lim and
Francesco Martorella
Ciboulette
1312 Spruce Street
Philadelphia PA 19107
215-790-1210

Jimella Lucas and Nanci Main
The Ark
P.O. Box 95
Nahcotta WA 98637
206-665-4134

Nanci Main and Jimella Lucas of the nationally acclaimed Ark Restaurant, overlooking Willapa Bay in southwest Washington, present new awareness and innovative styles in Northwest cuisines. They also share their bounty by being leading regional cookbook authors, restaurant consultants and culinary instructors.

Sirio Maccioni
Le Cirque
58 East 65th Street
New York NY 10021
212-794-9292

Dennis MacNeil
Fresno Place
East Hampton NY 11937
516-324-0727

Mark Malicki
Truffles
234 South Main Street
Sebastopol CA 95472
707-823-8448

Waldy Malouf
La Cremaillere Restaurant
Greenwich Road
Banksville NY 10506
914-234-9647

Anthony Mantuano
Spiaggia
980 North Michigan Avenue
Chicago IL 60604
312-280-2750

Valentino Marcattilii
San Domenico
240 Central Park South
New York NY 10019
212-265-5959

Zarela Martinez
Zarela Restaurant
953 Second Avenue
New York NY 10022
212-644-6740

Francesco Martorella and
Bruce Lim
Ciboulette
1312 Spruce Street
Philadelphia PA 19107
215-790-1210

Nobuyuki Matsuhisa
Matsuhisa
129 North La Cienega Boulevard
Beverly Hills CA 90211
213-659-9639

Michael McCarty
Adirondacks
901 Larimer
Denver CO 80204
303-573-8900

Frank McClelland
L'Espalier
30 Gloucester Street
Boston MA 02116
617-262-3023

Philip McGrath
Doubles Club International
783 Fifth Avenue
New York NY 10022
212-751-9595

Robert McGrath
Four Seasons Hotel
Houston Center
1300 Lamar Street
Houston TX 77010
713-650-1300

Moncef Meddeb
Harvard Bookstore Cafe
190 Newbury Street
Boston MA 02116
617-536-0097

Jean-Francois Meteigner
L'Orangerie
903 North La Cienega Boulevard
Los Angeles CA 90069
213-652-9770

Mark Miller
Coyote Cafe
132 West Water Street
Santa Fe NM 87501
505-983-1615

**Mary Sue Milliken and
Susan Feniger**
Border Grill
7407 1/2 Melrose Avenue
Los Angeles 90046
213-938-2155
City Restaurant
180 South La Brea Avenue
Los Angeles CA 90036
213-658-7495

Paul Minnillo
Baricelli Inn
Cornell Road
Cleveland OH 44106
216-791-6500

Richard Moonen
The Water Club
500 East 30th Street
New York NY 10016
212-683-3333

Gregg Mosberger
Richard Perry Restaurant
1019 Pine Street
St. Louis MO 63101
314-436-2355

Bill Neal
Crook's Corner
610 West Franklin
Chapel Hill NC 27514
919-9299-7643

Wayne Nish
La Colombe d'Or Restaurant
134-136 East 26th Street
New York NY 10010
212-689-0666

John Novi
DePuy Canal House
Route 213
High Falls NY 12440
914-687-7700

Patrick O'Connell
The Inn at Little Washington
Middle and Main Streets
Washington VA 22747
703-675-3800

Rick O'Connell
Rosalie's
1415 Van Ness Avenue
San Francisco CA 94109
415-928-7188

Bradley Ogden
Lark Creek Inn
234 Magnolia
Larkspur CA 94939
415-924-7766

Antonio Orlando
Fresco Ristorante
514 South Brand Boulevard
Glendale CA 91204
818-247-5541

Jean-Louis Palladin
Jean-Louis at the Watergate
2650 Virginia Avenue NW
Washington DC 20037
202-298-4488

Charles Palmer
Aureole
34 East 61st Street
New York NY 10021
212-319-1660

Jean-Claude Parachini
La Grenouille
3 East 52nd Street
New York NY 10022
212-752-1495

Chris Pardue
L'Americain
2 Hartford Square West
Hartford CT 06106
203-522-6500

Roland Passot
La Folie
2316 Polk Street
San Francisco CA 94109
415-776-5577

Alex Patout
Alex Patout's Louisiana Restaurant
221 Royal Street
New Orleans LA 70130
504-525-7788

Cindy Pawlcyn
Mustards Grill
7399 St. Helena Highway
Napa CA 94558
707-944-2424

Kaprial Pence
Fullers
Seattle Sheraton
1400 Sixth Avenue
Seattle WA 98101
206-447-5544

Georges Perrier
Le Bec Fin
1523 Walnut Street
Philadelphia PA 19102
215-567-1000

Richard Perry
Richard Perry Restaurant
Hotel Majestic
1019 Pine Street
St. Louis MO 63101
314-436-2355

Harlan (Pete) Peterson
Tapawingo
9502 Lake Street
Ellsworth MI 49729
616-588-7971

Walter Plendner
American Harvest Restaurant
International Vista Hotel
3 World Trade Center
New York NY 10048
212-938-9100

Marc Poidevin
Maxim's
680 Madison Avenue
New York NY 10021
212-751-5111

William Poirier
Seasons
Bostonian Hotel
Faneuil Hall Marketplace
Boston MA 02109
617-523-4119

Brian Polcyn
Pike Street Restaurant
18 West Pike Street
Pontiac MI 48058
313-334-7878

Debra Ponzek
Montrachet
239 West Broadway
New York NY 10013
212-219-2777

Alfred Portale
The Gotham Bar and Grill
12 East 12th Street
New York NY 10003
212-620-4020

Stephen Poses
16th Street Bar and Grill
264 South 16th Street
Philadelphia PA 19102
215-735-3316

To Jim:
Somewhere over the

RAINBOW!

Greg Powell
Wooden Angel
West Bridgewater
Beaver PA 15009
412-774-7880

Paul Prudhomme
K-Paul's Louisiana Kitchen
416 Chartres Street
New Orleans LA 70130
504-942-7500
K-Paul's—New York
622 Broadway
New York NY 10012
212-460-9633

    Both the original K-Paul's Louisiana Kitchen in New Orleans and recently opened K-Paul's—New York offer Chef Paul Prudhomme's authentic Louisiana food in a casual setting. Menus at both establishments feature Chef Prudhomme's signature dishes (including Blackened Tuna, Cajun Popcorn), traditional Louisiana fare (gumbos, jambalayas) and special regional dishes combining fresh local ingredients with Chef Paul's masterful seasoning blends.
    Reservations are accepted at K-Paul's—New York only; K-Paul's Louisiana Kitchen maintains a no-reservation policy.

Wolfgang Puck
Spago
8795 Sunset Boulevard
Los Angeles CA 90069
213-652-33706

Stephan Pyles
Routh Street Cafe
3005 Routh Street
Dallas TX 75201
214-871-7161

Jean-Jacques Rachou
La Cote Basque
5 East 55th Street
New York NY 10022
212-688-6525

Leslee Reis
Cafe Provencal
1625 Hinman Avenue
Evanston IL 60201
708-475-2233

Andre Rene
The Rainbow Room
30 Rockefeller Plaza
New York NY 10112
212-632-5000

Seppi Renggli
The Four Seasons
99 East 52nd Street
New York NY 10022
212-754-9494

Leslie Revsin
Barbizon Hotel
140 East 63rd Street
New York NY 10021
212-838-5700

Maxime Ribera
Maxime's
Old Tomahawk Street
Routes 202 and 118
Granite Springs NY 10527
914-248-7200

Michel Richard
Citrus
6703 Melrose Avenue
Los Angeles CA 90038
213-857-0034

Giovanni Rigato
Capricio
846 Fawn Street
Baltimore MD 20202
301-685-2710

Michael Roberts
Trumps
8764 Melrose Avenue
Los Angeles CA 90069
213-855-1480

Jacky Roberts
Amelio's
1630 Powell Street
San Francisco CA 90133
415-397-4339

Judy Rodgers
Zuni Cafe
1658 Market Street
San Francisco CA 94102
415-552-2522

Olivier Roellinger
Julien Restaurant
Hotel Meridien
250 Franklin Street
Boston MA 02110
617-451-1900

Felipe Rojas-Lombardi
The Ballroom
253 West 28th Street
New York NY 10001
212-244-3005

The Ballroom is a restaurant/cabaret complex featuring a "tapas bar," a concept adapted from Spain by Ballroom Executive Chef Felipe Rojas-Lombardi. He is credited as being the first to bring these traditional foods to America. Lunch and Sunday brunch are spectacular buffets. Dinner is served daily and the tapas bar remains lively until long after midnight. The Cabaret, an adjacent but separate space, is a New York institution featuring major stars and exciting discoveries.

Michael Romano
Union Square Cafe
21 East 16th Street
New York NY 10003
212-243-4020

Mark Rosenstein
The Marketplace
10 North Market Street
Asheville NC 28801
704-252-4162

Anne Rosenzweig
Arcadia
21 East 62nd Street
New York NY 10021
212-223-2900

Yves Roubaud
Shaw's Crab House
21 East Hubbard Street
Chicago IL 60611
312-527-2722

David Ruggerio
La Caravelle
33 West 55th Street
New York NY 10019
212-586-4252

Timothy Ryan
American Bounty
Culinary Institute of America
Route 9
Hyde Park NY 12538
914-452-4600

Patrizio Sacchetto
Blue Fox
659 Merchant Street
San Francisco CA 94111
415-981-1177

Alain Sailhac
The Edwardian Room
The Plaza Hotel
768 Fifth Avenue
New York NY 10019
212-759-3000

Charles Saunders
Sonoma Mission Inn
P.O. Box 1447
Sonoma CA 95476
707-938-9000

Joseph Scarpati and Bruno Creglia
Giordano
409 West 39th Street
New York NY 10018
212-947-9811

Jay Schaeffer
Green Hills Inn
R.D. 11, Box 164
Reading PA 19607
215-777-9611

Green Hills Inn is a lovely country French restaurant. The 200-year-old coach stop serves superb food and has an excellent wine cellar. Chef-owner Jay Schaeffer and chef de cuisine Joseph Spangler lead their award-winning team to culinary heights. Aided by their classical training, they develop outstanding new dishes using American regional or international flavors. Susan Schaeffer oversees the dining rooms and service staff, and maintains the Inn's beautiful flowers and gardens.

Marco Schlenz
Baci Trattoria
138 West Pierpont Avenue
Salt Lake City UT 84101
801-328-1333

Chris Schlesinger
East Coast Grill
1271 Cambridge Street
Cambridge MA 02139
617-491-6568

Jimmy Schmidt
The Rattlesnake Club
300 River Place
Detroit MI 48207
313-567-4400

Heinz Schwab
Hedgerose Heights Inn
490 East Paces Ferry Road
Atlanta GA 30305
404-233-7673

John Sedlar
Saint Estephe
2640 Sepulveda Boulevard
Manhattan Beach CA 90266
213-545-1334

Guenter Seeger
The Dining Room
Ritz-Carlton Buckhead
3434 Peachtree Road NE
Atlanta GA 30326
404-237-2700

Hans George Seitz
The Arch
Route 22 North
Brewster NY 10509
914-279-5011

Piero Selvaggio
Primi
10543 West Pico Boulevard
West Los Angeles CA 90064
213-475-9235

Julian Serrano
Masa's
648 Bush Street
San Francisco CA 94108
415-989-7154

Jackie Shen
Jackie's
2478 North Lincoln Avenue
Chicago IL 60614
312-880-0003

Lydia Shire
Biba
272 Boylston Street
Boston MA 02116
617-426-7878

Stephen Simmons
Moreland's Restaurant
North 216 Howard Street
Spokane WA 99201
509-747-9830

Andre Soltner
Lutece
249 East 50th Street
New York NY 10022
212-752-2225

Gabino Sotelino
Ambria
Belden Stratford Hotel
2300 North Lincoln Park West
Chicago IL 60614
312-472-5959

Susan Spicer
The Bistro at Maison de Ville
733 Toulouse Street
New Orleans LA 70130
504-528-9206

Drew Stichter
Hamilton Plaza Hotel
Fourth and Hamilton
Allentown PA 18102
215-437-9876

Frank Stitt III
Highlands: A Bar and Grill
2011 Eleventh Avenue South
Birmingham AL 35205
205-939-1400

Paul Sturkey
The Restaurant at the Phoenix
812 Race Street
Cincinnati OH 45202
513-721-2255

Katsuo Sugiura
Grand Cafe
Grand South Bay Hotel
2669 Bayshore Drive
Coconut Grove FL 33133
305-858-0009

Jean-Francois Taquet
Taquet Restaurant
175 King of Prussia Road
Radnor PA 19087
217-293-9411

John Terczak
Terczak's Restaurant
2635 North Halstead Street
Chicago IL 60614
312-404-0171

Patrick Terrail
Ma Maison
8555 Beverly Boulevard
Los Angeles CA 90048
213-278-5444

Elizabeth Terry
Elizabeth on 37th
105 East 37th Street
Savannah GA 31401
912-236-5547

Jeremiah Tower
Stars
150 Redwood Alley
San Francisco CA 94102
415-861-7827

Barbara Tropp
The China Moon Cafe
639 Post Street
San Francisco CA 94109
415-775-4789

Charlie Trotter
Charlie Trotter's Restaurant
816 West Armitage
Chicago IL 60614
312-248-6228

Jeff Tunks
The River Club
3223 K Street NW
Washington DC 20007
202-333-8118

Charles Tutino
Capsouto Freres
451 Washington Street
New York NY 10013
212-966-4900

Norman Van Aken
Louie's Backyard
700 Waddell Avenue
Key West FL 33040
305-296-5595

Mauro Vincenti
Rex Il Ristorante
617 South Olive Street
Los Angeles CA 90014
213-627-2300

Jean-Georges Vongerichten
Restaurant Lafayette
The Drake Hotel
65 East 56th Street
New York NY 10022
212-832-1565

Brendan Walsh
(in transition)
131 East 93rd Street
New York NY 10128
212-876-4545

David Waltuck
Chanterelle
2 Harrison Street
New York NY 10013
212-966-6960

Alice Waters
Chez Panisse
1417 Shattuck Avenue
Berkeley CA 94709
415-548-5525

Jonathan Waxman
Hulot's
1007 Lexington Avenue
New York NY 10021
212-794-9800

Greg Westcott
D'Amico Cucina
100 North 6th Street
Minneapolis MN 55403
612-338-2401

Jasper White
Jasper's
240 Commercial Street
Boston MA 02109
617-523-1126

Andrew Wilkinson
Aurora
60 East 49th Street
New York NY 10017
212-692-9292

Steve Wilkinson
Fine Bouche
Centerbrook CT 06409
203-767-1277

Barry Wine
The Quilted Giraffe
550 Madison Avenue
New York NY 10022
212-593-1221

Danny Wisel
Rocco's
5 Charles Street South
Boston MA 02116
617-723-6800

Walter Zuromski
The Mill Falls Restaurant
Newton Upper Falls MA 02164
617-244-3080

The James Beard Foundation's Awards Programs

One of the first programs instituted at the Beard House was to select the country's greatest chefs and honor each of them with the title "Great American Chef." Larry Forgione and Wolfgang Puck were the first honorees when the program started in January 1987. The criteria for selection are that the chef must have made a significant contribution to fine cooking in America and have gained a national reputation for his or her own work.

The "Great American Cook" award is given to non-restaurant cooks. First to be honored with this award were Jacques Pepin and Madeleine Kamman.

A chef who has made outstanding contributions to fine cooking in America and has gained a regional reputation is honored as a "Great Regional Chef."

The "Rising Stars of American Cuisine" awards are given to chefs who have been recognized in their city by local critics and members of the food community. The program came into being to help young talents gain recognition and thus further their careers. Input is received from Beard Foundation members all over the country for this deservedly important category.

Other awards are given to the "Best American Cooking Teachers," those responsible for training future chefs and cooks and for shaping the American palate.

GREAT AMERICAN COOKS AT THE JAMES BEARD HOUSE

1988

Madeleine Kamman
Jacques Pepin

1989

Ken Hom
Christopher Idone

GREAT AMERICAN CHEFS AT THE JAMES BEARD HOUSE

1987

Yannick Cam
Michael Foley
Larry Forgione
Bradley Ogden
Jean-Louis Palladin
Walter Plendner
Wolfgang Puck
Stephan Pyles
Jimmy Schmidt
Jasper White

1988

Robert Del Grande
Marcel Desaulniers
Joyce Goldstein
Emeril Lagasse
Mark Miller
Felipe Rojas-Lombardi
Anne Rosenzweig
Jean-Georges Vongerichten
Jonathan Waxman

1989

Daniel Boulud
Richard Perry
Jimmy Schmidt
Jean-Georges Vongerichten

1990

Stephan Pyles
Leslee Reis
Anne Rosenzweig

GREAT REGIONAL CHEFS AT THE JAMES BEARD HOUSE

1989

Michel Attali
Patrick Clark
Andrew D'Amico
Thomas Keller
John Novi
Marc Poidevin
Debra Ponzek
Alfred Portale
David Ruggerio
Alain Sailhac
Brendan Walsh

1990

Sam Arnold
John Bennett
Vincent Guerithault

RISING STARS AT THE JAMES BEARD HOUSE

1987

Drew Schticter
Elizabeth Terry
Walter Zuromski

1988

John Bennett
Carolyn Buster
Jean-Louis Gerin
George Germon
Vincent Guerithault

Johanne Killeen
Marc Meyer
Rick O'Connell
Harlan Peterson
Stephen Simmons
Frank Stitt
Allen Susser

1989

Catherine Alexandrou
Keith Famie
Susan Feniger
Christopher Gross
Gordon Hamersley
Robert Marcelli
Mary Sue Milliken
Chris Schlesinger
Charles Tutino
Gina Zarrilli

1990

Todd English
Charlie Trotter

Spas and Spa Chains

This listing has been compiled with the aid of our consultant, Jeffrey Joseph, president of Jeffrey Joseph's Spa-Finders Travel Arrangements, Ltd., whose organization publishes The Spa Finder. This catalog lists 329 spas in nine categories, and SpaFinders offers a vast database to enable would-be spa-goers to select an appropriate resort to suit their needs. From this rich resource, Irena Chalmers selected the sampling given here, which is divided between spas offering regular and vegetarian regimes.

For complete information, contact Spa-Finders at 784 Broadway, New York NY 10003.

Aerobics Center Guest Lodge
12230 Preston Road
Dallas TX 75230
800-527-0362

The Ashram Health Resort
P.O. Box 8009
Calabasas CA 91302
818-888-0232

Cal-A-Vie
2249 Somerset Road
Vista CA 92083
619-945-2055

Canyon Ranch
8600 East Rockcliff Road
Tucson AZ 85715
800-742-9000

Doral Saturnia
8755 Northwest 36th Street
Miami FL 33178
800-331-7768

**Duke University Diet
& Fitness Center**
804 West Trinity Avenue
Durham NC 27701
919-684-6331

The Golden Door
P.O. Box 1567
Escondido CA 92025
619-744-5777

Green Mountain at Fox Run
Fox Lane
P.O. Box 164
Ludlow VT 05149
802-228-8885

The Greenbrier
Route 60
White Sulphur Springs WV 24986
800-624-6070

The Greenhouse
P.O. Box 1144
Arlington TX 76011
800-637-5882

The Heartland
18 East Chestnut Street
Chicago IL 60611
312-266-2050

Hilton Head Health Institute
P.O. Box 7138
Hilton Head Island SC 29928
800-292-2440

The Homestead
Route 220
Hot Springs VA 24445
800-336-5771

**Jane Fonda's Laurel
Springs Retreat**
369 South Robertson Boulevard
Beverly Hills CA 90211
805-964-9646

La Costa Hotel & Spa
Costa Del Mar Road
Carlsbad CA 92008
800-854-5000

Lake Austin Resort
1705 Quinlan Road
Austin TX 78732
800-847-5637

Lido Spa Hotel & Resort
40 Island Avenue
Venetian Causeway
Miami FL 33139
800-327-8363

National Institute of Fitness
202 North Snow Canyon Road
P.O. Box 938
Ivins UT 84738
801-628-4388

New Life Spa/Liftline Lodge
R.R. 1, Box 144
South Londonderry VT 05155
802-297-2534

Oaks at Ojai
122 East Ojai Avenue
Ojai CA 93023
805-646-5573

**Omega Institute
for Holistic Studies**
Lake Drive Road
R.D. 2, Box 377
Rhinebeck NY 12572
914-266-4301

Palm-Aire Hotel & Spa
2501 Palm-Aire Drive North
Pompano Beach FL 33069
800-327-4690

The Palms at Palm Springs
572 North Indian Avenue
Palm Springs CA 92262
619-325-1111

Pawling Health Manor
P.O. Box 401
Hyde Park NY 12538
914-889-4141

The Phoenix
111 North Post Oak Lane
Houston TX 77024
713-680-2626

**Safety Harbor Spa
& Fitness Center**
105 North Bayshore Drive
Safety Harbor FL 33572
800-237-0155

Sheraton Bonaventura Hotel & Spa
250 Racquet Club Road
Ft. Lauderdale FL 33326
800-327-8090

Structure House
3017 Pickett Road
Durham NC 27705
800-553-0052

Zane Haven
P.O. Box 2031
Palm Springs CA 92263
800-323-7537

VEGETARIAN SPAS

The Ashram Healthort
P.O. Box 8009
Calabasas CA 91302
818-888-0232

**Dr. Deal's Hawaiian
Fitness Holiday**
P.O. Box 1287
Koloa, Kauai HI 96756
808-332-9244

Evergreen Manor
P.O. Box 1154
Hot Springs National Park AR 71902
501-525-0600

The Expanding Light
14618 Tyler Foote Road
Nevada City CA 95959
800-346-5350

**Himalayan International
Institute of Yoga**
R.R. 1, Box 400
Honesdale PA 18431
717-253-5551

Hippocrates Health Institute
1443 Palmdale Court
West Palm Beach FL 33411
407-471-8876

Living Springs Retreat
Bryant Pond Road
Route 3
Putnam Valley NY 10579
914-526-2800

Lotus Center for Health
Route 1, Box 172A
Buckingham VA 23921
804-969-3300

Northern Pines Health Resort
Route 85, Box 279
Raymond ME 04071
207-655-7624

The Plantation Spa
51-550 Kamehameha Highway
Kaaawa HI 96730
808-237-8442

Regency Health Resort
2000 South Ocean Drive
Hallandale FL 33009
305-454-2220

Shangri-La Health Resort
P.O. Box 2328
Bonita Springs FL 33923
813-992-3811

Sharon Springs Health Spa
Chestnut Street
Sharon Springs NY 13459
518-284-2885

Shoshoni Yoga & Health Retreat Center
P.O. Box 307
Eldorado Springs CO 80025
303-494-3051

Sivananda Ashram
14651 Ballantree Lane
Grass Valley CA 95949
916-272-9322

White Lotus Foundation
2500 San Marcos Pass
Santa Barbara CA 93105
805-964-1944

Caterers

Catering has become one of the most creative areas in the business of food as the demand increases for firms to supply food in quantity that is also remarkable for its quality. Michael Roman, president of the National Institute for Off-Premise Catering, the largest association of professionals in this field, has made this selection among its members to achieve a nationwide representation and to include both established and up-and-coming caterers who do good work at a variety of price points, from moderate ($20 per head) to high-priced ($100 and upward). All offer a range of services, from self-service catering, in which the caterer supplies only the food (increasingly popular, especially in urban areas), all the way to complete party or banquet service with skilled professional help.

Rounding out the list are some catering firms who are not members of the institute, but whose reputations warrant their inclusion in such a professional listing as this.

The list is alphabetical by town or city within states.

More specific information and advice of all kinds—from how to select a caterer to assistance in locating an appropriate caterer in a specified area—is available from the institute at P.O. Box 14352, Chicago IL 60614.

ALASKA

Good Taste, Inc./Saucy Sisters
2000 West International Airport, Building C
Anchorage AK 99502
407-248-3522
Contact:
Connie S. Bennett

The Deli
P.O. Box 871540
Wasilla AK 99687
907-376-2914
Contact:
Marian Worrell

ARIZONA

Slight Indulgence
4730 East Indian School Road
Phoenix AZ 85018
602-840-0188
Contact:
Linda Bosse

Lewis Steven's Distinctive Catering
7601 East Gray Road, Suite C
Scottsdale AZ 85260
602-991-2799
Contact:
Lewis S. Medansky

Ames Catering Unlimited
88 East Broadway
Tucson AZ 85706
602-622-2275
Contact:
Keith Ames

Sutter's Catering Service
632 North Seventh Avenue
P.O. Box 12813
Tucson AZ 85732
602-622-7226
Contact:
David Sutter

ARKANSAS

Bon Appetit Catering, Inc.
509 Scott Street
Little Rock AR 72201
501-374-7556
Contact:
Pam Fendley

RSVP
3801 Bowman Road
Little Rock AR 72211
501-225-9594
Contact:
Mary Wildgen

Fabulous Foods, Inc.
5305 McClanahan, Suite E3
North Little Rock AR 72116
501-758-9005
Contact:
Maureen Christopher

CALIFORNIA

House of Catering
3331 East Orangethorpe Avenue
Anaheim CA 92806
714-996-1030
Contact:
Dan Wiencek

Beverly Hills Caterers
9030 West Olympic Boulevard
Beverly Hills CA 90211
213-278-8456
Contact:
William A. Pinkerson

Palate Pleasers
6531 Palmer Way, Suite B
Carlsbad CA 92008
619-931-7922
Contact:
Patti and Hank Kuemmel

Gai Klass Catering
10335 West Jefferson Boulevard
Culver City CA 90232
213-559-6777
Contact:
Gai Klass

Wonderful Parties Wonderful Foods
10848 Washington Boulevard
Culver City CA 90230
213-933-6211
Contact:
Don Ernstein

Elegant Delights Catering
169 East Prospect Avenue
Danville CA 94526
415-837-6661
Contact:
Jerry and Melanie McCarthy

American Hospitality
1607 63rd Street
Emeryville CA 94608
415-653-6699
Contact:
Joel Larson

Confetti
15913 South Halldale Avenue
Gardena CA 90247
213-532-6232
Contact:
Mina Semenza

Classic Catering
298 South Orange Avenue
Goleta CA 93117
805-683-3427
Contact:
Richard Wilson

Epicurean
8759 Melrose Avenue
Los Angeles CA 90069
213-659-5990
Contact:
Shelley Janson

L. A. Celebrations
1716 South Robertson Boulevard
Los Angeles CA 90035
213-837-8900
Contact:
Andrea Bell

Parties Plus, Inc.
3455 South La Cienega Boulevard
Los Angeles CA 90016
213-838-3800
Contact:
Tomiko Iwata

Steamers
50 University Avenue, Suite 38
Los Gatos CA 95030
408-354-4522
Contact:
Linda Matulich

Larimores
220 North Main Street
Manteca CA 95336
209-823-2776
Contact:
Richard Larimore

California Celebrations
4051 Glencoe Avenue, Suite 7
Marina Del Rey CA 90292
213-305-8849
Contact:
Steve Balfour

Sarah Scott Catering
1238 Orchard
Napa CA 94558
707-252-1578
Contact:
Sarah Scott

Mrs. P.J.'s Catering Company
106 Argall Way
Nevada City CA 95959
916-265-9091
Contact:
Martha Johnson

Mrs. P.J., the current six-year national grand champion in the Meat Platter Competition sponsored by the American Association of Meat Processors, has produced a 48-minute instructional videotape on how to create gourmet party platters with ease and originality. "Martha Johnson's Meat Platter Secrets" devotes careful attention to the importance of garnishes and color contrast, and also shows folding and displaying of meats and cheeses for the best visual impact. Telephone credit card orders are accepted.

Cheers Catering, Inc.
19431 Business Center Drive,
Suite 8
Northridge CA 91324
818-772-0233
Contact:
Carolyn Baer

Olsen Catering
1309 61st Street
Oakland CA 94608
415-655-9373
Contact:
Theresa Adams

Bridgehead Catering
Route 1, Box 64-A
Oakley CA 94561
415-757-0356
Contact:
Jeff and Cindy Lodge

Catering by Sharon
44-855 San Pablo Avenue, Suite 8
P.O. Box 2806 (92261)
Palm Desert CA 92260
619-568-9681
Contact:
Sharon Takacs

Starting its seventh year, Catering by Sharon enjoys a fine reputation for full-service catering to all areas of California, incorporating its fully licensed facility and liquor service to provide the finest in gourmet foods and beverages.

The company does all events, ranging from sit-down dinners to others, such as corporate catering, theme parties and grand openings. Our goal has always been to serve the best food, but always with that personal touch.

Castle Catering
50 East Green Street
Pasadena CA 91105
818-792-4444
Contact:
Ron Hobbs

Rose Catering, Inc.
P.O. Box 84
Petaluma CA 94952
707-778-6210
Contact:
Paul Pedroni

The Picnic People
8395 Camino Sante Fe, Suite C
San Diego CA 92121
619-587-1717
Contact:
Lisa and Rick Richards

Premier Food Services, Inc.
3500 Sports Arena Boulevard
San Diego CA 92110
619-223-8182
Contact:
George E. Karetas

Creative Catering
2800 Bryant Street
San Francisco CA 94110
415-285-2555
Contact:
Marie Pollard
Patra Cianciolo

Knight's Party Productions
550 Alabama Street
San Francisco CA 94110
415-861-3312
Contact:
Margaret and Ed McGovern

A Special Occasion
1080 Broadway
San Jose CA 95125
408-288-9054
Contact:
Jim Sweet

Miraglia Catering
2096 Burroughs Avenue
San Leandro CA 94577
415-483-5210
Contact:
Michael and Cheryl Miraglia

All Seasons Party Productions
58 Paul Drive, Suite 10
San Rafael CA 94903
415-435-6754
Contact:
Stan Vail

CaterMarin
911 Irwin Street
San Rafael CA 94901
415-453-0174
Contact:
Sarah Gordon

**A Classic Affair
(Creative Foods)**
1120 West 17th Street
Santa Ana CA 92706
714-834-0149
Contact:
Michael Hankey

Michael's Waterside Inn
50 Los Patos Way
Santa Barbara CA 93108
805-969-0307
Contact:
Michael Hutchings

Red Rose Catering Company
901 Philinda Avenue
Santa Barbara CA 93103
805-963-7550
Contact:
Cyndi Woo

Dorothy Wilson Caterers
303 Potrero, Suite 5
Santa Cruz CA 95060
408-425-0424
Contact:
Dorothy Wilson

Chef Klaus Catering, Inc.
946 Santa Rosa Avenue
Santa Rosa CA 95404
707-575-7211
Contact:
Klaus E. Scheftner

Bon Appetit of Lake Tahoe
P.O. Box 18366
South Lake Tahoe CA 95709
916-541-8797
Contact:
Charles and Debbie Elison

**The Alder Market & Catering
Company**
151 West Alder
Stockton CA 95204
209-943-1921
Contact:
Larry Ruhstaller

**Catering by Coast
Coordinators, Inc.**
1078 West Evelyn
Sunnyvale CA 94086
408-730-0500
Contact:
Ginger K. Miller

**Mon Cheri Cooking School &
Caterers**
461 South Murphy
Sunnyvale CA 94086
408-736-0892
Contact:
Sharon Shipley

Cowboy Catering
P.O. Box 853
Temecula CA 92390
714-699-4229
Contact:
Thomas G. Baum

Lisa's Bon Appetit
24032 Vista Montana
Torrance CA 90505
213-378-5284
Contact:
Susanne Alexander

Life's A Party
7848 Sepulveda Boulevard
Van Nuys CA 91405
818-989-1516
Contact:
Ilene McFadden
Andrea Marks
Charlie Scola

Dearmore's Bar-B-Que
P.O. Box 4685
Ventura CA 93004
805-485-3011
Contact:
Robert and Pat Dearmore

COLORADO

Denver's Catering
6810 North Broadway, Suite E
Denver CO 80221
303-426-4248
Contact:
Kathy Wood

CONNECTICUT

Epicurean Caterers
631 Grand Street
Bridgeport CT 06604
203-374-2745
Contact:
Richard J. LaManna Jr.

H. S. Blatt Presents, Inc.
136 Hamilton Avenue
Greenwich CT 06830
203-661-0646
Contact:
Helaine Blatt

Soiree, Ltd.
230 College Street
New Haven CT 06510
203-562-0821
Contact:
Tucker Sweitzer

**Wendland Catering/
A Thyme to Cook, Inc.**
426 Northwest Corner Road
North Stonington CT 06359
203-887-5932
Contact:
Linda S. Urbanetti

Cater, Inc.
6 Commerce Street
Norwalk CT 06850
203-838-9132
Contact:
Bruce Post

Special Occasions
320 Pomfret Street
Putnam CT 06260
203-928-7874
Contact:
Laura J. Cline

Judy Zagoren Catering, Inc.
540 Hopmeadow Street
Simsbury CT 06070
203-673-4759
Contact:
Judith Zagoren

Festivities
124 Washington Street
South Norwalk CT 06854
203-866-1616
Contact:
William Kaliff

Creative Catering
5665 Main Street
Trumbull CT 06611
203-452-1492
Contact:
Meg De'Ath

Cabbages & Kings
110 Lords Highway
Weston CT 06883
203-226-0531
Contact:
Sarah K. Gross

DELAWARE

Piane Caterers
2130 North Market Street
Wilmington DE 19802
302-658-4353
Contact:
Theresa Piane

DISTRICT OF COLUMBIA

Connecticut Avenue Caterers, Inc.
6303 Georgia Avenue NW
Washington DC 20011
202-291-5050
Contact:
Robert B. Eldridge

Swan Caterers
1532 U Street NW
Washington DC 20009
202-393-7926
Contact:
Milton Goldman

Lawson's Gourmet
1350 Connecticut Avenue NW,
Suite 307
Washington DC 20036
202-775-0400
Contact:
Ronald W. Hailey

Mattison & Company Caterers
P.O. Box 56119
Washington DC 20040
202-682-0502
Contact:
Gail A. Mattison

FLORIDA

HCA L. W. Blake Hospital
P.O. Box 25004
Bradenton FL 33506
813-792-6611
Contact:
Williams Evans

Catering by Lovables
4400 Ponce De Leon
Coral Gables FL 33146
305-445-7766
Contact:
Marilyn McSwiggan
Elizabeth Silverman

By Word of Mouth, Inc.
3200 Northeast 12th Avenue
Ft. Lauderdale FL 33334
305-564-3663
Contact:
Tom Ahlbrand

Food for Thought
3698 Northwest 16th Street
Ft. Lauderdale FL 33311
305-584-1925
Contact:
Sharon and Kevin Grim

Dale's Bar-B-Que
3362 South U. S. 1
Ft. Pierce FL 33482
407-461-0052
Contact:
Daniel Kinser

Spice of Life Caterers
122 Sixth Avenue North
Jacksonville Beach FL 32250
904-249-7667
Contact:
Bob Mark

Senter & Chess
7399 Southwest 45th Street
Miami FL 33155
305-262-2837
Contact:
Steven Chess
Al Senter

Contemporary Caterers, Inc.
275 Southwest 14th Avenue
Pompano Beach FL 33069
305-942-2617
Contact:
Gary Wisotzky

Lagrotte Catering/Leonard's
4207 South Tamiami Trail
Sarasota FL 34231
813-922-6500
Contact:
Sandra L. Lagrotte

Orange Blossom Catering
220 4th Street North
St. Petersburg FL 33701
813-822-6129
Contact:
Edward F. Shamas

Chavez Catering
915 South Howard
Tampa FL 33603
813-253-3269
Contact:
Timothe M. Chavez

Party Fare, Inc.
4820 North Armenia Avenue
Tampa FL 33606
813-875-8842
Contact:
Marsha Levine
Corinne Scanio

Port-A-Pit BBQ, Inc.
P.O. Box 15481
Tampa FL 33684
813-888-8252
Contact:
Scott Skornschek

Sierra's Catering
5802 North Armenia Avenue
Tampa FL 33603
813-873-1314
Contact:
Michael Sierra

Lupton's Fatman's Catering, Inc.
5299 East Busch Boulevard
Temple Terrace FL 33617
813-985-6963
Contact:
Ralph J. Lupton Jr.

Imagination!s Catering
1000A Old Okeechobee Road
West Palm Beach FL 33401
407-835-0003
Contact:
Dave Zylstra
Ken Best

William Gavigan, The Caterer, Inc.
2000 Wellington Road
West Palm Beach FL 33409
407-686-2096
Contact:
William J. Gavigan

GEORGIA

Top Bananas, Inc.
103 Roswell Street
Alpharetta GA 30201
404-475-8677
Contact:
Dave and Mary Ellen Shuppert

Celebrations
3024 Maple Drive NE
Atlanta GA 30305
404-261-5995
Contact:
Gail B. Prescott

Murphy's Catering
1019 Los Angeles Avenue
Atlanta GA 30306
404-872-6992
Contact:
Shelley Pedersen

Exclusively Anne
2649 Elkhorn Drive
Decatur GA 30034
404-243-3092
Contact:
Anne L. Willard

D & I Professional Caterers, Inc.
2692 Sandy Plains Road, Suite 2100
Marietta GA 30066
404-578-6640
Contact:
Doris Orndorff

Gourmet Tidbits, Inc.
3116-E Spring Hill Road
Smyrna GA 30080
404-432-3287
Contact:
Lauren Alanskas

ILLINOIS

Bob Knapp's Restaurant & Catering
1603 South Morrissey Drive
Bloomington IL 61704
309-663-8481
Contact:
Bob Knapp

D'Masti Events & Catering
11915 South Western Avenue
Blue Island IL 60406
708-388-0940
Contact:
Dan Mast

Carlyn Berghoff Catering
125 North Wabash Avenue
Chicago IL 60602
312-263-7564
Contact:
Carlyn Berghoff

Elegant Edge
2000 North Racine
Chicago IL 60614
312-549-5300
Contact:
Robert Giannetti

Intimate Affairs Catering
1360 West Randolph Street
Chicago IL 60607
312-942-0230
Contact:
Debra Cardinali

The Master Caterers
2110 West Grand Avenue
Chicago IL 60612
312-226-5545
Contact:
Louis Lonnecke

Barbecue on Wheels
67 Fountain Square
Elgin IL 60120
708-741-6374
Contact:
John Schalz

Prairie Path Catering
489 Spring Road, Unit C
Elmhurst IL 60126
708-833-1234
Contact:
Bob W. Gaudry

Catering by Michael's, Inc.
1434 Old Skokie Road
Highland Park IL 60035
708-831-9310
Contact:
Stewart Glass

Aller Cuisine, Ltd.
P.O. Box 445
Lake Bluff IL 60044
708-234-0232
Contact:
Nancy Kirby Harris

Peppercorn's Catering, Ltd.
564 West Main Street
Lake Zurich IL 60047
708-428-5563
Contact:
Arnold Deutchman

Hel's Kitchen Catering, Inc.
3015 Commercial Avenue
Northbrook IL 60062
708-433-1845
Contact:
David and Cari Borris

The Cater Inn
1224 West Pioneer Parkway
Peoria IL 61615
309-692-3990
Contact:
Richard and James Barrack

Stump's Catering
8104 South Archer Avenue
Willow Springs IL 60480
708-448-9400
Contact:
Todd Stump

Marie's Catering Service, Inc.
341 West 75th Street
Willowbrook IL 60521
708-655-3337
Contact:
Lorraine M. Hynek

INDIANA

Peachey's Catering, Inc.
P.O. Box 375
Cicero IN 46034
317-773-5447
Contact:
Lori Peachey

Goeglein's, Inc.
7311 Maysville Road
Ft. Wayne IN 46815
219-749-5192
Contact:
Larry and Jerry Goeglein

Dooley O'Toole's Catering
5960 East 10th Street
Indianapolis IN 46219
317-356-8478
Contact:
Paul H. Johnson III

Betty A. Jones Catering, Inc.
1805 Beechwood Avenue
New Albany IN 47150
812-944-3640
Contact:
Betty A. Jones

Bertsch Food Service
P.O. Box 815
Warsaw IN 46580
219-267-6051
Contact:
Larry Kinsey

IOWA

We 3 Catering/We 3 Markets, Inc.
412 River Avenue North
Belmond IA 50421
515-444-3871
Contact:
Joel Gabrielson

KANSAS

Kansas City Catering
3018 South 44th Street
Kansas City KS 66106
913-831-0764
Contact:
Brownie Simpson

Engroff Catering
410 West 18th Street
Topeka KS 66612
913-232-5993
Contact:
Jay Engroff

KENTUCKY

Grisanti Catering
1000 East Liberty Street
Louisville KY 40204
502-584-4379
Contact:
Jack Sedivy

Luckett & Associates, Ltd.
2035 South 3rd Street
P.O. Box 2600
Louisville KY 40201
502-637-9069
Contact:
Luckett Davidson

Prospect Store & Catering
P.O. Box 508
Prospect KY 40059
502-426-2864
Contact:
Shane Best

LOUISIANA

Boudin King, Inc.
P.O. Box 1267
Jennings LA 70546
318-824-6593
Contact:
Ellis Cormier

**Upper Crust Caterers
& Special Events**
5430 Magazine Street
New Orleans LA 70115
504-899-8065
Contact:
Margaret Marchese
Stephen Marchese

MARYLAND

Cameo Caterers, Inc.
5805 Oakleaf Avenue
Baltimore MD 21215
301-764-0808
Contact:
Rita Feinberg

Gail Kaplan's Classic Catering
5803 Oakleaf Avenue
Baltimore MD 21215
301-764-2715
Contact:
Gail Kaplan

Hoffman Quality Meats
Route 6, Box 5
Hagerstown MD 21740
301-739-2332
Contact:
Donald L. Hoffman

The Catering People
99C Painters Mill Road
Owings Mills MD 21117
301-363-3022
Contact:
Ansela and Michael Dopkin

Simply Elegant Catering, Inc.
10315 South Dolfield Road
Owings Mills MD 21117
301-363-3466
Contact:
Louis Bivona

Country Caterer
15537 New Hampshire Avenue
Silver Spring MD 20904
301-384-1123
Contact:
Marcia A. Buscher

MASSACHUSETTS

Morin's, Inc.
95 Frank Mossberg Drive
Attleboro MA 02703
508-226-6600
Contact:
R. Russell Morin Jr.

Sidell and Sasse
U.S. Trust Building
40 Court Street
Boston MA 02108
617-277-6565
Contact:
Stephanie Sidell

Seasoned To Taste, Inc.
7 Temple Street
Cambridge MA 02139
617-497-5262
Contact:
Donald R. Balcom

Creative Gourmets
529 Main Street, Suite 201
Charlestown MA 02129
617-242-7676
Contact:
Stephen Elmont

Robert Charles Caterers, Inc.
P.O. Box 318
Danvers MA 01923
508-774-5252
Contact:
Robert C. Tierney Jr.

The Catered Affair
Accord Park
P.O. Box 26
Hingham MA 02018
617-982-9333
Contact:
Holly P. Safford

The Party Specialist
530 Chestnut Street
Lynn MA 01904
617-592-0988
Contact:
Bruce Silverlieb

Barrett Restaurants
1235 Bedford Street
North Abington MA 02351
617-871-3025
Contact:
Francis M. Barrett

A Feast For All Reasons, Inc.
92 Reservoir Park Drive
Rockland MA 02370
617-878-0499
Contact:
Helen M. Saulia

Cafe in the Barn
1590 Fall River Avenue
Seekonk MA 02771
508-336-6330
Contact:
Guy Abelson

Elfman Caterers
27 Paul Revere Road
Sharon MA 02067
617-784-3720
Contact:
Rich Elfman

Creative Celebrations, Inc.
508 Medford Street
Somerville MA 02145
617-776-5800
Contact:
Alison Healy

Chanterelle Caterers
206 William Street
Springfield MA 01105
413-733-2309
Contact:
Joanne Parisi and Mark Antsel

Classics Capers Catering, Inc.
Tisbury Market Place
P.O. Box 2044
Tisbury MA 02568
508-695-4077
Contact:
Richard and Catherine Hayes

Hillcrest Caterers
220 Bear Hill Road
Waltham MA 02154
617-890-2282
Contact:
Bruce Potter

Fond Memories
76 School Street
Watertown MA 02172
617-926-8221
Contact:
Kathy Jannino

Sophie Serves, Inc.
26 Hyder Street
Westboro MA 01581
508-842-0434
Contact:
Albert V. Ferguson

MICHIGAN

Katherine's Catering, Inc.
24 Frank Lloyd Wright Drive
P.O. Box 985
Ann Arbor MI 48106
313-995-4270
Contact:
Katherine Curtis

Catering by Dennis
25740 Ford Road
Dearborn Heights MI 48127
313-563-7661
Contact:
Dennis Chatlin

Baker Catering
251 Page NE
Grand Rapids MI 49505
616-456-8824
Contact:
Randy Baker

Campbell Catering, Inc.
4616 North Grand River
Lansing MI 48906
517-321-3690
Contact:
Joe Campbell

Sterling Inn Catering
34911 Van Dyke
Sterling Heights MI 48077
313-979-1400
Contact:
Victor Martin

MINNESOTA

Perfect Host Catering
8949 University Avenue NE
Blaine MN 55434
612-780-8683
Contact:
Ron Bigley

Twin City Catering
9286 Wellington Lane
Maple Grove MN 55369
612-424-6543
Contact:
Jim Dolan

Allan Elias Custom Catering
323 East Franklin Avenue
Minneapolis MN 55404
612-871-4801
Contact:
Allan and Judy Elias

MISSISSIPPI

VIP Caterers
1841 County Line Road
Jackson MS 39213
601-366-7090
Contact:
Mildred Brown

Cantrell's Catering
2543 Jennifer Drive
Pearl MS 39208
601-353-5900
Contact:
Judy and Charles Cantrell

MISSOURI

The Prospect of Westport
1 Westport Square
Kansas City MO 64111
816-753-2227
Contact:
Don Anderson

Robert T. Salsman Caterers, Inc.
401 East 31st Street
Kansas City MO 64108
816-561-0266
Contact:
Robert T. Salsman

Richard Perry/Caterers, Inc.
The Hotel Majestic
1019 Pine Street
St. Louis MO 63101
314-436-2355
Contact:
Richard Perry

MONTANA

Butler's Kitchen
3233 Parkhill
Billings MT 59102
406-252-4684
Contact:
Paul N. Odegard

Cedric's Catering
3101 Russell Street
Missoula MT 59801
406-549-1191
Contact:
Cedric Hames

NEBRASKA

Catering by Elleven
NBC Center, 11th Floor
13th and O Streets
Lincoln NE 68508
402-472-4191
Contact:
Jenny DeBerg

NEW HAMPSHIRE

Capers of Amherst
6 Foundry Street
Amherst NH 03031
603-673-4802
Contact:
Sarah E. Ginsberg

NEW JERSEY

Growth Catering
55 South Finley Avenue
Basking Ridge NJ 07920
201-766-0660
Contact:
Jeff Beers

Hickory Steak House Catering
Carlls Corner
Bridgeton NJ 08302
609-451-6035
Contact:
Ross and Linda Capps

Chef Michael, Inc.
30 The Fairway
Cedar Grove NJ 07009
201-239-7206
Contact:
Paul P. Yurkosky

Catering by Lawrence
65 Main Street
Eatontown NJ 07724
201-544-1636
Contact:
Lawrence Feinberg

Insley Caterers, Ltd.
3-12 Fairlawn Avenue
Fair Lawn NJ 07410
201-797-4670
Contact:
James Fogg

Food Thoughts Catering & Event Planning, Inc.
177 Main Street, Suite 224
Ft. Lee NJ 07024
201-288-0951
Contact:
Jeffrey Kerne

Weinberg Caterers
30 Route 181
Lake Hopatcong NJ 07849
201-663-1999
Contact:
Elizabeth and Joel Weinberg

The Yellow Brick Toad
Route 179
Lambertville NJ 08530
609-397-3100
Contact:
W. David Duthie

Min Goldblatt & Sons
211 East Elizabeth Avenue
P.O. Box 533
Linden NJ 07036
201-925-3869
Contact:
Arnold J. Goldblatt

Demetrio's Catering, Inc.
10 Stuyvesant Avenue
P.O. Box 9029
Lyndhurst NJ 07071
201-935-0861
Contact:
James Kirkos

The Corporate Caterer
227 Freneau Avenue
Route 79
Matawan NJ 07747
201-583-9200
Contact:
Andy Bott

Collins and Barnes, Inc.
149 Valley Road
Montclair NJ 07042
201-744-3345
Contact:
David K. Barnes

Luberto's Caterer
55 Moonachie Avenue
Moonachie NJ 07074
201-438-4747
Contact:
Fred M. Luberto

Colonial Inn Caterers
545 Tappan Road
Norwood NJ 07648
201-767-1505
Contact:
Paul Guarino

Creative Catering by Ellen, Inc.
114 Pennington Avenue, Box E
Passaic NJ 07055
201-777-8504
Contact:
Ellen Trama

Lucille's Catering
47 Drummond Avenue
Red Bank NJ 07701
201-747-2458
Contact:
B. Lucille Allgood

Catering by Millard
902 Bay Shore Road
Villas NJ 08251
609-886-8605
Contact:
Stewart and Bonnie Millard

Club Car Catering Company
40 Washington Avenue
Westwood NJ 07675
201-666-6770
Contact:
Scott Tremble

NEW YORK

Abigail Kirsch Culinary Productions, Inc.
33 Plainfield Avenue
Bedford Hills NY 10507
914-666-7545
Contact:
Abigail Kirsch
Robert Kirsch

Marc Aaron Kosher Caterers
5652 Mosholu Avenue
Bronx NY 10471
212-548-0440
Contact:
Michael Pozit

Negev Caterers
1211 Avenue J
Brooklyn NY 11230
718-258-2875
Contact:
George Gross

Remember Basil, Ltd.
11 Cadman Plaza West
Brooklyn NY 11201
718-858-3000
212-753-3955
Contact:
Dounia Rathbone and
Donald Beckwith

Antun's of Westchester
35 Valley Avenue
Elmsford NY 10523
914-592-5260
Contact:
John M. Antun and Ron Stytzer

Arline Breskin, Ltd.
18 Old Farm Lane
Hartsdale NY 10530
914-946-3612
Contact:
Arline Breskin

Cornell Catering
77 Maplewood Road, Suite 3
Ithaca NY 14850
607-255-5555
Contact:
Mary Beth Swan

Anthony's
519 Hawkins Avenue
Lake Ronkonkoma NY 11779
516-981-8282
Contact:
Bart and Anthony Pellegrino

Culinary Classics, Inc.
27 Amy Todt Drive
Monroe NY 10950
914-782-5409
Contact:
Diane Soss

A Sense of Taste
217 East 85th Street, Suite 237
New York NY 10028
212-570-2928
Contact:
Susan Lippert

Claster and Company, Inc.
150 West 22nd Street,
10th Floor
New York NY 10011
212-633-0970
Contact:
Andrea Claster

   Claster and Company, Inc. is a full-service corporate event and gift-planning company. We take pride in our creative ability, coupled with our expertise in the fields of events and gifts to assure you distinctiveness and originality. We draw that originality from collaborations with an unlimited cadre of artists, entertainers, locations, chefs, designers and gift houses to match your goals. Product positioning and launches via custom baskets and events are our specialty.

The Cleaver Company, Inc.
229 West Broadway
New York NY 10013
212-431-3688
Contact:
Mary R. Cleaver

Fisher & Levy
1026 Second Avenue
New York NY 10022
212-832-3880
Contact:
Chip Fisher or Doug Levy

Glorious Food
172 East 75th Street
New York NY 10021
212-628-2320
Contact:
Sean Driscoll or Billye Hanan

Great Performances
125 Crosby Street
New York NY 10012
212-219-2800
Contact:
Liz Neumark

Indiana Market & Catering
80 Second Avenue
New York NY 10003
212-505-7290
Contact:
David Turk

Marcy L. Blum Associates, Inc.
251 East 51st Street
New York NY 10022
212-688-3057
Contact:
Marcy L. Blum

Neuman & Bogdonoff, Inc.
1385 Third Avenue
New York NY 10021
212-861-0303
Contact:
Stacy Bogdonoff

Perfect Touch Caterers
527 Third Avenue, Suite 293
New York NY 10016
212-860-7910
Contact:
Marty Levin

Restaurant Associates Caterers
36 West 44th Street
New York NY 10036
212-755-8300
Contact:
Mary Dearborn

Robbins Bianco Catering
501 East 87th Street, Suite 5A
New York NY 10128
212-772-6630
Contact:
Paula Wolfe

Taste Caterers
151 Hudson Street
New York NY 10013
212-925-5074
Contact:
Jon Gilman

Tentation
47 East 19th Street
New York NY 10003
212-353-0070
Contact:
Jean-Christophe Le Picart

Washington Street Cafe
433 Washington Street
New York NY 10013
212-925-5119
Contact:
Ronnie Davis

Wok on Wheels
666 Greenwich Street
New York NY 10014
212-727-0389
Contact:
Rosa Ross

Good & Plenty Catering, Inc.
10 Dorchester Road
Smithtown NY 11788
516-724-2209
Contact:
Frank and Paulette Salvia

Perfect Parties
1163 Forest Avenue
Staten Island NY 10310
718-727-8437
Contact:
Frank and Jean Cretella

Reeta Wolfsohn Party Designing & Catering
1338 Stony Brook Road
Stony Brook NY 11790
516-751-3114
Contact:
Reeta Wolfsohn

Yankel & Company Catering
303 Nottingham Plaza
Syracuse NY 13210
315-445-8120
Contact:
Howard Rosenthal

Laura-Fine Catering
33 Old Tappan Road
Tappan NY 10983
914-359-1110
Contact:
Laura Chersky

NORTH CAROLINA

A.V.S. Catering, Inc.
2045 North Fayetteville Street
Asheboro NC 27203
919-672-0927
Contact:
Michael W. Lee

C & C Catering
4416 East Monroe Road
Charlotte NC 28205
704-373-1392
Contact:
Melanie Culp

Eli's Catering
4301-B Stuart Andrew Boulevard
Charlotte NC 28217
704-529-1400
Contact:
Karen Smoots

Hieronymus Seafood Companies
610 Ravenswood Road
Hampstead NC 28443
919-392-6313
Contact:
Marlene Hieronymus

Plain and Fancy Caterers
P.O. Box 5237
High Point NC 27262
919-869-4842
Contact:
Margaret C. Schneider

Mitchell's Catering
P.O. Box 51111
Raleigh NC 27609
919-847-0135
Contact:
Craig W. Mitchell

OHIO

A. A. Executive Catering
4870 Frank Road NW
Canton OH 44720
216-497-1427
Contact:
Michael D. Kazes

Benson's Catering
4243 Hunt Road
Cincinnati OH 45242
513-891-5588
Contact:
Bob Sharp

The Chafer Caterers
4212 Plainfield Road
Cincinnati OH 45227
513-271-2500
Contact:
Richard and Bella Golden

Elegant Fare, Inc.
10700 Montgomery Road, Suite 220
Cincinnati OH 45242
513-489-4035
Contact:
Bert Kurinsky

Gourmet!
3866 Paxton Avenue
Cincinnati OH 45209
513-321-8100
Contact:
Claire T. Sillett

Ovations Catering & Special Events
5111 Rhode Island
Cincinnati OH 45212
513-731-5800
Contact:
Steven Shifman

Sammy's
1400 West 10th Street
Cleveland OH 44113
216-523-5560
Contact:
Denise M. Fugo

Sammy's, Cleveland's premier restaurant, brings world-class food, service, design and management to catered events within 200 miles of Cleveland. We will make your event for 2 to 2,000 guests one to be remembered. Every day Sammy's Corporate Catering division brings fine food to airplanes and boats as well as to conference rooms and sports events. Let Sammy's bring a five-star touch to your next party. Sammy's is a Fine Dining Hall of Fame inductee (1987), Wine Spectator Award of Excellence (1989) and Travel/Holiday Award winner.

Encore Catering, Inc.
P.O. Box 18693
Cleveland Heights OH 44118
216-321-3700
Contact:
Kim Pechak

Creative Cuisine
827 Busch Court
Columbus OH 43229
614-436-4949
Contact:
Shauna Chrisman
Kris Murphy

Eventmasters
3137 East 17th Avenue
Columbus OH 43219
614-471-1200
Contact:
Cheryl Richter

In Good Taste, Inc.
6161 Busch Boulevard
Columbus OH 43229
614-436-0220
Contact:
Arlene Levy

Buccalo Catering, Inc.
3020 Kenmore Avenue
Dayton OH 45420
513-228-9356
Contact:
David Buccalo

King Cole Restaurant & Catering
4 South Main Street, Suite 901
Dayton OH 45402
513-222-6771
Contact:
Uwe Knebelsberger

Sprenger Catering
600 East State Street
Fremont OH 43420
419-334-8266
Contact:
Rudy Sprenger

DeLuca's
6075 Middle Ridge Road
Lorain OH 44053
216-233-7272
Contact:
Leonard DeLuca

Lehr's Meats & Catering
740 Main Street
Milford OH 45150
513-831-3411
Contact:
Don Ackerman

Jagel's Catering Services, Inc.
2552 Airport Highway
Toledo OH 43609
419-382-7611
Contact:
Jim and Kevin Jagel

Meadowbrook Catering
4560 Heatherdowns Boulevard
Toledo OH 43614
419-382-8880
Contact:
Tom Thees

Bradley's, Inc.
26001 Miles Road, Suite 10
Warrensville Heights OH 44128
216-292-4530
Contact:
Daniel H. McElwain

Hall's Diversified Caterers
2645 North Maple Avenue
Zanesville OH 43701
614-453-0561
Contact:
Ed Hall

OKLAHOMA

Schaefer's Catering
209 South Bryant
Edmond OK 73034
405-340-6868
Contact:
Jim Sellers

Chisholm Trail Catering
1224 North Broadway
Moore OK 73160
405-793-9501
Contact:
Randie Harms

Chef John Bennett
1923 Northwest 42nd Street
Oklahoma City OK 73118
405-528-2832
Contact:
John Bennett

Cowboy's Tallgrass Grilled
Bobwhite Quail
Arbuckle Mountain "Oysters"
Blackbuck Antelope Chop, Mixed
Grill, Hot Whole Hog Sausage and
Sweet Corn Chowder
Mama Bennett's Coconut Cake
—and hundreds of other custom-
designed savory dishes available.
Chef John Bennett travels nationally
and internationally, creating specialized
luscious productions for large and small
occasions.
Over 25 years' experience as a
television personality and professional
food stylist.
Where you always find the most
unusual food and parties with style—
Chef John Bennett!

OREGON

The Best of Everything
9735 Southwest Sunshine Court,
Suite 900
Beaverton OR 97005
503-643-3711
Contact:
Maxine Borcherding

Catering Just For You
10580 Southwest McDonald Street,
Suite 103
Tigard OR 97223
503-620-9135
Contact:
Steve DeAngelo

PENNSYLVANIA

Brownie's Catering Service
Mountain Road, Box 253
Delaware Water Gap PA 18327
717-424-2254
Contact:
Frank M. Brown

Distinctive Affairs
119 Reese Avenue
Lancaster PA 17602
717-394-2475
Contact:
Ann E. Murray

Catering from the Hart
1347 South 7th Street
Philadelphia PA 19147
215-755-6064
Contact:
James W. Hart

David Lawrence Caterers, Inc.
14250 Bustleton Avenue
Philadelphia PA 19116
215-698-6600
Contact:
Larry Rashkow

Feast Your Eyes, Inc.
914-20 North 2nd Street
Philadelphia PA 19123
215-923-9449
Contact:
Seth Schwarzman

Food for Thought Caterers
Ivyridge Shopping Center
Philadelphia PA 19128
215-482-5874
Contact:
Stan and Larry Genkin

Tastefully Yours, Inc.
P.O. Box 28332
Philadelphia PA 19149
215-725-2176
Contact:
Faye Miller

Jardine's Farm Restaurant
499 Monroe Road
Sarver PA 16055
412-353-1551
Contact:
William Jardine

Jack Francis, Inc.
Road 1
Telford PA 18969
215-723-5825
Contact:
John D. Francis

Accomac Catering
P.O. Box 127
Wrightsville PA 17368
717-252-4058
Contact:
H. Douglas Campbell Jr.
Carol Lefever

RHODE ISLAND

Plantations Caterer
580 Thames Street
Newport RI 02840
401-846-4794
Contact:
Carol Smith and Chris Hartley

Gallimaufry
103 Point Street
P.O. Box 541
Providence RI 02901
401-521-4433
Contact:
Eric or Sally Godfrey

Michael's Catering
729 Hope Street
Providence RI 02906
401-421-9431
Contact:
Nick Kerras and Stephanie Masoian

SOUTH CAROLINA

TFI
P.O. Box 548
Laurens SC 29360
803-984-2131
Contact:
Tom Fischer

SOUTH DAKOTA

The Cater Cart
400 South Main Street
Sioux Falls SD 57102
605-336-2740
Contact:
Richard Kelly

TENNESSEE

Cotton Boll Catering
Route 3, Box 128
Brighton TN 38011
901-476-9698
Contact:
Andy L. Griffin

Charles Siskin Catering
P.O. Box 623
Chattanooga TN 37401
615-624-5853
Contact:
Charles Siskin

An Affair to Remember, Inc.
206 Sequoyah Trail
Hendersonville TN 37075
615-297-6609
Contact:
Jack and Dianne Keenan

The Copper Cellar Corporation
P.O. Box 50370
Knoxville TN 37950
615-637-6650
Contact:
Mary Alice Chase

Rothchild's Incorporated Catering
8807 Kingston Pike, Suite C
Knoxville TN 37923
615-690-0103
Contact:
Nathan and Susan Rothchild

Executive Chef Catering
2310 Airport Interchange
Memphis TN 38132
901-332-3223
Contact:
Judy Gupton

TEXAS

Bando's
4310 Calder
Beaumont TX 77706
409-898-8638
Contact:
Debbie Bando

Hathaway's Catering
P.O. Box 931
Bedford TX 76021
817-283-4575
Contact:
Mark Hurd

Classic Catering
903 Liberty Drive
Irving TX 75061
214-790-3646
Contact:
Colin Charles

Fresh Horizon Creative Catering
6514 New Braunfels
San Antonio TX 78209
512-828-5919
Contact:
Caryn H. Johnson

Robinette & Doyle Caterers
212 Kirby
Seabrook TX 77586
713-326-3663
Contact:
Pat Doyle
Brenda Robinette

Josephs of Tyler Catering
Troup Highway
Route 15, Box 264
Tyler TX 75707
214-581-7136
Contact:
Elias and Marnie Joseph

VERMONT

Truffles Catering
14 1/2 Railroad Street
Essex Junction VT 05452
802-879-4428
Contact:
Deborah Turner
Christie White

The Catering Company
3060 Williston Road
South Burlington VT 05403
802-863-6262
Contact:
Josh Patrick

VIRGINIA

Robertson's Catering Service, Inc.
5315 Macwood Drive
Dale City VA 22193
703-680-4120
Contact:
Linda Robertson

Feist Catering, Ltd.
64 Sycolin Road SE
Leesburg VA 22075
703-777-9068
Contact:
John Feist

Hart, McMurphy & Parks
102 West Washington
P.O. Box 1258
Middleburg VA 22117
703-687-5866
Contact:
G. Kimball Hart

Savories
339 West 21st Street
Norfolk VA 23517
804-640-1988
Contact:
Gloria Gibney

Commercial Cafe Catering
111 North Robinson Street
Richmond VA 23220
804-285-1116
Contact:
Ken Scott

Extra Billy's Steak & BBQ
5205 West Broad Street
Richmond VA 23230
804-288-5580
Contact:
Robert H. Harr

Commonwealth Caterers, Ltd.
207 East Holly Avenue, Suite 108
Sterling VA 22170
703-430-2673
Contact:
Marty Maykrantz

Clyde's of Tyson's Corner
8332 Leesburg Pike
Vienna VA 22180
703-734-1907
Contact:
Claude Anderson

Epicurean Events
8453-F Tyco Road
Vienna VA 22180
703-356-0217
Contact:
Leonard and Joyce Piotrowski

WASHINGTON

Sharon Snuffin's Catering
8817 Franklin Avenue
Gig Harbor WA 98335
206-851-2900
Contact:
Sharon and Dan Snuffin

Gretchen's Of Course
1333 Fifth Avenue
Seattle WA 98101
206-623-8194
Contact:
Gretchen Mathers

WEST VIRGINIA

Your Chef, Inc.
104 East Main Street, Suite 2E
Clarksburg WV 26301
304-623-3393
Contact:
C. Greg Lemunyon

WISCONSIN

TrimB's Restaurant & Catering
201 South Walnut Street
Appleton WI 54911
414-734-9204
Contact:
Carol Trimberger

Cajun Queen Enterprises, Inc.
69 Point Elkhart
Elkhart Lake WI 53020
414-876-3295
Contact:
Toni Haynes

Biebel's Supermarket & Catering
1234 Bellevue Road
Green Bay WI 54302
414-468-6828
Contact:
Paul Biebel

Theurich Catering Service
12345 West Janesville Road
Hales Corner WI 53130
414-425-0310
Contact:
Miles Theurich

Homeplate Catering
1523 Fond Du Lac Avenue
Kewaskum WI 53040
414-626-4982
Contact:
Kathy Krieser

Lo Becca
4319 Monona Drive
Madison WI 53716
608-222-2280
Contact:
Rebecca Hayter

Catering Complete, Inc.
8825 North Lake Drive
Milwaukee WI 53217
414-352-5887
Contact:
Kathleen M. Pandl

Shully's Catering
154 Green Bay Road
Thiensville WI 53092
414-242-6633
Contact:
Scott and Beth Shully

**Catering by Buck's Kinn/
A Special Event**
303 North Main Street
Oakhill Building, Suite 2A
West Bend WI 53095
414-338-2566
Contact:
Ron and Debbie Buck

131
100 Fine Wineries

135
Breweries

138
Wines and Spirits Importers

WANS STUDIO, INC. / PHOTOGRAPHY

Glen & Gayle Wans
325 West 40th Street
Kansas City, Missouri 64111
(816) 931-8905
FAX: (816) 931-6899

VICKI JOHNSON / FOOD STYLIST

8226 Cherokee Circle
Leawood, Kansas 66206
(913) 648-6015

100 Fine Wineries

Wine is now being produced in 45 out of the 50 states and there are many hundreds of vineyards that are making wines of top quality. This listing of 100 wineries has been selected from among those best known to the public and also most esteemed by connoisseurs and collectors of fine wines.

The selection has been made by Len Pickell, wine coordinator for The James Beard Foundation, who has been teaching wine appreciation for 15 years and heads a Les Amis du Vin chapter in New Jersey. The wineries are listed alphabetically by name, with the address and telephone number of the vineyard.

Acacia Winery
2750 Las Amigas Road
Napa CA 94558
707-226-9991

**Almaden Vineyards/
Inglenook Navalle
(Heublein, Inc.)**
12667 Road 24
Madera CA 93639
209-673-7071

Beaulieu Vineyard
100 St. Helena Highway South
Rutherford CA 94574
707-963-4480

Beringer Vineyards
2000 Main Street
St. Helena CA 94574
707-963-7115

Bonny Doon Vineyard
10 Pine Flat Road
Santa Cruz CA 95060
408-425-3625

Brotherhood Winery
35 North Street
Washingtonville NY 10992
914-496-3661

Burgess Cellars
1108 Deer Park Road
St. Helena CA 94574
707-963-4766

Cakebread Cellars
8300 St. Helena Highway
Rutherford CA 94574
707-963-5221

Callaway Vineyards
32720 Rancho California Road
Temecula CA 92390
714-676-4001

Caymus Vineyards
P.O. Box 268
Rutherford CA 94573
707-963-4204

Chalone Vineyard
P.O. Box 855
Soledad CA 93960
408-678-1717

Chateau Souverain
Independence Lane
Geyserville CA 95441
707-433-8281

Chappellet Winery
1581 Sage Canyon Road
St. Helena CA 94574
707-963-7136

Chateau Montelena
1429 Tubbs Lane
Calistoga CA 95415
707-942-5105

Chateau St. Jean
8555 Sonoma Highway
Kenwood CA 95452
707-833-4134

Chateau Ste. Michelle
1 Stimson Lane
Woodinville WA 98072
206-488-1133

The Christian Brothers
100 St. Helena Highway South
Rutherford CA 94574
707-963-4480

Clos du Bois Winery
5 Fitch Street
Healdsburg CA 95448
707-433-5576

Clos Du Val
5330 Silverado Trail
Napa CA 94558
707-252-6711

Clos Du Val, founded in 1972, has firmly established its label among the world's finest. Year in and year out, this winery produces outstanding wines, classically styled with finesse and elegance, which ideally complement great cooking. Estate-bottled Cabernet Sauvignon, Merlot and Zinfandel come from the Stag's Leap district of the Napa Valley, and Chardonnay and Pinot Noir from estate vineyards in Napa's Carneros district. Clos Du Val is available nationally through Areti Wines, Ltd.

Congress Springs Vineyard
23600 Congress Springs Road
Saratoga CA 95070
408-867-1409

Corbett Canyon Vineyards
P.O. Box 315
San Luis Obispo CA 93403
805-544-5800

Cuvaison Vineyard
4550 Silverado Trail
Calistoga CA 95415
707-942-6266

De Loach Vineyards
1791 Olivet Road
Santa Rosa CA 95401
707-526-9111

Domaine Chandon
California Drive
Yountville CA 94599
707-944-8844

Dry Creek Vineyard
3770 Lambert Bridge Road
Healdsburg CA 95448
707-433-1000

Dunn Vineyards
805 White Cottage Road
Angwin CA 94508
707-965-3642

Edna Valley Vineyard
2585 Biddle Ranch Road
San Luis Obispo CA 93401
805-544-9594

Eyrie Vineyards
935 East 10th
McMinnville OR 97128
503-472-6315

Fetzer Vineyards
P.O. Box 227
Redwood Valley CA 95470
707-485-7634

Firestone Vineyard
P.O. Box 244
Los Olivos CA 93441
805-688-3940

Franciscan Vineyards
1178 Galleron Road
Rutherford CA 94573
707-963-7111

E. & J. Gallo Winery
600 Yosemite Boulevard
Modesto CA 95353
209-579-3111

Geyser Peak Winery
22280 Chianti Road
Geyserville CA 95441
707-433-6585

Girard Winery
7717 Silverado Trail
Oakville CA 94562
707-944-8577

Glen Ellen Winery
1883 London Ranch Road
Glen Ellen CA 95442
707-935-3000

Grgich Hills Cellar
1829 St. Helena Highway
Rutherford CA 94573
707-963-2784

Grgich Hills Cellar was founded in 1977 by Miljenko "Mike" Grgich and Austin Hills, of Hills Brothers Coffee. Although Grgich Hills is best known as a house of Chardonnay, the cellar is also recognized for its crisp and elegant Fume Blanc, a delightful Johannisberg Riesling and a fine Zinfandel. Cabernet

Sauvignon was recently added and since then production has increased, placing red wines in the forefront of this prestigious winery's efforts.

Groth Vineyards and Winery
P.O. Box 412
Oakville CA 94562
707-255-7466

Guenoc Winery
2100 Butts Canyon Road
Middletown CA 95461
707-987-2385

Gundlach-Bundschu Winery
2000 Denmark Street
Vineburg CA 95487
707-938-5277

Heitz Wine Cellars
500 Taplin Road
St. Helena CA 94574
707-963-3542

Hess Collection
4411 Redwood Road
Napa CA 94558
707-255-1144

Heublein Wine
12667 Road 24
Madera CA 93629
209-673-7071

William Hill Winery
P.O. Box 3989
Napa CA 94558
707-224-6565

William Hill Winery, founded in 1974, produces premium varietal Chardonnay and Cabernet Sauvignon from vineyards owned and developed by the winery. Vineyards are paramount to our winemaking philosophy for one reason: We believe that wine character and quality are determined by the vineyard, not only through the very important day-to-day control of viticultural practices, but by the even more important absolute quality potential of the vineyard itself.

Inglenook-Napa Valley
100 St. Helena Highway South
Rutherford CA 94574
707-963-4480

Iron Horse Vineyards
9786 Ross Station Road
Sebastopol CA 95472
707-887-2913

Jekel Vineyard
40155 Walnut Avenue
Greenfield CA 93927
408-674-5522

Jordan Winery
1474 Alexander Valley Road
Healdsburg CA 95448
707-433-6955

Kalin Cellars
61 Galli Drive
Novato CA 94947
415-883-3543

Kendall Jackson Winery
700 Matthews Road
Lakeport CA 95453
707-263-9333

Kistler Vineyards
997 Madrone Road
Glen Ellen CA 95442
707-996-5117

Knudsen Erath Winery
Wardon Hill Road
Dundee OR 97115
503-538-3318

F. Korbel & Brothers
13250 River Road
Guerneville CA 95446
707-887-2294

Hanns Kornell Champagne Cellar
1091 Larkmead Lane
St. Helena CA 94574
707-963-9333

Charles Krug Winery
2800 St. Helena Highway
St. Helena CA 94574
707-963-2761

Laurel Glen Vineyard
P.O. Box 548
Glen Ellen CA 95442
707-526-3914

J. Lohr
1000 Lenzen Avenue
San Jose CA 95126
408-288-5057

Lyeth Vineyard and Winery
24625 Chianti Road
Geyserville CA 95441
707-857-3562

METHODE CHAMPENOISE

Vintage 1987 ALCOHOL 12% BY VOL.
750 ml

Piper Sonoma

SONOMA COUNTY
BRUT

SONOMA COUNTY SPARKLING WINE

PRODUCED AND BOTTLED BY PIPER SONOMA, HEALDSBURG, CA. IN THE METHODE CHAMPENOISE
UNDER THE DIRECT SUPERVISION OF CHAMPAGNE PIPER HEIDSIECK, REIMS, FRANCE.

Nestled in the gently rolling hills of California's Sonoma wine country, Piper Sonoma Cellars has, since 1980, created exclusively vintage-dated American sparkling wines in the tradition of the "grande marque" champagnes of France.

Using only the finest quality Sonoma County grapes and employing the strict production rules of the centuries-old "methode champenoise" process developed in France's Champagne region, Piper Sonoma's sparkling wines reflect the same meticulous care and devotion to excellence often associated with the champagnes of its French sister company - the esteemed House of Piper-Heidsieck.

Open to visitors 7 days a week, 10:00 a.m. to 5:00 p.m., Piper Sonoma Cellars and the sleek Visitors Center offer wine enthusiasts the unique experience of seeing California sparkling wines produced with the finesse and style of the great champagnes of France, as well as the opportunity of enjoying a glass of sparkling wine on the breezy terrace or a light lunch in the Cafe du Chai.

Piper Sonoma produces the following vintage-dated products: Brut, Blanc de Noirs, Brut Reserve and Tete de Cuvee.

Louis M. Martini
St. Helena Highway South
St. Helena CA 94574
707-963-2736

Paul Masson Winery
800 South Alta Street
Gonzales CA 93926
408-675-2481

Matanzas Creek Winery
6097 Bennett Valley Road
Santa Rosa CA 95401
707-542-8242

Mayacamas Vineyards
1155 Lokoya Road
Napa CA 94558
707-224-4030

Mirassou Vineyards
3000 Aborn Road
San Jose CA 95135
408-274-4000

Robert Mondavi Winery
7801 St. Helena Highway
Oakville CA 94562
707-963-9611

The Monterey Vineyards
800 South Alta Street
Gonzales CA 93926
408-675-2481

Monticello Cellars
4242 Big Ranch Road
Napa CA 94558
707-253-2802

Morgan Winery
526 Brunken Avenue, Unit E
Salinas CA 93901
408-484-1533

Newton Winery
2555 Madrona Avenue
St. Helena CA 94574
707-963-4613

Niebaum-Coppola Estate
1460 Niebaum Lane
Rutherford CA 94573
707-963-9435

Parducci Wine Cellars
501 Parducci Road
Ukiah CA 95482
707-462-3828

J. Pedroncelli Winery
1220 Canyon Road
Geyserville CA 95441
707-857-3531

Pheasant Ridge Winery
Route 3
Lubbock TX 79401
806-746-6033

Joseph Phelps Vineyards
200 Taplin Road
St. Helena CA 94574
707-963-2745

Pindar Vineyards
P.O. Box 332
Peconic, Long Island NY 11958
516-734-6200

Pine Ridge Winery
5901 Silverado Trail
Napa CA 94558
707-253-7500

Piper-Sonoma
11447 Old Redwood Highway
Healdsburg CA 95448
707-433-8843

STAG'S LEAP WINE CELLARS

◆

Napa Valley Premium Varietals Since 1972

Contact Us Regarding Wine Availability in your Area

Tasting 10 a.m.- 4 p.m. daily

Tours by Appointment

707/944-2020

Quady Winery
13181 Road 24
Madera CA 93637
209-673-8068

Ravenswood
21415 Broadway
Sonoma CA 95476
707-938-1960

Raymond Vineyard & Cellar
849 Zinfandel Lane
St. Helena CA 94574
707-963-3141

Ridge Vineyards
17100 Monte Bello Road
Cupertino CA 95014
408-867-3233

Rutherford Hill Winery
Rutherford Hill Road
Rutherford CA 94573
707-963-9694

Sakonnet Vineyards
162 West Main Road
Little Compton RI 02837
401-635-4356

Santa Barbara County Vintners' Association
P.O. Box WINE
Los Olivos CA 93441
805-688-0881

Santa Barbara County has emerged in recent years as one of California's premier wine regions. Its 23 wineries, producing outstanding Chardonnay, Cabernet Sauvignon, Pinot Noir, Sauvignon Blanc, Riesling and a dozen other varieties, include the following labels: Au Bon Climat, Austin, Babcock, Ballard Canyon, Brander, Byron, Cambria, J. Carey, Carrari, Firestone, Foxen, Gainey, Houtz, J. Kerr, Longoria, Mosby Qupe, Rancho Sisquoc, Sanford, Santa Barbara, Santa Ynez, Stearns Wharf and Zaca Mesa.

Contact: Pam Maines Ostendorf, Executive Director

Schramsberg Vineyards
1400 Schramsberg Road
Calistoga CA 95415
707-942-4558

Seghesio Winery
14730 Grove Street
Healdsburg CA 95448
707-433-3579

Silver Oak Cellars
915 Oakville Crossroad
Oakville CA 94562
707-944-8808

Silverado Vineyards
6121 Silverado Trail
Napa CA 94558
707-257-1770

Simi Winery
16275 Healdsburg Avenue
Healdsburg CA 95448
707-433-6981

Sonoma-Cutrer Vineyards
4401 Slusser Road
Windsor CA 95492
707-528-1181

Spottswoode Vineyard and Winery
1401 Hudson
St. Helena CA 94574
707-963-0134

Stag's Leap Wine Cellars
5766 Silverado Trail
Napa CA 94558
707-944-2020

Sterling Vineyards
1111 Dunaweal Lane
Calistoga CA 95415
707-942-5151

Sutter Home Winery
277 St. Helena Highway South
St. Helena CA 94574
707-963-3104

Taylor California Cellars
800 South Alta Street
Gonzales CA 93926
408-675-2481

Taylor Wine Company
Pleasant Valley Road
Hammondsport NY 14840
212-486-1800

Tepusquet
P.O. Box 142
Santa Maria CA 93454
415-863-2220

Trefethen Vineyards Winery
1160 Oak Knoll Avenue
Napa CA 94558
707-255-7700

Vichon Winery
1595 Oakville Grade
Oakville CA 94562
707-944-2811

Wente Brothers
5565 Tesla Road
Livermore CA 94550
415-447-3603

Whitehall Lane
1563 St. Helena Highway
St. Helena CA 94574
707-963-9454

Zaca Mesa Winery
Foxen Canyon Road
Los Olivos CA 93441
805-688-9339

ZD Wines
8383 Silverado Trail
Napa CA 94558
707-963-5188

Breweries

The growing popularity of beer has brought a corresponding increase in the number of smaller American breweries producing beers and ales that cater to individual tastes across the range from light to dark to steam. The selection that follows has been compiled by Fritz Maytag of Anchor Brewing Company. The listing is alphabetical, with the notation "Microbrewery" where appropriate.

Anheuser-Busch, Inc.
1 Busch Place
St. Louis MO 63118
314-577-2000
Other locations:
Fairfield CA
Los Angeles CA
Jacksonville FL
Tampa FL
Merrimack NH
Newark NJ
Baldwinsville NY
Columbus OH
Houston TX
Williamsburg VA

Abita Brewing Company, Inc.
P.O. Box 762
Abita Springs LA 70420
504-893-3143
Microbrewery

Albuquerque Brewing and Bottling Company
637 Broadway SE
Albuquerque NM 87102
505-242-9887
Microbrewery

Alpine Village Brewing Company
833 West Torrance Boulevard
Torrance CA 90502
213-329-8881
Microbrewery

Anchor Brewing Company
1705 Mariposa Street
San Francisco CA 94107
415-863-8350

Angeles Brewing Company
10009 Conoga Avenue
Chatsworth CA 91311
818-407-0340
Microbrewery

August Shell Brewing Company, Inc.
Shell's Park
New Ulm MN 56073
507-354-5528

Blitz-Weinhard Brewing (G. Heileman Brewing Company)
1133 West Burnside Street
Portland OR 97209
503-222-4351

Bohannon Brewing Company
134 Second Avenue North
Nashville TN 37201
615-255-7561
Microbrewery

The Boston Beer Company
230 Clarendon Street
Boston MA 02113
617-522-3400

Boulder Brewing Company
2880 Wilderness Place
Boulder CO 80301
303-444-8448

Bridgeport Brewing Company & Public House
1313 Northwest Marshall
Portland OR 97209
503-241-7179
Microbrewery

British Brewing Company
6759 Bay Meadow Drive
Glen Burnie MD 21061
301-760-1195
Microbrewery

Buffalo Bill's Brewery
1082 B Street
Hayward CA 94541
415-886-9823

Capital Brewery
7734 Terrace Avenue
Middleton WI 33562
608-836-7100
Microbrewery

Catamount Brewing Company
58 South Main Street
P.O. Box 457
White River Junction VT 05001
802-296-2248
Microbrewery

Chinook Alaskan Brewing & Bottling Company
P.O. Box 1053
Douglas AK 99824
907-780-5866
Microbrewery

Cold Spring Brewing Company, Inc.
219 North Red River Avenue
Cold Spring MN 56320
612-685-8686

Adolph Coors Company
Golden CO 80401
303-279-6565

Dixie Brewing Company, Inc.
2401 Tulane Avenue
New Orleans LA 70119
504-822-8711

Eastern Brewing Corporation
334 North Washington Street
Hammonton NJ 08037
609-561-2700

Electric Dave Brewery
1-A DD Street
Bisbee AZ 85603
602-432-3606
Microbrewery

Falstaff Brewing Corporation
P.O. Box 926
Ft. Wayne IN 46801
219-424-7232

Firestone-Fletcher Brewing Company
P.O. Box 244
Los Olivos CA 93441
805-688-3940
Microbrewery

Frankenmuth Brewery
425 South Main Street
Frankenmuth MI 48734
517-652-6183
Microbrewery

D. L. Geary Brewing Company
38 Evergreen Street
Portland ME 04103
207-878-2337
Microbrewery

The Genesee Brewing Company
445 St. Paul Street
Rochester NY 14605
716-546-1030

Golden Pacific Brewing Company
5155 Doyle Street
Emeryville CA 94608
415-547-8270
Microbrewery

Hale's Ales, Ltd.
410 Washington Street
Colville WA 99114
509-684-6503
Microbrewery

Hart Brewing Company
P.O. Box 1179
Kalama WA 98625
509-673-2962

G. Heileman Brewing Company
100 Harborview Plaza
La Crosse WI 54601
608-785-1000
Other locations:
Bessy GA
Belleville IL
Evansville IN
Baltimore MD
Frankenmuth MI
St. Paul MN
San Antonio TX

Hibernia Brewing, Ltd.
318 Elm Street
P.O. Box 143
Eau Claire WI 54701
715-836-2337

Honolulu Sake Brewery Company, Ltd.
2150 Booth Road
Honolulu HI 96813
808-537-9068

Hood River Brewing Company
506 Columbia Street
Hood River OR 97031
503-386-2281
Microbrewery

Joseph Huber Brewing Company
1208 14th Avenue
Monroe WI 53566
608-325-3191

Hudepohl-Schoenling Brewing Company
1625 Central Parkway
Cincinnati OH 45214
513-241-4344

Jones Brewing Company
P.O. Box 746
Smithton PA 15479
412-872-6626

Kalamazoo Brewing Company
315 East Kalamazoo Avenue
Kalamazoo MI 49007
616-382-2338
Microbrewery

Kemper Brewing Company
P.O. Box 46809
Rollingbay WA 98110
206-697-1446
Microbrewery

Koolau Brewery
411 Puuhale Road
Kalihi-Kai
Honolulu HI 96819
808-845-5050
Microbrewery

Lakefront Brewery
818-A East Chambers Street
Milwaukee WI 53212
414-372-8800
Microbrewery

Latrobe Brewing Company
119 Jefferson Street
Latrobe PA 15650
412-537-5545

Jacob Leinenkugel Brewing Company
1 Jefferson Avenue
Chippewa Falls WI 54729
715-723-5558

The Lion, Inc.
700 North Pennsylvania Avenue
Wilkes-Barre PA 18703
717-823-8801

Maine Coast Brewing
P.O. Box 1118
Portland ME 04101
207-773-7970

Manhattan Brewing Company
40-42 Thompson Street
New York NY 10013
212-219-9250

Massachusetts Bay Brewing Company
306 North Avenue
Boston MA 02210
617-574-9551
Microbrewery

Mendocino Brewing Company
13351 South Highway 101
P.O. Box 400
Hopland CA 95449
707-744-1015

Miller Brewing Company
3939 West Highland Boulevard
Milwaukee WI 53201
414-931-200
Other locations:
Irwindale CA
Albany GA
Fulton NY
Eden NC
Ft. Worth TX

Millstream Brewing Company
P.O. Box 283
Amana IA 52203
319-622-3672

Montana Beverage, Ltd.
1439 Harris Street
Helena MT 59601
406-449-6214

Nap Town Brewing Company
3250 North Post Road, Suite 285
Indianapolis IN 46226
317-898-1235
Microbrewery

Wm. S. Newman Brewing Company, Inc.
32 Learned Street
Albany NY 12207
518-465-8501

Oldenberg Brewery
I-75 and Buttermilk Pike
Ft. Michell KY 41017
606-341-2800
Microbrewery

Old New York Brewing Company
610 West 26th Street
New York NY 10001
212-255-4100

Oregon Trail Brewery
341 2nd Street, Box 70
Corvallis OR 97330
503-758-3527
Microbrewery

Pabst Brewing Company
917 West Juneau Avenue
Milwaukee WI 53201
414-223-3500
Other locations:
Tumwater WA

Pacific Brewing
380 Imi Kala Street
P.O. Box 1137
Wailuku
Maui HI 96793
808-244-0396
Microbrewery

James Page Brewing Company
1300 Quincy Street NE
Minneapolis MN 55413
612-331-2833
Microbrewery

Pavichevich Brewing Company
383 Romans Road
Elmhurst IL 60126
708-617-5252
Microbrewery

Pearl Brewing Company
603 East Brewery Street
P.O. Box 368
Shiner TX 77984
512-594-3852

Pittsburgh Brewing Company
3340 Liberty Avenue
Pittsburgh PA 15201
412-682-7400

Portland Brewing Company
1339 Northwest Flanders Street
Portland OR 97209
503-222-7150
Microbrewery

Rainier Brewing Company
3400 Phinney Avenue North
Seattle WA 98103
206-622-2600

Red Hook Ale Brewery, Inc.
4620 Leary Way NW
Seattle WA 98107
206-784-0800

Rhomberg Brewing Company
East 4th Street Extension
P.O. Box 1248
Dubuque IA 52001
319-582-1867

Saxton Brewery
11088 Midway
Chico CA 95928
916-893-5637
Microbrewery

Schirf Brewing Company
1250 Iron Horse Drive
P.O. Box 459
Park City UT 84060
801-645-9500
Microbrewery

Sierra Nevada Brewing Company
1075 East 20th Street
Chico CA 95928
916-893-3520

The Sierra Nevada Brewing Company produces world-class ales, using only traditional and authentic brewing methods. All of our ales are brewed naturally with barley malt, hops, water and yeast—no adjuncts, additives or preservatives. Our brands:
    Sierra Nevada Pale Ale
    Sierra Nevada Porter
    Sierra Nevada Stout
    Sierra Nevada Celebration Ale
    Sierra Nevada Bigfoot Barley-
    wine Ale
    Brewpub open Tuesday through Saturday!

Snake River Brewing Company
Route 5, Box 30-A
Caldwell ID 83605
208-459-7234

Sprecher Brewing Company
730 West Oregon Street
Milwaukee WI 53204
414-272-2337

Stanislaus Brewing Company
3454 Shoemake Avenue
Modesto CA 95351
415-422-7784

Stevens Point Brewery
2617 Water Street
Stevens Point WI 54481
715-344-9310

Stoudt Brewery
P.O. Box 809
Adamstown PA 19501
215-484-4387
Microbrewery

Straub Brewery, Inc.
303 Sorg Street
St. Mary's PA 15857
814-834-2875

The Stroh Brewery Company
100 River Place
Detroit MI 48207
313-446-2000
Other locations:
Van Nuys CA
Tampa FL
St. Paul MN
Winston-Salem NC
Allentown PA
Memphis TN
Longview TX

Summit Brewing Company
2264 University Avenue
St. Paul MN 55114
612-645-5029
Microbrewery

Tri-City Brewing Company
409 West Railroad Avenue
Kennewick WA 99336
509-586-1803
Microbrewery

Under the Oaks Brewery
415 East Villanova Road
Ojai CA 93023
805-646-4027
Microbrewery

**Val Blatz Brewing Company
(G. Heileman Brewing Company)**
1515 North 10th Street
Milwaukee WI 53205
414-263-8000

Vernon Valley Brewery
Route 94, Box 1100
Cobblestone Village
Vernon NJ 07462
201-827-0034
Microbrewery

Virginia Brewing Company
1373 London Bridge Road
Virginia Beach VA 23456
804-427-5230

**The West End Brewing Company/
F. X. Matt Brewing Company**
811 Edward Street
Utica NY 13502
315-732-3181

Widmer Brewing Company
1405 Northwest Lovejoy
Portland OR 97209
503-227-7276
Microbrewery

Yakima Brewing & Malting Company
25 North Front Street
Yakima WA 98901
509-575-1900

D. G. Yuengling & Son, Inc.
Fifth and Mahantongo Streets
Pottsville PA 17901
717-622-4141

Wines and Spirits Importers

This selection of United States wines and spirits importers has been compiled from several sources: the *National Beverage Marketing Directory*, published by Beverage Marketing, 2670 Commercial Avenue, Mingo Junction OH 43938; *Jobson's Liquor Handbook*, published by Jobson Publishing Corp., 352 Park Avenue South, New York NY 10010; and *Restaurants & Institutions 1989 Buyer's Guide*, published by Cahners Publications, 1350 East Touhy Avenue, Des Plaines IL 60017.

The listing is alphabetical by company name and includes the brand names of the major wines and spirits represented by each importer.

**Austin, Nichols & Company/
Pernod Ricard**
156 East 46th Street
New York NY 10017
212-455-9400
Brands include: Wild Turkey liqueur

Bacardi Imports, Inc.
2100 Biscayne Boulevard
Miami FL 33137
305-573-8511
Brands include: Bacardi rums, Martini & Rossi vermouth, Castillo rum, Don Emilio tequila, O'Darby liqueur, Nassau Royale liqueur

**Barton Brands, Ltd./
Amalgamated Distilled Products, Ltd.**
55 East Monroe Street
Chicago IL 60603
312-346-9200
Brands include: Very Old Barton, Kentucky Gentleman, Colonel Lee, Tom Moore bourbons and whiskies, Highland Mist and Glenfarclas single malt scotches, Camus cognac, Montezuma white and gold tequila and triple sec, Barton gin, rum, vodka and flavored schnapps

**James B. Beam Distilling Company/
American Brands, Inc.**
500 North Michigan Avenue
Chicago IL 60611
312-948-8888
Brands include: Jim Beam and Beam's Black Label bourbons, Aalborg akvavit, Beam's Choice bourbon, Beam's 8 Star blended whiskey, Jim Beam rye, Canadian Silk whisky, Cheverny brandy, Kamora imported coffee liqueur, Gammel Dansk bitters, Dark Eyes vodka

Brown-Foreman Beverage Company
P.O. Box 1080
Louisville KY 40201
502-774-7950
Brands include: Jack Daniels Tennessee whiskey, Korbel California champagne and brandy, Bols liqueurs, Southern Comfort liqueur, Early Times Kentucky whiskey, Noilly Prat vermouth, Canadian Mist Canadian whisky, Pepe Lopez tequila, Bolla wines

Carillon Importers, Inc.
Glenpointe Center West
Teaneck NJ 07666
201-836-7799
Brands include: Grand Marnier and Creme de Grand Marnier liqueurs, La Grande Passion liqueur, Marnier-Lapostolle VS and VSOP cognac and Armagnac XO, Absolut and Absolut Peppar vodkas, Bombay gin, Achaia Clauss ouzo, O. P. Anderson aquavit, Skane aquavit

Christian Brothers Sales Company

100 St. Helena Highway South,
Box 391
St. Helena CA 94574
707-963-4480
Brands include: Christian Brothers brandy, Otard cognac, Jacquart champagne, Chateau LaSalle wine, Christian Brothers wines, ports, sherries, vermouths, sparkling and premium wines, Mont LaSalle generic wines

The Distillers Somerset Group

1114 Avenue of the Americas
New York NY 10036
212-997-0900
Brands include: Appleton Jamaica rums, Johnny Walker Red Label and Black Label scotches, Tanqueray gin, Crawford's scotch, Bell's scotch, Pimm's cups, Cakebread Cellars wines, San Martin wines, Concannon wines, Cynar aperitif, Sambuca Sarti liqueur

Glenmore Distilleries Company

1700 Citizens Plaza
Louisville KY 40202
502-589-0130
Brands include: Kentucky Tavern, Yellowstone and Mellow Mash bourbons, Old Thompson blended whiskey, Glenmore gin and vodka, Mr. Boston brandy, flavored brandies, gin, vodka, rum and cocktails, Boston schnapps and cordials, Felipe II brandy, Gavilan tequila, Corbett Canyon wines

Fleischmann Distilling Company (Glenmore Distilleries Company)

Brands include: Fleischmann's gin, Royal vodka, brandy, Preferred 90 and 80 blended whiskies, Canadian Ltd. U.S.-bottled Canadian, Amaretti de Amore liqueur, Bourbon Supreme, Dunphy's Irish Cream liqueur, Denaka imported vodka

Heublein, Inc. National Accounts Division

16 Munson Road
Farmington CT 06032
203-240-5000
Brands include: Smirnoff, Silver, de Czar and Special Reserve vodkas, Wild Turkey bourbon and rye, Arrow cordials, schnapps and flavored brandies, Heublein cocktails, Club cocktails, Popov vodka, Milshire gin, Black Velvet Canadian whisky, Jose Cuervo tequila, Irish Mist liqueur, Inglenook Vineyards Napa Valley, Inglenook Navalle, Beaulieu Vineyards and Almaden Vineyards wines

Kobrand Corporation

134 East 40th Street
New York NY 10016
212-490-9300
Brands include: Taittinger champagne, Alize de France, Louis Jadot burgundies, Deinhard German wines, Taylor port, Bollini Italian wines, Bouvet brut, Cakebread Cellars of California, Maitre d'Estournel, Albert Pic chablis

McCormick Distilling Company/ Universal Importing Company

Box 41
Weston MO 64098
816-386-2276
Brands include: McCormick Gold Label, Green Label and Signature X bourbons, McCormick scotch, Canadian and blended whiskies, gin, vodka, rum, tequila, brandy and grain alcohol, B. J. Holladay bourbon, Platte Valley corn whiskey, Stillbrook bourbon, Ron Rio rum, Rio Grande tequila

Premiere Wine Merchants

888 Seventh Avenue
New York NY 10106
212-246-7770
Brands include: Remy Martin cognacs, Champagne Krug, Charles Heidsieck champagne, Piper Heidsieck champagne, Piper Sonoma California sparkling wines, Mt. Gay rum, Macallan single malt scotch, Cointreau and Galliano liqueurs

Schenley Industries

12770 Merit Drive
Dallas TX 75251
214-450-6500
Brands include: Old Charter, Charter 10 and I. W. Harper bourbons, George Dickel Nos. 8 and 12 Tennessee whiskey, Schenley Reserve blended whiskey, Schenley vodka, 90-proof gin and cordials, Coronet brandy, Cruzan and Old St. Croix rums, Dewar's White Label, 12-year-old Ancestor and Peter Dawson scotches, Ole tequila, Dubonnet aperitif

Schieffelin and Somerset Company

30 Cooper Square
New York NY 10003
212-477-7711
Brands include: Moet & Chandon champagne, Hennessy cognac, Sichel German wine, Blue Nun, Sichel French wine, Simi, Domaine Chandon sparkling wine, Glenmorangie scotch, Petite liqueur, Dom Ruinart champagne, Marie Brizard liqueurs

The House of Seagram

375 Park Avenue
New York NY 10152
212-572-7000
Brands include: Seagram's V.O., Seagram's 7 Crown and Crown Royal whiskies, Seagram's gin, Seagram's imported vodkas, The Glenlivet scotch, Myers' Original dark rum, Jameson and Jameson 1780 Special Reserve Irish whiskies, Mumm VSOP cognac, Chivas Regal, Calvert gin, Four Roses whiskey, Leroux brandy, Lord Calvert Canadian whisky, Passport scotch, Ronrico rum, Burnett's gin

The Seagram Classics Wine Company (House of Seagram)

3 Gannett Drive
White Plains NY 10604
914-641-4372
Brands include: Monterey Vineyards, Sterling Vineyards, Mumm champagnes, Barton & Guestier, Domaine Mumm

Hiram Walker, Inc.

P.O. Box 33006
Detroit MI 48232
313-965-6611
Brands include: Imperial blended whiskey, Walker's Deluxe bourbon, Ten High bourbon, Lauder's scotch, Royal Canadian whisky, Two Fingers tequila, Hiram Walker cordials and fruit-flavored brandies, Canadian Club whisky, Praline liqueur

The Buckingham Wile Company/ Whitbread, Inc.

1 Hollow Lane
Lake Success NY 11042
516-222-8142
Brands include: Cutty Sark Scots whisky, Molinari Sambuca and Waterford Irish Cream liqueurs, Dry Sack sherry, Bollinger champagne, Metaxa liqueurs, Montgomery Calvados apple brandy, Murphy's Irish whisky, Robertson's port

143
Cooking Schools
Professional;
Professional & Avocational

151
University Home Economics
Departments

155
University Restaurant and
Hotel Management Schools

Help yourself...

IRENA CHALMERS, INC.

M·E·N·U

Irena Chalmers

Compiled this "Food Professional's Guide."
"Wittiest lecturer and wisest forecaster of food trends."
Author of "The Great American Food Almanac."
Winner of nine Tastemaker awards for cookbook excellence.
President elect of the
International Association of Culinary Professionals.
Winner of 1989 Woman of the Year in Food Award.

NEWSLETTERS

We will design, write and produce
a newsletter for your company, restaurant, association, school
or business. Our clients include The Rockefeller Center Club,
The Rainbow Room, La Varenne (Paris) and IACP.

BOOKS

**Cookbook
Consultant
Custom-Made
books
Directories
Translations**
Everything to do with food
in print, from concept to
bound books. Our clients
include Waldenbooks,
Harper & Row,
Viking/Penguin, Barrons,
Publications International,
Prentice Hall, General
Electric, Donvier, Le Creuset.

FOOD RESEARCH

Our experienced staff will find answers
to your questions. We will conduct a
survey, compile a study or write an after-
dinner speech.
**Facts about Food.
People, Products and
Services located
promptly...**

INFORMATION

Write to Irena Chalmers, 305 Second
Avenue, New York, N.Y. 10003 or call
(212) 529-4666.

Cooking Schools

These days, American chefs are training at American schools and displaying their credentials with pride, and more and more professional schools are offering avocational training as well. Accordingly, this listing has three divisions: schools that offer professional training with a diploma or certificate; schools that grant professional qualifications and also accept students with an avocational interest in cooking; and schools that are for avocational cooks only.

The first two lists are alphabetical by name of cooking school; for convenience, the avocational list is alphabetical by name within regions. A few overseas schools that are almost exclusively patronized by Americans are also included, with their United States contact addresses.

The lists have been compiled by Peter Kump, founder of Peter Kump's New York Cooking School and president of The James

Beard Foundation, from schools listed in *The Guide to Cooking Schools*, and those who are members of the national organization of cooking schools, the International Association of Cooking Professionals (IACP), 304 West Liberty Street, Suite 301, Louisville KY 40202. The IACP grants certification to qualified teachers; IACP Certified Cooking Professionals are indicated by CCP in the lists.

The Guide to Cooking Schools is published by Shaw Associates, 625 Biltmore Way, Suite 1406FP, Coral Gables FL 33134.

PROFESSIONAL

**Academy of Culinary Arts—
Atlantic Community College**
Mays Landing NJ 08330
609-343-4944
Contact:
Frank Verheul, Director

**Baltimore's International
Culinary College**
19-21 South Gay Street
Baltimore MD 21202
301-752-4710
Contact:
Roger Chylinski, President

**Boston University Seminars
in the Culinary Arts**
Boston University Metropolitan College
755 Commonwealth Avenue, Suite B-3
Boston MA 02215
617-353-4130
Contact:
Rebecca Alssid, Director

California Culinary Academy
625 Polk Street
San Francisco CA 94102
415-771-3555
Contact:
Thomas Bloom, President

**The Cambridge School
of Culinary Arts**
2020 Massachusetts Avenue
Cambridge MA 02140
617-354-3836
Contact:
Roberta Dowling, Executive
and Owner

**Clark College
Culinary Arts Department**
1800 East McLoughlin Boulevard
Vancouver WA 98663
206-699-0304
Contact:
Larry Maines, Director

The French Culinary Institute
462 Broadway
New York NY 10013
212-219-8890
Contact:
Dorothy Cann, President

The French Culinary Institute offers a six-month intensive course in classical technique under the guidance of master chef, author and educator Jacques Pepin. Our European curriculum, developed in conjunction with the Ferrandi Parisian cooking school, emphasizes small classes and hands-on training. Students practice in our SoHo restaurant **L'Ecole**, with direction from renowned sommelier Roger Dagorn.

National accreditation. Classes offered day, evening and weekend, full or part-time. Financial and placement assistance available to qualified students.

**Johnson & Wales University
Culinary Arts Division**
1 Washington Avenue
Providence RI 02905
401-456-1130
Contact:
Paula Keogh, Director of
Communications

New England Culinary Institute
250 Main Street
Montpelier VT 05602
802-223-6324
Contact:
Francis Voigt, President

The School for American Chefs

Directed by internationally known chef, author and PBS television personality Madeleine Kamman, the School for American Chefs provides graduate study programs for professional American chefs. The chefs are selected as a result of competition in regional menu design and state-ment of professional goals.

❑

Ten two-week scholarship classes, limited to four chefs per seminar, are held annually. Wine and food pairing is discussed, as well as a focus on learning to "cook to the wine."

❑

Also, intimate three day "Wine Country Cuisine" seminars are held throughout the year for amateur enthusiasts.

"Without a doubt, she's the best cooking teacher in the country. And to top it off, she's a brilliant cook."
Michael Bauer
Executive Food Editor
San Francisco
Chronicle

For further information:
Antonia Allegra
Director of
Culinary Programs
Beringer Vineyards
P.O. Box 111
St. Helena,
California 94574
707-963-7115

New York Food and Hotel Management School
154 West 14th Street
New York NY 10011
212-675-6655
Contact:
Joseph M. Monaco, President

New York Restaurant School
27 West 34th Street
New York NY 10001
212-947-7097
Contact:
J. R. McCarthen, President

The Restaurant School
2129 Walnut Street
Philadelphia PA 19103
215-561-3446
Contact:
Daniel Liberatoscioli,
President

Rhode Island School of Design Culinary Arts Apprenticeship
55 Angell Street
Providence RI 02903
Contact:
Terrence Thompson, Assistant Director,
Culinary Arts Program

School for American Chefs
P.O. Box 111
St. Helena CA 94574
707-963-7115
Contact:
Antonia Allegra, Director
of Culinary Programs

Scottsdale Culinary Institute
4141 North Scottsdale Road,
Suite 110
Scottsdale AZ 85251
602-990-3773
Contact:
Elizabeth Liete, President

Western Culinary Institute
1316 Southwest 13th Avenue
Portland OR 97201
503-223-2245
Contact:
Nick Fluge, Director

Wine World, Inc.
Beringer Vineyards
P.O. Box 111
St. Helena CA 94574
707-963-7115
Contact:
Antonia Allegra, Director of
Culinary Programs

PROFESSIONAL & AVOCATIONAL

The Chocolate Gallery
34 West 22nd Street
New York NY 10010
212-675-2253
Contact:
Joan Mansour, President

Connecticut Culinary Institute
230 Farmington Avenue
Farmington CT 06032
203-677-7869
Contact:
David M. Tine, President

The Cooking and Hospitality Institute of Chicago
858 North Orleans
Chicago IL 60610
312-944-0882
Contact:
Linda Califiore, President

Culinary Arts Program Department UCLA Extension
10995 Le Comte Avenue, Suite 414
Los Angeles CA 90024
213-206-8120
Contact:
Deb Mincey, Director

UCLA Extension's Culinary Arts Program provides professional culinary and hospitality education to individuals entering the foodservice industry. Students may apply to certificate programs in either catering or profes-sional cooking. Courses range from basic principles in cooking and catering to specific disciplines, such as garde-manger, advanced baking, and computer applications in the foodservice industry.

Graduates have been placed in such noted restaurants as Spago and L'Orangerie, and instructors are all well-known industry professionals.

The Culinary Institute of America (CIA)
North Road
P.O. Box 53
Hyde Park NY 12538
914-452-9430
Contact:
Ferdinand Metz, President

The Culinary School of Kendall College

2408 Orrington Avenue
Evanston IL 60201
708-866-1300
Contact:
John Draz, Director

International Pastry Arts Center

525 Executive Boulevard
Elmsford NY 10523
914-347-3737
Contact:
Jean M. Harper, Director

L'Academie de Cuisine, Inc.

5021 Wilson Lane
Bethesda MD 20814
301-986-9490
Contact:
Francois Dionot, CCP, President

La Varenne Cooking School, USA

P.O. Box 25574
Washington DC 20007
202-333-9077
Contact:
Anne Willan, CCP, Director

Libby Hillman Cooking School

P.O. Box 135
Whitingham VT 05361
802-368-7128
Contact:
Libby Hillman, Director

Memphis Culinary Academy

1252 Peabody Avenue
Memphis TN 38104
901-722-8892
Contact:
Joseph Carey,
    President and Director
Elaine Wallace-Carey,
    President and Director

The Natural Gourmet Cookery School

48 West 21st Street, 2nd Floor
New York NY 10010
212-645-5170
Contact:
Annemarie Colbin, Director

The Natural Gourmet Cookery School, known as "the Cordon Bleu of health-supportive cooking," offers a wide variety of cooking classes and lectures covering natural foods, vegetarian, fish, high-fiber, "zero" cholesterol, sugar-free, macrobiotic and "alternative" dietary topics.

Evening and daytime classes. Professional chefs and teaching pro-

grams. Menu consulting and recipe development. Catalog available.

Culinary Arts at the New School

100 Greenwich Avenue
New York NY 10011
212-255-4141
Contact:
Gary Goldberg, Director

Peter Kump's New York Cooking School

307 East 92nd Street
New York NY 10128
212-410-4601
Contact:
Peter Kump, CCP, President

The Postilion School of Culinary Art

220 Old Pioneer Road
Fond du Lac WI 54935
414-922-4170
Contact:
Liane Kuony, Director

Tante Marie's Cooking School

271 Francisco Street
San Francisco CA 94133
415-788-6699
Contact:
Mary Risley

Wilton School of Cake Decorating and Confectionery Art

2240 West 75th Street
Woodridge IL 60517
708-963-7100
Contact:
Zella Junkin, Director

Zona Spray Cooking School

140 North Main Street
Hudson OH 44236
216-650-1665
Contact:
Zona Spray, CCP, Owner

AVOCATIONAL

NORTHEAST

CONNECTICUT

The Complete Kitchen

863 Post Road
Darien CT 06820
203-655-4055
Contact:
Anne Brown, Director

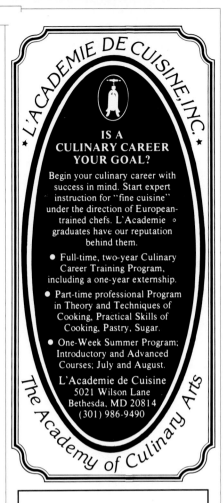

Entertaining Seminars with Martha Stewart
10 Saugatuck Avenue
Westport CT 06880
203-222-7332
Contact:
Carolyn Kelly, Director

Hay Day's Cooking School
907 Post Road East
Westport CT 06880
203-227-4258
Contact:
Sallie Van Rensselaer, Owner

Hsu's Cookery
37 Old Avon Village
Avon CT 06001
203-677-1350
Contact:
Hsu S. Chiang, Director

International Cooking with Polly Stewart Fritch
1 Scott Lane
Greenwich CT 06831
203-661-7742
Contact:
Polly Stewart Fritch, Director

Ronnie Fein School of Creative Cooking
438 Hunting Ridge Road
Stamford CT 06903
203-322-7114
Contact:
Ronnie Fein, Director

The Silo, Inc.
44 Upland Road
Hunt Hill Farm, RR 3
New Milford CT 06776
203-355-0300
Contact:
Ruth Henderson, Owner
Sandra Daniels, Director
   of Cooking School

The Wood Creek Cooking School
71 Judson Lane
Bethlehem CT 06751
203-266-5904
Contact:
Terry Frank, Owner/Director

MAINE

The Whip and Spoon
161 Commercial Street
Portland ME 04101
207-774-4020
Contact:
Sonia Robertson, Director

MASSACHUSETTS

Jin Mi Oriental Cooking School
313 Walnut Street
Newton MA 02160
617-965-0515
Contact:
J. Soon Cho, Owner/Director

Marge Cohen
P.O. Box 53
Needham Heights MA 02194
617-449-2688
Contact:
Marge Cohen, Director

Peggy Glass Cooking School
72 Williston Road
Newton MA 02166
617-964-8171
Contact:
Peggy K. Glass, Owner

NEW HAMPSHIRE

A Taste of the Mountains
Snow Village Inn
Box T.O.M.
Snowville NH 03849
603-447-2818
Contact:
Steven Raichlen, Director

NEW JERSEY

Carole Walter
8 Murphy Court
West Orange NJ 07052
Contact:
Carole Walter, CCP

Cooktique
9 West Railroad Avenue
Tenafly NJ 07670
201-568-7990
Contact:
Cathy McCauley, Owner
Al Cappellini, Owner

Kings Cookingstudio
2 Dedrick Place
West Caldwell NJ 07006
201-575-3320
Contact:
Mary Lantz, Director

Peter Kump's New York Cooking School in New Jersey
36 Orchard Drive
Saddle River NJ 07458
201-934-7025
Contact:
Gaynor Grant, Instructor

NEW YORK

A La Bonne Cocotte
23 Eighth Avenue
New York NY 10014
212-675-7736
Contact:
Lydie P. Marshall, Owner

Anna Amendolara Nurse Cooking Classes
414 East 2nd Street
Brooklyn NY 11218
718-436-1054
Contact:
Anna Amendolara Nurse

Carol's Cuisine, Inc.
1571 Richmond Road
Staten Island NY 10304
718-979-5600
Contact:
Carol Frazzetta, Director

Club Cuisine
244 Madison Avenue
New York NY 10016
212-286-0214
Contact:
Michele Lyster, Owner

De Gustibus at Macy's
343 East 74th Street, Suite 9G
New York NY 10021
212-439-1714
Contact:
Arlene Feltman, Director

Giuliano Bugialli's Cooking in Florence
53 Wooster Street
New York NY 10013
212-334-6430
Contact:
Patrice Morini, Director

New Mexican Tex-Mex Cookery School
500 East 77th Street, Suite 2324
New York NY 10162
212-628-5374
Contact:
Jane Butel Associates

Richard Grausman
155 West 68th Street
New York NY 10023
212-873-2434
Contact:
Richard Grausman

The Wire Whisk
155 Main Street
Northport NY 11768
516-757-5050
Contact:
Kathryn Sedlock, Director

PENNSYLVANIA

Charlotte Ann Albertson's Cooking School
P.O. Box 27
Wynnewood PA 19096
215-649-9290
Contact:
Charlotte Ann Albertson, Director

Jacqualin et Cie
Route 202
P.O. Box 303
Lahaska PA 18931
215-794-7316
Contact:
Jacqualin Giles, Director

The Kitchen Shoppe and Cooking School
101 Shady Lane
Carlisle PA 17013
717-243-0906
Contact:
Suzanne Hoffman, Owner

Rania's To Go
100 Central Square
Pittsburgh PA 15228
412-531-2222
Contact:
Rania Harris, Director

SOUTH

ALABAMA

Southern Living Cooking School
P.O. Box 2581
Birmingham AL 35202
205-877-6576
Contact:
Martha Johnston, Director

DELAWARE

Creative Cooking: The Cooking School
Branmar Plaza
1812 Marsh Road
Wilmington DE 19810
302-475-0390
Contact:
Pat Tabibian, Director

FLORIDA

Ariana's Cooking School
7251 Southwest 57th Court
Miami FL 33143
305-667-5957
Contact:
Ariana Kumpis, President/Owner

Cuisine Classics Cooking School
401 Burns Court
Sarasota FL 34236
813-349-7626
Contact:
Sally Fine, Director

Mimi's
1984 San Marco Boulevard
Jacksonville FL 32207
904-399-1218
Contact:
Mimi Kersun, Owner

GEORGIA

Diane Wilkinson's Cooking School
4365 Harris Trail
Atlanta GA 30327
404-233-0366
Contact:
Diane Wilkinson, Owner

Kitchen Fare Cooking School
2385 Peachtree Road NE
Atlanta GA 30305
404-233-8849
Contact:
Laura Shapiro, Owner

Things Are Cooking!
5475 Chamblee Dunwoody Road
Dunwoody GA 30338
404-394-2665
Contact:
Jana Graves, Director

LOUISIANA

Kay Ewing's Everyday Gourmet
9259 Florida Boulevard
Baton Rouge LA 70815
504-927-4371
Contact:
Kay Ewing, Director

The New Orleans School of Cooking
620 Decatur Street
New Orleans LA 70130
504-525-2665
Contact:
Joe Cahn and Karen Cahn, Owners

Now in their eleventh year, our nationally acclaimed three-hour Cajun/Creole cooking classes are concise and educational. We can arrange more intensive, week-long programs for professionals, or bring Louisiana cuisine to your location. We are often viewed as a comprehensive resource on the state's products and cuisine and offer the largest selection of Louisiana cookbooks, food products and music available anywhere. Wholesale prices are available. Call or write for our Louisiana Products Catalog.

Tout de Suite a la Microwave, Inc.
P.O. Box 30121
Lafayette LA 70593
318-984-2903
Contact:
Jean Kellner Durkee, Director

Wok and Whisk, Inc.
6301 Perkins Road
Baton Rouge LA 70808
504-769-5122
Contact:
Barbara Peterson, Director

MARYLAND

Cake Cottage, Inc.
Putty Hill Plaza
7918 Belair Road
Baltimore MD 21236
301-882-9232
Contact:
Donna Parish and Charlie Parish, Directors

The Chinese Cookery, Inc.
14209 Sturtevant Road
Silver Spring MD 20904
301-236-5311
Contact:
Joan Shih

NORTH CAROLINA

Cooks Corner, Ltd.
401 State Street
Greensboro NC 27405
919-272-2665
Contact:
Mary James Lawrence, Owner

The Kitchen Cupboard
654 Arlington Boulevard
Greensville NC 27858
919-756-1310
Contact:
Betty Grossnickle, CCP, Director

The Stocked Pot & Company
111-B Reynolda Village
Winston Salem NC 27106
919-722-3663
Contact:
Donald C. McMillan, President

SOUTH CAROLINA

In Good Taste
1124 Sam Rittenberg Boulevard
Charleston SC 29407
803-763-5597
Contact:
Jackie Boyd, Owner

TENNESSEE

Conte-Philips Cooking School
73 White Bridge Road
Nashville TN 37205
615-352-5837
Contact:
Andrea Conte, Owner

Cooking With Class
9700 Kingston Pike West
Knoxville TN 37922
615-693-9866
Contact:
Kathy L. Dittmar, Director

Culinary Classics Cooking School
1145 Balbade Drive
Nashville TN 37215
615-297-3893
Contact:
Gloria Olson, Owner

VIRGINIA

Dolores Kostelni Cooking School
Turtle Brook, Route 4
P.O. Box 251
Lexington VA 24450
703-261-2304
Contact:
Dolores Kostelni, Owner/Director

Dolores Kostelni Cooking School
Christ Episcopal Church
Franklin Road and Washington Street
Roanoke VA 24014
703-343-0159
Contact:
Dolores Kostelni, Owner/Director

World of Cuisine
5833 Colfax Avenue
Alexandria VA 22311
703-998-3079
Contact:
Marcia Fox, Owner/Director

WEST VIRGINIA

The Greenbrier Cooking School
White Sulphur Springs WV 24986
304-536-7809
Contact:
Julie Dannenbaum, Director

The Greenbrier Culinary Apprenticeship Program requires two seasons at the hotel. To enter, the apprentice must have completed at least three years of practical experience after graduating from high school or higher education in a food-related curriculum. The program includes: demonstrations, lectures, specialized kitchen work, a culinary competition and performance evaluations. Job opportunities are available to graduates. Submit applications, references and recommendations to Hartmut Handke, C.M.C., Executive Chef.

MIDWEST

ILLINOIS

Chez Madelaine
211 North Washington Street
Hinsdale IL 60521
708-325-4177
Contact:
Madelaine Bullwinkel, Owner

Chez Madelaine holds weekly technique-oriented classes in home cooking for six students, following a mixed demonstration and participation format. Attention is given to health issues, taste awareness and food chemistry.

An eight-page bimonthly newsletter, *Madelaine's Kitchen Secrets*, complements the school program with simple but elegant recipes seasoned with technical notes, nutrition news and historical asides. (Sample issues available upon request.)

Cooking Classes with Nancy Eichler
29455 Baker Lane
Lake Fairfield Estates
Mundelein IL 60060
708-526-1461
Contact:
Nancy C. Eichler, Owner

Dumas Pere L'Ecole de la Cuisine Francaise
1129 Depot Street
Glenview IL 60025
708-729-4823
Contact:
Chef Juan Snowden, Director

Kitchen Conservatory
6930 West Main Street
Belleville IL 62223
708-398-2665
Contact:
Carol Hess, Owner

La Cucina Italiana, Inc.
1 Prudential Plaza
130 East Randolph Drive
Chicago IL 60601
312-819-4121
Contact:
Maria Battaglia, President

Oriental Food Market and Cooking School
2801 West Howard Street
Chicago IL 60645
312-274-2826
Contact:
Pansy and Chu-Yen Luke, Owners

La Venture
5100 West Jarlath
Skokie IL 60077
708-679-8845
Contact:
Sandra Bisceglie, Director

What's Cooking
226 Birchwood Road
Hinsdale IL 60521
708-986-1595
Contact:
Ruth Law, Owner

INDIANA

Country Kitchen
3225 Wells Street
Fort Wayne IN 46808
219-482-4835
Contact:
Vi Whittington, Owner

IOWA

Chez Mimi Gormezano Cooking School
621 Holt
Iowa City IA 52246
319-351-2778
Contact:
Mimi Gormezano, Director

Cooking with Liz Clark
116 Concert Street
Keokuk IA 52632
319-524-4716
Contact:
Elizabeth M. Clark, Director

MICHIGAN

Kitchen Glamour...The Cook's World
26770 Grand River
Redford Township MI 48240
313-537-1300
Contact:
Toula Patsalis, Director

Nell Benedict Cooking Classes
The Community House
380 South Bates Street
Birmingham MI 48009
313-644-5832
Contact:
Nell Benedict, Instructor

MINNESOTA

**Hotel Sofitel School of
French Culinary Skills**
5601 West 78th Street
Bloomington MN 55435
612-835-1900
Contact:
Diane Papin, Admissions Director

Thrice Cooking School
850 Grand Avenue
St. Paul MN 55105
612-228-1333
Contact:
Lois Lee, Director

MISSOURI

Dierbergs School of Cooking
11481 Olive Street Road
Creve Coeur MO 63141
314-432-6561
Contact:
Jeannie Rader, Director

Dierbergs School of Cooking
1322 Clarkson/Clayton Center
Ellisville MO 63011
314-394-2254
Contact:
Nancy Lorenz, Director

Dierbergs School of Cooking
12420 Tesson Ferry Road
St. Louis MO 63128
314-849-3600
Contact:
Lorene Edwards, Director

Dierbergs School of Cooking
290 Mid Rivers Drive
St. Peters MO 63376
314-928-1117
Contact:
Kathy Hasick, Director

**Suzanne Corbett—
Culinary Concepts**
1602 Locust Street, Suite 214
St. Louis MO 63103
314-487-5205
Contact:
Suzanne Corbett, Director

Take Pleasure in Cooking
8612 East 84th Street
Kansas City MO 64138
816-353-6022
Contact:
Gloria Martin, Director

OHIO

American Cooking School
1701 East 12th Street,
Suite 4JW
Cleveland OH 44114
216-771-1001
Contact:
Donna Adams, Owner/President

La Belle Pomme
Lazarus
P.O. Box 16538
Columbus OH 43216
614-463-2665
Contact:
Betty G. Rosbottom, Director

Gourmet Curiosities, Etc.
Starlite Plaza
5700 Monroe Street
Sylvania OH 43560
419-882-2323
Contact:
Bruce C. Williams, Owner

WISCONSIN

Creative Cuisine—Karen Maihofer
9458 North Regent Court
Milwaukee WI 53217
414-352-0975
Contact:
Karen Maihofer, Owner

SOUTHWEST

ARIZONA

Les Gourmettes Cooking School
6610 North Central Avenue
Phoenix AZ 85012
602-240-6767
Contact:
Barbara Pool Fenzl, Director

The Tasting Spoon
P.O. Box 44013
Tucson AZ 85733
602-327-8174
Contact:
Virginia Selby, Director

TEXAS

Cooking with Amber, Inc.
6211 West Northwest Highway,
Suite C-120
Dallas TX 75225
214-363-3687
Contact:
Amber C. Robinson, Director

The Cooking School
6003-A Berkshire Lane
Dallas TX 75225
214-361-9848
Contact:
Ellen S. McDowell, Director

**The French Apron School
of Cooking**
1424 Shady Oaks Lane
Fort Worth TX 76107
817-877-0838
Contact:
Louise Lamensdorf, Director

Judy Terrell's School of Cooking
2405 Clublake Trail
McKinney TX 75070
214-542-1530
Contact:
Judy Terrell, Owner

Le Panier
7275 Brompton Road
Houston TX 77025
713-664-9848
Contact:
LaVerl Daily, Director

Macrobiotics Center of Texas
3815 Garrott
Houston TX 77006
713-523-0171
Contact:
Janice Jamail, Co-Owner
Catherine Willhite, Co-Owner

MOUNTAIN STATES

COLORADO

Healy-Lucullus School of French Cooking
840 Cypress Drive
Boulder CO 80303
303-494-9222
Contact:
Bruce Healy, Director

The Little Kitchen
Broadmoor Hotel
Colorado Springs CO 80901
719-577-5751
Contact:
Nancy Gilbert, Director

Nonesuch, Ltd.
257 Filmore Street
Denver CO 80206
303-388-0959
Contact:
Bernice Lane, Director

WEST COAST

CALIFORNIA

Bonnie Renoir's Cordon Bleu Cooking School
Le Meridien Hotel
4500 MacArthur Boulevard
Newport Beach CA 92660
714-850-4131
Contact:
Bonnie Renoir, President

Epicurean Cooking School
8759 Melrose Avenue
Los Angeles CA 90069
213-659-5990
Contact:
Shelley Janson, Owner

Flo Braker Baking
1441 Edgewood Drive
Palo Alto CA 94301
415-327-1015
Contact:
Flo Braker, Owner

The Great Chefs at Robert Mondavi Winery
P.O. Box 106
Oakville CA 94562
707-944-2866
Contact:
Axel Fabre, Director

More than a cooking school...**The Great Chefs at the Robert Mondavi**

Winery is an ongoing series of events where the elegant presentation of wine and food in a convivial atmosphere is enhanced by a unique and intimate learning experience. We offer week events with two-, three- and five-day segments, as well as long weekend and weekend events featuring world-renowned chefs. Four to six programs are featured each year during Spring and Fall.

Judi Kaufman & Company
400 South Beverly Drive,
Suite 214
Beverly Hills CA 90210
213-858-7787
Contact:
Judi Kaufman, President

Judith Ets-Hokin Culinary Company
3525 California Street
San Francisco CA 94118
415-668-3191
Contact:
Judy Ets-Hokin, Owner

A professional cooking school especially for the home cook.

Hotel-restaurant chefs have an easier time than the home chef, because entire staffs help to get out a single dish.

At Judith Ets-Hokin's we appreciate that students may be juggling a career, children, household chores, daily cooking and entertaining. You will learn more efficient, professional methods and techniques, adapted especially for the home cook.

We don't just teach recipes. We teach how to cook—and you'll have fun learning. We guarantee it.

Kake Kreations
21835 Sherman Way
Canoga Park CA 91303
818-346-7621
Contact:
Hilda Garlock, Owner

La Bernice Cooking School
4360 Marconi Avenue
Sacramento CA 95821
916-972-7082
Contact:
Bernice Hagen, Owner

Le Kookery
4158 Benedict Canyon Drive
Sherman Oaks CA 91423
818-995-0568
Contact:
Mitzie Cutler, CCP, Director

Let's Get Cookin'
4643 Lakeview Canyon Road
Westlake Village CA 91361
818-991-3940
Contact:
Phyllis Vaccarelli, Owner

Louise's Pantry
859 Santa Cruz Avenue
Menlo Park CA 94025
415-325-1712
Contact:
Louise Fiszer, Director

Marcella's Taste of Nature
360 South Shoreline Boulevard
Mountain View CA 94041
415-969-9838
Contact:
Marcella Lynch, Owner

Mon Cheri Cooking School & Caterer
461 South Murphy
Sunnyvale CA 94086
408-736-0892
Contact:
Sharon Shipley, Director

Montana Mercantile
1500 Montana Avenue
Santa Monica CA 90403
213-451-1418
Contact:
Rachel Dourec, Director

The San Francisco School of Cooking
2801 Leavenworth Street
San Francisco CA 94133
415-474-3663
Contact:
Shirley Cano, Owner

Yan Can International Cooking School
Charter Square
1064G Shell Boulevard
Foster City CA 94404
415-574-7788
Contact:
Judith Dunbar Hines, Owner

OREGON

Cloudtree & Sun School of Cookery
112 North Main Street
Gresham OR 97030
503-666-8495
Contact:
Mary Jo Hessel, Director

Hot Pots Cooking School
The Market Place at Salisham
P.O. Box 7
Lincoln City OR 97367
503-764-2000
Contact:
Ellie Kringer, Owner

WASHINGTON

Bon Vivant School of Cooking
4925 Northeast 86th Street
Seattle WA 98115
206-525-7537
Contact:
Louise Hasson, Director

**Everyday Gourmet School
of Cooking**
5053 Northeast 178th Street
Seattle WA 98155
206-363-1602
Contact:
Beverly Gruber, Owner

**Everyday Gourmet School of
Cooking** emphasizes the techniques
and principles of cooking in its 15-
session Cooking Basics Certificate
Course, 12-session Advanced Certificate
Course and Apprentice/Teacher
Training Program. Various special
interest courses are also offered.

Everyday Gourmet is a Business
member of the International Association
of Culinary Professionals (IACP). Its
director is Beverly Gruber, cum laude
graduate of Madeleine Kamman's two-
year professional cooking school and an
IACP Certified Teacher with over 10
years' experience.

Larry's Market Cooking School
12321 120th Place NE
Kirkland WA 98034
206-821-7696
Contact:
Nancy Varriale, Director

**Magnolia Kitchen Shoppe
& Cooking School, Inc.**
3214 West McGraw
Seattle WA 98199
206-282-2665
Contact:
Linda Johnson, Owner

HAWAII

Creative Cookery, Ltd.
947 Kaluanui Road
Honolulu HI 96825
808-395-5882
Contact:
Lavonne S. Tollerud, Director

University Home Economics Departments

Each of the institutions that follow offers an undergraduate program in home economics that is accredited by the American Home Economics Association. The list is organized regionally, then alphabetically by institution within each state.

NORTHEAST

MASSACHUSETTS

Framingham State College
Department of Home Economics
P.O. Box 2000
Framingham MA 01701
617-620-1220

The department offers a four-year
Bachelor of Science degree in food and
nutrition, in the areas of general
dietetics, community nutrition and
foodservice management. There is also a
coordinated program that fulfills the
academic and experience requirements of
the American Dietetics Association. The
department has three food laboratories.

Framingham State also offers an
M.Ed. degree with a concentration in
nutrition and a Master of Science degree
in food science and nutrition.

NEW JERSEY

Montclair State College
Department of Home Economics
Upper Montclair NJ 07043
201-893-5116

NEW YORK

Queens College
City University of New York
Department of Home Economics
65-30 Kissena Boulevard
Flushing NY 11367
718-520-7749

State University of New York
College at Oneonta
Department of Home Economics
Oneonta NY 13820
607-431-2524

PENNSYLVANIA

Indiana University
of Pennsylvania
College of Human Ecology
and Health Sciences
105 Ackerman Hall
Indiana PA 15701
412-357-2230

SOUTH

ALABAMA

Alabama A&M University
Division of Home Economics
Normal AL 35762
205-859-7468

Auburn University
School of Human Sciences
Auburn AL 36849
205-826-4080

University of Alabama
College of Human Environmental
Sciences
P.O. Box 1488
Tuscaloosa AL 35487
205-348-5666

University of Montevallo
Department of Home Economics
Station 101
Montevallo AL 35115
205-665-6457

ARKANSAS

University of Arkansas at
Fayetteville
Department of Home Economics
118 Home Economics Building
Fayetteville AR 72701
501-575-5346

University of Arkansas at
Pine Bluff
Department of Home Economics
UAPB P.O. Box 4128
Pine Bluff AR 71601
501-541-6542

DISTRICT OF COLUMBIA

Howard University
School of Human Ecology
2400 6th Street NW
Washington DC 20059
202-636-6150

FLORIDA

Florida State University
College of Home Economics
Tallahassee FL 32306
904-644-6200

GEORGIA

Fort Valley State College
Department of Home Economics
P.O. Box 4622
Fort Valley GA 31030
912-825-6307

Georgia Southern College
Division of Home Economics
Statesboro GA 30458
912-681-5531

University of Georgia
College of Home Economics
Athens GA 30602
404-542-2112

LOUISIANA

Louisiana State University and
Agricultural & Mechanical College
School of Home Economics
Baton Rouge LA 70803
504-388-1175

Louisiana Tech University
College of Home Economics
P.O. Box 3167
Ruston LA 71270
318-257-3036

Nicholls State University
Department of Home Economics
P.O. Box 2014
Thibodaux LA 70310
504-446-8111

Northeast Louisiana University
Department of Home Economics
Monroe LA 71209
318-342-4170

Southern University and
A & M College
College of Agriculture and
Home   Economics
P.O. Box 11342
Baton Rouge LA 70813
504-771-2430

University of Southwestern
Louisiana
School of Home Economics
P.O. Box 40399
Lafayette LA 70504
318-231-6474

MARYLAND

Hood College
Department of Home Economics
Rosemont Avenue
Frederick MD 21701
301-663-3131

MISSISSIPPI

Delta State University
Division of Home Economics
P.O. Box 3273
Cleveland MS 38733
601-846-4655

Mississippi State University
Department of Home Economics
P.O. Drawer HE
Mississippi State MS 39762
601-325-2224

Mississippi University for Women
Division of Home Economics and
Human Services
P.O. Box W-1310
Columbus MS 39701
601-329-4750

In the Home Economics unit of the division students may major in home economics education, family and human development, or clothing, textiles and merchandising. The home economics curriculum offers a variety of food and nutrition courses including food science, quantity food production, experimental and evaluative food, foodservice management and advanced human nutrition.

University of Mississippi
Department of Home Economics
110 Meek Hall
University MS 38677
601-232-7226

MISSOURI

**Central Missouri
State University**
Department of Home Economics
250 Grinstead Hall
Warrensburg MO 64093
816-429-4761

Fontbonne College
Department of Home Economics
6800 Wydown Boulevard
St. Louis MO 63105
314-889-1400

**Northeast Missouri State
University**
Division of Home Economics
Violette Hall 176
Kirksville MO 63501
816-785-4114

**Northwest Missouri
State University**
Department of Home Economics
Maryville MO 64468
816-562-1587

**Southwest Missouri
State University**
Department of Home Economics
634 South National, Suite 608
Springfield MO 65804
417-836-5517

University of Missouri—Columbia
College of Environmental Sciences
113 Gwynn Hall
Columbia MO 65211
314-882-7786

Established in 1900, the College of
Environmental Sciences is ranked seventh out of more than 350 similar units
in the country. It is also among the
largest.

The college offers a B.S. degree in
human environmental sciences. The two
areas of emphasis are human nutrition
and foods, and dietetics. M.A. and M.S.
degrees in human nutrition and foods,
and a Ph.D. degree in human environmental sciences are also offered.

NORTH CAROLINA

Appalachian State University
Department of Home Economics
Boone NC 28608
704-262-2120

East Carolina University
Department of Home Economics
Greenville NC 27834
919-757-6640

**North Carolina Agricultural and
Technical State University**
Department of Home Economics
Benbow Hall
Greensboro NC 27411
919-379-7946

**University of North Carolina
at Greensboro**
School of Human Environmental
Sciences
213 Stone Building
Greensboro NC 27412
919-379-5243

Western Carolina University
Department of Home Economics
Belk Building
Cullowhee NC 28723
704-272-7317

SOUTH CAROLINA

South Carolina State College
School of Home Economics and
Human Services
P.O. Box 1686
Orangeburg SC 29117
803-536-7185

TENNESSEE

Carson-Newman College
Department of Home Economics
P.O. Box 1881
Jefferson City TN 37760
615-475-9061

Middle Tennessee State University
Department of Home Economics
P.O. Box 86
Murfreesboro TN 37132
615-898-2111

Tennessee State University
Department of Home Economics
3500 John Merritt Boulevard
Nashville TN 37203
615-320-3420

University of Tennessee—Knoxville
College of Human Ecology
Knoxville TN 37916
615-974-2184

University of Tennessee—Martin
Department of Home Economics
Gooch Hall, Suite 340
Martin TN 38238
901-587-7020

VIRGINIA

James Madison University
Department of Living Sciences
Moody 210
Harrisonburg VA 22807
703-586-6147

**Virginia Polytechnic Institute and
State University**
College of Human Resources
216 Wallace Hall
Blacksburg VA 24061
703-961-6267

MIDWEST

ILLINOIS

Eastern Illinois University
School of Home Economics
Charleston IL 61920
217-581-2223

Illinois State University
Department of Home Economics
Turner Hall
Normal IL 61761
309-428-2181

Northern Illinois University
Department of Human
and Family Resources
Wirtz Hall
DeKalb IL 60115
815-753-0446

**University of Illinois at
Urbana—Champaign**
School of Human and Family
Resource Studies
274 Bevier Hall
905 South Goodwin
Urbana IL 61801
217-333-0302

INDIANA

Ball State University
Department of Home Economics
Practical Arts Building, Suite 150
Muncie IN 47306
317-285-5000

Indiana State University
Department of Home Economics
Terre Haute IN 47809
812-237-2121

IOWA

Iowa State University
College of Family and Consumer
Sciences
122 MacKay Hall
Ames IA 50011
515-294-5836

University of Northern Iowa
Department of Home Economics
Wright Hall, Suite 216B
Cedar Falls IA 50614
319-273-2281

KANSAS

Kansas State University
College of Home Economics
119 Justin Hall
Manhattan KS 6506
913-532-6250

MICHIGAN

Andrews University
Department of Home Economics
Berrien Springs MI 49104
616-471-3303

Eastern Michigan University
Department of Human Environmental
and Consumer Resources
108 Roosevelt Hall
Ypsilanti MI 48197
313-487-3060

NEBRASKA

University of Nebraska at Lincoln
College of Home Economics
Lincoln NE 68584
402-472-7211

NORTH DAKOTA

North Dakota State University
College of Home Economics
Fargo ND 58105
701-237-8643

OHIO

Miami University
Department of Home Economics
and Consumer Sciences
260 McGuffey Hall
Oxford OH 45056
513-529-2531

Ohio University
School of Home Economics
Tupper Hall 108
Athens OH 45701
614-594-5174

University of Akron
School of Home Economics
and Family Ecology
215 Schrank Hall South
Akron OH 44325
216-375-7100

SOUTH DAKOTA

South Dakota State University
College of Home Economics
Brookings SD 57007
605-688-4121

SOUTHWEST

NEW MEXICO

New Mexico State University
Department of Home Economics
P.O. Box 30003 Department 3470
Las Cruces NM 88003
505-64-3121

OKLAHOMA

Oklahoma State University
College of Home Economics
Home Economics West
Stillwater OK 74078
405-624-6857

TEXAS

Prairie View A&M University
Department of Home Economics
P. O. Drawer M
Prairie View TX 77446
409-857-2423

Southwest Texas State University
Department of Home Economics
San Marcos TX 78666
512-245-2343

Stephen F. Austin State University
Department of Home Economics
P.O. Box 13014 SFA
Nacogdoches TX 75962
409-569-2504

Texas Tech University
College of Home Economics
P.O. Box 4170
Lubbock TX 79409
806-742-3661

University of Texas at Austin
Department of Home Economics
Austin TX 78712

MOUNTAIN STATES

MONTANA

Montana State University
Department of Health and
Human Development
221 Herrick Hall
Bozeman MT 59717
406-994-2452

NEVADA

University of Nevada—Reno
School of Home Economics
Reno NV 89557
702-784-6865

UTAH

Utah State University
College of Family Life
FL 203 UMC 29
Logan UT 84322
801-750-1092

WEST

CALIFORNIA

California State University—Chico
School of Home Economics
Chico CA 95929
916-895-6321

**California State University—
Los Angeles**
Department of Family Studies
and Consumer Sciences
5151 State College Avenue
Los Angeles CA 90032
213-224-2192

**California State University—
Northridge**
Department of Home Economics
18111 Nordoff Street
Northridge CA 91324
818-885-3777

San Francisco State University
Department of Consumer and
Family Studies/Dietetics
1600 Holloway Education 331
San Francisco CA 94132
415-469-2014

OREGON

Oregon State University
College of Home Economics
Corvallis OR 97331
503-754-4411

University Restaurant and Hotel Management Schools

This brief listing of graduate programs in this field is organized into regions, for convenience. More comprehensive information is obtainable by writing to the National Restaurant Association, 150 North Michigan Avenue, Suite 2000, Chicago IL 60601.

NORTHEAST

CONNECTICUT

University of New Haven
Hotel, Restaurant Management, Dietetics & Tourism Administration
300 Orange Avenue
West Haven CT 06516
203-932-7362

MASSACHUSETTS

University of Massachusetts
Department of Hotel, Restaurant & Travel Administration
101 Flint Laboratory
Amherst MA 01003
413-545-2535

NEW JERSEY

Fairleigh Dickinson University
Hotel & Restaurant Management School
College of Business
Rutherford NJ 07070
201-460-5362

The school offers a four-year Bachelor of Science degree in hotel, restaurant and tourism management. It forms part of the College of Business and courses are offered on such subjects as financial management, business policy and marketing. Food-related courses include food and beverage management and quantity food production. Students gain hands-on experience through supervised 400-hour internships each summer, generally undertaken in major hotels or test kitchens. The school will soon have its own foodservice management laboratory.

NEW YORK

Cornell University
School of Hotel Administration
Statler Hall
Ithaca NY 14853
607-256-5106

New York University
Foodservice Management
239 Greene Street
537 East Building
New York NY 10003
212-598-2369

SOUTH

FLORIDA

Florida International University
School of Hospitality
Tamiami Trail
Miami FL 33199
305-554-2591

MARYLAND

University of Maryland
Institution Administration
Department of Food, Nutrition & Institution Administration
College Park MD 20742
301-454-2143

TENNESSEE

University of Tennessee
Tourism, Food & Lodging Administration
220 CHE College of Human Ecology
Knoxville TN 37996
615-974-5445

VIRGINIA

Virginia Polytechnic Institute & State University
Hotel, Restaurant & Institutional Management
18 Hillcrest Hall
Blacksburg VA 24061
703-961-6783

MIDWEST

ILLINOIS

University of Illinois
Restaurant Management School
274 Bevier Hall
Urbana IL 61801
217-333-1326

The school, which forms part of the university's Foods and Nutrition Division, offers a four-year B.S. degree course in restaurant management. With a strong scientific base, areas covered include food preparation, quantity food production and hotel management, as well as various hospitality-linked courses. The program is small but select, admitting only 125 students who must meet the university's high admission standards.

The program focuses strongly on practical experience gained through internship programs and use of on-campus facilities.

Graduate programs in foodservice systems and nutrition are available.

INDIANA

Purdue University
Department of Restaurant, Hotel & Institutional Management
Stone Hall
West Lafayette IN 47907
317-494-4643

IOWA

Iowa State University
Hotel, Restaurant & Institution Management
11 MacKay Hall
Ames IA 50011
515-294-1730

MICHIGAN

Michigan State University
School of Hotel, Restaurant
& Institutional Management
425 Eppley Center
East Lansing MI 48824
517-353-9211

SOUTHWEST

NEVADA

University of Nevada, Las Vegas
College of Hotel Administration
4505 Maryland Parkway
Las Vegas NV 89154
702-739-3230

MOUNTAIN STATES

UTAH

Brigham Young University
Food Systems Administration
2218 SFLC
Provo UT 84602
801-378-6677

159
Kitchen Designers

162
Major Kitchen Appliances

164
Small Electric Appliances

167
Cookware and Cooking Accessories

Concept to Creation...

Kitchen Designers

This selection of kitchen designers has been made to offer as broad a geographic representation as possible and is organized alphabetically by town or city within regions. All the designers listed here are members of the Society of Certified Kitchen Designers who have qualified for its professional accreditation of CKD. (For a complete listing, contact the Society at 124 Main Street, Hackettstown, NJ 07840.) Unless a firm is indicated as undertaking only residential work, these designers accept both commercial and residential commissions. Where several qualified designers work for a firm, all names are included.

NORTHEAST

CONNECTICUT

St. Charles Kitchens by Deane
1267 East Main
Stamford CT 06902
203-327-7008
Designer:
Kelly Stewart

**Signature Kitchen and Bath/
M. A. Peterson, Inc.**
P.O. Box 10324
West Hartford CT 06110
203-232-4407
Designer:
Timothy J. Bates

MASSACHUSETTS

Lee Kimball Kitchens
276 Friend Street
Boston MA 02114
617-227-0250
Designer:
Leon K. Johnson

St. Charles Kitchens of Boston
473 Winter Street
Waltham MA 02154
617-890-2324
Designer:
Chester H. Sandford

NEW HAMPSHIRE

The Kitchen Showcase, Inc.
94 Granite Street
Manchester NH 03101
603-622-4776
Designer:
James C. Callanan

NEW JERSEY

Mike Kelly's Kitchens
Landis Avenue
RR 8, Box 229
Bridgeton NJ 08302
609-455-8160
Designer
Michael R. Kelly

**National Kitchen
& Bath Association**
124 Main Street
Hackettstown NJ 07840
201-852-0033
Designers:
Francis Jones
William R. Mathisen
David H. Newton
Russell W. Platek

Kitchens by A & B, Inc.
279 Franklin Avenue
Wyckoff NJ 07481
201-891-0313
Designers:
Herman Brandes
Randy J. Brandes
William F. Earnshaw

NEW YORK

Mayfair Kitchen Center, Inc.
87 Homestead Avenue
Albany NY 12203
518-482-7056
Designer:
Jesse Mendelsohn

Creative Kitchens & Baths
331 Main Street
Binghamton NY 13905
607-729-1576
Designer:
Arthur H. Andrews

**Herbert P. Bisulk, Inc./
Kitchens of Distinction**
295 Nassau Boulevard South
Garden City NY 11530
516-483-0377
Residential only
Designer:
Monte G. Berkoff

Kitchen Associates, Inc.
324 East 81st Street
New York NY 10028
212-239-8210
Designers:
John F. Hammill
Lawrence N. Newman

**Sleepy Hollow Custom
Kitchens, Inc.**
42 River Street
North Tarrytown NY 10591
914-631-3101
Designer:
Joseph S. Bracchitta

PENNSYLVANIA

Kitchens by Wieland, Inc.
4210 Tilghman Street
Allentown PA 18104
215-395-2074
Residential only
Designer:
Robert L. Wieland

Cogan & Gordon, Inc.
2200 North American Street
Philadelphia PA 19133
215-425-1556
Designers:
Bert (Bud) Fleet
Sidney Haifetz
James S. Kaufer

Kitchen and Bath Concepts of Pittsburgh
7901 Perry Highway North
Pittsburgh PA 15237
412-369-2900
Residential only
Designers:
Julia A. Lorentz
Thomas D. Trzcinski

VERMONT

Kitchen Professionals
1 Blair Park, Suite 13
Williston VT 05495
802-878-7822
Designer:
Paul L. Hackel

SOUTH

ARKANSAS

Smith/Osburn Design
10020 Rodney Parham Road
Little Rock AR 72207
501-225-4478
Designer:
Kaye M. Osburn

DISTRICT OF COLUMBIA

The Kitchen Guild
5027 Connecticut Avenue NW
Washington DC 20008
202-362-7111
Designers:
Robert W. Baur
Randi J. Place
Robert D. Schafer
Louis E. Schucker

FLORIDA

Kitchen Center, Inc.
3968 Curtiss Parkway
Miami Springs FL 33166
305-871-4147
Designer:
Ivan Parron

Kitchen Design Studio
924 4th Street North
St. Petersburg FL 33701
813-823-5080
Designer:
Fred Grove

BMW Designer Kitchens, Inc.
1860 Old Okeechobee Road,
Suite 510
West Palm Beach FL 33409
407-478-3033
Designer:
Beverly M. Wolfe

GEORGIA

Enlightened Homes
9401 Roberts Drive, Suite 20A
Atlanta GA 30350
404-993-0399
Designer:
Maggi Hughes

KENTUCKY

Kitchen Planning Center, Inc.
101 West Loudon Avenue
Lexington KY 40508
606-252-0866
Designer:
Robert B. Cornett

The House of Kitchens, Inc.
106 Bauer Avenue
Louisville KY 40207
502-897-2505
Designer:
Philip M. Pittenger

LOUISIANA

Kitchens by Cameron
8019 Palm Street
New Orleans LA 70125
504-486-3759
Designers:
Belva M. Johnson
Gerald C. Johnson

Kitchens, Inc.
352 Warren Avenue
Portland LA 04103
207-878-2124
Designer:
Roger R. Goding Jr.

MARYLAND

Stuart Kitchens, Inc.
1858 Reisterstown Road
Baltimore MD 21208
301-486-0500
Designer:
Robert O. Geddes

Creative Kitchens, Inc.
1776 East Jefferson Street
Rockville MD 20852
301-984-4477
Designer:
Jay Dobbs

MISSISSIPPI

Kitchen Kreators
1513 Lakeland Drive
Jackson MS 39216
601-982-2325
Designer:
Raymond A. Sanders

NORTH CAROLINA

Triangle Design Kitchens, Inc.
5216 Hollyridge Drive
Raleigh NC 27612
919-787-0256
Designer:
John H. G. Raiser

Amarr Kitchens
1001 North Liberty Street
Winston-Salem NC 27101
919-724-1754
Designer:
Stanley C. Gilfoyle

SOUTH CAROLINA

Hampton Kitchens
P.O. Box 7273
Columbia SC 29202
803-779-0670
Designer:
W. Hampton Oliver

TENNESSEE

Carruthers Kitchens, Inc.
2665 Broad Avenue
Memphis TN 38112
901-324-8588
Designer:
Wilson M. Carruthers
Carolyn M. Poore

Dean's Kitchen Center, Inc.
1023 16th Avenue South
Nashville TN 37212
615-242-3106
Designer:
Howard P. Dean

VIRGINIA

Kitchen Towne
2600 Hampton Boulevard
Norfolk VA 23517
804-622-3800
Designers:
Eugene E. Bryant
Benton Flax
Robert G. Games

Kitchen Art, Inc.
2337 West Broad Street
Richmond VA 23220
804-353-2775
Designers:
Robert G. Baker
Dayton Leadbetter

WEST VIRGINIA

Creative Kitchens, Inc.
1242 Fifth Avenue
Huntington WV 25701
304-529-2537
Designer:
Robert E. Stepp

MIDWEST

ILLINOIS

Karlson Kitchens
1815 Central Street
Evanston IL 60201
708-931-2646
Designer:
Ben E. Karlson

C & A Custom Kitchens
3500 Clear Lake
Springfield IL 62702
217-523-0170
Designer:
Kathryn E. Schultz

INDIANA

Jordan Showplace Kitchens
2206 Lafayette Road
Indianapolis IN 46222
317-639-2003
Residential only
Designer:
James S. Jordan

IOWA

Miller Kitchens
335 Kirkwood Avenue
Iowa City IA 52240
319-337-5226
Designer:
Jane A. Miller

KANSAS

The Kitchen Place, Inc.
1634 East Central
Wichita KS 67214
316-263-2249
Designers:
Sherman Culbertson
Jan E. Parker

MICHIGAN

Gallery of Kitchens, Inc.
5243 Plainfield NE
Grand Rapids MI 49505
616-363-4881
Designer:
Jack M. Damstra

Royal Oak Kitchens
4518 North Woodward Avenue
Royal Oak MI 48072
313-549-2944
Designers:
Cheryl A. Felt
Rex E. Holton

MINNESOTA

Kitchens by Krengel, Inc.
International Market Square
275 Market Street, Suite 120
Minneapolis MN 55405
612-698-0844
Designer:
Richard J. Gorman

NEBRASKA

Nebraska Custom Kitchens
4601 Dodge Street
Omaha NE 68132
402-556-1000
Designers:
Bard Goedeker
Ed M. Honke

OHIO

**H & C Kitchens
and Bathrooms, Inc.**
1290 West Broad Street
Columbus OH 43222
614-279-1855
Designer:
William A. Hagedorn

**McKimmy & Elliot Kitchen
Design Plus**
5250 Renwyck
Toledo OH 43615
419-536-6605
Designer:
Richard A. McKimmy

OKLAHOMA

Fred H. Young Jr. & Associates
P.O. Box 18916
Oklahoma City OK 73154
405-525-9005
Designers:
Donald G. Dobbs
Glenn C. Snook

WISCONSIN

Kitchen Design Studio
8932 West North Avenue
Wauwatosa WI 53226
414-774-8266
Designer:
Eugene L. Delfosse

MOUNTAIN STATES

COLORADO

Thurston, Inc.
2920 East Sixth Avenue
Denver CO 80206
303-399-4564
Designers:
Catherine Dulacki
Seth T. Fordham
Helen D. Francis
Bill Kline
Kathleen A. Turner
Ed Winger

NEVADA

Kitchen Studio, Inc.
610 1/2 East Sahara Avenue
Las Vegas NV 89104
702-369-8474
Designer:
Sidney B. Wechter

UTAH

Carlson Kitchens
2261 East 3300 South
Salt Lake City UT 84109
801-486-4651
Designers:
Larry A. Carlson, Owner
Michael G. Russotto

SOUTHWEST

ARIZONA

American Kitchens, Inc.
5802 South 25th Street
Phoenix AZ 85040
602-276-8445
Designer:
Rita L. Phillips

Kitchens of Distinction
1940 East Winsett
Tucson AZ 85719
602-623-5891
Designers:
Harold S. Denny
Patty R. Klassen
John H. Klassen
Michael P. O'Brien

TEXAS

Kitchen Planners
3300 Airport Freeway
Ft. Worth TX 76111
817-831-4483
Designers:
Walter J. Chambless
Beth M. Stribling
Emil K. Test

Kitchens by Beldon
P.O. Box 13380
San Antonio TX 78213
512-341-3100
Designer:
Robert G. Thompson

WEST COAST

CALIFORNIA

Showcase Kitchens
2317 Westwood Boulevard
Los Angeles CA 90064
213-470-3222
Residential only
Designer:
Gary A. Bishop

The Kitchen Specialist
10643 West Pico Boulevard
Los Angeles CA 90064
213-470-6727
Designer:
Michael Goldberg

Carlene Anderson Kitchen Design, Inc.
5818 Balboa Drive
Oakland CA 94611
415-339-2530
Residential only
Designer:
Carlene F. Anderson

Ultimate Kitchens
4010 Morena Boulevard
San Diego CA 92117
619-581-9400
Designer:
Scott G. Grandis

OREGON

Neil Kelly Company
804 North Alberta
Portland OR 97217
503-288-7461
Designer:
J. Lynette Black

WASHINGTON

Kitchen Designs and Interiors
9702 South Tacoma Way
Tacoma WA 98499
206-581-0990
Designer:
Margaret S. Jensen

ALASKA & HAWAII

HAWAII

Kitchen Concepts Plus, Inc.
845 Cooke Street
Honolulu HI 96813
808-545-5655
Designer:
Michael L. Smith

Major Kitchen Appliances

Almost all the manufacturers on this list belong to the National Kitchen & Bath Association, America's major organization of kitchen planners, and are nationally known as specialists in making appliances for the home kitchen.

The list is alphabetical by name of manufacturer and the addresses given are in most cases those of the public relations contact, from which an interested food professional or consumer can obtain additional information about a specific product or its distribution.

AEG/Andi-Co Appliances, Inc.
65 Campus Plaza
Edison NJ 08837
201-225-8837
Contact:
Amir Miremadi

Aga Cookers
Cooper & Turner
RFD 1, Box 477
Stowe VT 05672
802-253-9727
Contact:
Cate McHugh

Amana Refrigeration, Inc.
Main Street
Middle Amana IA 52204
319-622-2731
Contact:
Ann Humbert

Brewmatic Company
3828 South Main Street
Los Angeles CA 90037
213-233-8204
Contact:
Ed Raives

Dacor
950 South Raymond Avenue
Pasadena CA 91109
818-799-1000
Contact:
Candy Abney

Gaggenau USA
5 Commonwealth Avenue
Woburn MA 01801
617-255-1766
Contact:
Ronald Rhinerson

Gaggenau's newest collection of German-designed built-in kitchen appliances has been designed for people who find preparing a meal an enjoyable hobby and who care about their kitchen's appearance and efficiency. Each Gaggenau appliance is distinguished by its high quality of materials and workmanship and the unpretentious beauty of its functional design.

Gaggenau manufactures more than 30 sophisticated, innovative products that can be combined to suit your needs.

Garland Commercial Industries
185 East South Street
Freeland PA 18224
717-636-1000
Contact:
Ann Williams

General Electric
Appliance Park
Louisville KY 40225
502-452-4616
Contact:
Jeffrey Dick

In-Sink-Erator
4700 21st Street
Racine WI 53406
441-554-5432
Contact:
Todd Eber

Jenn-Air Corporation
3035 Shadeland
Indianapolis IN 46226
317-545-2271
Contact:
Consumer Relations Department

KitchenAid, Inc.
701 Main Street
St. Joseph MI 49085
616-982-4500
Contact:
Don Stuart

Since 1919, the name of KitchenAid has meant performance, durability and quality—from the first KitchenAid stand mixers to today's full line of premium products. Led by the sleek Architect Series, KitchenAid offers tools for the serious cook who also values style. Its product line includes built-in and free-standing refrigerators, built-in cooktops and ovens, drop-in ranges, dishwashers, microwave ovens and microwave hood combinations, hot water dispensers, stand mixers...and more.

The Maytag Company
1 Dependability Square
Newton IA 50208
515-792-7000
Contact:
Susan Martin

Modern Maid
110 East 59th Street, Suite 1515
New York NY 10022
212-753-4311
Contact:
Ed Falk

Ron-Matic Systems, Inc.
100 Pennsylvania Avenue
Paterson NJ 07509
201-523-3434
Contact:
Anthony Sabbatino

Tappan Appliances
WCI Major Appliance Group
6000 Perimeter Road
Dublin OH 43017
614-792-4100
Contact:
M. W. Challburg

Thermador/Waste King

A. Masco Company
5119 District Boulevard
Los Angeles CA 90040
213-562-1133
Contact:
Cap Hendrix

Traulsen & Company, Inc.
114-02 15th Avenue
College Point NY 11356
718-463-9000
Contact:
Bob Pirrone

Weber-Stephen Products Company
200 East Daniels Road
Palatine IL 60067
708-934-5700
Contact
Barbara Camm

Welbilt Corporation
3333 New Hyde Park Road
New Hyde Park NY 11042
516-365-5040
Contact:
Ron Moser

Whirlpool Corporation
Administration Center
2000 M 63
Benton Harbor MI 49022
616-926-3164
Contact:
Joy Schrage

Whirlpool Corporation and its subsidiaries worldwide manufacture and market a full line of major home appliances. In the United States the corporation markets its products under the Whirlpool, KitchenAid and Roper brand names.

Product lines that are food-related include dishwashers, refrigerators, freezers, ranges, built-in ovens and surface units, microwave ovens, hot water dispensers and icemakers.

Small Electric Appliances

The listing that follows was compiled from the list of exhibitors at the 1989 International Housewares Exposition, the annual trade show sponsored by the National Housewares Manufacturers' Association.

The selection, by Elaine Yannuzzi, founder of Expression unltd., includes all those American exhibitors manufacturing and/or distributing products related to food preparation. The listing is alphabetical by name of the firm. To help both potential sellers and buyers in using the list, the major product specialties listed by each firm are also included.

Copies of the most recent show catalog may be available from the National Housewares Manufacturers' Association, 1324 Merchandise Mart, Chicago IL 60654.

**Alton Electric
(Antilles International, Inc.)**
2225 Northwest 70th Avenue
Miami FL 33122
305-592-6281
Can openers, electric knives, hand mixers, juicers, percolators, rice cookers, sandwich waffle makers, toasters

**Betty G Appliances
(Abbott Industries)**
95-25 149th Street
Jamaica NY 11435
718-291-0800
Can openers, deep-fryers, electric kettles, mixers, slowcookers, table ranges

**Black & Decker
(Household Products Group)**
6 Armstrong Road
Shelton CT 06484
203-926-3020
Coffeemakers, electric kettles, electric knives, food processors, mixers, blenders, ovens, popcorn makers, skillets, slicers, peelers, mincers, toaster ovens, wafflebakers

For most of us, the name of Black & Decker used to be synonymous with good-quality reliable handyman's electrical tools. Some years ago, the firm expanded from the workshop into the kitchen, where it is now famous for a flourishing line of electric items such as cordless beaters, knife sharpeners, can openers and chopper/mincers—though its best known contribution may still be the invaluable Dustbuster. Black & Decker products are exported worldwide.

Robert Bosch Corporation
2800 South 25th Avenue
Broadview IL 60153
708-865-5200
Coffee makers & grinders, deep-fryers, food processors, grain mills, grills, juicers, mixers, slicers, toasters, waffle irons

Braun, Inc.
66 Broadway
Route 1
Lynnfield MA 01940
617-596-7300
Coffeemakers, food processors, grinders, hand blenders, juicers, mills

**Broil-King
(Hudson Standard Corporation)**
90 South Street
Newark NJ 07114
201-589-6140
Deep-fryers, grills & wafflers, hot electric serving trays, rotisseries, tabletop ranges, toaster ovens, broilers

Brother International Corporation
8 Corporate Place
Piscataway NJ 08854
201-981-0300
Electric housewares, microwave ovens

Bunn-O-Matic Corporation
1400 Stevenson Drive
P.O. Box 3227
Springfield IL 62708
217-529-6601
Coffee brewers & warmers, coffee filters & decanters

Capitol Products Corporation
35 Willow Street
P.O. Box 710
Winsted CT 06098
203-379-3393
Electric broilers, multipurpose kitchen electrics, portable electric table stoves, sandwich grills

Chaney Instrument Company
P.O. Box 72
Lake Geneva WI 53147
414-248-4449
Thermometers & timers

Component Design Northwest, Inc.
2658 Northwest Cornell Road
P.O. Box 10141
Portland OR 97210
503-242-9337
Electronic timers, mechanical timers, thermometers

Cuisinarts, Inc.
15 Valley Drive
P.O. Box 2150
Greenwich CT 06836
203-622-4600
Cookware, cordless hand mixers, food choppers, grinders, food processors & accessories, food thermometers, kitchen accessories, kitchen scales, pressure cookers

Dazey Corporation
1 Dazey Circle
Industrial Airport KS 66031
913-782-7500
Coffee-soup-beverage warmers, electric toasters, fruit juicers, fryers, steamers, slow

cookers, glass percolators, knife-scissor sharpeners, toaster oven broilers, waffle iron grills

DeLonghi America, Inc.
625 Washington Avenue
Carlstadt NJ 07072
201-507-1110
Coffeemakers, deep-fryers, espresso makers, microwave ovens, toaster ovens, toasters

DeLonghi manufactures the finest kitchen and comfort appliances from Europe. DeLonghi's product line ranges from the Alfredo Toaster Oven to the exclusive Roto-Fryer rotating deep-fryer. The Bar espresso/cappuccino maker is one of the finest in the industry.

DeLonghi also has a complete line of oil-filled electric radiators and convection and fan-forced heaters. For the summer, DeLonghi offers a complete line of fans as well as Pinguino, the windowless air conditioner.

Deni/Keystone Manufacturing, Inc.
P.O. Box 863
Buffalo NY 14240
716-875-6680
Can openers, electric & rechargeable appliances, kitchen appliances, kitchen gadgets, spacesaver appliances

Donvier/Nikkal Industries, Ltd.
562 Lynnhaven Parkway
P.O. Box 2636
Virginia Beach VA 23452
804-431-2818
Cordial makers, diet shakemakers, ice cream makers

European Electrics Corporation
236 East Avenue
Norwalk CT 06855
203-866-5165
Food processors & accessories

Evaco Import Services, Inc.
16 Golden Gate Drive
P.O. Box 2687
San Rafael CA 94901
415-457-3133
Electric appliances, kitchenware, slicing machines, teakettles

Farberware, Inc.
(Hanson Industries)
1500 Bassett Avenue
Bronx NY 10461
212-863-8000
Can openers, convection-turbo ovens, drip coffeemakers, electric broiler-rotisseries, griddles, hand mixers, microwave cookware,

percolators, stainless steel cookware, teakettles, toasters, woks

Fujiware America, Inc.
230 Fifth Avenue, Suite 300
New York NY 10001
212-684-6328
Coffee percolators, enamel servingware, enamel teakettles, porcelain enamel cookware, stainless steel items

General Electric Appliances
Appliance Park, Building 4-242
Louisville KY 40225
502-452-7208
Compact refrigerators, microwave ovens

Global Marketing/Kenwood
156 Halsey Road
Parsippany NJ 07054
201-839-4333
Blenders, can openers, cord/cordless knives, electric mixers, food processors, fryers, juicers, juice extractors, toasters

Hamilton Beach Company
(Glen Dimplex)
Spring Road, Highway 17 North
P.O. Box 1158
Washington NC 27889
919-975-2121
Blenders, can openers, choppers, coffeemakers, cookers, drink mixers, electric knives, food processors, hand & stand mixers, slow cookers, toaster ovens, toasters

Hitachi Sales Corporation
of America
401 West Artesia Boulevard
Compton CA 90220
213-537-8383
Food steamers, rice cookers, home bakeries, knife sharpeners, rotation grill fans

Hudson Standard Corporation
90 South Street
Newark NJ 07114
201-589-6140
Deep-fryers, slow cookers, grills, waffle irons, hot electric serving trays, rotisseries, tabletop ranges, toaster oven broilers

Iwatani International Corporation
of America
2050 Center Avenue, Suite 425
Fort Lee NJ 07024
201-585-2442
Electric steamers, toasters, portable gas cooking stoves

KitchenAid, Inc.
(Whirlpool Corporation)
701 South Main Street
St. Joseph MI 49085
616-982-4500
Electric stand mixers, food processors

Robert Krups, North America
7 Reuten Drive
Closter NJ 07624
201-767-5500
Automatic teamakers, coffee grinders, coffeemakers, espresso/cappuccino makers, food processors, juicers, kitchen electric mixers, slicers, toasters, waffle irons

Lello Appliances Corporation
355 Murray Hill Parkway
East Rutherford NJ 07073
201-939-2555
Electric ice cream makers, electric pasta makers, espresso/cappuccino makers, manual ice cream makers

Lello Appliances imports Simiac pasta makers, ice cream makers and espresso machines from Italy. This well-designed, upscale collection of small appliances features Simiac Pastamatics, which can produce fresh dough in your choice of 24 shapes, and Il Gelataio ice cream makers for concocting just about any type of frozen dessert, while Caffe Simiac makes delicious espresso or cappuccino in minutes. Simiac appliances are available in department and specialty stores.

Maverick Industries, Inc.
265 Raritan Center Parkway
Edison NJ 08857
201-417-9666
Broilers, electric kitchen message centers, food warmers, griddles, indoor electric grills

Maxim Company
164 Delancy Street
Newark NJ 07105
201-344-4600
Convection ovens, crepe makers, espresso makers, indoor broilers, milk shakemakers, mini choppers, toasters, warming trays, woks

Meyer Corporation, U.S.
601 Gateway Boulevard,
Suite 1150
South San Francisco CA 94080
415-871-2444
Electric appliances, hard anodized cookware, nonstick aluminum cookware, stainless steel cookware

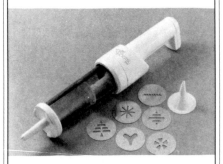
Morris Stuhl, Inc.
220 West Crescent Avenue
Allendale NJ 07401
201-327-9500
Electric hot pots, electric percolators, hot plates

Mr. Coffee, Inc.
24700 Miles Road
Bedford Heights OH 44146
216-464-4000
Coffee decanters, coffee filters, coffee machines

Munsey Products, Inc.
9911 Interstate 30
P.O. Box 9830
Little Rock AR 72219
501-568-7870
Small kitchen electric appliances

National Presto Industries, Inc.
3925 North Hastings Way
Eau Claire WI 54703
715-839-2121
Electric coffeemakers/teakettles, electric corn poppers, electric fry pans, deep-fryers, electric griddles, electric ice cream makers, food processors, pressure cookers & canners

Norelco Consumer Products Company (North American Philips Corporation)
High Ridge Park
P.O. Box 10166
Stamford CT 06904
203-329-5700
Automatic drip coffeemakers, electric mixers, ice cream makers, juicers

Oster/Sunbeam Appliance Company
5505 North Lydell Avenue
Milwaukee WI 53217
414-332-8300
Blenders, toasters, can openers, coffeemakers, food meat slicers, ice cream makers, ice crushers, juice extractors, knife sharpeners, meat/food grinders, toasters

Palmer Manufacturing, Inc.
P.O. Box 220
West Newton PA 15089
Belgian cookie irons, electric mountain pie irons, hot dog toasters, ravioli forms, sandwich toasters, waffle irons

Panasonic
2 Panasonic Way
Secaucus NJ 07094
201-348-7824
Kitchen electrics, microwave ovens

Proctor-Silex/Wear-Ever
4421 Waterfront Drive
Glen Allen VA 23060
804-273-9777
Automatic drip coffeemakers, can openers, coffee mills, hot air poppers, juicers, electric/nonelectric mixers, nonstick aluminum cookware, percolators, toasters & toaster ovens

Regal Ware, Inc.
1675 Reigle Drive
Kewaskum WI 53040
414-626-2121
Cast aluminum cookware, coffeemakers, food processors, microwave cookware, stainless steel accessories

Rival Manufacturing Company
3601 Bennington
Kansas City MO 64129
816-861-1000
Electric can openers, electric mixers, electric skillets, food slicers, hot pots, ice cream freezers, pizzelle makers, serving trays, slow cookers, steamer rice cookers, toasters, waffler grills

Rival Manufacturing Company is a leading producer of portable electric household appliances, with a product line that includes the original **Crock-** pot stoneware slow cooker. Rival also manufactures countertop and under-cabinet can openers, electric skillets, hand mixers, food grinders, ice cream freezers, ice crushers and warming trays.

Rowenta, Inc.
281 Albany Street
Cambridge MA 02139
617-661-1600
Can openers, coffeemakers, electric knives, espresso makers, toasters

Russell Hobbs, Inc.
1951 Hamburg Turnpike, Site 1,
FT2 No. 23
P.O. Box 1472
Buffalo NY 14218
Coffeemakers, cookware, electric kettles, electric toasters, fryers

Salton Housewares, Inc.
550 Business Center Drive
Mt. Prospect IL 60656
708-803-4600
Coffee filters, coffee grinders, electric can openers, electric drip coffeemakers, electric juicers, electric knives, electric mixers, espresso/cappuccino machines, hot plates, ice cream machines, toasters

Salton has been steadily developing its line of advanced technology espresso/cappuccino makers to achieve espressos with ease and cappuccino on demand. Designed, engineered and manufactured in West Germany, Switzerland and Italy, the various models use steam and pump drives and offer continuous steam modes and patented exclusive frothing devices.

Sanyo Fisher (USA) Corporation
200 Riser Road
Little Ferry NJ 07643
201-641-2333
Kitchen appliances

Shetland Corporation
100 Justin Drive
Chelsea MA 02150
617-884-7744
Can openers, coffee machines, electric coffeemakers, espresso machines

Sunbeam Appliance Company
1333 Butterfield Road
Downers Grove IL 60515
708-719-5000
Can openers, electric knives, food choppers, food processors, hand & stand mixers, hot beverage makers, ovens, toasters

Swing-A-Way Manufacturing Company
4100 Beck Avenue
St. Louis MO 63116
314-773-1487
Can openers, ice crushers, jar openers, kitchen tools & gadgets

Tappan/WCI Appliance Group (WCI)
300 Phillipi Road
P.O. Box 182056
Columbus OH 43218
614-272-4417
Microwave ovens

Tefal Appliance Company
23 Kulick Road
Fairfield NJ 07006
201-575-1060
Broiler-toaster ovens, deep-fryers, electric kettles, indoor barbecues, steam ovens, toasters

Toastmaster, Inc.
1801 North Stadium Boulevard
Columbia MO 65201
314-445-8666
Buffet ranges, can openers, convection ovens, electric knives, food processors, food slicers, hand mixers, microwave ovens, oven-broilers, pizzelle makers, toaster-oven broilers, toasters, griddles, under-cabinet broilers, toasters, waffle bakers, Belgian wafflers

Waring Products (Dynamics Corporation of America)
283 Main Street
New Hartford CT 06057
203-379-0731
Blenders, can openers, coffeemakers, coffee mills/grinders, drink mixers, food dehydrators, food processors, food steamers, hand-held blenders, hand mixers, extractors, juicers, stand mixers, toasters

Waring Products, a division of Dynamics Corporation of America, manufactures small electric appliances and is currently expanding its line of commercial foodservice equipment for restaurants, bars and institutional kitchens.

Waring recently introduced **Waring Professional**, a line of commercial-quality products for the home. This new upscale line currently features more than ten items, including kitchen blenders, bar blenders, juice extractors, toasters and food processors.

Welbilt Appliance Company
3333 New Hyde Park Road
New Hyde Park NY 11042
516-365-5040
Automatic bread machines, espresso machines, microwave ovens, refrigerators

West Bend Company
400 Washington Street
P.O. Box 278
West Bend WI 53095
414-334-2311
Choppers, corn poppers, deep-fryers, drip coffeemakers, electric timers, electric woks, food processors, griddles, percolators, skillets, slow cookers, special electrics

A leading seller of small appliances, the West Bend Company has been manufacturing items designed for convenience and style in the home kitchen since 1911. Its current best-seller is a six-quart electric wok, though the Stir-Crazy Corn Popper is also a popular gift item. West Bend recently introduced an updated quick-drip coffeemaker featuring a timer, automatic shutoff and a pause-and-pour mechanism.

Xcell International Corporation (Trendex International)
1540 Merchandise Mart
Chicago IL 60654
312-644-7756
Ceramic tableware, coffee filters & grinders, electric drip coffeemakers, espresso/cappuccino machines

Zephyr Convection Cooking Systems Company, Inc.
1550 Bryant Street, Suite 850
San Francisco CA 94103
415-558-9890
Convection oven systems

Zojirushi America Corporation
5628 Bandini Boulevard
Bell CA 90201
213-264-6270
Carafes, electric air pots, electric cookware, electric grills, thermal servers

Cookware and Cooking Accessories

The listing that follows was compiled from those American manufacturers and/or distributors who exhibited kitchen tools and gadgets and cookware of all kinds at the 1989 International Housewares Exposition, the annual trade show sponsored by the National Housewares Manufacturers Association.

The selection, by Elaine Yannuzzi, founder of Expression unltd., is alphabetical by name of the firm. To assist both potential sellers and buyers, the major product specialties listed by each are also included.

Copies of the most recent show catalog may be available from the National Housewares Manufacturers' Association, 1324 Merchandise Mart, Chicago IL 60654.

Acme Metal Goods Manufacturing Company

2 Orange Street
Newark NJ 07102
201-623-0725
Baking cups, cookie cutters, gadgets

Founded early in the century as a metal stamping company, Acme now makes kitchen gadgets such as potato peelers and cookie cutters. Home bakers will be familiar with Acme baking cups, which come in prints and pastel colors as well as foil. The company also makes kitchen organizers such as vinyl-coated hooks.

Your mother probably had (or wished she had) an Acme safety grater in her kitchen but this invaluable tool, guaranteed to prevent scraped knuckles, is alas! no longer manufactured.

Alco Industries, Inc.

490 Nepperhan Avenue
Yonkers NY 10701
914-969-7722
Cookware, dinnerware, wicker products, wooden giftware

All-Clad Metalcrafters, Inc.

Road 2
Canonsburg PA 15317
412-745-8300
Stainless aluminum cookware

The All-Clad range of pans is well known to professional chefs and serious home cooks. An aluminum or copper exterior, a stainless steel interior and a core of pure aluminum ensure even heat distribution and eliminate the infamous "hot spot." All-Clad also makes a range of **Magna-core** seven-ply pans for use on induction as well as conventional ranges. Products include frying pans, casseroles, stock pots, au gratin and omelette pans as well as saucepans in various sizes.

Alumaline Cutlery Company, Inc.

2nd and State Streets
P.O. Box 156
Dike IA 50624
319-989-2531

Aluminum Housewares

11700 Fairgrove Independence Boulevard
P.O. Box 1599
Maryland Heights MO 63043
314-872-8855
Can & jar openers, canning equipment, cutlery, cutting boards, graters & choppers, household hardware, kitchen tools & gadgets, knife sharpeners, nonelectrics, rangetop drip pans, scissors & shears, slicers & juicers, steamers, woodenware

Ambras International Trading Company

230 Fifth Avenue
New York NY 10001
212-679-5060
Cookware, giftware, housewares

Amco Corporation

901 North Kilpatrick Avenue
Chicago IL 60651
312-379-2100
Barbecue products, gadgets, roast racks, storage products, wire shelving

American Harvest/Harvest Maid

4064 Peavey Road
Chaska MN 55318
612-448-4400
Food dehydrators, jet-stream oven

American Housewares Manufacturing Company

385 Gerard Avenue
P.O. Box 121
Bronx NY 10451
212-665-9500
Colanders, food strainers, fry baskets, kitchen tools, splatter screens

American International Trading Company

S.W.C. Ellis Street and New Jersey Avenue
P.O. Box 400
Glassboro NJ 08028
Cookware, giftware, housewares, porcelain dinnerware

Arjon Manufacturing Corporation

100 Hoffman Place
Hillside NJ 07205
201-372-3500
Kitchen gadgets

A. Aronson, Inc.

889 Broadway
New York NY 10003
212-505-9551
Barbecue products, bar accessories, can & jar openers, cutlery, kitchen gadgets & tools, scissors & shears, wooden tools

American Profile, Inc.

1239 Peterson Drive
Wheeling IL 60090
708-520-1555
Coffee filters, stainless steel cookware

Atlantic Representations, Inc.

141 North Clark, Suite 2
Los Angeles CA 90048
213-261-2660
Barbecue tools, home & kitchen organizers, housewares, kitchen gadgets & tools

Atlas Metal Spinning Company

470 South Airport Boulevard
South San Francisco CA 94080
415-871-6710
Champagne/wine buckets, copper cookware, stainless steel cookware, steamers, steel cookware, woks & accessories

Automatic Wire Goods Manufacturing Company

385 Gerard Avenue
P.O. Box 121 GPO
Bronx NY 10451
212-665-9500
Colanders, food strainers, fry baskets, kitchen tools, splatter screens

Back to Basics Products, Inc.

11660 South State Street
Sandy UT 84070
801-571-7349
Bakeware, canning equipment, food processing equipment, juicers, gadgets, steamers

Beem California Corporation

18319 Sherman Way
Reseda CA 91335
818-708-2828
Barbecues, breadbakers, chinaware, teamakers, meat grinders, food choppers, rice cookers, sausage stuffers, tea & coffee accessories, vegetable shredders

Bendow, Ltd., (Lewis L. Salton Company)

1120 Federal Road
Brookfield CT 06804
203-775-6341
Permanent coffee & tea filters, nonelectric coffeemakers, nonelectric teamakers

Berndes U.S.

872 Thomas Drive
Bensenville IL 60106
708-228-1907
Bakeware, coated cookware, cast aluminum cookware, stainless steel, multipurpose cookpots, whistling kettles

Best Manufacturers
P.O. Box 20091
Portland OR 97220
503-253-1528
Hand kitchen tools

If you have a collection of wire whisks, it's likely at least one was manufactured by Best. Founded more than 30 years ago, the company makes whisks in 45 different sizes: long or short, balloon or flat, with a handle of metal, wood or plastic—you name it, Best makes it. Other products are a heavy-duty masher (preferred by Tex-Mex enthusiasts when mashing beans, for which a regular potato masher is too flimsy) and a tool for popping bubbles in pizza dough to ensure the smooth crust the American public prefers.

Better Housewares Corporation
25-12 41st Avenue
Long Island City NY 11101
718-392-2123
Bakeware, gourmet housewares, kitchen gadgets

Big Time/Prime Marketing
5 Terminal Road
West Hempstead NY 11552
516-489-3300
Gadgets

Bonny Products, Inc.
10 Peninsula Boulevard
Lynbrook NY 11563
516-887-3737
Colanders & strainers, cookware, corkscrews, egg boilers & slicers, food scoops, kitchen cutlery, kitchen tools & gadgets, knife sharpeners, pastry brushes & dough blenders, scissors, seafood & nut crackers, shredders, graters, choppers, stainless steel flatware, thermometers

BRA USA, Inc.
195 Redneck Avenue
Little Ferry NJ 07643
201-641-7220
Cookware, stainless steel, kitchen utensils

Brabantia Division of Loroman Company (Abbott Company)
95-25 149th Street
Jamaica NY 11435
718-291-0800
Cookware, countertop items, gadgets, utensils

Bradshaw International, Inc.
9303 Greenleaf Avenue
Santa Fe Springs CA 90670
213-946-7466
Cookware, kitchen tools & gadgets, mugs

Brewmatic Company
3828 South Main Street
Los Angeles CA 90037
213-233-8204
Coffee brewing equipment, coffee dispensers, coffee serving decanters, vacuumware

Bromwell Housewares, Inc.
601 North Carroll Street
P.O. Box 797
Michigan City IN 46360
219-874-6447
Bakeware, camping equipment cookware, fry pans, graters & sifters, popcorn makers

Max Burton Enterprises, Inc.
502 Puyallup Avenue
Tacoma WA 98421
206-627-2665
Burner covers, mixing bowls, stovetop grills, teakettles, trivets

C. M. International
P.O Box 60127
Colorado Springs CO 80934
719-390-0505
Smoker & cooker accessories

Century Cookware/Birmingham Stove
P.O. Box 2647
Birmingham AL 35202
205-252-7800
Cast-iron cookware, cast-iron outdoor furniture, charcoal barbecues

Chantal by Lentrade
2030 West Belt
Houston TX 77043
713-467-9949
Cookware

Chantry/Victor
P.O. Box 3039
Clearwater FL 34630
813-446-1960
Cast-iron cookware & accessories, cookbooks, knives & knife sharpeners, yogurt & cheese makers

Chefmate Housewares Corporation (Herald Housewares)
3928 North Rockwell
Chicago IL 60618
312-586-2188
Aluminum & nonstick cookware, electric skillets, fry pans & electric woks

Chef Aid
385 Gerard Avenue
P.O. Box 121 GPO
Bronx NY 10451
212-665-9600
Food strainers & colanders, fry baskets, splatter screens, kitchen tools

Chemex (International Housewares)
1 Monument Mills
Housatonic MA 01236
413-274-3396
Automatic & manual coffeemakers, bonded coffee filters, double boilers, French press coffeemakers, glass mugs & teakettles, measuring cups, microwave & ovenproof cookware, souffle casseroles

Chicago Cutlery Company
5420 North County Road 18
Minneapolis MN 55428
612-533-0472
Cutlery, kitchen accessories

Chicago Metallic
800 Ela Road
Lake Zurich IL 60047
708-438-3400
Disposable aluminum foil bakeware, nonstick bakeware, professional bakeware, Silverstone on steel bakeware, tinned steel bakeware

Chip Clip Corporation
1608 West Parklane Towers
Dearborn MI 48126
313-593-3884
Kitchen gadgets, microwave accessories

Chuppa Knife Manufacturing, Inc.
Industrial Road
P.O. Box 356
Dyersburg TN 38024
901-286-4777
Stainless steel cutlery

Clipper Mill
P.O. 376
San Francisco CA 94101
415-552-5005
Housewares, kitchen gadgets

Colonial Kitchen (Bemis Manufacturing Company)
300 Mill Street
Sheboygan Falls WI 53085
414-467-4621
Cutting & chopping boards, knife holders

Commercial Aluminum Cookware Company

P.O. Box 583
Toledo OH 43693
419-666-8700
Barbecue tools, copper & aluminum cookware, nonstick fry pans, pot racks

Concord Shear Corporation

38 Leuning Street
South Hackensack NJ 07606
201-489-2400
Poultry shears, scissors, shears

Looking for egg-cutting shears shaped like a chicken? Then contact Concord Shear. Since 1945, the company has produced a wide range of "pivotal cutting instruments," the term it prefers to "scissors." In addition to the gold-plated carbon steel egg shears, there are decorative grape shears, poultry shears and all kinds of kitchen and general household scissors. (And fishing enthusiasts find Concord Shear's applique scissors ideal for tying flies.)

Cooktime by Eastern

175 Getty Avenue
Paterson NJ 07503
201-684-3033
Anodized aluminum cookware, canister sets, copperware, measuring cup sets, mixing bowl sets, roast pans, salt & pepper shakers, stainless steel cookware, steamers, stock pots & woks, teakettles

Cooper Instrument Corporation

Reeds Gap Road
Middlefield CT 06455
203-347-2256
Basters, electric thermometers & timers, thermometers

Copco, Inc. (Wilton Enterprises)

2240 West 75th Street
Woodridge IL 60517
708-963-7100
Casual serveware, kitchen tools & gadgets, plastic kitchenware, teakettles

Coppersource

3427 Enterprise Avenue
Hayward CA 94545
415-786-4200
Chafing dishes, teapots, copper bakeware, copper cookware, copper decorative pieces, copper serving pieces

Peter Cora Sr., Specialty Equipment

4304 West 63rd Street
Chicago IL 60629
312-767-7154
Aluminum cookware, copper cookware, electric gelato ice cream makers, electric pasta machines, espresso/cappuccino machines, pasta cookers, slicers

Corning, Inc.

Houghton Park, Building B
Corning NY 14831
607-974-8146
Cookware, dinnerware, flatware, serveware, drinkware, stemware

Corning...for the best in food-contact surfaces. **Pyrex**® glass and **Corning Ware**® and **Visions**® glass-ceramic cookware. **Revere Ware**® stainless steel cookware and bakeware. **Corelle**® and **Comcor**® laminated glass and **Pyroceram**® glass-ceramic dinnerware. Trusted, versatile names in any kitchen. Prepare, cook, serve and store—all in one dish. And all but **Revere Ware** are microwave-compatible.

All this and spokesperson Cornelius O'Donnell, too, for media appearances, guest cooking instruction, cooking demonstrations.

Creative House

11 Humphreys Drive
Ivyland PA 18974
215-357-5620
Bakeware, cookie cutters, kitchen gadgets, thermometers

Creative Kitchen, Inc.

110 Meadowlands Parkway
Secaucus NJ 07094
201-866-9560
Bakeware, gadgets, home products housewares, kitchen tools, teakettles

Creative Specialty Manufacturing

194 Skokie Boulevard
Highland Park IL 60035
708-831-4775
Glass ovenware, microwave accessories

Cuisine Cookware Company

1239 Peterson Drive
Wheeling IL 60090
708-541-6640
Coffee filters, stainless steel cookware

Davidcraft Corporation

7040 North Lawndale
Lincolnwood IL 60645
708-674-8700
Cook & bakeware, electric housewares, kitchen tools & gadgets

Deflecto Corporation, Housewares Division

P.O. Box 50057
Indianapolis IN 46250
317-849-9555
Magnetic kitchen accessories, magnets, spice racks, paper towel bars, towel bars, knife & tool racks

Diamond Overseas Trading Company

1125 East St. Charles Road
Lombard IL 60148
708-916-7775
Aluminum cookware, flatware, fry pans, porcelain enamel cookware, salad & mixing bowls, salt & pepper shakers, stainless steel cookware, stock pots, teakettles

Dong Chang International, Inc.

8214 Lehigh Avenue
Morton Grove IL 60053
708-965-8778
Cast-iron cookware, mugs, portable folding tables, stainless steel cookware, stainless steel vacuum bottles

Drexel/Cook'n Cajun

P.O. Box 3726
Shreveport LA 71133
318-925-6933
Heavy-gauge aluminum cookware, outdoor cookers & smokers

Enclume Design Products, Inc.

P.O. Box 700
Port Hadlock WA 98339
206-385-6100
Culinary accessories, pot & pan racks

Ekco Housewares, Inc.

9234 West Belmont Avenue
Franklin Park IL 60131
708-678-8600
Barbecue gadgets, bakeware, beaters, can openers, cutlery, cutting boards, gadgets, kitchen tools, microwave accessories, rolling pins, step stools, strainers, woodenware

Felknor International, Inc.

Route 1, Airport Road
Loudon TN 37774
615-458-4616
Green bean frenchers, popcorn poppers

Fernanda Manufacturing, Inc. Designs by Jerry Abrams

965 Wellwood Avenue
North Lindenhurst NY 11757
516-957-8452
Carving & cutting boards, salt & pepper mills, stemware holders, wine racks, wooden kitchen helpers

Fiskars Manufacturing Corporation
7811 West Stewart Avenue
P.O. Box 8027
Wausau WI 54402
715-842-2091
Kitchen cutlery, kitchen gadgets, scissors

**Foley Company, Cookware-Bakeware
(Newell Group)**
P.O. Box 1330
Manitowoc WI 54221
414-684-4421
Aluminum cookware & bakeware, nonstick coated bakeware, nonstick coated cookware, teakettles

Forever Cookware
P.O. Box 50579
New Orleans LA 70005
504-831-9907
Anodized cookware, indoor-outdoor cookware, polished aluminum cookware

Fouineteau USA, Inc.
1200 Waterway Boulevard
Indianapolis IN 46202
317-634-6767
Food dehydrators, kitchen gadgets, nonelectric grills, nonstick cookware, spice racks, stainless steel cookware, steamers

Fox Run Craftsmen
1907 Stout Drive, Warwick Commons
Industrial Park
P.O. Box 2727
Ivyland PA 18974
215-675-7700
Bakeware, cake decorating supplies, ceramics, cookie cutters, kitchen gadgets, woodenware

**G & S International Products/
Four Star International**
3330 East 79th Street
Cleveland OH 44127
216-441-0700
Barbecue tools and accessories, bar accessories, cast-iron cookware, gadgets

**G & S Metal Products
Company, Inc.**
3330 East 79th Street
Cleveland OH 44127
216-441-0700
Aluminum bakeware, Silverstone bakeware, heavyweight steel bakeware, nonstick silicone, cast-iron cookware, gadgets, woodenware

GTC International, Inc.
7131 West 61st Street
Chicago IL 60638
312-586-1400
Bakeware, cookware, glass cutting boards, glassware, microwave accessories, serving trays

**General Housewares Corporation,
Cookware Group**
1536 Beech Street
P.O. Box 4066
Terre Haute IN 47804
812-232-1000
Aluminum & enamel bakeware, canning equipment, cookware, fry pans, steamers

**Gerber Legendary Blades
(Fiskars Company)**
14200 Southwest 72nd Avenue
P.O. Box 23088
Portland OR 97223
503-639-6161
Gadgets, hand tools, kitchen knives, scissors

Gourmac, Inc.
Route 7 & Grace Way
P.O. Box 988
Canaan CT 06018
203-824-5117
Kitchen gadgets, plastic bakeware

H & P Mayer Corporation
621 Route 46 West
P.O. Box 621
Hasbrouck Heights NJ 07604
201-288-8550
Gourmet accessories, kitchen gadgets

In business for more than 50 years, H & P Mayer markets an extensive line of kitchenware that includes wooden lemon reamers (a best-seller), strawberry hullers, french-fry makers, potato peelers and kitchen tool sets in olive wood or one-piece, professional-standard stainless steel. Two popular devices are a **Frosty Cup**, designed for chilling drinks in the freezer, and a **Stay-Kool Pitcher** with a freezable core. Some items are manufactured domestically; most are imported.

Hallmark Housewares Company
1923 South Santa Fe Avenue
Los Angeles CA 90021
213-489-5150
Cookware, cutlery, flatware, gadgets

**Harbortown Division,
IBR Corporation**
1250 South Grove Avenue,
Suite 304
Barrington IL 60010
708-381-2133
Chrome rangetop drip pans, nonstick rangetop drip pans, specialty bakeware items

Harper-Lee International, Inc.
P.O. Box 279
Roan Mountain TN 37687
615-772-3233
Baskets, kitchen gadgets, magnetics

J. A. Henckels
9 Skyline Drive
Hawthorne NY 10532
914-592-7370
Flatware, gadgets, scissors

M. E. Heuck Company
3274 Beekman Street
P.O. Box 23036
Cincinnati OH 45223
513-681-1774
Barbecue tools, kitchen tools & gadgets

Hill Design, Inc.
7 Eagle Square
Concord NH 03301
603-934-2650
Cookie art, shortbread pans

This company specializes in designing ceramic shortbread pans and cookie molds, which are sold together with recipe booklets. Among some 40 designs are several with seasonal themes, such as snowmen, holly wreaths, valentines, lambs and Easter eggs. The pans are sold in specialty and department stores and through mail-order catalogs. The firm also conducts a thriving export trade, chiefly with England, Finland and Japan.

Hillside Metal Ware Company
1060 Commerce Avenue
Union NJ 07083
201-964-3080
Aluminum bakeware, aluminum cookware

Hoan Products, Ltd.
820 Third Avenue
Brooklyn NY 11232
718-499-9500
Baking accessories, baking papers, cutlery, kitchen gadgets & accessories, kitchen tools, wood cutting boards

**Hobart Products Company
(G & S Metal Products, Inc.)**
3330 East 79th Street
Cleveland OH 44127
216-441-0700
Aluminum bakeware, steel bakeware, cast-iron cookware, Silverstone bakeware

Hoffritz International
515 West 24th Street
New York NY 10011
212-924-7300
Carving sets, gadgets, kitchen cutlery, knives, steak knives

Holliston Corporation
107 Trumbull Street, K Building
Elizabeth NJ 07206
201-351-7979
Flatware, nonstick cookware, stainless steel cookware, teakettles

**Hutzler Manufacturing
Company, Inc.**
Route 7 & Grace Way
Canaan CT 06018
203-824-5117
Kitchen gadgets, plastic bakeware

IMEX Enterprise
110 Gerstley Road
Hatboro PA 19040
215-672-2887
Cookware, gadgets

Imperial Schrade Corporation
1776 Broadway
New York NY 10019
212-757-1814
Flatware, gadgets, cutlery

Intermarket Corporation
2056 Milan Avenue
P.O. Box 685
South Pasadena CA 91030
818-441-4555
Gadgets

International Cookware Company
1239 Peterson Drive
Wheeling IL 60090
708-520-3040
Coffee filters, stainless steel cookware

J & F Imports, Inc.
2626 Humboldt Street
Los Angeles CA 90069
213-221-4000
Cook & bakeware, gadgets

Jennex Company
5222 Tractor Road
Toledo OH 43612
419-478-4300
Knife sharpeners

Jericho America, Inc.
2181 Northwest Nicolai
P.O. Box 10191
Portland OR 97210
503-227-1560
Coffee & tea brewers, filters, grinders, servers

Joyce Chen Products
411 Waverly Oaks Road
Waltham MA 02154
617-894-9020
Bamboo kitchen tools, steamers, cutlery, cutting boards, scissors, stir-fry cookware & accessories

K-Co., Inc.
P.O. Box 82013
Lincoln NE 68501
402-474-6043
Can & jar openers, aluminum bakeware, kitchen tools & gadgets, food thermometers

Kalkus-Hirco, Inc., Ursula
8405 West 45th Street
Lyons IL 60534
708-442-5232
Cookie cutters, rosette molds, small kitchen gadgets, woodenware

Keter Plastic (USA), Inc.
1140 Broadway
New York NY 10001
212-679-5260
Cutting boards, food & storage carts, food storage containers, insulated coolers & jugs, insulated flasks, gadgets, picnic items

Kitchen Hardware, Ltd.
6670-C Jones Mill Court
Norcross GA 30092
404-441-1385
Peppermills, specialty bakeware, vegetable slicers

Kitchen Supply Company
209 South Lombard
Oak Park IL 60302
708-383-5990
Kitchen gadgets, kitchen textiles, knife guards, pizza baking stones, pizza-making utensils

L.D.E., Inc.
2716 Kearney Street
P.O. Box 701399
East Elmhurst NY 11369
718-476-2255
Gadgets, housewares

L K Manufacturing Corporation
P.O. Box 634
Westbury NY 11590
516-420-8777
Baking products, bar accessories, cookie cutters, gadgets, refrigerator magnets, wire baking & roast racks

Lasso Corporation of America
1075 West Belt Drive North,
Suite 210
Houston TX 77043
713-827-7809
Kitchen cutlery, kitchen gadgets

Le Creuset of America, Inc.
P.O. Box 575
Yemassee SC 29945
803-589-6211
Enameled cast-iron cookware

**Leifheit Sales
(S. J. International Corporation)**
1140 Broadway
New York NY 10001
212-679-5260
Canning products, gadgets

Lentrade, Inc./Chantal
2030 West Belt
Houston TX 77043
713-467-9949
Chantal cookware

Lifetime Cutlery Corporation
820 Third Avenue
Brooklyn NY 11232
718-499-9500
Colored-handle flatware, cutlery, cutting boards, gadgets, golden flatware, kitchen tool sets, stainless flatware, wood knife blocks

Lodge Manufacturing Company
6th Street at Railroad Avenue
P.O. Box 380
South Pittsburg TN 37380
615-837-7181
Cast-iron bakeware, cast-iron cookware

Lexco Corporation
5900 M. L. King Way South
Seattle WA 98118
206-721-5425
Gadgets

M B R Industries, Inc.
4600 Northwest 128th Street Road
Miami FL 33054
305-769-1000
Cookware, small appliances

Madison, Ltd.
(Davis Brothers Wholesalers, Inc.)
111 Midtown Bridge Road
Hackensack NJ 07601
201-845-8600
Housewares, gadgets

Mark Louis Company
2225 Northwest 29th Street
Oakland Park FL 33311
305-739-9769
*Bakeware, gadgets, knives, peppermills,
teakettles*

Megaware, Inc. of California
5301 Beethoven Street, Suite 101
Los Angeles CA 90066
213-578-5939
*Stainless steel cookware, steel enameled
cookware*

Melitta USA, Inc.
1401 Berlin Road
P.O. Box 900
Cherry Hill NJ 08003
609-428-7202
*Coffee, coffee filters, coffee grinders, coffee
warmers, drip coffeemakers*

Mendix Corporation
12601 Southwest 130th Street
Miami FL 33186
305-233-9866
*Cookware, cutlery, plastic housewares &
flatware*

The Metal Ware Corporation
1700 Monroe Street
Two Rivers WI 54241
414-793-1368
*Coffeemaker urns, electric housewares, hot
cups, roaster oven cookers*

Micromeals, Inc.
2406 North Court Street
Rockford IL 61103
815-964-5841
Microwave cooking-related products

Microwise Cookware USA
5801 Lee Highway
Arlington VA 22207
703-533-8555
Microwave cookware accessories

Mirro/Foley Company
(The Newell Group)
P.O. Box 1330
Manitowoc WI 54221
414-684-4421
*Aluminum cookware-bakeware, canning
equipment, kitchen accessories, nonstick
cookware-bakeware, pressure cookers
& canners, Silverstone cookware-bakeware,
teakettles*

Nevco Housewares, Inc.
174 Passaic Street
P.O. Box 160
Garfield NJ 07026
201-778-2311
*Cookware, kitchenware, gadgets & utensils,
woodenware*

Nordic Ware, Inc.
(Northland Aluminum Products)
Highway 7 at #100
Minneapolis MN 55416
612-920-2888
*Bakeware, cookware, gas barbecues, ice cream
makers, microwave bake-cookware, specialty
bake-cookware, waffle irons*

Normandy Distributors
(National Housewares, Inc.)
135 Rowayton Avenue
Rowayton CT 06853
203-838-1755
*Cast-iron cookware, enamel cookware, kitchen
tools, roasting pans, stainless steel cookware,
teakettles*

Norpro, Inc.
6306 215th Street NW
Mountlake Terrace WA 98043
206-771-3717
*Barbecue tools, bakeware, canning accessories,
coffee accessories, cookie cutters, copperware,
kitchen gadgets, kitchen utensils, pasta
accessories, teakettles, thermometers, timers,
woks, woodenware*

P. J. Enterprises
International, Inc.
4701 West Schroeder Drive, Suite 180
P.O. Box 17109
Milwaukee WI 53223
414-357-7100
*Cutting boards, scissors, stainless steel
bakeware*

Paulware
(Paulshin International, Inc.)
7330 North Clark Street
Chicago IL 60626
312-262-6300
*Nonstick cookware, mixing bowls, porcelain
roasters, stock pots, teakettles, stainless steel
cookware, roasters, steamers*

Pedrini USA, Inc.
273 Edison Avenue
West Babylon NY 11704
516-293-0810
Food processors, kitchen gadgets

R. E. Phelon Company, Inc.
(Magnagrip Division)
2342 Boston Road
Wilbraham MA 01095
413-596-3760
*Gadgets, racks, knife & tool holders, write-
on/wipe-off memo boards*

Phoenixware
4022 South 20th Street
Phoenix AZ 85040
602-233-1000
*Bakeware molds, bar accessories & gadgets,
chrome giftware, flasks, flatware, ice buckets,
ice cream sets, pizza accessories*

The Pot Shop
P.O. Box 101
Hanover Station
Boston MA 02113
617-523-9210
Black iron cookware, omelette pans

Primex International Trading
Corporation
230 Fifth Avenue, Suite 711
New York NY 10001
212-679-5060
*Bakeware, ceramics, coffee thermoses,
cookware, giftware, housewares*

Prodyne Enterprises, Inc.
P.O. Box 212
Montclair CA 91763
714-628-1316
*Cheese keepers, cheese slicers, nutcrackers,
serveware, wooden cheese boards*

Profit Targets, Inc.
3191 Commonwealth, Suite 200
Dallas TX 75247
214-634-4412
*Gadgets, magnets, microwave accessories,
nonelectric can openers*

Progressive International Corporation

8300 Military Road South
Seattle WA 98108
206-762-8300
Coffee & tea carafes & accessories, copper cookware, plasticware, stainless cookware & bakeware

Progressus Company

40 St. Mary's Place
Freeport NY 11520
516-623-8300
Aluminum foilware, bakeware, gadgets, plastic cutlery, woodenware

R.S.V.P. International

451 North 34th Street
Seattle WA 98103
206-547-6850
Barbecue tools, coffee & tea makers, copper-ware, grill baskets, stainless steel bowls, stainless steel colanders & cookware, stovetop popcorn poppers

Raadvad American, Ltd.

5378 Fairlawn Shores Trail
Prior Lake MN 55372
612-447-8553
Bread cutters, cookware, cutlery, flatware, knives, scissors

Range Kleen Manufacturing, Inc.

4240 East Road
Lima OH 45807
419-331-8000
Electric range reflector bowls & pans, trim rings, gas range reflector bowls & pans

Reco International Corporation

150 Haven Avenue
Port Washington NY 11050
516-767-2400
Clay bakeware & cookware, coffee filters, copper cookware & molds

Regent-Sheffield, Ltd. (Wiltshire International)

70 Schmitt Boulevard
P.O. Box 219
Farmingdale NY 11735
516-293-8200
Cutlery, gourmet cutlery, kitchen tools, knife blocks, self-sharpening scissors, sport knives, steak knife sets, wooden accessories

Rema Bakeware, Inc.

625 East North Street
Salina KS 67401
913-823-1682
Insulated bakeware, pizza bakeware

Rema is famous for its innovative insulated bakeware. Constructed from two layers of aluminum that trap a layer of air between them, the designs ensure even browning on the bottom as well as the top of any baked item. The firm initially made cookie sheets, then added brownie, jelly-roll, pizza, muffin and cake pans. Its latest invention is a pizza pan of single-layer aluminum pierced with 800 holes that let all the steam escape, banishing soggy crusts forever.

Reston Lloyd, Ltd.

335 Victory Drive
P.O. Box 2302
Reston VA 22070
703-437-0003
Glazed clay pots, microwave bakeware, porcelain-on-steel cookware, stock pots, stove burner covers, teakettles, thermal carafes

Revere Ware Corporation

1000 South Sherman Street
P.O. Box 250
Clinton IL 61727
217-935-3111
Anodized aluminum cookware, cutlery, microwave cookware, plastic, stainless steel bakeware, stainless steel cookware, teakettles

The Richard Group

815 North La Brea, Suite 416
Inglewood CA 90302
213-324-6082
Gas lighters, scissors, jar & bottle openers, gadgets, magnets, saws, knife sharpeners, mechanical timers, plastic cutting boards, poultry shears

Roshco, Inc.

2560 North Elston Avenue
Chicago IL 60647
312-235-8500
Nonstick bakeware, stainless steel bakeware, woks

Rosti (USA), Inc.

18 Sidney Circle
Kenilworth NJ 07033
201-964-6555
Canisters, coffee filters, nonelectric drip coffeemakers, espresso/cappuccino machines, flatware, glass bakeware & cookware, gadgets, microwave accessories, serving & buffet accessories

Rowoco, Homecraft Consumer Products Group (Dynacast)

2 Glenshaw Road
Orangeburg NY 10962
914-365-1900
Barbecue tools, bakeware, barware, gadgets, pasta accessories, peppermills, woks, woodenware

Royal Household Products, Inc.

1444 178th Street
Gardena CA 90248
213-323-5366
Cookware, cutlery, gadgets

Sanyei America Corporation, Household Division

450 Harmon Meadow Boulevard
Secaucus NJ 07094
201-864-4848
Ceramic ware, coffee mugs, cookware, kitchen tools, teakettles, tinware

Scanpan USA, Inc.

4 Pearl Court
Allendale NJ 07401
201-327-9299
Combination cold carriers, nonstick cookware

Schiller & Asmus, Inc.

P.O. Box 575
Yemassee SC 29945
803-589-6211
Coffeemakers, cookware, food storage containers

SCI Scandicrafts, Inc.

4550 Calle Alto
P.O. Box 659
Camarillo CA 93010
805-482-0791
Bakeware, gadgets, kitchen tools

Sitram USA, Inc.

1 Eves Drive, Suite 111
Marlton NJ 08053
609-985-9323
Cookware, copper cookware

Spanek Enterprises

19135 Brook Lane
Saratoga CA 95070
408-446-3000
Cutting boards, wire roasting products, portable barbecues

Stanco Metal Products, Inc.

105 Fulton Street
P.O. Box 307
Grand Haven MI 49417
616-842-5000
Electric & gas range bowls, range burner pans, stove covers & trivets

**Swissmar Imports
(Gra-Mic, Inc.)**
8300 Quarry Road
Niagara Falls NY 14304
*Fondue sets, kitchen gadgets, raclette
equipment*

Taylor & Ng
1212-B 19th Street
Oakland CA 94607
415-834-2754
*Espresso/cappuccino accessories, espresso/
cappuccino makers, kitchen textiles, mugs, pot
racks, woks*

T-Fal Corporation
23 Kulick Road
Fairfield NJ 07006
201-575-1060
*Nonstick cookware & bakeware, stainless steel
pressure cookers*

Tops Manufacturing Company, Inc.
83 Salisbury Road
Darien CT 06820
203-655-9367
*Bacon presses, beverage warmers, broiling
racks, coffee dispensers, cookware knobs &
handles, drip coffeemakers, glass mugs, glass
whistling teakettles, percolators, replacement
percolator parts, tea strainers*

Tops markets a wide variety of useful
kitchen gadgets. Under the Fitz-All
brand name, the firm makes replacement
parts—principally knobs and handles—
for cookware, and a simple wire heat
diffuser, which protects glass pots from
cracking when heated on a gas or electric
range. About two-thirds of Tops'
products are manufactured at its factory
in Rockaway, New Jersey; the remainder
are imported.

Trend Products Company
7417 Van Nuys Boulevard, Suite H
Van Nuys CA 91405
818-787-8844
*Canister sets, stainless steel cookware &
bakeware, steamer pots, stainless steel stovetop
percolators, teakettles*

Trendex International, Inc.
1540 Merchandise Mart
Chicago IL 60654
312-644-7754
Espresso coffee pots, cutlery, kitchen accessories

Vandel International, Inc.
150 Ethel Road West
Piscataway NJ 08854
201-572-7400
*Aluminum cookware, enamel cookware,
espresso coffeemakers, Hispanic specialty items,
pressure cookers*

Villaware Manufacturing Company
1420 East 36th Street
Cleveland OH 44114
216-891-6650
*Cheese graters, electric baking irons, espresso
coffee pots, Italian ceramic bowls & platters,
kitchen gadgets, meat grinders, pasta
machines, ravioli makers*

Vitantonio Manufacturing Company
34355 Vokes Drive
Eastlake OH 44094
216-946-1661
*Espresso coffeemakers, kitchen gadgets, pasta
& canning equipment, small electric
appliances*

Vollmer Products, Inc.
4522 Macro
San Antonio TX 78218
512-661-4181
*Aluminum cookware, barbecue smoker pits &
grills, enameled cookware, gadgets*

Weatherbee Company
9 Old Littleton Road
P.O. Box 297
Harvard MA 01451
617-456-8488
*Cook's charts, jar vises, recipe easels, recipe
wheels*

Westwood International
2274 Davis Avenue
P.O. Box 5018
Hayward CA 94545
415-887-1000
*Cutting boards, decorative baskets &
ceramics, barbecue & kitchen ceramics,
household ceramics, kitchenware*

Wilkinson Sword, Inc., USA
7012 Best Friend Road
Atlanta GA 30340
404-441-3030
*Household cutters & snips, self-sharpening
cutlery*

Wilton Enterprises
2240 West 75th Street
Woodridge IL 60517
708-963-7100
*Cake decorating products, candymaking
products, cook & bakeware, decorating kits &
accessories, party goods*

**Wisconsin Aluminum Foundry
Company, Inc.**
838 South 16th Street
P.O. Box 246
Manitowoc WI 54220
414-682-8627
*Bakeware, cookware, griddles, pressure
canners, pressure cookers, stock pots*

Wingknife, Inc.
3112 South Andrews Avenue
P.O. Box 6506
Ft. Lauderdale FL 33316
305-467-8707
Citrus tools, kitchen gadgets

Wooco International Corporation
1182 Broadway, Suite 603
New York NY 10001
212-685-5716
*Aluminum fry pans, bakeware, ceramic ware,
colanders, kitchen gadgets, mixing bowls,
roast pans, steamers, stock pots, teakettles*

**John Wright
(Donsco)**
North Front Street, Suite C-40
Wrightsville PA 17368
717-252-3661
*Muffin & cookie molds, porcelain-coated
cookware, cast-iron teakettles, teakettles*

A division of Donsco, this Pennsylvania company specializes in decorative
cast-iron cookie molds. The "sweetheart"
pan with its nine hearts and a harvest
mold with fruit and vegetable designs
are based on antique models; others,
such as the dinosaur, teddy bear and
alphabet molds, are contemporary. John
Wright also makes cast-iron pans and
heavy teakettles, designed primarily to
sit on wood stoves and put humidity
into the air—as well as others for
actually making tea.

Wusthof/Trident Cutlery Company
113 North 1st Street
Minneapolis MN 55401
612-332-0332
*Kitchen cutlery & accessories, kitchen gadgets,
knife blocks & knife sets*

The Zanger Company
295 Ella Grasso Turnpike
P.O. Box 3306
Windsor Locks CT 06096
203-627-7467
*Kitchen & tableware cutlery, plastic cutting
boards*

Zani America, Inc.
7399 South Tucson Way, Unit A-5
Englewood CO 80112
303-792-2665
Espresso coffee machines, stainless steel cookware, stainless steel serveware, tabletop kitchen acrylics

Zim Manufacturing Company
2850-56 West Fulton Street
Chicago IL 60612
312-722-6622
Aluminum drip trays, can, bottle & jar openers, stainless steel basters

Zivi Hercules, Inc.
50 Kerry Place
Norwood MA 02062
617-762-8310
Barbecue accessories, choppers, forged & stamped cutlery, knives

Food
PROMOTION

179
Food Associations and Institutes

183
Product Promotion Associations
Beverages; Cheese, Eggs & Dairy/Deli;
Fruit & Nuts; Meat; Poultry; Potatoes,
Pasta, Rice & Beans; Sauces & Season-
ings; Seafood; Sweets & Snacks; Vegetables

188
Public Relations and Advertising

192
TV and Radio Networks

Matthew Klein   *Telephone (212) 255-6400 FAX (212) 242-6149*   *Photography*

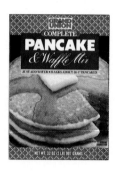

Matthew Klein Studio, 104 West 17th Street, No. 2E, New York, New York 10011

Represented by Michael Crecco (212) 682-3422

Food Associations and Institutes

This listing has been compiled from many sources and may well be a "first" of its kind. It includes the names of organizations representing people who are active in the food industry. Some are groupings of professionals, some of semiprofessionals and others have members in both categories. In each case their members are knowledgeable in a specific topic.

For convenience, the list is organized alphabetically by the name of the organization and includes the name and title of the executive currently responsible for it.

American Bakers' Association
1111 14th Street NW, Suite 300
Washington DC 20005
202-296-5800
Contact:
Paul Abenante, President

American Culinary Federation
P.O. Box 3466
St. Augustine FL 32085
904-824-4468
Contact:
Ron Wolf, Public Relations
Director

American Frozen Food Institute
1764 Old Meadow Lane, Suite 350
McLean VA 22102
703-821-0770
Contact:
Steve Anderson, Executive
Vice President

American Home Economics Association
1555 King Street
Alexandria VA 22314
703-706-4600
Contact:
Carole Fromer, President

American Home Economists in Business
5008 Pine Creek Drive
Blendonview Office Park
Westerville OH 43081
614-890-4342
Contact:
Marlissa Banister,
Executive Director

American Hotel and Motel Association
1201 New York Avenue NW,
Suite 600
Washington DC 20005
202-289-3100
Contact:
Kenneth F. Hine, Executive
Vice President

American Institute of Food Distribution
28-12 Broadway
Fair Lawn NJ 07410
201-791-5570
Contact:
Jack Rengstorff, Executive
Vice President

American Institute of Wine and Food
1550 Bryant Street, Suite 700
San Francisco CA 94103
415-255-3000
Contact:
Kerry Parker, Membership
Director

American School Food Service Association
5600 South Quebec, Suite 300B
Englewood CO 80111
303-220-8484
Contact:
Pat Bayer, Executive Director

Arizona Women in Food and Wine
4209 North 33rd Place
Phoenix AZ 85018
602-956-7647
Contact:
Sylvia Smith, President

Association of Food Industries
177 Main Street
P.O. Box 776
Matawan NJ 07747
201-583-8188
Contact:
Richard Sullivan, Executive
Vice President

Chefs in America
Hearst Building, Suite 324
Market and 3rd Streets
San Francisco CA 94103
415-541-7773
Contact:
Jesse W. Sartain, National Director

Chicago Culinary Guild
c/o The Cooking & Hospitality
Institute of Chicago
858 North Orleans Street
Chicago IL 60610
312-944-0882
312-280-1181
Contact:
Linda Calafiore, President

Cleveland Society for Culinary Professionals
33755 Chagrin Boulevard
Moreland Hills OH 44022
216-831-2279
Contact:
Holly Collins, President

Club Managers' Association of America
P.O. Box 26308
Alexandria VA 22313
703-739-9500
Contact:
James Schuping, Executive
Director

Commercial Food Equipment Service Association, Inc.
9240 North Meridian, Suite 355
Indianapolis IN 46260
317-844-4700
Contact:
Carla Helm, Executive
Director

Connecticut Women's Culinary Alliance
770 Reef Road
Fairfield CT 06430
203-254-2463
Contact:
Mary Goodbody, President

Council for Regional Culinary Organizations (CORCO)
401 East 80th Street, Suite 4K
New York NY 10021
212-879-2709
Contact:
Susy Davidson, Coordinator

Council on Hotel/Restaurant and Institutional Education
1200 17th Street NW
Washington DC 20036
202-331-5990
Contact:
Doug Adair, Executive
Vice President

Culinary Guild of Chicago
812 South Kensington
La Grange IL 60525
708-579-9453
Contact:
Tobe Lemoine, President

Culinary Historians of Ann Arbor
1207 West Madison Street
Ann Arbor MI 48103
313-663-4894
Contact:
Jan Longone, Chair

Culinary Historians of Boston
3 Evergreen Lane
Hingham MA 02043
617-740-1548
Contact:
Joan Kriegstein, Liaison

Culinary Historians of New York
New York Public Library
Fifth Avenue at 42nd Street
New York NY 10018
212-930-0577
Contact:
Reynaldo Alejandro, Curator,
Culinary Collection

Delaware Valley Association of Cooking Professionals
69 Lowry Drive
Wilmington DE 19805
302-475-0390
Contact:
Pat Tabibian

The Educational Foundation of the National Restaurant Association
250 South Wacker Drive,
Suite 1400
Chicago IL 60606
312-715-1010
Contact:
Charles H. Sandler, Director,
Public Relations

Food Equipment Manufacturers' Association
111 East Wacker Drive
Chicago IL 60601
312-644-6610
Contact:
Maxine Lee Couture,
Executive Secretary

Food Marketing Institute (FMI)
1750 K Street NW,
Suite 700
Washington DC 20006
202-452-8444
Contact:
Charlie Bray,
Senior Vice President

Food Marketing Communicators
P.O. Box 19117
Lenexa KS 66215
913-888-8814
Contact:
George Selders,
Executive Director

Food Processing Machinery and Supplies Association
200 Daingerfield Road
Alexandria VA 22314
202-684-1080
Contact:
George Melnykovich, President

Food Service & Packaging Institute
1025 Connecticut Avenue NW,
Suite 513
Washington DC 20036
202-347-0020
Contact:
Joseph W. Bow, President

Foodservice Consultants' Society International
12345 30th Avenue NE, Suite A
Seattle WA 98125
206-367-3274
Contact:
C. Russell Nickle, Executive
Vice President

Foodservice Equipment Distributors' Association
332 South Michigan Avenue,
Suite 1840
Chicago IL 60604
312-427-9605
Contact:
Raymond Herrick,
Executive Director

Grocery Manufacturers of America
1010 Wisconsin Avenue NW,
Suite 800
Washington DC 20007
202-337-9400
Contact:
Kathleen Ramsey, Vice President,
Legislation & Administration

Heartland Food Society
2315 Huron Street
Chicago IL 60612
312-278-1661
Contact:
Kay Zubow, President

Houston Culinary Guild
1708 Sunset Boulevard
Houston TX 77005
713-528-2264
Contact:
Eloise Cooper, President

In-Flight Food Service Association
304 West Liberty Street,
Suite 301
Louisville KY 40202
502-583-3783
Contact:
Phillip S. Cooke, President

International Association of Cooking Professionals (IACP)
304 West Liberty Street,
Suite 301
Louisville KY 40202
502-583-3783
Contact:
Anne Willan, President

International Caterers' Association
220 South State Street,
Suite 1416
Chicago IL 60604
312-922-1271
Contact:
Robert Kolinek, President

International Chefs' Association
50 Hidden Glen Road
Upper Saddle River NJ 07458
201-825-8455
Contact:
Helmut Hamann, President

**International Food, Wine
and Travel Writers' Association**
1020 Via Vadera
Palm Springs CA 92262
619-322-4717
Contact:
Don Jackson, President

**International Foodservice
Editorial Council (IFEC)**
82 Osborne Lane
East Hampton NY 11937
516-324-2725
Contact:
Betty Bastion, Director

**International Foodservice
Executives' Association**
3017 West Charleston Boulevard,
Suite 50
Las Vegas NV 89102
702-736-4332
Contact:
Van Heffner, Executive
Vice President

**International Foodservice
Manufacturers' Association**
321 North Clark Street,
Suite 2900
Chicago IL 60610
312-644-8989
Contact:
Mike Licata, President

International Franchise Association
1350 New York Avenue, Suite 900
Washington DC 20005
202-628-8000
Contact:
William Cherkasky, President

**International Institute of Foods
and Family**
225 West Ohio Street
Chicago IL 60610
312-670-0200
Contact:
Lucille Lampman, President

**International Microwave
Power Institute (IMPI)**
13542 Union Village Circle
Clifton VA 22024
703-830-5588
Contact:
Robert C. LaGasse,
Executive Director

Institute of Food Technologists
221 North La Salle Street
Chicago IL 60601
312-782-8424
Contact:
Howard Mattson, President

The James Beard Foundation
167 West 12th Street
New York NY 10011
212-675-4984
Contact:
Peter Kump, President

Les Dames d'Escoffier, Chicago
270 Arden Shore Road
Lake Bluff IL 60044
708-234-0346
Contact:
Nancy Kirby Harris, President

Les Dames d'Escoffier, Dallas
1545 West Mockingbird Lane,
Suite 1047
Dallas TX 75235
214-688-0906
Contact:
Rebecca Murphy, President

Les Dames d'Escoffier, New York
c/o Joseph Baum &
Michael Whiteman Company
186 Fifth Avenue
New York NY 10010
212-206-7110
Contact:
Rozanne Gold, President

**Les Dames d'Escoffier,
Philadelphia**
1810 Rittenhouse Square,
Suite 2010
Philadelphia PA 19103
215-732-2607
Contact:
Claire Boasi, President

Les Dames d'Escoffier, Seattle
c/o Larry's Markets
14900 Interurban Avenue South
Seattle WA 98168
206-243-2951
Contact:
Nancy Lazara

Les Dames d'Escoffier, Washington
3802 Jocelyn Street NW
Washington DC 20015
202-362-8228
Contact:
Ann Harvey Yonkers, President

**Los Angeles Women's Culinary
Alliance**
8033 Sunset Boulevard,
Suite 3504
Los Angeles CA 90046
213-285-3856
Contact:
Debbie Slutsky, President

**Marketing Agents for the Food
Service Industry**
111 East Wacker Drive, Suite 600
Chicago IL 60601
312-644-6610
Contact:
Jim Dickenson, Executive Director

**Mexican-American Grocers'
Association**
405 North San Fernando Road
Los Angeles CA 90031
213-227-1565
Contact:
Steve Soto, President

**National-American Wholesale
Grocers' Association (NAWGA)**
201 Park Washington Court
Falls Church VA 22046
703-532-9400
Contact:
John Block, President

**National Association of Catering
Executives (NACE)**
5757 West Century Boulevard,
Suite 512
Los Angeles CA 90045
213-417-8072
Contact:
Raymond Delrich, Executive
Director

National Association of College and University Food Services
Manly Miles Building
1405 South Harrison Road,
Suite 303
East Lansing MI 48824
517-332-2494
Contact:
Clark E. DeHaven, Executive
Director

National Association of Concessionaires
35 East Wacker Drive, Suite 1545
Chicago IL 60601
312-236-3858
Contact:
Charles A. Winans, Executive
Director

National Association of Food Equipment Manufacturers
111 East Wacker Drive, Suite 600
Chicago IL 60601
312-644-6610
Contact:
William Carpenter, President

National Association of Meat Purveyors
8365-B Greensboro Drive
McLean VA 22102
703-827-5754
Contact:
Stanley Emerling, Executive
Vice President

National Association for the Specialty Food Trade, Inc. (NASFT)
215 Park Avenue South
New York NY 10003
212-505-1770
Contact:
Edith Friedland, President

National Automatic Merchandising Association
20 North Wacker Drive, Suite 3500
Chicago IL 60606
312-346-0370
Contact:
James A. Rost, President

National Candy Wholesalers' Association
1120 Vermont Avenue NW,
Suite 1120
Washington DC 20001
202-463-2124
Contact:
Ernie May, President

National Caterers' Association
P.O. Box 4510
Akron OH 44310
800-848-FOOD
Contact:
Tony Rubino, President

National Food Brokers' Association (NFBA)
1010 Massachusetts Avenue NW,
6th Floor
Washington DC 20001
202-789-2844
Contact:
Bob Schwarre, President

National Food Distributors' Association (NFDA)
111 East Wacker Drive
Chicago IL 60601
312-644-6610
Contact:
Arthur H. Klawans, President

National Grocers' Association
1825 Samuel Morse Drive
Reston VA 22090
703-437-5300
Contact:
Thomas K. Zaucha, President

National Housewares Manufacturers' Association
1324 Merchandise Mart
Chicago IL 60654
312-644-3333
Contact:
Kimberly Rawn, Director
of Communications

National Institute for Off-Premise Catering
2555 North Clark Street,
Suite 302
Chicago IL 60614
312-525-6800
Contact:
Michael Roman, President

National Nutritional Foods Association (NNFA)
125 East Baker Avenue, Suite 230
Costa Mesa CA 92626
714-966-6632
Contact:
Emil Mahler, President

National Restaurant Association
311 1st Street NW
Washington DC 20001
202-331-5900
Contact:
Jeffry Prince, Director
of Public Relations

National Retail Merchants' Association (NRMA)
100 West 31st Street
New York NY 10001
212-244-8780
Contact:
James William, President

Newspaper Food Editors' and Writers' Association
c/o Food Day
The Oregonian
1320 Broadway SW
Portland OR 97201
503-221-8384
Contact:
Barb Durbin, President

New York Association of Cooking Teachers
c/o Carole Walter
8 Murphy Court
West Orange NJ 07052
201-325-0119
Contact:
Carole Walter, President

New York Women's Culinary Alliance
142 East 13th Street
New York NY 10003
212-923-7023
Contact:
Susan Pomerantz, President

Northwest Culinary Alliance
1613 Fourth Avenue North
Seattle WA 98109
206-284-1780
Contact:
Diane Hazen, President

Philadelphia Women's Culinary Guild
1201 East Moyamensing Avenue
Philadelphia PA 19147
215-468-6776
Contact:
Cindy Ayers, President

Pizza Industry Manufacturers' Association
P.O. Box 80279
Chicago IL 60680
312-938-0127
Contact:
Drew Axelrod, President

Private Label Manufacturers' Association (PLMA)
41 East 42nd Street, Suite 1500
New York NY 10017
212-972-3131
Contact:
Brian Sharoff, President

Produce Marketing Association, Inc.
1500 Casho Mill Road
Newark DE 19714
302-738-7100
Contact:
Steve Ahlberg, Food Service
Vice President

San Francisco Professional Food Society
P.O. Box 410990
San Francisco CA 94141
415-327-1015
Contact:
Flo Braker, President

Society for the Advancement of Foodservice Research
304 West Liberty Street, Suite 301
Louisville KY 40202
502-583-3783
Contact:
Phillip S. Cooke, Executive
Vice President

Society for Cuisine in America
304 West Liberty Street, Suite 301
Louisville KY 40202
502-583-3783
Contact:
Daniel Maye, Executive Director

Society for Foodservice Management
304 West Liberty Street, Suite 301
Louisville KY 40202
502-583-3783
Contact:
Phillip S. Cooke, President

Southern California Culinary Guild
4158 Benedict Canyon Drive
Sherman Oaks CA 91423
818-784-7019
Contact:
Mitzie Cutler, Co-President

St. Louis Culinary Society
130 South Bemiston Boulevard,
Suite 304
St. Louis MO 63105
314-721-2221
Contact:
Lila Spencer, President

United Fresh Fruit & Vegetable Association
727 North Washington Street
Alexandria VA 22314
703-836-3410
Contact:
John M. Addy, Director,
Member Services

**W.I.N.E.
The Wine Information & News Exchange**
201 Summer Street
Stanford CT 06901
800-327-4442
Contact:
Elizabeth Oremus, Director

Wisconsin Cheese & Specialty Food Merchants' Association
302 East Washington Avenue,
Suite 200
Madison WI 53703
608-255-0373
Contact:
Tom Dohm, President

Women's Culinary Guild of New England
50 Hartford Street
Natick MA 01760
508-653-5188
Contact:
Denise Schorr, President

Product Promotion Associations

The promotion of food products is one of the most active areas of the food industry. Almost all major products are represented by an association or commission or board that exists to disseminate information and improve a specific product's sales. Some are regional, others are sponsored by cooperative organizations of producers or by a state department of agriculture. Many such groups have pictures and promotional aids available and all are prime sources of accurate information about the products they represent.

Other helpful resources in this field are: *National Trade and Professional Associations of the United States*, Columbia Books, Inc., 1350 New York Avenue NW, Suite 207, Washington DC 20005; *Thomas Grocery Register*, Thomas Publishing Company, 1 Penn Plaza, New York NY 10119; and *The Encyclopedia of Associa-*

tions, Gale Research, Inc., 835 Penobscot Building, Detroit MI 48226.

BEVERAGES

Coffee Development Group
1400 Eye Street NW, Suite 650
Washington DC 20005
202-682-4034

Coffee, Sugar & Cocoa Exchange
4 World Trade Center SE
New York NY 10048
212-938-2800

National Coffee Association of the USA
110 Wall Street
New York NY 10005
212-344-5596

National Soft Drink Association
1101 16th Street NW
Washington DC 20036
202-463-6732

Specialty Coffee Association of America
1133 15th Street NW, Suite 1000
Washington DC 20005
202-293-5913

Tea Association of the USA, Inc.
230 Park Avenue
New York NY 10169
212-986-9415

CANNED FOODS

Canned Food Information Council
National Food Processors Association
1401 New York Avenue NW
Washington DC 20005
312-836-7279

The council, affiliated with the National Food Processors Association, was created in 1984 to promote canned food. Funded annually by contributions from manufacturers and industry suppliers, it markets canned foods through spokesperson tours, press materials, consumer cookbooks, recipes and information for foodservice operators.

The council also coordinates the February Canned Food Month trade promotion each year, distributing

information nationally and supporting regional committees planning local activities. Manufacturers, retailers, wholesalers, food brokers and media are encouraged to participate.

CHEESE, EGGS & DAIRY/DELI

American Dairy Association
6300 North River Road
Rosemont IL 60018
708-696-1880

American Egg Board
1460 Renaissance Drive
Park Ridge IL 60068
708-296-7044

California Egg Commission
1150 North Mountain Avenue,
Suite 114
Upland CA 91786
714-961-4923

California Milk Advisory Board
400 Oyster Point Boulevard,
Suite 214
South San Francisco CA 94080
415-871-6455

Cheese Importers' Association
460 Park Avenue
New York NY 10022
212-753-7500

Eastern Dairy-Deli Association, Inc.
P.O. Box 156
Great Neck NY 11021
516-487-4640

National Dairy Council
6300 North River Road
Rosemont IL 60018
708-696-1020

National Yogurt Association
1764 Old Meadow Lane, Suite 350
McLean VA 22102
703-821-0770

New England Dairy-Deli Association
420 Washington Street, Suite 102
Braintree MA 02184
617-849-1334

United Dairy Industry Association
6300 North River Road
Rosemont IL 60018
708-696-1860

Wisconsin Cheese Makers' Association
P.O. Box 2133
Madison WI 53701
608-255-2027

Wisconsin Milk Marketing Board Dairy Farmers of Wisconsin
4337 West Beltline Highway
Madison WI 53711
608-271-1021

FRUIT & NUTS

Almond Board of California
1900 Point West A
P.O. Box 15920
Sacramento CA 95852
916-929-6506

Blue Diamond Growers
1802 C Street
Sacramento CA 95814
916-442-0771

California Apricot Advisory Board
1280 Boulevard Way
Walnut Creek CA 94595
415-937-3660

Ninety-seven percent of all domestically grown apricots come from California, and 100 percent of the processed fruit comes from the golden state. The board promotes and publicizes its apricot products—fresh, canned, dried, frozen, concentrate and nectar— for all its 500 apricot growers.

Materials available for distribution include point-of-sale items for grocery stores and restaurants; quantity recipe cards for restaurants and health maintenance organizations; recipes and nutritional information for schools and consumers.

California Granny Smith Association
1941 North Gateway Boulevard,
Suite 102
Fresno CA 93727
209-456-0900

California Kiwifruit Commission
1540 River Park Drive, Suite 110
Sacramento CA 95815
916-929-5314

California Pistachio Commission
1915 North Fine Avenue
Fresno CA 93727
209-252-3345

California Prune Board
World Trade Center, Suite 103
San Francisco CA 94111
415-984-6193

California Raisin Advisory Board
55 Union Street
San Francisco CA 94111
415-984-6100

California Table Grape Commission
P.O. Box 5498
Fresno CA 93755
209-224-4997

California is the top producer of table grapes in the United States and its growers fund the California Table Grape Commission. This nonprofit organization helps to increase awareness, sales and consumption of California table grapes through market development, research and education programs. The commission has promotional items such as recipes, point-of-purchase materials and informational pieces oriented to consumers, foodservice professionals and retailers. They are available free of charge, while supplies last.

California Tree Fruit Agreement
P.O. Box 255383
Sacramento CA 95865
916-483-9261

Canned Fruit Promotion Service
P.O. Box 7111
San Francisco CA 94120
415-541-0100

**Dried Fruit Association
of California**
303 Brokaw Road
Santa Clara CA 95052
408-727-9302

Florida Department of Citrus
P.O. Box 148
Lakeland FL 33802
813-682-0171

**Florida Gift Fruit Shippers'
Association**
521 North Kirkman Road
Orlando FL 32808
407-295-1491

**Florida Lime Administrative
Committee**
P.O. Box 188
Homestead FL 33090
305-247-0848

Georgia Peanut Commission
P.O. Box 967
Tifton GA 31793
912-386-3470

International Apple Institute
P.O. Box 1137
McLean VA 22101
703-442-8850

**Michigan Blueberry Growers'
Association**
P.O. Box B
Grand Junction MI 49056
616-434-6791

Michigan Cherry Committee
2220 University Drive, Suite 200
Okemos MI 48864
517-321-1231

Michigan Plum Advisory Board
P.O. Box 23218
Lansing MI 48909
517-323-7000

National Cherry Foundation
190 Queen Anne Avenue North
Seattle WA 98109
206-285-7082

National Red Cherry Institute
2220 University Drive, Suite 200
Okemos MI 48864
517-321-1231

National Sunflower Association
4023 North State Street
Bismarck ND 58501
701-224-3019

**New York Cherry Growers'
Association, Inc.**
P.O. Box 350
Fishers NY 14453
716-924-2171

North American Blueberry Council
P.O. Box 166
Marmora NJ 08223
609-399-1559

Oregon Cherry Growers
P.O. Box 439
The Dalles OR 97058
503-296-5487

**Oregon-Washington-California
Pear Bureau**
813 Southwest Alder, Suite 601
Portland OR 97205
503-223-8139

**Pacific Coast Canned Pear
Service, Inc.**
P.O. Box 7111
San Francisco CA 94120
415-541-0100

This nonprofit organization represents the Bartlett pear growers of California, Oregon and Washington. The Pacific Coast Canned Pear Service's mission is to increase awareness, sales and consumption of U.S. canned Bartlett pears. It has promotional materials such as recipe cards, nutritional information, posters and product information for consumers, foodservice professionals (a category including restaurant, school and healthcare operators) and distributors. Materials are available free of charge, while supplies last.

Papaya Administrative Committee
2211 Hacienda Boulevard
Hacienda Heights CA 91745
818-961-1856

Peanut Advisory Board
1950 North Park Place, Suite 525
Atlanta GA 30339
404-933-0357

**Pineapple Growers' Association
of Hawaii**
1150 South King Street,
Suite 901 D
Honolulu HI 96814
808-531-5395

Rare Fruit Council International
P.O. Box 561914
Miami FL 33256
305-663-2852

Sunkist Growers, Inc.
14130 Riverside Drive
Sherman Oaks CA 91423
818-986-4800

South Carolina Peach Board
P.O. Box 13413
Columbia SC 29201
803-253-4036

Sun Diamond Growers
5568 Gibraltar Drive
Pleasanton CA 94566
415-463-8200

Walnut Marketing Board
55 Union Street
San Francisco CA 94111
415-984-6240

**Washington State Apple
Commission**
190 Queen Anne Avenue North
Seattle WA 98109
206-285-5625

**Washington Rhubarb Growers'
Association**
P.O. Box 887
Sumner WA 98390
206-863-7333

**Washington State Fruits
Commission**
1005 Tieton Drive
Yakima WA 98902
509-453-4837

**Western New York Apple Growers'
Association, Inc.**
P.O. Box 350
Fishers NY 14453
716-924-2171

MEAT

American Lamb Council
200 Clayton Street
Denver CO 80206
303-771-3500

The American Lamb Council is a
producer-funded organization dedicated
to promoting the extraordinary quality,
flavor and value of fresh American lamb.
The council has extensive educational
and promotional materials, including
point-of-purchase kits, nutritional
information, recipes and usage ideas for
foodservice professionals, retailers and
consumers. Six regional marketing
directors welcome your inquiries.

For more information, contact Robin
Ganse at 303-771-3500.

American Meat Institute (AMI)
17 North Moore Street
Arlington VA 22209
703-841-2400

**American Sheep Industry
Association**
200 Clayton Street
Denver CO 80206
303-771-3500

California Beef Council
551 Foster City Boulevard,
Suite A
Foster City CA 94404
415-571-7100

Iowa Beef Council
Box 451
Ames IA 50010
515-232-0428

National Livestock & Meat Board
444 North Michigan Avenue
Chicago IL 60611
312-467-5520

**National Pork Producers' Council,
Division of the National Livestock
& Meat Board**
P.O. Box 10383
Des Moines IA 50306
515-223-2600

Pork Industry Group
444 North Michigan Avenue
Chicago IL 60611
312-467-5520

POULTRY

National Broiler Council
1155 15th Street NW
Washington DC 20005
202-296-2622

National Turkey Federation
11319 Sunset Hills Road
Reston VA 22090
703-435-7206

Poultry Science Association
309 West Clark Street
Champaign IL 61820
217-356-3182

POTATOES, PASTA, RICE & BEANS

**California Dried Bean
Advisory Board**
531-D North Alta
Dinuba CA 93618
209-591-4866

California Rice Promotion Board
335 Teegarden Street
Yuba City CA 95991
916-674-1227

Frozen Potato Product Institute
1764 Old Meadow Lane, Suite 350
McLean VA 22102
703-821-0770

Idaho Bean Commission
P.O. Box 9433
Boise ID 83707
208-334-3520

Idaho Potato Commission
P.O. Box 1068
Boise ID 83701
208-334-2350

Michigan Bean Commission
P.O. Box 473
Leslie MI 49251
517-694-0581

Maine Potato Board
744 Main Street
Presque Isle ME 04769
207-769-5061

National Pasta Association
1901 North Fort Myer Drive,
Suite 1000
Arlington VA 22209
703-841-0818

Oregon Potato Commission
700 Northeast Multnomah, Suite 460
Portland OR 97232
503-238-7500

The Potato Board
1385 South Colorado Boulevard,
Suite 512
Denver CO 80222
303-758-7783

Rice Council of America
P.O. Box 740121
Houston TX 77274
713-270-6699

**Rice Growers' Association
of California**
P.O. Box 958
Sacramento CA 95812
916-371-6941

**Washington State Potato
Commission**
108 Interlake Road
Moses Lake WA 98837
509-765-8845

The nonprofit Washington State
Potato Comission represents all the
state's potato growers, shippers and
processors. Its primary responsibility is
advertising and promoting Washington

state potatoes in the United States and export markets, primarily the Pacific Rim.

An extensive inventory of promotional items such as recipes, point-of-purchase materials and information pieces is oriented to consumers, foodservice operators, school foodservice directors, and distributors. All are available free while supplies last.

SAUCES & SEASONINGS

Association for Dressing & Sauces
5775 Peachtree-Dunwoody Road,
Suite 500-D
Atlanta GA 30342
404-252-3663

American Spice Trade Association
P.O. Box 1267
Englewood Cliffs NJ 07632
201-568-2163

The Vinegar Institute
5775 Peachtree-Dunwoody Road,
Suite 500-D
Atlanta GA 30342
404-252-3663

SEAFOOD

Alaska Seafood Marketing Institute
P.O. Box DX
Juneau AK 99811
907-586-2902

Bi-State Seafood Development Conference
1 World Trade Center, Suite 64-E
New York NY 10048
212-466-2757

California Fisheries Association/ California Seafood Institute
1715 Capitol Avenue
Sacramento CA 95814
916-441-5560

Catfish Farmers of America
P.O. Box 34
Jackson MS 39205
601-353-7916

Halibut Association of North America
2208 Northwest Market Street,
Suite 311
Seattle WA 98107
206-784-8317

Maine Department of Marine Resources
State House Station 22
Augusta ME 04333
207-289-2291

National Fisheries Institute, Inc.
200 M Street NW, Suite 580
Washington DC 20036
282-296-3428

New England Fisheries Development Foundation, Inc.
280 Northern Avenue
Boston MA 02210
617-542-8890

North Atlantic Seafood Association
1422 Euclid Avenue, Suite 333
Cleveland OH 44115
216-781-6400

Rhode Island Seafood Council
406A Main Street
Wakefield RI 02879
401-783-4200

Virginia Marine Products Board
97 Main Street, Suite 103
Newport News VA 23601
804-594-7261

SWEETS & SNACKS

Biscuit & Cracker Distributors' Association
111 East Wacker Drive
Chicago IL 60601
312-644-6610

Chocolate Manufacturers' Association
7900 Westpark Drive,
Suite A-320
McLean VA 22102
703-790-5011

Flavor & Extract Manufacturers
1620 I Street NW, Suite 925
Washington DC 20006
202-293-5800

National Association of Fruits, Flavors & Syrups
177 Main Street
Matawan NJ 07747
201-583-8272

National Association of Specialty Food & Confection Brokers
6501 Poco Court
Fort Worth TX 76133
817-292-8495

National Candy Brokers' Association
P.O. Box 486
North Andover MA 01845
508-685-3893

National Candy Wholesalers' Association
1120 Vermont Avenue NW,
Suite 1120
Washington DC 20005
202-463-2124

National Confectioners' Association
7900 Westpark Drive, Suite A320
McLean VA 22102
703-790-5750

National Honey Board
421 21st Avenue, Suite 203
Longmont CO 80501
303-776-2337

Popcorn Institute
111 East Wacker Drive
Chicago IL 60601
312-644-6610

Sugar Association, Inc.
1101 15th Street NW, Suite 600
Washington DC 20005
202-785-1122

Vanilla Information Bureau
928 Broadway
New York NY 10010
212-420-8808

VEGETABLES

American Mushroom Institute
907 East Baltimore Pike
Kennett Square PA 19348
215-388-7806

Belgian Endive Marketing Board
745 Fifth Avenue
New York NY 10151
212-980-3881

California Artichoke Advisory Board
P.O. Box 747
Castroville CA 95012
408-633-4411

The California Artichoke Advisory Board is a nonprofit organization that represents artichoke growers in California. Its principal responsibility is the advertising and promotion of California artichokes in the United States and export markets. The commission has promotional materials such as recipe cards, posters, product information and usage ideas for consumer and foodservice professional use. Materials are available free of charge while supplies last.

California Avocado Commission
1251 East Dyer Road, Suite 200
Santa Ana CA 92705
714-558-6761

California Fresh Market Tomato Advisory Board
531-D North Alta
Dinuba CA 93618
209-591-0437

California Fresh Produce Council
1601 East Olympic Boulevard,
Suite 360
Los Angeles CA 90021
213-629-4171

California Iceberg Lettuce Commission
P.O. Box 3354
Monterey CA 93942
408-375-8277

The California Iceberg Lettuce Commission is an industry-funded promotion program representing iceberg lettuce producers in California and Arizona. Its primary purpose is to build a long-term base of loyal consumers. A consistent year-round educational program is conducted, which emphasizes care, handling and usage ideas. All types of promotional materials are available upon request.

California Olive Industry
1903 North Fine Avenue,
Suite 102
Fresno CA 93727
209-456-9096

Canned Food Information Council
500 North Michigan Avenue,
3rd Floor
Chicago IL 60611
312-836-7142

Florida Avocado Administrative Committee
P.O. Box 188
Homestead FL 33090
305-247-0848

Florida Celery Exchange
P.O. Box 140067
Orlando FL 32814
407-894-2911

Florida Tomato Committee
P.O. Box 140635
Orlando FL 32814
407-894-3071

Fresh Garlic Association
P.O. Box 2151
Gilroy CA 95021

Idaho-Oregon Promotion Committee
P.O. Box 909
Parma ID 83660
208-722-5111

Michigan Asparagus Advisory Board
P.O. Box 23218
Lansing MI 48909
517-323-7000

National Onion Association
1 Greeley National Plaza,
Suite 510
Greeley CO 80631
303-353-5895

North Carolina Yam Commission, Inc.
108 West Main Street
Benson NC 27504
919-894-2166

Washington Asparagus Growers
P.O. Box 150
Sunnyside WA 98944
509-837-6022

Wisconsin Canned Vegetables
P.O. Box 5258
Madison WI 53705
608-231-2250

Wisconsin Potato/Vegetable Growers' Association
P.O. Box 327
Antigo WI 54409
715-623-7683

Public Relations and Advertising

Like many other areas of the food industry, this field is constantly in motion, which makes it hard to track down who represents whom. Many of the larger food companies divide account responsibilities among several public relations firms and advertising agencies, while some smaller companies use consultants for advice and representation in these areas.

The list of public relations firms that handle food accounts, as well as accounts in other areas, is too lengthy to give here, so a selection has been made by Irena Chalmers of those firms and consultants particularly noted for their work in the field of food. For a comprehensive listing that includes the names of accounts currently represented by each company and/or its subsidiaries, consult *O'Dwyer's Directory of Public Relations Firms*, published by J.R. O'Dwyer Company, Inc., 271 Madison Avenue, New

York NY 10016, which is updated annually.

In the even larger field of advertising, almost all agencies will welcome a food account, so that a similarly limited listing would be of very little value. The best source of information here is *The Standard Directory of Advertising Agencies*, familiarly called "The Red Book of Advertising," published by the National Register Publishing Company, Macmillan Directory Division, 3004 Glenview Road, Wilmette IL 60091; this, too, is updated annually.

Ayer Public Relations
1345 Avenue of the Americas
New York NY 10105
212-708-6650

Gail Becker Associates
111 Great Neck Road
Great Neck NY 11021
516-829-3260

Gail Becker Associates, experts in food, nutrition and health communications, offers creative public relations strategies designed to match clients' interests—product introduction and publicity, media campaigns and placement, special events and seminars, professional and consumer communications and toll-free consumer information systems. A staff of home economists, dietitians and marketing and consumer affairs specialists is headed by Gail Becker, a public relations professional, registered dietitian and author of several cookbooks, including *Heart Smart* (Simon & Schuster).

Burrell Public Relations, Inc.
20 North Michigan Avenue
Chicago IL 60602
312-443-8700

Burson-Marsteller
230 Park Avenue South
New York NY 10003
212-614-4000

Creative Net-work, Inc.
1125 Northeast 125th Street, Suite A
North Miami FL 33161
305-892-8307

Dorf & Stanton Communications, Inc.
111 Fifth Avenue
New York NY 10003
212-420-8100

Daniel J. Edelman, Inc.
211 East Ontario Street
Chicago IL 60611
312-280-7000

Lisa Ekus Public Relations Company
57 North Street
Hatfield MA 01038
413-247-9325

Lisa Ekus Public Relations Company offers full-service national and local publicity for publishers and authors. We create press kits and materials, organize national tours including TV, radio and press interviews, and plan radio campaigns, in-store promotions, press events and demonstrations. Our specialization is cookbooks and food authors, food events and select food products. One- to three-day media training programs for food professionals are offered. For further information, contact Lisa Ekus, President.

Evans/Kraft Bean Public Relations
190 Queen Anne North
Seattle WA 98109
206-285-2222

Fish Works!
Fishermen's Terminal
C-10 Building
Seattle WA 98119
206-283-7566

Fleishman Hillard, Inc.
200 North Broadway
St. Louis MO 63102
314-982-1700

Gautsch & Associates, Inc.
P.O. Box 22939
Seattle WA 98122
206-325-1780

Gilbert Whitney and Johns, Inc.
1501 Broadway 505B
New York NY 10036
212-921-2488

Gilbert, Whitney & Johns, Inc., has proven expertise in designing and implementing strategic marketing-driven communications programs for food, health and nutrition-related products and associations. Strengths include special events, sponsorships, media tours, video news releases, copywriting, promotions, surveys, sweepstakes and product publicity campaigns that get attention.

Golin/Harris
500 North Michigan Avenue
Chicago IL 60611
312-836-7100

Gordon Hanrahan, Inc.
180 North Michigan Avenue
Chicago IL 60601
312-372-0935

Gordon Hanrahan specializes in food industry advertising and public relations. Services include creative development, promotions, media planning, full public relations representation and corporate strategy formulation.

HDM
810 Seventh Avenue
New York NY 10019
212-408-2100

From press kits, videos and recipes to product sampling, media tours and special events, HDM offers food and food-related clients a complete range of public relations services. As part of a leading New York-based full-service advertising agency that, in turn, is part of one of the largest worldwide agency networks, HDM brings clients immediate and personal contact with agency professionals along with access to an international network of resources.

Hill and Knowlton
420 Lexington Avenue
New York NY 10017
212-697-5600

Jenkins Communications, Inc.
150 Spear Street
San Francisco CA 94105
415-777-0604

Nathana Josephs Public Relations
205 West End Avenue, Suite 19A
New York NY 10023
212-769-2198

Ketchum Public Relations
1133 Avenue of the Americas
New York NY 10036
212-536-8800

Lewis & Neale, Inc.
928 Broadway
New York NY 10010
212-420-8808

Lewis & Neale, Inc. specializes in national food publicity and new product introduction programs, nutrition information campaigns and supermarket point-of-purchase materials reaching the consumer. In addition the agency develops complete foodservice and food industry publicity programs. The agency staff includes food marketing specialists, food writers, publicity specialists, registered dietitians and home economists.

Clients include major national food manufacturers, produce boards, food trade associations and food importers. Facilities include a test kitchen and a food photography studio.

The Londre Company Public Relations
3340 Barham Boulevard
Los Angeles CA 90068
213-851-8230

Since 1982, "TLC" has become one of the nation's leading resources for innovative, skilled, successful food public relations. This award-winning agency offers national and regional capabilities, including valuable Hispanic marketing expertise. Client experience includes Kahlua, Lawry's Foods, Mrs. Fields Cookies, Knox Gelatine, California Egg Commission, Frieda's Finest/Produce Specialties, Beatrice/Hunt-Wesson, Ballantine's Scotch, Baskin-Robbins Ice Cream, Kentucky Fried Chicken, Pepsi-Cola USA, and more.

Manning, Selvage & Lee, Inc.
79 Madison Avenue
New York NY 10016
212-213-0909

Ruth Morrison Associates, Inc.
19 West 44th Street
New York NY 10036
212-302-8886

Noble Tennant
500 North Michigan Avenue
Chicago IL 60611
312-644-4600

Noble is a strategic food marketing and communications company. Expert knowledge of the food consumer, channels of distribution and the one food dollar has helped Noble grow clients' businesses. Services include advertising; sales promotion; recipe development; the *Food Channel* newsletter; public relations; food photography; access to proprietary research and trend reports; consultation from leading manufacturers through Noble's broker panel; food media databases; package design; convenience stores and deli consultation; and an express product development service.

Ogilvy & Mather Public Relations (Ogilvy Public Relations Group)
40 West 57th Street
New York NY 10019
212-977-9400

The Plummer Group
Werner, Bicking & Fenwick
Advertising
866 United Nations Plaza,
Suite 4007
New York NY 10017
212-759-8434

The Plummer Group is well known for advertising, public relations and marketing in the hospitality field, ranging from hotels, resorts and restaurants to food and beverage and gourmet/retail products. It is equally renowned for creative design and innovative concepts in restaurants and menu development. The group has been responsible for the creation of many new restaurants and its redesigns of existing menus for restaurants have resulted in increased sales success.

Primavera PR
2718 Hickory Street
Yorktown Heights NY 10598
914-245-5390

Ruder-Finn, Inc.
301 East 57th Street
New York NY 10022
212-593-6400

Niki Singer, Inc.
400 Madison Avenue
New York NY 10017
212-751-9720

Smith & Hemingway Associates
49 South Elliott Place
Brooklyn NY 11217
718-403-0418

Smith & Hemingway Associates is a public relations and promotion firm specializing in food products, food personalities, wine and spirits, restaurants, hotels, inns, related trade associations and publications. A full-service agency in all media areas, Smith & Hemingway provides all press/media materials, campaign designs, product introductions and media tours. The firm is well known in the industry for joint product/event promotions, nationally and internationally. Multilingual, Smith & Hemingway works with clients around the world.

Dian Thomas Company
4360 South Diana Way
Salt Lake City UT 84124
801-277-4332

Full-service communications company specializing in food and consumer product marketing, spokesperson tours, collateral material preparation, recipe development, tradeshow product presentations and lectures. Emphasis on lifestyle marketing and unique creative approaches to marketing challenges.

Dian Thomas is a best-selling author, lecturer and company spokesperson. She is regularly featured on ABC-TV's *Home Show* and NBC-TV's *Today Show*. Dian has authored four books, including *The New York Times* best-seller, *Roughing It Easy*.

Marian Tripp Communications, Inc.
70 East Walton Place, Suite 5B
Chicago IL 60611
312-751-1440

Dean Weller & Company
138 West 74th Street
New York NY 10023
212-873-2316

Western Research Kitchens
45 South Fairfax Avenue,
Suite 301
Los Angeles CA 90008
212-938-3300

Western Research Kitchens is extremely active in the daily routine of contacting and working with TV and radio news directors and talk-show producers, as well as food editors, to arrange product tie-ins and media exposure.

Formed as a subsidiary of Lee & Associates, Inc., Los Angeles, California, in 1950, Western Research Kitchens is often contracted on a project basis by Midwest and East Coast agencies and food companies to represent their interests on the West Coast.

TV and Radio Networks

Promotion through the use of TV and radio is a field in which it is almost impossible to operate without professional help from a knowledgeable consultant or public relations firm.

Cable TV's growing share of the national market means that independent stations have varying importance in each viewing area. Accordingly, this listing includes only those stations operated by the three networks in the 30 major market areas as identified by *Bacon's Radio/ TV Directory*, published by Bacon's Publishing Company, Inc., 332 South Michigan Avenue, Chicago IL 60604. In each case, programming changes so much that the best source of information is the station's PR contact, who will know those specific shows where food-related topics will be welcome.

In the area of radio, a great deal of exposure is possible. Here again, though, experienced assistance is essential. Only someone with specialized knowledge of the field will know exactly which shows are syndicated nationally and which have proved to be significant aids in promotion—whether it be of a specific product, or of food knowledge or cooking expertise, or information. For this reason, no listing of radio stations is included here; for specific details, consult *Bacon's Radio/TV Directory*.

ATLANTA

WAGA-TV, Channel 5
P.O. Box 4207
Atlanta GA 30302
404-875-5551
Network: CBS

WSB-TV, Channel 2
1601 West Peachtree Street NE
Atlanta GA 30309
404-897-7500
Network: ABC

WXIA-TV, Channel 11
1611 West Peachtree Street NE
Atlanta GA 30309
404-892-1611
Network: NBC

BALTIMORE

WBAL-TV, Channel 11
3800 Hooper Avenue
Baltimore MD 21211
301-467-3000
Network: CBS

WJZ-TV, Channel 13
Television Hill
Baltimore MD 21211
301-466-0013
Network: ABC

WMAR-TV, Channel 2
6400 York Road
Baltimore MD 21212
301-377-2222
Network: NBC

BOSTON

WBZ-TV, Channel 4
1170 Soldiers Field Road
Boston MA 02134
617-787-7000
Network: NBC

WCVB-TV, Channel 5
5 TV Place, Needham Branch
Boston MA 02192
617-449-0400
Network: ABC

WNEV-TV, Channel 7
7 Bulfinch Place
Government Center
Boston MA 02114
617-725-0777
Network: CBS

CHICAGO

WBBM-TV, Channel 2
630 North McClurg Court
Chicago IL 60611
312-944-6000
Network: CBS-O&O

WLS-TV, Channel 7
190 North State Street
Chicago IL 60601
312-750-7777
Network: ABC-O&O

WMAQ-TV, Channel 5
Merchandise Mart
Chicago IL 60654
312-861-5555
Network: NBC-O&O

CINCINNATI

WCPO-TV, Channel 9
500 Central Avenue
Cincinnati OH 45202
513-721-9900
Network: CBS

WKRC-TV, Channel 12
1906 Highland Avenue
Cincinnati OH 45219
513-651-1200
Network: ABC

WLWT-TV, Channel 5
140 West 9th Street
Cincinnati OH 45202
513-352-5000
Network: NBC

CLEVELAND

WEWS-TV, Channel 5
Euclid at 30th
Cleveland OH 44115
216-431-5555
Network: ABC

WJKW-TV, Channel 8
5800 South Marginal Road
Cleveland OH 44103
216-431-8888
Network: CBS

WKYC-TV, Channel 3
1403 East 6th Street
Cleveland OH 44114
216-344-3333
Network: NBC-O&O

COLUMBUS

WBNS-TV, Channel 10
P.O. Box 1010
Columbus OH 43216
614-460-3700
Network: CBS

WCMH-TV, Channel 4
P.O. Box 4
Columbus OH 43216
614-263-4444
Network: NBC

WSYX-TV, Channel 6
1261 Dublin Road
Columbus OH 43216
614-481-6666
Network: ABC

DALLAS

KDFW-TV, Channel 4
400 North Griffin Street
Dallas TX 75202
214-720-4444
Network: CBS

WFAA-TV, Channel 8
Communications Center
Dallas TX 75202
214-748-9631
Network: ABC

KXAS-TV, Channel 5
4300 MacArthur Avenue, Suite 100
Dallas TX 75209
214-745-5555
Network: NBC

DENVER

KCNC-TV, Channel 4
P.O. Box 5012
Denver CO 80217
303-861-4444
Network: NBC

KMGH-TV, Channel 7
123 Speer Boulevard
Denver CO 80203
303-832-7777
Network: CBS

KUSA-TV, Channel 9
1089 Bannock Street
Denver CO 80204
303-893-9000
Network: ABC

KUSA's 6:00 a.m. morning show, produced by Jack Maher, has guests who may occasionally be food people.

The station also runs a syndicated show at 12 noon, *Mr. Food*. Mr. Food, whose real name is Art Ginsberg, cooks on the show and gives his viewers quick recipes.

KUSA is part of the ABC network.

DETROIT

WDIV-TV, Channel 4
550 West Lafayette Boulevard
Detroit MI 48231
313-222-0444
Network: NBC

WJBK-TV, Channel 2
P.O. Box 2000
Southfield MI 48037
313-557-2000
Network: CBS

WXYZ-TV, Channel 7
P.O. Box 789
Southfield MI 48037
313-827-7777
Network: ABC-O&O

HOUSTON

KHOU-TV, Channel 11
1945 Allen Parkway
Houston TX 77019
713-526-1111
Network: CBS

KPRC-TV, Channel 2
P.O. Box 2222
Houston TX 77252
713-771-4631
Network: NBC

KTRK-TV, Channel 13
P.O. Box 13
Houston TX 77001
713-666-0713
Network: ABC

INDIANAPOLIS

WISH-TV, Channel 8
P.O. Box 7088
Indianapolis IN 46207
317-924-4381
Network: CBS

WRTV-TV, Channel 6
1330 North Meridian Street
Indianapolis IN 46206
317-635-9788
Network: ABC

WTHR-TV, Channel 13
1000 North Meridian Street
Indianapolis IN 46204
317-636-1313
Network: NBC

KANSAS CITY

KCTV-TV, Channel 5
P.O. Box 5555
Kansas City MO 64109
913-677-5555
Network: CBS

KMBC-TV, Channel 9
1049 Central Street
Kansas City MO 64105
816-221-9999
Network: ABC

WDAF-TV, Channel 4
3030 Summit
Kansas City MO 64108
816-753-4567
Network: NBC

LOS ANGELES

KABC-TV, Channel 7
4151 Prospect Avenue
Los Angeles CA 90027
213-557-7777
Network: ABC-O&O

KCBS-TV, Channel 2
6121 Sunset Boulevard
Los Angeles CA 90028
213-460-3000
Network: CBS-O&O

KNBC-TV, Channel 4
3000 West Alameda Avenue
Burbank CA 91523
818-840-3425
Network: NBC-O&O

MIAMI

WPLG-TV, Channel 10
3900 Biscayne Boulevard
Miami FL 33137
305-576-1010
Network: ABC

WSVN-TV, Channel 7
1401 79th Street Causeway
Miami FL 33141
305-751-6692
Network: NBC

WTVJ-TV, Channel 4
316 North Miami Avenue
Miami FL 33128
305-379-4444
Network: CBS

MILWAUKEE

WISN-TV, Channel 12
P.O. Box 402
Milwaukee WI 53201
414-342-8812
Network: ABC

WITI-TV, Channel 6
9001 North Green Bay Road
Milwaukee WI 53217
414-355-6666
Network: CBS

WTMJ-TV, Channel 4
P.O. Box 693
Milwaukee WI 53201
414-332-9611
Network: NBC

MINNEAPOLIS/ ST. PAUL

KARE-TV, Channel 11
8811 Olson Memorial Highway
Minneapolis MN 55427
612-546-1111
Network: NBC

KSTP-TV, Channel 5
3415 University Avenue
St. Paul MN 55114
612-646-5555
Network: ABC

WCCO-TV, Channel 4
90 South 11th Street
Minneapolis MN 55403
612-339-4444
Network: CBS

NEW ORLEANS

WDSU-TV, Channel 6
520 Royal Street
New Orleans LA 70130
504-527-0666
Network: NBC

WVUE-TV, Channel 8
P.O. Box 13847
New Orleans LA 70185
504-486-6161
Network: ABC

WWL-TV, Channel 4
1024 North Rampart Street
New Orleans LA 70176
504-529-4444
Network: CBS

NEW YORK

WABC-TV, Channel 7
7 Lincoln Square
New York NY 10023
212-887-7777
Network: ABC-O&O

WCBS-TV, Channel 2
524 West 57th Street
New York NY 10019
212-975-4321
Network: CBS-O&O

WNBC-TV, Channel 4
30 Rockefeller Plaza
New York NY 10112
212-664-4444
Network: NBC-O&O

PHILADELPHIA

KYW-TV, Channel 3
Independence Mall East
Philadelphia PA 19106
215-238-4700
Network: NBC

WCAU-TV, Channel 10
Monument City Avenue
Philadelphia PA 19131
215-668-5500
Network: CBS-O&O

WPVI-TV, Channel 6
4100 City Line Avenue
Philadelphia PA 19131
215-878-9700
Network: ABC

PHOENIX

KPNX-TV, Channel 12
P.O. Box 711
Phoenix AZ 85001
602-257-1212
Network: NBC

KTSP-TV, Channel 10
511 West Adams Street
Phoenix AZ 85003
602-257-1234
Network: CBS

KTVK-TV, Channel 3
3435 North 16th Street
Phoenix AZ 85016
602-263-3333
Network: ABC

PITTSBURGH

KDKA-TV, Channel 2
1 Gateway Center
Pittsburgh PA 15222
412-392-2200
Network: CBS

WPXI-TV, Channel 11
P.O. Box 1100
Pittsburgh PA 15230
412-237-1100
Network: NBC

WTAE-TV, Channel 4
400 Ardmore Boulevard
Pittsburgh PA 15221
412-242-4300
Network: ABC

PORTLAND

KATU-TV, Channel 2
P.O. Box 2
Portland OR 97207
503-231-4222
Network: ABC

KGW-TV, Channel 8
1501 Southwest Jefferson Street
Portland OR 97201
503-226-5000
Network: NBC

KOIN-TV, Channel 6
222 Southwest Columbia Street
Portland OR 97201
503-243-6666
Network: CBS

SACRAMENTO

KCRA-TV, Channel 3
3 Television Circle
Sacramento CA 95814
916-444-7300
Network: NBC

KOVR-TV, Channel 13
1216 Arden Way
Sacramento CA 95815
916-927-1313
Network: ABC

KXTV-TV, Channel 10
P.O. Box 10
Sacramento CA 95801
916-441-2345
Network: CBS

ST. LOUIS

KMOV-TV, Channel 4
One Memorial Drive
St. Louis MO 63102
314-621-4444
Network: CBS

KSDK-TV, Channel 5
1000 Market Street
St. Louis MO 63101
314-421-5055
Network: NBC

Part of the NBC network, this station's 12 o'clock News program includes a segment called *New Nutrition* which covers a variety of food-related stories. The show is run by Connie Deikman and information should be sent to Ara Ehrlich.

A morning newscast, *Today in St. Louis*, sometimes covers food stories and may feature guests from the food world.

KTVI-TV, Channel 2
5915 Berthold Avenue
St. Louis MO 63110
314-647-2222
Network: ABC

SAN DIEGO

KCST-TV, Channel 39
8330 Engineer Road
San Diego CA 92111
619-279-3939
Network: NBC

KFMB-TV, Channel 8
7677 Engineer Road
San Diego CA 92111
619-571-8888
Network: CBS

KGTV-TV, Channel 10
P.O. Box 85347
San Diego CA 92138
619-237-1010
Network: ABC

SAN FRANCISCO

KGO-TV, Channel 7
900 Front Street
San Francisco CA 94111
415-954-7777
Network: ABC-O&O

KOFY-TV, Channel 20
2500 Marin Street
San Francisco CA 94124
415-821-2020
Network: CBS, NBC

KPIX-TV, Channel 5
855 Battery Street
San Francisco CA 94111
415-362-5550
Network: CBS

KPIX has a show entitled *People Are Talking* which covers a single issue during its one-hour time frame. If the subject is appropriate, guests from the food world may be invited. For example, a program on heart disease might include a doctor, a nutritionist and a guest such as the Slim Gourmet. Ideas should be submitted to Jan Landis.

KPIX is part of the CBS network.

KRON-TV, Channel 4
P.O. Box 3412
San Francisco CA 94119
415-441-4444
Network: NBC

SEATTLE

KING-TV, Channel 5
P.O. Box 24525
Seattle WA 98124
206-448-5555
Network: NBC

KIRO-TV, Channel 7
2807 Third Avenue
Seattle WA 98121
206-728-7777
Network: CBS

KOMO-TV, Channel 4
100 Fourth Avenue North
Seattle WA 98109
206-443-4000
Network: ABC

TAMPA/ ST. PETERSBURG

WTSP-TV, Channel 10
P.O. Box 10000
St. Petersburg FL 33733
813-577-1010
Network: ABC

WTVT-TV, Channel 13
P.O. Box 31113
Tampa FL 33631
813-876-1313
Network: CBS

WXFL-TV, Channel 8
905 Jackson Street
Tampa FL 33602
813-228-8888
Network: NBC

WASHINGTON

WJLA-TV, Channel 7
4461 Connecticut Avenue NW
Washington DC 20008
202-364-7777
Network: ABC

WRC-TV, Channel 4
4001 Nebraska Avenue NW
Washington DC 20016
202-885-4000
Network: NBC-O&O

WUSA-TV, Channel 9
4001 Brandywine Street NW
Washington DC 20016
202-364-3900
Network: CBS

Food
GRAPHICS

199
Food Photographers

204
Food Stylists

210
Food Illustrators

218
Graphic Designers

221
Food Videos
Food Celebrity Videos; Cooking Technique Videos; Video Shopping/ Supermarket Services

V I N C E N T   L E E

PHOTOGRAPHER

155 WOOSTER ST.
NEW YORK, NY
1 0 0 1 2
(212) 254-7888

Food Photographers

Fine photography has become an essential element of almost every publication connected with food, from advertisements to posters to cookbooks and brochures. The listing that follows is a wide-ranging selection of some outstanding photographers currently working in the field of food.

It is alphabetical by last name and includes a contact address and telephone number, which are often those of the photographer's representative. These reps are useful sources of information and can also help in suggesting appropriate photographers for a specific assignment or geographical location.

Robert Ammirati Studio
568 Broadway
New York NY 10012
212-925-5811

Paul Aresu
Aresu-Goldring Studio
568 Broadway
New York NY 10012
212-334-9494

Donna Aristo
City Limit Productions
360 Manville Road
Pleasantville NY 10570
914-747-1422

Dan Barba
305 Second Avenue, Suite 322
New York NY 10003
212-420-8611

Jim Bathie
1473 Alford Avenue
Birmingham AL 35226
205-822-5722

Myron Beck
611 South Burlington
Los Angeles CA 90057
213-933-9883

Hank Benson
653 Bryant Street
San Francisco CA 94107
415-543-8153

David Bishop
251 West 19th Street
New York NY 10011
212-929-4355

Henry Bjoin
146 North La Brea Avenue
Los Angeles CA 90036
213-937-4097

Dennis Blachut
145 West 28th Street
New York NY 10001
212-947-4270

Peter Bosch
477 Broome Street
New York NY 10013
212-925-0707

Matt Bowman
1345 Chemical Street
Dallas TX 75207
214-637-0211

Bob Brody Photography, Inc.
5 West 19th Street
New York NY 10011
212-741-0013

Ron Brello Jr.
400 Lafayette Street
New York NY 10003
212-982-0490

Steve Bronstein
Big City Productions
5 East 19th Street
New York NY 10003
212-473-3366

Bruno Photography, Inc.
43 Crosby Street
New York NY 10012
212-925-2929

Victor Budnik
125 King Street
San Francisco CA 94107
415-541-9050

Tom Bufas
534 West 35th Street
New York NY 10001
212-927-4678

Burke/Triolo
940 East 2nd Street
Los Angeles CA 90012
213-687-4730

John Campos
132 West 21st Street
New York NY 10011
212-675-0601

Skip Caplan
124 West 24th Street
New York NY 10011
212-463-0541

Ed Carey
60 Federal Street
San Francisco CA 94107
415-621-2349

Dennis Chalkin Studio, Inc.
5 East 16th Street
New York NY 10003
212-929-1036

Lisa Charles
119 West 23rd Street
New York NY 10011
212-807-8600

Walt Chrynwski
154 West 18th Street
New York NY 10011
212-675-1906

James Cohen, Inc.
36 East 20th Street
New York NY 10003
212-533-4400

Marc David Cohen
5 West 19th Street
New York NY 10011
212-741-0015

Ric Cohn
137 West 25th Street
New York NY 10001
212-924-4450

Corinne Colen
519 Broadway, 5th Floor
New York NY 10012
212-431-7425

Chris Collins
35 West 20th Street
New York NY 10011
212-633-1670

Earl Culberson
Big City Productions
5 East 19th Street
New York NY 10003
212-473-3366

Michael Datoli
121 West 17th Street, Suite 4C
New York NY 10011
212-633-1672

Bill Debold
2320 Donley Drive, Suite C
Austin TX 78758
512-337-1177

De Gennaro Associates
902 South Norton Avenue
Los Angeles CA 90019
213-935-5179

Silva Devarj
116 West Illinois Street
Chicago IL 60610
312-266-1358

Rick Diaz Photography, Inc.
4884 Southwest 74th Court
Miami FL 33155
305-264-9761

David Dobbs
Photo Accents
2632-C Mountain Industrial Boulevard
Atlanta GA 30084
404-938-9200

John Dominis
252 West 102nd Street
New York NY 10025
212-222-9890

T. Mike Fletcher
7467 Kingsbury Boulevard
St. Louis MO 63130
314-721-2279

Lois Ellen Frank
Fine Food Photography
3109 Beverly Boulevard
Los Angeles CA 90057
213-663-7630

Dennis Galante
133 West 22nd Street
New York NY 10011
212-463-0938

Dennis Galante has produced award-winning photographs in his state-of-the-art studio for over 10 years. His advertising and editorial food photography is considered among the most accomplished of the day. A photographer of unique style, he is always in pursuit of creative excellence.

For a visual presentation please call for the food portfolio, or FAX 212-463-0943. A sample of Dennis's work appears on page 68.

Michael Geiger, Ltd.
R.D. 3, Box 692
New Paltz NY 12561
212-431-5205

Andre Gillardin
6 West 20th Street,
6th Floor
New York NY 10011
212-675-2950

Ken Glaser and Associates
5270 Annunciation Street
New Orleans LA 70115
504-895-7170

Maybe it's our Creole heritage, but we see food in a special light. And that's the way we shoot food. Because the essential ingredient in great food photography is lighting. Tasteful presentation is important, too, and in New Orleans we take that for granted.

Our recipe has produced gourmet images for Finlandia Vodka, Popeyes Famous Fried Chicken, Columbo Yogurt, the Louisiana Seafood Promotion Board, and *Food Management* magazine, among others. Call us for an appetizer.

Charles Gold, Inc.
56 West 22nd Street
New York NY 10010
212-242-2600

Scrumptious, delicious, appetizing, yummy, mouth-watering, appealing, delectable, aromatic, tantalizing, crunchy, crispy, sparkling, effervescent, sizzling, hot, steamy, cool, buttery, creamy, juicy, well-done, rare, spreadable, eatable, tasty, succulent, stimulating, spicy, sweet, perfect, luscious, decadent, strong, chewy, flavorful, tempting, sinful, sticky, savory, award-winning, tangy, hearty, fruity, tart, zesty, tasty, basic, sumptuous, fancy, simple, elegant, colorful, saucy, lusty, robust, sexy, fresh, peppery, delicate, professional—some of the words art directors use to describe Charley's food photography.

Peter Gollo Photography
1238 Callowhill Street
Philadelphia PA 19123
215-925-5230

Dennis M. Gottlieb Studio, Inc.
137 West 25th Street
New York NY 10001
212-620-7050

Walter Gray Photography, Inc.
1035 West Lake Street
Chicago IL 60607
312-733-3800

Brian Hagiwara
504 La Guardia Place
New York NY 10012
212-674-6026

Ted Hardin
119 West 23rd Street, Suite 505
New York NY 10011
212-307-6208

Michael Harris
18 West 21st Street
New York NY 10010
212-255-3377

Hashi Studio, Inc.
49 West 23rd Street
New York NY 10011
212-675-6902

Christopher Hawker Photography
1025 West Madison Street
Chicago IL 60607
312-829-4766

Brian Healy
541 Netoma Street
San Francisco CA 94103
415-861-1008

Buck Holzemer Photography
3448 Chicago Avenue
Minneapolis MN 55407
612-824-2905

Tom Hopkins
15 Orchard Park, Box 7A
Madison CT 06443
203-245-0824

Tom Hopkins Studio has specialized in food photography for the past seven years. Among the studio's advertising and editorial credits is the illustration of six cookbooks, including *The Art of Cooking, Volumes 1 and 2*, by Jacques Pepin and *Tapas* by Penelope Casas.

The studio features a complete operating kitchen, approximately 2,000 square feet of shooting area, and film formats ranging from 35mm to 8 by 10.

Ross M. Horowitz
206 West 15th Street
New York NY 10011
212-206-9216

William Hubbell
99 East Elm Street
Greenwich CT 06830
203-629-9629

Steven Huszar
377 Park Avenue South
New York NY 10016
212-532-3772

Martin Jacobs
34 East 23rd Street,
5th Floor
New York NY 10010
212-475-1160

Bruno Joachim Photography
326 A Street
Boston MA 02210
617-451-6156

Seth Joel
440 Park Avenue South
New York NY 10016
212-685-3179

Peter Johansky
27 West 20th Street
New York NY 10011
212-242-7013

Spencer Jones
23 Leonard Street,
5th Floor
New York NY 10013
212-914-8165

David Jordano Photography
1335 North Wells Street
Chicago IL 60610
312-787-8834

Katrina
286 Fifth Avenue
New York NY 10001
212-279-2838

Moshe Katvan
40 West 17th Street
New York NY 10011
212-242-4895

Yutaka Kawachi
33 West 17th Street
New York NY 10011
212-929-4825

Susan Kinast Photography
1035 West Lake Street
Chicago IL 60607
312-738-0067

Matthew Klein
104 West 17th Street
New York NY 10011
212-255-6400

Jeff Kosta Studio
256 South 3rd Street
San Francisco CA 94103
415-285-7002

Dan Kozan Studio
32 West 22nd Street
New York NY 10011
212-691-2288

James Kozyra
568 Broadway
New York NY 10012
212-431-1911

Jim Krantz Studios, Inc.
5017 South 24th Street
Omaha NE 68107
402-734-4848

Carin Krasner Photography
3239 Helms Avenue
Los Angeles CA 90034
213-280-0082

Rick Kroninger
Illustrated Photographs
P.O. Box 15913
San Antonio TX 78212
512-733-9931

Alan Krosnick
2800 20th Street
San Francisco CA 94110
415-285-1819

Advertising, point-of-sale and collateral photography. From prepared dishes in large sets to single ingredients in limbo. Our 7,000-square-foot studio includes a professional working kitchen.

Clients: Bon Appetit, Dole, Beringer, Del Monte, Diamond Walnuts, Hidden Valley Ranch, Amy's Kitchen, Christian Brothers, Golden Grain, Beef Council, Raisin Board, Prune Board, Seagram's, Dreyer's, Sees Candies, Perrier.

For portfolio and information, call Vicki Vandamme, 415-285-1819.

Don Kushnick
245 East 40th Street
New York NY 10018
212-687-8296

Lamar Photographics
P.O. Box 1470
Framingham MA 01701
508-881-3881

Chuck Lamonica
121 East 24th Street
New York NY 10010
212-673-4848

Michael Lamotte Studios, Inc.
828 Mission Street
San Francisco CA 94103
415-777-1443

John Lawder Photography
2672 South Grand Avenue
Santa Ana CA 92705
714-557-3657

Brian Leatart
520 North Western Avenue
Los Angeles CA 90004
213-856-0121

Paul Lecat Photography
820 North Franklin Street
Chicago IL 60610
312-664-7122

Vincent B. Lee
155 Wooster Street, Suite 3F
New York NY 10012
212-254-7888

Advertising and editorial food photography. Partial client list: *The New York Times, Cook's* magazine, *McCall's* magazine, Pottery Barn, Dansk International Designs, Perdue Chicken, Cognac Information Bureau, 21 Brands, Courvoisier Cognac, William Morrow Publishers, Harper and Row, Random House, Ritter Foods. Portfolio and photomatic reel available upon request. See ad on page 198.

John Lehn and Associates
Advertising Photography, Inc.
1601 East Franklin Avenue
Minneapolis MN 55406
612-338-0257

Richard Levy
5 West 19th Street
New York NY 10011
212-243-4220

David Luttrell
1500 Highland Drive
Knoxville TN 37918
615-588-5775

Fred Lyon
237 Clara Street
San Francisco CA 94107
415-974-5645

Macuch Studio
1133 Spring Street
Atlanta GA 30309
404-432-6309

Charles Masters
212-688-9510

Tom McCarthy
8960 Southwest 114th Street
Miami FL 33176
305-233-1703

Ned McCormick
55 Hancock Street
Lexington MA 02173
617-862-2552

Nancy McFarland
3 Tuck Lane
Westport CT 06880
203-227-6178

Meisels Photography, Ltd.
334 South La Brea Avenue
Los Angeles CA 90036
213-939-3011

George Menda, Inc.
36 West 20th Street
New York NY 10011
212-675-5561

Gordon Meyer
216 West Ohio Street
Chicago IL 60610
312-642-9303

Joe Morello
40 West 28th Strreet
New York NY 10001
212-684-2340

Steven Mark Needham
111 West 19th Street,
2nd Floor
New York NY 10011
212-206-1914

Terry Niefield Studio
12 West 27th Street
New York NY 10001
212-686-8722

Steve Nozicka Photography, Ltd.
314 West Institute Place
Chicago IL 60610
312-787-8925

Rick Ofentoski
13 East 31st Street,
4th Floor
New York NY 10016
212-679-5919

William Oquendo
4680 Southwest 27th Avenue
Ft. Lauderdale FL 33312
305-981-2823

Complete food and beverage photography in studio or on location, from fresh seafood to hearty Western beef. Partial client list includes: Kellogg Company, Beatrice Foods, Taco Viva, Golden Greek Restaurants, Dockside Seafood, *Cook's* magazine, *Restaurant Business* magazine, Florida Restaurant Association.

Call or write for additional food samples or see *American Photography Showcase*, Vol. 12, 13.

Stock available through Southern Stock Photos USA; 305-486-7117.

Randy O'Rourke
578 Broadway
New York NY 10012
212-226-7424

Diane Padys Studio
Stockland Martel
5 Union Square West
New York NY 10003
212-972-4747

Ray Perkins Photography
222 South Morgan Street
Chicago IL 60607
312-944-5116

Petrucelli Associates
17522 Von Karman Avenue
Irvine CA 92714
714-250-8591

Bernard Phillips Photography
3100 Stonybrook Drive, Suite N8
Raleigh NC 27604
919-878-1611

Twenty-three years shooting food, drink, still life in London, San Francisco, Raleigh. United States clients include: California Prune Board, California Raisin Advisory Board, California Strawberry Advisory Council, Del Monte, Bahlsen, Seapak, Farm Rich, Libby's, Idaho Potatoes, *Image* magazine, U.K. Oxo, Pickering Foods, Heritage Cheese, Outline, Birdseye, Campbell's, John West, Kraft, Quaker, Heinz, Egg Board, Mathews Turkeys, Uncle Ben's Rice.

With fully equipped studio, all formats, large kitchen, gas range. Portfolio flies; FAX 919-878-1602.

Judd Pilossof
142 West 26th Street
New York NY 10001
212-989-8971

Paul Poplis Photography
3599 Refugee Road
Columbus OH 43232
614-231-2942

Paul Poplis Photography produces beautifully lit, well-composed images of food that are shot in a state-of-the-art studio with articulate lighting, video image monitoring, a complete kitchen, extensive prop and background collection. (See our ad on page 284.)

For a portfolio you will appreciate and a client list you will recognize—Call Paul: 614-231-2942.

Michael Pruzan
1181 Broadway
New York NY 10001
212-686-5505

Aaron Rezny, Inc.
119 West 23rd Street
New York NY 10011
212-691-1894

Jack Richmond
12 Farnsworth Street
Boston MA 02210
617-482-5974

Rita Marie & Friends
405 North Wabash Avenue,
Suite 2709
Chicago IL 60611
312-222-0339

Kathryn Russell Photography
4002 Burbank Boulevard
Burbank CA 91505
818-841-3883

Michael W. Rutherford
Rutherford Studios
623 Sixth Avenue South
Nashville TN 37203
615-242-5953

Kathy Sanders Studios, Inc.
411 South Sangamon Street, Suite 2B
Chicago IL 60607
312-935-1707

Teri Sandison
1545 North Wilcox Avenue
Hollywood CA 90028
213-461-3529

Susumu Sato Photography, Inc.
109 West 27th Street
New York NY 10001
212-741-0688

Heimo Schmitt
517 South Jefferson Street
Chicago IL 60607
312-772-7586

Barry Seidman
85 Fifth Avenue
New York NY 10003
212-255-6666

Charles Shotwell Photography
2111 North Clinton Street
Chicago IL 60614
312-929-0168

Ellen Silverman
126 West 25th Street, Suite 5-F
New York NY 10001
212-627-5911

Jerry Simpson
244 Mulberry Street
New York NY 10012
212-941-1255

Michael Skott
244 Fifth Avenue
New York NY 10001
212-686-4807

Ralph Smith Photography
2211 Beall Street
Houston TX 77008
713-862-8301

With three professional photographers on staff, Ralph Smith Photography is a full-service studio specializing in food photography. The 8,000-square-foot studio houses a complete commercial-style kitchen, in-house film processing and an extensive prop selection.

Our major clients include: Coca-Cola Foods, Sysco, Armour Meats, Ralston Purina, Bacardi, Uncle Ben's Rice, Stop-N-Go, Granada Foods, Rice Council of America and Westin Hotels.

A portfolio of work is available upon request.

Dan Springston
135 Madison Avenue,
Penthouse South
New York NY 10016
212-689-0685

Lynn St. John
St. John Associates
308 East 59th Street
New York NY 10022
212-308-7744

Cynthia Stern
515 Broadway
New York NY 10012
212-925-2677

Taryn Stinnett Photography
305 Second Avenue
New York NY 10003
212-533-0613

Two of my greatest passions in life are photography and food. Thus it was a natural compulsion that I would strive to capture on film food as delectable and oh! so edible as it is in life.

Clients: Random House, Dell, *Town*

& Country, *Prevention*, *Better Nutrition*, *Today's Living*, Mas, Ketchum Communications, KCS&A.

A sample of my work appears on page 2.

Studio 400
760 Burr Oak Drive
Westmont IL 60559
708-323-3616

Studio 400 is a comprehensive marketing/design and photography firm. We specialize in the concept, design and production of exceptional food and product photography as well as marketing communication materials for the food industry.

Our studio has a fully equipped set, complete kitchen and a creative team of photographers, designers, food stylists, illustrators, copywriters and other design communication talents.

For a sample of our work, see page 158.

Mark Thomas
141 West 26th Street
New York NY 10001
212-741-7252

Janis Tracy Photography
213 West Institute Place
Chicago IL 60610
312-787-7166

John Uher Photography
529 West 42nd Street
New York NY 10036
212-594-7377

Andrew Unangst
Ken Mann and Robin Dictenberg
20 West 46th Street
New York NY 10036
212-944-2853

Jan Van Gorder Studios
63 Unquowa Road
Fairfield CT 06430
203-255-6622

Michael Waine
873 Broadway
New York NY 10003
212-533-4200

Lou Wallach
Marge Casey & Associates
245 East 63rd Street
New York NY 10021
212-486-9575

Wans Studio, Inc.
325 West 40th Street
Kansas City MO 64111
816-931-8905

Glen and Gayle Wans shoot food and still-life photography in their spacious Kansas City studio. With over 15 years' experience in commercial photography, they have won numerous national and local awards.

Wans Studio specializes in food and still-life tabletop photography for advertising, consumer and trade (including foodservice), cookbooks, editorial and packaging.

For further information, contact Gayle Wans, or FAX 816-931-6899.

For samples of their work, see page 130.

Les Ward Photography, Inc.
21477 Bridge Street,
Suites C & D
Southfield MI 48034
313-350-8666

Michael Watson Studio
133 West 19th Street
New York NY 10011
212-620-3125

In film or print, award-winning photographer Michael Watson transforms food visuals to dynamic photographs which capture a mood...tell a story. Large studio, equipped with professional chef's kitchen, is the ideal place to create mouth-watering images. A professional group of stylists and assistants is on hand to help you and Michael bring your layouts to life. FAX us a layout...we'll produce and shoot the job!

Call for Michael's portfolio, or FAX us at 212-627-3798.

Bill White
34 West 17th Street
New York NY 10011
212-243-1780

Douglas Whyte
519 Broadway
New York NY 10012
212-431-1667

Bret Wills Photography
245 West 29th Street
New York NY 10001
212-629-4878

Bruce Wolf
123 West 28th Street
New York NY 10001
212-947-0570

Ron Wu
179 St. Paul Street
Rochester NY 14604
716-454-5600

Dan Wynn
170 East 73rd Street
New York NY 10021
212-535-1551

Zan Productions
108 East 16th Street
New York NY 10003
212-477-3333

Gerald Zanetti Associates, Inc.
536 West 50th Street
New York NY 10019
212-767-1717

Carl Zapp
Menken Studios
119 West 22nd Street
New York NY 10011
212-924-4240

David Zimmerman Studio
119 West 23rd Street
New York NY 10011
212-268-6130

Food Stylists

Good food styling is absolutely integral to fine food photography, and most photographers have skilled stylists with whom they like to work. Certain stylists will have particular skills. Styling for advertising, for example, demands a different approach from styling for editorial purposes, just as a setup for a family magazine will differ from that for a coffee-table cookbook.

This selection of stylists' names has been compiled from several sources. For convenience, it is arranged by region, then alphabetically by town or city within states. There are a number of source books available which give comprehensive listings of professionals working in all categories of this "creative" area. Individual photographers can also provide reliable referrals.

NORTHEAST

CONNECTICUT

Mary Divett
34 Tory Hole Road
Darien CT 06820
203-655-8594

Sara Foster
374 1/2 Greenwich Avenue
Greenwich CT 06830
203-869-9545

Marina P. Freyer
30 Northway
Old Greenwich CT 06870
203-637-5045

Grace Manney
c/o Maria Walsh
65 Glenbrook Road
Stamford CT 06902
203-358-8598

Paul E. Piccuito
16 Olmstead Place
East Norwalk CT 06855
203-866-6993

MASSACHUSETTS

John Carafoli
1 Hawes Road
Sagamore Beach MA 02562
508-888-1557

NEW JERSEY

Anne Disrude
230 3rd Street
Jersey City NJ 07302
201-659-8394

Alice Cronk
10 Mohigan Way
Mahwah NJ 07430
201-327-2982

Ann McKenna
41 DeKalb Place
Morristown NJ 07960
201-267-8693

Marianne Langan
536 West Saddle River
Upper Saddle River NJ 07458
201-327-2666

NEW YORK

Jane Curtin
114 Clinton Street, Apartment 5F
Brooklyn NY 11201
718-237-2438

Deborah Mintcheff
Food Style, Inc.
24 Monroe Place
Brooklyn NY 11201
718-855-6672

Marianne Zanzarella
245 Henry Street, Apartment 6D
Brooklyn NY 11201
718-858-0911

Maret Price
7 Gramaton Court
Bronxville NY 10708
914-779-8546

Davie Raphael
P.O. Box 169
Brookhaven NY 11719
516-286-2143

Kathy De Villeneuve
5 Whispering Court
Dix Hills NY 11746
516-595-2710

Carol Brock
303 Arleigh Road
Douglaston NY 11363
718-428-3172

Food/Entertaining Consultant/
Writer. Over 25 years' experience in the
food and beverage industry specializing
in recipe development, food writing and
coordination of corporate and home
entertaining. Have written articles for
national magazines, major newspapers
and corporations promoting food and
beverage products. Co-edited the *Good
Housekeeping Party Book*, published by
Harper & Row (a national best-seller).
Have made numerous appearances on
radio and television and have served both
as a spokesperson and keynote speaker.
Was formerly Food Reporter for the
New York *Daily News* and Hostess
Editor, *Good Housekeeping*.

Ann Broder
30 East Beacon Lane
East Northport NY 11731
516-368-2454

Polly Talbott
44 Talfor Road
East Rockaway NY 11518
516-887-1497

Suki Cannon
210 Springville Road
Hampton Bays NY 11946
516-728-7136

Pat Croce
R.D. 7, Box 286
Hopewell Junction NY 12533
914-226-7266

A. J. Battifarano
230 West 76th Street
New York NY 10023
212-877-7138

Dyne Benner
311 East 60th Street
New York NY 10022
212-688-7571

Benicia Berman
399 East 72nd Street
New York NY 10021
212-737-9627

Jacqueline Buckner
399 East 72nd Street, Suite 10F
New York NY 10021
212-737-5746

Sidney Burstein
348 West 36th Street
New York NY 10018
212-967-0547

Sidney Burstein is a food writer,
chef and stylist. His first cookbook, *The
Only 25 Recipes You'll Ever Need* (Doubleday), will appear in Spring 1990. His
work has taken him to London, Lisbon
and the Philippines. Clients include:
Sheila Lukins, Julee Rosso, *The New York
Times*, the New York *Daily News*, *Parade*
magazine, Time Life Books, *Woman's
Day, Elle, Chocolatier*, Agnes de Mille and
the late James Beard. He was Test Kitchen Director of *Good Food* magazine.

John F. Carafoli
106 Lexington Avenue
New York NY 10016
212-532-6387

Food styling/writing/recipe develop-
ment and lectures. Accounts include:
Ocean Spray, Knorr's, and campaigns for
Parade magazine, Howard Johnson's,
Pepperidge Farm, Ground Round,
Bally's, McDonald's and Friendly's.
Carafoli has been featured along with his
work in *Ladies' Home Journal, Better
Homes and Gardens, Bon Appetit, 1001
Home Ideas, Prevention, The Boston Globe*
and *P.M. Magazine*.

He has studied with Madeleine
Kamman and other professional chefs.

Vicki Cheung
301 East 22nd Street
New York NY 10010
212-254-4404

Fay Chin
67 Vestry Street
New York NY 10013
212-219-8770

Vickie Emerson Cooke
380 Lafayette Street
New York NY 10003
212-674-5547

Delores Custer
80 North Moore Street,
Apartment 4W
New York NY 10013
212-285-1410

Susan Culver Darrin
5 East 22nd Street, Suite 30F
New York NY 10010
212-228-7200

Rick Ellis & Associates
1 University Place
New York NY 10003
212-228-3624

Food prepared for the camera—print, TV and film—by established and multifaceted staff. Wide experience with challenging styling problems—from boring brown meatloaves to fast-melting ice creams, with equal attention paid to jobs large and small. Also: recipe development, writing, editing and spokesperson work.

Carol Gelles
545 West End Avenue
New York NY 10024
212-580-3485

Dale Goday
55 East 11th Street
New York NY 10003
212-254-4062

Sarah Greenberg
65 West 69th Street, Apartment 5B
New York NY 10023
212-873-1764

Marilinda Hodgdon
225 East 95th Street
New York NY 10128
212-735-6583

Susan Huberman
242 East 19th Street
New York NY 10003
212-674-2748

Cheryle Jaffe Janelli
200 East 82nd Street
New York NY 10028
212-861-7728

Judy Lieberman
30 Waterside Plaza,
Apartment 23D
New York NY 10010
212-686-2076

Barbara J. D. Listenik
146 Reade Street, Penthouse
New York NY 10013
212-925-2683

Zabel Meshejian
125 Washington Place
New York NY 10014
212-242-2459

Russell Pritchard
308 West 40th Street
New York NY 10018
212-956-8020

Ricki Rosenblatt
77 Perry Street
New York NY 10014
212-206-8383

Linda Sampson
431 West Broadway
New York NY 10012
212-925-6821

Mariann Sauvion
129 West 85th Street,
Apartment 1R
New York NY 10024
212-496-6009

Joan Scherman
450 West 24th Street
New York NY 10011
212-620-0475

Karen Temple
337 West 21st Street
New York NY 10011
212-924-7870

Helga Weinrib
880 Lexington Avenue
New York NY 10021
212-628-9509

Susan West
59 East 7th Street
New York NY 10003
212-982-8228

Patricia Winters
215 East 68th Street
New York NY 10021
212-249-6337
213-475-9368

Yoshiko
30 Waterside Plaza,
Apartment 21-J
New York NY 10010
212-725-0175

Ann Zekauskas
21 West 89th Street
New York NY 10024
212-879-7909

Marlene Maggio
Aura Productions
55 Waterview Circle
Rochester NY 14625
716-381-8053

Bette Harris Friedman
187 Parkside Drive
Roslyn Heights NY 11577
516-621-7941

Experienced Food Stylist/Consultant
Home economics and M.B.A. degrees
Experienced in styling *all* foods, with special expertise in baking and cake decorating
Styling for packaging, editorials and advertising
Recipe testing and development
Knowledge of latest food trends
Will assist media spokespersons visiting the New York area with food styling and preparation
Clients (details upon request):
National food companies and distributors
Major cookbook publishers and catalog companies
National food magazines

Barbara Pullo
30 Scenic Drive
Suffern NY 10901
914-354-3247

Lynn Cantor
6 Danville Court
West Nyack NY 10994
914-623-9471

Rita L. Barrett
73 Grandview Avenue
White Plains NY 10605
914-948-1290

Ann Harrington
495 Odell Avenue
Yonkers NY 10703
212-581-6470

PENNSYLVANIA

Paul Grimes
742 South Harshaw Street,
Suite P
Philadelphia PA 19146
215-732-2549

SOUTH

ALABAMA

Kay E. Clarke
P.O. Box 2262
Birmingham AL 35201
205-877-6491

FLORIDA

Mary Ruden
Reelistic Productions, Inc.
6467 Southwest 48th Street
Miami FL 33155
305-284-9989

Marina Polvay
c/o Creative Network, Inc.
1125 Northeast 125th Street,
Suite A
North Miami FL 33161
305-892-8307

Laura Ciffone
2140 Southwest 52nd Terrace
Plantation FL 33317
305-321-8422

GEORGIA

Dianne Simmons
3895 High Green Place
Marietta GA 30068
404-977-1858

Patti Matheney
3108-H Spring Hill Road
Smyrna GA 30080
404-434-1707

LOUISIANA

Linda Sampson
827 Ursulines
New Orleans LA 70116
504-523-3085

NORTH CAROLINA

Janet Grennes
2706 Rosedale Avenue
Raleigh NC 27607
919-828-7067

VIRGINIA

**Susan Bond Foresman—
Foodworks**
1541 Colonial Terrace
Arlington VA 22209
703-524-2606

MIDWEST

ILLINOIS

Teri Ernst
4125 Landing Drive
Aurora IL 60504
708-898-5319

Walter L. Moeller
7420 Cove Drive
Cary IL 60013
708-639-5848

Amy Andrews
2815 West Fargo Avenue
Chicago IL 60645
312-465-0619

Janice Bell
915 West Gunnison Street
Chicago IL 60640
312-769-2458

Kathy M. Aragaki
Jacqueline Motooka & Associates
1516 West Edgewater Avenue
Chicago IL 60660
312-271-5092

James Boardman
1372 West Grand Avenue
Chicago IL 60622
312-829-8410

Donna Coates
3850 North Lawndale Avenue
Chicago IL 60618
312-588-0929

Kathleen Fitzsimmons
3737 North Paulina Street
Chicago IL 60613
312-327-0248

Pat Martin Godsted
8931 South Oakley Avenue
Chicago IL 60620
312-881-4897

Lori Hartnett
6219 North Caldwell Avenue
Chicago IL 60646
312-774-6129

Nancy Heller
1834 West Berteau Avenue
Chicago IL 60613
312-549-4486

Lois Willecke Hlavak
2020 Lincoln Park West
Chicago IL 60614
312-248-0278

Janet Howerton
720 Gordon Terrace
Chicago IL 60613
312-525-8760

**International Institute
of Foods**
225 West Ohio Street
Chicago IL 60610
312-670-0200

Gail Klatt
2628 North Tallman Avenue
Chicago IL 60647
312-489-0438

Jane Kuoni
400 East Ohio Street, Suite 4803
Chicago IL 60611
312-923-1906
312-222-9266

Kimberley Loughlin
5541 West Cullom Avenue
Chicago IL 60641
312-685-5455

I do beautifully executed work for advertising and editorial photography, plus historical research in food and food-related props.

Please call to see my portfolio and reel. They include a wide range of work: from a simple bowl of cereal or elegant environmental images to complex technical styling such as pastry and meats.

Wendy Mary
719 West Wrightwood Avenue
Chicago IL 60614
312-871-5476

**Jacqueline Motooka
and Associates**
1516 West Edgewater Avenue
Chicago IL 60660
312-271-5092

Josephine Orba
1418 West Addison Street
Chicago IL 60613
312-337-1901

Fran Paulson Picture Foods
155 North Harbor Point
Chicago IL 60601
312-943-2540

Bonnie Rabert—Food Consultant
3838 North Alta Vista Terrace
Chicago IL 60613
312-929-0047

As a home economist, I have been working in the area of food for 25 years. As a freelance consultant since 1979, I have specialized in food styling for photography, recipe development, personal appearances, new product concepts, teaching and some writing. An extensive Chicago network enables me to put together teams of professionals for large projects. A sample book and rate schedule are available.

Carol Smoler
1825 North Sedgwick Street
Chicago IL 60614
312-266-1133

Experienced food stylist for print and film; creative consultant for recipe development and product presentation; media spokesperson; food publicity; extensive corporate background in food marketing and promotion. Available locally, on location and in own large kitchen facility. Also available to coordinate freelance associates for large projects.

Mary-Helen Steindler
3543 North Wilton Avenue
Chicago IL 60657
312-525-3802

Dalia Tatoris
651 West Belmont Avenue
Chicago IL 60657
312-248-6131

Kathy Thomas
2830 West Fargo Avenue
Chicago IL 60645
312-338-7428

JoAnn Witherell
4943 North Leavitt Street
Chicago IL 60625
312-334-7593

Work of Art Cakes
642 West Diversey Parkway
Chicago IL 60614
312-528-6507

Gail O'Donnell
1103 Park Avenue
Deerfield IL 60015
708-945-8186

The Food Company
2723 North 75th Court
Elmwood Park IL 60635
708-453-4054

Donna Lafferty
2733 North 75th Court
Elmwood Park IL 60635
708-456-8415

She's cool, she's hot, she'll work nonstop.
If that's what it takes to get the shot.
Call the food stylist who can **prop** that "pic,"
Design the **concept**
And **garnish** the schtick,
Write the **copy** and **recipe** well...
She'll put it together so it's sure to sell.
So make that call to Chicago today.
You'll be a hit with your clients, who'll say,
"We like that stylist you hired to do...
A job and a half...I'll say she's **cool!**"

Dorothy Peterson
1838 North 78th Court
Elmwood Park IL 60635
708-453-0051

Caroline Kriz
544 Michigan Avenue
Evanston IL 60202
708-475-4799

Jane Ellis
1256 Brentwood Court
Flossmoor IL 60422
708-799-4563

Beth Kent Puett
2208 Collett Lane
Flossmoor IL 60422
708-957-5887

Barbara Kohout
23 West 256 Windsor Drive
Glen Ellyn IL 60137
708-858-4543

Pat Nagel
72 North Parkside Avenue
Glen Ellyn IL 60137
708-469-5502

Coena Coffee
118 West 2nd Street
Hinsdale IL 60521
708-986-8949

Florence French
6414 Pontiac Drive
LaGrange IL 60525
708-246-5851

**Judy Vance, Food Stylist and
Consultant**
720 South Stone
LaGrange IL 60525
708-354-6196

A degreed home economist and active member of the Chicago Culinary Guild.
Former food stylist for *Cuisine* magazine, with 14 years' experience in freelance creative food styling for print, film and media tours, and in securing prop food.
Judy Vance is an expert in recipe development, baked goods, dairy products, pasta and ethnic cuisines. She has studied in Italy and France, and has presented programs at the Minneapolis HEIB Food on Film.

Yvonne Sutton and Associates
2222 South Stewart, Apartment 5B
Lombard IL 60148
708-932-1101

Mim Hinske
710 Windsor
Mt. Prospect IL 60056
708-506-0754

Tobe Le Moine
329 South Oak Park Avenue
Oak Park IL 60302
708-386-7045

Diane Leo/Calico Cook
118 East Norman
Palatine IL 60067
708-359-7117

Becky Roller
801 South Chester
Park Ridge IL 60068
708-825-1353

Marge Lichtenberg
8733 North Kedvale Avenue
Skokie IL 60076
708-673-5163

Foodcraft/Cathy German
2 South 185 Williams Road
Warrenville IL 60555
708-393-1269

Judith Larwill
402 East Evergreen Street
Wheaton IL 60187
708-682-9134

Jeff Anthony Food Styling
918 10th Street
Wilmette IL 60091
708-256-1448

Carol Parik
2727 Vernon Court
Woodridge IL 60517
708-969-2259

INDIANA

Incredible Edibles/Sue Spitler
2107 Avondale
Long Beach IN 46360
219-874-5644

Incredible Edibles is a food consultant firm that offers a wide range of editorial services for the production of cookbooks and instruction manuals. Services include recipe development and testing, preparation of type-ready manuscript, editing and proofreading, indexing and food styling for photography.

Other services include specialized recipe development for public relations and advertising agencies, recipe development for foodservice accounts and food product appliance testing for national manufacturers.

KANSAS

Vicki Johnson—Food Stylist
8226 Cherokee Circle
Leawood KS 66206
913-648-6015

Graduate home economist with 14 years' food-styling experience.

Specializes in print, film and video photography.

Assignments have included recipe illustration for cookbooks, magazines, national ad campaigns, press releases and brochures, greeting cards and puzzles.

Will assist with media presentations and other public relations events.

Skilled in recipe development, product introductions, focus groups and trade shows.

Located in metropolitan Kansas City area. Can be FAXed at 913-894-2086.

MINNESOTA

Mary Kiesau
8717 Penn Avenue South
Bloomington MN 55431
612-884-4674

Donnie Flora
5805 Hansen Road
Edina MN 55436
612-929-2402

Lynn C. Boldt
2524 36th Avenue NE
Minneapolis MN 55418
612-789-1042

Jill Broadfoot
1785 Bryant Avenue, Suite 7
Minneapolis MN 55403
612-377-5930

Marilyn S. Krome
6032 Golden Valley Road
Minneapolis MN 55422
612-546-2961

Susan Olson
5200 Knox Avenue South
Minneapolis MN 55419
612-920-3991

Susan Zechmann
5613 Xerxes Avenue South
Minneapolis MN 55410
612-922-2942

Barb Standal
4115 Juneau Lane
Plymouth MN 55446
612-553-0185

Bev Lundgren
14349 Watersedge Trail NE
Prior Lake MN 55372
612-445-8086

OHIO

Carmen Himes
3918 Bramford Road
Columbus OH 43220
614-451-4014

WISCONSIN

Cindy Greaves
Image Studios
1100 South Lyndale
Appleton WI 54914
414-739-7824

Mary K. Franz
4349 Hillside Road
Slinger WI 53086
414-644-5784

SOUTHWEST

ARIZONA

Barbara Fenzl
6610 North Central Avenue
Phoenix AZ 85012
602-240-6767

TEXAS

Fran Gerling
2000 Meadowbrook Drive
Austin TX 78703
512-476-8290

Cosette McGee
3219 Camelot Drive
Dallas TX 75229
214-357-7921

Lenore (Lenny) Angel
1111 River Park
San Antonio TX 78216
512-493-8810

MOUNTAIN STATES

UTAH

Dian Thomas
The Dian Thomas Company
4360 South Diana Way
Salt Lake City UT 84124
801-277-4332

Food Illustrators

WEST COAST

CALIFORNIA

Marilyn Granas
220 South Palm Drive
Beverly Hills CA 90212
213-278-3773

Kim Adams
909 Ford Street
Burbank CA 91505
818-508-4792

Barbara Berry Foodstyling
79 Franciscan Way
Kensington CA 94707
415-524-4760

Justine Frank
8243 West 4th Street
Los Angeles CA 90048
213-651-5695

Tobi Frank-Martin
373 North La Cienega Boulevard
Los Angeles CA 90048
213-552-7921

Judy Peck Prindle
106 North Mansfield
Los Angeles CA 90036
213-939-7009

Norman Stewart
937 North Vista Street
Los Angeles CA 90046
213-285-8361

Susan DeVaty
423 Pennsylvania Street, Apartment 4
San Francisco CA 94107
415-285-6536

Sandra Griswald
963 North Point
San Francisco CA 94109
415-775-4272

Amy Nathan
463 1/2 Bryant Street
San Francisco CA 94107
415-243-0470

Sara Slavin
463 1/2 Bryant Street
San Francisco CA 94107
415-243-0545

Weinberg and James Foodstyle
3888 Woodcliff Road
Sherman Oaks CA 91403
213-274-2383

Stephen Shern, Creative Food Stylist
1330 North Sweetzer Avenue
West Hollywood CA 90069
213-654-6543

OREGON

Carolyn Schirmacher Gerould
3307 Southwest Dosch Road
Portland OR 97201
503-222-4266

Taste 1, Inc.
P.O. Box 30371
Portland, OR 97230
503-254-5309

A highly respected, well-known company that is unequaled in the food industry. Best known for work in new product research development, authoring recipes, recommending usage ideas for finished products (commercial, foodservice and retail). Experienced in food-styling techniques and presentations for still and video photography. Consultations for start-up companies or ideation sessions for large corporations. We have access to a large network of resourceful individuals and enterprising companies to draw from.

Illustration is another area of vital importance for any first-class publication about food or foodstuffs, and the range of styles and approaches is even broader than for food photography. Some illustrators represent themselves; many prefer to be contacted through their representatives and in the alphabetical listing that follows, artists' names are frequently followed by their agents' names and addresses.

Others belong to the Graphic Artists Guild, an organization that supports professionals in the field, which can be contacted at 11 West 20th Street, New York NY 10011. A valuable source of comprehensive information is *American Showcase Illustration*, 724 Fifth Avenue, New York NY 10019, which is updated regularly.

Kathie Abrams
548 9th Street
Brooklyn NY 11215
718-499-3308
Member, Graphic Artists Guild

Anatoly
Represented by:
Ella, Photographers' & Artists' Representative
229 Berkeley Street
Boston MA 02116
617-266-3858

Robert Anderson
Represented by:
Jack Jernigan Representing Artists
4209 Canal Street
New Orleans LA 70119
504-821-4005

The Art Bunch, Inc.
230 North Michigan Avenue
Chicago IL 60601
312-368-8777
Member, Graphic Artists Guild

Bob August
Represented by:
Kirsch Represents
7316 Pyramid Drive
Hollywood CA 90046
213-651-3706

Pat Bailey
Represented by:
Bernstein & Andriulli, Inc.
60 East 42nd Street
New York NY 10165
212-682-1490

Don Baker,
Kolea Baker
2815 Alaskan Way, Suite 37-A
Seattle WA 98121
206-443-0326

Barbara Banthien
Represented by:
Lindgren & Smith
41 Union Square
New York NY 10003
212-929-5590

Ken Barr
Represented by:
Jerry Leff Associates, Inc.
420 Lexington Avenue
New York NY 10170
212-697-8525

Jeffrey Bellantuono
292 Britannia Street, Unit A
Meriden CT 06450
203-639-0665
Member, Graphic Artists Guild

Janice Belove
46 Carolin Road
Upper Montclair NJ 07043
201-744-3760
Member, Graphic Artists Guild

Norm Bendell
Represented by:
David Goldman Agency
41 Union Square West
New York NY 10003
212-807-6627

Robert Bergin
Represented by:
Incandescent Ink, Inc.
111 Wooster Street
New York NY 10012
212-925-0491

Semyon Bilmes
Represented by:
Jerry Leff Associates, Inc.
420 Lexington Avenue
New York NY 10170
212-697-8525

Deborah Blackwell
3 River Street
Sandwich MA 02563
508-888-4019
Member, Graphic Artists Guild

Garie Blackwell
Represented by:
Bernstein & Andriulli, Inc.
60 East 42nd Street
New York NY 10165
212-682-1490

Alice M. Block
Represented by:
Ron Puhalski, Inc.
1133 Broadway
New York NY 10010
212-242-2860

Joan Blume
25 Monroe Place, Apartment 12A
Brooklyn Heights NY 11201
718-858-9595

Robin Brickman

Food and Garden Illustrations for:

The New York Times
Gourmet
Horticulture
Delftree Mushrooms
Rodale Press
Little, Brown, & Co.
D.R. Godine
Doubleday
Harper & Row

413-458-9853 *FAX available (also see listing)*

Alex Boies
Represented by:
Jerry Leff Associates, Inc.
420 Lexington Avenue
New York NY 10170
212-697-8525

Bernard Bonhomme
Represented by:
Incandescent Ink, Inc.
111 Wooster Street
New York NY 10012
212-925-0491

Wendy Braun
Represented by:
Pamela Korn and Associates
321 East 12th Street
New York NY 10003
212-529-6389

Steve Brennan
Represented by:
Mendola Ltd.
Graybar Building
420 Lexington Avenue,
Penthouse
New York NY 10170
212-986-5680

Robin Brickman
32 Fort Hoosac Place
Williamstown MA 01267
413-458-9853
Member, Graphic Artists Guild

Ralph Brillhart
Represented by:
Hankins + Tegenborg
Artist's Representatives
60 East 42nd Street
New York NY 10165
212-867-8092

Andrea Brooks
99 Bank Street, Apartment 3-G
New York NY 10014
212-633-1477
Member, Graphic Artists Guild

Bradford Brown
Represented by:
Jerry Leff Associates, Inc.
420 Lexington Avenue
New York NY 10170
212-697-8525

John Burgoyne
Represented by:
Katherine Tise
Illustrator's Representative
200 East 78th Street
New York NY 10021
212-570-9069

Dana Burns
Represented by:
Burns-Pizer
580 Patten Avenue, Suite 19
Long Branch NJ 07740
201-870-6807

Lon Busch
Represented by:
Gerald & Cullen Rapp, Inc.
108 East 35th Street, Suite 1
New York NY 10016
212-889-3337

Jim Butcher
Represented by:
Frank & Jeff Lavaty
& Associates
509 Madison Avenue, Suite 1014
New York NY 10022
212-355-0910

Mark Cable
Represented by:
Clare Jett and Associates
21 Theater Square, Suite 200
Louisville KY 40202
502-561-0737

Thomas Cain
Represented by:
Sarah Perry
968 Homewood Court
Decatur GA 30033
404-634-2349

Wende Caporale
Represented by:
John Brewster/Creative Services
597 Riverside Avenue
Westport CT 06880
203-226-4724

Wayne Carey
Represented by:
Will Sumpter and Associates
1728 North Rock Springs Road NE
Atlanta GA 30324
404-874-2014

Michael Carpenter
Represented by:
Kolea Baker
2815 Alaskan Way, Suite 37-A
Seattle WA 98121
206-443-0326

Bunny Carter
Represented by:
Katherine Tise
Illustrator's Representative
200 East 78th Street
New York NY 10021
212-570-9069

Penny Carter
430 East 66th Street
New York NY 10021
212-772-3715
Member, Graphic Artists Guild

Steve Carver
Represented by:
Susan Gomberg
Artists Representative
145 East 22nd Street
New York NY 10010
212-473-8747

Cheryl Chalmers
Represented by:
The Ivy League of Artists
156 Fifth Avenue
New York NY 10010
212-243-1333

Ellis Chappell
Represented by:
Ron Puhalski, Inc.
1133 Broadway
New York NY 10010
212-242-2860

David Chestnutt
Represented by:
Artists International
7 Dublin Hill Drive
Greenwich CT 06830
203-869-8010

Garry Ciccarelli
Represented by:
American Artists'
Representatives, Inc.
353 West 53rd Street, Suite 1W
New York NY 10019
212-682-2462

Bradley Clark
Represented by:
Lindgren & Smith
41 Union Square
New York NY 10003
212-929-5590

Judy Clifford
24 West 90th Street, Apartment 3B
New York NY 10024
212-799-9040

Rob Cline
Represented by:
Ella, Photographers' &
Artists' Representative
229 Berkeley Street
Boston MA 02116
617-266-3858

Elaine Cohen
Represented by:
Kolea Baker
2815 Alaskan Way, Suite 37-A
Seattle WA 98121
206-443-0326

William Colrus
Represented by:
The Ivy League of Artists
156 Fifth Avenue
New York NY 10010
212-243-1333

Anne Cook
Represented by:
Artco
232 Madison Avenue, Suite 600
New York NY 10016
212-889-8777

Esky Cook
Represented by:
Joel Harlib Associates
405 North Wabash Avenue
Chicago IL 60611
312-329-1370

Jeff Cornell
Represented by:
Artco
232 Madison Avenue, Suite 600
New York NY 10016
212-889-8777

Richard Cowdrey
Represented by:
Ella, Photographers' &
Artists' Representative
229 Berkeley Street
Boston MA 02116
617-266-3858

Daniel Craig
Represented by:
Bernstein & Andriulli, Inc.
60 East 42nd Street
New York NY 10165
212-682-1490

Robert Crawford
Represented by:
Pushpin Associates
215 Park Avenue South, 13th Floor
New York NY 10003
212-674-8080

Alicia Czechowski
Represented by:
Pushpin Associates
215 Park Avenue South, 13th Floor
New York NY 10003
212-674-8080

Bob Dacey
Represented by:
Artco
232 Madison Avenue, Suite 600
New York NY 10016
212-889-8777

Don Daily
Represented by:
Frank & Jeff Lavaty
& Associates
509 Madison Avenue, Suite 1014
New York NY 10022
212-355-0910

Robert Dale
Represented by:
Susan Gomberg
Artists Representative
145 East 22nd Street
New York NY 10010
212-473-8747

Larry Daste
Represented by:
Evelyne Johnson Associates
201 East 28th Street
New York NY 10016
212-532-0928

Larry Daste, an award-winning artist, has an impressive list of clients. Some are: 7-Up, Frito-Lay, Borden's Foods, Borden's Milk, Bennigan's Restaurant, Xerox, Met Life, CitiCorp, Sharp, Philip Morris, Greyhound Bus, Braniff, American Airlines, Texas Instruments, Northwest Airlines, Radio Shack and Finnair. His illustration appears in books from Random House, Macmillan, Harper & Row and other publishers. His work can currently be seen in magazines such as *Ski* magazine, *Woman's World*, *Games* magazine and others. See a sample of his work on page 226.

Everett Davidson
Represented by:
Bernstein & Andriulli, Inc.
60 East 42nd Street
New York NY 10165
212-682-1490

Greg Dearth
Represented by:
Scott Hull Associates
68 East Franklin Street
Dayton OH 45459
513-433-8383

Jim Deigan
Represented by:
Cliff Knecht Representing Artists
309 Walnut Road
Pittsburgh PA 15202
412-761-5666

Ric Del Rossi
Represented by:
The Ivy League of Artists
156 Fifth Avenue
New York NY 10010
212-243-1333

Bob Deschamps
Represented by:
Gerald & Cullen Rapp, Inc.
108 East 35th Street, Suite 1
New York NY 10016
212-889-3337

Danilo Ducak
Represented by:
Hankins + Tegenborg
Artist's Representatives
60 East 42nd Street
New York NY 10165
212-867-8092

Chris Duke
Represented by:
Frank & Jeff Lavaty
& Associates
509 Madison Avenue, Suite 1014
New York NY 10022
212-355-0910

Nina Duran
Represented by:
Bernstein & Andriulli, Inc.
60 East 42nd Street
New York NY 10165
212-682-1490

Jon Ellis
Represented by:
Mendola Ltd.
Graybar Building
420 Lexington Avenue,
Penthouse
New York NY 10170
212-986-5680

Jan Evans
Represented by:
Carol Chislovsky, Inc.
853 Broadway
New York NY 10003
212-677-9100

Deresa Fasolino
Represented by:
Jacqueline Dedell, Inc.
58 West 15th Street
New York NY 10011
212-741-2539

Vivienne Flesher
Represented by:
VMA
194 Third Avenue
New York NY 10003
212-475-0440

Tony Gabriele
Represented by:
Ron Puhalski, Inc.
1133 Broadway
New York NY 10010
212-242-2860

Gervasio Gallardo
Represented by:
Frank & Jeff Lavaty
& Associates
509 Madison Avenue, Suite 1014
New York NY 10022
212-355-0910

Allen Garns
Represented by:
Susan Gomberg
Artists Representative
145 East 22nd Street
New York NY 10010
212-473-8747

Jackie Geyer
Represented by:
Cliff Knecht Representing Artists
309 Walnut Road
Pittsburgh PA 15202
412-761-5666

Ralph Giguere
Represented by:
Susan Gomberg
Artists Representative
145 East 22nd Street
New York NY 10010
212-473-8747

Byron Gin
Represented by:
Carolyn Potts & Associates
4 East Ohio Street, Suite 11
Chicago IL 60611
312-935-1707

Randy Glass
Represented by:
Gerald & Cullen Rapp, Inc.
108 East 35th Street, Suite 1
New York NY 10016
212-889-3337

Dale Glasser
Dale Glasser Graphics, Inc.
124 West 24th Street, Suite 2A
New York NY 10011
212-929-2151

Bob Gleason
Represented by:
Carolyn Potts & Associates
4 East Ohio Street, Suite 11
Chicago IL 60611
312-935-1707

Penelope Gottlieb
Represented by:
Jerry Leff Associates, Inc.
420 Lexington Avenue
New York NY 10170
212-697-8525

Cheryl Griesbach/Stanley Martucci
Represented by:
Jacqueline Dedell, Inc.
58 West 15th Street
New York NY 10011
212-741-2539

William Harrison
324 West State Street
Geneva IL 60134
708-232-7733

Ray Harvey
Represented by:
Hankins + Tegenborg
Artist's Representatives
60 East 42nd Street
New York NY 10165
212-867-8092

John Harwood
Represented by:
Bernstein & Andriulli, Inc.
60 East 42nd Street
New York NY 10165
212-682-1490

Karel Havlicek
Represented by:
Joel Harlib Associates
405 North Wabash Avenue
Chicago IL 60611
312-329-1370

Joe and Kathy Heiner
Represented by:
VMA
194 Third Avenue
New York NY 10003
212-475-0440

Lisa Henderling
Represented by:
Artco
232 Madison Avenue, Suite 600
New York NY 10016
212-889-8777

Doug Henry
Represented by:
American Artists'
Representatives, Inc.
353 West 53rd Street, Suite 1-W
New York NY 10019
212-682-2462

Ginnie Hofmann
Represented by:
Gerald & Cullen Rapp, Inc.
108 East 35th Street, Suite 1
New York NY 10016
212-889-3337

Phil Howe
Represented by:
Kolea Baker
2815 Alaskan Way, Suite 37-A
Seattle WA 98121
206-443-0326

Stan Hunter
Represented by:
Frank & Jeff Lavaty
& Associates
509 Madison Avenue, Suite 1014
New York NY 10022
212-355-0910

Mitch Hyatt
Represented by:
American Artists'
Representatives, Inc.
353 West 53rd Street, Suite 1-W
New York NY 10019
212-682-2462

Jacobson/Fernandez
Represented by:
Susan Gomberg
Artists Representative
145 East 22nd Street
New York NY 10010
212-473-8747

Lauren Jarrett Watercolors
25 Harborview Lane, Box 1081
East Hampton NY 11937
516-324-5523

I grew up surrounded by the arts of cooking, gardening and living. My grandfather was an art director, painter, naturalist and farmer, my grandmother taught me to cook, garden and arrange flowers. They nurtured my childhood passions for beauty, orderliness and good food.

A deep appreciation for nature and the domestic arts fills my life and directs my efforts; drawing and painting for cookbooks and gardening books bring together my real loves and skills.

Dave Jonason
Represented by:
Pushpin Associates
215 Park Avenue South, 13th Floor
New York NY 10003
212-674-8080

Hal Just
Represented by:
Anita Grien Representing Artists
155 East 38th Street
New York NY 10016
212-697-6170

Joyce Kitchell
Represented by:
Mendola Ltd.
Graybar Building
420 Lexington Avenue,
Penthouse
New York NY 10170
212-986-5680

Kristin Knutson
Represented by:
Susan Trimpe Representing Artists
2717 Western Avenue
Seattle WA 98121
206-728-1300

Laszlo Kubinyi
Represented by:
Gerald & Cullen Rapp, Inc.
108 East 35th Street, Suite 1
New York NY 10016
212-889-3337

Tom LaPadula
Represented by:
Evelyne Johnson Associates
201 East 28th Street
New York NY 10016
212-532-0928

Beth Whybrow Leeds
Represented by:
Janice Stefanski
2022 Jones Street
San Francisco CA 94133
415-928-0457

Marsha E. Levine
140-55 34th Avenue, Apartment 4-P
Flushing NY 11354
718-445-9410
Member, Graphic Artists Guild

Lemuel Line
Represented by:
Frank & Jeff Lavaty
& Associates
509 Madison Avenue, Suite 1014
New York NY 10022
212-355-0910

Francis Livingston
Represented by:
Jerry Leff Associates, Inc.
420 Lexington Avenue
New York NY 10170
212-697-8525

Todd Lockwood
Represented by:
Bernstein & Andriulli, Inc.
60 East 42nd Street
New York NY 10165
212-682-1490

Roberta Ludlow
Represented by:
Incandescent Ink, Inc.
111 Wooster Street
New York NY 10012
212-925-0491

Turi MacCombie
Represented by:
Evelyne Johnson Associates
201 East 28th Street
New York NY 10016
212-532-0928

Turi MacCombie enjoys successful careers both in fine arts and in commercial art. Her work is in many famous collections, including clients such as Chemical Bank, Paine Webber, the Juilliard School of Music and Fidelity Trust, as well as in numerous private collections. Her commercial clients include Godiva Chocolates, Metropolitan Life Insurance and General Motors. She illustrated *Chocolate Dreams* published by Lothrop Lee, as well as books for Random House, Western Publishing, Bantam and Macmillan. See a sample of her work on page 226.

Dennis Magdich
Represented by:
Jerry Leff Associates, Inc.
420 Lexington Avenue
New York NY 10170
212-697-8525

Michele Manning
Represented by:
Jerry Leff Associates, Inc.
420 Lexington Avenue
New York NY 10170
212-697-8525

Shelley Matheis
534 East Passaic Avenue
Bloomfield NJ 07003
201-338-9506
Member, Graphic Artists Guild

Dan McGowan
Represented by:
Susan Gomberg
Artists Representative
145 East 22nd Street
New York NY 10010
212-473-8747

Julia McLain
Represented by:
Incandescent Ink, Inc.
111 Wooster Street
New York NY 10012
212-925-0491

Mark McMahon
Represented by:
Mendola Ltd.
Graybar Building
420 Lexington Avenue,
Penthouse
New York NY 10170
212-986-5680

Frank Miller
Represented by:
Pushpin Associates
215 Park Avenue South, 13th Floor
New York NY 10003
212-674-8080

Celia Mitchell
Represented by:
Jerry Leff Associates, Inc.
420 Lexington Avenue
New York NY 10170
212-697-8525

Linda Y. Miyamoto
P.O. Box 022310
Brooklyn NY 11202
718-596-4787
Member, Graphic Artists Guild

Jacqui Morgan
692 Greenwich Street
New York NY 10014
212-463-8488
Member, Graphic Artists Guild

David Moses
Represented by:
Woody Coleman Presents, Inc.
490 Rockside Road
Cleveland OH 44131
216-661-4222

Margo Z. Nahas
Represented by:
Lindgren & Smith
41 Union Square
New York NY 10003
212-929-5590

Marlies Merk Najaka
241 Central Park West
New York NY 10024
212-580-0058
Member, Graphic Artists Guild

Will Nelson
Represented by:
Sweet Represents
716 Montgomery Street
San Francisco CA 94111
415-433-1222

Richard Newton
Represented by:
Renard Represents, Inc.
501 Fifth Avenue
New York NY 10017
212-490-2450

Jeff Nishinaka
Represented by:
Bernstein & Andriulli, Inc.
60 East 42nd Street
New York NY 10165
212-682-1490

Kathy O'Brien
Represented by:
Lindgren & Smith
41 Union Square
New York NY 10003
212-929-5590

Carlos Ochagavia
Represented by:
Frank & Jeff Lavaty
& Associates
509 Madison Avenue, Suite 1014
New York NY 10022
212-355-0910

Richard A. Olson
85 Grand Street
New York NY 10013
212-925-1820
Member, Graphic Artists Guild

Earl Parker
Represented by:
Artists International
7 Dublin Hill Drive
Greenwich CT 06830
203-869-8010

Edward Parker
Represented by:
Jacqueline Dedell, Inc.
58 West 15th Street
New York NY 10011
212-741-2539

John Parsons
Represented by:
Jerry Leff Associates, Inc.
420 Lexington Avenue
New York NY 10170
212-697-8525

Joyce Patti
Represented by:
VMA
194 Third Avenue
New York NY 10003
212-475-0440

Judy Pelikan
Represented by:
Katherine Tise
Illustrator's Representative
200 East 78th Street
New York NY 10021
212-570-9069

Roy Pendleton
Represented by:
Pushpin Associates
215 Park Avenue South, 13th Floor
New York NY 10003
212-674-8080

Fred Pepera
Represented by:
Joel Harlib Associates
405 North Wabash Avenue
Chicago IL 60611
312-329-1370

Laura Phillips
Represented by:
Bernstein & Andriulli, Inc.
60 East 42nd Street
New York NY 10165
212-682-1490

Deborah Pinkney
Represented by:
Irmeli Holmberg, Artist Agent
280 Madison Avenue, Room 1402
New York NY 10016
212-545-9155

Herb Reed
Represented by:
The Ivy League of Artists
156 Fifth Avenue
New York NY 10010
212-243-1333

Jean Restivo
Represented by:
Artco
232 Madison Avenue, Suite 600
New York NY 10016
212-889-8777

Mark Riedy
Represented by:
Scott Hull Associates
68 East Franklin Street
Dayton OH 45459
513-433-8383

Ellen Rixford
Represented by:
Anita Grien Representing Artists
155 East 38th Street
New York NY 10016
212-697-6170

Ray Roberts
Represented by:
Bernstein & Andriulli, Inc.
60 East 42nd Street
New York NY 10165
212-682-1490

Robert Rodriguez
Represented by:
Renard Represents, Inc.
501 Fifth Avenue
New York NY 10017
212-490-2450

Lilla Rogers
483 Henry Street
Brooklyn NY 11231
718-624-6862
Member, Graphic Artists Guild

Delro Rosco
Represented by:
Mendola Ltd.
Graybar Building
420 Lexington Avenue,
Penthouse
New York NY 10170
212-986-5680

Masao Saito
Represented by:
Renard Represents, Inc.
501 Fifth Avenue
New York NY 10017
212-490-2450

Katherine Salentine
Represented by:
Janice Stefanski
2022 Jones Street
San Francisco CA 94133
415-928-0457

Elizabeth Sayles
16 East 23rd Street
New York NY 10010
212-777-7012
Member, Graphic Artists Guild

Dana Schreiber
89 St. James Place
Brooklyn NY 11238
718-638-3505
Member, Graphic Artists Guild

Ward Schumaker
Represented by:
VMA
194 Third Avenue
New York NY 10003
212-475-0440

Hisashi Sekine
Represented by:
Daniele Collignon
200 West 15th Street
New York NY 10011
212-243-4209

Marla Shega
Represented by:
Bernstein & Andriulli, Inc.
60 East 42nd Street
New York NY 10165
212-682-1490

Al Skaar
Represented by:
Kolea Baker
2815 Alaskan Way, Suite 37-A
Seattle WA 98121
206-443-0326

Stan Skardinski
Represented by:
Evelyne Johnson Associates
201 East 28th Street
New York NY 10016
212-532-0928

Chuck Slack
Represented by:
Bernstein & Andriulli, Inc.
60 East 42nd Street
New York NY 10165
212-682-1490

Vicki Smith
Represented by:
Maud Geng Represents Artists
25 Gray Street
Boston MA 02116
617-236-1920

Kirsten Soderland
Represented by:
Incandescent Ink, Inc.
111 Wooster Street
New York NY 10012
212-925-0491

Rosalind Solomon
Represented by:
Artists International
7 Dublin Hill Drive
Greenwich CT 06830
203-869-0491

Tommy Soloski
Represented by:
Incandescent Ink, Inc.
111 Wooster Street
New York NY 10012
212-925-0491

Peter Stallard
Represented by:
Bernstein & Andriulli, Inc.
60 East 42nd Street
New York NY 10165
212-682-1490

Pat Stewart
Represented by:
Evelyne Johnson Associates
201 East 28th Street
New York NY 10016
212-532-0928

Pat Stewart is a noted illustrator of cookbooks and trade books. Some of her books are *Living a Beautiful Life* (Random House), *Visions of Sugar Plums* (Mimi Sheraton, Harper & Row), *The Great East Coast Seafood Book* (Yvonne Young Tarr, Random House), *Betty Crocker's International Cookbook* (Random House), *The Complete Chicken* (Carl Jerome, Random House) and many other best-selling cookbooks. Pat's art is exhibited at local galleries and her works can be found in notable private collections. See a sample of her work on page 226.

Maria Stroster
Represented by:
Incandescent Ink, Inc.
111 Wooster Street
New York NY 10012
212-925-0491

Robert Stuhmer
Represented by:
Andy Badin
210 East 67th Street
New York NY 10021
212-532-1222

Jozef Sumichrast
Represented by:
Renard Represents, Inc.
501 Fifth Avenue
New York NY 10017
212-490-2450

Judy Sutton
Represented by:
Incandescent Ink, Inc.
111 Wooster Street
New York NY 10012
212-925-0491

Plato Taleporos
333 East 23rd Street
New York NY 10010
212-689-3138
Member, Graphic Artists Guild

Paul Tankersley
Represented by:
Ron Puhalski, Inc.
1133 Broadway
New York NY 10010
212-242-2860

Phyllis Tarlow
42 Stratford Road
New Rochelle NY 10804
914-235-9473
Member, Graphic Artists Guild

Cathleen Toelke
Represented by:
Lindgren & Smith
41 Union Square
New York NY 10003
212-929-5590

Ron Toelke
Represented by:
Ella, Photographers' &
Artists' Representative
229 Berkeley Street
Boston MA 02116
617-266-3858

Cynthia Torp
Represented by:
Clare Jett and Associates
21 Theater Square, Suite 200
Louisville KY 40202
502-561-0737

James Tughan
Represented by:
Susan Gomberg
Artists Representative
145 East 22nd Street
New York NY 10010
212-473-8747

Jeff Tull
Represented by:
Clare Jett and Associates
21 Theater Square, Suite 200
Louisville KY 40202
502-561-0737

Clay Turner
Represented by:
Bernstein & Andriulli, Inc.
60 East 42nd Street
New York NY 10165
212-682-1490

Paul Vaccarello
Represented by:
Artists International
7 Dublin Hill Drive
Greenwich CT 06830
203-869-8010

Monte Varah
Represented by:
Woody Coleman Presents, Inc.
490 Rockside Road
Cleveland OH 44131
216-661-4222

Rhonda Voo
Represented by:
Carolyn Potts & Associates
4 East Ohio Street, Suite 11
Chicago IL 60611
312-935-1707

Sarah Waldron
Represented by:
Incandescent Ink, Inc.
111 Wooster Street
New York NY 10012
212-925-0491

Pam Wall
Represented by:
Bernstein & Andriulli, Inc.
60 East 42nd Street
New York NY 10165
212-682-1490

Kurt Wallace
Represented by:
Jerry Leff Associates, Inc.
420 Lexington Avenue
New York NY 10170
212-697-8525

Brent Watkinson
Represented by:
Bernstein & Andriulli, Inc.
60 East 42nd Street
New York NY 10165
212-682-1490

Marcia Wetzel
Represented by:
Aldridge Reps, Inc.
755 Virginia Avenue
Atlanta GA 30306
404-872-7980

Willardson and Associates
Represented by:
VMA
194 Third Avenue
New York NY 10003
212-475-0440

Amanda Wilson
346 East 20th Street
New York NY 10003
212-260-7567
Member, Graphic Artists Guild

Phil Wilson
Represented by:
Cliff Knecht Representing Artists
309 Walnut Road
Pittsburgh PA 15202
412-761-5666

Kris Wiltse
Represented by:
Kolea Baker
2815 Alaskan Way, Suite 37-A
Seattle WA 98121
206-443-0326

Alan Witschonke
Represented by:
The Artery
68 Agassiz Avenue
Belmont MA 02178
617-484-8023

Paul Wolf
Represented by:
Clare Jett and Associates
21 Theater Square, Suite 200
Louisville KY 40202
502-561-0737

John Youssi
Represented by:
Hankins + Tegenborg
Artist's Representatives
60 East 42nd Street
New York NY 10165
212-867-8092

Brian Zick
Represented by:
VMA
194 Third Avenue
New York NY 10003
212-475-0440

Dennis Ziemienski
Represented by:
Incandescent Ink, Inc.
111 Wooster Street
New York NY 10012
212-925-0491

Darryl Zudeck
Represented by:
Lindgren & Smith
41 Union Square
New York NY 10003
212-929-5590

Matt Zumbo
Represented by:
Bernstein & Andriulli, Inc.
60 East 42nd Street
New York NY 10165
212-682-1490

Graphic Designers

Here are some graphic design firms that have been recent award-winners in the areas of food and beverage packaging. The list was compiled with the aid of *Graphis* Packaging Design Annual, Volume 5, and *Communication Arts* Design Annual. It is organized alphabetically by the name of the company.

Primo Angeli, Inc.
590 Folsom Street
San Francisco CA 94105
415-974-6100
Contact:
Primo Angeli

Jann Church Partners
110 Newport Center Drive,
Suite 160
Newport Beach CA 92660
714-640-6224
Contact:
Jann Church

Design Team One, Inc.
49 East 4th Street,
10th Floor
Cincinnati OH 45202
513-281-4774
Contact:
Dan Bittan

Drentell Doyle Partners
1123 Broadway
New York NY 10010
212-463-8787
Contact:
Stephen Doyle

The Duffy Design Group
701 Fourth Avenue South
Minneapolis MN 55415
612-339-3247
Contact:
Joe Duffy

The Dunlavey Studio, Inc.
3576 McKinley Boulevard
Sacramento CA 95816
916-451-2170
Contact:
Linda Dunlavey

First Class Productions
119 West 23rd Street, Room 1003
New York NY 10011
212-727-1528
Contact:
Mara Rogers

Complete publishing production
from concept and design through
camera-ready mechanicals. A one-stop
service for publishers, public relations
firms and corporations. We specialize in
food writing, ranging from point-of-
purchase pamphlets to cookbooks. Production services include: research,
writing, recipe development and testing,
food styling and propping of photographs, food photography and illustration.

Frazier Design
173 7th Street
San Francisco CA 94103
415-863-9613
Contact:
Craig Frazier

Josh Freeman Associates
8019 1/2 Melrose Avenue
Los Angeles CA 90046
213-653-6466
Contact:
Josh Freeman

Gerstman & Meyers, Inc.
111 West 57th Street,
7th Floor
New York NY 10019
212-586-2535
Contact:
Larry Riddell

Giovanitti Design Group, Inc.
16 East 23rd Street
New York NY 10010
212-777-7012
Contact:
Sara Giovanitti

Tim Girvin Design, Inc.
911 Western Avenue, Suite 408
Seattle WA 98104
206-623-7808
Contact:
Tim Girvin

Milton Glaser, Inc.
207 East 32nd Street
New York NY 10016
212-242-5357
Contact:
Milton Glaser

Bruce Hale Design
2916 Fifth Avenue West
Seattle WA 98119
206-282-1191
Contact:
Bruce Hale

Harte Yamashita & Forest
5735 Melrose Avenue
Los Angeles CA 90038
213-462-6486
Contact:
Tets Yamashita

Hermsen Design Associates, Inc.
5151 Beltline Road, Suite 825
Dallas TX 75240
214-233-5090
Contact:
Jack Hermsen

The Hively Agency, Inc.
520 Post Oak Boulevard,
Suite 800
Houston TX 77027
713-961-2888
Contact:
Charles Hively

**Jonson Pirtle Pedersen Alcorn
Metzdorf & Hess**
35 East 20th Street
New York NY 10003
212-353-0101
Contact:
Lyle Metzdorf

Koppel & Scher
156 Fifth Avenue
New York NY 10003
212-627-9330
Contact:
Paul Scher

Landor Associates
1001 Front Street
San Francisco CA 94111
415-955-1200
Contact:
Walter Landor

The Leonhardt Group
411 First Avenue South,
Suite 315
Seattle WA 98104
206-624-0551
Contact:
Carolyn Leonhardt

Michael Mabry Design
212 Sutter Street
San Francisco CA 94108
415-982-7336
Contact:
Michael Mabry

Morren Design
2200 North Lamar, Suite 308
Dallas TX 75202
214-720-0220
Contact:
Virginia Morren

Peckolick & Partners
108 East 31st Street
New York NY 10016
212-532-6166
Contact:
Alan Peckolick

Pentagram Design
212 Fifth Avenue
New York NY 10010
212-683-7000
Contact:
Woody Pirtle

The Michael Peters Group
800 Third Avenue, 27th Floor
New York NY 10022
212-371-1919
Contact:
Alan Hill

The Pushpin Group
215 Park Avenue South
New York NY 10003
212-674-8080
Contact:
Seymour Chwast

Gerald Reis & Company
560 Sutter Street
San Francisco CA 94102
415-421-1232
Contact:
Gerald Reis

Richards, Brock, Miller, Mitchell & Associates
7007 Twin Hills, Suite 200
Dallas TX 75231
214-987-4800
Contact:
Luis Acevedo

Richardson or Richardson
1301 East Bethany Home
Phoenix AZ 85014
602-266-1301
Contact:
Forrest and Valerie Richardson

Richardson/Smith, Inc.
139 Lewis Wharf
Boston MA 02110
617-367-1491
Contact:
Michael Westcott

Ross Culbert Holland & Lavery, Inc.
15 West 20th Street
New York NY 10011
212-206-0044
Contact:
Peter Ross

The Schechter Group, Inc.
212 East 49th Street
New York NY 10017
212-752-4400
Contact:
Alvin Schechter

Tracey Shiffman Roland Young Design Group
7421 Beverly Boulevard, Suite 4
Los Angeles CA 90036
213-930-1816
Contact:
Tracey Shiffman

Sidjakov, Berman & Gomez Partners
1725 Montgomery Street
San Francisco CA 94111
415-931-7500
Contact:
Nicolas Sidjakov

Source, Inc.
116 South Michigan Avenue
Chicago IL 60603
312-236-7620
Contact:
Kim Read-Vallone

Michael Stanard, Inc.
996 Main Street
Evanston IL 60202
708-869-9820
Contact:
Michael Stanard

Studio 400
760 Burr Oak Drive
Westmont IL 60559
708-323-3616
Contact:
Jennifer Billman

Studio 400 is a comprehensive marketing/design and photography firm. We specialize in the concept, design and production of exceptional food and product photography as well as marketing communication materials for the food industry.

Our studio has a fully equipped set, complete kitchen and a creative team of photographers, designers, food stylists, illustrators, copywriters and other design communication talents.

For a sample of our work, see page 158.

Sullivan/Perkins
5207 McKinney, Suite 10
Dallas TX 75205
214-528-7510
Contact:
Ron Sullivan

Tharp Did It
50 University Avenue, Suite 21
Los Gatos CA 95030
408-354-6726
Contact:
Rick Tharp

Weber Design
1439 Larimer Square
Denver CO 80202
303-892-9816
Contact:
Christina Weber

Dean Weller & Company
138 West 74th Street
New York NY 10023
212-873-2316
Contact:
Dean Weller

The Weller Institute for the Cure of Design, Inc.
1398 Aerie Drive
Park City UT 84060
801-649-9859
Contact:
Don Weller

Woods & Woods
1810 Harrison Street
San Francisco CA 94103
415-863-6533
Contact:
Paul and Allison Woods

Bruce Yelaska Design
1546 Grant Avenue
San Francisco CA 94133
415-392-0717
Contact:
Bruce Yelaska

Lloyd Ziff Design Group
114 East 32nd Street, Suite 1103
New York NY 10016
212-689-6455
Contact:
Lloyd Ziff

Food Videos

With more than 67 million VCRs currently operating in American homes, the production and sale of food videos is a burgeoning field of activity, but a surprisingly hard one to encapsulate.

The selected listing that follows, therefore, has been divided into three categories: a sampling of videos made by food celebrities, almost always in connection with books or television programs; a selection of the videos on cooking techniques made as teaching aids by the Culinary Institute of America; and a short list of sources to contact for information in the expanding field of video shopping and supermarket services.

Most video stores stock a very limited range of food videos and major cooking supply stores may be of more help in locating specific videos. By far the most comprehensive source of information is the catalog published (price $3.00) and regularly updated by Video-takes, a video software marketing service at 187 Parker Avenue, Manasquan NJ 08736 (see ad on page 223).

According to our consultant Lee Kraft, founder/president of Videocraft Classics, the major producer of cooking-related videos, this is an extremely hard field to break into. To be a candidate for making a food video that will sell, it is necessary to be well known in the food field, have had a television show or published at least two successful cookbooks. The procedure varies greatly: it usually begins with submitting a detailed written proposal to an established video producer, as one would to a book publisher. If the producer likes the proposal, a master video is made from which the producer manufactures copies to be bought for mass sale by the distributor.

Finding a producer will be difficult and may well be expensive. A good way to circumvent the problem without risking major investment is to make a deal with a local TV station with cooking facilities to help make a master video in return for an agreed fee.

For information on producers and distributors, consult *The Video Source Book*, published by Gale Research,

Inc., 835 Penobscot Building, Detroit MI 48226, which has breakdowns by subject. This is also a good way to find the names of videos to rent or buy.

FOOD CELEBRITY VIDEOS

Sam Arnold
Trails West Cookin'
Videocraft Classics
1790 Broadway
New York NY 10019
212-246-9849

Rose Levy Beranbaum
Cookies, Cakes and Pies
Videocraft Classics

Paul Bocuse
Bocuse a la Carte
Kartes Video Communications
7225 Woodland Drive
Indianapolis IN 46278
317-297-1888

Giuliano Bugialli
A Guide to Italian Cooking
Videocraft Classics

Jane Butel
A Guide to Tex-Mex Cooking
Videocraft Classics

Julia Child
The Way to Cook
Random House Video
201 East 50th Street
New York NY 10022
212-572-7778

Julia Child
The French Chef
Random House Video

Chris and Geofreddo
International Gourmet Delights
Videocraft Classics

Craig Claiborne
Craig Claiborne's New York Times Cookbook
Warner Home Video
4000 Warner Boulevard
Burbank CA 91510
818-846-9090

Craig Claiborne and Pierre Franey
The Master Cooking Course
MCA Home Video
70 Universal City Plaza
Universal City CA 91608
818-777-4300

Dom DeLuise
Eat This—The Video
Healing Arts Home Video
1229 3rd Street, Suite C
Santa Monica CA 90401
213-458-9795

Pierre Franey and Bryan Miller
Cuisine Rapide
Breger Video, Inc.
915 Broadway
New York NY 10010
212-254-3900

Breger Video specializes in the production of food- and cooking-related television and home video programs. PBS series include Pierre Franey's *Cuisine Rapide* and *Madeleine Cooks*, which stars Madeleine Kamman; home video projects include *Madeleine Kamman Cooks, Volumes 1, 2 and 3*, *Judith Olney on Chocolate* and Richard Sax's *Secrets for Great Dinner Parties*.

Jane Freiman
The Food Processor Video Cookbook
Videocraft Classics

Barbara Gibbons
The Slim Gourmet
Media Home Entertainment
5730 Buckingham Parkway
Culver City CA 90230
213-216-7900

Bert Greene
The Vegetable Lover's Video Cookbook, Volumes 1 and 2
Videocraft Classics

Ken Hom
A Guide to Chinese Cooking
Videocraft Classics

Martin Johnson
Chocolate
McGraw-Hill Productions
1221 Avenue of the Americas
New York NY 10020
212-997-6572

Madeleine Kamman
Madeleine Cooks
Breger Video, Inc.

Martin Katahn
The Rotation Diet
New World Video
1140 South Sepulveda Boulevard
Los Angeles CA 90025
213-444-8500

Shirley King
A Guide to Seafood Cookery
Videocraft Classics

Abe Lebewohl
The Art of New York Deli Cooking
Videocraft Classics

Judith Olney
Judith Olney on Chocolate
Breger Video, Inc.

Jacques Pepin
A Guide to Good Cooking, Volumes 1, 2 and 3
Videocraft Classics

Kathleen Perry
The Everyday Gourmet
Kartes Video Communications

Paul Prudhomme
Chef Paul Prudhomme's Louisiana Kitchen
J2 Communications
10850 Wilshire Boulevard, Suite 1000
Los Angeles CA 90024
213-474-5252

Wolfgang Puck
Spago Cooking with Wolfgang Puck
Warner Home Video

Lynn Redgrave
Weight Watchers' Guide to Dining and Cooking
Vestron Video
P.O. Box 10382
Stamford CT 06901
203-978-5400

Lynn Redgrave
Weight Watchers' Guide to a Healthy Lifestyle
Vestron Video

Seppi Renggli
The Four Seasons Spa Cuisine Video Cookbook
Videocraft Classics

The Romagnolis
The Wonderful World of Pasta
Videocraft Classics

Julie Rosso and Sheila Lukins
Silver Palate: The Good Times Live
Simon & Schuster Video
108 Wilmot Road
Deerfield IL 60015
708-940-1260

Richard Sax
Secrets for Great Dinner Parties
Breger Video, Inc.

San Francisco Firemen's Cookbook
Academy Home Entertainment
1 Pine Haven Shore Road
P.O. Box 788
Shelburne VT 05482
802-985-8403

Thelma Snyder
Mastering Microwave Cookery
Videocraft Classics

Martha Stewart
Secrets of Entertaining
Crown/A Division of Random House
201 East 50th Street
New York NY 10022
212-572-2387

Chef Tell
Caribbean Cuisine
Interfin Video Productions
1400 Post Oak Boulevard
Houston TX 77056
713-840-5400

Anne Willan
Classic French Cooking
Videocraft Classics

Steven Yan
Wok Before You Run; Wok on the Wild Side
Embassy Home Entertainment
1901 Avenue of the Stars
Los Angeles CA 90067
213-553-3600

Video Cooking Library
Kartes Video Communications

Donovan Jon Fandre
Yes You Can Microwave
JCI Video
5308 Derry Avenue, Suite P
Agoura Hills CA 91301
800-223-7479

COOKING TECHNIQUE VIDEOS

**Culinary Institute of America
Learning Resources Center**
North Road
Hyde Park NY 12538
914-452-9600
Boning a Leg of Veal
Braising
Breakfast Cookery
Cheese Identification (slides on tape)
Chicken Breakdown
Cous Cous
Duck Galantine
How to Fillet Flatfish
How to Fillet Roundfish
Knife Skills: Vegetables
Lamb: Leg, Loin, Rack & Shoulder
The Lobster
*Onions: Rings, Halving, Slicing & Mincing
  (slides on tape)*
Poaching & Steaming
Puff Pastry 1 and 2
Roasting
Sandwiches: Dinner, Tea & Canape,
Scandinavian
Shish Kebab & Shish Taouk
Stocks: White, Brown & Fish
Table-Side Cooking: Entrees
Table-Side Cooking: Flaming Desserts
Tortillas & Tacos
Vegetable Art 1 through 5
The Way to Saute

VIDEO SHOPPING/ SUPERMARKET SERVICES

Food Marketing Institute (FMI)
1750 K Street NW
Washington DC 20006
202-452-8444

Inter-Ad, Inc.
52 Marway Circle
Rochester NY 14624
716-247-7860

Prodigy Services
445 Hamilton Avenue
White Plains NY 10601
914-993-8000

Howard Solganik & Associates
2305 Far Hills Avenue
Dayton OH 45419
513-296-1414

Food
PUBLICATIONS

227

Cookbook and Foodbook Publishers

228

Literary Agents

231

**Specialized Cookbook Stores
and Dealers**

232

**Specialized Libraries and Sources of
Information on Food**

234

Consumer Food Magazines

235

Food Trade Magazines

238

Professional Food Journals

240

Food Newsletters

243

Food Authors

248

Food Journalists

*Newspaper & Wire Service Editors;
Writers & Columnists*

Tasty Food Illustrations

Turi MacCombie

Pat Stewart

Larry Daste

Cookbook and Food Book Publishers

All the publishers in the list that follows include cookbooks among their specialties described in *Literary Market Place*, published by R. R. Bowker Company, 245 West 17th Street, New York NY 10011. Each house has an actual cookbook list, and the names given are those of the editors currently responsible for cookbook acquisitions.

As the market for cookbooks is virtually saturated, no houses will accept unsolicited manuscripts. The best course for a hitherto unpublished author is to try to obtain the services of a literary agent, who can advise on content and presentation and also submit the final proposal to the house or houses most suitable for it.

Acropolis Books, Inc.
Colortone Building
2400 17th Street NW
Washington DC 20009
202-387-6805
Contact:
Judy Mollen

Aris Books
1621 5th Street
Berkeley CA 94710
415-527-5171
Contact:
John Harris

Atheneum Publishers
115 Fifth Avenue
New York NY 10003
212-702-2000
Contact:
Pam Hoenig

Ballantine Books
201 East 50th Street
New York NY 10022
212-751-2600
Contact:
Robert B. Wyatt

Bantam Books
666 Fifth Avenue
New York NY 10103
212-765-6500
Contact:
Coleen O'Shea

Barron's Educational Series, Inc.
250 Wireless Boulevard
Hauppauge NY 11788
516-434-3311
Contact:
Grace Freedson

Irena Chalmers Cookbooks, Inc.
305 Second Avenue, Suite 316
New York NY 10003
212-529-4666
Contact:
Irena Chalmers

Chartwell Books
110 Enterprise Avenue
Secaucus NJ 07094
201-864-6341
Contact:
Editorial Staff

Chronicle Books
275 5th Street
San Francisco CA 94103
415-777-7240
Contact:
William Le Blond

Contemporary Books, Inc.
180 North Michigan Avenue
Chicago IL 60601
312-782-9181
Contact:
Nancy Crossman

Dell Publishing Company
1 Dag Hammarskjold Plaza
New York NY 10017
212-765-6500
Contact:
Jodi Rein

Doubleday & Company
666 Fifth Avenue
New York NY 10103
212-765-6500
Contact:
John Duff

Michael Friedman Publishing Group, Inc.
15 West 26th Street
New York NY 10010
212-685-6610
Contact:
Michael Friedman

Globe Pequot Press
138 West Main Street
Chester CT 06412
203-526-9571
Contact:
Eric Newman

Grove Weidenfeld
841 Broadway
New York NY 10003
212-614-7860
Contact:
Editorial Staff

Harmony Books
225 Park Avenue South
New York NY 10003
212-254-1600
Contact:
Harriet Bell

Harper & Row Publishers, Inc.
10 East 53rd Street
New York NY 10022
212-207-7000
Contact:
Susan Friedland

Houghton Mifflin Company
1 Beacon Street
Boston MA 02108
617-725-5000
Contact:
Frances Penenbaum

Interlink Publishing Group
99 Seventh Avenue
Brooklyn NY 11215
718-797-4292
Contact:
Michelle Moushabeck

The Knapp Press
5900 Wilshire Boulevard
Los Angeles CA 90036
213-937-5486
Contact:
Editorial Staff

Alfred A. Knopf, Inc.
201 East 50th Street
New York NY 10022
212-751-2600
Contact:
Judith Jones

William Morrow & Company, Inc.
105 Madison Avenue
New York NY 10016
212-889-3050
Contact:
Maria Guarnaschelli

North Point Press
850 Talbot Avenue
Berkeley CA 94706
415-527-6260
Contact:
Jenny MacDonald

Clarkson N. Potter, Inc.
225 Park Avenue South
New York NY 10003
212-254-1600
Contact:
Carole Southern

Ortho Books
Ortho Information Services
575 Market Street
San Francisco CA 94105
415-894-0277
Contact:
Sallly W. Smith

Prentice Hall Press
1 Gulf + Western Plaza
New York NY 10023
212-373-8000
Contact:
Toula Polygalaktos

Random House, Inc.
201 East 50th Street
New York NY 10022
212-751-2600
Contact:
Judith Jones

Rodale Press, Inc.
33 East Minor Street
Emmaus PA 18049
215-567-5171
Contact:
William Gottlieb

Scribner Book Companies, Inc.
Macmillan Publishing Company
866 Third Avenue
New York NY 10022
212-702-2000
Contact:
Pam Hoenig

Schocken Books, Inc.
201 East 50th Street
New York NY 10022
212-572-2517
Contact:
Wendy Wolf

Simon & Schuster, Inc.
1230 Avenue of the Americas
New York NY 10020
212-698-7000
Contact:
Editorial Staff

Stewart, Tabori & Chang, Publishers
740 Broadway
New York NY 10003
212-460-5000
Contact:
Roy Finamore

Ten Speed Press
P.O. Box 7123
Berkeley CA 94707
415-845-8414
Contact:
Editorial Staff

Times Books
Subsidiary of Random House, Inc.
201 East 50th Street
New York NY 10022
212-751-2600
Contact:
Ruth Fecych

Van Nostrand Reinhold Company, Inc.
115 Fifth Avenue
New York NY 10003
212-254-3232
Contact:
Pam Scott

John Wiley & Sons, Inc.
605 Third Avenue
New York NY 10158
212-850-6777
Contact:
Katherine C. Schowalter

Workman Publishing Company, Inc.
1 West 39th Street
New York NY 10018
212-254-5900
Contact:
Suzanne Rafer

Literary Agents

This listing includes *only* those literary agents listed in *Literary Market Place* who are prepared to represent cookbook authors. They caution that the cookbook market is flooded and only a superlative, very unusual, or specialized book on food is likely to be accepted. Retaining the services of an agent is essential for an unpublished author.

No agents will consider unsolicited manuscripts. In each case, a query with a self-addressed stamped envelope should be submitted, followed by an outline and sample chapters, with return postage included. The listing is alphabetical by the agency name; most agencies are in the New York area but represent authors nationwide.

Carole Abel Literary Agent
160 West 87th Street
New York NY 10024
212-724-1168

Dominick Abel
Literary Agency, Inc.
146 West 82nd Street, Suite 1B
New York NY 10024
212-877-0710

Elizabeth H. Backman & Company
491 Pacific Street
Brooklyn NY 11217
718-330-0949

Alison M. Bond
171 West 79th Street
New York NY 10024
212-362-3350

Andrea Brown, Literary Agent
319 East 52nd Street,
2nd Floor
New York NY 10022
212-581-7068

Marie Brown Associates
412 West 154th Street
New York NY 10032
212-690-7613

Pema Browne, Ltd.
185 East 85th Street
New York NY 10028
212-369-1925

Connie Clausen Associates
250 East 87th Street
New York NY 10128
212-427-6135

**Diane Cleaver, Inc.
(Affiliated with Sanford J.
Greenburger Associates)**
55 Fifth Avenue
New York NY 10003
212-206-5600

The Connor Literary Agency
640 West 153rd Street
New York NY 10031
212-491-5233

Robert Cornfield Literary Agency
145 West 79th Street
New York NY 10024
212-874-2465

Liz Darhansoff
1220 Park Avenue
New York NY 10128
212-534-2479

Joan Daves
21 West 26th Street
New York NY 10010
212-685-2663

**Anita Diamant
(Subsidiary, The Writers
Workshop, Inc.)**
310 Madison Avenue
New York NY 10017
212-687-1122

Sandra Dijkstra Literary Agency
1237 Camino del Mar, Suite 515-C
Del Mar CA 92014
619-755-3115

Vicki Eisenberg Literary Agency
4514 Travis Street, Suite 217
Dallas TX 75205

Elek International Rights Agents
P.O. Box 223
Canal Street Station
New York NY 10013
212-431-9368

Ethan Ellenberg, Literary Agent
548 Broadway, Suite 5-C
New York NY 10012
212-431-4554

John Farquharson, Ltd.
250 West 57th Street, Suite 1007
New York NY 10107
212-245-1993

Marje Fields
165 West 46th Street, Suite 1205
New York NY 10036
212-764-5740

Jay Garon-Brooke Associates, Inc.
415 Central Park West, Suite 17-E
New York NY 10025
212-866-3654

Goodman Associates
500 West End Avenue
New York NY 10024
212-873-4806

Charlotte Gordon
235 East 22nd Street
New York NY 10010
212-679-5363

**Sanford J. Greenburger
Associates, Inc.**
55 Fifth Avenue, 15th Floor
New York NY 10003
212-206-5600

Reece Halsey Agency
8733 Sunset Boulevard
Los Angeles CA 90069
213-652-2409

The Mitchell J. Hamilburg Agency
292 South La Cienega Boulevard,
Suite 312
Beverly Hills CA 90211
213-657-1501

Heacock Literary Agency, Inc.
1523 6th Street, Suite 14
Santa Monica CA 90401
213-393-6227

Heinle & Heinle Enterprises, Inc.
29 Lexington Road
Concord MA 01742
508-369-4858

Alice Hilton Literary Agency
13131 Welby Way, Suite B North
Hollywood CA 91606
818-982-2546

John L. Hochmann Books
320 East 58th Street
New York NY 10022
212-319-0505

Sidney B. Kramer
Mews Books, Ltd.
20 Bluewater Hill
Westport CT 06880
203-227-1836

Lucy Kroll Agency
390 West End Avenue
New York NY 10024
212-877-0627

Michael Larsen/Elizabeth Pomada
1029 Jones Street
San Francisco CA 94109
415-673-0939

The Adele Leone Agency, Inc.
26 Nantucket Place
Scarsdale NY 10583
914-961-2965

Susan Lescher
Lescher & Lescher
67 Irving Place
New York NY 10003
212-529-1790

Ray Lincoln Literary Agency
Elkins House Apartments
7900 Old York Road,
Apartment 107B
Elkins Park PA 19117
215-635-0827

**Barbara Lowenstein
Associates, Inc.**
121 West 27th Street, Suite 601
New York NY 10001
212-206-1630

McIntosh & Otis, Inc.
310 Madison Avenue
New York NY 10017
212-687-7400

Janet Wilkens Manus Literary Agency, Inc.
370 Lexington Avenue, Suite 906
New York NY 10017
212-685-9558

Denise Marcil Literary Agency, Inc.
685 West End Avenue, Apartment 9C
New York NY 10025
212-932-3110

Toni Mendez, Inc.
141 East 56th Street
New York NY 10022
212-838-6740

Scott Meredith Literary Agency, Inc.
845 Third Avenue
New York NY 10022
212-245-5500

Jean V. Naggar Literary Agency
216 East 75th Street
New York NY 10021
212-794-1082

Charles Neighbors, Inc.
7600 Blanco Road, Suite 3607
San Antonio TX 78216
512-342-5324

B. K. Nelson Literary Agency
303 Fifth Avenue
New York NY 10016
212-889-0637

The Betsy Nolan Literary Agency (Division of The Betsy Nolan Group, Inc.)
50 West 29th Street, Suite 9-W
New York NY 10001
212-779-0700

Fifi Oscard Associates, Inc. (FOA Inc.)
19 West 44th Street
New York NY 10036
212-764-1100

Susan Ann Protter Literary Agent
110 West 40th Street, Suite 1408
New York NY 10018
212-840-0480

Helen Rees Literary Agency
308 Commonwealth Avenue
Boston MA 02116
617-262-2401

The Robbins Office, Inc.
2 Dag Hammarskjold Plaza
866 Second Avenue, 12th Floor
New York NY 10017
212-223-0720

The Mitchell Rose Literary Agency
799 Broadway, Suite 410
New York NY 10003
212-418-0747

Jane Rotrosen Agency
318 East 51st Street
New York NY 10022
212-593-4330

Russell & Volkening, Inc.
50 West 29th Street
New York NY 10001
212-684-6050

SBC Enterprises, Inc.
11 Mabro Drive
Denville NJ 07834
201-366-3622

Schaffner Associates, Inc.
264 Fifth Avenue, 4th Floor
New York NY 10001
212-689-6888

Rita Scott—Marje Fields
165 West 46th Street, Suite 1205
New York NY 10036
212-764-5740

Evelyn Singer Agency, Inc.
P.O. Box 594
White Plains NY 10602
914-949-1147
212-799-5203

Slawson Communications, Inc.
165 Vallecitos de Oro
San Marcos CA 92069
619-744-2299

Michael Snell Literary Agency (Subsidiary, H. Michael Snell, Inc.)
P.O. Box 655
Truro MA 02666
617-349-3718

Nat Sobel Associates, Inc.
146 East 19th Street
New York NY 10003
212-420-8585

F. Joseph Spieler
410 West 24th Street
New York NY 10011
212-242-7152

Lyle Steele & Company, Literary Agents
511 East 73rd Street, Suite 7
New York NY 10021
212-288-2981

Stepping Stone Literary Agency, Inc.
59 West 71st Street
New York NY 10023
212-362-9277

Gloria Stern Agency
1230 Park Avenue
New York NY 10128
212-289-7698

Marianne Strong Literary Agency
65 East 96th Street
New York NY 10128
212-249-1000

Roslyn Targ Literary Agency, Inc.
105 West 13th Street, Suite 15E
New York NY 10011
212-206-9390

Watkins, Loomis Agency, Inc.
150 East 35th Street, Suite 530
New York NY 10016
212-532-0080

Rhoda Weyr Agency
216 Vance Street
Chapel Hill NC 27514
919-942-0770

Wieser & Wieser, Inc.
118 East 25th Street,
2nd Floor
New York NY 10010
212-260-0860

Ruth Wreschner, Authors' Representative
10 West 74th Street
New York NY 10023
212-877-2605

Writers' Representatives, Inc.
25 West 19th Street
New York NY 10011
212-620-9009

Wylie, Aitken & Stone, Inc.
250 West 57th Street, Suite 2106
New York NY 10107
212-246-0069

A Frank Young Enterprise
P.O. Box 1205
Elmhurst IL 60126
708-530-8818

Specialized Cookbook Stores and Dealers

The bookstores and dealers listed alphabetically here are all specialists in the field of books that are related in any way to food and wine. The list has been selected by Nach Waxman, founder/ owner of Kitchen Arts and Letters, a unique store that stocks just about everything on paper that has a relationship with food—from cookbooks to posters.

Several of the book dealers specialize in the field of antique cookbooks and almost all are prepared to conduct free searches for a fee arranged in advance and payable when the book is found.

Books for Cooks
301 South Light Street
Harvard Place
Baltimore MD 21202
301-547-9066
Current cookbooks
Contact:
Arlene Gillis

Cornucopia/Carol A. Greenberg
RD Box 2108
Edge Road
Syosset NY 11791
516-921-4813
Antiquarian and out-of-print books
Visitors by appointment only
Contact:
Carol A. Greenberg

M. M. Einhorn Maxwell, Books
At the Sign of the Dancing Bear
80 East 11th Street
New York NY 10003
212-477-5066
212-228-6767
Antiquarian books
Visitors by appointment only
Contact:
Marilyn Einhorn

This whimsically named establishment deals in hard-to-find and out-of-print books and has a stock of more than 10,000 titles. Business is conducted by means of a 36-page catalog which goes out four times a year to clients such as libraries and historians, as well as to individuals who have an interest in a particular subject. Appointments are required for personal visits.

The catalog includes books on food and wine as well as some on restaurants and hotels. A book search service is offered.

Marian L. Gore
P.O. Box 433
San Gabriel CA 91775
818-287-2946
Antiquarian books

Hoppin' Johns
30 Pinckney Street
Charleston SC 29401
803-577-6404
Current, rare and out-of-print books

John Martin Taylor

Household Words
284 Purdue
Berkeley CA 94708
415-524-8859
Antiquarian books
Contact:
Kathleen Caughren

Kitchen Arts and Letters
1435 Lexington Avenue
New York NY 10128
212-876-5550
Current cookbooks
Orders taken for rare and out-of-print books
Contact:
Nahum Waxman

Dedicated food professionals rejoiced when this store opened in 1983. As well as its impressive stock of cookbooks (5,500 titles), it provides the armchair gourmet an ample supply of straight reading material on all aspects of food and wine. The shop offers a free search service for out-of-print books and is building up a solid inventory of imported books, mainly from France and Britain.

Jan Longone
The Wine and Food Library
1207 West Madison
Ann Arbor MI 48103
313-663-4894
Rare and out-of-print books

Pro Libris
88 Ossipee Road
Somerville MA 02144
617-628-7487
Out-of-print cookbooks
Contact:
Gertrude B. Toll

Charlotte F. Safir
1349 Lexington Avenue, Suite 9B
New York NY 10128
212-534-7933
Antiquarian books

Season to Taste
911 School Street
Chicago IL 60657
312-327-0210
Current, rare and out-of-print books
Contact:
Barry Bluestein

Libraries and Sources of Information on Food

All the resources in this selected list have collections specializing in food from various specific perspectives, such as history, preparation, composition and/or nutritive values. The listing is regional, then alphabetical within states, with a very brief description of the types of materials and services available.

For comprehensive information on specialized libraries and the specific materials available at each, the basic reference source is the *Directory of Special Libraries and Information Sources*, published by Gale Research, Inc., 835 Penobscot Building, Detroit MI 48226-4094. Also well worth consulting is *Who's Who in Special Libraries*, newly published by the Special Libraries Association, 1700 18th Street NW, Washington DC 20009.

CONNECTICUT

Westreco, Inc. Technical Library
140 Boardman Road
New Milford CT 06776
203-355-0911
3,700 books. Food science and technology. Open to the public by arrangement. Interlibrary loans.

The Progressive Grocer Research Library
4 Stamford Forum
Stamford CT 06901
203-977-2913
Grocery industry history, trends, statistics. Open to professionals only.

MASSACHUSETTS

Arthur and Elizabeth Schlesinger Library on the History of Women
Radcliffe College
3 James Street
Cambridge MA 02138
617-495-8647
Includes the Chamberlain collection on French cuisine and important contributions from Julia Child and M.F.K. Fisher. Old and rare books on microfilm. Open to the public. Noncirculating.

The Schlesinger Library's extensive collection of cookbooks is housed in the newly designated Julia Child Research Area. In addition to the Chamberlain collection it includes historic and current works of interest to culinary scholars and social scientists. Julia Child and M.F.K. Fisher have donated their papers to the library and Eleanor Lowenstein, a rare book dealer in New York, bequeathed her correspondence, which includes records of outstanding food people from the 1940s to the 1970s.

NEW JERSEY

CPC International/Best Foods Research & Information Center
1120 Commerce Avenue
P.O. Box 1534
Union NJ 07083
201-688-9000
Food technology and microbiology, food analysis. Open to the public by arrangement. Interlibrary loans.

RJR/Nabisco Technology Center Library
200 River Road
P.O. Box 1944
East Hanover NJ 07936
201-503-3467
12,000 volumes. Food science. Open to the public. Interlibrary loans.

NEW YORK

Katharine Angell Library
Culinary Institute of America
North Road
Hyde Park NY 12538
914-452-9600
The culinary arts. Open to the public by appointment. Interlibrary loans.

Cornell University School of Hotel Administration Library
Statler Hall
Ithaca NY 14853
607-255-3673
Primarily restaurant and hospitality-oriented. Collections of rare cookbooks, historical menus. Open to the public for reference. Research service for a fee.

New York Botanical Garden Library
Bronx NY 10458
212-220-8751
Horticulture, environmental sciences, food. Collections include nursery catalogs and seed lists. Open to the public. Interlibrary loans.

New York Public Library Culinary Collection
Room 121
Fifth Avenue at 42nd Street
New York NY 10018
212-930-0573
Cookbooks, periodicals, historical menus, rare books and manuscripts. Open to the public.

The New York Public Library houses 80,000 items relating to all aspects of food and drink. The Culinary Collection is located throughout the divisions of the library. The historical resources include manuscripts and rare books dating from the 15th century. The New York Public Library is open six days a week.

SOUTH

DISTRICT OF COLUMBIA

National Restaurant Association Information Service and Library
1200 17th Street NW
Washington DC 20001
800-424-5156
Current and historical information about all aspects of foodservice industry. Specialists respond primarily to NRA members' queries; other inquiries answered as time permits.

FLORIDA

University of Florida Central Science Library
Gainesville FL 32611
904-392-0342
Food and agricultural sciences. Open to the public. Interlibrary loans.

GEORGIA

Atlanta Historical Society
Box 12423
Atlanta GA 30355
404-261-1837
Antique cookbooks donated by The Coca-Cola Company. Primarily Southern cookbooks. Reference only.

The Coca-Cola Company Technical Information Services
P.O. Drawer 1734
Atlanta GA 30301
404-676-2008
Food technology and nutrition; beverages. Open to the public by arrangement. Interlibrary loans.

MARYLAND

National Agricultural Library
U.S. Department of Agriculture
10301 Baltimore Boulevard
Beltsville MD 20705
301-344-3755
1.9 million volumes. Food and food science; agriculture; nutrition. Open to the public. Interlibrary loans.

MIDWEST

ILLINOIS

A. E. Staley Manufacturing Company Technical Information Center
2200 East Eldorado Street
Decatur IL 62525
217-421-2543
Fats, oils, carbohydrates, sweeteners. Open to the public by arrangement. Interlibrary loans.

Archer Daniels Midland Company Library
4666 Faries Parkway
Decatur IL 62526
217-424-5397
Food and nutrition; fats and oils; agribusiness. Open to the public by arrangement. Interlibrary loans.

Quaker Oats Company Research Library
617 West Main Street
Barrington IL 60010
708-304-2055
Food science. Open to the public by arrangement. Interlibrary loans.

INDIANA

Central Soya Company Food Research Library
P.O. Box 1400
Ft. Wayne IN 46801
219-425-5906
Food science. Open to the public. Interlibrary loans.

KANSAS

Farrell Library
Kansas State University
Manhattan KS 66506
913-532-7455
Historical and rare cookbooks; books on food. Reference only. Phone queries accepted.

OHIO

Ohio State University Agriculture Library
45 Agriculture Building
2120 Fyffe Road
Columbus OH 43210
614-292-6125
Food science and nutrition; animal and poultry science. Open to the public. Interlibrary loans.

WISCONSIN

Oscar Mayer Foods Corporation Research & Development Library
910 Mayer Avenue
P.O. Box 7188
Madison WI 53707
Food science, technology, engineering; meat and poultry science. Open to the public by arrangement. Interlibrary loans.

SOUTHWEST

TEXAS

Texas Department of Agriculture Library
Stephen F. Austin Building
P.O. Box 12847
Austin TX 78711
412-463-7476
Major recipe clipping file. Written queries accepted. Free Xerox copies sent out.

Texas Woman's University Special Collections
P.O. Box 23715
TWU Station
Denton TX 76204
918-898-3700
Includes historical cookbooks and special diet collection. Extensive pamphlet vertical file. Open to the public.

WEST COAST

CALIFORNIA

Merck & Company, Inc. Literature and Information Services
8355 Aero Drive
San Diego CA 92123
619-292-4900, Ext. 641
4,000 volumes. Food science. Open to the public by arrangement. Interlibrary loans.

Alice Statler Library
City College of San Francisco
Hotel and Restaurant Department
50 Phelan Avenue
San Francisco CA 94112
415-239-3460
Contemporary cookbooks. Historical menu collection. Open to the public for reference.

Stanford University Food Research Institute Library
Encina Building West
Stanford CA 94305
415-723-3943
76,000 volumes emphasizing food supply and population. Open to the public for reference. Interlibrary loans.

WASHINGTON

University of Washington Fisheries/Oceanography Library
151 Oceanography Teaching Building
University of Washington
Seattle WA 98195
206-543-4279
Fisheries; food science and technology. Open to the public for reference. Interlibrary loans.

Food Magazines

All the major consumer publications whose subject matter is confined to the food field are listed here, in alphabetical order, with the name of the current editorial director. (No general magazines have been selected, although almost all of them have food departments.) Each magazine's masthead lists the appropriate section or subject editor to contact for information in a specific area.

As each magazine has its own range of topics and style of dealing with them, it is advisable to study the field carefully when considering a possible submission, before sending a query to the appropriate editor to find out whether the magazine might be interested.

There are three excellent sources of comprehensive information about periodicals, whether in the field of consumer and trade magazines, or professional journals. They are: *Magazines for Libraries* and *Ulrich's Inter-* *national Periodicals Directory*, both published by R. R. Bowker, 245 West 17th Street, New York NY 10011; and *The Standard Periodical Directory*, published by Oxbridge Communications, Inc., 150 Fifth Avenue, Suite 301, New York NY 10011.

Bon Appetit
5900 Wilshire Boulevard
Los Angeles CA 90036
213-965-3600
Contact:
William J. Garry, Editor-in-Chief
Monthly—$30.00 per year (see page 262 for special offer to the trade)
Circulation:
1,300,000

Chocolatier Magazine
45 West 34th Street, Suite 500
New York NY 10001
212-239-0855
Contact:
Barbara Albright, Editor-in-Chief
Bimonthly—$14.97 per year
Circulation:
350,000

Cook's Magazine
2710 North Avenue
Bridgeport CT 06604
203-366-4155
Contact:
Christopher Kimball, Publisher
& Editorial Director
10 times a year—$30.00 per year
Circulation:
250,000

Cook's is a national food magazine dedicated to the serious hobby of cooking. Its articles, accompanied by full-color original photography, are in-depth treatments of techniques illustrated by recipes. The magazine also covers trends in food and wine and keeps its readers up to date on people of note in the food business.

Cooking Light: The Magazine of Food and Fitness
2100 Lakeshore Drive
Birmingham AL 35209
205-877-6000
Contact:
Katherine M. Eakin, Editor
Bimonthly—$12.00 per year
Circulation:
600,000

Food & Wine Magazine
1120 Avenue of the Americas
New York NY 10036
212-382-5628
Contact:
Carole Lalli, Editor-in-Chief
Monthly—$24.00 per year
Circulation:
800,000

Food & Wine Magazine is one of the most popular cooking magazines on the market. Its articles, most of which include recipes, emphasize holidays, entertaining, trends, chefs and seasonal foods. All are accompanied by original color photographs. The magazine also has a number of regular columns.

Gourmet Magazine
560 Lexington Avenue
    New York NY 10022
212-371-1330
Contact:
Jane Montant, Editor-in-Chief
Monthly—$18.00 per year
Circulation:
806,300

Kashrus Magazine
P.O. Box 96
Brooklyn NY 11204
718-998-3201
Contact:
Rabbi Yosef Wikler
5 times a year—$15.00 per year
Circulation:
10,000

Mazal Magazine
KGM Publications, Inc.
P.O. Box 963
Planetarium Station
New York NY 10024
212-595-1714
Contact:
Gil Marks, Editor
Bimonthly—$18.00 per year
Circulation:
9,000

Organic Gardening Magazine

Rodale Press, Inc.
33 East Minor Street
Emmaus PA 18098
215-967-5171
Contact:
Stevie Daniels, Executive Editor
10 times a year—$18.00 per year
Circulation:
1,000,000

Petits Propos Culinaires

PPC North America
5311 42nd Street NW
Washington DC 20015
202-362-6986
Contact:
Jennifer Davidson,
    North American Representative
Nic Spencer,
    North American Representative
3 times a year—$22.50 per year

Vegetarian Times

P.O. Box 570
Oak Park IL 60303
708-848-8100
Contact:
Sally Cullen, Editor
Monthly—$24.95 per year
Circulation:
165,000

Food Trade Magazines

This alphabetical listing has been compiled by Irena Chalmers to include all the major trade journals serving professionals in various aspects of the food industry. For convenience, each entry gives the name of the current editorial director, specifics of frequency, cost and circulation, and whether subscriptions are restricted or available to interested food professionals outside the specific topic or membership area.

For more detailed information, consult *Magazines for Libraries* and *Ulrich's International Periodicals Directory*, both published by R. R. Bowker, 245 West 17th Street, New York NY 10011; and *The Standard Periodical Directory*, published by Oxbridge Communications, Inc., 150 Fifth Avenue, Suite 301, New York NY 10011.

Bakery Production & Marketing

Gorman Publishing Company
8750 West Bryn Mawr Avenue
Chicago IL 60631
312-693-3200
Contact:
Ray Lahvic, Editor
Monthly—$64.00 per year
Circulation:
42,000

Catering Today

P.O. Box 222
Santa Claus IN 47579
812-937-4464
Contact:
Gerry Durnell, Publisher
Bimonthly—$18.00 per year
Circulation:
36,000

Culinary Review

1246 North State Parkway
Chicago IL 60610
312-944-6200
Contact:
Edward Robert Brooks, Editor
and Publisher
Monthly—Members only
Circulation:
35,000

Dairy Field

Cummins Publishing Company
26011 Evergreen Road
Southfield MI 48076
313-358-4900
Contact:
Robert A. Elliott, Editor
Monthly—$48.00 per year
Circulation:
18,000

Dairy Foods Magazine

Gorman Publishing Company
8750 West Bryn Mawr Avenue
Chicago IL 60631
312-693-3200
Contact:
Wendy Kimbrell, Editor
Monthly—$64.00 per year

Entree

P.O. Box 5148
Santa Barbara CA 93108
805-969-5848
Contact:
William Tomicki, Editor
Monthly—$59.00 per year
Circulation:
7,500

F & B Marketplace
Food Marketing Communicators
P.O. Box 19117
Lenexa KS 66215
913-888-8814
Contact:
Nancy A. Parsons, Editor
Quarterly—Free to association
members
Circulation:
5,000

Fancy Food Magazine
1414 Merchandise Mart
Chicago IL 60654
312-670-0800
Contact:
Larry Natta, Editor
Monthly—$26.00 per year
Circulation:
22,000

Food & Nutrition
U.S. Department of Agriculture
U.S. Government Printing Office
Washington DC 20402
202-756-3297
Contact:
Jan Kern, Editor
Quarterly—$5.00 per year
Circulation:
6,000

Food Broker Quarterly
National Food Brokers' Association
1010 Massachusetts Avenue NW
Washington DC 20001
202-789-2844
Contact:
Alan Goldstein, Editor
Quarterly—$30.00 per year
Circulation:
3,000

Food Distributors Magazine
Gro Com Group Publishers
P.O. Box 10378
Clearwater FL 34617
813-443-2723
Contact:
Waveney Ann Moore, Editor
Monthly—$49.00 per year
Circulation:
30,000

Food Management Magazine
747 Third Avenue
New York NY 10017
212-418-4163
Contact:
Donna Boss, Editor
Monthly—Controlled circulation
to institutional foodservice
personnel
Circulation:
62,170

Food Technology
Institute of Food Technologists
221 North La Salle Street, Suite 300
Chicago IL 60601
312-782-8424
Contact:
John B. Klis, Editor
Monthly—$60.00 per year
Circulation:
25,587

Foodservice Director
633 Third Avenue
New York NY 10017
212-984-2356
Contact:
Walter Schruntek, Editor
Monthly—Controlled circulation
to noncommercial foodservice
personnel
Circulation:
45,000

The Foodservice Distributor
1100 Superior Avenue
Cleveland OH 44114
216-696-7000
Contact:
John Lawn, Editor
Monthly—$40.00 per year
Circulation:
32,000

Foodservice Equipment and
Supplies Specialist
Cahners Publishing
1350 East Touhy Avenue
P.O. Box 5080
Des Plaines IL 60017
708-635-8800
Contact:
Gregory Richards, Editor-in-Chief
Monthly—$55.00 per year
Circulation:
20,268

Gastronome
980 Madison Avenue, Suite 202
New York NY 10021
212-570-1302
Contact:
Thomas R. Moore, Editor-in-Chief
2 times a year—$30.00 per year

The Gourmet Retailer Magazine
1450 Northeast 123rd Street
North Miami FL 33161
305-893-8771
800-327-3736
Contact:
Susan Friedman, Executive Editor
Monthly—$24.00 per year
Circulation:
23,000

Gourmet Today
26011 Evergreen Road, Suite 204
Southfield MI 48076
313-358-4900
Contact:
Eric Nordwall, Managing Editor
Bimonthly—$25.00 per year
Circulation:
20,000

Grocery Distribution Magazine
Grocery Market Publications
307 North Michigan Avenue
Chicago IL 60601
312-263-1057
Contact:
Thomas Smith, Editor
6 times a year—$30.00 per year
Circulation:
16,000

Health Food Business
Howark Publishing
Corporation, Inc.
567 Morris Avenue
Elizabeth NJ 07208
201-353-7373
Contact:
Gina Geslewitz, Editor
Monthly—$30.00 per year
Circulation:
13,000

Hotel & Motel Management
7500 Old Oak Boulevard
Cleveland OH 44130
216-891-2797
Contact:
Robert Nozar, Editor
Bimonthly—$25.00 per year
Circulation:
45,000

Hotels & Restaurants International

Cahners Publishing
1350 East Touhy Avenue
Des Plaines IL 60018
708-635-8800
Contact:
Mary Scoviak-Lerner, Editor
Monthly—$50.00 per year
Circulation:
40,000

Institutional Distribution

633 Third Avenue
New York NY 10017
212-986-4800
Contact:
Dana Tanyeri, Senior Editor
14 times a year—$70.00 per year
Circulation:
35,000

Kashrus Magazine

P.O. Box 96
Brooklyn NY 11204
718-998-3201
Contact:
Rabbi Yosef Wikler
5 times a year—$15.00 per year
Circulation:
10,000

Market Watch

387 Park Avenue South
New York NY 10016
212-684-4224
Contact:
Marvin Shanken, Editor
Monthly—$60.00 per year
Circulation:
40,000

N.A.S.F.T. Showcase

National Association
for the Specialty Food Trade
215 Park Avenue South, Suite 1606
New York NY 10003
212-505-1770
Contact:
Ronald Tanner, Editor
Bimonthly—Free to members
Circulation:
11,000

Nation's Restaurant News

425 Park Avenue
New York NY 10022
212-371-9400
Contact:
Charles Bernstein, Chief Editor
Weekly—$50.00 per year
Circulation:
100,000

Natural Foods Merchandiser

New Hope Communications
1301 Spruce Street
Boulder CO 80302
303-939-8440
Contact:
Stephen Hoffman, Editor
Monthly—$40.00 per year
Circulation:
13,018

Pasta Journal

National Pasta Association
1901 North Fort Myer Drive,
Suite 1000
Arlington VA 22209
703-841-0818
Contact:
Jula Kinnaird, Editor
Bimonthly—$28.00 per year
Circulation:
900

Pizza and Pasta

Talcott Corporation
1414 Merchandise Mart
Chicago IL 60654
312-670-0800
Contact:
M. Edward Paulson, Editor
Bimonthly—$18.00 per year
Circulation:
35,000

Pizza Today Magazine

P.O. Box 114
Santa Claus IN 47579
812-937-4464
Contact:
Amy Lorton, Editor
Monthly—$18.00 per year
Circulation:
45,000

Prepared Foods Magazine

Gorman Publishing Company
8750 West Bryn Mawr Avenue
Chicago IL 60631
312-693-3200
Contact:
Michael Pehanich, Editor
13 times a year—$64.00 per year
Circulation:
60,000

Progressive Grocer

4 Stamford Forum
Stamford CT 06901
203-325-3500
Contact:
Michael Sansolo, Managing Editor
Monthly—$55.00 per year
Circulation:
90,000

Restaurant & Hotel Design International

633 Third Avenue
New York NY 10017
212-986-4800
Contact:
Mary Jane Madigan, Editor-in-Chief
Monthly—$40.00 per year
Circulation:
35,773

Restaurants & Institutions

Cahners Publishing
1350 East Touhy Avenue
P.O. Box 5080
Des Plaines IL 60018
708-635-8800
Contact:
Michael Bartlett, Editor-in-Chief
Biweekly—$99.00 per year
Circulation:
143,000

Restaurants & Institutions is written for commercial and noncommercial high-volume operations. Its readers are responsible for restaurant chains, independent restaurants, food services for school districts, hospitals, prisons and so on. Columns and articles address trends in marketing, merchandising, menu concepts, equipment and food legislation. The subscription includes a once-a-year Buyers' Guide.

Restaurant Business

633 Third Avenue
New York NY 10017
212-986-4800
Contact:
Peter R. Berlinski, Editor
18 times a year—$79.00 per year
Circulation:
130,000

The goal of this trade magazine is to help restaurant owners, managers, chefs, regional chain officers and national chain officers successfully run their businesses. Sixty percent of the readers are independents and 40 percent are chain operators. Articles and columns cover topics ranging from food legislation and garbage problems to labor problems.

Restaurant Business is distributed without charge to a controlled list of restaurant operators.

Restaurant Hospitality

1100 Superior Avenue
Cleveland OH 44114
216-696-7000
Contact:
Stephen Michaelides, Editor
Monthly—$50.00 per year
Circulation:
150,000

Restaurants USA

National Restaurant Association
1200 17th Street NW
Washington DC 20036
202-331-5900
Contact:
William P. Fisher
11 times a year—$125.00 per year
Circulation:
27,000

Science of Food and Agriculture

Council for Agricultural Science
137 Lynn Avenue
Ames IA 50010
515-292-2125
Contact:
Bob Ver Straeten
Semiannual—$4.00 for 4 issues
Circulation:
23,000

Seafood Leader

1115 Northwest 46th Street
Seattle WA 98107
206-789-6506
Contact:
Peter Redmayne
6 times a year—$18.00 per year
Circulation:
15,000

As one of the major international seafood industry trade publications, *Seafood Leader* is published for top-end decision makers including importers, exporters, restaurateurs, processors and retailers. The magazine puts out six focused issues annually: the whole seafood catalog; the seafood buyers' guide; international seafoods; food services; aquaculture and retail; and the shrimp and Alaska issue.

Special Events Magazine

Miramar Publishing
P.O. Box 3640
Culver City CA 90231
213-337-9717
Contact:
Lisa Gardner, Editor
Monthly—$36.00 per year
Circulation:
29,000

Supermarket News

7 East 12th Street
New York NY 10003
212-741-4343
Contact:
Tim Simmons, Editor-in-Chief
Weekly—$18.00 per year for wholesalers;
$60.00 per year for manufacturers; $100.00
per year for the public
Circulation:
56,776

Taste Magazine

Culinary Institute of America
Route 9
Hyde Park NY 12538
914-452-9600
Contact:
Lisa Tippett, Editor
Quarterly—Free to members

Vegetarian Journal

The Vegetarian Resource Group
P.O. Box 1463
Baltimore MD 21203
301-752-8348
Contact:
Charles Stahler, Co-founder
Bimonthly—Free to members
$18.00 per year for nonmembers
Circulation:
3,500

Professional Food Journals

The listing that follows has been compiled from a variety of sources, representing specialized interests across the field of food and nutrition. The listing is alphabetical and includes the name of the journal's editor as well as specifics of cost and frequency.

For more detailed information, consult *Magazines for Libraries* and *Ulrich's International Periodical Directory*, both published by R. R. Bowker, 245 West 17th Street, New York NY 10011; and *The Standard Periodical Directory*, published by Oxbridge Communications, Inc., 150 Fifth Avenue, Suite 301, New York NY 10011.

American Journal of Clinical Nutrition

American Society for Clinical Nutrition
9650 Rockville Pike
Bethesda MD 20814
301-530-7050
Contact:
Dr. Albert I. Mendeloff, Editor
Monthly—$70.00 per year/individual
$95.00 per year/institutional

American School Food Service Journal

5600 South Quebec Street,
Suite 300B
Englewood CO 80111
303-220-8484
Contact:
Denny McLarn
11 times a year—$80.00 per year

Journal of Food Biochemistry

Food & Nutrition Press, Inc.
6527 Main Street
P.O. 374
Trumbull CT 06611
203-261-8587
Contact:
John R. Whitaker, Editor
Bimonthly—$110.00 per year

Journal of Food Distribution Research

Food Distribution Research Society
P.O. Box 441110
Ft. Washington MD 20744
301-292-1970
Contact:
Dr. Carl Toensmeyer, Editor
Semiannual—$25.00-$100.00 per year

Journal of Food Process Engineering

Food & Nutrition Press, Inc.
6527 Main Street
P.O. Box 374
Trumbull CT 06611
203-261-8587
Contact:
Dennis Heldman
R. P. Singh
Quarterly—$92.00 per year

Journal of Food Processing and Preservation

Food & Nutrition Press, Inc.
6527 Main Street
P.O. Box 374
Trumbull CT 06611
203-261-8587
Contact:
Daryl B. Lund
Bimonthly—$110.00 per year

Journal of Food Quality

Food & Nutrition Press, Inc.
6527 Main Street
P.O. Box 374
Trumbull CT 06611
203-261-8587
Contact:
Rob L. Shewfelt
Bimonthly—$122.00 per year

Journal of Food Safety

Food & Nutrition Press, Inc.
6527 Main Street
P.O. Box 374
Trumbull CT 06611
203-261-8587
Contact:
Art Miller, Co-editor
Tom J. Montville, Co-editor
Quarterly—$87.00 per year

Journal of Food Service Systems

Food & Nutrition Press, Inc.
6527 Main Street
P.O. Box 374
Trumbull CT 06611
203-261-8587
Contact:
Oscar P. Snyder, Editor
Quarterly—$65.00 per year

Journal of Gastronomy

American Institute of Wine & Food
1515 Bryant Street
San Francisco CA 94103
415-255-3000
Contact:
Nancy Jenkins, Editor
Quarterly—$60.00 per year to members

Journal of Home Economics

American Home Economics Association
1555 King Street
Alexandria VA 22314
703-706-4600
Contact:
Lisa Garbus, Editor
Quarterly—Free to members; $20.00 per year to nonmembers

Journal of Muscle Foods

Food & Nutrition Press, Inc.
6527 Main Street
P.O. Box 374
Trumbull CT 06611
203-261-8587
Contact:
Norman G. Marriot, Editor
Quarterly—$85.00 per year

Journal of Nutrition

American Institute of Nutrition
9650 Rockville Pike
Bethesda MD 20814
301-530-7050
Contact:
Dr. Willard J. Visek
Monthly—$160.00 per year

Journal of Sensory Studies

Food & Nutrition Press, Inc.
6527 Main Street
P.O. Box 374
Trumbull CT 06611
203-261-8587
Contact:
Maximo Gacula Jr., Editor
Quarterly—$92.00 per year

Journal of Texture Studies

Food & Nutrition Press, Inc.
6527 Main Street
P.O. Box 374
Trumbull CT 06611
203-261-8587
Contact:
Malcolm Bourne, Co-editor
Phillip Sherman, Co-editor
Quarterly—$115.00 per year

Food Newsletters

This is another field that is in a state of constant movement, chiefly expansion, as interest in a particular food topic becomes sufficiently widespread to suggest it would be worthwhile publishing a newsletter in that area. Some die fast, but more succeed.

This list of food newsletters currently being published covers a wide range of topics, some extremely specialized, others quite general in approach. Irena Chalmers' selection is alphabetical and includes the name of the editorial director and specifics of each newsletter's frequency and cost.

For more detailed information, consult *The Oxbridge Directory of Newsletters*, an annual publication from Oxbridge Communications, Inc., 150 Fifth Avenue, Suite 301, New York NY 10011, and *Newsletters in Print*, published by Gale Research, Inc., 835 Penobscot Building, Detroit MI 48226-4094.

AFI Newsletter
Association of Food Industries
P.O. Box 776
Matawan NJ 07747
201-583-8188
Contact:
Eli Hall, Editor
6 times a year—$100.00 per year

AHEA Action
American Home Economics Association
1555 King Street
Alexandria VA 22314
703-706-4600
Contact:
Kitty Barber, Editor
6 times a year—Free to members;
$7.50 a year to nonmembers

American Wine & Food:
The American Institute of Wine
& Food Monthly
The American Institute
of Wine & Food
1550 Bryant Street
San Francisco CA 94103
415-255-3000
Contact:
Robert Clark, Editor
10 times a year—$20.00
of members' dues

Anderson Report
Anderson Publications
320 North Michigan Avenue, Suite 1305
Chicago IL 60601
312-726-3268
Contact:
Mary Jane Anderson, Editor
Monthly—$125.00 per year

The Art of Eating
H.C.R. 30, Box 3
Peacham VT 05862
802-592-3491
Contact:
Edward Behr, Editor
Quarterly—$22.00 per year

The Art of Eating is a 12-page newsletter directed at people who are curious about food and interested in acquiring a better understanding of what constitutes good food. The focus is on in-depth articles on a specific food topic—for example, a round-up of the best small cheese producers in the United States or a piece on wild boar. Each issue includes two or three recipes, as well as cookbook reviews. Circulation is a select 600.

Breakin' Bread
Greyhound Food Management, Inc.
Greyhound Tower, Suite 1431
Phoenix AZ 85077
602-248-6070
Contact:
Ed Sirhal, Editor
Quarterly—Free

Briefing: The Restaurateur's
News Digest
Walter Matthews Associates, Inc.
28 West 38th Street
New York NY 10018
212-869-4680
Contact:
Walter Matthews, Editor
10 times a year—$45.00 per year

Seymour Britchky's
Restaurant Letter
P.O. Box 155
New York NY 10276
Contact:
Seymour Britchky, Editor
Monthly—$25.00 per year

Cheese Importers' Association
of America Bulletin
430 Park Avenue
New York NY 10022
212-753-7500
Contact:
Richard Kabyco, Co-editor
Virginia Sheahan, Co-editor
Monthly—Free to members

Cheesemakers' Journal
New England Cheesemaking
Supply Company
P.O. Box 85
Ashfield MA 01330
413-628-3808
Contact:
Robert L. Carroll
6 times a year—$12.00 per year

Commentary
International Association of
Cooking Professionals
304 West Liberty Street
Louisville KY 40202
Contact:
Mary Goodbody, Managing Editor
6 times a year—Free to members
$30.00 per year for nonmembers

Commentary is a 6- to 12-page newsletter published for members of the International Association of Cooking Professionals. It offers items of general interest to food professionals, with coverage of food trends, new products and nutritional developments. News of the association's members, regional group activities and committees is also included, together with extensive coverage of the association's annual convention.

Cooking Contest Chronicle

P.O. Box 10792
Merrillville IN 46411
219-887-6983
Contact:
Karen Martis, Editor-in-Chief
Monthly—$16.00 per year

Variety is the keynote of this eight-page newsletter, which is read not only by food contest regulars but also by food professionals and, in fact, by anyone interested in cooking prize-winning recipes. Topics covered include food trends, contest listings, monthly cookbook reviews, tips for contest entrants and, of course, winning recipes. The *Cooking Contest Chronicle* has a circulation of 1,400.

Cranberry Station Newsletter

Cranberry Experiment Station
Glen Charlie Road
P.O. Box 569
East Wareham MA 02538
508-295-2212
Contact:
Irving E. Demoranville, Editor
Periodic—Free

Cranberry Vine

Washington State University,
Long Beach Research &
Extension Unit
Route 1, Box 570
Long Beach WA 98631
206-642-2031
Quarterly—Free

Culinary Arts News

Culinary & Fine Arts Club, Ltd.
P.O. Box 153
Western Springs IL 60558
708-246-5845
Contact:
Camille J. Cook, Editor-in-Chief
Semiannual—$15.00 per 2 years

Fish News

New England Fisheries Development
Association, Inc.
280 Northern Avenue
Boston MA 02210
617-542-8890
Contact:
Kenelm Coons, Executive Director
Monthly—Free to members
$25.00 per year for nonmembers

Food Business Mergers & Acquisitions

American Institute of Food
Distribution
28-12 Broadway
Fair Lawn NJ 07410
201-791-5570
Contact:
Frank Pangko, Editor
Annual—$340.00 per issue

The Food Channel Newsletter

3 Corporate Center
Springfield MO 65804
417-882-5050
Contact:
Chris Wolf, Editor
Bimonthly—$80.00 per year

Food Chemical News

1101 Pennsylvania Avenue SE
Washington DC 20003
202-544-1980
Contact:
Lewis Rothchild Jr., Editor
Weekly—$695.00 per year

The Food Industry Newsletter

Newsletters, Inc.
13234 Pleasantview Lane
Fairfax VA 22033
703-631-2322
Contact:
Max Busetti, Editor
22 times a year—$195.00 per year

The Food Institute Report

American Institute of Food
Distribution, Inc.
28-12 Broadway
Fair Lawn NJ 07410
201-791-5570
Contact:
Roy Harrison, Editor
Weekly—$395.00 per year

Food Protection Report

Charles Felix Associates
P.O. Box 1581
Leesburg VA 22075
703-777-7448
Contact:
Charles W. Felix, Editor
Monthly—$125.00 per year

The 12-page *Report* includes some photographs and artwork and covers all aspects of food safety from the perspective of the retail side of food service and selling. It is aimed chiefly at government officials, food consultants and members of corporations with responsibility for food safety.

Food Talk

Charles Felix Associates
P.O. Box 1581
Leesburg VA 22075
703-777-7448
Contact:
Charles W. Felix, Editor
Quarterly—$110.00 per year

Food Talk

P.O. Box 6543
San Francisco CA 94101
415-386-3067
Contact:
Elaine Douglas Cahn,
Editor-in-Chief
Quarterly—$18.00 per year

Foods by Mail

Anderson Publications
320 North Michigan, Suite 1305
Chicago IL 60601
312-726-3268
Contact:
Mary Jane Anderson, Editor
Monthly—$85.00 per year

Foodservice Information Abstracts

National Restaurant Association
1200 17th Street NW
Washington DC 20036
202-331-5900
Contact:
Information Service Library
Biweekly—$80.00 per year

Foodservice Report

International Foodservice
Distributors Association
201 Park Washington Court
Falls Church VA 22046
703-532-9400
Contact:
John Thompson, Editor
Monthly—Free to members

Gorman's New Product News

8750 West Bryn Mawr Avenue
Chicago IL 60631
312-693-3200
Contact:
Martin Friedman, Editor
Monthly—$295.00 per year

Herbalgram

American Botanical Council
P.O. Box 201660
Austin TX 78720
512-331-8868
Contact:
Mark Blumenthal, Editor
4 times a year—$25.00 per year

Information Service Abstract

National Restaurant Association
1200 17th Street NW
Washington DC 20036
202-331-5900
Contact:
Linda Smith, Editor
*Semimonthly—$40.00 per year
for members
$80.00 per year for nonmembers*

Kitchen Times

185 Marlborough Street
Boston MA 02116
617-266-2453
Contact:
Howard Wilson, Editor
Monthly—$36.00 per year

Madelaine's Kitchen Secrets

P.O. Box 3512
Oak Brook IL 60522
708-325-4177
Contact:
Madelaine Bullwinkel, Editor
and Publisher
Bimonthly—$15.00 per year

Microwave Times

Recipes Unlimited, Inc.
P.O. Box 1271
Burnsville MN 55337
612-890-6655
Contact:
Janet L. Sadlack, Editor
6 times a year—$9.95 per year

N.A.C.U.F.S. Facts & Findings

National Association of College and
University Food Services
Manly Miles Building, Suite 303
1405 South Harrison
East Lansing MI 48824
517-332-2499
Contact:
Mary Jo Custer, Editor
Quarterly—Free to members

National Coffee Association of the USA, Inc. Newsletter

110 Wall Street
New York NY 10005
212-344-5596
Weekly—$25.00 per year

N.A.W.G.A. Review

National-American Wholesale
Grocers' Association
201 Park Washington Court
Falls Church VA 22046
703-532-9400
Contact:
John Thompson, Editor
Monthly—Free to members

News from the Beard House

The James Beard Foundation
167 West 12th Street
New York NY 10011
212-675-4984
Contact:
Dorie Greenspan, Editor
*12 times a year—$35.00
of members' dues*

Nutrition Action Healthletter

Center for Science in the
Public Interest
1501 15th Street NW
Washington DC 20036
Contact:
Stephen Schmidt, Editor
10 times a year—$19.95 per year

Pastahhh

National Pasta Association
1901 North Fort Myer Drive,
Suite 1000
Arlington VA 22209
703-841-0818
Contact:
Jula Kinnaird, Editor
4 times a year—$5.00 per year

Peanut Butter and Nut Processors Association Bulletin

9005 Congressional Court
Potomac MD 20854
301-365-4080
Contact:
James E. Mack, Editor
1-2 times a month—Free to members

Pecan-E-Gram

Southeastern Pecan Growers'
Association
1104 Friar Tuck Road
Starkville MS 39759
601-323-5873
Contact:
Sarah H. Hines, Editor
Quarterly—Free to members

Pecan Report

Federal-State Market News Service
P.O. Box 1447
Thomasville GA 31799
912-228-1208
Contact:
Richard DeMenna,
Local Representative
Semiweekly—$36.00 per year

Pork Industry Group Letter

National Livestock and Meat Board
444 North Michigan Avenue
Chicago IL 60611
312-467-5520
Contact:
Sharlet Brown, Editor
Semimonthly—Free

Pork Pro

Professional Farmers
of America, Inc.
219 Parkade
Cedar Falls IA 50613
319-277-1278
Contact:
Douglas Harper, Editor
*50 times a year—$88.00 per year
for members
$115.00 per year for nonmembers*

The Potato Museum's Peelings

Potato Museum
704 North Carolina Avenue SE
Washington DC 20003
202-544-1558
Contact:
Meredith Hughes, Editor
*Bimonthly—included in
$20.00 per year membership*

This newsletter, covering all subjects related to the humble potato, goes to the several hundred members of the Potato

Museum. Food-related items such as potato varieties or sweet potatoes are covered, but articles on such topics as the potato in art or potato sacking also appear. There is a regular section on potato news from all over the world and the newsletter runs one or two recipes in each issue.

The Practical Gourmet
Healthy Gourmet, Inc.
7 Putter Lane
Middle Island NY 11953
516-924-8555
Contact:
Roger Dextor, Director
of Public Relations
Monthly—$48.00 per year

Promotion
National Restaurant Association
1200 17th Street NW
Washington DC 20036
202-331-5900
Contact:
David Slater, Editor
*6 times a year—$15.00 per year
for members
$25.00 per year for nonmembers*

R.B.I. Executive Report
633 Third Avenue
New York NY 10017
212-986-4800
Contact:
Norma Vavolizza, Editor
50 times a year—$95.00 per year

Reference Point: Food Industry Abstracts
Food Marketing Institute
1750 K Street NW
Washington DC 20006
202-452-8444
Contact:
Information Service Department
Monthly—$70.00 per year

Restaurant Management Today
Atcom, Inc.
2315 Broadway, Suite 300
New York NY 10024
212-873-5900
Contact:
Michael Schau, Editor
Weekly—$250.00 per year

Mimi Sheraton's Taste
P.O. Box 1396
Old Chelsea Station
New York NY 10011
212-484-2494
Contact:
Mimi Sheraton, Editor
10 times a year—$48.00 per year

Shrimp Notes
417 Eliza Street
New Orleans LA 70114
504-368-1571
Contact:
William D. Chauvin, President
Monthly—$155.00 per year

Simple Cooking
Jackdaw Press
P.O. Box 371
Essex Station
Boston MA 02112
Contact:
John Thorne, Editor
Monthly—$12.00 per year

The Upper Crust
361 Virginia Street
Crystal Lake IL 60014
815-459-0100
Contact:
Sharon R. Myers, Editor-in-Chief
Bimonthly—$12.00 per year

Whole Foods
WFC, Inc.
3000 Hadley Road
South Plainfield NJ 07080
201-494-2889
Contact:
Daniel McSweeney, Editor
Monthly—$30.00 per year

Food Authors

This listing is a selection of current and classic authors who are writing about food, arranged alphabetically by last name. The book title given is that of the author's most recent or most distinguished work.

The majority of the books are cookbooks, but there is also a wide selection of writings on food, viewed from aspects as varied as nutrition, anthropology or restaurant reviewing. The only topic not fairly or fully covered is wine.

In each case, the publisher's name is also included, as a means of getting in touch with the author.

Marcia Adams
Cooking from Quilt Country
Clarkson N. Potter, Inc.

Jean Anderson
The Food of Portugal
William Morrow & Company, Inc.

Elizabeth Andoh
An Ocean of Flavor
Alfred A. Knopf, Inc.

Colman Andrews
Catalan Cuisine
Atheneum Publishers

Nancy Baggett
The International Cookbook
Stewart, Tabori & Chang

Lee Bailey
Lee Bailey's Soup Meals
Clarkson N. Potter, Inc.

Bruce Ballenger
The Lobster Almanac
Globe Pequot Press

Melanie Barnard and Brooke Dojny
Sunday Suppers
Prentice Hall Press

Rose Levy Beranbaum
The Cake Bible
William Morrow & Company, Inc.

**James Beard with
Helen Evans Brown**
The Complete Book of Outdoor Cookery
Perennial Library

George Berkowitz and Jane Doerfer
The Legal Seafoods Cookbook
Doubleday & Company

**Maurice and
Jean-Jacques Bernachon**
A Passion for Chocolate
William Morrow & Company, Inc.

Raymond Blanc
*Recipes from Le Manoir aux
Quat' Saisons*
Van Nostrand Reinhold
Company, Inc.

Fred Brack and Tina Bell
Tastes of the Pacific Northwest
Doubleday & Company

Flo Braker
The Simple Art of Perfect Baking
William Morrow & Company, Inc.

Jane Brody
Jane Brody's Good Food Book
W. W. Norton & Company, Inc.

Ruth Adams Bronz
Miss Ruby's American Cooking
Harper & Row, Publishers, Inc.

Ellen Brown
The Gourmet Gazelle Cookbook
Bantam Books

Giuliano Bugialli
Bugialli on Pasta
Simon & Schuster, Inc.

Marian Burros
20-Minute Menus
Simon & Schuster, Inc.

Jane Butel
Tex-Mex Cookbook
Harmony Books

Anna Teresa Callen
*Anna Teresa Callen's Menus
for Pasta*
Crown Publishers, Inc.

Hugh Carpenter
*Pacific Flavors: Oriental Recipes
for a Contemporary Kitchen*
Stewart, Tabori & Chang

Mary Harrison Carroll
Elegant Low-Calorie Cooking
Ortho Books

Penelope Casas
The Foods and Wines of Spain
Alfred A. Knopf, Inc.

Irena Chalmers
The Food Professional's Guide
American Showcase, Inc.

Sarah Leah Chase
Nantucket Open House Cookbook
Workman Publishing Company, Inc.

Bernard Clayton Jr.
The Complete Book of Soups and Stews
Fireside Books

Laura Chenel and Linda Siegfried
American Country Cheese
Aris Books

Julia Child
The Way to Cook
Alfred A. Knopf, Inc.

Craig Claiborne
Craig Claiborne's Southern Cooking
Times Books

Laurie Colwin
Home Cooking
Alfred A. Knopf, Inc.

**Marcia Cone and
Thelma Snyder**
Mastering Microwave Cooking
Simon & Schuster, Inc.

Bruce Cost
Asian Ingredients
William Morrow & Company, Inc.

Susan Costner
Good Friends, Great Dinners
Crown Publishers, Inc.

Rosalind Cready
Cooking from the Garden
Sierra Club Books

Marion Cunningham
The Breakfast Book
Alfred A. Knopf, Inc.

Andre Daguin and Anne de Ravel
*Foie Gras, Magret, and Other Good Food
from Gascony*
Random House, Inc.

Elizabeth David
Elizabeth David Classics
Alfred A. Knopf, Inc.

Alan Davidson
*Seafood: A Connoisseur's Guide and Cook-
book*
Simon & Schuster, Inc.

Anna del Conte
Gastronomy of Italy
Prentice Hall Press

Julia della Croce
Pasta Classica
Chronicle Books

Lorenza de' Medici
The Renaissance of Italian Cooking
Fawcett Columbine

Huntley Dent
The Feast of Santa Fe
Simon & Schuster, Inc.

Marcel Desaulniers
The Trellis Cookbook
Weidenfeld & Nicolson

Yamuna Devi
The Art of Indian Vegetarian Cooking
Bala Books/E.P. Dutton

**Hallie Donnelly and
Janet Kessel Fletcher**
Menus for Entertaining
Ortho Books

Nathalie Dupree
New Southern Cooking
Alfred A. Knopf, Inc.

Anton Edelman
The Savoy Food and Drink Book
Salem House

John Egerton
Southern Food
Alfred A. Knopf, Inc.

Rose Elliot
The Complete Vegetarian Cuisine
Pantheon Books, Inc.

Mary Emmerling
Mary Emmerling's American Country Cooking
Clarkson N. Potter, Inc.

Engel and Engel
Food Finds
Harper & Row, Publishers, Inc.

Florence Fabricant
Pleasures of the Table
Harry N. Abrams

Joe Famularo
The Joy of Grilling
Barron's Educational Series, Inc.

Dean Fearing
The Mansion on Turtle Creek
Weidenfeld & Nicolson

**Susan Feniger and
Mary Sue Milliken**
City Cuisine
William Morrow & Company, Inc.

Carol Field
The Italian Baker
Harper & Row, Publishers, Inc.

**Lynn Fischer and
W. Virgil Brown, M.D.**
Low-Cholesterol Gourmet
Acropolis Books Ltd.

M. F. K. Fisher
The Physiology of Taste
North Point Press

Helen S. Fletcher
The New Pastry Cook
William Morrow & Company, Inc.

Jim Fobel
Old-Fashioned Baking Book
Ballantine Books, Inc.

Leslie Forbes
A Taste of Tuscany
Little, Brown & Company, Inc.

Margaret S. Fox and John Dear
Cafe Beaujolais
Ten Speed Press

Pierre Franey and Bryan Miller
Cuisine Rapide
Times Books

Jane Freiman
Dinner Party: The New Entertaining
Harper & Row, Publishers, Inc.

Betty Fussell
I Hear America Cooking
Viking

Barbara Gibbons
Light and Spicy: Low-Calorie, Full Flavor Recipes
Harper & Row, Publishers, Inc.

Sal Gilbertie
Kitchen Herbs
Bantam Books

Peggy K. Glass
Home-Cooking Sampler
Prentice Hall Press

Joyce Goldstein
The Mediterranean Kitchen
William Morrow & Company, Inc.

Sharda Gopal
Step-by-Step Indian Cooking
Barron's Educational Series, Inc.

Richard Grausman
At Home with the French Classics
Workman Publishing Company, Inc.

Patience Gray
Honey from a Weed
Harper & Row, Publishers, Inc.

Bert Greene
The Grains Cookbook
Workman Publishing Company, Inc.

Anne Lindsay Greer
Foods of the Sun
Harper & Row, Publishers, Inc.

Jane Grigson
Jane Grigson's Vegetable Book
Penguin Books

Barbara Grunes and Phyllis Magida
Poultry on the Grill
Dell Publishing Company

John Hadamuscin
Special Occasions
Harmony Books

Jessica B. Harris
Iron Pots and Wooden Spoons
Atheneum Publishers

Marcella Hazan
The Classic Italian Cookbook
Alfred A. Knopf, Inc.

Nika Hazelton
Ups and Downs: Memoirs of Another Time
Harper & Row, Publishers, Inc.

Maida Heatter
Maida Heatter's New Book of Great Desserts
Alfred A. Knopf, Inc.

Beth Hensberger
Bread
Chronicle Books

Howard Hillman
Kitchen Science
Houghton Mifflin Company

Moira Hodgson
Keeping Company
Prentice Hall Press

Geraldene Holt
Recipes from a French Herb Garden
Simon & Schuster, Inc.

Ken Hom
Fragrant Harbor Taste
Simon & Schuster, Inc.

Jane Watson Hopping
The Pioneer Lady's Country Kitchen
Villard Books

Jane Horn
Cooking A to Z
Ortho Books

Judith Benn Hurley
Healthy Microwave Cooking
Rodale Press Inc.

Christopher Idone
Salad Days
Random House, Inc.

Madhur Jaffrey
Madhur Jaffrey's Far Eastern Cookery
Harper & Row, Publishers, Inc.

Evan Jones and Judith Jones
The Book of Bread
Harper & Row, Publishers, Inc.

Barbara Kafka
The Microwave Gourmet Healthstyle Cookbook
William Morrow & Company, Inc.

Madeleine Kamman
Madeleine Kamman's Savoie
Atheneum Publishers

Mollie Katzen
The Enchanted Broccoli Forest
Ten Speed Press

Diana Kennedy
The Cuisines of Mexico
Harper & Row, Publishers, Inc.

Robert Lambert
Fantasy Chocolate Desserts
Chronicle Books

Leslie Land
The New England Epicure
Dell Publishing Company

George Lang
The Cuisine of Hungary
Atheneum Publishers

Jenifer Harvey Lang
Larousse Gastronomique
Crown Publishers, Inc.

Faye Levy
Dinner Inspirations
E. P. Dutton

Edna Lewis
In Pursuit of Flavor
Alfred A. Knopf, Inc.

Anne Lindsay
The American Cancer Society Cookbook
Hearst Books

Eileen Yin-Fei Lo
Eileen Yin-Fei Lo's Cantonese Cooking
Viking

Susan Herrman Loomis
The Great American Seafood Cookbook
Workman Publishing Company, Inc.

Pino Luongo
A Tuscan in the Kitchen
Clarkson N. Potter, Inc.

Michael McCarty
Michael's
Macmillan Publishing Company

Kelly McCune
The Fish Book
Harper & Row, Publishers, Inc.

Harold McGee
On Food and Cooking
Scribner Book Companies, Inc.

Deborah Madison
The Greens Cookbook
Bantam Books

Nick Malgieri
Nick Malgieri's Perfect Pastry
Macmillan Publishing Company

Abby Mandel
More Taste Than Time
Simon & Schuster, Inc.

Lydie Marshall
Cooking with Lydie Marshall
Alfred A. Knopf, Inc.

Phyllis Meras
The New Carry-Out Cuisine
Houghton Mifflin Company

Perla Myers
Perla Myers' Peasant Kitchen
Simon & Schuster, Inc.

Carlo Middione
The Food of Southern Italy
William Morrow & Company, Inc.

Mark Miller
Coyote Cafe Cookbook
Ten Speed Press

Marian Morash
The Victory Garden Cookbook
Alfred A. Knopf, Inc.

Joan Nathan
The Jewish Holiday Kitchen
Schocken Books, Inc.

Duane Newcomb and Karen Newcomb
New Complete Vegetable Gardener's Sourcebook
Prentice Hall Press

Beatrice Ojakangas
The Great Scandinavian Baking Book
Little, Brown & Company

Judith Olney
Summer Food
Atheneum Publishers

Richard Olney
Ten Vineyard Lunches
Interlink Books

Jean-Louis Palladin
Jean-Louis: Cooking with the Seasons
Thomasson-Grant, Inc.

Jean Pennington and Helen Church
Food Values of Portions Commonly Used
Perennial Library

Jacques Pepin
A Fare for the Heart
Cleveland Clinic Foundation

Thelma Pressman
365 Quick and Easy Microwave Recipes
Harper & Row, Publishers, Inc.

Johanna Pruess
The Supermarket Epicure
William Morrow & Company, Inc.

Paul Prudhomme
The Prudhomme Family Cookbook
William Morrow & Company, Inc.

Wolfgang Puck
The Wolfgang Puck Cookbook
Random House, Inc.

Susan G. Purdy
A Piece of Cake
Atheneum Publishers

Mardee Haidin Regan
Great Desserts
Stewart, Tabori & Chang

Rose Reisman
Manhattan's Dessert Scene
Lymas Publications

Michael Roberts
Secret Ingredients
Bantam Books

Laurel Robertson, Carol Flinders and Brian Ruppenthal
The New Laurel's Kitchen
Ten Speed Press

Greg Robinson and Max Schofield
The Icing on the Cake
E. P. Dutton

Felipe Rojas-Lombardi
Soup, Beautiful Soup
Random House, Inc.

Betty Rosbottom
Betty Rosbottom's Cooking School Cookbook
Workman Publishing Company, Inc.

David Rosengarten and Joshua Wesson
Red Wine with Fish
Simon & Schuster, Inc.

Julee Rosso and Sheila Lukins
The New Basics Cookbook
Workman Publishing Company, Inc.

Harriet Roth
Harriet Roth's Cholesterol Control Cookbook
New American Library

Nichole Routhier
The Foods of Vietnam
Stewart, Tabori & Chang

Julie Sahni
Classic Indian Cooking
William Morrow & Company, Inc.

Lorna J. Sass
Cooking Under Pressure
William Morrow & Company, Inc.

Jean-Michel Savoca and Boyce Brawley
New York Parties: The Art of Hosting
Rizzoli International Publications, Inc.

Richard Sax with Sandra Gluck
From the Farmers' Market
Harper & Row, Publishers, Inc.

Stephen Schmidt
Master Recipes
Fawcett Columbine

Elizabeth Schneider
Uncommon Fruits and Vegetables
Harper & Row, Publishers, Inc.

Phillip Stephen Schulz
As American As Apple Pie
Simon & Schuster, Inc.

John Sedlar
Modern Southwest Cuisine
Simon & Schuster, Inc.

Martha Rose Shulman
Supper Club Chez Martha Rose
Atheneum Publishers

Mary Taylor Simeti
Pomp and Sustenance: 25 Centuries of Sicilian Food
Alfred A. Knopf, Inc.

Marie Simmons
365 Ways to Cook Pasta
Harper & Row, Publishers, Inc.

Jeff Smith
The Frugal Gourmet Cooks Three Ancient Cuisines
William Morrow & Company, Inc.

Raymond Sokolov
The Jewish-American Kitchen
Alfred A. Knopf, Inc.

Marlene Sorosky
Easy Entertaining with Marlene Sorosky
Harper & Row, Publishers, Inc.

Jane and Michael Stern
A Taste of America
Andrews, McMeel & Parker

Sally Stone and Martin Stone
The Brilliant Bean
Bantam Books

Martha Stewart
Entertaining
Clarkson N. Potter, Inc.

Christopher Styler
Primi Piatti
Harper & Row, Publishers, Inc.

Reay Tannahill
Food in History
Crown Publishers, Inc.

Yvonne Young Tarr
The New York Times Bread and Soup Cookbook
Times Books

Patricia Tennison
Sumptuous Sauces in the Microwave
Contemporary Books, Inc.

Sylvia Thompson
Feasts and Friends: Recipes from a Lifetime
North Point Press

Emelie Tolley and Chris Mead
Cooking with Herbs
Clarkson N. Potter, Inc.

Jeremiah Tower
New American Classics
Harper & Row, Publishers, Inc.

Barbara Tropp
The Modern Art of Chinese Cooking
William Morrow & Company, Inc.

Miriam Ungerer
Summertime Food
Random House, Inc.

Schuyler Ungle and Sharon Kramis
Northwest Bounty
Simon & Schuster, Inc.

Norman Van Aken
Norman Van Aken's Feast of Sunlight
Ballantine Books

James Villas
Villas at Table
Harper & Row, Publishers, Inc.

Margaret Visser
Much Depends on Dinner
Collier Books

Jeanne Voltz
Community Suppers
Scribner Book Companies, Inc.

Hilary Walden
The Encyclopedia of Creative Cuisine
Chartwell Books, Inc.

Carole Walter
Great Cakes
Ballantine Books, Inc.

Alice Waters
The Chez Panisse Menu Cookbook
Random House, Inc.

Jack Weatherford
Indian Givers
Crown Publishers, Inc.

Patricia Wells
Bistro Cooking
Workman Publishing Company, Inc.

Anne Willan
La Varenne Pratique
Crown Publishers, Inc.

Jasper White
Jasper White's Cooking from New England
Harper & Row, Publishers, Inc.

Helen Witty
Fancy Pantry
Workman Publishing Company, Inc.

Richard Wolfe, M.D., and Edward Giobbi
Eat Right, Eat Well—The Italian Way
Alfred A. Knopf, Inc.

Paula Wolfert
Paula Wolfert's World of Food
Harper & Row, Publishers, Inc.

Diane Rossen Worthington
The Taste of Summer
Bantam Books

William Woys Weaver
America Eats
Harper & Row, Publishers, Inc.

Susan Wyler
Cooking for a Crowd
Harmony Books

Eugene H. Zagat and Nina S. Zagat
Restaurant Surveys
Zagat Surveys
Arizona
Boston
Chicago
Dallas
Houston
Los Angeles
New Orleans
New York City
Philadelphia
San Francisco
Washington/Baltimore

Food Journalists

This listing represents a selection of the country's major newspapers that provide regular food coverage in their pages, followed by the names of those food journalists who write most frequently for newspapers and magazines.

In the first section, the newspapers are listed regionally, then alphabetically within each state by the name of the city in which they are published. The contact names are those of the feature editors currently responsible for food coverage; most papers have a specific food or lifestyles editor. It is worth noting that the food contact at the local paper is the most accurate source of information on regional food events, the best restaurants in town, and what's happening locally in the field of food.

For a complete rundown of the major national and local newspapers, consult the *Gale Directory of Publications*, which is reissued annually by Gale Research, Inc., 835 Penobscot Building, Detroit MI 48226-4094. Another source of detailed information is *Editor and Publisher International Yearbook*, published by Editor and Publisher, 11 West 19th Street, New York NY 10011, which is also updated each year.

The second section contains an additional selection of journalists who are not currently heading newspaper food sections, but whose work constantly appears in magazines and newspapers, in the form of regular columns, restaurant reviews, or articles on food topics of all kinds. The list is alphabetical by name only; letters to writers listed here and addressed c/o Irena Chalmers Books, Inc., 305 Second Avenue, New York NY 10003, will be forwarded.

NEWSPAPER & WIRE SERVICE EDITORS

NORTHEAST

CONNECTICUT

Bridgeport Post-Telegram
410 State Street
Bridgeport CT 06604
203-333-0161
Contact:
Karen Berman, Food Editor

The Hartford Courant
285 Broad Sreet
Hartford CT 06115
203-241-6452
Contact:
Linda Giuca, Food Editor

New Haven Register
40 Sargent Drive
New Haven CT 06511
203-562-1121
Contact:
Carla Van Kampen, Food Writer

The Daily Republican
389 Meadow Street
P.O. Box 2090
Waterbury CT 06722
203-574-3636
Contact:
Rosemary Jackson, Food Editor

MAINE

The Bangor News
491 Main Street
Bangor ME 04401
207-942-4881
Contact:
Cheryl Olsen, Food Editor

Lewiston Daily Sun
104 Park Street
Lewiston ME 04240
207-784-5411
Contact:
Ursula Albert, Living Page Editor

Portland Press Herald
390 Congress Street
P.O. Box 1460
Portland ME 04104
207-780-9000
Contact:
Andrea R. Philbrick, Food Editor

MASSACHUSETTS

The Boston Globe
P.O. Box 2378
Boston MA 02107
617-929-2802
Contact:
Gail Perrin, Food Editor

The Boston Herald
1 Herald Square
Boston MA 02106
617-426-3000
Contact:
Jane Lichtenstein, Food Editor

The Christian Science Monitor
1 Norway Street
Boston MA 02115
617-450-2000
Contact:
Phyllis Hanes, Food Editor

Cape Cod Times
319 Main Street
Hyannis MA 02601
508-775-1200
Contact:
Alicia Blaisdell-Bannon,
Food Editor

The Lowell Sun
15 Kearney Square
P.O. Box 1477 (01852)
Lowell MA 01853
508-458-7100
Contact:
David Haynes, Food Editor

The Standard-Times
555 Pleasant Street
New Bedford MA 02742
508-997-7411
Contact:
Brad Hathaway, Food Editor

Springfield Union-News
1860 Main Street
Springfield MA 01102
413-788-1000
Contact:
Jean O'Connell, Food Editor

Worcester Telegram and Gazette
20 Franklin Street
P.O. Box 15012
Worcester MA 01615
508-793-9100
Contact:
Barbara Houle

NEW HAMPSHIRE

The Keene Sentinel
60 West Street
P.O. Box 546
Keene NH 03431
603-352-1234
Contact:
Arlie Corday, Women's Editor

Manchester Union-Leader
35 Amherst Street
P.O. Box 780
Manchester NH 03105
603-668-4321
Contact:
Ed Chapman, Food Editor

NEW JERSEY

The Courier-Post
301 Cuthbert Boulevard
P.O. Box 5300
Cherry Hill NJ 08034
609-663-6000
Contact:
Ruth Olis, Food Editor

The Record
150 River Street
Hackensack NJ 07601
201-646-4351
Contact:
Rosemary Black, Food Editor

Asbury Park Press
3601 Highway 66
P.O. Box 1550
Neptune NJ 07754
201-922-6000
Contact:
Teresa Kline, Food Editor

The Home News
123 How Lane
P.O. Box 551
New Brunswick NJ 08903
201-246-5500
Contact:
Patricia Ferrara, Food Editor

Newark Star-Ledger
Star-Ledger Plaza
Newark NJ 07101
201-877-4040
Contact:
Ann Lerner, Food Editor

The *Newark Star-Ledger* is a prominent New Jersey newspaper with a daily circulation of 400,000, increasing to 600,000 for the Sunday edition.

The *Star-Ledger* runs three to four food columns each week, on Wednesdays and Sundays. These include a Slim Gourmet column, some health articles, recipes and book reviews.

The Bergen News
111 Grand Avenue
Palisades Park NJ 07650
201-947-5000
Contact:
Sue Perkins, Food Editor

The Atlantic City Press
1000 West Washington Avenue
Pleasantville NJ 08232
609-645-1234
Contact:
Alice Post, Food Editor

The Trenton Times
500 Perry Street
P.O. Box 847
Trenton NJ 08605
609-396-3232
Contact:
Joan Belknap, Food Editor

The Trentonian
600 Perry Street
Trenton NJ 08602
609-989-7800
Contact:
Diane Dixon, Food Editor

News Tribune
1 Hoover Way
Woodbridge NJ 07095
201-442-0400
Contact:
Patricia Mack, Food Editor

NEW YORK

Albany Times-Union
News Plaza
P.O. Box 15000
Albany NY 12212
518-454-5479
Contact:
James Gray, Food Editor

Press & Sun-Bulletin
P.O. Box 1270
Binghamton NY 13902
607-798-1190
Contact:
Sharon Eurich, Food Editor

The Buffalo News
1 News Plaza
P.O. Box 100
Buffalo NY 14240
716-849-4468
Contact:
Janice Okun, Food Editor

Elmira Star-Gazette
201 Baldwin Street
P.O. Box 285
Elmira NY 14902
607-734-5151
Contact:
Tom Beiswenger, Food Editor

Newsday
235 Pinelawn
Melville NY 11747
516-454-2975
Contact:
Peggy Katalinich, Food Editor

Newsday has extensive food coverage. In addition to an eight-page section on

Wednesdays, the Long Island Sunday edition includes a four-page food section, while the Sunday magazine regularly features local chefs. Columns cover various health-related topics (Fit and Fast, Good For You) as well as items of seasonal interest such as barbecue cooking.

Restaurant reviews covering Long Island as well as New York City appear on Fridays and Sundays. The paper also runs a syndicated column from *The Los Angeles Times* on food styles.

Times Herald-Record
40 Mulberry Street
Middletown NY 10940
914-343-2181
Contact:
Brenda Gilhooly, Food Editor

Associated Press
50 Rockefeller Plaza
New York NY 10020
212-621-1500
Contact:
Carol Deegan, Food Editor

King Features Syndicate
235 East 45th Street
New York NY 10017
212-455-4000
Contact:
Jean Jones, Food Editor

New York Daily News
220 East 42nd Street
New York NY 10017
212-210-1654
Contact:
Arthur Schwartz, Food Editor

The New York Times
229 West 43rd Street
New York NY 10036
212-556-7422
Contact:
Angela Dodson, Editor,
Living Section

New York Post
210 South Street
New York NY 10002
212-815-8637
Contact:
Pucci Meyer, Food Editor

The Poughkeepsie Journal
85 Civic Center Plaza
Poughkeepsie NY 12602
914-454-2000
Contact:
Carol Trapani, Food Editor

Democrat and Chronicle
55 Exchange Boulevard
Rochester NY 14614
716-232-7100
Contact:
Reoma McGinnis, Food Editor

The Rochester Times-Union
55 Exchange Boulevard
Rochester NY 14614
716-232-7100
Contact:
Kathy Lindsley, Food Editor

Schenectady Gazette
332 State Street
Schenectady NY 12301
518-374-4141
Contact:
Gail Shufelt, Food Editor

The Staten Island Advance
950 Fingerboard Road
Staten Island NY 10305
718-981-1234
Contact:
Jane Milza, Food Editor

The Post-Standard
P.O. Box 4818
Syracuse NY 13221
315-470-2146
Contact:
Margaret McCormick, Food Editor

Syracuse Herald-Journal
P.O. Box 4915
Syracuse NY 13221
315-470-2238
Contact:
William Robinson, Assistant
Managing Editor, Features

PENNSYLVANIA

The Morning Call
6th and Linden Streets
P.O. Box 1260
Allentown PA 18105
215-820-6526
Contact:
Diane Stoneback, Food Editor

The Patriot-News
P.O. Box 2265
Harrisburg PA 17105
717-255-8100
Contact:
Nance Woodward, Food Editor

Lancaster New Era
8 West King Street
Lancaster PA 17603
717-291-8733
Contact:
Jean Korten, Food Editor

Bucks County Courier Times
8400 Route 13
Levittown PA 19057
215-752-6881
Contact:
Paul Davenport, Food Editor

Inquirer
400 North Broad Street
Philadelphia PA 19101
215-854-5743
Contact:
Ken Bookman, Food Editor

The *Philadelphia Inquirer* has a daily circulation of 500,000, increasing to 1,100,000 for the Sunday edition.

The paper runs a regular 8- to 16-page food section on Wednesdays and food-related items appear on Sundays also. Topics covered in regular columns include health and nutrition (The Savvy Shopper, Health Watch) and best produce buys (The Monthly Market Basket). Features on local chefs appear from time to time. The newspaper also uses many syndicated columnists, including Jean Mayer and Jeanne Goldberg.

Philadelphia Daily News
P.O. Box 7788
Philadelphia PA 19101
215-854-5879
Contact:
Deborah Licklider, Food Editor

Pittsburgh Press
34 Boulevard of the Allies
Pittsburgh PA 15230
412-263-1409
Contact:
Marilyn McDevitt Rubin,
Food Editor

Pittsburgh Post-Gazette
50 Boulevard of the Allies
P.O. Box 957
Pittsburgh PA 15222
412-263-1666
Contact:
Marsha Bennett, Food Editor

Reading Eagle
P.O. Box 582
Reading PA 19603
215-371-5055
Contact:
Mary Jo Fox, Food Editor

Times
P.O. Box 3311
Scranton PA 18505
717-348-9127
Contact:
Terry B. Avery, Food Editor

RHODE ISLAND

Providence Bulletin
75 Fountain Street
Providence RI 02902
401-277-7268
Contact:
Donna Lee, Food Editor

VERMONT

The Free Press
191 College Street
Burlington VT 05401
802-863-3471
Contact:
Debbie Salomon, Food Editor

SOUTH

ALABAMA

Birmingham News
P.O. Box 2553
Birmingham AL 35202
205-325-2436
Contact:
Jo Ellen O'Hara, Food Editor

Birmingham Post-Herald
P.O. Box 2553
Birmingham AL 35202
205-325-2322
Contact:
Mitchell Diggs, Food Editor

The Mobile Press-Register
P.O. Box 2488
Mobile AL 36630
205-433-1551
Contact:
Janice Hume, Food Editor

Montgomery Advertiser
P.O. Box 100
Montgomery AL 36101
205-262-1611
Contact:
Beth Barmettler, Food Editor

ARKANSAS

Arkansas Democrat
Capitol Avenue and Scott Street
P.O. Box 2221
Little Rock AR 72203
501-378-3497
Contact:
Helen Austin, Food Editor

Arkansas Gazette
Gazette Building
P.O. Box 1821
Little Rock AR 72203
501-371-3737
Contact:
Harriett Aldridge, Food Editor

DELAWARE

The News-Journal
950 West Basin Road
New Castle DE 19720
302-324-2500
Contact:
Al Mascitti, Food Editor

DISTRICT OF COLUMBIA

Gannett News Service
P.O. Box 7858
Washington DC 20044
703-276-5800
Contact:
Angie Terrell, Food Editor

United Press International
1400 Eye Street
Washington DC 20005
202-898-8000
Contact:
Michele Mundth, Features Editor

USA Today
P.O. Box 500
Washington DC 20044
703-276-6532
Contact:
Nancy Hellmich, Health & Behavior,
Diet & Fitness Editor

The Washington Post
1150 15th Street NW
Washington DC 20071
202-334-7590
Contact:
Robert Kelleter, Food Editor

The Washington Times
3600 New York Avenue NE
Washington DC 20002
202-636-3000
Contact:
John Rosson, Food Editor

FLORIDA

Daytona Beach News-Journal
P.O. Box 431
Daytona Beach FL 32015
904-252-1511
Contact:
Louise Lindley, Food Editor

News and Sun-Sentinel
101 North New River Drive
Ft. Lauderdale FL 33301
305-761-4000
Contact:
Susan Puckett, Food Editor

News-Press
2442 Anderson Avenue
Ft. Myers FL 33901
813-335-0369
Contact:
Lillian Austin, Food Editor

The Gainesville Sun
P.O. Drawer A
Gainesville FL 32602
904-378-1411
Contact:
Diane Chun, Food Editor

The Florida Times-Union
1 Riverside Avenue
Jacksonville FL 32202
904-359-4583
Contact:
Linda Hanks Stem, Food Editor

Florida Today
Gannett Plaza
P.O. Box 363000
Melbourne FL 32936
407-242-3784
Contact:
Amy Clark, Food Editor

Florida Today has a circulation of 100,000. The paper runs a regular food section on Thursdays covering a broad spectrum of food-related topics. These include local events and produce news. Local restaurants are mentioned from time to time but are not reviewed.

The Miami Herald
1 Herald Plaza
Miami FL 33132
305-376-3636
Contact:
Linda Cicero, Food Editor

The Orlando Sentinel
633 North Orange Avenue
Orlando FL 32801
407-420-5498
Contact:
Heather McPherson, Food Editor

News-Journal
1 News-Journal Plaza
Pensacola FL 32501
904-435-8550
Contact:
Sue Lutz, Food Editor

St. Petersburg Times
490 First Avenue South
P.O. Box 1121
St. Petersburg FL 33731
813-893-8111
Contact:
Chris Sherman, Food Editor

Sarasota Herald Tribune
P.O. Drawer 1719
Sarasota FL 34230
813-953-7755
Contact:
Linda Brandt, Food Editor

The Tampa Tribune
202 South Parker Street
P.O. Box 191
Tampa FL 33601
813-272-7679
Contact:
Ann McDuffie, Food Editor

The Palm Beach Post
2751 South Dixie Highway
West Palm Beach FL 33405
407-837-4737
Contact:
Jan Norris, Food Editor

GEORGIA

The Atlanta Journal-Constitution
72 Marietta Street NW
Atlanta GA 30303
404-526-5443
Contact:
Anne Byrn, Food Editor

The afternoon edition of the newspaper, *The Journal*, runs a 10-page food section each Wednesday. *The Constitution* is the morning edition and runs a Thursday food section. John Egerton, a Nashville-based Southern food writer, is a regular columnist. Cookbook reviews and a wine column also appear regularly.

The newspaper offers a Dial-a-Dietician service. Monday through Friday, from 8:00 a.m. to 6:00 p.m., readers can call 404-266-4512 with questions for a representative of the Atlanta Dietetic Association.

The Augusta Chronicle
P.O. Box 1928
Augusta GA 30913
404-724-0851
Contact:
Roger Whibdons, Features Editor

Macon Telegraph and News
P.O. Box 4167
Macon GA 31208
912-744-4200
Contact:
Michelle Bell, Food Editor

Savannah News
111 West Bay Street
P.O. Box 1088
Savannah GA 31402
912-236-9511
Contact:
Mary Mayle, Food Editor

KENTUCKY

Lexington Herald-Leader
100 Midland Avenue
Lexington KY 40508
606-231-3321
Contact:
Sharon Thompson, Food Editor

The Courier-Journal
525 West Broadway
Louisville KY 40202
502-582-4203
Contact:
Sarah Fritschner, Food Editor

Although the paper has no formal food section, the food pages of the *Courier-Journal* offer readers a combination of features and food news.

Best buys and inexpensive recipes are featured regularly, as well as a syndicated column, Slim Gourmet. The Sunday color magazine has a food page with recipes and photographs. Restaurant reviews appear in the paper's Saturday weekend section.

Readers have access to recipes, food information and cooking tips by calling 502-582-4617.

LOUISIANA

Morning Advocate
P.O. Box 588
Baton Rouge LA 70821
504-383-1111
Contact:
Pat Baldridge, Food Editor

The Times-Picayune
3800 Howard Avenue
New Orleans LA 70140
504-826-3279
Contact:
Dale Curry, Food Editor

Shreveport Times
222 Lake Street
P.O. Box 30222
Shreveport LA 71130
318-459-3200
Contact:
Martha Fitzgerald, Food Editor

MARYLAND

The Sun
501 North Calvert Street
Baltimore MD 21278
301-332-6156
Contact:
Karol Menzie, Food Editor

The Baltimore *Sun* has a daily circulation of 232,000, rising to 500,000 on Sundays. With two regular, full-color food sections on Wednesdays and Sundays, the paper offers its readers a variety of topics including food news and recipes. Health-related items are covered in a regular syndicated column, The Happy Eater, by Rob Kasper. In addition, a nutrition column appears in the newspaper's Thursday health section.

MISSISSIPPI

The Sun Herald
P.O. Box 4567
Biloxi MS 39535
601-896-2357
Contact:
Lue Rogers, Food Editor

Clarion-Ledger/Jackson Daily News
311 East Pearl Street
Jackson MS 39205
601-961-7000
Contact:
Orly Hood, Food Editor

NORTH CAROLINA

The Charlotte Observer
600 South Tyron Street
P.O. Box 32188
Charlotte NC 28232
704-379-6407
Contact:
Caroline Beyray, Food Editor

The Durham Herald
115 Market Street
Durham NC 27702
919-687-6664
Contact:
Jim Wise, Features Editor

The Greensboro News & Record
P.O. Box 20848
Greensboro NC 27420
919-373-7057
Contact:
Lynn Burnette, Assistant
Features Editor

The News & Observer
215 South McDowell Street
P.O. Box 191
Raleigh NC 27602
919-829-4500
Contact:
Marilyn Spencer, Food Editor

Winston-Salem Journal
P.O. Box 3159
Winston-Salem NC 27102
919-727-7392
Contact:
Beth Tartan-Sparks, Food Editor

The *Journal*'s food section appears on Wednesdays and, in addition, the paper runs regular food columns on Sundays and Tuesdays. These offer readers local food news as well as syndicated columns by Pierre Franey, Jean Jones and Susan Caulwalder. Restaurants are mentioned from time to time, but not reviewed.

In addition, readers can call 919-727-7392 and reach a home economist who is available to answer questions.

SOUTH CAROLINA

The News and Courier
134 Columbus Street
Charleston SC 29403
803-577-7111
Contact:
Elizabeth Moye, Food Editor

The State
P.O. Box 1333
Columbia SC 29202
803-771-8572
Contact:
Fran Zupan, Food Editor

The News
South Main Street
P.O. Box 1688
Greenville SC 29602
803-298-4100
Contact:
Al Clark, Food Editor

TENNESSEE

Chattanooga News-Free Press
400 East 11th Street
P.O. Box 1447
Chattanooga TN 37401
615-756-6900
Contact:
Helen Exum, Food Editor

The Knoxville News-Sentinel
208 West Church Avenue
P.O. Box 59038
Knoxville TN 37950
615-523-3131
Contact:
Louise Durman, Food Editor

The Commercial Appeal
495 Union Avenue
Memphis TN 38103
901-529-2368
Contact:
Christine Arpe Gang, Food Editor

Nashville Banner
1100 Broadway
Nashville TN 37203
615-259-8233
Contact:
Bernie Arnold, Food Editor

The Tennessean
1100 Broadway
Nashville TN 37202
615-259-8051
Contact:
Beverly Garrison, Food Editor

VIRGINIA

Fairfax Journal
6883 Commercial Avenue
Springfield VA 22159
703-750-8782
Contact:
Raymond M. Lane, Food Editor

The Daily Press
7505 Warwick Boulevard
Newport News VA 23607
804-247-4600
Contact:
Carolyn West, Food Editor

The Ledger-Star
150 West Brambleton Avenue
Norfolk VA 23510
804-446-2417
Contact:
Ann Hoffman, Food Editor

The Virginian Pilot
150 West Brambleton Avenue
Norfolk VA 23510
804-446-2417
Contact:
Ann Hoffman, Food Editor

Richmond News Leader
P.O. Box C-32333
Richmond VA 23293
804-649-6432
Contact:
Louis Mahoney, Food Editor

Richmond Times-Dispatch
P.O. Box C-32333
Richmond VA 23293
804-649-6820
Contact:
Jann Malone, Food Editor

The *Times-Dispatch* runs two regular food sections, with the Thursday section running as long as 10 pages; the Sunday paper runs a full food page. Local food news, activities and events are covered. A regular nutrition column, Eat Smart, appears biweekly. The newspaper also runs syndicated columns by Marian Burros and Rob Kasper. Restaurant reviews appear in the paper's weekender section.

The paper offers an unusual service called Trading Secrets: Readers who have enjoyed a dish at a restaurant can call in and the paper will obtain the recipe.

Roanoke Times & World News
P.O. Box 2491
Roanoke VA 24010
703-981-3253
Contact:
Toni Burks, Food Editor

WEST VIRGINIA

Charleston Daily Mail
1001 Virginia Street East
Charleston WV 25301
304-348-4806
Contact:
Julianne Kemp, Food Editor

News-Register
1500 Main Street
Wheeling WV 26003
304-233-0100
Contact:
Mary Ann Menendez, Food Editor

MIDWEST

ILLINOIS

The Pantagraph
301 West Washington Street
P.O. Box 2907
Bloomington IL 61702
309-829-9411
Contact:
Nancy Gordon, Food Editor

The News-Gazette
P.O. Box 677
Champaign IL 61820
217-351-5221
Contact:
Jack Tanner, Food Editor

The Chicago Tribune
435 North Michigan Avenue
Chicago IL 60611
312-222-4533
Contact:
Carol Haddix, Food Editor

This leading Chicago newspaper has a circulation of 800,000-plus. On Thursdays, the *Tribune* has a 30-page food section covering all aspects of food news including restaurant reviews.

Chicago Sun-Times
401 North Wabash Avenue
Chicago IL 60611
312-321-2132
Contact:
Beverly Bennett, Food Editor

Herald and Review
P.O. Box 311
Decatur IL 62525
217-429-5151
Contact:
Steve Metsch, Food Editor

Journal Star
1 News Plaza
Peoria IL 61643
309-686-3000
Contact:
Sharon Oberholtzer, Food Editor

State Journal-Register
1 Copley Plaza
P.O. Box 219
Springfield IL 62705
217-788-1300
Contact:
Bob Gonko, Food Editor

INDIANA

The Journal Gazette
600 West Main Street
P.O. Box 88 (46801)
Ft. Wayne IN 46802
219-461-8304
Contact:
Sandy Thorn Clark, Food Editor

The News-Sentinel
600 West Main Street
P.O. Box 102 (46801)
Ft. Wayne IN 46802
Contact:
Virginia French, Features Editor

The Post-Tribune
1065 Broadway
Gary IN 46402
219-881-3145
Contact:
Barbara Thomas, Food Editor

The Indianapolis News
P.O. Box 145
Indianapolis IN 46206
317-633-9130
Contact:
Marge Hanley, Food Editor

The Indianapolis Star
307 North Pennsylvania Street
Indianapolis IN 46204
317-633-9403
Contact:
Donna Salle Segal, Food Editor

IOWA

The Cedar Rapids Gazette
500 Third Avenue SE
P.O. Box 511
Cedar Rapids IA 52406
319-398-8286
Contact:
Kathy Torburg, Food Editor

The Des Moines Register
P.O. Box 957
Des Moines IA 50304
515-284-8000
Contact:
Cynthia Mitchell, Food Editor

Every Wednesday, this daily paper, with a circulation of 215,000, offers its readers a one-page food section. The section regularly includes an article on nutrition.

Sioux City Journal
6th and Pavonia Streets
Sioux City IA 51102
712-279-5079
Contact:
Marcia Poole, Food Editor

KANSAS

The Topeka Capital-Journal
616 Jefferson Street
Topeka KS 66607
913-295-1111
Contact:
Nancy Stoetzer, Food Editor

The Wichita Eagle-Beacon
825 East Douglas
P.O. Box 820
Wichita KS 67201
913-268-6000
Contact:
Kathleen Kelly, Food Editor

MICHIGAN

Detroit Free Press
321 West Lafayette Boulevard
Detroit MI 48231
313-222-6549
Contact:
John Tanasychuck, Food Writer

The Detroit News
615 Lafayette Boulevard
Detroit MI 48231
313-222-2480
Contact:
Robin Mather, Food Editor

The Grand Rapids Press
155 Michigan Street NW
Grand Rapids MI 49503
616-459-1503
Contact:
Ann Wells, Food Editor

Kalamazoo Gazette
401 South Burdick Street
Kalamazoo MI 49007
616-345-3511
Contact:
Peggy Guthaus, Food Editor

State Journal
120 East Lenawee
Lansing MI 48919
517-377-1073
Contact:
Janet Watson, Food Editor

The Saginaw News
203 South Washington Avenue
Saginaw MI 48605
517-752-7171
Contact:
Mary Foreman, Food Editor

MINNESOTA

Duluth News-Tribune
424 West 1st Street
P.O. Box 169000
Duluth MN 55816
218-723-5353
Contact:
Gordy Behrens, Food Editor

Minneapolis Star & Tribune
425 Portland Avenue
Minneapolis MN 55488
612-372-4423
Contact:
Mary Hart, Food Editor

St. Paul Pioneer Press Dispatch
345 Cedar Street
St. Paul MN 55101
612-222-5011
Contact:
Holly Mullen, Food Editor

MISSOURI

The Kansas City Star
1729 Grand Avenue
Kansas City MO 64108
816-234-4395
Contact:
Andy Badecker, Food Editor

The *Star* provides its readers with a food section of six to eight pages every Wednesday. The emphasis is on recipes and there is a regular health and nutrition column as well. Interviews with local chefs, together with recipes, appear from time to time. There are no syndicated columns. The newspaper has a circulation of 170,000.

The Kansas City Times
1729 Grand Avenue
Kansas City MO 64108
816-234-4900
Contact:
Jeanne Meyer, Food Editor

St. Louis Post-Dispatch
900 North Tucker Boulevard
St. Louis MO 63101
314-622-7570
Contact:
Barbara G. Ostmann, Food Editor

NEBRASKA

Omaha World-Herald
World-Herald Square
Omaha NE 68102
402-444-1000
Contact:
Jane Palmer, Food Editor

NORTH DAKOTA

The Forum
P.O. Box 2020
Fargo ND 58107
701-235-7311
Contact:
Cathy Mauk, Food Editor

OHIO

Beacon Journal
44 East Exchange Street
Akron OH 44328
216-375-8520
Contact:
Jane Snow, Food Editor

The Enquirer
617 Vine Street
Cincinnati OH 45201
513-369-1985
Contact:
Toni Cashnelli, Food Editor

Cincinnati Post
125 East Court Street
Cincinnati OH 45202
513-352-2753
Contact:
Joyce Rosencrans, Food Editor

The Plain Dealer
1801 Superior Avenue NE
Cleveland OH 44114
216-344-4553
Contact:
Iris Bailin, Food Editor

The Columbus Dispatch
34 South 3rd Street
Columbus OH 43216
614-461-5000
Contact:
Sue Dawson, Food Editor

Dayton Daily News
4th and Ludlow Streets
Dayton OH 45401
513-225-2419
Contact:
Ann Heller

The Toledo Blade
541 Superior Street
Toledo OH 43660
419-245-6155
Contact:
Mary Alice Powell, Food Editor

The Vindicator
Vindicator Square
P.O. Box 780
Youngstown OH 44501
216-747-1471
Contact:
Tricia McChesney, Food Editor

OKLAHOMA

The Oklahoman
P.O. Box 25125
Oklahoma City OK 73125
405-231-3304
Contact:
Sharon Dowell, Food Editor

The Tulsa Tribune
315 South Boulder Avenue
P.O. Box 1770
Tulsa OK 74102
918-581-8400
Contact:
JoAnn Bond, Food Editor

The Tulsa World
315 South Boulder Avenue
Tulsa OK 74102
918-581-8340
Contact:
Pat Morris, Food Editor

SOUTH DAKOTA

Argus Leader
200 South Minnesota Avenue
P.O. Box 5034
Sioux Falls SD 57117
605-331-2300
Contact:
Coletta Bly, Food Editor

WISCONSIN

The Press-Gazette
Walnut and Madison Streets
P.O. Box 19430
Green Bay WI 54307
414-435-4411
Contact:
Dian Page, Food Editor

Wisconsin State Journal
P.O. Box 8058
Madison WI 53708
608-252-6180
Contact:
Sandy Kallio, Food Editor

The Milwaukee Journal
P.O. Box 661
Milwaukee WI 53201
414-224-2385
Contact:
Tom Sietsema, Food Editor

Milwaukee Sentinel
P.O. Box 371
Milwaukee WI 53201
414-224-2184
Contact:
Lee Aschoff, Food Editor

SOUTHWEST

ARIZONA

The Phoenix Gazette
P.O. Box 1950
Phoenix AZ 85001
602-271-8948
Contact:
Jane Baker, Food Editor

The Arizona Daily Star
P.O. Box 26807
Tucson AZ 85726
Contact:
Colette Bancroft, Food Editor

Tucson Citizen
P.O. Box 26767
Tucson AZ 85726
602-573-4630
Contact:
Paul Schwalbach, Assistant
Features Editor

NEVADA

Las Vegas Review-Journal
P.O. Box 70
Las Vegas NV 89125
702-383-0304
Contact:
Pat Morgan, Food Editor

Las Vegas Sun
P.O. Box 4275
Las Vegas NV 89127
702-385-3111
Contact:
Muriel Stevens, Food Editor

Reno Gazette-Journal
P.O. Box 22000
Reno NV 89520
702-788-6338
Contact:
Sandra Macias

NEW MEXICO

Albuquerque Journal
7777 Jefferson NE
Albuquerque NM 87109
505-823-3926
Contact:
Susan Stiger, Food Editor

TEXAS

Abilene Reporter-News
P.O. Box 30
Abilene TX 79604
915-673-4271
Contact:
Celia Davis, Food Editor

Austin American-Statesman
166 East Riverside Drive
P.O. Box 670
Austin TX 78767
512-445-3656
Contact:
Kitty Crider, Food Editor

Beaumont Enterprise
P.O. Box 3071
Beaumont TX 77704
409-833-3311
Contact:
Elaine Wittstrom, Food Editor

Caller-Times
P.O. Box 9136
Corpus Christi TX 78469
512-884-2011
Contact:
Mary Sherwood, Food Editor

The Dallas Morning News
Communications Center
P.O. Box 655237
Dallas TX 75265
214-977-8417
Contact:
Dotty Griffith, Food Editor

The newspaper has a daily circulation of 350,000, rising to 500,000 on Sunday. A regular Wednesday food section features a health and nutrition page as well as a market report on meat, seafood and poultry and includes recipes. The emphasis is currently shifting to quick, easy and nutritious food.

Restaurant reviews appear in *The Guide*, which comes out on Fridays and is separate from the food section. One page of food news also appears in *Dallas Life*, the paper's Sunday magazine.

Dallas Times Herald
1101 Pacific Avenue
Dallas TX 75202
214-720-6777
Contact:
Ron Ruggless, Food Editor
Candy Sagon, Food Editor

El Paso Times
401 Mills Avenue
El Paso TX 79901
915-546-6154
Contact:
Jose Cantu-Weber, Food Editor

Fort Worth Star-Telegram
400 West 7th Street
Fort Worth TX 76102
817-429-4571
Contact:
Beverly Bundy, Food Editor

The Houston Chronicle
801 Texas Avenue
Houston TX 77002
713-220-7373
Contact:
Ann Criswell, Food Editor

The *Chronicle*'s 8- to 12-page food section appears on Wednesdays. It regularly includes articles by a local dietician and a wine expert, as well as syndicated columns covering a variety of food topics such as microwave cooking, light and nutritious food and gourmet diets. On Tuesdays, readers can call in with food questions. In addition, profiles of local restaurants appear in the paper's monthly magazine, *Texas Life*.

Daily circulation is 440,000, rising to 518,000 on Sundays.

The Houston Post
P.O. Box 4747
Houston TX 77210
713-840-6709
Contact:
Ann Valentine, Food Editor

San Antonio Light
P.O. Box 161
San Antonio TX 78291
512-271-2736
Contact:
Ron Bechtol, Food Editor

Waco Tribune-Herald
P.O. Box 2588
Waco TX 76702
817-757-5757
Contact:
Teresa Johnson, Food Editor

MOUNTAIN STATES

COLORADO

The Gazette Telegraph
30 South Prospect
P.O. Box 1779 (80903)
Colorado Springs CO 80901
719-636-0271
Contact:
Leslie Weddell, Food Editor

The Denver Post
1560 Broadway
P.O. Box 1709 (80201)
Denver Co 80202
303-820-1440
Contact:
Helen Dollaghan, Food Editor

Rocky Mountain News
400 West Colfax Avenue
Denver CO 80204
303-892-5229
Contact:
Marty Meitus, Food Editor
Linda Castrone, Acting Food Editor

IDAHO

The Idaho Statesman
1200 North Curtis Road
P.O. Box 40
Boise ID 83707
208-377-6444
Contact:
Bill Roberts, Food Editor

MONTANA

The Billings Gazette
401 North Broadway
P.O. Box 36300 (59107)
Billings MT 59103
406-657-1200
Contact:
Joyce Michels, Food Editor

UTAH

The Deseret News
30 East 1st South Street
P.O. Box 1257
Salt Lake City UT 84110
801-237-2150
Contact:
Ann Whiting Allen, Food Editor

Salt Lake City Tribune
P.O. Box 867
Salt Lake City UT 84110
801-237-2075
Contact:
Donna Lou Morgan, Food Editor

WEST COAST

CALIFORNIA

The Bakersfield Californian
P.O. Box 440
Bakersfield CA 93302
805-395-7369
Contact:
Joan Swenson, Food Editor

San Diego County Times-Advocate
207 East Pennsylvania Avenue
Escondido CA 92025
619-745-6611
Contact:
Laura Grouch

The Fresno Bee
1626 E Street
Fresno CA 93786
209-441-6111
Contact:
Gail Marshall, Food Editor

Long Beach Press-Telegram
604 Pine Avenue
Long Beach CA 90844
213-435-1161
Contact:
Debbie Arrington, Food Editor

The Los Angeles Times
Times Mirror Square
Los Angeles CA 90053
213-237-5000
Contact:
Betsy Balsley, Food Editor

This leading California newspaper offers its readers a large food section every Thursday. At 50 pages, it is probably the biggest in the country and covers the full range of food-related topics.

The Modesto Bee
14th and H Streets
P.O. Box 3928
Modesto CA 95352
209-578-2314
Contact:
Dan Herrera, Food Editor

The readership of *The Modesto Bee* is 80,000. The newspaper has a regular food section appearing on Wednesdays which generally focuses on recipes but includes local food stories from time to time.

The Oakland Tribune
409 13th Street
Oakland CA 94612
415-645-2000
Contact:
Wendy Miller, Features Editor

Peninsula Times-Tribune
245 Lytton Avenue
Palo Alto CA 94301
415-833-1200
Contact:
Lou Pappas, Food Editor

Pasadena Star-News
525 East Colorado Boulevard
Pasadena CA 91109
818-578-6300
Contact:
Mary Andrek, Food Editor

The Sacramento Bee
21st and Q Streets
P.O. Box 15779
Sacramento CA 95852
916-321-1052
Contact:
Elaine Corn, Food Editor

One of Sacramento's two newspapers, *The Bee* has a regular 16-page food section. It covers a broad range of food-related items.

The Sacramento Union
301 Capitol Mall
Sacramento CA 95812
916-442-7811
Contact:
Gloria Glyer, Food Editor

The San Bernardino County Sun
399 North D Street
San Bernardino CA 92401
714-889-9666
Contact:
Jackie Richard, Food Editor

The San Diego Union
Union-Tribune Publishing Company
P.O. Box 191
San Diego CA 92112
619-299-3131
Contact:
Maureen Clancy, Food Editor

The San Diego Tribune
P.O. Box 191
San Diego CA 92112
619-299-3131
Contact:
Linda Dudley, Food Editor

San Francisco Chronicle
901 Mission Street
San Francisco CA 94103
415-777-7044
Contact:
Michael Bauer, Food Editor

San Francisco Examiner
925 Mission Street
P.O. Box 7260 (94120)
San Francisco CA 94103
415-777-7934
Contact:
Lynn Forbes, Food Editor

San Jose Mercury/News
750 Ridder Park Drive
San Jose CA 95190
408-920-5000
Contact:
Carolyn Snyder, Food Editor

Orange County Register
625 North Grand Avenue
P.O. Box 11626
Santa Ana CA 92711
714-953-2278
Contact:
Joel Crea, Food Editor

The Press-Democrat
427 Mendocino Avenue
Santa Rosa CA 95402
707-546-2020
Contact:
George Hower, Food Editor

The Stockton Record
P.O. Box 900
Stockton CA 95201
209-943-6397
Contact:
Joan Simpson, Food Editor

Ventura County Star-Free Press
5250 Ralston
P.O. Box 6711
Ventura CA 93003
805-655-5831
Contact:
Rita Moran, Food Editor

Contra Costa Times
2640 Shadelands Drive
P.O. Box 5088
Walnut Creek CA 94596
415-935-2525
Contact:
Deborah Byrd, Food Editor

OREGON

The Register-Guard
P.O. Box 10188
Eugene OR 97440
503-485-1234
Contact:
Jim Godbold, Food Editor

The Oregonian
1320 Southwest Broadway
Portland OR 97201
503-221-8384
Contact:
Ginger Johnston, Food Editor

The newspaper's 20-page food section appears on Tuesdays. Subjects covered include cooking for children, food labeling, growing your own produce, nutritional analyses of recipes, vegetarian cooking and cooking for one. A wine review appears weekly, a beer review monthly. Advice is given on the week's best produce. Local chefs are featured from time to time, and readers can call in on Mondays, Tuesdays and Wednesdays with food questions.

The Statesman-Journal
280 Church Street NE
Salem OR 97309
503-399-6610
Contact:
Andrea Howry, Food Editor

WASHINGTON

Seattle Post-Intelligencer
101 Elliott Avenue West
Seattle WA 98119
206-448-8356
Contact:
Nancy Erickson, Assistant
Features Editor

Seattle Times
P.O. Box 70
Seattle WA 98111
206-464-2305
Contact:
Sharon Lane, Food Editor

The Spokesman-Review
West 999 Riverside
P.O. Box 2160
Spokane WA 99210
509-459-5440
Contact:
Jamie Neely, Food Editor

The Morning News Tribune
1950 South State Street
P.O. Box 11000
Tacoma WA 98411
206-597-8675
Contact:
Robin Newcomer, Food Editor

ALASKA & HAWAII

ALASKA

Anchorage Daily News
1001 Northway Drive
P.O. Box 149001 (99514)
Anchorage AK 99508
907-257-4316
Contact:
Linda Sievers, Food Editor

HAWAII

Honolulu-Star Bulletin
P.O. Box 3080
Honolulu HI 96802
808-525-8660
Contact:
Betty Shimabukuro, Food Editor

FOOD WRITERS & COLUMNISTS

Molly Abraham

Ann Whiting Allen

Jean Anderson

Colman Andrews

Gerald Asher

Nancy Verde Barr

Lee Bailey

Jane Benet

Alexis Bespaloff

Andy Birsch

Mark Bittman

Anthony Dias Blue

Carol Brock

Jane Brody

Ellen Brown

Pat Bruno

Marian Burros

Paul Camp
Laura Chenel

Craig Claiborne

Philomena Corradeno

Barbara Costikyan

Marian Cunningham

Sharon Delano

Merle Ellis

Ella Elvin

Barbara Ensrud

Jerry Etter

Florence Fabricant

Fred Ferretti

Michael Foley

Valerie Foster

Pierre Franey

Jane Freiman

Betty Fussell

Peter Gianutti

Howard Goldberg

Mary Goodbody

Gael Greene

Suzanne Hamlin

Zack Hanle

Joanne Hayes

Mindy Heiferling

Janice Wald Henderson

Nancy Harmon Jenkins

Barbara Kafka

Mike Kalina

Rob Kasper

Alan Katz

Corby Kummer

Cecile Lamalle

Jenifer Harvey Lang

Bob Lape

Preston Lerner

Elliott Mackle

Karen MacNeil

Abby Mandel

John Mariani

Ellin McCoy

Michael McLaughlin

Bryan Miller

Marian Morash

Jinx and Jefferson Morgan

Molly O'Neill

Eleanor Ostman

Robert M. Parker Jr.

Jacques Pepin

Peggy Rahn

Mardee Haidin Regan

Ruth Reichl

William Rice

Phyllis Richman

Hank Rubin

Irene Sax

Richard Sax

Elizabeth Schneider

Sallie Schneider

Stan Sesser

Laura Shapiro

Mimi Sheraton

Regina Schrambling

Sylvia Schur

Marie Simmons

Jeffrey Steingarten

Jane and Michael Stern

Waltrina Stovill

Stendahl (Bill Bernal)

Carol Sugarman

Elaine Tait

Calvin Trillin

Geri Trotta

Patricia Unterman

Charlyne Varkonyi

James Villas

John Frederick Walker

Patricia Wells

Thayer Wine

Clark Wolf

Jim Wood

Scientific and
GOVERNMENT INFORMATION SOURCES

263
Scientific Research Centers
Food Science & Technology; Agriculture; Meat,
Poultry & Dairy Products; Fisheries/Aquaculture

265
Nutrition Study Centers,
Associations and Action Groups
267
Federal Government Agencies

270
State Government Agencies

273
Chambers of Commerce

276
Consumer Advocacy and
Environmental Resource Groups

278
Registered Food Lobbyists

Scientific Research Centers

Universities across the country house research centers working on many aspects of the food world, ranging from truck gardening or sugar cane culture to oenology. The list that follows is a mere sampling of some of the centers where researchers are investigating areas of major interest. For convenience, they are listed alphabetically by center name within the following categories: Food Science & Technology; Agriculture; Meat, Poultry & Dairy Products; Fisheries/Aquaculture.

For a complete and more comprehensive account of the work going on in food research throughout the United States, consult the *Research Centers Directory* published by Gale Research, Inc., 835 Penobscot Building, Detroit MI 48226, which is the major resource in this field and updated each year.

FOOD SCIENCE & TECHNOLOGY

Cornell University Institute of Food Science
114 Stocking Hall
Ithaca NY 14853
607-255-7915
Contact:
Dr. Richard A. Ledford

Mississippi State University Department of Food Science and Human Nutrition
P.O. Drawer NH
Mississippi State MS 39762
601-325-3200
Contact:
Dr. Gale R. Ammerman

Ohio State University Food Industries Center (FIC)
2001 Fyffe Court
Howlett Hall, Suite 140
Columbus OH 43210
614-292-7004
Contact:
Dr. Winston D. Bash

Purdue University Food Sciences Institute
Smith Hall
West Lafayette IN 47907
317-494-8256
Contact:
Professor P. E. Nelson

In terms of undergraduate training, Purdue University has one of the larger food science departments in the country. Research covers areas such as aseptic processing and process optimization. The Whistler Center for Carbohydrate Research focuses on research into the molecular structure of food components such as starches, gums, sweeteners and noncaloric bulking agents. The center is also researching the use of carbohydrates in the development of biodegradable plastics.

Rutgers University Center for Advanced Food Technology
College Farm Road & Dudley Road
Food Science Building
P.O. Box 231
New Brunswick NJ 08903
201-932-8306
Contact:
Dr. Myron Solberg

AGRICULTURE

Institute for Alternative Agriculture
9200 Edmonston Road, Suite 117
Greenbelt MD 20770
301-441-8777
Contact:
Dr. I. Garth Youngberg

Michigan State University Pesticide Research Center
East Lansing MI 48824
517-353-9430
Contact:
Robert M. Hollingworth

Ohio State University Ohio Agricultural Research and Development Center
Wooster OH 44691
216-263-3700
Contact:
Dr. Kirklyn M. Kerr

Purdue University Agricultural Experiment Station
Lafayette IN 47907
317-494-8360
Contact:
Dr. B. R. Baumgardt

Richard B. Russell Agricultural Research Center (RRC)
College Station Road
P.O. Box 5677
Athens GA 30613
404-546-3541
Contact:
Dr. David E. Zimmer

Rutgers University Agricultural Experiment Station
New Brunswick NJ 08903
201-932-9447
Contact:
Dr. Stephen S. Kleinschuster

University of Arizona Environmental Research Laboratory
Tucson International Airport
Tucson AZ 85706
602-621-7962
Contact:
Carl N. Hodges

University of California, Davis
Plant Growth Laboratory
Davis CA 95616
916-752-6160
Contact:
Dr. R. W. Breidenbach

Work at the laboratory focuses on the basic physiology of growing plants. Among the physiological processes under study are the uptake of nitrogen or nitrates through plant root systems; the composition of plant membranes; plant hormones; and biological stresses, such as virus attacks, to which plants may be subjected.

More specifically, studies have been conducted on the freeze or chill tolerance of tomatoes and on nitrogen uptake through the root system of barley.

University of Connecticut, Storrs
Agricultural Experiment Station
Storrs CT 06268
203-486-2919
Contact:
Dr. Kirvin L. Knox

MEAT, POULTRY & DAIRY PRODUCTS

Colorado State University
Animal Reproduction Laboratory
College of Veterinary Medicine
Fort Collins CO 80523
303-491-6666
Contact:
G. D. Niswender

Dairy Research, Inc.
6300 North River Road
Rosemount IL 60018
708-696-1870
Contact:
Dr. Anthony J. Luksas

As part of the United Dairy Industry Association, whose mission is to promote dairy products, Dairy Research Inc. develops new products and technologies for the dairy industry and finds manufacturers for any product reaching prototype stage. Recent products to look out for on the supermarket shelves include "light" butter and carbonated milk. And the research team's work on freeze concentration technology could mean that in the future reconstituted milk will taste a lot more like the Real Thing.

Fats and Protein Research
Foundation, Inc.
2250 East Devon Avenue
Des Plaines IL 60018
708-827-0139
Contact:
Dr. Larry E. Davis

Roman L. Hruska U.S. Meat
Animal Research Center
USDA, Agricultural Research Service
P.O. Box 166
Clay Center NE 68933
402-762-3241
Contact:
Dr. Robert R. Oltjen

Kansas State University
Thomas B. Avery Research Center
(Poultry Science)
Call Hall
Manhattan KS 66506
913-539-5041
Contact:
Kenneth E. Anderson

Michigan State University
Beef Cattle Research Center
East Lansing MI 48824
517-353-2245
Contact:
Dr. Steven Rust

Michigan State University
Dairy Research and Teaching Center
Department of Animal Science
4075 College Road
Lansing MI 48910
517-355-7473
Contact:
Dr. Mary Schmidt

Mississippi State University
Meat Laboratory
P.O. Drawer 5228
Mississippi State MS 39762
601-325-3566
Contact:
Dr. Robert W. Rogers

Ohio State University
Meat Laboratory-Animal Science
2029 Fyffe Road
Columbus OH 43210
614-292-2201
Contact:
Dr. H. W. Ockerman

Ohio State University Dairy Center
2027 Coffey Road
Columbus OH 43210
614-422-6851
Contact:
Dr. David L. Zartman

Purdue University
Calvert-Purdue Beef Research and
Teaching Center
6203 West 750 North
West Lafayette IN 47906
317-494-4817
Contact:
Ronald P. Lemenager

University of Hawaii Livestock
Research Station
58-160 Kam Highway
Haleiwa HI 96712
808-948-8295
Contact:
C. W. Weems

University of Wisconsin, Madison
Center for Dairy Research
Babcock Hall
1605 Linden Drive
Madison WI 53706
608-262-5970
Contact:
Dr. Norman F. Olson

FISHERIES/ AQUACULTURE

Auburn University International
Center for Aquaculture
Auburn AL 36849
205-826-4786
Contact:
Dr. E. W. Shell

Institute for Fisheries Research
212 Museums Annex
Ann Arbor MI 48109
313-663-3554
Contact:
W. C. Latta

Oregon State University
Hatfield Marine Science Center
Marine Science Drive
Newport OR 97365
503-867-3011
Contact:
Dr. Lavern Weber

Oregon State University Seafoods Laboratory
250 36th Street
Astoria OR 97103
503-325-4531
Contact:
Dr. David L. Crawford

Rhode Island Sea Grant Marine Advisory Service
University of Rhode Island
Narragansett Bay Campus
Narragansett RI 02882
401-792-6211
Contact:
Edward Richardson

Rutgers University Shellfish Research Laboratory
P.O. Box 587
Port North Norris NJ 08349
609-785-0074
Contact:
Dr. Richard A. Lutz

The laboratory conducts research into a variety of areas connected with shellfish, including the development of disease-resistant oysters, soft crab shedding systems and the biology of hard clams. Rutgers' Fisheries and Aquaculture Technology Extension Center is concerned with the practical application of the laboratory's shellfish research and with seafood marketing.

University of Alaska, Fairbanks Institute of Marine Science
Fairbanks AK 99775
907-474-7531
Contact:
Dr. Vera Alexander

University of California, Davis Marine Food Science Group
Davis CA 95616
916-752-2506
Contact:
Norman F. Haard

University of Connecticut Marine Sciences Institute
Avery Point
Groton CT 06340
203-446-1020
Contact:
Dr. Donald F. Squires

University of Florida Florida Sea Grant College
Building 803
Gainesville FL 32611
904-392-5870
Contact:
Dr. James C. Cato

University of Hawaii, Manoa Sea Grant College Program
1000 Pope Road, MSB 220
Honolulu HI 96822
808-948-7031
Contact:
Dr. Jack R. Davidson

University of Oklahoma Aquatic Ecology and Fisheries Research Center
Norman OK 73019
405-325-4821
Contact:
Dr. Alan P. Covich

University of Oklahoma Aquatic Biology Center
Zoology Department
730 Van Vleet Oval
Norman OK 73019

University of Wisconsin, Madison Aquaculture & Food Engineering Laboratories
123 Babcock Hall
Madison WI 53706
608-263-2003
Contact:
Dr. C. H. Amundson

Nutrition Study Centers, Associations and Action Groups

Considerable knowledge has been gained in the field of nutrition in recent years, much of it of particular value to older people. Research has also led to major advances in the understanding and treatment of bulimia and anorexia nervosa, the two major eating disorders prevalent in young people.

The listing that follows, compiled from several sources, identifies major groups in the United States currently concerned with research in nutrition studies and eating disorders. The list is alphabetical by group name, and includes the name of a contact person and, where appropriate, a brief indication of the area of research activity.

Another aspect of the nutrition story is the issue of hunger in America. A directory entitled *Who's Involved with Hunger*, listing governmental and private agencies with a national focus as well as numerous regional organizations active in this field, can be obtained from World Hunger Education Service, 3018 4th Street NE, Washington DC 20017.

American Anorexia/Bulimia Association

133 Cedar Lane
Teaneck NJ 07666
201-836-1800
Contact:
Lisa Galper

The association is concerned with education, information, referrals and self-help groups for those suffering from eating disorders. Members, who pay a $50.00 annual membership fee, receive a newsletter at least twice a year which offers up-to-date information about eating disorders and their treatment. The association coordinates self-help/ support group meetings for sufferers and their families each month and the referral of individuals for help both nationally and internationally is an important part of its activities.

American Dietetic Association

216 West Jackson Boulevard,
Suite 800
Chicago IL 60606
312-899-0040
Contact:
Rhona Frankfort
Direction for research on health through nutrition

American Dietetic Association Foundation

216 West Jackson Boulevard, Suite 800
Chicago IL 60606
312-899-4825
Contact:
Philip J. Skeris
Fund-raising for ADA programs

American Institute of Nutrition

9650 Rockville Pike
Bethesda MD 20814
301-530-7050
Contact:
Richard G. Allison
Promotes research in nutrition

American Medical Association

535 North Dearborn Street
Chicago IL 60610
312-645-5070
Contact:
Information Services
Publishes materials, sets up a referral directory

Anorexia Nervosa and Related Eating Disorders (ANRED)

P.O. Box 5102
Eugene OR 97405
503-344-1144
Contact:
Jean Rubel

Calorie Control Council

5775 Peachtree-Dunwoody Road,
Suite 500-D
Atlanta GA 30342
404-252-3663
Contact:
Robert H. Kellen

Center for the Study of Anorexia and Bulimia

1 West 91st Street
New York NY 10024
212-595-3449
Contact:
Jane Supino

Dietary Managers' Association

400 East 22nd Street
Lombard IL 60148
708-932-1444
Contact:
William St. John

National Association of Anorexia Nervosa and Associated Disorders (ANAD)

P.O. Box 7
Highland Park IL 60035
708-831-3438
Contact:
Dawn Ries

National Nutritional Foods Association

125 East Baker Street,
Suite 230
Costa Mesa CA 92626
714-966-6632
Contact:
Patricia Heydlauff

Food Sciences Department, Purdue University

Smith Hall
West Lafayette IN 47907
317-494-8256
Contact:
P. E. Nelson
Effects of processing, packaging and storage on nutrient content

Georgia Institute of Human Nutrition, Medical College of Georgia

Augusta GA 30912
404-721-4861
Contact:
Elaine B. Feldman
Nutrition and disease

Human Nutrition Option, Mississippi State University

Drawer NH
Mississippi State MS 39762
601-325-3200
Contact:
Janet McNaughton
Alternate foods; biochemistry and the aging process

National Anorexic Aid Society

5796 Karl Road
Columbus OH 43229
614-436-1112
Contact:
Arline Iannicello

National Association to Advance Fat Acceptance (NAAFA)

P.O. Box 188620
Sacramento CA 95818
916-443-0303
Contact:
Sally Smith
Promotes tolerance and understanding of fat people

National Obesity Research Foundation

c/o David L. Margules
Weiss Hall 867, Temple University
Philadelphia PA 19122
215-787-8841
Contact:
David Margules
Disseminates information and funds research on obesity

North Dakota State University Food & Nutrition Research Laboratory

College of Home Economics
Fargo ND 58105
701-237-7567
Contact:
Susan Crockett
Food and nutrition research

Nutritional Effects Foundation

c/o Winrock International
Route 3, Box 376, Petit Jean Mountain
Morrilton AR 72110
501-727-5435
Contact:
Frank H. Baker
Provision of healthier, leaner, safer meat and other food products for consumers

Nutrition Information Center

515 East 71st Street,
Room 904
New York NY 10021
212-746-1617
Contact:
Barbara Levine
Nutritional education of physicians; clinical nutrition and nutritional research

Obesity Foundation

5600 South Quebec, Suite 160-D
Englewood CO 80111
303-779-4834
Contact:
Clair Williams
Educates health professionals and public on obesity

Ohio State University Human Nutrition Research Laboratory

265 Campbell Hall
1787 Neil Avenue
Columbus OH 43210
614-292-4485
Contact:
Wayne A. Johnson
Lipid, nitrogen and energy status of humans

Oklahoma State University Human Nutrition Center

Department of Food, Nutrition & Institution Administration
Stillwater OK 74078
405-744-5040
Contact:
Lea Ebro
Fiber and human nutrition, nutritional education for the elderly, nutritional analyses

Oregon State University Nutrition Research Institute

Corvallis OR 97331
503-737-2211
Contact:
James E. Oldfield
Coordinates university research in nutritional areas such as food processing and consumption for specific needs; publishes materials on nutrition

Overeaters Anonymous

P.O. Box 92870
Los Angeles CA 90009
213-542-8363
Contact:
Jorge Sever
Obesity control and recovery based on 12-step program

Society for Nutrition Education

1700 Broadway, Suite 300
Oakland CA 94612
415-444-7133
Contact:
Gwyn Donchin
Provides general reference services primarily for members; on contract basis to others

University of Texas Human Nutrition Center

P.O. Box 20186
Houston TX 77225
713-792-4660
Contact:
Milton Z. Michaman
Information on community, national and international health issues

World Hunger Education Service

3018 4th Street NE
Washington, DC 20017
202-347-4441

This agency was founded in 1976 to enable concerned individuals to find out how they can help combat hunger. The focus is on information and education and the program includes a model hunger action project based on work in the District of Columbia, which serves as a model for other cities.

As well as books and research reports, the agency publishes a bimonthly newsletter, *Hunger Notes*, which provides up-to-date information on world food problems and current policies. The agency's library may be used by appointment.

Federal Government Agencies

In this listing, information on the major federal agencies and those subsidiary services that are likely to be of interest to food professionals has been selected from the most recent edition of the *United States Government Manual*, which is updated annually.

The listings are given in alphabetical order with a suggested contact route and, where appropriate, a note of the materials that are available. Branches of the Food and Drug Administration are listed alphabetically by state, as are the retail bookstores operated by the Government Printing Office in individual states.

Center for Food Safety and Applied Nutrition

200 Independence Avenue SW
Washington DC 20201
202-673-6800

Department of Agriculture

14th Street & Independence Avenue SW
Washington DC 20250
202-447-2791
Contact:
Press Secretary

Department of Agriculture (cont'd.)

Food and Nutrition Service
3101 Park Center Drive
Alexandria VA 22302
703-756-3276
Contact:
Public Information Officer

Food Safety and Inspection Service
14th and Independence Avenue SW
Washington DC 20250
202-447-7943
Contact:
Director of Information
and Legislative Affairs

Human Nutrition Information
Service
6505 Belcrest Road
Hyattsville MD 20782
301-436-7725

Office of the Consumer Advisor
14th and Independence Avenue SW
Washington DC 20250
202-382-9681

Photography Division
Office of Governmental
and Public Affairs
14th and Independence Avenue SW
Washington DC 20250
202-447-6633
Priced film strips and slide sets

Video and Film
Office of Governmental
and Public Affairs
14th and Independence Avenue SW
Washington DC 20250
202-447-6072
Video and film rentals

Department of Health and Human Services
Food and Drug Administration

5600 Fishers Lane
Rockville MD 20857
301-443-1544
Consumer Affairs Officers
301-443-5006

BRANCH OFFICES:

California

1521 West Pico Boulevard
Los Angeles CA 90015
213-252-7597

50 United Nations Plaza,
Suite 506
San Francisco CA 94102
415-556-1457

Colorado

Denver Federal Center,
Building 20
P.O. Box 25087
Denver CO 80225
303-236-3031

Florida

7200 Lake Ellenor Drive,
Suite 120
Orlando FL 32809
305-855-0900

Georgia

60 8th Street NE
Atlanta GA 30309
404-347-7355

Illinois

1222 Main Post Office Building
and 433 West Van Buren Street
Chicago IL 60607
312-353-7126

Indiana

575 North Pennsylvania Street,
Suite 693
Indianapolis IN 46204
317-269-6500

Louisiana

4298 Elysian Fields Avenue
New Orleans LA 70122
504-589-6341

Maryland

900 Madison Avenue
Baltimore MD 21201
301-962-3731

Massachusetts

1 Montvale Avenue
Stoneham MA 02180
617-279-1479

Michigan

1560 East Jefferson Avenue
Detroit MI 48207
313-226-6274

Minnesota

240 Hennepin Avenue
Minneapolis MN 55401
612-334-4103

Missouri

1009 Cherry Street
Kansas City MO 64106
816-374-3817

808 North Collins Alley
St. Louis MO 63102
314-425-5021

Nebraska

200 South 16th Street
Omaha NE 68102
402-221-4675

New Jersey

61 Main Street
West Orange NJ 07052
201-645-3265

New York

599 Delaware Avenue
Buffalo NY 14202
716-846-4483

850 Third Avenue
Brooklyn NY 11232
718-965-5043

Ohio

1141 Central Parkway
Cincinnati OH 45202
513-684-3501

3820 Center Road
P.O. Box 838
Brunswick OH 44212
216-273-1038

Pennsylvania

2nd and Chestnut Streets,
Suite 900
Philadelphia PA 19106
215-597-0837

Tennessee

297 Plus Park Boulevard
Nashville TN 37217
615-738-2088

Texas

3032 Bryan Street
Dallas TX 75204
214-767-5433

1445 North Loop West
Houston TX 77008
713-229-3530

727 East Durango, Suite B-406
San Antonio TX 78206
512-229-6737

Washington

909 First Avenue
Seattle WA 98174
206-442-5265

Library of Congress
Science and Technology Division
101 Independence Avenue SE
Washington DC 20540
202-287-5639

United States Government
Printing Office
Superintendent of Documents
Washington DC 20402
202-783-3238
Free and priced publications

The Printing Office prints and distributes books and pamphlets published by Congress and the various agencies of the federal government. A free catalog is published regularly describing the books available. Titles are grouped by subject and include publications on agricultural, food and health topics. Books can be purchased by mail order or via a nationwide network of government bookstores at the locations listed below.

RETAIL BOOKSTORES:

Alabama
O'Neill Building
2021 Third Avenue North
Birmingham Al 35203
205-731-1056

California
ARCO Plaza, C Level
505 South Flower Street
Los Angeles CA 90071
213-894-5841

Federal Building, Suite 1023
450 Golden Gate Avenue
San Francisco CA 94102
415-556-0643

Colorado
Federal Building, Suite 117
1961 Stout Street
Denver CO 80294
303-844-3964

World Savings Building
720 North Main Street
Pueblo CO 81003
719-544-3142

District of Columbia
U.S. Government Printing Office
710 North Capitol Street NW
Washington DC 20401
202-275-2091

1510 H Street NW
Washington DC 20005
202-653-5075

Florida
Federal Building, Suite 158
400 West Bay Street
Jacksonville FL 32202
904-791-3801

Georgia
Federal Building, Suite 100
275 Peachtree Street NE
P.O. Box 56445
Atlanta GA 30343
404-331-6947

Illinois
Federal Building, Suite 1365
219 South Dearborn Street
Chicago IL 60604
312-353-5133

Maryland
Warehouse Sales Outlet
8660 Cherry Lane
Laurel MD 20707
301-953-7974

Massachusetts
Thomas P. O'Neill Building,
Suite 179
10 Causeway Street
Boston MA 02222
617-565-6680

Michigan
Federal Building, Suite 160
477 Michigan Avenue
Detroit MI 48226
313-226-7816

Missouri
120 Bannister Mall
5600 East Bannister Road
Kansas City MO 64137
816-765-2256

New York
26 Federal Plaza, Suite 110
New York NY 10278
212-264-3825

Ohio
Federal Building, Suite 1653
1240 East 9th Street
Cleveland OH 44199
216-522-4922

Federal Building, Suite 207
200 North High Street
Columbus OH 43215
614-469-6956

Oregon
1305 Southwest First Avenue
Portland OR 97201
503-221-6217

Pennsylvania
Robert Morris Building
100 North 17th Street
Philadelphia PA 19103
215-597-0677

Federal Building, Suite 118
1000 Liberty Avenue
Pittsburgh PA 15222
412-644-2721

Texas
Federal Building, Suite 1C46
1100 Commerce Street
Dallas TX 75242
214-767-0076

Texas Crude Building, Suite 120
801 Travis Street
Houston TX 77002
713-653-3100

Washington
Federal Building, Suite 194
915 Second Avenue
Seattle WA 98174
206-442-4270

Wisconsin
Federal Building, Suite 190
517 East Wisconsin Avenue
Milwaukee WI 53202
414-291-1304

State Government Agencies

This listing has been compiled from the United States Department of Agriculture publication, *Directory of State Departments of Agriculture*. The list is organized regionally, then alphabetically by state, and the contact name given is either that of the official in charge of public relations or the director of the department or agency.

Many states offer a variety of specialized services under the general supervision of their agricultural departments. These are listed in detail in the *Directory*, which is obtainable from the Financial Management Division, Agricultural Marketing Service, Washington DC 20250.

ALABAMA

Department of Agriculture and Industries
Richard Beard Building
1445 Federal Drive
P.O. Box 3336
Montgomery AL 36193
205-261-5872
Contact:
Gale Norman, Publications & Information

ALASKA

Division of Agriculture
P.O. Box 949
Palmer AK 99645
907-745-7200
Contact:
Frank Mielke, Director

ARIZONA

Arizona Commission of Agriculture and Horticulture
1688 West Adams, Room 421
Phoenix AZ 85007
602-542-4373
Contact:
I. J. Tiny Shield, Director

ARKANSAS

Arkansas State Plant Board
1 Natural Resources Drive
P.O. Box 1069
Little Rock AR 72203
501-225-1598
Contact:
Gerald King, Director

Livestock and Poultry Commission
1 Natural Resources Drive
Little Rock AR 72205
501-225-5138
Contact:
Taylor Woods, Director

CALIFORNIA

Department of Food and Agriculture
1220 N Street
P.O. Box 942871
Sacramento CA 94271
916-445-7126
Contact:
Jan Wessell, Communications Director

COLORADO

Department of Agriculture
1525 Sherman Street,
4th Floor
Denver CO 80203
303-866-2811
Contact:
Steven W. Horn, Commissioner

CONNECTICUT

Department of Agriculture
State Office Building
Hartford CT 06106
203-566-4667
Contact:
Kenneth B. Andersen, Commissioner

DELAWARE

State Department of Agriculture
2320 South DuPont Highway
Dover DE 19901
302-736-4811
Contact:
Roland Derrickson, Director

FLORIDA

Department of Agriculture and Consumer Services
The Capitol
Tallahassee FL 32399
904-488-3022
Contact:
Doyle Conner, Commissioner

GEORGIA

Department of Agriculture
Agriculture Building
Capitol Square
Atlanta GA 30334
404-656-3600
Contact:
Thomas T. Irvin, Commissioner

HAWAII

Department of Agriculture
P.O. Box 22159
Honolulu HI 96822
808-548-7101
Contact:
Yukio Kitagawa, Chair,
Board of Agriculture

IDAHO

Department of Agriculture
2270 Old Penitentiary Road
P.O. Box 790
Boise ID 83701
208-334-3240
Contact:
Richard R. Rush, Director

ILLINOIS

Department of Agriculture
State Fairgrounds
Springfield IL 62706
217-782-2172
Contact:
Larry A. Werries, Director

INDIANA

**Division of Agriculture,
Indiana Department of Commerce**
1 North Capitol Street,
Suite 700
Indianapolis IN 46204
317-232-8770
Contact:
Gary O. Swaim, Director

IOWA

**Department of Agriculture and Land
Stewardship**
Wallace Building
Des Moines IA 50319
515-281-5322
Contact:
Bill Brewer, Chief,
Public Information

KANSAS

State Board of Agriculture
109 Southwest 9th Street
Topeka KS 66612
913-296-3556
Contact:
Sam Brownback, Secretary

KENTUCKY

Department of Agriculture
Capitol Plaza Tower,
7th Floor
Frankfort KY 40601
502-564-4696
Contact:
Scott Willett, Director,
Communications Division

LOUISIANA

**Department of Agriculture and
Forestry**
P.O. Box 94302
Baton Rouge LA 70804
504-922-1234
Contact:
Bob Odom, Commissioner

MAINE

**Department of Agriculture, Food
and Rural Resources**
Augusta ME 04333
207-289-3871
Contact:
Peter Kress, Director of
Planning & Information

The numerous divisions in Maine's
Department of Agriculture, Food and
Rural Resources reflect the breadth of
the state's agricultural concerns. Among
them are the Division of Plant Industry,
the Maine Seed Potato Board, the State
Horticulturist, the Division of Quality
Assurance, the Grain and Apple
Inspection Department, the Consumer
Food Inspection & Returnable Contain-
ers Department, the Board of Pesticides
Control, the Dairy Inspection Depart-
ment and the Animal Welfare Board.

MARYLAND

Department of Agriculture
50 Harry S. Truman Parkway
Annapolis MD 21401
301-841-5880
Contact:
Harold Kanarek, Public
Information Officer

MASSACHUSETTS

Department of Food and Agriculture
Leverett Saltonstall Building
100 Cambridge Street
Boston MA 02202
617-727-3000
Contact:
August Schumacher Jr.,
Commissioner

MICHIGAN

Department of Agriculture
Ottawa Building North,
4th Floor
P.O. Box 30017
Lansing MI 48909
517-373-1050
Contact:
Margie Cooke, Director,
Press & Public Affairs

MINNESOTA

Department of Agriculture
90 West Plato Boulevard
St. Paul MN 55107
612-296-9310
Contact:
Jim Nichols, Commissioner

MISSISSIPPI

**Department of Agriculture and
Commerce**
P.O. Box 1609
Jackson MS 39215
601-359-7075
Contact:
Billy Cox, Public Information Officer

Just some among the many divisions
of the Mississippi Department of
Agriculture and Commerce are the
Catfish Marketing Division, the Farmers
Central Market, the Grain Warehouse
Division, the Market Development
Division, the Seed Laboratory, the Swine
Health Division, the Plant Industry
Division and the State Fair Commission.

MISSOURI

Department of Agriculture
1616 Missouri Boulevard
P.O. Box 630
Jefferson City MO 65102
314-751-4211
Contact:
Charles E. Kruse, Director

MONTANA

Department of Agriculture
Agriculture/Livestock Building
Capitol Station
Helena MT 59620
Contact:
Everett M. Snortland,
Director

NEBRASKA

Department of Agriculture
301 Centennial Mall South,
4th Floor West
P.O. Box 94947
Lincoln NE 68509
402-471-2341
Contact:
Stan Garbacz, Manager, Agricultural
Promotion & Development

NEVADA

Department of Agriculture
350 Capitol Hill Avenue
P.O. Box 11100
Reno NV 89510
702-789-0180
Contact:
Thomas W. Ballow,
Executive Director

NEW HAMPSHIRE

Department of Agriculture
Caller Box 2042
Concord NH 03302
603-271-3551
Contact:
Stephen H. Taylor,
Commissioner

NEW JERSEY

Department of Agriculture
John Fitch Plaza
CN 330
Trenton NJ 08625
609-292-3976
Contact:
Arthur R. Brown Jr., Secretary

NEW MEXICO

Department of Agriculture
P.O. Box 30005
Las Cruces NM 88003
505-646-3007
Contact:
Frank A. Dubois, Director/Secretary

NEW YORK

Department of Agriculture and Markets
Capital Plaza
1 Winner's Circle
Albany NY 12235
518-457-4188
Contact:
Gerald A. Moore, Director,
Public Information Services

NORTH CAROLINA

Department of Agriculture
P.O. Box 27647
Raleigh NC 27611
919-733-7125
Contact:
James F. Devine, Acting Director,
Public Affairs Division

NORTH DAKOTA

Department of Agriculture
600 East Boulevard, 6th Floor
State Capitol
Bismarck ND 58505
701-224-2231
Contact:
Ellen Crawford, Director,
Public Information

OHIO

Department of Agriculture
65 South Front Street
Columbus OH 43215
614-466-2732
Contact:
Alice Walters, Chief, Division of
Marketing & Communications

OKLAHOMA

Department of Agriculture
2800 North Lincoln
Oklahoma City OK 73105
405-521-3864
Contact:
Jack D. Craig, Commissioner

OREGON

Department of Agriculture
Salem OR 97310
503-378-4665
Contact:
Bruce Andrews, Director

PENNSYLVANIA

Department of Agriculture
Agriculture Building
2301 North Cameron Street
Harrisburg PA 17110
717-783-0133
Contact:
H. Eugene Schenck, Press
Secretary

RHODE ISLAND

Department of Environmental Management
9 Hayes Street
Providence RI 02908
401-277-2771
Contact:
Frances Segerson, Chief, Office of
Information & Education

SOUTH CAROLINA

Department of Agriculture
Wade Hampton Office Building
P.O. Box 11280
Columbia SC 29211
803-734-2210
Contact:
Robert B. Rogers, Assistant Commis-
sioner, Marketing Services

SOUTH DAKOTA

Department of Agriculture
445 East Capitol
Pierre SD 57501
605-773-3375
Contact:
Jay C. Swisher, Secretary

TENNESSEE

Department of Agriculture and Markets
Box 40627
Melrose Station
Nashville TN 37204
615-360-0103
Contact:
Tom Womack, Administrative
Assistant-Public Affairs

TEXAS

Department of Agriculture
P.O. Box 12847
Capitol Station
Austin TX 78711
512-463-7665
Contact:
Andy Welch, Coordinator,
Public Information

UTAH

Department of Agriculture
350 North Redwood Road
Salt Lake City UT 84116
801-538-7100
Contact:
Elwood Shaffer, Information Officer

VERMONT

Department of Agriculture
116 State Street
State Office Building
Montpelier VT 05602
802-832-2430
Contact:
Ronald A. Allbee, Commissioner

VIRGINIA

Department of Agriculture and Consumer Services
P.O. Box 1163
Richmond VA 23209
804-786-3501
Contact:
S. Mason Carbaugh, Commissioner

WASHINGTON

Department of Agriculture
406 General Administration Building
Olympia WA 98504
206-753-5063
Contact:
C. Alan Pettibone, Director

WEST VIRGINIA

Department of Agriculture
State Capitol
Charleston WV 25305
304-348-2201
Contact:
Howard Knotts, Director, Printing & Information

WISCONSIN

Department of Agriculture, Trade and Consumer Protection
801 West Badger Road
P.O. Box 8911
Madison WI 53708
608-266-7100
Contact:
Howard C. Richard, Secretary

WYOMING

Department of Agriculture
2219 Carey Avenue
Cheyenne WY 82002
307-777-7321
Contact:
Don Rolston, Commissioner

Chambers of Commerce

In addition to the United States Chamber of Commerce, the national organization in Washington DC, this listing includes one chamber in each state—either that of the state itself, if it has one, or that of its capital city. A complete listing of local chambers of commerce in every state can be found in the *World Chamber of Commerce Directory*, from which this selection was made. It is published annually in June and can be ordered from P.O. Box 1029, Loveland CO 80539.

United States Chamber of Commerce
1615 H Street NW
Washington DC 20062
202-659-6000
Contact:
Dr. Richard Lesher, President

The mission of the United States Chamber of Commerce is to represent its 850,000 members on all legislative issues which have an impact on small- to medium-sized businesses. Acting as a lobbyist, the chamber reviews such issues and develops policies as appropriate. These positions are then articulated to the general public as well as to Congress, the White House and the press.

A monthly magazine, *Nation's Business*, is sent to members and sold on newsstands.

ALABAMA

Montgomery Area Chamber of Commerce
41 Commerce Street
P.O. Box 79
Montgomery AL 36101
205-834-5200
Contact:
Randall L. George, Executive Vice President

ALASKA

Alaska State Chamber of Commerce
310 2nd Street
Juneau AK 99801
907-586-2323
Contact:
George Krusz, President

ARIZONA

Arizona State Chamber of Commerce
1366 East Thomas Road, Suite 202
Phoenix AZ 85012
602-248-9172
Contact:
Lowell Reese, President

ARKANSAS

Arkansas State Chamber of Commerce
100 Main Street, Suite 510
P.O. Box 3645 (72203)
Little Rock AR 72201
501-374-9225
Contact:
Bob Lamb, Executive Vice President

CALIFORNIA

California State Chamber of Commerce
P.O. Box 1736
Sacramento CA 95812
916-444-6670
Contact:
Kirk West, President

COLORADO

**Colorado Association
of Commerce & Industry**
1860 Lincoln Street, Suite 550
Denver CO 80295
303-831-7411
Contact:
George S. Dibble Jr., President

CONNECTICUT

**Greater Hartford Chamber
of Commerce**
250 Constitution Plaza
Hartford CT 06103
203-525-4451
Contact:
Timothy J. Moynihan, President

DELAWARE

**Delaware State Chamber
of Commerce**
1 Commerce Center, Suite 200
Wilmington DE 19801
302-655-7221
Contact:
William C. Wyer, President

DISTRICT OF COLUMBIA

**District of Columbia
Chamber of Commerce**
1411 K Street NW
Washington DC 20005
202-347-7201
Contact:
Marcus M. Griffith, President

FLORIDA

Florida State Chamber of Congress
136 South Bronough Street
P.O. Box 11309
Tallahassee FL 32302
904-222-2831
Contact:
Frank M. Ryll Jr., Executive
Vice President

GEORGIA

Business Council of Georgia
233 Peachtree Street, Suite 200
Atlanta GA 30303
404-223-2264
Contact:
Gene Dyson, President

HAWAII

Hawaii Chamber of Commerce
735 Bishop Street
Honolulu HI 96813
808-522-8800
Contact:
Robert B. Robinson, President

IDAHO

Boise Area Chamber of Commerce
711 West Bannock Street
P.O. Box 2368 (83701)
Boise ID 83702
208-344-5515
Contact:
Jay M. Clemens, President

ILLINOIS

**Illinois State Chamber
of Commerce**
20 North Wacker Drive
Chicago IL 60606
312-372-7373
Contact:
Lester W. Brann Jr., President

INDIANA

**Indiana State Chamber
of Commerce**
1 North Capitol Avenue, Suite 200
Indianapolis IN 46204
317-634-6407
Contact:
John W. Walls, President

IOWA

**Greater Des Moines Chamber
of Commerce**
309 Court Avenue, Suite 300
Des Moines IA 50309
515-286-4950
Contact:
Dr. Michael Reagen, President

KANSAS

**Kansas Chamber of Commerce
and Industry**
500 Bank IV Tower
Topeka KS 66603
913-357-6321
Contact:
Edward G. Brusko, President

KENTUCKY

**Kentucky State Chamber
ofCommerce**
452 Versailles Road
P.O. Box 817
Frankfort KY 40601
502-695-4700
Contact:
James Wiseman, Executive
Vice President

LOUISIANA

**Louisiana Association of
Business and Industry**
3113 Valley Creek Drive
P.O. Box 80258 (70898)
Baton Rouge LA 70808
Contact:
Maridel Avery, President

MAINE

Maine State Chamber of Commerce
126 Sewall Street
Augusta ME 04330
207-623-4568
Contact:
John S. Dexter Jr., President

MARYLAND

**Maryland State Chamber
of Commerce**
275 West Street, Suite 400
Annapolis MD 21401
301-269-0642
Contact:
Peter J. Lombardi, President

MASSACHUSETTS

**Greater Boston Chamber
of Commerce**
Federal Reserve Building
600 Atlantic Avenue
Boston MA 02210
617-227-4500
Contact:
James L. Sullivan, President

MICHIGAN

**Michigan State Chamber
of Commerce**
600 South Walnut Street
Lansing MI 48933
517-371-2000
Contact:
James Barrett, President

MINNESOTA

Minnesota State Chamber of Commerce
480 Cedar Street, Suite 300
St. Paul MN 55101
612-292-4650
Contact:
Winston Borden, President

MISSISSIPPI

Mississippi Economic Council, The State Chamber of Commerce
P.O. Box 1849
Jackson MS 39215
601-969-0022
Contact:
Bob W. Pittman, President

MISSOURI

Missouri State Chamber of Commerce
428 East Capitol Avenue
P.O. Box 149
Jefferson City MO 65102
314-634-3511
Contact:
Ron D. Roberson, President

MONTANA

Montana State Chamber of Commerce
2030 11th Avenue
P.O. Box 1730
Helena MT 59624
406-442-2405
Contact:
F. H. Boles, President

NEBRASKA

Nebraska Chamber of Commerce and Industry
1320 Lincoln Mall
P.O. Box 95128 (68509)
Lincoln NE 68508
402-474-4422
Contact:
Jack Swartz, President

NEVADA

Nevada State Chamber of Commerce
P.O. Box 3499
Reno NV 89505
702-786-3030
Contact:
Fred Davis, Executive Director

NEW HAMPSHIRE

Greater Concord Chamber of Commerce
244 North Main Street
Concord NH 03301
603-224-2508
Contact:
Steven D. Sade, President

NEW JERSEY

New Jersey State Chamber of Commerce
5 Commerce Street
Newark NJ 07102
201-623-7070
Contact:
Frederick A. Westphal, President

NEW MEXICO

Association of Commerce and Industry of New Mexico
2309 Renard Place SE, Suite 402
Albuquerque NM 87106
505-842-0644
Contact:
Mark Douglas, President

NEW YORK

New York State Chamber of Commerce
1 Commerce Plaza
Albany NY 12245
518-474-6950
Contact:
Vincent Tese, Commissioner

NORTH CAROLINA

North Carolina Association of Chamber of Commerce Executives
P.O. Box 1001
Raleigh NC 27602
919-828-0758
Contact:
Cynthia Cover, Executive Director

NORTH DAKOTA

North Dakota State Chamber of Commerce
808 Third Avenue South
P.O. Box 2467 (58108)
Fargo ND 58103
701-237-9461
Contact:
Dale O. Anderson, President

OHIO

Ohio State Chamber of Commerce
35 East Gay Street
Columbus OH 43215
614-228-4201
Contact:
John Reimers, President

OKLAHOMA

Oklahoma State Chamber of Commerce
4020 North Lincoln Boulevard
Oklahoma City OK 73105
405-424-4003
Contact:
Richard P. Rush, President

OREGON

Salem Area Chamber of Commerce
220 Cottage Street NE
Salem OR 97301
503-581-1466
Contact:
John Irelan, Executive
Vice Presdent

PENNSYLVANIA

Pennsylvania Chamber of Business and Industry
222 North 3rd Street
Harrisburg PA 17101
717-255-3252
Contact:
Clifford L. Jones, President

RHODE ISLAND

Greater Providence Chamber of Commerce
30 Exchange Terrace
Providence RI 02903
401-521-5000
Contact:
James G. Hagan, President

SOUTH CAROLINA

South Carolina State Chamber of Commerce
1301 Gervais Street
P.O. Box 11278 (29211)
Columbia SC 29201
803-799-4601
Contact:
Kenneth H. Oischager, Executive
Vice President

SOUTH DAKOTA

Industry and Commerce Association of South Dakota
P.O. Box 190
Pierre SD 57501
605-224-6161
Contact:
Julie Johnson, President

TENNESSEE

Nashville Area Chamber of Commerce
161 Fourth Avenue North
Nashville TN 37219
615-259-3900
Contact:
Keel Hunt, Executive
Vice President

TEXAS

Texas State Chamber of Commerce
300 West 15th Street, Suite 875
Austin TX 78701
512-472-1594
Contact:
Rex Jennings, President

UTAH

Utah State Chamber of Commerce Association
777 South State Street
Orem UT 84058
801-224-3636
Contact:
Steve T. Densley, President

VERMONT

Vermont State Chamber of Commerce
P.O. Box 37
Montpelier VT 05602
802-223-3443
Contact:
Christopher G. Barbieri,
President

VIRGINIA

Virginia State Chamber of Commerce
9 South 5th Street
Richmond VA 23219
804-644-1607
Contact:
Edwin C. Luther III, Executive
Vice President

WASHINGTON

Olympia/Thurston County Chamber of Commerce
1000 Plum Street SE
P.O. Box 1427 (98507)
Olympia WA 98501
206-357-3362
Contact:
Jacquie Kelley, Executive
Director

WEST VIRGINIA

West Virginia State Chamber of Commerce
300 Capitol Street, Suite 100
P.O. Box 2789 (25330)
Charleston WV 25301
304-342-1115
Contact:
John D. Hurd, President

WISCONSIN

Wisconsin Association of Manufacture and Commerce
501 East Washington Avenue
P.O. Box 352 (53701)
Madison WI 53703
608-258-3400
Contact:
James Haney, President

WYOMING

Greater Cheyenne Chamber of Commerce
301 West 16th Street
P.O. Box 1147 (82003)
Cheyenne WY 82001
Contact:
Larry T. Atwell, Executive
Vice President

Consumer Advocacy and Environmental Resource Groups

This alphabetical listing brings together the names of some of the major organizations concerned with advocating consumer rights and safety in various areas connected with food. It covers a wide range of interests from worrisome questions about the quality and safety of food to fears about irradiation. Environmental issues are addressed as are increasing consumer interests in alternative agriculture and concerns over the use of pesticides.

For every question there is a society devoted to finding answers.

Americans for Safe Food, Center for Science in the Public Interest
1501 16th Street NW
Washington DC 20036
202-332-9110
Contact:
Michael Jacobson, Executive Director
Food safety, diet, nutrition, alcohol-related concerns

Boycott McDonald's and Burger King Coalition

P.O. Box 1836 G.M.F.
Boston MA 02205
617-734-4068
Contact:
Heather Schofield, President

Coalition for Food Irradiation

1401 New York Avenue NW
Washington DC 20005
202-639-5994
Contact:
Ellen Morton, Executive Director

Community Nutrition Institute

2001 S Street NW
Washington DC 20009
202-462-4700
Contact:
Rodney Leonard, Executive Director

Concern, Inc.

1947 Columbia Road NW
Washington DC 20009
202-328-8160
Contact:
Susan Boyd, Executive Director
Environmental education association offering guidelines for community action

Conference of Consumer Organizations

P.O. Box 1158
Newton Center MA 02159
617-552-8184
Contact:
Robert J. McEwen, Chair

Congress Watch

215 Pennsylvania Avenue SE
Washington DC 20003
202-546-4996
Contact:
Craig McDonald, Director

Consumer Federation of America

1424 16th Street NW,
Suite 604
Washington DC 20036
202-387-6121
Contact:
Stephen J. Brobeck, Executive Officer

Consumers' Union of the United States

256 Washington Street
Mt. Vernon NY 10553
914-667-9400
Contact:
Rhoda H. Karpatkin, Executive Director

Environmental Defense Fund

257 Park Avenue South
New York NY 10010
212-505-2100
Contact:
Becky Duffrat, Media Liaison

Food & Drug Law Institute

1000 Vermont Avenue NW
Washington DC 20005
202-371-1420
Contact:
Frank A. Duckworth, President
Nonprofit educational association promoting public knowledge of laws and regulations

Food Research and Action Center

1319 F Street NW, Suite 500
Washington DC 20004
202-393-5060
Contact:
Robert J. Fersh, Executive
Director
Monitors federal food programs to alleviate hunger

Gross National Waste Product Forum

4201 South 31st Street, Suite 616
Arlington VA 22206
703-578-4627
Contact:
Dana D. Reynolds, Coordinator

This group is researching the economic effects of wasteful practices in the areas of agriculture, food and the environment. They are collecting data on a wide range of diverse but related subjects, including soil erosion, pesticides, pollution of water and the displacement of small farmers.

Institute for Alternative Agriculture

9200 Edmonston Road, Suite 117
Greenbelt MD 20770
301-441-8777
Contact:
Garth Youngberg, Executive Director
Compiles and publishes scientifically reliable information on alternative farming systems

The Land Institute

Route 3
Salina KS 67401
913-823-8967
Contact:
Jon Piper, Research Coordinator

The institute is one of many groups conducting research into the development of ecology-based agriculture. Its main focus is on how plants relate to each other in the natural ecosystem and how some of these relationships can be developed for agricultural use. Current projects include the development of new grain crops derived from perennial plants which currently grow wild.

National Alliance of Supermarket Shoppers

2 Broadlawn Avenue
Great Neck NY 11024
516-487-9750
Contact:
Martin Sloane, Executive Officer

If you want to become a smart shopper, this organization is for you. The Alliance publishes a weekly column, syndicated to 300 newspapers, which is full of tips on how to get the best value for money when you shop. It also helps shoppers who have had problems with supermarket coupons or refunds.

National Coalition Against the Misuse of Pesticides

530 7th Street NW
Washington DC 20003
202-543-5450
Contact:
Jane Cochersperger, Information Coordinator
Information clearinghouse on alternative pest-control methods

National Coalition to Stop Food Irradiation

P.O. Box 59-0488
San Francisco CA 94159
415-626-2734
Contact:
Mary Carol Randall

Natural Food Associates

P.O. Box 210
Atlanta TX 75551
214-796-4136
Contact:
Bill Francis, Executive Director

Natural Resources Defense Council

40 West 20th Street
New York NY 10011
212-727-2700
Contact:
Jennifer Steuzel, Membership Associate
A nonprofit group with 125,000 members, the Natural Resources Defense Council works on major environmental issues such as the use of pesticides in food and the quality of drinking water. The staff includes lawyers and scientists who help evaluate data which is then used to produce reports on diverse environmental

concerns. The council has offices in Washington, San Francisco and Los Angeles as well as New York City.

Public Voice for Food and Health Policy
1001 Connecticut Avenue NW, Suite 522
Washington DC 20036
202-659-5930
Contact:
Ellen Haas, Executive Director

Registered Food Lobbyists

This alphabetical listing of lobbyists currently registered in Washington is selected from those groups that are listed as lobbying for the food industry in the *1989 Washington Representatives*, published by Columbia Books, Inc., 1212 New York Avenue NW, Suite 330, Washington DC 20005. In most cases, we have selected institutes, associations and some Political Action Committees who represent more general food interests; companies marketing specific products have not been included here. For a more comprehensive listing, consult the *Directory*.

American Butter Institute
699 Prince Street, Suite 102
Alexandria VA 22314
703-549-2230
Contact:
Floyd D. Gaibler

American Cocoa Research Institute
7900 Westpark Drive, Suite A-320
McLean VA 22102
703-790-5011
Contact:
Richard T. O'Connell

American Fisheries Society
5410 Grosvenor Lane
Bethesda MD 20814
301-897-8616
Contact:
Carl R. Sullivan

American Frozen Food Institute
1764 Old Meadow Lane, Suite 350
McLean VA 22102
703-821-0770
Contact:
Steven C. Anderson

American Meat Institute
P.O. Box 3556
Washington DC 20007
703-841-2400
Contact:
Sara Lilygren

American Peanut Product Manufacturers' Institute
1055 Thomas Jefferson Street NW
Washington DC 20007
202-342-8525
Contact:
Richard Silverman

American Soybean Association
1300 L Street NW, Suite 950
Washington DC 20005
202-371-5511
Contact:
Nancy E. Foster

American Sugar Beet Growers' Association
1156 15th Street NW, Suite 1020
Washington DC 20005
202-833-2398
Contact:
Luther Markwart

Apple Processors' Association
1629 K Street NW, Suite 1100
Washington DC 20006
202-785-6715
Contact:
Paul S. Weller Jr.

Biscuit and Cracker Manufacturers' Association
1400 L Street NW, Suite 400
Washington DC 20005
202-898-1636
Contact:
Francis P. Rooney

Can Manufacturers' Institute
1625 Massachusetts Avenue NW, Suite 500
Washington DC 20036
202-232-4677
Contact:
J. Michael Dunn

Center for Science in the Public Interest
1501 16th Street NW
Washington DC 20036
202-332-9110
Contact:
Michael F. Jacobson

Chocolate Manufacturers' Association of the USA
7900 Westpark Drive, Suite A-320
McLean VA 22101
703-790-5011
Contact:
Susan Snyder Smith

Dairy and Food Industries Supply Association
6245 Executive Boulevard
Rockville MD 20852
301-984-1444
Contact:
Bruce D'Agostino

Dairy Industry Committee
6245 Executive Boulevard
Rockville MD 20852
301-984-1444
Contact:
Burke Wilford

Food and Drug Law Institute
1000 Vermont Avenue NW, Suite 1200
Washington DC 20005
202-371-1420
Contact:
Frank A. Duckworth

Food Industry Association Executives
1001 Connecticut Avenue NW, Suite 800
Washington DC 20036
202-296-8951
Contact:
Laura Devlin

Food Marketing Institute
1750 K Street NW, Suite 700
Washington DC 20006
202-452-8444
Contact:
Dagmar T. Farr

Food Marketing Institute Political Action Committee
1750 K Street NW, Suite 700
Washington DC 20006
202-452-8444
Contact:
Pat Davis

Food Processing Machinery and Supplies Association
200 Daingerfield Road
Alexandria VA 22314
703-684-1080
Contact:
George O. Melnykovich

The Food Processors' Institute
1401 New York Avenue NW
Washington DC 20005
202-393-0890
Contact:
Jill P. Strachan

Food Research and Action Center
1319 F Street NW, Suite 500
Washington DC 20004
202-393-5060
Contact:
Robert J. Fersh

Foodservice and Lodging Institute
1919 Pennsylvania Avenue NW, Suite 504
Washington DC 20006
202-659-9060
Contact:
Pam Sedarholm

Frozen Potato Products Institute
1764 Old Meadow Lane
McLean VA 22102
703-821-0770
Contact:
Steven C. Anderson

Future Farmers of America
P.O. Box 15160
Alexandria VA 22309
703-360-3600
Contact:
Larry D. Case

Grocery Manufacturers of America
1010 Wisconsin Avenue NW, Suite 800
Washington DC 20007
202-337-9400
Contact:
Jeffrey Nedelman

Institute of Shortening and Edible Oils
11750 New York Avenue NW
Washington DC 20006
202-783-7960
Contact:
Robert M. Reeves

International Apple Institute
P.O. Box 1137
McLean VA 22101
703-442-8850
Contact:
Derl I. Derr

International Banana Association
1101 Vermont Avenue NW, Suite 306
Washington DC 20005
202-371-1620
Contact:
Robert M. Moore

International Foodservice Distributors' Association
201 Park Washington Court
Falls Church VA 22046
703-532-9400
Contact:
Denis R. Zegar

International Frozen Food Association
1764 Old Meadow Lane
McLean VA 22102
703-821-0770
Contact:
Thomas B. House

International Ice Cream Association
888 16th Street NW
Washington DC 20006
202-296-4250
Contact:
Becky L. Davenport

Meat Industry Suppliers' Association
7297 Lee Highway, Suite N
Falls Church VA 22042
703-533-1159
Contact:
Clay D. Tyeryar

National-American Wholesale Grocers' Association
201 Park Washington Court
Falls Church VA 22046
703-532-9400
Contact:
Stephen P. Bower

National Anti-Hunger Coalition
1319 F Street NW, Suite 500
Washington DC 20004
202-393-5060
Contact:
Michele Tingling-Clemmons

National Association of Margarine Manufacturers
1005 E Street NW
Washington DC 20005
202-785-3232
Contact:
Charles E. Ehrhart

National Association of Meat Purveyors
8365-B Greensboro Drive
McLean VA 22102
703-827-5754
Contact:
Stanley J. Emerling

National Broiler Council
1155 15th Street NW, Suite 614
Washington DC 20005
202-296-2622
Contact:
Mary M. Colville

National Candy Wholesalers' Association
1120 Vermont Avenue NW,
Suite 1120
Washington DC 20005
202-463-2124
Contact:
Dennis Lavallee

National Cheese Institute
P.O. Box 20047
Alexandria VA 22320
703-549-2230
Contact:
Floyd D. Gaibler

National Coffee Service Association
4000 Williamsburg Square
Fairfax VA 22032
703-273-9008
Contact:
G. Dean Wood

National Confectioners' Association
7900 Westpark Drive, Suite A-320
McLean VA 22102
703-790-5750
Contact:
Philips H. Kimball

National Fisheries Institute
2000 M Street NW, Suite 580
Washington DC 20036
202-296-5090
Contact:
Lee Weddig

National Food Processors' Association
1401 New York Avenue NW,
Suite 400
Washington DC 20005
202-639-5900
Contact:
Lawrence T. Graham

National Food Processors' Association Political Action Committee
1401 New York Avenue NW,
Suite 400
Washington DC 20005
202-639-5900
Contact:
Lawrence T. Graham

National Frozen Food Association
204 E Street NE
Washington DC 20002
202-547-6340
Contact:
Mike Giuffrida

National Frozen Pizza Institute
1764 Old Meadow Lane, Suite 350
McLean VA 22102
703-821-0770
Contact:
Francis G. Williams

National Grocers' Association
1825 Samuel Morse Drive
Reston VA 22090
703-437-5300
Contact:
Richard A. Brown

National Pasta Association
1901 North Ft. Myer Drive, Suite 1000
Arlington VA 22209
703-841-0818
Contact:
Joseph M. Lichtenberg

National Peanut Council
1500 King Street, Suite 301
Alexandria VA 22314
703-838-9500
Contact:
Kimberly Cutchins

National Pork Board
1015 15th Street NW, Suite 402
Washington DC 20005
202-789-5607
Contact:
Jim Smith

National Pork Producers' Council
1015 15th Street NW, Suite 402
Washington DC 20005
202-789-5606
Contact:
Karen Coble

Peanut Butter and Nut Processors' Association
9005 Congressional Court
Potomac MD 20854
301-365-4080
Contact:
James E. Mack

Popcorn Institute
1101 Connecticut Avenue NW,
Suite 700
Washington DC 20036
202-857-1100
Contact:
Robert H. Wilbur

Salt Institute
206 North Washington Street
Alexandria VA 22314
703-549-4648
Contact:
Louis V. Priebe

Snack Food Association
1711 King Street, Suite 1
Alexandria VA 22314
703-836-4500
Contact:
Stephen E. Eure

Sweetener Users' Association
2100 Pennsylvania Avenue NW,
Suite 695
Washington DC 20037
202-872-8676
Contact:
Thomas A. Hammer

United Egg Producers
2501 M Street NW, Suite 410
Washington DC 20037
202-833-3123
Contact:
Kathy McCharen

United Fresh Fruit and Vegetable Association
727 North Washington Street
Alexandria VA 22314
703-836-3410
Contact:
John Addy

United Fresh Fruit and Vegetable Association Political Action Committee
727 North Washington Street
Alexandria VA 22314
703-836-3410
Contact:
John McClung

Food Fairs & FESTIVALS

285
State Fairs

288
Food Festivals

291
Cook-Offs and Competitions

State Fairs

This listing is alphabetical for those 40 states that hold annual statewide fairs. It includes the mailing address and telephone number for each fair's contact person and the month in which the event usually takes place. Alaska, Connecticut, Hawaii, Idaho, Massachusetts, New Hampshire, Pennsylvania, Rhode Island, Washington and the District of Columbia do not have state fairs; district or regional fairs are alternatives in several states. In major agricultural areas, county fairs also attract exhibitors and attendance on a grand scale.

State chambers of commerce are useful sources of additional information.

ALABAMA

Alabama State Fair
P.O. Box 3800-B
Birmingham AL 35208
205-787-2641
Contact:
M. L. House
Held in October

ARIZONA

Arizona State Fair
1826 West MacDowell Road
P.O. Box 6728 (85005)
Phoenix AZ 85007
602-252-6771
Contact:
Gary Montgomery
Held in October

ARKANSAS

Arkansas State Fair
P.O. Box 166660
Little Rock AR 72216
501-372-8341
Contact:
Sheila Magdlin
Held in October

CALIFORNIA

California State Fair
P.O. Box 15649
Sacramento CA 95852
916-924-2032
Contact:
Judy King
Held in August/September

COLORADO

Colorado State Fair
Colorado State Fairgrounds
Pueblo CO 81004
719-561-8484
Contact:
Jerry Robbe
Held in August/September

DELAWARE

Delaware State Fair
Delaware State Fairgrounds
P.O. Box 28
Harrington DE 19952
302-398-3269
Contact:
Gary Simpson
Held in July

FLORIDA

Florida State Fair
P.O. Box 11766
Tampa FL 33680
813-621-7821
Contact:
Tom Umiker
Held in February

GEORGIA

Georgia State Fair
P.O. Box 5260
Macon GA 31208
912-746-7184
Contact:
Charles Inman
Held in October

ILLINOIS

Illinois State Fair
P.O. Box 576
Springfield IL 62705
217-782-6661
Contact:
Merle S. Miller
Held in August

INDIANA

Indiana State Fair
Indiana State Fairgrounds
1202 East 38th Street
Indianapolis IN 46205
317-923-3431
Contact:
Donald W. Moreau Sr.
Held in August

IOWA

Iowa State Fair
State House
Des Moines IA 50319
515-262-3111
Contact:
Marion Lucas
Held in August

KANSAS

Kansas State Fair
Kansas State Fairgrounds
2000 North Poplar
Hutchinson KS 67502
316-662-6611
Contact:
Robert A. Gottschalk
Held in September

KENTUCKY

Kentucky State Fair
P.O. Box 37130
Louisville KY 40233
502-366-9592
Contact:
Harold Workman
Held in August

The Kentucky State Fair is held every August in the Bluegrass State. In addition to livestock shows, agriculture-related demonstrations, craft exhibits, rides and games, the Fair always features a canning and baking competition. Since 1985, the winners' recipes have been published in the *Official Kentucky State Fair Cookbook*. Flavor, texture and appearance are primary judging criteria. Blue-ribbon recipes are as varied as taco bread, pecan cake and the traditional Pride of Kentucky Pie.

LOUISIANA

Louisiana State Fair
P.O. Box 9100
Shreveport LA 71139
318-635-1361
Contact:
C. Ed Nelson
Held in October

MARYLAND

Maryland State Fair
P.O. Box 188
Timonium MD 21093
301-252-0200
Contact:
Howard M. Mosner
Held in August/September

MICHIGAN

Michigan State Fair
1120 West State Fair
Detroit MI 48203
313-368-1000
Contact:
Bernie Lennon
Held in August/September

The Michigan State Fair is held in August or early September to celebrate the agricultural bounty of the state. *Michigan State Fair Blue Ribbon Recipes* offers a compilation of winning recipes judged during the annual event. The second edition of the cookbook included blue-ribbon winners from 1980 to 1985. The recipes, primarily for baking and canning, cover a wide range of breads, cookies and cakes, as well as all manner of jams, preserves, condiments and salad dressings.

MINNESOTA

Minnesota State Fair
Minnesota State Fairgrounds
St. Paul MN 55108
612-642-2200
Contact:
Jim Sinclair
Held in August/September

MISSISSIPPI

Mississippi State Fair
P.O. Box 892
Jackson MS 39205
601-961-4000
Contact:
Billy J. Orr
Held in October

MISSOURI

Missouri State Fair
P.O. Box 111
Sedalia MO 65301
816-826-0570
Contact:
Arlene Rouchka
Held in August

MONTANA

Montana State Fair
P.O. Box 1524
Great Falls MT 59403
406-727-8900
Contact:
Bill Ogg
Held in July/August

NEBRASKA

Nebraska State Fair
P.O. Box 81223
Lincoln NE 68501
402-474-5371
Contact:
John Skold
Held in August/September

NEVADA

Nevada State Fair
1350-A North Wells Avenue
Reno NV 89512
702-322-4424
Contact:
Kim Peterson
Held in August

NEW JERSEY

New Jersey State Fair
P.O. Box 8174
Trenton NJ 08650
609-587-6300
Contact:
Elva Hausser
Held in August

NEW MEXICO

New Mexico State Fair
P.O. Box 8546
Albuquerque NM 87198
505-265-1791
Contact:
Sam Hancock
Held in September

NEW YORK

New York State Fair
New York State Fairgrounds
State Fair Boulevard
Syracuse NY 13209
315-487-7711
Contact:
Wayne H. Gallagher
Held in August/September

NORTH CAROLINA

North Carolina State Fair
1025 Blue Ridge Boulevard
Raleigh NC 27607
919-733-2626
Contact:
Sam G. Rand
Held in October

NORTH DAKOTA

North Dakota State Fair
P.O. Box 1796
Minot ND 58702
701-852-3113
Contact:
Gerald Iverson
Held in July

OHIO

Ohio State Fair
632 East 11th Avenue
Columbus OH 43211
614-644-3247
Contact:
Jack Foust
Held in August

OKLAHOMA

Oklahoma State Fair
P.O. Box 74943
Oklahoma City OK 73147
405-948-6700
Contact:
Don Hotz
Held in September

OREGON

Oregon State Fair
2330 17th Street NE
Salem OR 97310
503-378-3247
Contact:
Don Hillman
Held in August/September

SOUTH CAROLINA

South Carolina State Fair
P.O. Box 393
Columbia SC 29202
803-799-3387
Contact:
Gary Goodman
Held in October

SOUTH DAKOTA

South Dakota State Fair
P.O. Box 1275
Huron SD 57350
605-352-1431
Contact:
Robert Osborne
Held in August/September

TENNESSEE

Tennessee State Fair
P.O. Box 40208
Melrose Station
Nashville TN 37204
615-259-1960
Contact:
Alice Jackson
Held in September

TEXAS

Texas State Fair
P.O. Box 26010
Dallas TX 75226
214-565-9931
Contact:
Errol McKoy
Held in October

UTAH

Utah State Fair
155 North 1000 West
Salt Lake City UT 84116
801-538-8440
Contact:
Judy Terry
Held in September

VERMONT

Vermont State Fair
175 South Main Street
Rutland VT 05701
802-775-5200
Contact:
Beverly Davidson
Held in September

VIRGINIA

Virginia State Fair
P.O. Box 26805
Richmond VA 23261
804-228-3200
Contact:
Corris L. Teachworth
Held in September

WEST VIRGINIA

West Virginia State Fair
P.O. Drawer 986
Lewisburg WV 24901
304-645-1090
Contact:
E. W. Rock
Held in August

WISCONSIN

Wisconsin State Fair
State Fair Park
Milwaukee WI 53214
414-257-8800
Contact:
James W. Greiner
Held in August

WYOMING

Wyoming State Fair
P.O. Drawer 10
Douglas WY 82633
307-358-2398
Contact:
Dave Noble
Held in August

Food Festivals

This list of 64 of the food festivals that take place annually in the United States is organized alphabetically by state, with the dates currently set for 1990. The selection was made to establish a fair geographical distribution and includes all the regularly held major festivals connected with food.

Festivals, a distinctly American form of enjoyment, frequently include music, sideshows, beauty pageants, parades and contests of all kinds. New gatherings sprout up each year while others wither; these are the stalwarts that remain and are well worth visiting.

ALABAMA

National Peanut Festival
National Peanut Festival Association
1691 Ross Clark Circle SE
Dothan AL 36301
205-793-4323
Held in October

National Shrimp Festival
Gulf Shores Chamber of Commerce
Gulf Shores AL 36542
205-968-7511
Held in October

Sorghum Sopping Days
Town of Waldo, Route 3
Talladega AL 35160
205-362-9075
Held in September

ALASKA

Seward Silver Salmon Derby
Seward Chamber of Commerce
P.O. Box 749
Seward AK 99664
907-224-3046
Held in August

ARKANSAS

Arkansas Rice Festival
Weiner City Hall
P.O. Box 338
Weiner AR 72479
501-684-2284
Held in October

Pink Tomato Festival
Bradley County Chamber of Commerce
Municipal Building
206 North Myrtle Street
Warren AR 71671
501-226-5225
Held in June

Watermelon Festival
Hope-Hempstead County Chamber of Commerce
P.O. Box 250
Hope AR 71801
501-777-3640
Held in August

CALIFORNIA

Brussels Sprouts Festival
Santa Cruz Beach Boardwalk
400 Beach Street
Santa Cruz CA 95060
408-423-5590
Held in October

California Avocado Festival
Carpinteria Chamber of Commerce
5036 Carpinteria Avenue
P.O. Box 956
Carpinteria CA 93013
805-684-4101
Held in October

Carrot Festival
Holtville Chamber of Commerce
P.O. Box 185
Holtville CA 92250
619-356-2923
Held in January/February

Castroville Artichoke Festival
P.O. Box 1041
Castroville CA 95012
408-633-2465
Held in September

Castroville bills itself as the Artichoke Center of the World. Every year on the second weekend of September, Castroville hosts an Artichoke Festival. The streets of this little town, some 110 miles south of San Francisco and 16 miles north of Monterey, are lined with booths selling artichoke delicacies of every kind. Other attractions are a beauty pageant, a foot race, a parade and a flea market.

Gilroy Garlic Festival
Garlic Festival Association
P.O. Box 2311
Gilroy CA 95021
408-842-1625
Held in July

Lodi Grape Festival
Grape Festival Grounds
413 East Lockford
Lodi CA 95241
209-369-2771
Held in September

Mushroom Mardi Gras
Morgan Hill Chamber of Commerce
P.O. Box 786
Morgan Hill CA 95038
408-779-9444
Held in May

National Date Festival
P.O. Drawer NNNN
Indio CA 92202
619-342-8247
Held in February

The National Date Festival is the only fair in the country with camel and ostrich races. Celebrating the date harvest, the festival welcomes nearly 200,000 visitors to the tiny town of Indio, deep in California's fertile Coachella Valley. Date palms were planted here at the turn of the century and today the groves bring forth nearly all the dates consumed in the western world. Following an elaborate Moorish theme, the festival crowns a Queen Scheherazade and stages an Arabian Nights Pageant.

Oxnard Strawberry Festival
Oxnard Chamber of Commerce
325 South A Street
Attn:Commerce Service Department/
Special Events Office
Oxnard CA 93030
805-984-4715
Held in May

Sebastopol Apple Blossom Festival
Sebastopol Chamber of Commerce
P.O. Box 178
Sebastopol CA 95473
707-823-3032
Held in April

CONNECTICUT

Windsor Shad Derby
Windsor Chamber of Commerce
43 Poquonock Avenue
Windsor CT 06095
203-688-5165
Held in May

DELAWARE

Delmarva Chicken Festival (Delmarva Poultry Industry, Inc.)
R.D. 2, Box 47
Georgetown DE 19947
302-856-9037
Held in June

Each year in early June, one of the towns on the Delmarva Peninsula—a 200-mile area located in the states of Delaware, Maryland and Virginia— hosts the Delmarva Chicken Festival. The weekend affair includes a Poultry Princess pageant, a chicken plucking contest and exhibits on the chicken- raising industry. Without question, the festival's highlight is the cook-off, and the creator of the winning recipe subse- quently competes in the finals of the National Chicken Cook-Off in Dallas.

FLORIDA

Boggy Bayou Mullet Festival
Niceville Chamber of Commerce
P.O. Box 231
Niceville FL 32578
904-678-2323
Held in October

Swamp Cabbage Festival
P.O. Box 2081
La Belle FL 33935
813-675-1717
Held in February

GEORGIA

Fall on the Flint Festival
Albany Chamber of Commerce
P.O. Box 308
Albany GA 31701
912-883-6900
Held in September

HAWAII

Kona Coffee Festival
Kailua-Kona Chamber of Commerce
75-5737 Kuakini Highway, Suite 206
Kailua-Kona HI 96740
808-329-1758
Held in November

ILLINOIS

Burgoo Festival
P.O. Box 278
Utica IL 61373
815-667-4861
Held in October

INDIANA

Maple Sugaring Days
Prairie Creek Park
Terre Haute IN 47808
812-238-8413
Held in February

Persimmon Festival
City of Mitchell Chamber
of Commerce
P.O. Box 216
Mitchell IN 47446
812-849-2151
Held in September

The native American fruit, little known to most Americans and quite unlike the cultivated Asian persimmon, is celebrated every September in this small midwestern town. During the festival, cooks make persimmon pud- ding and pie to sell at the booths lining Mitchell's streets (plenty of other typical fair-type food is available, too). The major event of the week-long festival is the cooking contest. Persimmon aficio- nados develop recipes for two categories: pudding and everything else!

KANSAS

Beefiesta
221 West Fifth
Scott City KS 67871
316-872-3525
Held in August

KENTUCKY

Marion County Ham Days
Lebanon-Marion County Chamber
of Commerce
Lebanon KY 40033
502-692-2661
Held in September

LOUISIANA

Breaux Bridge Crawfish Festival
Crawfish Festival Merchants
Association, Inc.
117 North Main Street
Breaux Bridge LA 70517
318-332-2345
Held in May

Gumbo Festival
P.O. Box 9069
Bridge City LA 70094
504-436-4712
504-436-9360
Held in October

The second weekend in October is the time for some good, down-home gumbo served up annually at the fair- grounds in Bridge City, self-proclaimed as the world's gumbo capital. The tradi- tional Creole and Cajun stew, thickened with okra or file powder, comes in many guises, among them seafood gumbo and chicken and andouille sausage gumbo. Both are highly seasoned and beg to be washed down with beer, sodas and a regional, strawberry-flavored soft drink called "pop rouge."

Jambalaya Festival
Jambalaya Festival Association
P.O. Box 1243
Gonzales LA 70737
504-647-7487
Held in June

Louisiana Pecan Festival
Colfax LA 71417
318-627-3711
Held in November

MAINE

Central Maine Egg Festival
Central Maine Egg Festival
Corporation
Pittsfield ME 04967
207-487-3259
Held in July

Maine Lobster Festival
Winter Harbor Chamber of Commerce
Winter Harbor ME 04693
207-963-2235
Held in August

State of Maine Blueberry Festival
Union Fair
Knox Agricultural Society
Union ME 04862
207-785-4173
Held in August

MARYLAND

National Hard Crab Derby
National Hard Crab Derby
& Fair
P.O. Box 215
Crisfield MD 21817
301-968-2500
Held in August/September

Crisfield, a small town at the southern tip of Maryland on the Chesapeake Bay, hosts the annual National Hard Crab Derby & Fair. The event, honoring Maryland's famous blue crab, includes an actual derby in which live crabs compete in the Governor's Cup Race. It also features a crab-picking contest, parades and fireworks. Crabs for eating are abundantly evident, notably Maryland steamed crabs cooked with a coating of peppery Chesapeake Bay seasoning.

St. Mary's County Oyster Festival
P.O. Box 198
Hollywood MD 20636
301-373-5242
Held in October

MASSACHUSETTS

Ipswich Strawberry Festival
20 North Main Street
Ipswich MA 01938
508-356-5660
Held in June

Shaker Kitchen Festival
Hancock Shaker Village
P.O. Box 898
Pittsfield MA 01202
413-443-0188
Held in July

Every August the Hancock Shaker Village holds its week-long Kitchen Festival during which traditional Shaker dishes are demonstrated. Available for sampling are such tempting items as quick breads, molasses candy and fried cakes.

World's People's Dinners are an important part of the festival. These are family-style meals served in a simple Shaker setting—the Believers Dining Room in the village's 1830 Brick Dwelling—for which all the food is prepared according to original Shaker recipes.

MICHIGAN

Harrison Mushroom Festival
Harrison Chamber of Commerce
P.O. Box 682
Harrison MI 48625
517-539-6011
Held in May

National Asparagus Festival
P.O. Box 117
Shelby MI 49455
616-861-5530
Held in June

National Cherry Festival
Traverse City Chamber of Commerce
P.O. Box 141
Traverse City MI 49684
616-947-5075
Held in July

National Mushroom Hunting Championship
Boyne City Chamber of Commerce
28 South Lake Street
Boyne City MI 49712
616-582-6222
Held in May

MINNESOTA

Minnesota Wild Rice Festival
Wild Rice Festival Committee
Kelliher MN 56650
218-647-8236
Held in July

MISSISSIPPI

World Catfish Festival
Belzoni Chamber of Commerce
P.O. Box 268
Belzoni MS 39038
601-247-4838
Held in April

NEBRASKA

Applejack Festival
Nebraska City Chamber of Commerce
P.O. Box 245
Nebraska City NE 68410
402-873-6654
Held in September

NEVADA

National Basque Festival
Elko Chamber of Commerce
P.O. Box 470
Elko NV 89801
702-738-7135
Held in June/July

NEW MEXICO

Hatch Chile Festival
Hatch Valley Chamber of Commerce
P.O. Box 38
Hatch NM 87937
505-267-3021
Held in September

NORTH CAROLINA

Lexington Barbecue Festival
P.O. Box 1642
Lexington NC 27293
704-243-2629
Held in October

Strange Seafood Exhibition
120 Turner
Beaufort NC 28516
919-728-7317
Held in August

OHIO

Circleville Pumpkin Show
P.O. Box 288
Circleville OH 43113
614-474-4923
Held in October

OREGON

Tillamook Swiss Festival
Tillamook County Chamber
of Commerce
3705 Highway 101 North
Tillamook OR 97141
503-842-7525
Held in March

PENNSYLVANIA

McClure Bean Soup Festival
McClure Bean Soup Committee
McClure PA 17841
717-658-8425
Held in September

SOUTH CAROLINA

Crawfish Festival
Georgetown County Chamber
of Commerce
P.O. Box 569
Pawleys Island SC 29585
803-546-8436
Held in April

Okra Strut
Town of Irmo
1239 Columbia Avenue
P.O. Box 406
Irmo SC 29063
803-781-7050
Held in October

TENNESSEE

Cosby Ramp Festival
Newport-Cocke County Chamber
of Commerce
803 Prospect
Newport TN 37821
615-623-7201
Held in May

TEXAS

Black-Eyed Pea Jamboree
Athens Chamber of Commerce
P.O. Box 608J
Athens TX 75751
214-675-5181
Held in July

The Black-Eyed Pea Jamboree takes
place every June in Athens, Texas, the
capital of the black-eyed pea world. As
might be expected, there is a black-eyed
reci-pea contest, with contestants in four
categories. Other activities at this well-
attended festival include a parade, a
swim meet, a pea-shelling contest, a
bicycle race and an arts and crafts show.

VERMONT

Vermont Maple Festival
Vermont Maple Festival
Council, Inc.
P.O. Box 255
St. Albans VT 05478
802-524-5800
Held in April

VIRGINIA

Chincoteague Oyster Festival
Chincoteague Chamber
of Commerce
P.O. Box 258
Chincoteague Island VA 23336
804-336-6161
Held in October

Eastern Shore Seafood Festival
Chincoteague Chamber of Commerce
P.O. Box 258
Chincoteague Island VA 23336
804-336-6161
Held in May

Pork, Peanut and Pine Festival
Chippokes State Park
Surry VA 23883
804-294-3021
Held in July

WASHINGTON

Indian-Style Salmon Bake
Sequim Chamber of Commerce
P.O. Box 907
Sequim WA 98382
206-683-6197
Held in August

WEST VIRGINIA

Apple Butter Festival
Berkley Springs-Morgan County
Chamber of Commerce
204 North Washington Street
Berkley Springs WV 25411
304-258-3738
Held in October

**West Virginia Black
Walnut Festival**
P.O. Box 77
Spencer WV 25276
304-927-1780
Held in October

Cook-Offs and Competitions

Cook-offs were probably
the original drawing
cards for state fairs. When
the menfolk came to exhibit
their prize cattle or turnips,
farm women brought their
pies and pickles and ex-
changed recipes for those
they thought the best. Once
the American spirit of competition came of age, the
housewives started doing
their baking and cooking in
public—and the cook-off
was born.

Though some cook-offs
still survive as the basis for
country food festivals, these
days most of them are sponsored by various organizations as promotions for a specialty food or foods. The alphabetical listing that follows gives the names of those
associations or companies
that are currently sponsoring
cook-offs, with the name and
title of the person to contact
for further information.

American Dry Pea & Lentil Association

Stateline Office
5071 Highway 8 West
Moscow ID 83843
208-882-3023
Contact:
Merilee Frets, Director,
U.S. Market Development

American Lamb Council

6911 South Yosemite Street
Englewood CO 80112
303-771-3500
Contact:
Arlene Brockel, Secretary, Lamb Product
Publicity Department

Borden, Inc.

180 East Broad Street
Columbus OH 43215
614-225-4037
Contact:
Veronica Petta, Manager,
Product Publicity

California Beef Council

551 Foster City Boulevard,
Suite A
Foster City CA 94404
415-571-7100
Contact:
Mary Ryan, Director of
Communications

The National Beef Cook-Off has been
held since the mid-1970s, always in
different locations across the United
States. Now the contest has evolved to
include three categories: indoor cooking,
barbecue and microwave. Winners in
each category receive $5,000. A grand
winner is awarded an additional $10,000
and his or her recipe represents the "Best
of Beef" for that year. The recipes are
judged by a panel of 10 nationally
known food authorities.

California Fresh Market Tomato Advisory Board

531-D North Alta Avenue
Dinuba CA 93618
209-591-0437
Contact:
Ed Beckman, Manager,
Market Development

Catfish Farmers of America

1100 Highway 82 East, Suite 202
Indianola MS 38751
601-887-2699
Contact:
Hugh Warren, Executive
Vice President

Indiana Beef Council

8770 Guion Road, Suite A
Indianapolis IN 46268
317-872-2333
Contact:
Susan E. Jackson,
Consumer Affairs Director

Indiana Pork Producers Association

8645 Guion Road, Suite I
Indianapolis IN 46268
317-872-7500
Contact:
Julie Miller,
Consumer Affairs Coordinator

International Chili Society

P.O. Box 2966
Newport Beach CA 92663
714-631-1780
Contact:
Jim West, Executive Director

Since its very humble beginnings in
1967 with only two cooks, the World's
Championship Chili Cook-Off has
grown into a major event. With as many
as 2 million attendees and 9,000 contestants, the annual contest at the Tropico
Goldmine in Rosamond, California, has
become a pilgrimage for chiliheads from
around the world. The International
Chili Society, which runs the cook-off,
annually sanctions some 300 events that
raise more than $2 million for charity.

Kraft, Inc.

Kraft Court
Glenview IL 60025
708-998-2000
Contact:
Kim Ward Burson,
Publicity Department

March of Dimes Birth Defects Foundation

1275 Mamaroneck Avenue
White Plains NY 10605
914-428-7100
Contact:
Elaine Whitelaw, Special Assistant to
the President

Since it began in 1976 as part of the
Bicentennial celebration, the March of
Dimes Gourmet Gala has raised millions
of dollars. Approximately 40 annual
galas are held each year across the country. At each one, celebrities from the
arts, government and media prepare
dishes, which are judged by a panel of
prominent food professionals. Guests
pay from $100 to $750 a ticket to dine
on these celebrity creations. In 1988

alone, the galas, for which the expenses
are completely underwritten, raised $5
million for the March of Dimes.

National Beef Cook-Off

444 North Michigan Avenue
Chicago IL 60611
312-467-5520
Contact:
Jane Lindeman,
Beef Cook-Off Coordinator

National Orange Show

689 South E Street
P.O. Box 5749 (92412)
San Bernardino CA 92408
714-383-5444
Contact:
Eileen Tillevy,
Coordinator, Home Arts

National Pork Producers Council

P.O. Box 10383
Des Moines IA 50306
515-223-2600
Contact:
Robin Kline, Director of
Consumer Affairs

New Jersey Department of Agriculture Fisheries Development Advisory Council

CN 330
Trenton NJ 08625
609-984-1608
Contact:
Tracy R. Bacek, Fish and
Seafood Development Program

To encourage more home cooking of
local fish and seafood, the New Jersey
Department of Agriculture sponsors the
Fabulous "Fishing for Compliments"
recipe contest. The contest is held during the summer months and is publi-
cized by point-of-purchase displays and
newspapers. From the hundreds of entries a panel of experts selects five finalists, each of whom receives a $200 prize.
An overall winner is selected at a celebration dinner and winning recipes are
featured in newspapers and magazines.

North Dakota Wheat Commission

4023 North State Street
Bismarck ND 58501
701-224-2498
Contact:
Margie Martin,
Product Promotion Specialist

The Pillsbury Company
2727 Pillsbury Center
Minneapolis MN 55402
612-330-4719
Contact:
Marlene Johnson, Manager, Product
Communications

From 1949 until 1975 The Pillsbury
Bake-Off Contest was held annually; it is
now held in the winter of every other
year. Pillsbury solicits recipes from
consumers through Pillsbury products,
point-of-purchase display advertisements and media exposure. An independent judging organization selects
100 finalists, who are flown to that year's
host city for the three-day event, where
they compete for $100,000 in cash prizes
awarded by a panel of eight judges emi-
nent in the food world.

Planters LifeSavers Company
1100 Reynolds Boulevard
Winston-Salem NC 27102
919-741-2000
Contact:
Charles F. Wallington,
Manager of Communications

Started in 1987, the Planters Holiday
Baking Contest encourages the use of
nuts in desserts. The grand prize of
$100,000 in savings bonds is thought to
be the largest single prize awarded in a
recipe contest. Entry forms are available
late in the year in supermarkets or can be
obtained from Planters Recipe Contest,
P.O. Box 1928, East Hanover NJ
07937. Entries are judged on the basis of
originality, creativity, ease of preparation, apprearance, taste, availability of
ingredients and clarity.

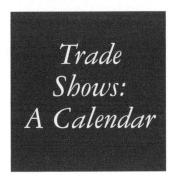

Trade Shows: A Calendar

1990

JANUARY

14 - 17
National Housewares Manufacturers' Association
International Housewares Exposition
McCormick Place
Chicago IL

Exhibits: 1,900   *Attendance:* 60,000

Contact:
Brian Casey
Show Manager
1324 Merchandise Mart
Chicago IL 60654
312-644-3333

14 - 17
Northwest Food Processors' Association
Northwest Food Processors' Convention
and Exposition
Washington State Convention Center
Seattle WA

Exhibits: 325   *Attendance:* 3,000

Contact:
Patricia Wolvert
Convention Manager
2300 Southwest First Avenue
Portland OR 97201
503-226-2848

21 - 24
National Grocers' Association
1990 Convention: The Winner's Edge
San Antonio Convention Center
San Antonio TX

Exhibits: 400   *Attendance:* 5,000

Contact:
Linda Leiby
Vice President, Conventions and Meetings
1825 Samuel Morse Drive
Reston VA 22090
703-437-5300

22 - 24
International Caterers' Association
International Caterers' Show and Conference
Mirage Hotel
Las Vegas NV

Exhibits: 75   *Attendance:* 1,600

Contact:
Robert Kolinek
Executive Director
220 South State Street, Suite 1416
Chicago IL 60604
312-922-1271

24 - 27
National Association of Pizza Operators
Pizza Expo '90
Las Vegas Convention Center
Las Vegas NV

Exhibits: 700   *Attendance:* 5,000

Contact:
Vera Adkins
Show Manager
Box 114
Santa Claus IN 47579
812-937-4464

FEBRUARY

2 - 4
National Food Distributors' Association
Midwinter Conference
San Antonio Hilton and Convention Center
San Antonio TX

Exhibits: 200   *Attendance:* 600 - 800

Contact:
Irene Condon
Convention Manager
111 East Wacker Drive
Chicago IL 60601
312-644-6610

7 - 9
International Seafood Exposition
Seafood International 1990
Long Beach Convention Center
Long Beach CA

Exhibits: 550   *Attendance:* 14,000

Contact:
John Cooksey
General Manager
454 North 34th Street
Seattle WA 98103
206-547-6030

11 - 13

United Fresh Fruit and Vegetable Association
86th Annual Convention and Exposition
San Antonio Convention Center
San Antonio TX

Exhibits: 400   *Attendance:* 7,000

Contact:
Jessica Grace
Exhibits and Meetings Coordinator
727 North Washington Street
Alexandria VA 22314
703-836-3410

14 - 18

National Candy Wholesalers' Association
31st National Winter Convention and Exposition
Moscone Center
San Francisco CA

Exhibits: 550   *Attendance:* 7,000

Contact:
Dottie Russell
Convention Manager
1120 Vermont Avenue NW, Suite 1120
Washington DC 20005
202-463-2124

24 - 28

American Frozen Food Institute
Western Frozen Food Convention
Hyatt Regency
Monterey CA

Exhibits: none   *Attendance:* 1,600

Contact:
Traci Vasilik
Manager of Communications
1764 Old Meadow Lane, Suite 350
McLean VA 22102
703-821-0770

M A R C H

4 - 7

National American Wholesale Grocers' Association
Dollars and Sense 1990
Rivergate Center
New Orleans LA

Exhibits: 450   *Attendance:* 3,000

Contact:
Rob Milko
Convention Coordinator
201 Park Washington Court
Falls Church VA 22046
703-532-9400

4 - 6

National Association for the Specialty Food Trade
International Fancy Food and Confection Show
Moscone Center
San Francisco CA

Exhibits: 800 - 900   *Attendance:* 18,000 - 25,000

Contact:
Show Manager
215 Park Avenue South, Suite 1606
New York NY 10003
212-505-1770

10 - 12

Natural Foods Exposition West
Anaheim Convention Center
Anaheim CA

Exhibits: 550   *Attendance:* 13,000

Contact:
Pam Breen
Events Director
1301 Spruce Street
Boulder CO 80302
303-939-8440

10 - 13

Retail Bakers of America
Anniversary Convention and Exhibition
Hynes Veterans' Memorial Convention Center
Boston MA

Exhibits: 800   *Attendance:* 9,000

Contact:
Richard C. Gohla
Executive Vice President
6525 Belcrest Road, Suite 250
Hyattsville MD 20782
301-277-0990

10 - 13

Snack Food Association
Snaxpo '90
Marriott Hotel and Convention Center
San Diego CA

Exhibits: 175 - 200   *Attendance:* 2,000

Contact:
Peggy Batchelor
Meeting Planner
1711 King Street, Suite 1
Alexandria VA 22314
703-836-4500

A P R I L

22 - 25
George Little Management, Inc.
The Gourmet Show
Moscone Center and Civic Auditorium/Brooks Hall
San Francisco CA

Exhibits: 600 *Attendance:* 10,000

Contact:
Susan G. Corwin
Show Manager
577 Airport Boulevard, 4th Floor
Burlingame CA 94010
415-344-5171

29 - May 1
Specialty Coffee Association of America
Specialty Coffee Conference and Trade Show
Claremont Resort
Oakland CA

Exhibits: 40 *Attendance:* 500

Contact:
Daryl Davidson
1101 14th Street NW, Suite 1100
Washington DC 20005
202-371-1347

M A Y

6 - 9
Food Marketing Institute
Supermarket Industry Education Exposition
McCormick Place
Chicago IL

Exhibits: 850 Attendance: 34,000

Contact:
Brian E. Tully
Director
1750 K Street NW, Suite 700
Washington DC 20006
202-452-8444

19 - 23
National Restaurant Association
Restaurant-Hotel-Motel Show
McCormick Place
Chicago IL

Exhibits: 2,000 *Attendance:* 106,000

Contact:
Theresa Struppa
Convention Services Manager
150 North Michigan Avenue
Chicago IL 60601
312-853-2525

J U N E

3 - 5
International Dairy-Deli Association
Annual Convention
Baltimore Convention Center
Baltimore MD

Exhibits: 260 *Attendance:* 2,500

Contact:
Carol Christison
Executive Director
313 Price Place
P.O. Box 5528
Madison WI 53705
608-238-7908

9 - 12
Tradexpo
New York Pizza and Fast Food Show
Jacob Javits Center
New York NY

Exhibits: 400 *Attendance:* 10,000

Contact:
Hal Barry
Marketing Director
P.O. Box 802079
Chicago IL 60680
800-722-9995

16 - 18
Retail Confectioners International
Retail Confectioners' Convention and Industry
Exposition
Omni Shoreham
Washington DC

Exhibits: 125 *Attendance:* 1,500

Contact:
Evans Billington
Executive Director
1807 Glenview Road, Suite 204
Glenview IL 60020
708-724-6120

J U L Y

2 - 6
National Association of College and University Food
Services
Star-Spangled Future
Baltimore Convention Center
Baltimore MD

Exhibits: 150 *Attendance:* 500

Contact:
Clark DeHaven
Executive Director
1405 South Harrison Road, Suite 303
Manly Miles Building
East Lansing MI 48824
517-332-2494

21 - 24
National Nutritional Foods Association
Trade Show
Hynes Veterans' Memorial Convention Center
Boston MA

Exhibits: 500   *Attendance:* 7,500

Contact:
Tammy Simpson
Exhibition Manager
125 East Baker Avenue, Suite 230
Costa Mesa CA 92626
714-966-6632

22 - 25
American Culinary Federation
National Convention
New Orleans Hilton and Riverside Towers
New Orleans LA

Exhibits: 120   *Attendance:* 1,300

Contact:
Ron Wolf
P.O. Box 3466
St. Augustine FL 32084
904-824-4468

OCTOBER

14 - 17
National Frozen Food Association
National Frozen Food Convention and Exposition
San Francisco Hilton
San Francisco CA

Exhibits: 125   *Attendance:* 2,500

Contact:
Shirley Spahr
P.O. Box 398
Hershey PA 17033
717-534-1601

29 - 31
Midwest Food Processors' Association
Midwest Food Processors' Convention and Exposition
Hyatt Regency Milwaukee
Milwaukee WI

Exhibits: 200   *Attendance:* 1,100

Contact:
Sue Wiggen
Program Director
P.O. Box 1297
Madison WI 53701
608-255-9946

NOVEMBER

2 - 4
Natural Foods Exposition East
Philadelphia Civic Center
Philadelphia PA

Exhibits: 500   *Attendance:* 9,000

Contact:
Pam Breen
Events Director
1301 Spruce Street
Boulder CO 80302
303-939-8440

11 - 14
Private Label Manufacturers' Association
The Great Store Brand Treasure Hunt
O'Hare Expo Center
Chicago IL

Exhibits: 750   *Attendance:* 3,000

Contact:
Roberta Friedman
Director of Advertising and Promotion
41 East 42nd Street, Suite 1500
New York NY 10017
212-972-3131

DECEMBER

7 - 12
National Food Brokers' Association
Annual Convention
Wacker Hall
Chicago IL

Exhibits: 170   *Attendance:* 15,000

Contact:
Mary Weekley
Director of Convention Services
1010 Massachusetts Avenue NW
Washington DC 20001
202-789-2844

Janice Copple
Suzanne Corbett
David Corcoran
Anita Corey
Michael Corsello
Lisa Costanzo
Beatrice Cowan
Candace Cox
Patrick B. Crane
Dorothy Crebo
Elizabeth Crossman
Mark J. Crowell
Mildred Cruickshank
Bob Cuillo
Martha Culbertson
Cathy Culver
Joanna Cumberland
Ruth D. Cuming
Marion Cunningham
Carol R. Cutler
Andrew D'Amico
Anna D'Onafrio
Howard Dalrymple
Julie Dannenbaum
Paul Danziger
Deborah Darlington
Sally Darr
Suzanne Dasilva
Maureen Daume
Rebecca Davidson
Susy Davidson
Linda Davies
Jack Davis
Stephen Davis
Julie Dawn
Gail Dawson
Giorgio DeLuca
Robert De Natale
Len H. De Pas
Anne de Ravel
Lorna DeVris
Betsy Dean
Charles Dean
Joel Dean
Irene Deichman
Robert Del Grande
Noreen Delaney
Bunny Dell
Jeff Dell
Julia della Croce
Christian Delouvrier
Susan Dempsey
William Denton
Wesley Depp
Marcel Desaulniers
Flavia Destefanis
Lee M. Dick
Ruth B. Diebold
Jerry Dillard
Jane Dillon
Patrice Dionot
Gladys Dobelle

Eric Doescher
Gary Dolgins
Jill Thayer Don
Bruce B. Donnell
Nichole Donnelley
Mark Dorian
June A. Douglass
Irene Douler
Kathleen Dowd
Mary Downing
Lacy D. Doyle
Judith A. Drake
Carrie Drazin
Lydia Driscoll
Lisa Dubin
Jere L. Dudley
Charles Dulos
Teresa Dunn
Bonnie Dupy
Jean K. Durkee
Kim E. Ebert
Ann Eber
Ima Rose Ebong
Kathleen Ecker
William Eddy
Ivana Edwards
Michael Ehrenpreis
Natalie Eigen
Carole R. Eisner
Mary C. Ekstrom
Rick Ellis
Roberta Elson
Ronald Elvena
Rosa Lee Emerson
Donald Engel
Ann-Elise Engleton
Jules I. Epstein
Joseph Erena
Richard Esner
Michele Esposito
Jane Ethe
Joan Everett
Bill Eyre
Florence Fabricant
Al Falk
Keith Famie
Paul A. Farago
Ali Farrell
Donald Fass
Norma Feder
Lisa S. Feder-Feitel
Jill Feinberg
Dolores Feinswog
Lynn Feld
Catherine Felix
Arlene Feltman
Susan Feniger
Barbara Fenzl
Eleanor E. Ferguson
Elizabeth Ferguson
James G. Ferguson
William Ferguson

Kenneth Ferrin
John Ferrone
Beverly Fetner
Donald Feuerstein
Anita Fial
Carol Fiederlein
Elizabeth Field
Ruth Field
Natalie Fielding
Bette B. Filip
Mary Filip
Beth S. Fillman
Sue Findlay
Frances T. Fischer
Sue Fischer
Irene Fischl
William Fish
Virginia Fitzgerald
Kathleen Fitzpatrick
Edwin Fivekiller
Marjorie Flanagan
Patrick Flanagan
Susan Flanagan
Bobby Flay
Linda Florio
James Fobel
Karen Fohrhaltz
James B. Foley
Michael Foley
Vincent Foley
Terry Ford
Larry Forgione
Diane Forley
Silvi Forrest
Margaret Fox
Eva M. Franqui
Andrew Frappolli
Catherine Fredman
William J. Freedman
Belmont Freeman
Marlena Freeman
Jane Freiman
Eleanor Friede
Susan Friedland
Bea Friedman
Linda Friedman
Sara Friedman
Nina Friscia
Polly Fritch
Jacklyn Fusco
Randy Fusfeld
Betty Fussell
Nancy Gahles
Barry M. Gaines
Evelyn Galen
James J. Gallagher
Keith Garber
Ronald A. Garfunkel
Aggie Garibaldi
Robert Garritti
Justin Gasarch
Gail Gaston

James Gaston
Marjorie Gatanzaro
Sue Geisler
Patricia S. Geiss
Carol Gelles
Natalie Gerardi
Sheila Gerber
Jean-Louis Gerin
George Germon
Jean Gershunoff
Judie Gerstein
Daniele Gespert
Deborah Gesser
Steven Gethers
Charmain Gibson
Ted Miles Gidaly
Gino Giglio
Ame Gilbert
James Gilbert
Lelia Gilchrist
Emily K. Gilder
Andre Gillardin
Carol Gillot
Sarah E. Ginsberg
Catherine Giordano
Marcia Glickman
Adam Glinert
Peter Goatley
Ellen Harrison Godkin
Alan Gold
Ruth B. Gold
Lesley E. Goldberg
Lisa Goldberg
Esta Sue Golden
Sylvia Golden
Katja B. Goldman
Lilyan Goldman
Mitchell Goldman
Rachelle Goldman
Gerald Goldsmith
Al Goldstein
Joyce Goldstein
Michael Goldstein
Michelle Goldstein
Philip Goldstein
Susan A. Goldstein
Daniel Gonnella
Elaine L. Gonzalez
Max Goree
Marion Gorman
Willard A. Gortner
Edward Gottlieb
Jean Gottlieb
John C. Gould
Ines T. Govoni
Mark Grace
Sharon F. Grana
Gaynor Grant
Richard Grausman
Matthew Green
Mary Ann Green-Tedeschi
Fern Greenberg

Freddi Greenberg
Gael Greene
John D. Greene
Michael Greenspan
Manya Greif
Gerald G. Griffin
Joanne Griffin
Ben Grim
Paul Grimes
William Grose
Eileen Grossman
Laura Gruber
Stephanie Gubelin
Vincent Guerithault
Ronald J. Gumbaz
Dorothy Gupton
Robert Gutenstein
Farha Joyce Haboucha
Sara Hacala
Carter H. Hale
Julie Hall
Susan Hallman
Michael Halperin
Daniel Halpern
Raizel Halpin
Mary Hamblett
Jacques Hamburger
Judith Hamer
Robert Hamilton
Stella Hamilton
Burks L. Hammer
Phyllis Hanes
Dorothea Hanil
Carolyn P. Hansard
Hank Hansen
C. Thomas Happer III
Adlai S. Hardin Jr.
Carol P. Harless
Joan S. Harlow
James Harpel
Amanda Harris
Andrew Harris
Dale Harris
Nancy Harris
Lawrence Hatterer
Olga Hatterer
Joanne L. Hayes
Julia Hayes
Toni Hayes
Jan T. Hazard
Nika Hazelton
Tena Heller
Norma Helwege
Ruth Henderson
Gayle Hennesey
Frank Heron
Rhona Hershkowitz
Jean Hewitt
William J. Hexamer
Sheila Hicks
Georgia Hiden
Emile Hiesiger, M.D.

Hildegarde Hiestos
Prudence Hilburn
Libby Hillman
Michele Hillman
David Hirsch
Yocheved Hirsch
Alisa Hixson
Lewis J. Hober
Tobi Hochman
Fred P. Hockberg
Lisa Hoffman
Suzanne Hoffman
Diana Hoguet
Deena Hohle
Jean S. Hollis
Daniel W. Homan
Mary Homi
Tim Horan
Josefina Howard
Peter D. Howell
Idelle A. Howitt
Alice T. Hozumi
Peter Humes
Janet Hummel
Allyson Huskisson
Genevieve Huss
Jerry Huven
Dale Hytholt
Susan J. Ichikawa
Lillian M. Imbeli
Paul Inveen
June Iseman
Arnold Israel
Inaki Izaguirre
Dana Jacobi
Arlene Jacobs
Anita Jacobson
Beverly Jacobson
Elin Jacobson
Phyllis Jaffe
Cathie Jenkins
John Jenkins
Laura Jennings
Pat Jennings
Julie Jensen
Morris Jgalen
Kay Johnson
Miriam P. Johnson
Evan Jones
Judith Jones
William Jones
Kae Jonsons
Gay Jordan
Carol Joseph
Barbara Josephson
Rosemary Joyce
Sheryl Julian
Martha Kaemmer
Barbara Kafka
Joy Kagele
Joseph F. Kahmann III
Peter J. Kalata

Ursula Kalish
Judith Kaminski
Madeleine Kamman
Alixanne Kaplan
Laura Kaplan
Louise Kaplan
Sylvia B. Kaplan
Joanne Karlinsky
Barbara Kasman
Helen Kasner
Alexia Kasper
Wilhelm Kast
Peggy Katalinich
Allan S. Katz
Arlene Katz
Robert Katz
John Kaufman
R. L. Kaufman
Janice Kaye
Michele Keith
Patricia L. Keller
Thomas Keller
Doris Kelly
Kathy Kelly
Daniel Kenneally
K. E. Kennedy
Diane D. Kern
Laibe A. Kessler
Paul R. Kessler
Susan Kessler
Lisa Ketchum
Georgianna Khatib
Reza Khatib
Johanne Killeen
Phyllis Kinett
Charles King
Paul King
Shirley King
Garrett Kirk Jr.
Stuart Kirkpatrick
Carol Kitman
Enid Klass
Laura Kleber
Claire S. Klein
Barbara Klion
Edmond A. Knopp, M.D.
Elana Kobrick
David Kolatch
Stephen Kolkey
Patricia Konrad
Sharon Korman
Robert L. Korus
Pamela Koslow
Mayburn Koss
Kyle Koszowski
Paul Kovi
Sharon Kramar
Selma Krasner
Cindy Krivosheiw
Teresa Krsulich
Joann Kruger
Janet I. Kuhl

Melvin W. Kuiyper
Peter Kump
Charles T. La Punzina
Michelle Labow
Lynn Lacava
Edward Lafaye
Emeril Lagasse
Jerry Lamb
Michael Landes
Deborah Lang
Jenifer Harvey Lang
Hope Lange
Susan Langhorne
Charles J. Larson
Judy Lasardo
Richard Launer
Richard Lavin
David R. Lawson
Bonnie T. Leblang
Joseph B. Ledbetter
Lucky Lee
Fran Castigan Leeds
Sylvia Lehrer
Bobbie Leigh
David L. Leigh
Jane LeMaster
Christine Lemley
Ann J. Lemon
Ron Leonard
Barbara Leopold
Robert Lescher
John Lese
Steven Leventhal
Vicki Levey
Carolyn Levin
Michael T. Levine
Sarabeth Levine
Norman Levy
Lisa Lewin
Edna Lewis
Bernard Liberman
Patricia Liddy
Richard Lieward
Nickolas Lim
Robin LoGuidice
Gasbarro Lombard
Lori Longbotham
Jan Longone
Felix Lopez
Anthony Loscalzo
Michele H. Loth
Richard Love
Mary Lou Lowenthal
Maureen Luchejko
D. Lukshus
Priscilla Lunden
Claire Lussier-Pogue
Mary Lutky
Stephanie Lyness
Michele Lyster
Alice MacDonald
Karen Mack

Troye Mackie	Darlene McKinney	Nancy Newman	Roger Philip
Francis MacVeagh	MaeJean McLemore	Tom Ney	Robert C. Philipson
Mary A. MacVean	Alice B. McReynolds	Michael Nichter	Estelle Phillips
Patsy Madden	Bruce McWilliams	Janice R. Nieder	Paul Piccuito
Charlotte Maeder	Vincent Meade	Drew Nieporent	Leonard Pickell
Michele S. Magazine	J. B. Meaders	Judy A. Nies	Judy Pickens
Janet Mager	Lynn Medlin	Atsuko Nishiyama	Michael Pieiss
Paul Magnusson	Robert Mei	Robert Noah	Charles Pierce
Anthony Mahn	Emiel Meisel	Mary Noble	Linda Piggott
Fred Malanczuk	Barbara Meltsner	Paulette Cooper Noble	Anne Pipping
Josephine Malandro	Julie A. Mendoza	Lucinda Noguera	Robert S. Pirie
Nicholas Malgieri	Paul D. Mesenheimer	Patricia C. Nolan	Lillian Pitta
Judith Mallin	Christopher Metz	Anna Amendolara Nurse	Linda Pizzurro
Anita C. Malugani	Karen Metz	Joanne Ellison Nydegger	Carol Plaquet
Abby Mandel	Daniel Meyer	Rick O'Connell	Linda Platzer
Rosemary Manell	Anthony Micheleti	Doris O'Donnell	Walter Plendner
Edith Manfredi-Zoppi	Paula Michtom	Molly O'Neill	Geraldine Pluenneke
Bruce C. Manson	William Mickley	Michael O'Reilly	Nicole Polak
Fred J. Marchini	Margot W. Milch	Mimi D. C. Oatland	Stanley Poll
Debra S. Marcus	Robert Milch	Leslie Ochs	Daniel Pollitz
Jean Marcus	Mary Sue Milliken	Bradley Ogden	Toula Polygalaktos
Jeffrey Marcus	Eileen R. Milioti	Judith Olney	Mae L. Pontoni
Claire Margiotta	Bryan Miller	Paul Olivo	Nanette Porcelli
Lynn Margulies	Joseph M. Miller	Michelle Oltman	Marie Portella
John Mariani	L. J. Miller	Jane Orans	Maureen Pothier
Anna R. Marinaccio	Mark Miller	Jerrie Ortega	Thomas Potter
Ronald Marion	Patricia A. Miller	Robert Osborn	Alice Prabst
James D. Marks	Jane Milza	Diane Ostermann	Marilyn Pred
Robin Markowitz	Burt Minkoff	Jane Owens	Ada Press
Barbara Marmo	Vincent Minuto	Judith Pacht	Dana Preston
Lydie Marshall	Harvey Mirsky	Donna Packer	Jose Prud'homme
Mary A. Marshall	Jean-Louis Missud	Bernard P. Palinkas	Dorothy Ptacek
Carla Martin	Sherri Mitchell	Jean-Louis Palladin	Bette Publicker
Nancy Martin	Judith D. Mitchener Jr.	Peter Pallotta	Wolfgang Puck
Zarela Martinez	Wes Mobley	Muriel L. Palmer	Walter D. Pugh
Alison Marx	Marci Mondavi	Susan K. Panagos	Sybille Pump
James W. Mason	Rona Monlu	Tony Paris	Susan G. Purdy
Jill S. Massa	Rick Moonen	Glen King Parker	Jean M. B. Purvis
Stephanie Massey	Lisa R. Morell	Joan Post Parker	Stephan Pyles
John R. Massie	Margaret Morgan	Sophie Parker	Marion E. Pyne
Mary Massie	Richard Morganstern	Jennifer Parkinson	George A. Rada
David Master	Robert Morris	Richard J. Parmley	Harvey Radler
Cheryl Matalene	Spencer Morris	Allen B. Parsons	Susan M. Rafaj
Carol Matorin	Ruth Morrison	Mark E. Pasquerilla	Patrick M. Raffaele
Dee Mattox	Steven H. Mosenson	Dan Paul	Lena Rafter
Glen Maulden	Phyllis Mossberg	Mel Pell	Tina Raia
Alice Maurer	Sanford Mossberg	Jacques Pepin	James B. Ramsey
Mary J. Maxwell	Nancy B. Mott	Olga Perillo	Richard A. Rapaport
Fritz Maytag	Kathleen Mulhern	Sue Perkins	Justin Rashid
Amy McAllister	Georgene Munger	Gail Perrin	Ruth Joan Rather
Marina E. McCabe	Bennet Murtha	Bernard T. Perry	Ruth B. Rattner
Barbara K. McCarthy	Ann C. Myatt	Kathleen Perry	Leonard Reed
Michael McCarty	Nancy Myers	Joseph A. Perry	Marjorie Reed
Cathy McCauley	Willard Nagel	Richard Perry	John R. Reen
Sara McGinnis	Ingrid W. Naidech	Leah Peters	Katharine Rees
Dianne McConnell	Joseph Napolitano	Elizabeth Peterson	Myrna Reich
John I. B. McCulloch	Rose Nastasi	Harlan Peterson	Herman Reimer
Robert R. McElman	John Neal	Gregory Petrick	Herb Rein
Jean McGillion	Nancy Noble	Marybeth Petscheck	Betty Reiser
Philip McGrath	Susan W. Nelson	M. Pfiefer	Melanie Ress
Lynn McKay	Rick Neves	Robert R. Pflueger	Humberto Restrepo
Winston McKellar	Leslie Newman	Robert S. Phelps	Leslie Revsin

Luther Reynolds	Victor Samrock	Wilma K. Shiffman	Mary Stark
Lisa Rhodes	Carlos Sanchez-Sierle	Fran Shinagel	Rusty Staub
Judy R. Richardson	Betty J. Sancholtz	Stuart Shoprio	Willard Stearns
Edwin R. Ridgway	Jeffrey Sandhaus	Martha Shulman	H. Lisa Steele
Judith M. Rifkin	Alice B. Sandler	Crescencia Siao	Robert Stein
Charles Riggs	Richard Sanford	Chizuko Sievers	David S. Steiner
Mary Risley	Ann Sargent	Frances Signorile	Sylvia Steiner
Glenn Rispaud	Janeen Sarlin	Geoffrey Silagy	Dorothea Steins
David Ritter	Mark Sarrazin	Joan Silinsh	Larry Sterner
Marie Ritter	Jesse Sartain	Hope Silvera	Gale Steves
Beverly Rivers	Ilda Sauberlich	Arlyn B. Silverman	Renie Steves
Robert Robinson	Charles P. Saunders	Marsha Silverman	Cathleen Stewart
Ellen Rochford	Dennis Sauter	Steven Silverman	Judy Stewart
Lynn Roddy	Ellen Sax	Vera Silverman	Anne Still
Linda Rodman	Irene Sax	Stephen Simmons	Pascal W. Stingone
Carole Rodnick	Richard Sax	Dolores S. Simon	Taryn Stinnett
Juan Rodriguez	Nina B. Scerbo	Jeffrey Lee Simons	Frank Stitt
Ted Rodriguez	Janet Schachtel	Eileen B. Simpson	Stewart Stoliz
Debora Rogan	Steven Schaem	Richard Simpson	Robert Strada
Frank A. Rogers	Elizabeth Schaible	R. B. Simpson Jr.	Caroline Stuart
Felipe Rojas-Lombardi	Harry P. Schaller	Bonnie K. Singer	Bobbi Sturgis
Renate Romano	Eric L. Schawaroch	J. Matthew Singleton	Greg Sujeta
Neil E. Romanoff	Lucille H. Schechter	Kathryn Singleton	Elsa B. Sullivan
Betty G. Rose	Christine Schefman	Martin Sinkoff	Martha Sullivan
Carol Rose	Ron Scher	Linda L. Sinsar	Noriya Sumihara
Shery Rosefield	Aileen Schlef	Alain Sinturel	Tilly Supor
Shirley Roseman	Christopher Schlesinger	Garlan Sisco	Allen Susser
Barry Rosenberg	Sally Schlosberg	Senya D. Sisk	Margaret Suter
Alan Rosenblatt	Carol Schmetz	Jonathan Siskin	Jayne Sutton
Alfred Rosenthal	Jimmy C. Schmidt	John G. Sisson	Leslie L. Sutton
Alvin Rosenthal	Stephen Schmidt	Robert A. Skinnick	Shelby H. Swatek
Bruce Rosenthal	Irene Schoen	Eileen Slater	Janice Swearingen
Anne Rosenzweig	Harold Schonberg	Leslie Slaughter	Blake Swihart
Edith Ross	Helen Schonberg	Robert R. Slaughter	Barrie Switzen
Joan H. Ross	Ellen Schottenfeld	Randy Slifka	Lynda Sylvester
Rosa Ross	Joan Schottmuller	Susan M. Small	Deszo Szonntagh
Sarah Ross	Paul Schrade	William Small Jr.	Linda P. Taber
Stanley Ross	June K. Schulman	Allen R. Smith	Jeffrey Talbert
Suzanne Rossi	Jane Schultze	Candida Smith	Kathleen Talbert
Earle Rothbell	Phillip S. Schulz	J. Allen Smith	Rebecca Talbert
Martin Rothman	Roger Schulz	Kimberly Smith	Christine Tallackson
Ruth B. Rothseid	Sylvia Schur	Sylvia Smith	Anne Tallman
Gerald A. Rothstein	Arthur Schwartz	Victoria Smith	Kazukiro Tanaka
S. Rubenstein	Peggy Schwartz	Jean Snoddy	Helen Tandler
Joseph Rubin	Sandra Schwartz	Dolores Snyder	Ilene Tanen
Karen Rubin	Terry Schwerin	Thelma Snyder	Norman Tanen
Stacey Rudbart	Michele Scicolone	Carol Sobel	Mark J. Tanenbaum
Jeffrey Ruesch	David A. Segal	Dorothy Sobel	Anna-mai Tanttu
David Ruggerio	Judith Segal	Peter Sobel	Yvonne Y. Tarr
Jerry Ruotolo	Milan Segall, D.D.S.	Sandy Sobel	Andrew Tauber
Arthur Ruskin	Philip Seldon	Barbara Somers	Bruce Tavors
Leslie Russell	June Seligman	Carl Sontheimer	Fatima Taylor
Marie S. Russo	Jeane Semon	Williams Sorvino	Harold Taylor
Paul Ryan	Claude Serebuykoff	Toni Sosnoff	Elaine Taylor-Gordon
Charlotte Safir	Mann Seymour	Ann L. Sottong	Christine Tegtmeier
Jeanette Saget	David Shack	Reka Souwapawong	Arnold Tennbaum
Beverly Salaff	Hortense Shair	Janet Spector	Eleanor Termine
Joan Salomon	Lisa Shatz	Stanley Spivak	Elizabeth Terry
Mikelynn Salthouse	Stuart Sheinbrot	Marsha St. Lifer	Ruby Thalman
Sandra Saltzman	Les Shenkel	Nancy St. Liter	Elizabeth Thatcher
Patrice Samara	Pamela Sherman	Ila Stanger	Barbara Thomas
Elizabeth Sample	Lew Sherwood	Regina Stanley	Marilyn Thomas

Shelagh Thomee
David T. Thompson
Anne Thomson
Ava C. Thorin
David Thorn
Lisa S. Thornton
Wellington Tichenor
Elissa Tinchler
Barbara Tirola
Jeffrey Tischler
James Tissot
Suzanne Tobias
Naomi Tobol
Molly Totoro
Jeremiah Tower
Susanne Townsend
Fulvio Tramotina
David Trenk
George F. Trescher Jr.
Calvin Trillin
Clay Triplette
Marian Tripp
Frederick Tripp Jr.
Aukse Trojanas
Alexandra Troy
Gerald F. Tucci
Cathie Tuchy
Jane Tucker
Nancy Tuckerman
John P. Tuke
David Turk
Charles Tutino
Regina Ullendorff
Mary C. Uslander
Carrie Valinsky
Eric Valinsky
Gwen M. Valley
Lester J. Van Ess
Joseph R. Vicarisi, Esq.
Valerie Vickers-Kutsch
Toni W. Viertel
Diane Vigilante
Bill Virgin
Lawrence Vitale
Robert Vitale
Francis Voigt
Anthony Volpe
Jeanne Voltz-MacKnight
Jean-Georges Vongerichten
Judith Wahl
Maggie Waldron
Sue E. Wallace
Cornelia Walmsley
Carole Walter
Gary Walther
Arlene Ward
Bryan Warren
Donald Warriner
Linda C. Waterman
Victoria L. Watson
Nach Waxman
Judith Weber

Nicholas Weber
Pat Weckerly
Terry Weeks
Robert J. Wegner Jr.
Annie M. Wehner
Sheila E. Weil
Barbara M. Weiner
Gary Weiner
Edmund Weinmann
Angela C. Weinroth
Michael Weinstein
Michael Weinstein
Norman Weinstein
Lawrence D. Weis
Doris Weisberg
Alan Weisman
Kathy Weissberger
Patricia Wells
Norma J. Wheat
Bernadette Wheeler
Jasper White
Alice Henry Whitmore
Gunther Wiest
Sandra G. Wilde
Jeanne Wilensky
John M. Wiler
Crosby Wiley
Arnold Wilkerson
William F. Wilkinson
Anne Willan
Nagel Willard
Frances B. William
Stephanie Williams
Richard Winger
Margo S. Winterstein
Pamela J. Wischkaemper
Coreze N. Wise
Thelma Wise
Alice B. Wittsten
Nancy Wittwer
Joann M. Wleklinski
Clark Wolf
Paula Wolfert
Leslie R. Wolff
Mark Woltin
Eileen Wong
Matthew Wood
Laura Lee Woods
Lawrence Woodson
Gregory Woodworth
Peter Wyhof
Dan Wynn
Elaine Yannuzzi
Esther Yntema
Barry Young
Kathy Young
Reggie Young
David Yudkin
Tim Zagat
Beverly Zakarian
John Zeiler
Mary Zick

Beverly Zimmerman
Gloria Zimmerman
Marvin Zimmerman
Mary Ann Zimmerman
Toby Zimmerman
Jane Zimmy
Sidney A. Zineibel
M. Zullo
Rona Zwerling

Additional Food Professionals Who Are Members of The James Beard Foundation

Bob Allen
Food Squad/Famous Affairs
760 Greenwich Street
New York NY 10014
212-807-9544
Caterer, gourmet store owner

Irma Lee Anapol
1115 Tucker Road
North Dartmouth MA
02747
508-228-1749
Organic/health food information resources

Samuel P. Arnold
2221 South Filmore Street
Denver CO 80210
303-758-1896
Food historian

Frank C. Baker
416 East 84th Street
New York NY 10028
212-353-2995

Barbara Bassett
The Healthy Gourmet®
P.O. Box 2167
Carson City NV 89702
702-882-1537
Cookbook author/editor

Ronald Beaumont
Preferred Hotels
Association, Inc.
1901 South Meyers Road,
Suite 220
Oakbrook Terrace IL 60181
708-953-0404
Hotel operations

Nancy Bloom
32 Perry Street
New York NY 10014
212-645-7124
Cooking teacher, nutrition

Diane H. Brown
Harris Brown Caterers
333 Pearl Street,
Suite 19-K
New York NY 10038
212-732-0541
Caterer

Mead M. Brownell
21 Sweetser Road
Cumberland Center ME
04021
207-829-6988
Writer

Julie Brumlik
58 Morton Street
New York NY 10014
212-966-3560
Chef

Jacques O. Burdick
145 East 16th Street,
Apartment 18-F
New York NY 10003
212-982-2621
Food writer

Davis C. Burroughs III
Rent-A-Chef
80 Wood Avenue
Bridgeport CT 06605
203-331-0380
Caterer

Winnie Burwell
Frederick Wildman & Sons
21 East 69th Street
New York NY 10021
212-288-8000
Wholesale wine sales

Carolyn Buster
525 Torrence Avenue
Calumet City IL 60409
708-891-3900
*Restaurant operations,
catering, food promotion*

Joanne Callahan
The Bostonian Hotel
Faneuil Hall Marketplace
Boston MA 02109
617-523-3600
Hotel public relations

Anne L. Casale
369 Mountain Boulevard
Watchung NJ 07060
201-756-9328
Writer/teacher

Barbara Conwell
Folly Farm
Box 219, Route 1
Accord NY 12404
914-687-9823
Caterer

Elizabeth Crossman
Henry Holt & Company
115 West 18th Street
New York NY 10001
212-886-9330
Editor/food writer

Mark J. Crowell
Director of Foodservice
Host International, Inc.
15 Engle Street, Suite 302
Englewood NJ 07631
201-894-0200
Foodservice, airport restaurants

Joanna Cumberland
J. B. Cumberland &
Associates
370 Lexington Avenue
New York NY 10017
212-953-0600
Public relations

Julie Dannenbaum
1816 Delancey Place
Philadelphia PA 19103
215-732-1850
Writer/author

Deborah Darlington
1118 First Avenue,
Apartment 5-C
New York NY 10021
212-751-0654
Caterer

Jere L. Dudley
84 James Avenue,
Apartment 2
Cranford NJ 07016
201-272-3497
Supermarket operations

**Eleanor E. Ferguson
James G. Ferguson**
P.O. Box 869
Chapel Hill NC 27514
919-929-8851
Writers, editors, photographers

William J. Ferguson Jr.
Coral House Restaurant and
Caterers
70 Milburn Avenue
Baldwin NY 11510
516-223-6500
Restaurant proprietor, caterer

Beth S. Fillman
P.O. Box 2059
Sag Harbor NY 11963
516-725-2136
Public relations

Bobby Flay
Executive Chef
Miracle Grill
112 First Avenue
New York NY 10009
212-254-2353
Chef

Catherine Fredman
Diversion Magazine
60 East 42nd Street
New York NY 10165
212-297-9652
Editor

Ted Miles Gidaly
Executive Chef
Loews Glen Pointe Hotel
100 Frank W. Burr
Boulevard
Teaneck NJ 07666
201-836-0600
Chef

Peter Goatley
Peter's Palate Pleaser, Inc.
1087 West Long Lake Road
Bloomfield Hills MI 48013
313-540-2266
Specialty food retailer

Sharon F. Grana
Connecticut Cooking
School
29 Liberty Street
Clinton CT 06413
205-669-5539
Teacher, restaurant consultant

Prof. Gerald G. Griffin
Department of Hotel and
Restaurant Management
New York City Technical
College
300 Jay Street
Brooklyn NY 11201
718-643-8383
Teacher, department chairman

Julie Hall
Culinary Jewels
44-20 Douglaston Parkway
Douglaston NY 11363
718-423-5836
*Caterer, specialty food
wholesaler*

Joan S. Harlow
Harlow's Bread and Cracker
Company
Epping NH 03042
603-679-8883
Specialty food retailer

Joanne L. Hayes
Country Living Magazine
224 West 57th Street,
Seventh Floor
New York NY 10019
212-649-3514
Food editor

Jan Turner Hazard
Ladies' Home Journal
100 Park Avenue
New York NY 10017
212-953-7070
*Editor, women's service
publication*

Jean Hewitt
Family Circle Magazine
110 Fifth Avenue
New York NY 10011
212-463-1720
Food editor

Yocheved Hirsch, CCP
172 Chestnut Street
Englewood Cliffs NJ 07632
201-567-5711
Teacher

Jean Hollis
3013 Walnut Road
Norman OK 73072
405-321-2225
Food consultant

Anita Jacobson
221 Fairway Road
Lido Beach NY 11561
516-432-4585
Teacher

Gay Jordan
Gay Jordan, Inc./Bespoke
Food
1065 Lexington Avenue
New York NY 10021
212-794-2248
Caterer

Mayburn Koss
167 Putnam Park
Greenwich CT 06830
203-869-8553
Food promotion

Susan Kessler
910 Park Avenue,
Apartment 6-N
New York NY 10021
212-744-5536

Janet Kuhl
32 Leroy Street, Suite 6
New York NY 10014
212-741-2392
Caterer

Michael Landes
1900 Broadway, Eighth
Floor
New York NY 10023
212-769-6366
Restaurant investments

Lucky Lee
Vice President, Sales
Sunrise Sun-Ripened
Tomatoes, Inc.
G.P.O. 2017
New York NY 10116
212-725-1775
Specialty foods wholesaler

Christine P. Lemley
WFYI, Channel 20
1401 North Meridian
Street
Indianapolis IN 46202
317-636-2020
Radio and television

Judith Young Mallin
983 Park Avenue, Apart-
ment 5-A
New York NY 10028
212-288-4199
Writer

J. B. Meaders
B & B/Benedictine
Liqueurs
45 West 45th Street
New York NY 10036
212-398-7172
Specialty wine/liqueur sales

Barbara Meltsner
1220 Park Avenue
New York NY 10128
Teacher

Margaret Morgan
The Peninsula, New York
700 Fifth Avenue
New York NY 10019
212-938-9100
Hotel operations

Leslie Newman
300 Central Park West
New York NY 10024
212-595-2451
Writer

Tom Ney
Prevention Magazine
Rodale Press, Inc.
33 East Minor Street
Emmaus PA 18098
215-967-5171
Food editor

Joanne Ellison Nydegger
985 Kingston Drive
Cherry Hill NJ 08034
609-795-7841
Teacher

Judith Pacht
910 Gretna Green Way
Los Angeles CA 90049
213-826-9787
Food writer/cookbook author

Joseph Perry
Route 100B
White Plains NY 10607
914-592-6600
Country club

Nanette Porcelli
2207 Pine Lane
Saugerties NY 12477
914-246-5832
Caterer

Maureen Pothier
Blue Point Oyster Bar
99 North Main Street
Providence RI 02903
401-272-6145
Executive chef

Ada Press
383 Oak Avenue
Cedarhurst NY 11516
516-239-1775
Food publications

Dorothy Ptacek
335 Archers Mead
Williamsburg VA 23185
804-220-4946
Cookbook author

Alfred Rosenthal
By Invitation Only, Ltd.
110 East 87th Street,
Suite 2-B
New York NY 10128
Food consultant

Patrice Samara
President, Patrice Samara
Productions
29 Fifth Avenue,
Apartment 7-A
New York NY 10003
212-777-0788
Food video producer

Janeen Sarlin
Cooking with Class, Inc.
110 East End Avenue
New York NY 10028
212-517-8514
Teacher

Mark Sarrazin
DeBragga & Spitler
826-D Washington Street
New York NY 10014
212-924-1311
Specialty meats

Lucille Haley Schechter
The Wandering Spoon
340 East 57th Street
New York NY 10022
212-751-4532
Food publications, teacher

Sally Schlosberg
The Pillsbury Company
311 2nd Street SE
Minneapolis MN 55414
402-330-4966
Research and development

Judith Segal
880 Fifth Avenue
New York NY 10021
212-737-3016
Writer

Pamela Sherman
Pam Sherman Bakery
2914 Hennepin Avenue
South
Minneapolis MN 55408
612-824-0604
Specialty food retailer

Barbara Somers
176 New Road
Ridgefield CT 06877
203-431-3674
Freelance editor/writer

Carl Sontheimer
P.O. Box 4780
Greenwich CT 06830
203-629-5880
Publisher

Ila Stanger
Travel & Leisure
1120 Avenue of the
Americas
New York NY 10036
212-382-5600
Editor-in-chief

Rusty Staub
Rusty's Restaurant
1271 Third Avenue
New York NY 10021
212-861-4518
Restaurant operations

Caroline Stuart
47 Will Merry Lane
Greenwich CT 06831
203-622-6821
Writer

Marilyn Thomas
Marilyn Thomas School of
Cooking
29 Afterglow Way
Montclair NJ 07042
201-746-5578
Teacher

David T. Thompson
Master Chefs Institute
20 Waterside Plaza,
Suite 34-A
New York NY 10010
212-545-8270
*Chairman, restaurant
association, and publisher,
Master Chef Magazine*

Ava C. Thorin
100 Manhattan Avenue,
Apartment 161-J
Union City NJ 07087
Public relations

Alexandra Troy
Culinary Architect, Inc.
Catering
P.O. Box 1072
Manhasset NY 11030
516-883-7885
212-410-5474

Gary Walther
Travel & Leisure
1120 Avenue of the
Americas
New York NY 10036
212-382-5600
Senior editor

Arlene Ward, CCP
Adventures in Cooking
66 Heights Road
Wayne NJ 07470
201-694-5115
Teacher

Annie M. Wehner
Annie M's Bakery
3785 L. Honoapiilani
Highway,
Suite 405
Lahaina Maui HI 96761
Chef/owner

Norman Weinstein
Norman Weinstein's
Hot Wok
412 East 2nd Street
Brooklyn NY 11218
718-438-0577
Cooking teacher

Doris Weisberg
145 East 92nd Street
New York NY 10128
212-831-1690
Food educator

Gunther Wiest
35 River Drive South,
Apartment 207
Jersey City NJ 07310
201-626-2653
Caterer

Jeanne S. Wilensky
716 Ocean Parkway
Brooklyn NY 11230
718-435-5569
Public relations consultant

William F. Wilkinson
Ayala Hotels
340 Stockton Street
San Francisco CA 94108
415-956-3773
Luxury hotel operations

Arnold Wilkerson
Little Pie Company, Inc.
424 West 43rd Street
New York NY 10036
212-736-4780
*Specialty food retailer, food
promotion*

Gloria Zimmerman
17 Horseshoe Road
Guilford CT 06437
203-453-6127
Teacher

Index

Since the *Food Professional's Guide* lists are arranged alphabetically or alphabetically by region, we have not duplicated our entire book of listings here. Categories such as Chambers of Commerce, Publications, Spas, TV Networks, etc. can easily be located by using the Table of Contents or appropriate section divider.

This Index will assist you in locating companies or individuals that may not be readily identifiable as part of a particular category (i.e. wholesaler or retailer; illustrator or graphic designer; contract foodservice or fast food company).

A

A.A. Executive Catering, 124
Aaron, Marc, Kosher Caterers, 122
Abbott Company, 169
Abbott Industries, 164
Abeles & Heymann, 63
Abel & Schafer, Inc., 63
Abilene Reporter-News, 256
Abraham, Molly, 259
Abrams, Jerry, 170
Abrams, Kathie, 211
ABV & Associates, 98
Academy of Culinary Arts—Atlantic Community College, 143
Acadiane Piggly Wiggly, 44
Acapulco (Restaurant Associates Industries, Inc.), 81
Accomac Catering, 125
Ace Pecan Company, 49
Acme Candy Company, Inc., 25
Acme Metal Goods Manufacturing Company, 168
Actuelle, 104
Adams, James, & Associates, Inc., 99
Adams, Kim, 210
Adirondacks, 106
Adrienne, 105
AEG/Andi-Co Appliances, Inc., 162
An Affair to Remember, Inc., 126
Aga Cookers, Cooper & Turner, 162
Agri-Pack, Division of Liberty Carton Company, 33
Agway, Inc., 71
Ahler's Organic Date Garden, 58
Aiello Associates, 98
AIRCOA, 79
Air La Carte, 91
A La Bonne Cocotte, 146
Alaska Honey Farm, 59
Alaska Seafood Marketing Institute, 187
Albany Times-Union, 250
Albert, Ursula, 249
Albertson, Charlotte Ann, Cooking School, 147

Albertson's, 74
Albitz Design, Inc., 98
Albuquerque Journal, 256
Alco Industries, Inc., 168
Al Dente, Inc., 35, 47
The Alder Market & Catering Company, 116
Aldridge, Harriett, 251
Alex Patout's Louisiana Restaurant, 107
Al Forno/Lucky's, 104, 105
All-Clad Metalcrafters, Inc., 168
Allegro, 102
Allen, Ann Whiting, 257, 259
Aller Cuisine, Ltd., 119
Allied International Corporation/European Chocolate Shops, 25
All Seasons Party Productions, 116
Almond Board of California, 184
Alton Electric (Antilles International, Inc.), 164
Alumaline Cutlery Company, Inc., 168
Aluminum Housewares, 168
Amana Refrigeration, Inc., 163
Amarr Kitchens, 160
Ambassador Grill, 102
Ambras International Trading Company, 168
Ambria, 110
Ambrosia, 46
Amco Corporation, 168
Amelio's, 109
American Airlines, 90
American Anorexia/Bulimia Association, 266
American Bakers' Association, 179
American Bounty, 105, 109
American Butter Institute, 278
American Cocoa Research Institute, 278
American Cooking School, 149
American Crystal Sugar Company, 72
American Culinary Federation, 179
American Dairy Association, 184
American Dietetic Association, 266
American Dietetic Association Foundation, 266
American Dry Pea & Lentil Association, 292
American Egg Board, 184
American Festival Cafe. *See Restaurant Associates Industries, Inc.*
American Fisheries Society, 278
American Frozen Food Institute, 179, 278
American Harvest/Harvest Maid, 168
American Harvest Restaurant, 107
American Home Economics Association, 179
American Home Economists in Business, 179
American Home Products Corporation, 72
American Hospitality, 115
American Hotel and Motel Association, 179
American Housewares Manufacturing Company, 168
American Institute of Food Distribution, 179
American Institute of Nutrition, 266
American Institute of Wine and Food, 179
American International Trading Company, 168

American Kitchens, Inc., 161
American Lamb Council, 186, 292
American Maize-Processing Company, 73
American Meat Institute, 278
American Meat Institute (AMI), 186
American Medical Association, 266
American Mushroom Institute, 187
American Peanut Product Manufacturers' Institute, 278
An American Place, 104
American Profile, Inc., 168
American Restaurant Group, Inc., 81, 87, 88
American Roland Food Corporation, 29
American School Food Service Association, 179
American Sheep Industry Association, 186
American Soybean Association, 278
American Spice Trade Association, 187
American Spoon Foods, 36, 51, 57
Americans for Safe Food, Center for Science in the Public Interest, 276
American Stores, 74
American Sugar Beet Growers' Association, 278
Ames Catering Unlimited, 114
Ammirati, Robert, Studio, 199
Anatoly, 211
Anchorage Daily News, 259
Anco Foods Corporation, 26
Anderson, Carlene, Kitchen Design, Inc., 162
Anderson, Jean, 259
Anderson, Lee, Covalda Date Company, 58
Anderson, Robert, 211
Andree's Wine, Cheese & Things, 43
Andrek, Mary, 258
Andrews, Amy, 207
Andrews, Colman, 259
Angel, Lenore (Lenny), 209
Angeli, Primo, Inc., 218
Angeli Caffe, 105
Anheuser-Busch Companies, Inc., 69
Annie's Enterprises, Inc., 25
Anorexia Nervosa and Related Eating Disorders (ANRED), 266
Anthony, Jeff, Food Styling, 209
Anthony's, 122
Antilles International, Inc., 164
Antonio's Pizza. *See Levy Restaurants, Inc.*
Antun's of Westchester, 122
A & P, 74
Aphrodisia Products, 49
Apple Butter Festival, 291
Applejack Festival, 290
Apple Jacks Cider Mill, 54
Apple Processors' Association, 278
Aquaculture Marketing Service, 60
Aquavit, 106
Aragaki, Kathy M., 207
Arby's, Inc., 87
Arcadia, 109
The Arch, 110
Archer Daniels Midland Company, 69
Archisis Design Corporation, 99
Aresu, Paul, 199
Argus Leader, 256
Ariana's Cooking School, 147
Aristo, Donna, 199

The Arizona Daily Star, 256
Arizona Women in Food and Wine, 179
Arjon Manufacturing Corporation, 168
Arjoy Acres, 57
The Ark, 106
Arkansas Democrat, 251
Arkansas Gazette, 251
Arkansas Rice Festival, 288
Arnold, Bernie, 253
Aronson, A., Inc., 168
Arrington, Debbie, 257
Arrowhead Mills, Inc., 35, 58
ARA Services, Inc., 77, 79
The Art Bunch, Inc., 211
Artifax Design International, 97
Art Mart & Art Mart Foods, 45
Asbury Park Press, 249
Ascher, Inc., 97
Aschoff, Lee, 256
Asher, Gerald, 259
Associated Hosts, Inc., 77
Associated Milk Products, Inc., 70
Associated Press, 250
Association for Dressing & Sauces, 187
Association of Food Industries, 179
Astor Restaurant Group, Inc., 82
Atalanta Corporation, 29
Atlanta Family Restaurants, Inc., 77
The Atlanta Journal-Constitution, 252
Atlanta State Farmers' Market, 20
Atlantic Bedford Paper Bag Company, 33
Atlantic Can Company, Inc., Division of Centennial Industries, Inc., 33
The Atlantic City Press, 249
Atlantic Community College, 143
Atlantic Representations, Inc., 168
Atlas Metal Spinning Company, 168
Auberge Argenteuil, 103, 105
Auburn University International Center for Aquaculture, 264
August, Bob, 211
The Augusta Chronicle, 252
Augusta State Farmers' Market, 20
Aujourd'hui, 100
Aumiller Youngquist, P.C., 97
Aureole, 107
Auricchio Cheese, Inc., 26
Aurora, 111
Austin, Helen, 251
Austin, Lillian, 252
Austin American-Statesman, 256
Automatic Wire Goods Manufacturing Company, 168
Avery, Terry B., 251
A.V.S. Catering, Inc., 123
A&W Restaurants, Inc., 87
Ayer Public Relations, 189

B

Babcock & Schmid Associates, Inc., Design Management, 98
Baci Trattoria, 109
Back to Basics Products, Inc., 168
Badecker, Andy, 255
Bagcraft Corporation of America, 33
Bahlsen, Inc., 23, 65
Bailey, Lee, 259
Bailey, Pat, 211
Bailin, Iris, 255
Bainbridge's Festive Foods, 51

Baker, Don, 211
Baker, Jane, 256
Baker, Kolea, 211
Baker Catering, 121
The Bakersfield Californian, 257
Bakers Square Restaurants
    (VICORP Restaurants, Inc.), 82
Baldridge, Pat, 253
Balducci's, 42, 51
Baldwin Hill Bakery, 50, 60
Ballard, Walter M., Ltd., SPGA
    Group, Inc., 95
The Ballroom, 109
Bally's Grand (Las Vegas). See Bally
    Manufacturing Corporation
Bally's Grand (Reno). See Bally
    Manufacturing Corporation
Bally's Park Place. See Bally
    Manufacturing Corporation
Bally Manufacturing
    Corporation, 80
Balsley, Betsy, 257
Baltimore's International Culinary
    College, 143
Bancroft, Colette, 256
Bando's, 126
The Bangor News, 249
Banks/Eakin Architects, 97
Banthien, Barbara, 211
Barba, Dan, 199
Barbecue on Wheels, 118
Barbetta, 102
Barbizon Hotel, 108
Baricelli Inn, 107
Barmettler, Beth, 251
Barr, Ken, 211
Barr, Nancy Verde, 259
Barrett, Rita L., 207
Barrett Restaurants, 120
Barrie House Gourmet Coffee, 28
Barrows Tea Company, 28
Barry Design Associates, Inc., 98
Barth-Spencer, 49
Bartley, Bronstein, Long &
    Mirenda, 96
Baskin-Robbins Ice Cream
    Company, 77
Bathie, Jim, 199
Battaglia & Company, Inc., 26
Battifarano, A.J., 205
Bauer, Michael, 258
Bay Street. See S&A Restaurant
    Corporation
Bay Window Deli, 43
Bazzini, A.L., Company, Inc., 39
BDG, Inc., 95
Beacon Journal, 255
Beall, Edward Carson, &
    Associates, 99
Beard, James, Foundation, 181
Beatrice Company, 70
Beaumont Enterprise, 256
Bechtol, Ron, 257
Beck, Myron, 199
Becker, Gail, Associates, 189
Beckham/Eisenman, 98
Beech Hill Farm, 54
Beefiesta, 289
Beem California Corporation, 168
Behrens, Gordy, 255
Beiswenger, Tom, 250
Bel Air Marketplace, 47
Bel Canto Fancy Foods, 29
Beldon, Kitchens by, 162
Belgian Endive Marketing
    Board, 187

Belknap, Joan, 250
Bell, Janice, 207
Bell, Michelle, 252
Bellantuono, Jeffrey, 211
Bellevue Gardens Organic
    Farm, 55
Bell's Suprecentre, 42
Belove, Janice, 211
Bel Paese Sales Company, Inc., 26
Bemis Manufacturing Com-
    pany, 169
Bendell, Norm, 211
Bendow, Ltd., (Lewis L. Salton
    Company), 168
Benedict, Nell, Cooking
    Classes, 149
Benet, Jane, 259
Benihana of Tokyo, Inc., 82
Benner, Dyne, 205
Bennett, Beverly, 254
Bennett, Chef John, 125
Bennett, Marsha, 251
Bennigan's. See S&A Restaurant
    Corporation
Benson, Hank, 199
Benson's Catering, 124
Benton Harbor Fruit Market,
    Inc., 21
The Bergen News, 249
Berghoff, Carlyn, Catering, 118
Bergin, Robert, 211
Beringer Vineyards, 144
Berman, Benicia, 205
Berman, Karen, 248
Bernal, Bill, 259
Berndes U.S.A., 168
Berry, Barbara, Foodstyling, 210
Berry Best Farm, Inc., 36
Bertolli USA, Inc., 29
Bertrand, 101
Bertsch Food Service, 119
Besnier USA, 27
Bespaloff, Alexis, 259
The Best of Everything, 125
Best Manufacturers, 169
Best Quality Breadsticks, 63
Better Foods Foundation,
    Inc., 49, 55
Better Housewares Corpora-
    tion, 169
Betty G Appliances (Abbott
    Industries), 164
Beverly Enterprises, 90
Beverly Hills Caterers, 115
Bewley Irish Imports, 29
Beyray, Caroline, 253
Biba, 110
Biebel's Supermarket &
    Catering, 127
Big Bear Stores, 75
Big Boy. See Marriott Corporation
The Big Cheese, 45
Big Time/Prime Marketing, 169
Big Wheel. See Consolidates Specialty
    Restaurants, Inc.
The Billings Gazette, 257
Bill Knapp's Michigan, Inc., 82
Billy Ogden's Lovejoy Grill, 103
Bilmes, Semyon, 211
Birmingham News, 251
Birmingham Post-Herald, 251
Birmingham Stove, 169
Birsch, Andy, 259
Biscuit & Cracker Distributors'
    Association, 187

Biscuit and Cracker Manufacturers'
    Association, 278
Bishop, David, 199
Bishop Buffets, Inc. (Furr's/Bishop's
    Cafeterias LP.), 86
Bishop's Cafeterias LP., 86
Bissinger's Sweet Tooth, 48
Bi-State Seafood Development
    Conference, 187
The Bistro at Maison de Ville, 110
Bisulk, Herbert P., Inc./Kitchens of
    Distinction, 159
Bittman, Mark, 259
Bjoin, Henry, 199
BK Root Beer Drive Inns, Inc. See
    DeNovo Corporation
Blachut, Dennis, 199
Black, Rosemary, 249
Black Cloud Farm, 54
Black & Decker (Household
    Products Group), 164
Black-Eyed Pea Jamboree, 291
Blackeyed Pea Restaurant. See
    Unigate Restaurants, Inc.
Blackwell, Deborah, 211
Blackwell, Garie, 211
Blaisdell-Bannon, Alicia, 249
Blanchard & Blanchard, 39
Blatt, H.S., Presents, Inc., 117
Blimpie. See Astor Restaurant
    Group, Inc.
Block, Alice M., 211
Bloom's Kosher Candy, 63
Blue, Anthony Dias, 259
Blueberry Ledge Farm, 54
Blue Corn Connection, 30
Blue Diamond Growers, 73, 184
Blue Fox, 109
Blue Heron Farm, 58
Blue Ridge Farms, Inc., 63
Blue Ridge Food Service, 59
Blum, Marcy L., Associates,
    Inc., 123
Blume, Joan, 211
Bly, Coletta, 256
BMW Designer Kitchens, Inc., 160
Boardman, James, 207
Bobby McGee's USA, Inc., 77
Bockwinkel's Incorporated, 45
Bocock-Stroud Company, 50
Boddie-Noell Enterprises, Inc., 87
Boggy Bayou Mullet Festival, 289
Boies, Alex, 211
Bojangle's Chicken & Biscuits. See
    The Horn & Hardart Company
Boldt, Lynn C., 209
Bonanza Family Restaurants. See
    USA Cafes
Bon Appetit Catering, Inc., 115
Bon Appetit of Lake Tahoe, 116
Bon Appetit Management
    Company, 79
Bond, JoAnn, 256
Bongrain International (American)
    Corporation, 27
Bonhomme, Bernard, 211
A La Bonne Cocotte, 146
Bonny Products, Inc., 169
Bonsignore, Brignati & Mazzotta,
    P.C., 95
Bon Vivant School of Cooking, 151
Bookman, Ken, 251
Bordeaux, H.R., Ltd., Cheese, 63
Borden, Inc., 70, 292
The Border Cafe. See Astor Restaurant
    Group, Inc.

Border Grill, 103, 107
Borel's. See Stouffer Restaurant
    Company
Borman's, 75
Bosch, Peter, 199
Bosch, Robert, Corporation, 164
The Boston Globe, 249
The Boston Herald, 249
Boston Tea Company, 28
Boston University Seminars in the
    Culinary Arts, 143
Botero, Samuel, Associates,
    Inc., 95
Boudin King, Inc., 119
Bouley's, 101
Bowlby Candy Company, 49
Bowman, Matt, 199
The Box Tree, 102
Boycott McDonald's and Burger
    King Coalition, 277
Brabantia Division of Loroman
    Company (Abbott
    Company), 169
Braden's Inc., 42
Bradley's, Inc., 124
Bradshaw International, Inc., 169
Brandt, Linda, 252
Braniff, Inc., 90
Brans Nut Company, 33
Braselle Design Company, 99
Brasserie. See Restaurant Associates
    Industries, Inc.
Braswell, A.M., Jr. Food Company,
    Inc., 36
Braum Ice Cream and Dairy Stores
    Company, 77
Braun, Inc., 164
Braun, Wendy, 211
Bread Alone, 60
Bread & Circus, 54
Breaux Bridge Crawfish
    Festival, 289
Bredflats, J.J., Inc., 29
Brello, Ron, Jr., 199
Bremen House, 51
Bremner Biscuit Company, 29
Brennan, Steve, 211
Breskin, Arline, Ltd., 122
Bresse Bleu, 27
Brewmatic Company, 163, 169
Bricker's Organic Farm, Inc., 59
Brickman, Robin, 212
Bridel USA, 27
Bridgehead Catering, 115
Bridgeport Post-Telegram, 248
Brier Run Farm, 60
Bries, Dennis, 57
Brightwaters, 45
The Brigittine Monks Gourmet
    Confections, 48
Brigtsen's, 101
Brillhart, Ralph, 212
Bristol. See Restaurant Enterprises
    Group, Inc.
Broadbent's B & B Products, 50
Broadfoot, Jill, 209
Brock, Carol, 205, 259
Broder, Ann, 205
Brody, Bob, Photography,
    Inc., 199
Brody, Jane, 259
Broil-King (Hudson Standard
    Corporation), 164
Bromwell Housewares, Inc., 169
Bronstein, Steve, 199

Brookes, Christopher Reeves, Company, 30
Brook-Hill Restaurants. *See The Happy Steak, Inc.*
Brooks, Andrea, 212
Brother International Corporation, 164
Brown, Bradford, 212
Brown, Ellen, 259
Brown, George C., Biscuit and Confectioners, Inc., 25
Brown Derby, Inc., 82
Brown-Forman Corporation, 72
Brownie's Catering Service, 125
Brown & Portillo, Inc., 87
Brown's Chicken. *See Brown & Portillo, Inc.*
Brownville Mills, 49
Bruni Farm, 41
Bruno, Pat, 259
Bruno Photography, Inc., 199
Bruno's, 74
BRA USA, Inc., 169
Brussels Sprouts Festival, 288
Buccalo Catering, Inc., 124
Buckner, Jacqueline, 205
Bucks County Courier Times, 251
Budnik, Victor, 199
Bufas, Tom, 199
The Buffalo News, 250
Buffets, Inc., 77
Bugialli, Giuliano, Cooking in Florence, 146
Bundy, Beverly, 257
Bunn-O-Matic Corporation, 164
Buon Appetito, 46
Burger Chef. *See Hardee's Food Systems, Inc.*
Burger King Corporation, 87. *See also U.S. Restaurants, Inc.*
Burger's Market, 44
Burgoo Festival, 289
Burgoyne, John, 212
Burke/Triolo, 199
Burks, Toni, 254
Burnette, Lynn, 253
Burns, Dana, 212
Burrell Public Relations, Inc., 189
Burros, Marian, 259
Burson-Marsteller, 189
Burstein, Sidney, 205
Burton, Max, Enterprises, Inc., 169
Busch, Lon, 212
Busy Bee Gourmet Food and Wine, Inc., 45
Butcher, Jim, 212
Butler's Kitchen, 121
The Butlery, Ltd., 44
Butt, H.E., Grocery Company, 74
Buxman, Paul A., 58
Bwarie's Emporium, 47
Byrd, Deborah, 258
Byrd Cookie Company, Inc., 23
Byrn, Anne, 252
By Word of Mouth, Inc., 117

C

Cabbages & Kings, 117
Cable, Mark, 212
Cactus Restaurants and Clubs. *See El Chico Corporation*
C & A Custom Kitchens, 161
Cadbury Schweppes, Inc., 72
Caesar's World, Inc., 80
Cafe Annie, 103
Cafe des Artistes, 104

Cafe in the Barn, 120
Cafe Beaujolais, 105
Cafe Beaujolais Bakery, 23, 50
Cafe Pierre, 104
Cafe Provencal, 108
Cafe Sport, 103, 105
Cafe 21, 104
Cain, Thomas, 212
Cairo State Farmers' Market, 20
Cajun Queen Enterprises, Inc., 127
Cake Cottage, Inc., 147
The Cake Stylists, Inc., 23
Calder, Nicholas A., Interiors, Ltd., 95
Calico Cook, 209
California Apricot, 184
California Artichoke Advisory Board, 188
California Avocado Commission, 188
California Avocado Festival, 288
California Beef Council, 186, 292
California Celebrations, 115
California Certified Organic Farmers, 58
California Culinary Academy, 143
California Dried Bean Advisory Board, 186
California Egg Commission, 184
California Fisheries Association/ California Seafood Institute, 187
California Fresh Market Tomato Advisory Board, 188, 292
California Fresh Produce Council, 188
California Granny Smith Association, 184
California & Hawaiian Sugar Company, 72
California Hi-Lites, Inc., 33
California Iceberg Lettuce Commission, 188
California Kiwifruit Commission, 184
California Milk Advisory Board, 184
California Olive Industry, 188
California Pistachio Commission, 185
California Prune Board, 185
California Raisin Advisory Board, 185
California Rice Promotion Board, 186
California Seafood Institute, 187
California Soleil Vineyards, 36
California Sunshine Fine Foods, 32
California Table Grape Commission, 185
California Treats, Inc., 39
California Tree Fruit Agreement, 185
Callebaut, 25
Caller-Times, 256
Calorie Control Council, 266
Caltex Foods, Division of Caltex Trading, Inc., 30
Caltex Trading, Inc., 30
The Cambridge School of Culinary Arts, 143
Cameo Caterers, Inc., 119
American International, 62
Cameron, Kitchens by, 160
Camp, Paul, 259
Campbell Catering, Inc., 121
Campbell Soup Company, 69

Campos, John, 199
The Candy Jar, 25
Can Manufacturers' Institute, 279
Canned Food Information Council, 184, 188
Canned Fruit Promotion Service, 185
Cannon, Suki, 205
Canteen Company (TW Services, Inc.), 79, 82
Cantina Laredo. *See El Chico Corporation*
Cantor, Lynn, 206
Cantrell's Catering, 121
Cantu-Weber, Jose, 257
Cape Cod Times, 249
Capers of Amherst, 121
Capital District Cooperative, Inc. (Menands Market), 19
Capitol Products Corporation, 164
Caplan, Skip, 199
Caporale, Wende, 212
Capricio, 108
Capsouto Freres, 110
Captain D's. *See Shoney's, Inc.*
Carafoli, John, 205
Carafoli, John F., 205
Caravali Coffees, 28
Cardwell's, 102
Carey, B.J., Provisions, 42
Carey, Ed, 199
Carey, Wayne, 212
Carlos Sweeney's. *See Consolidated Specialty Restaurants, Inc.*
Carl's Jr. *See Carl Karcher Enterprises, Inc.*
Carlson Companies, Inc., 80
Carlson Kitchens, 161
Carmel Kosher Food Products, 62
Carol's Cuisine, Inc., 146
Carolyn Candies, 61
Carolyn Collins Caviar Company, Inc., 32
Carpenter, Michael, 212
Carpenter Farms, 55
Carrols Corporation, 87
Carrot Festival, 288
Carruthers Kitchens, Inc., 160
Carson/Smith Fine Foods, 41
Carson Pirie Scott & Company, 77
Carter, Bunny, 212
Carter, Penny, 212
Carvel Corporation, 77
Carver, Steve, 212
Casa Bonita. *See Unigate Restaurants, Inc.*
Casa DiLisio Products, Inc., 40
Casa Gallardo. *See Restaurant Enterprises Group, Inc.*
Casbah/Sahara Natural Foods, Inc., 30
Cascade Seafoods, 32
Cascadian Farm, 59
Cashnelli, Toni, 255
Caspian Star Caviar, Inc., 32
Castle Catering, 116
Castle & Cooke, Inc., 70
Castrone, Linda, 257
Castroville Artichoke Festival, 288
Cater, Inc., 117
The Cater Cart, 125
The Catered Affair, 120
Catering by Buck's Kinn/A Special Event, 127
Catering by Coast Coordinators, Inc., 116

The Catering Company, 126
Catering Complete, Inc., 127
Catering by Dennis, 121
Catering by Elleven, 121
Catering from the Hart, 125
Catering Just For You, 125
Catering by Lawrence, 121
Catering by Lovables, 117
Catering by Michael's, Inc., 119
Catering by Millard, 122
The Catering People, 120
Catering by Sharon, 116
The Cater Inn, 119
CaterMarin, 116
Cates, Charles F., & Sons, Inc., 65
Catfish Farmers of America, 187, 292
Cavanaugh Lakeview Farms, 50
Cavey's, 102
Caviar Direct, Caspian Imperial Caviar, 32
Caviarteria, 49
C & C Catering, 123
The C&C Organization, 77
The Cedar Rapids Gazette, 254
Cedric's Catering, 121
Celebrations, 118
Centennial Industries, Inc., 33
Center for Food Safety and Applied Nutrition, 267
Center for Science in the Public Interest, 276, 279
Center for the Study of Anorexia and Bulimia, 266
Central Maine Egg Festival, 290
Central New York Regional Market Authority, 19
Central Soya Company, Inc., 70
Century Cookware/Birmingham Stove, 169
Cero's, 45
Certified Prime, Inc., 37
C'est Bon, 41
C'est Croissant, 50
The Chafer Caterers, 124
Chalet Suzanne Foods, Inc., 40, 51
Chalif, Inc., 25
Chalkin, Dennis, Studio, Inc., 199
Chalmers, Cheryl, 212
Champagne, 104
Chaney Instrument Company, 164
Chantal, 172
Chantal by Lentrade, 169
Chanterelle, 110
Chanterelle Caterers, 120
Chanterelle Specialty Foods, Inc., 47
Chantry, 52
Chantry/Victor, 169
Chapman, Ed, 249
Chappell, Ellis, 212
Charcuterie & Cheese Market, 47
Charcuterie Tour Eiffel, Inc., 37
Charles, Lisa, 199
Charles & Company, 51
Charleston Daily Mail, 254
Charleston Farmers' Market, 21
Charley Brown's. *See Restaurant Enterprises Group, Inc.*
Charlie Brown's (Restaurant Associates Industries, Inc.), 82
Charlie Trotter's Restaurant, 110
Charlotte Charles, Inc., 33
The Charlotte Observer, 253
Chateau Souverain, 103
Chateau Specialties, 43

Chattanooga News-Free Press, 253
Chavez Catering, 118
CHE, Inc., 77
The Cheddar Box, 44
Cheers Catering, Inc., 115
The Cheese Haus, 47
Cheese House, 46
Cheese Importers' Association, 184
Cheese Shop International,
    Inc., 41, 46
The Cheese Shop of Vail, 47
The Cheese Shop of Virginia, 44
Chef Aid, 169
Chef Klaus Catering, Inc., 116
Chefmate Housewares Corporation
    (Herald Housewares), 169
Chef Michael, Inc., 121
Chefs in America, 179
Chelsea Trattoria, 101
Chemex (International House-
    wares), 169
Chen, Joyce, Products, 172
Chenel, Laura, 259
Cher-Make Sausage Company, 37
Chestnutt, David, 212
Cheung, Vicki, 206
Chez Catherine, 100
Chez Madelaine, 148
Chez Panisse, 101, 110
Chez Raphael, 105
Chicago Culinary Guild, 179
Chicago Cutlery Company, 169
Chicago Metallic, 169
Chicago Sun-Times, 254
The Chicago Tribune, 254
Chi-Chi's, Inc., 82. See also
    Foodmaker, Inc.
Chick-fil-A, Inc., 87
Chili's, Inc., 82
Chin, Fay, 206
The China Moon Cafe, 110
Chincoteague Oyster Festival, 291
The Chinese Cookery, Inc., 147
Chip Clip Corporation, 169
Chipurnoi Incorporated, 25
Chisholm Trail Catering, 124
The Chocolate Catalogue, 48
The Chocolate Gallery, 144
Chocolate Manufacturers'
    Association, 187, 279
Chocolate Photos, 63
Christian, Peter, Specialty Food
    Company, 39
The Christian Science
    Monitor, 249
Christopher's, 104
CHRO, Inc., 99
Chrynwski, Walt, 199
Chun, Diane, 252
Chuppa Knife Manufacturing,
    Inc., 169
Church, Jann, Partners, 218
Ci'Bella, 40
Ciboulette, 106
Ciccarelli, Garry, 212
Cicero, Linda, 252
Ciffone, Laura, 207
Cincinnati Post, 255
Cinco de Mayo, 105
Cinnabon World-Famous
    Cinnamon Rolls. See Restaurants
    Unlimited, Inc.
The Circle K Corporation, 77
Circleville Pumpkin Show, 290
Citrus, 108
Citrus World, Inc., 73

Citterio USA Corporation, 37
City Market, 21
City Market of Los Angeles (Ninth
    Street), 22
City Restaurant, 103
Claiborne, Craig, 259
Clancy, Maureen, 258
Clarion-Ledger/Jackson Daily
    News, 253
Clark, Al, 253
Clark, Amy, 252
Clark, Bradley, 212
Clark, Liz, Cooking with, 148
Clark, Sandy Thorn, 254
Clark College, Culinary Arts
    Department, 143
Clarke, Kay E., 207
A Classic Affair (Creative
    Foods), 116
Classic Catering, 115, 126
Classics Capers Catering, Inc., 120
Claster and Company, Inc., 122
Clearbrook Farms, 36
Clearview Baking, 62
Clearview Farm, 57, 60
The Cleaver Company, Inc., 123
Cleveland Society for Culinary
    Professionals, 179
Clifford, Judy, 212
Cline, Rob, 212
Clipper Mill, 169
Cloudtree & Sun School of
    Cookery, 150
Club Car Catering Company, 122
Club Corporation of America, 77
Club Cuisine, 146
Club Managers' Association of
    America, 179
Clyde's of Tyson's Corner, 126
C.M. International, 169
The Coach Farm, 27
The Coach House Restaurant, 106
Coalition for Food Irradiation, 277
Coates, Donna, 207
Coca-Cola USA, 69
Cocolat, Inc., 25
Coco's. See Restaurant Enterprises
    Group, Inc.
Coffee, Coena, 208
Coffee, Sugar & Cocoa
    Exchange, 184
Coffee Bean International, Inc., 28
Coffee Development Group, 184
Cogan & Gordon, Inc., 159
Cohen, Elaine, 212
Cohen, James, Inc., 199
Cohen, Marc David, 200
Cohen, Marge, 146
Cohn, Ric, 200
Cole and Goyette, Architects and
    Planners, Inc., 95
Colen, Corinne, 200
Collins, Chris, 200
Collins and Barnes, Inc., 122
Collins Foods International,
    Inc., 77
Colonial Inn Caterers, 122
Colonial Kitchen (Bemis
    Manufacturing Company), 169
The Colony, 105
Colony Resorts, Inc. (Carlson
    Companies, Inc.), 80
Colorado State University Animal
    Reproduction Laboratory, 264
Colrus, William, 212

Columbia State Farmers'
    Market, 21
The Columbus Dispatch, 256
Columbus State Farmers'
    Market, 20
Colvada Date Company, 49
Commander's Palace, 106
Commerce Foods, Inc., 30
Commercial Aluminum Cookware
    Company, 170
The Commercial Appeal, 253
Commercial Cafe Catering, 126
Commercial Food Equipment
    Service Association, Inc., 179
Commonwealth Caterers, Ltd., 126
Community Coffee Kitchen, The
    Art of Food, 48
Community Kitchens, 28
Community Mill and Bean, 55
Community Nutrition
    Institute, 277
The Complete Kitchen, 145
Component Design Northwest,
    Inc., 164
ConAgra, Inc., 69
Concept Development, Inc. See
    Pantera's Corporation
Concern, Inc., 277
Concord Shear Corporation, 170
Confection Connection, 45
Conference of Consumer
    Organizations, 277
Confetti, 115
Congress Watch, 277
Connecticut Avenue Caterers,
    Inc., 117
Connecticut Culinary
    Institute, 144
Connecticut Regional Market, 19
Connecticut Women's Culinary
    Alliance, 180
Consolidated Products, Inc., 82
Consolidated Specialty Restaurants,
    Inc., 82
Constantin's, 102
Consul Restaurant Corporation, 82
Consumer Federation of
    America, 277
Consumers' Union of the United
    States, 277
Conte, George, Design Consult-
    ants, Inc., 96
Contemporary Caterers, Inc., 118
Conte Philips, 44
Conte-Philips Cooking School, 148
Continental Airlines, 91
Continental Cheese
    Corporation, 27
The Continental Companies, 77
Contra Costa Times, 258
Contri Brothers' Gift Basket, 43
Convenient Food Marts, 77
Cook, Anne, 212
Cook, Esky, 212
Cooke, Vickie Emerson, 206
Cookie Man Company, 23
Cooking with Amber, Inc., 149
Cooking With Class, 148
The Cooking and Hospitality
    Institute of Chicago, 144
The Cooking School, 149
Cook'n Cajun, 170
Cook's Classics, 39
Cooks Corner, Ltd., 147
Cook's Nook, 47
Cooktime by Eastern, 170

Cooktique, 146
Cooper Instrument
    Corporation, 170
Cooper & Turner, 162
Coors, Adolph, Company, 71
Copco, Inc. (Wilton
    Enterprises), 170
Copeland, A., Enterprises, Inc., 87
Copeland Krieger Associates, 96
Copeland's. See A. Copeland
    Enterprises, Inc.
The Copper Cellar
    Corporation, 126
Coppersource, 170
Cora, Peter, Sr., Specialty
    Equipment, 170
Corbett, Suzanne, Culinary
    Concepts, 149
Corday, Arlie, 249
Cordele State Farmers' Market, 20
Corn, Elaine, 258
Cornell, Jeff, 213
Cornell Catering, 122
Cornell University Institute of
    Food Science, 263
Corning, Inc., 170
The Corporate Caterer, 122
Corporate Food Services,
    Inc., 77, 79
Corradeno, Philomena, 259
Cosby Ramp Festival, 291
Costikyan, Barbara, 259
The Cottage Restaurant, 102
Cotton Boll Catering, 125
Council on Hotel/Restaurant and
    Institutional Education, 180
Council for Regional Culinary
    Organizations, 180
Country Caterer, 120
The Country Cupboard, 46
Country Epicure, Inc., 23
Country Hospitality, Inc., 77
Country Kitchen, 148
Country Life Natural Foods, 57
The Courier-Journal, 252
The Courier-Post, 249
The Courtyard, 47
Cowan & Fransman, Division of
    Jaret International, Inc., 30
Cowboy Catering, 116
Cowdrey, Richard, 213
Coyote Cafe, 107
CPC International, Inc., 69
The CPG, 23
Crabtree & Evelyn, Ltd., 36, 51
Cracker Barrel Old Country
    Store, Inc., 77
Craig, Daniel, 213
The Crate and Barrel, 52
Crawfish Festival, 291
Crawford, Robert, 213
Crayton Cove Gourmet, Inc., 43
Crea, Joel, 258
Creative Catering, 116, 117
Creative Catering by Ellen,
    Inc., 122
Creative Celebrations, Inc., 120
Creative Cookery, Ltd., 151
Creative Cookie Company, 61
Creative Cooking: The Cooking
    School, 147
Creative Cuisine, 124
Creative Foods, 116
Creative Gourmets, 120
Creative House, 170
Creative Kitchen, Inc., 170

Creative Kitchens, Inc., 160, 161
Creative Kitchens & Baths, 159
Creative Kosher Foods, Inc., 61
Creative Net-work, Inc., 189
Creative Specialty Manufacturing, 170
Crider, Kitty, 256
Crinklaw Farms—Gourmet Decoratives, 33
Criswell, Ann, 257
Croce, Pat, 205
Cronk, Alice, 205
Crook's Corner, 107
Crossroad Farm, 54
Crowley Cheese, 48
Crowne Plaza (Holiday Corporation), 80
Croxton Collaborative, 95
Crumpets, 42
Crystal Food Import Corporation, 27
Crystal's Pizza & Spaghetti. *See Unigate Restaurants, Inc.*
CSO Interiors, 97
Cuisinarts, Inc., 164
Cuisine Classics Cooking School, 147
Cuisine Cookware Company, 170
Cuisine Perel, 39
Culberson, Earl, 200
Culinary Arts at the New School, 145
Culinary Arts Program Department, UCLA Extension, 144
Culinary Classics, Inc., 122
Culinary Classics Cooking School, 148
Culinary Concepts, 149
The Culinary Emporium, 46
Culinary Guild of Chicago, 180
Culinary Historians of Ann Arbor, 180
Culinary Historians of Boston, 180
Culinary Historians of New York, 180
The Culinary Institute of America (CIA), 144
The Culinary School of Kendall College, 145
Cullum Companies, 75
Cunningham, Marian, 259
Curry, Dale, 253
Curtice-Burns, Inc., 72
Curtin, Jane, 205
Custer, Delores, 206
Czechowski, Alicia, 213

D

Dacey, Bob, 213
Dach Ranch, 58
Dacor, 163
Dae-Julie, Inc., 25
Dagorim Tahorim, 63
Daily, Don, 213
The Daily Press, 254
The Daily Republican, 249
Dairy and Food Industries Supply Association, 279
Dairy Industry Committee, 279
Dairy Isle. *See DeNovo Corporation*
Dairymen, Inc., 71
Dairy Research, Inc., 264
daka, 80
Dakin Farm, 50
Dale, Robert, 213
Dale's Bar-B-Que, 117

Dallas Market, 21
The Dallas Morning News, 256-257
Dallas Times Herald, 257
Dalts. *See TGI Friday's, Inc.*
D'Amico Cucina, 111
Dana Import, 30
Daniels & Stine, 96
Darci's, 46
Daroff Design, Inc., 96
Darrin, Susan Culver, 206
D'Artagnan, Inc., 38
Daste, Larry, 213
Datoli, Michael, 200
Davenport, Paul, 251
Davidcraft Corporation, 170
Davidson, Everett, 213
David's Specialty Foods, 78
Davis, Celia, 256
Davis Brothers Cafeterias, 87
Davis Brothers Wholesalers, Inc., 173
Dawson, Sue, 256
Days Inns of America, Inc., 80
Daytona Beach News-Journal, 252
Dayton Daily News, 256
Dayton Hudson Department Store Company, 78
Day & Young, 50
Dazey Corporation, 164-165
D.B. Kaplan's Deli. *See Levy Restaurants, Inc.*
Dean & DeLuca, 42, 51
  Imports, Inc., 30
Dean Foods Company, 70
Dean's Kitchen Center, Inc., 160
Dean Weller & Company, 191
Dear, Hugh W., & Associates, Inc., 97
Dearborn Farms, Inc., 41
Dearmore's Bar-B-Que, 116
Dearth, Greg, 213
Debold, Bill, 200
De Choix Specialty Foods Company, 30
Deegan, Carol, 250
Deer Creek Wild Rice Company, Inc., 35
Deer Park Baking Company, 25
Deer Valley Farm, 54, 59, 60
Deflecto Corporation, Housewares Division, 170
De Gennaro Associates, 200
De Gustibus at Macy's, 146
DeHaan, Norman, Associates, Inc., 97
Deigan, Jim, 213
DeKalb Farmers' Market, 56
Delano, Sharon, 259
DeLaurenti Specialty Food Market, 47
Delaware North Companies, Inc., 91
Delaware Valley Association of Cooking Professionals, 180
Delftree Shitake, 30
The Deli, 47, 114
The Deli Gourmet Food & Wine, 45
Delmarva Chicken Festival (Delmarva Poultry Industry, Inc.), 289
DeLonghi America, Inc., 165
Del Rossi, Ric, 213
Delta Airlines, Inc., 91

Del Taco, Inc. (American Restaurant Group, Inc.), 88
DeLuca's, 124
De Medici Imports, Ltd., 39
Demetrio's Catering, Inc., 122
Democrat and Chronicle, 250
DeMoulas/Market Basket, 75
Deni/Keystone Manufacturing, Inc., 165
Denny's, Inc., 88
DeNovo Corporation, 88
The Denver Post, 257
Denver's Catering, 117
Department of Agriculture (U.S.), 267-268
Department of Health and Human Services, Food and Drug Administration, 268
The Depot Market, 41
DePuy Canal House, 107
Deschamps, Bob, 213
The Deseret News, 257
Desert Rose Salsa Corporation, 30
Design & Associates, Inc., 98
Design Continuum, 97
Design Development, 99
Designers II, Inc., 97
Design Interpretation, Inc., 99
Design 1 Interiors, 98
Design Restaurant Systems, 99
Design Services, Inc., 98
Design Solutions, Inc., 97
Design Team One, Inc., 218
Design Works, Inc., 97
The Des Moines Register, 255
DeSoto Confectionery & Nut Company, 39, 49
Desserts by David Glass, Inc., 23
Detroit Free Press, 255
The Detroit News, 255
Detroit Produce Terminal, 21
Deux Cheminees, 101
Devarj, Silva, 200
DeVaty, Susan, 210
De Villeneuve, Kathy, 205
Devon. *See Restaurant Enterprises Group, Inc.*
Dial-A-Gift, 44
Diamond K. Enterprises, 57
Diamond Overseas Trading Company, 170
Diamond Ridge Farms, 59
Diane's, 43
Diaz, Rick, Photography, Inc., 200
Di Camillo Baking Company, Inc., 23, 50
The Dickinson Family, Inc., 36
Dierbergs School of Cooking, 149
Dietary Managers' Association, 266
Diggs, Mitchell, 251
DiLeonardo International, Inc., 96
Dimensional Interiors, 98
The Dining Room, 104, 110
Dinkel's Bakery, Inc., 23
DiOrio, Al, Design, 95
D & I Professional Caterers, Inc., 118
DiSalvo's Deli & Italian Store, 46
Disney, Walt, Company, 79
Disrude, Anne, 205
Distinctive Affairs, 125
Divett, Mary, 205
Dixie House. *See Unigate Restaurants, Inc.*
Dixon, Diane, 250
D'Masti Events & Catering, 118

Dobbs, David, 200
Dobbs Houses, Inc., 88
Dobbs International Services, Inc., 88, 91. *See also Greyhound Food Management, Inc.*
Dodson, Angela, 250
D'oeuvres by Dottie, 45
Dog n Suds, Inc. *See DeNovo Corporation*
Dolefam Corporation, 30
Dole Nut Company, 39
Dollaghan, Helen, 257
Dominick's Finer Foods, 74
Dominique Gourmet Foods, Inc., 40
Dominis, John, 200
Domino's Pizza, Inc., 88
Dong Chang International, Inc., 170
Donghia Associates, 95
Donsco, 175
Don's Finest Foods, 45
Donvier/Nikkal Industries, Ltd., 165
Dorf Associates, 95
Dorf & Stanton Communications, Inc., 189
Dorman-Roth Foods, Inc., 27
Dorothy Lane Market, 46
Doubles Club International, 106
Doubletree, Inc., 80
Dowell, Sharon, 256
Downey's Products, Inc., 23
Downing, G. "Skip," Architects, 99
Drake Bakeries, 62
Draper, Dorothy, & Company, Inc., 95
Dream Confectioners, Ltd., 62
Drentell Doyle Partners, 218
Drexel/Cook'n Cajun, 170
Dried Fruit Association of California, 185
Drink Tyme Vending, 63
Driver's Seat Restaurant, 100
Druther's International, Inc., 88
Ducak, Danilo, 213
Duck & Decanter, 46
Dudley, Linda, 258
The Duffy Design Group, 219
Dufour Pastry Kitchens, Inc., 23
Dugan's Ingredients, 39
Duke, Chris, 213
Duluth News-Tribune, 255
Dumas Pere L'Ecole de la Cuisine Francaise, 148
Dunkin' Donuts, Inc., 88
The Dunlavey Studio, Inc., 219
Duran, Nina, 213
The Durham Herald, 253
Durman, Louise, 253
Dynacast, 174
Dynamics Corporation of America, 167
Dyna-Pak Corporation, Retail Packaging, 33

E

Eagle Agricultural Products, 55
Eagle Provisions Company, Inc., 42
Earth Natural Foods, 57
Earth Natural Foods Deli, 57
Earth's Harvest, 55
East 48th Street Market/Italian Food Specialties, 43
East Coast Grill, 109

Eastern Airlines, 91
Eastern Dairy-Deli Association, Inc., 184
Eastern Shore Seafood Festival, 291
Eastern Shore Tea Company, Inc., 28
Eastman, Jerome, Inc., 97
E.A.T., 51
Eat'N Park Restaurants, Inc., 83
Edelman, Daniel J., Inc., 189
Eden Foods, Inc., 56
The Educational Foundation of the National Restaurant Association, 180
The Edwardian Room, 109
Edwards, S. Wallace, & Sons, Inc., 38
Edwards Design Group, 97
Edwards' Virginia Ham Shoppe, 44
EFCO Importers, 30
Eichler, Nancy, Cooking Classes with, 148
The Eight Mice, 45
Ekco Housewares, Inc., 170
Ekus, Lisa, Public Relations Company, 189
El Chico Corporation, 83
Elegant Delights Catering, 115
Elegant Edge, 118
Elegant Fare, Inc., 124
Elfman Caterers, 120
Elias, Allan, Custom Catering, 121
Elias Brothers Restaurants, Inc., 83
Eli's Catering, 123
Eli's Chicago's Finest, Inc., 61
Elizabeth on 37th, 110
Elki Corporation, 31
Elliot, Barbara, Interiors, Inc., 98
Elliott, Russell, Organic Gardens, 59
Ellis, Jane, 208
Ellis, Jon, 213
Ellis, Merle, 259
Ellis, Rick, & Associates, 206
Elmira Star-Gazette, 250
Elmore Roots Nursery, 55
The El Paso Chili Company, 31
El Paso Times, 257
El Pollo Loco, 88
El Torito. See Restaurant Enterprises Group, Inc.
Elvin, Ella, 259
Embassy Suites (Holiday Corporation), 80
Emmental Cheese Corporation, 27
Empire Coffee & Tea Company, 48
Empire Kosher Poultry, Inc., 65
Empire Market, 42
Enclume Design Products, Inc., 170
Encore Catering, Inc., 124
Engroff Catering, 119
Enlightened Homes, 160
The Enquirer, 255
Ensrud, Barbara, 259
Entertainment One, 83
Environmental Defense Fund, 277
Epicurean, 115
Epicurean Caterers, 117
Epicurean Cooking School, 150
Epicurean Events, 126
Epicurean International, Inc., 32
Epicure Foods Corporation, 27
The Epicures' Club, 51
Equipment Planners, Inc., 97

Erickson, Nancy, 258
Erickson Associates, Inc., 98
Ernst, Teri, 207
Estee Candy Company, 48
Estee Corporation, 31
Ets-Hokin, Judith, Culinary Company, 150
Etter, Jerry, 259
Eurich, Sharon, 250
The Euro Market, 46
Europa Foods, Ltd., 31
European Chocolate Shops, 25
European Electrics Corporation, 165
European Home Products, 52
European Imports, Ltd., 31
Evaco Import Services, Inc., 165
Evans, Bob, Farms, Inc., 77
Evans, Jan, 213
Evans/Kraft Bean Public Relations, 189
Eventmasters, 124
The Everest Room, 105
Everyday Gourmet School, 151
Evian Waters of France, Inc., 22
Ewing, Kay, Everyday Gourmet, 147
Exclusively Anne, 118
Executive Chef Catering, 126
Expression unltd., 41
Extra Billy's Steak & BBQ, 126
Exum, Helen, 253

F

Faber Enterprises (Greyhound Food Management, Inc.), 78
Fabio Imports, 25
Fabricant, Florence, 259
Fabulous Foods, Inc., 115
F & A Farm, 54
Fairfax Journal, 253
Fairmont Hotel Company, 80
The Fairmount Restaurant, 101
Fairwinds Gourmet Coffee Company, 28
Fall on the Flint Festival, 289
Famous Fish. See Famous Restaurants, Inc.
The Famous Pacific Dessert Company, 23
Famous Restaurants, Inc., 83
Fantasia Confections, 51
Farberware, Inc. (Hanson Industries), 165
Fare with Flair, 47
The Farm Basket, 44
Farmers' Market/Shelby County Growers' Association, Inc., 21
Farmers' Wholesale Cooperative, 59
Farm Fresh, 76
Farmland Industries, Inc., 72
Fasolino, Deresa, 213
Fats and Protein Research Foundation, Inc., 264
FBC Foods International, 47
FDL Foods, Inc., 72
Fearn International, Inc., 49
A Feast For All Reasons, Inc., 120
Feast Your Eyes, Inc., 125
Federal Market, 43
Fein, Ronnie, School of Creative Cooking, 146
Feist Catering, Ltd., 126
Felidia Ristorante, 100
Felknor International, Inc., 170

Fenix, 104
Fennel, 101
Fenzl, Barbara, 209
Fernanda Manufacturing, Inc., Designs by Jerry Abrams, 170
Ferrara, Patricia, 249
Ferrara Foods & Confections, 51
Ferrero Specialty Food Division, 31
Ferretti, Fred, 259
Feste Foods, Inc., 65
Festivities, 117
Fiddler's Green Farm, 53
Fifth Quarter Steak House. See Shoney's, Inc.
Fight, Loyd, 56
Figi's, 51
Fike's Finer Foods, 47
Fine Bouche, 111
Fini USA Corporation, 35
Finnfoods, Inc., 31
Fiorucci Foods Corporation, 38
Firehouse Bar-B-Que, 40
First American Marketing Group, Ltd., 22
First Class Productions, 219
First Colony Coffee & Tea Company, 28
First National Supermarkets (Eastern Division), 75
First National Supermarkets (Ohio Division), 75
First Ranch. See The Happy Steak, Inc.
Fisheries Development Advisory Council, New Jersey Department of Agriculture, 292
Fisher & Levy, 123
Fish Works!, 189
Fiskars Company, 171
Fiskars Manufacturing Corporation, 171
Fitzgerald, Martha, 253
Fitzsimmons, Kathleen, 207
Flavorbank Company, Inc., 36
Flavorchem Corporation, 36
Flavor & Extract Manufacturers, 187
Fleishman Hillard, Inc., 189
Flesher, Vivienne, 213
Fletcher, T. Mike, 200
Fleur de Lait Foods, Ltd., 27
Fleur de Lys, 105
FLIK International Corporation, 79
Flo Braker Baking, 150
Flora, Donnie, 209
Florenz. See Jerrico, Inc.
Florida Avocado Administrative Committee, 188
Florida Celery Exchange, 188
Florida City/State Farmers' Market, 20
Florida Department of Citrus, 185
Florida Gift Fruit Shippers' Association, 185
Florida Lime Administrative Committee, 185
The Florida Times-Union, 252
Florida Today, 252
Florida Tomato Committee, 188
Flowers Industries, Inc., 72
Flyer's Island Express. See Chili's, Inc.
Foah Enterprises, Inc., 31
Foley, Michael, 259
Foley Company, Cookware-Bakeware (Newell Group), 171

Fond Memories, 120
The Food Company, 208
Foodcraft/Cathy German, 209
Food Dimensions, Inc., 79
Food and Drug Administration, 268
Food and Drug Law Institute, 277, 279
Food Equipment Manufacturers' Association, 180
Food Industry Association Executives, 279
Food Lion, 74
Foodmaker, Inc., 88
Food Marketing Communicators, 180
Food Marketing Institute, 279
Food Marketing Institute (FMI), 180
Political Action Committee, 279
Food of Our Own Design, 23
Food Processing Machinery and Supplies Association, 180, 279
The Food Processors' Institute, 279
Food Research and Action Center, 277, 279
Foods of All Nations, 44-45
Food Sciences Department, Purdue University, 266
Foodservice Consultants' Society International, 180
Foodservice Equipment Distributors' Association, 180
Foodservice and Lodging Institute, 279
Food Service & Packaging Institute, 180
Food Stuffs, 42
Food for Thought, 117
Food for Thought Caterers, 125
Food Thoughts Catering & Event Planning, Inc., 122
Foodworks, 207
Forbes, Lynn, 258
Forbes-Ergas Design Associates, 95
Foreman, Mary, 255
Foresman, Susan Bond, 207
Forever Cookware, 171
Forte Hotels International, 80
Fort Pierce State Farmers' Market, 20
Fort Worth Star-Telegram, 257
40 Village Place Gourmet, 45
The Forum, 255
Forum Architecture & Planning, 97
Foster, Sara, 205
Foster, Valerie, 259
Fosters Freeze International, 78
Fouineteau USA, Inc., 171
The Fountain Restaurant, 106
The Four Seasons, 108
Four Seasons Hotel, 106
Four Star International, 171
Fowler's Food Store of Durham, 44
Fox, Mary Jo, 251
Fox Run Craftsmen, 171
Francis, J., Company, 57
Francis, Jack, Inc., 125
Franey, Pierre, 259
Frank, Justine, 210
Frank, Lois Ellen, 200
Frank-Martin, Tobi, 210
Franz, Mary K., 209
Fraser-Morris Fine Foods, 51
Frazier Design, 219

Freeman, Josh, Associates, 219
The Free Press, 251
Freiman, Jane, 259
French, Florence, 208
French, Virginia, 254
The French Apron School of
Cooking, 149
French Bakery & Cafe. *See Vie de
France Restaurant Corporation*
The French Culinary Institute, 143
French Meadow Bakery, 23
Fresco Ristorante, 107
Fresh Garlic Association, 188
Fresh Horizon Creative
Catering, 126
Fresh Mark, Inc., 73
The Fresno Bee, 257
Fresno Place, 106
Freyer, Marina P., 205
Frieda's Finest Produce
Specialties, 31
Friedman, Bette Harris, 206
Fritch, Polly Stewart, International
Cooking with, 146
Fritschner, Sarah, 252
Frontera Grill, 100
Frozen Potato Product
Institute, 186
Frozen Potato Products
Institute, 279
Fudge 'n' Such Gourmet
Shoppe, 43
Fujiware America, Inc., 165
Fulford Brothers Nursery, 54
Fullers, 107
Furr's, 75
Furr's/Bishop's Cafeterias LP., 86
Fussell, Betty, 259
Future Farmers of America, 279

G

Gabriele, Tony, 213
Gadsden County State Farmers'
Market, 20
Gage & Tollner, 106
Gaggenau USA, 163
The Gainesville Sun, 252
Galante, Dennis, 200
Galardi Group, 88
Gallardo, Gervasio, 214
Gallery of Kitchens, Inc., 161
Gallimaufry, 125
Gang, Christine Arpe, 253
Gannett News Service, 251
Garcia's of Scottsdale, Inc. *See
Famous Restaurants, Inc.*
Garden Spot Distributors, 55
Garland Commercial
Industries, 163
Garns, Allen, 214
Garrison, Beverly, 253
Garry Packing, Inc., 33
Gaspar's Sausage Company, 50
Gaston Dupre, Inc., 35
Gautsch & Associates, Inc., 190
Gavigan, William, The Caterer,
Inc., 118
Gaylord Specialties
Corporation, 34
The Gazette Telegraph, 257
Gazin's, Inc., 51
GB Design, Inc., 98
Geiger, Michael, Ltd., 200
Gelles, Carol, 206
General Cinema Corporation, 72
General Electric, 163

General Electric Appliances, 165
General Foods, 64
General Housewares Corporation,
Cookware Group, 171
General Mills, Inc., 70
General Mills Restaurant
Group, Inc., 83
The General Store, 45
Genesee Valley Regional Market
Authority, 19
Gensler & Associates, 99
Georgetown Coffee, Tea and
Spice, 48
Georgia Institute of Human
Nutrition, Medical College of
Georgia, 266
Georgia Organic Growers'
Association, 56
Georgia Peanut Commission, 185
Gerbeaud, Inc., 31
Gerber Legendary Blades (Fiskars
Company), 171
Gerber Products Company, 73
Gerling, Fran, 209
German, Cathy, Foodcraft, 209
Gerould, Carolyn
Schirmacher, 210
Gerstman & Meyers, Inc., 219
Geyer, Jackie, 214
GFM Public Service Division. *See
Greyhound Food Management, Inc.*
Ghirardelli Chocolate
Company, 25
Giant Eagle, 75
Giant Food Inc., 74
Gianutti, Peter, 259
Gift Basket Supplies, Inc., 34
The Gift Company, 47
The Gifted Line, John Grossman,
Inc., 34
Giguere, Ralph, 214
Gilbert Whitney and Johns,
Inc., 190
Gilhooly, Brenda, 250
Gillardin, Andre, 200
Gill/G'Dam Kosher Cheese
Company, 62
Gillies Coffee Company, 28
Gilroy Garlic Festival, 288
The Gilway Company Limited, 31
Gin, Byron, 214
Giordano, 102, 109
Giovanitti Design Group,
Inc., 219
Giovanni's, 100
Girvin, Tim, Design, Inc., 219
Giuca, Linda, 249
Glaser, Ken, and Associates, 200
Glaser, Milton, Inc., 219
Glass, David, Desserts by, Inc., 23
Glass, Peggy, Cooking School, 146
Glass, Randy, 214
Glasser, Dale, 214
Gleason, Bob, 214
Glen Dimplex, 165
Glenn Foods, Inc., 63
Glerup-Revere Company, Inc., 34
Global Marketing/Kenwood, 165
Globe Products (Holly Farms
Corporation), 62
Glorious Food, 123
Glyer, Gloria, 258
Goday, Dale, 206
Godbold, Jim, 258

Godfather's Pizza, Inc. (The
Pillsbury Company Restaurant
Group), 88
Godiva Chocolatier, Inc., 25, 48
Godsted, Pat Martin, 207
Goeglein's, Inc., 119
Gold, Charles, Inc., 200
Goldberg, Howard, 259
Goldblatt, Min, & Sons, 122
Golden Acres Apiary, 56
Golden Acres Orchard, 56
Golden Corral Corporation. *See
Investors' Management Corporation*
Golden Fluff Popcorn
Company, 62
Golden Gate Produce Terminal, 22
Golden Glow Cookie Company, 63
Golden Key Farm, 56
The Golden Mushroom, 102
Golden Nugget. *See Bally
Manufacturing Corporation*
Golden Simcha Poultry, Inc., 63
Golden Skillet. *See International
Dairy Queen, Inc.*
Gold Kist, Inc., 71
Goldman's Dairy, 62
Gold Mine Natural Food
Company, 58
Gold Pure Food Products
Company, Inc., 63
Gold Rush. *See Consolidated Specialty
Restaurants, Inc.*
Goldrush Sourdough Mix, 23
Gold Star Smoked Fish, Inc., 32
Go Lightly Candy
Company, 25, 62
Golin/Harris, 190
Gollo, Peter, Photography, 200
Gonko, Bob, 254
Goodbody, Mary, 259
Goodfellow's, 100
Good & Plenty Catering, Inc., 123
Good Taste, Inc./Saucy Sisters, 114
Gordon, Nancy, 254
Gormezano, Mimi, Chez, Cooking
School, 148
The Gotham Bar and Grill, 107
Gottlieb, Dennis M., Studio,
Inc., 200
Gottlieb, Penelope, 214
Gourmac, Inc., 171
Gourmet!, 124
Gourmet America, Inc., 31
Gourmet Curiosities, Etc., 149
Gourmet Decoratives, 33
Gourmet Emporium, 46
Gourmet Nut Center, 49
Gourmet Produce Company, 55
The Gourmet Shop, Inc., 44
Gourmet's Market, Inc., 44
Gourmet Take-Away, 41
Gourmet Tidbits, Inc., 118
Grace's Marketplace, 42
Grace Tea Company, Ltd., 28
Graham-Solano, Ltd., 95
Gra-Mic, Inc., 175
Granas, Marilyn, 210
Grand Cafe, 110
Grandesign Architects, 95
Grandma's Pantry, 43
The Grand Rapids Press, 255
Grand Union, 74
Grandy's. *See Restaurant Manage-
ment Company*
Grate Things, 43
Gratzi. *See Jerrico, Inc.*

Grausman, Richard, 146
Graven, J.M., Company, 99
Gray, Ann Milligan, Inc., 97
Gray, James, 250
Gray, Walter, Photography,
Inc., 200
The Great Chefs at Robert
Mondavi Winery, 150
Great Date in the Morning, 58
Great Performances, 123
Greaves, Cindy, 209
Greca, William A., Company, 26
Green & Ackerman Baking
Company, 63
Greenberg, Sarah, 206
The Greenbrier, 45
The Greenbrier Cooking
School, 148
Green County Foods, Inc., 33
Greene, Gael, 259
The Green Earth, 56
Greengrass, Barney, "The Sturgeon
King," 41
Green Hills Inn, 109
Green Lake Grill, 101
Green Parrot Restaurant, 102
The Greensboro News &
Record, 253
Greenville State Farmers'
Market, 21
Grell, G., 58
Grennes, Janet, 207
Gretchen's Of Course, 126
Greyhound Food Management,
Inc., 78, 79, 88
Griesbach, Cheryl, 214
Griffith, Dotty, 256
The Grill Room, 104
Grimes, Paul, 207
Grisanti Catering, 119
Griswald, Sandra, 210
Grocery Manufacturers of
America, 180, 279
Grogan's, 44
Grossman, John, Inc., 34
Gross National Waste Product
Forum, 277
Grosvenor Marketing, Ltd., 28
Grouch, Laura, 257
The Ground Round, Inc., 83
Growth Catering, 121
Gruwell-Pheasant-Design, 99
G & S International Products/Four
Star International, 171
G & S Metal Products Company,
Inc., 171, 172
GSO, Inc., 63
GTC International, Inc., 171
Guckenheimer Enterprises, Inc., 79
Guest Services, Inc., 80
Gulliver's. *See Canteen Company*
Gumbo Festival, 289
Gump's Mail Order, 51
Guthaus, Peggy, 255
Gwathmey Siegel & Associates, 96

H

Haagen-Dazs Company, Inc. (The
Pillsbury Company Restaurant
Group), 78
Haddix, Carol, 254
Haddon House Food Products,
Inc., 31
Hagiwara, Brian, 200
Hale, Bruce, Design, 219
Hale Indian River Groves, 49

Halibut Association of North America, 187
Hallmark Housewares Company, 171
Hall's Diversified Caterers, 124
Hamburger Hamlets, Inc., 88
Hamersley's Bistro, 104
Hamilton, Thomas, & Associates, 97
Hamilton Beach Company (Glen Dimplex), 165
Hamilton Plaza Hotel, 110
Hamlin, Suzanne, 259
Hammacher Schlemmer, 52
Hampton Kitchens, 160
Hanes, Phyllis, 249
Hanle, Zack, 259
Hanley, Marge, 254
Hannaford Brothers, 75
Hanrahan, Gordon, Inc., 190
Hansen Caviar Company, Inc., 32
Hanson Industries, 165
Happy Herman's, 43
The Happy Steak, Inc., 83
Happy Steak Restaurants. *See The Happy Steak, Inc.*
Happy Town Farm, 54, 59
Haram-Christensen Corporation, 31
Harbortown Division, IBR Corporation, 171
Hardee's Food Systems, Inc., 88
Hardin, Ted, 200
Hardscrabble Enterprises, Inc., 56
Harper-Lee International, Inc., 171
Harrah's Hotels and Casinos (Holiday Corporation), 80
Harrington, Ann, 207
Harrington's, 50
Harris, Michael, 200
Harrison, William, 214
Harrison Mushroom Festival, 290
Harry & David, 49
Harry's Market, 55
Hart, Mary, 255
Hart, McMurphy & Parks, 126
Harte Yamashita & Forest, 219
The Hartford Courant, 249
Hartnett, Lori, 207
Harvard Bookstore Cafe, 106
Harvest Maid, 168
Harvest Time Foods, 65
Harvey, Ray, 214
Harwood, John, 214
Hashi Studio, Inc., 200
Hatch Chile Festival, 290
Hathaway, Brad, 249
Hathaway's Catering, 126
Haverson/Rockwell Architects, 95
Havlicek, Karel, 214
Hawaiian Plantations, 31
Hawaii Holiday Macadamia Nut Company, Inc., 49
Hawker, Christopher, Photography, 200
Hawkins Creek Farm, 58
Hawthorne Valley Farm, 59, 60
Hay Day's Cooking School, 146
Hayes, Joanne, 259
Haynes, David, 249
Hay's Farm Stand, 59
HCA L. W. Blake Hospital, 117
H & C Kitchens and Bathrooms, Inc., 161
HDM, 190
Healy, Brian, 201

Healy-Lucullus School of French Cooking, 150
Heartland Food Society, 180
Hebrew National Kosher Foods, Inc., 63
Hedgerose Heights Inn, 109
Heiferling, Mindy, 259
Heileman, G., Brewing Company, Inc., 71
Heiner, Joe and Kathy, 214
Heinz, H.J., Company, 65, 69
Helen's Tropical-Exotics, Inc., 40
Heller, Ann, 256
Heller, Nancy, 207
Hellmich, Nancy, 251
Hellmuth, Obata & Kassabaum, 97
Helms Foods, 43
Hel's Kitchen Catering, Inc., 119
Hena, Inc., 28
Henckels, J.A., 171
Henderling, Lisa, 214
Henderson, Janice Wald, 259
Henry, Carolyn, & Associates, Inc., 98
Henry, Doug, 214
Herald Housewares, 169
Herald and Review, 254
Herb Pharm, 59
Herman Goelitz, Inc., 25
Hermsen Design Associates, Inc., 219
Herrera, Dan, 258
Herr Foods, Inc., 65
Hershey Foods Corporation, 70
Hershey Import Company, Inc., 39
Hershey's Chocolate World, 48
Hetherington, William, & Associates, Inc., 98
Heuck, M.E., Company, 171
Hickory Farms, 48
Hickory Steak House Catering, 121
Hidden Valley Farm, 53, 59
Hieronymus Seafood Companies, 123
Highlands: A Bar and Grill, 110
High Valley Farm, Inc., 38, 50
Hillary's. *See Levy Restaurants, Inc.*
Hillcrest Caterers, 120
Hillcrest Farms, 55
Hill and Dale Farms, 55
Hill Design, Inc., 171
Hill and Knowlton, 190
Hillside Farm, 53
Hillside Metal Ware Company, 171
Hilton Hotels Corporation, 80
Himes, Carmen, 209
Hinske, Mim, 208
Hirsch/Bedner and Associates, 99
Hitachi Sales Corporation of America, 165
The Hively Agency, Inc., 219
Hlavak, Lois Willecke, 207
Hoan Products, Ltd., 171
Hobart Products Company (G & S Metal Products, Inc.), 172
Hochheiser-Elias Design Group, 95
Hodgdon, Marilinda, 206
Hoffman, Ann, 254
Hoffman Quality Meats, 120
Hoffritz International, 172
Hofmann, Ginnie, 214
Holiday Corporation, 80

Holiday Inn Hotel Group (Holiday Corporation), 80
Hollenbach, Charles, Inc., 37
Holliston Corporation, 172
Holly Farms Corporation, 62, 70
Holzemer, Buck, Photography, 201
Homarus, Inc., 32
Homecraft Consumer Products Group (Dynacast), 174
Homegrown Produce Company, 56
The Home News, 249
Homeplate Catering, 127
Honey Acres, Inc., 36
Honolulu-Star Bulletin, 259
Hood, Orly, 253
Hope's Specialty Foods, Inc., 31
Hopkins, Tom, 201
Hormel, George A., & Company, 70
The Horn & Hardart Company, 88
Horowitz, Ross M., 201
Horsepower Farm, 53
Hospital Corporation of America, 90
Hospitality International, Inc., 80
Hospital Purchasing Services, 90
Host International. *See Marriott Corporation*
Hotel Sofitel School of French Culinary Skills, 149
Hot Pots Cooking School, 151
Houle, Barbara, 249
Houlihan's. *See Restaurant Enterprises Group, Inc.*
House of Catering, 115
The House of Hasenfratz, 34
Household Products Group, 164
The House of Kitchens, Inc., 160
House of Tsang, Inc., 31
House of Webster, Inc., 33
The Houston Chronicle, 257
Houston Culinary Guild, 180
Houston Foods, 33
The Houston Post, 257
Houston Produce Center, 21
Houston's Restaurants, 83
Howard, Jeffrey, & Associates, 97
Howe, Phil, 214
Hower, George, 258
Howerton, Janet, 207
Howry, Andrea, 258
H & P Mayer Corporation, 171
HRI-Purchase Connection, 78
Hruska, Roman L., U.S. Meat Animal Research, 264
H.S.F. Enterprises, 29
Hsu's Cookery, 146
Hubbell, William, 201
Huberman, Susan, 206
Hubert's, 100
Hudson Foods, Inc., 72
Hudson Standard Corporation, 164, 165
Hughes Market, 76
Hulot's, 110
Humana, Inc., 90
Human Nutrition Option, Mississippi State University, 266
Hume, Janice, 251
Hungry's. *See The Jan Companies*
The Hunt Club, 104
Hunter, Stan, 214
Hunts Point Terminal Produce Cooperative Market, 19
Hurd, Kenneth E., & Associates, 95

Huszar, Steven, 201
Hutzler Manufacturing Company, Inc., 172
Hyatt, Mitch, 214
Hyatt Hotels Corporation, 80
Hye Quality Bakery, 29
Hyplains Dressed Beef, Inc., 73
Hy-Vee Food Stores, 75

IBP, Inc., 69
IBR Corporation, 171
Idaho Bean Commission, 186
Idaho-Oregon Promotion Committee, 188
Idaho Potato Commission, 186
The Idaho Statesman, 257
Ideal Cheese, 48
Ideal Cheese Shop, 42
Idle Wild Foods, Inc., 71
IHOP Corporation, 83
Image Design, Inc., 97
Imagination!s Catering, 118
IMEX Enterprise, 172
Immokalee State Farmers' Market, 20
Imperial Holly Corporation, 72
Imperial Schrade Corporation, 172
Incredible Edibles/Sue Spitler, 209
Index The Design Firm, 98
Indiana Beef Council, 292
Indiana Market & Catering, 123
The Indianapolis News, 254
The Indianapolis Star, 254
Indiana Pork Producers Association, 292
Indian-Style Salmon Bake, 291
Indian Summer, Inc., 39
In-Flight Food Service Association, 180
In Good Taste, Inc., 44, 124, 148
The Inn at Little Washington, 107
Inquirer, 251
In-Sink-Erator, 163
Insley Caterers, Ltd., 121
Institute for Alternative Agriculture, 263, 277
Institute for Fisheries Research, 264
Institute of Food Technologists, 181
Institute of Shortening and Edible Oils, 279
Integra Hotel and Restaurant Company, 80, 88
Inter-Continental Hotels Corporation, 80
Interior Design Force, Inc., 95
Interior Design International, 95
Intermarket Corporation, 172
Intermili, Inc., 62
International Apple Institute, 185, 279
International Association of Cooking Professionals (IACP), 180
International Banana Association, 279
International Beverages, Inc., 22
International Caterers' Association, 180
International Chefs' Association, 181
International Chili Society, 292
International Cookware Company, 172

International Dairy Queen, Inc., 88
International Design Concepts, 98
International Food, Wine and
	Travel Writers' Association, 181
International Foodservice
	Distributors' Association, 279
International Foodservice Editorial
	Council (IFEC), 181
International Foodservice
	Executives' Association, 181
International Foodservice
	Manufacturers' Association, 181
International Franchise Associa-
	tion, 181
International Frozen Food
	Association, 279
International Housewares, 169
International Ice Cream
	Association, 279
International Institute of
	Foods, 207
International Institute of Foods
	and Family, 181
International King's Table,
	Inc., 83
International Marketing
	Services, 31
International Microwave Power
	Institute (IMPI), 181
International Multifoods
	Corporation, 71
International Pastry Arts
	Center, 145
Interstate Bakeries Corporation, 71
Interstate Hotels Corporation, 80
Intimate Affairs Catering, 118
Intradesign, Inc., 99
Investors' Management Corpora-
	tion, 83
Iowa Beef Council, 186
Iowa State Natural Food
	Associates, 56
Ipswich Strawberry Festival, 290
Iron Gate Products Company,
	Inc., 32, 49
Iwatani International Corporation
	of America, 165

J

Jablum USA, 28
Jackie's, 110
Jack In The Box. See Foodmaker, Inc.
Jackson, Rosemary, 249
Jacksonville Farmers' Market, 20
Jacobs, Martin, 201
Jacobson/Fernandez, 214
Jacobs Suchard Brach, Inc., 25
Jacqualin et Cie, 147
Jacquet USA, 29
Jaffe Brothers, 59
Jagel's Catering Services, Inc., 124
Jake's Famous Products, Inc., 23
Jambalaya Festival, 289
Jamco, Ltd./Mr. Steak, 83
James Taverns. See Stouffer
	Restaurant Company
The Jan Companies, 83
Janelli, Cheryle Jaffe, 206
Janeric Products of Vermont,
	Inc., 65
Jane's Bar and Grill, 100
Jardine's Farm Restaurant, 125
Jardine's Texas Foods, 31
Jaret International, Inc., 25, 30
Jarrett, Lauren, Watercolors, 214
Jasper's, 111

J.B.'s Restaurants, Inc., 84
J.B. Winberie's. See Stouffer
	Restaurant Company
J.D. Mercantile, 43
Jean-Louis at the Watergate, 107
Jefferson County Truck Growers'
	Association—Farmers'
	Market, 20
Jenkins, Nancy Harmon, 259
Jenkins Communications,
	Inc., 190
Jenn-Air Corporation, 163
Jennex Company, 172
Jerbeau Chocolate Classics, 26
Jeremiah Sweeney's. See Consolidated
	Specialty Restaurants, Inc.
Jericho America, Inc., 172
Jerrico, Inc., 84
Jerry's Caterers, 91
Jerry's Restaurants. See Jerrico, Inc.
Jessica's Biscuit Cookbook
	Catalog, 52
J & F Imports, Inc., 172
Jimmy's Harborside
	Restaurant, 105
Jin Mi Oriental Cooking
	School, 146
J.M. Specialties, 36
Joachim, Bruno, Photography, 201
Joel, Seth, 201
Joe's Restaurant, 103
Johansky, Peter, 201
John Ash & Company, 100
John Clancy's, 102
Johnny's Selected Seeds, 53
Johnson, Teresa, 257
Johnson, Vicki, Food Stylist, 209
Johnson & Wales University,
	Culinary Arts Division, 143
Johnston, Ginger, 258
Jojo's. See Restaurant Enterprises
	Group, Inc.
Jolly Porpoise. See daka
Jolly Roger. See Trans/Pacific
	Restaurants, Inc.
Jonason, Dave, 214
Jones, Betty A., Catering, Inc., 119
Jones, Jean, 250
Jones, Spencer, 201
Jonson Pirtle Pedersen Alcorn
	Metzdorf & Hess, 219
Jordano, David, Photography, 201
Jordan Showplace Kitchens, 161
Jordan Virginia Ham
	Company, 50
Josephs, Nathana, Public
	Relations, 190
Josephs of Tyler Catering, 126
The Journal Gazette, 254
Journal Star, 254
Joyner, Jim, 56
Joyva Corporation, 31
Judyth's Mountain, Inc., 40
Julien Restaurant, 100, 109
JungDesigns, Inc., 99
Jurgensen's Grocery Company, 51
Just, Hal, 214

K

Kafka, Barbara, 259
Kake Kreations, 150
Kalamazoo Gazette, 255
Kalina, Mike, 259
Kalkus-Hirco, Inc., Ursula, 172
Kallio, Sandy, 256
Kampen, Carla Van, 249

Kansas City, Missouri, Terminal
	Market, 21
Kansas City Catering, 119
The Kansas City Star, 255
The Kansas City Times, 255
Kansas State University Thomas B.
	Avery Research Center (Poultry
	Science), 264
Kaplan, Gail, Classic Catering, 119
Karcher, Carl, Enterprises, Inc., 87
Karlson Kitchens, 161
Karmelkorn. See International Dairy
	Queen, Inc.
Kasilof Fish Company, 32
Kasler & Associates, Inc., 97
Kasota Fruit Terminal, 21
Kasper, Rob, 259
Katalinich, Peggy, 250
Katherine's Catering, Inc., 121
Katrina, 201
Kattman, J., Associates, 98
Katvan, Moshe, 201
Katz, Alan, 259
Kaufman, Judi, & Company, 150
Kaufman's Fancy Fruits &
	Vegetables, 44
Kaukauna Cheese, 27
Kawachi, Yutaka, 201
Kaye, Sheila, Candies, 26
K-Bob's Steak Houses, Inc., 84
K-Co., Inc., 172
Keebler Company, 71
The Keene Sentinel, 249
Keller-Charles of Philadelphia, 34
Kelleter, Robert, 251
Kellogg Company, 70
Kelly, Kathleen, 255
Kelly, Mike, Kitchens, 159
Kelly, Neil, Company, 162
Kemach Food Products
	Corporation, 63
Kemp, Julianne, 254
Kencraft, Inc., 26
Kendall-Brown Foods, 39
Kendall College, The Culinary
	School of, 145
Kennedy's Natural Foods, 56
Kenwood, 165
Ketchum Public Relations, 190
Keter Plastic (USA), Inc., 172
Kettle Restaurants, Inc., 84
Key West Grill. See S&A Restaurant
	Corporation
KFC Corporation (PepsiCo
	Foodservice Division), 88
Kiesau, Mary, 209
Kimball, Lee, Kitchens, 159
Kinast, Susan, Photography, 201
Kineret Foods Corporation, 63
King Cole Restaurant &
	Catering, 124
King David Knishes, 63
King Features Syndicate, 250
King Hill Farm/Hay's Farm
	Stand, 53, 59
King Kullen, 76
Kings Cookingstudio, 146
Kings Super Markets, Inc., 42
Kirsch, Abigail, Culinary
	Productions, Inc., 122
Kitchell, Joyce, 215
KitchenAid, Inc., 163
KitchenAid, Inc. (Whirlpool
	Corporation), 165
Kitchen Art, Inc., 161
Kitchen Associates, Inc., 159

Kitchen and Bath Concepts of
	Pittsburgh, 160
Kitchen Center, Inc., 160
Kitchen Concepts Plus, Inc., 162
Kitchen Conservatory, 148
The Kitchen Cupboard, 147
Kitchen Designs and Interiors, 162
Kitchen Design Studio, 160, 161
Kitchen Fare Cooking School, 147
Kitchen Glamour...The Cook's
	World, 149
The Kitchen Guild, 160
Kitchen Hardware, Ltd., 172
Kitchen Kreators, 160
The Kitchen Place, Inc., 161
Kitchen Planners, 162
Kitchen Planning Center, Inc., 160
Kitchen Professionals, 160
Kitchens, Inc., 160
Kitchens by A & B, Inc., 159
Kitchens of Distinction, 159, 162
The Kitchen Shoppe and Cooking
	School, 147
The Kitchen Showcase, Inc., 159
The Kitchen Specialist, 162
Kitchen Studio, Inc., 161
Kitchen Supply Company, 172
Kitchen Towne, 160
Klass, Gai, Catering, 115
Klatt, Gail, 207
Klein, Matthew, 201
Kline, Teresa, 249
K Mart Corporation, 78
Knapp, Bob, Restaurant &
	Catering, 118
Knight's Party Productions, 116
Knorr, Torin/ Shari Pulcrano,
	Interior Design, 99
Knott's Berry Farm, 51
	Foods, 36
Knouse Foods, Inc., 65
The Knoxville News-Sentinel, 253
Knudsen Company, 58
Knutson, Kristin, 215
Koeze Specialty Foods, Inc., 45
Kohout, Barbara, 208
Kojel Food Company (V.I.P
	Foods), 64
Kolb-Lena Cheese Company, 48
Kona Coffee Festival, 289
Kona Kai Farms, 29
Konriko Company Store, 51
Koppel & Scher, 219
Kopper's Chocolate Specialty
	Company, Inc., 26, 63
Korn, Carole, Interiors, Inc., 97
Korten, Jean, 251
Kosta, Jeff, Studio, 201
Kostelni, Dolores, Cooking
	School, 148
Kovacs and Associates, Inc., 99
Kozan, Dan, Studio, 201
Kozlowski Farms, 51
	Sonoma County Classics, 36
Kozyra, James, 201
K-Paul's Louisiana Kitchen, 108
Kraft, Inc., 69, 292
Krane & Rush, 46
Krantz, Jim, Studios, Inc., 201
Krasner, Carin, Photography, 201
Kreiner Imports, 31
Krengel, Kitchens by, Inc., 161
Kriz, Caroline, 208
The Kroger Company, 70, 74
Krome, Marilyn S., 209
Kron Chocolatier, Inc., 26, 48

Kroninger, Rick, 201
Krosnick, Alan, 201
Krum's Chocolatiers, 26, 64
Krups, Robert, North America, 165
The Krystal Company, 88
Krystal Wharf Farms, 55
Kubinyi, Laszlo, 215
Kuhn's Imports, Inc., 31
Kummer, Corby, 259
Kump, Peter, New York Cooking School in New Jersey, 146
Kuoni, Jane, 207
Kushnick, Don, 201

L

La Belle Pomme, 149
La Bernice Cooking School, 150
L'Academie de Cuisine, Inc., 145
La Caravelle, 109
L.A. Celebrations, 115
La Colombe d'Or Restaurant, 107
La Cote Basque, 108
La Cremaillere Restaurant, 106
La Cucina Italiana, Inc., 148
Lafayette Gourmet, 45
Lafferty, Donna, 208
La Folie, 107
La Grenouille, 107
Lagrotte Catering/Leonard's, 118
Lamalle, Cecile, 259
Lamar Photographics, 201
La Martinique, 39
L'Americain, 107
Lamonica, Chuck, 201
Lamotte, Michael, Studios, Inc., 201
Lancaster New Era, 251
Lance, Inc., 73
The Land Institute, 277
Land O'Lakes, Inc., 71
Landor Associates, 219
Lane, Raymond M., 253
Lane, Sharon, 259
Lang, Jenifer Harvey, 259
Langan, Marianne, 205
LaPace Imports, Inc., 31
LaPadula, Tom, 215
La Patisserie, 41
Lape, Bob, 259
La Petite Boulangerie. See Mrs. Field's Cookies
La Piccolina & Company, Inc., 24
La Preferida Inc. of New York, 32
La Reserve, 104
Larimores, 115
Lark Creek Inn, 107
Larkin, Inc., 98
Larry's Brown Deer Market, 46
Larry's Market Cooking School, 151
Larwill, Judith, 209
Lasso Corporation of America, 172
Las Vegas Review-Journal, 256
Las Vegas Sun, 256
La Tempesta, 24
La Tour, 105
La Tulipe, 103
L'Auberge Bretonne, 104
Laughner Brothers, Inc., 87
Laura-Fine Catering, 123
La Varenne Cooking School, USA, 145
La Venture, 148
La Villa Taxco, 84
Lavosh-Hawaii, 29

Lawder, John, Photography, 201
Lawler Foods, Inc., 65
Lawrence, David, Caterers, Inc., 125
Lawrence's Smoke House, 50
Lawson's Gourmet, 117
L.D.E., Inc., 172
Leaf, Inc., 73
Leatart, Brian, 201
Le Bec Fin, 107
Le Bernardin, 106
Lecat, Paul, Photography, 201
Le Chocolatier Manon, 26
Le Cirque, 101, 106
Le Creuset of America, Inc., 172
The Ledger-Star, 254
Lee, Donna, 251
Lee, Tom, Ltd., 95
Lee, Vincent B., 202
Leeds, Beth Whybrow, 215
Lee's Famous Recipe Chicken. See Shoney's, Inc.
Lee's Turkey Farm, 54
Le Francais, 106
Legal Sea Foods, Inc., 49, 84
Legume, Inc., 62
Lehn, John, and Associates, 202
Lehr's Meats & Catering, 124
Leibman's Wine & Fine Foods, 46
Leifheit Sales (S.J. International Corporation), 172
Le Kookery, 150
Le Lion D'Or, 104
Lello Appliances Corporation, 165
Lello Ristorante, 100
Lentrade, Inc./Chantal, 172
Leo, Diane, Calico Cook, 209
Leonard's, 118
The Leonhardt Group, 219
Le Panier, 149
Le Pavillon, 102
Le Perigord, 101
Le Restaurant de la Tour Eiffel, 101
L'Ermitage, 101
Lerner, Ann, 249
Lerner, Preston, 259
Le Ruth's, 106
Les Auteurs—An American Bistro, 103
Les Dames d'Escoffier, Chicago, 181
Les Dames d'Escoffier, Dallas, 181
Les Dames d'Escoffier, New York, 181
Les Dames d'Escoffier, Philadelphia, 181
Les Dames d'Escoffier, Seattle, 181
Les Dames d'Escoffier, Washington, 181
Les Gourmettes Cooking School, 149
L'Espalier, 106
Lessirard, Michelle, Designs, Inc., 97
Le Steak Gourmet International, Ltd., 39
Les Trois Petits Cochons Pate Company, 38
Letier, Charles W., 96
L'Etoile, 101
Let's Get Cookin', 150
Lettuce Entertain You, 84
Levine, Marsha E., 215
Levy, Richard, 202

Levy Restaurants, Inc., 84
Lewis & Neale, Inc., 190
Lewis Steven's Distinctive Catering, 114
Lewiston Daily Sun, 249
Lexco Corporation, 172
Lexington Barbecue Festival, 290
Lexington Herald-Leader, 252
Libby Hillman Cooking School, 145
Liberty Carton Company, 33
Liberty Richter, Inc., 32
Library of Congress, Science and Technology Division, 269
Lichtenberg, Marge, 209
Lichtenstein, Jane, 249
Licklider, Deborah, 251
Lieberman, Judy, 206
Lieber's Kosher Food Specialties, 64
Life's A Party, 116
Lifestyle Restaurants, Inc., 84
Lifetime Cutlery Corporation, 172
Lightlife Foods, Inc., 54, 62
Li-Lac Chocolates, Inc., 48
Lindley, Louise, 252
Lindsley, Kathy, 250
Lindt & Sprungli (USA), Inc., 26
Line, Lemuel, 215
Lion's Rock, 101
Lipton, Thomas J., Inc., 49, 71
Lisa's Bon Appetit, 116
Listenik, Barbara J.D., 206
The Litchfield Food Company, Inc., 41
Little Caesar Enterprises, Inc., 88
The Little Kitchen, 150
Littlewood Farm, 55
Livingston, Francis, 215
L K Manufacturing Corporation, 172
L&N Seafood Grill. See Morrison's, Inc.
Loaf 'n' Ladle, 45
Lo Becca, 127
Lockwood, Todd, 215
Lodge Manufacturing Company, 172
Lodi Grape Festival, 288
Loews Hotels, 81
The Londre Company Public Relations, 190
Lone Pine Farm, 56
Long Beach Press-Telegram, 257
Long Island Cheese Specialties, Inc., 27
Long John Silver. See Restaurant Management Company
Long John Silver's. See Jerrico, Inc.
Lopata, Sam, Inc., 96
L'Orangerie, 106
Loroman Company (Abbott Company), 169
The Los Angeles Times, 257
Los Angeles Union Terminal, Inc. (Seventh Street), 22
Los Angeles Wholesale Produce Market, 22
Los Angeles Women's Culinary Alliance, 181
Loughlin, Kimberley, 207
Louie's Backyard, 110
Louis, Mark, Company, 173
Louise's Pantry, 150
Louisiana Pecan Festival, 289
Louisville Produce Terminal, 21

Love At First Bite, 27
Love & Quiches, Ltd., 24
The Lowell Sun, 249
Lubbert's Organic Products, 57
Luberto's Caterer, 122
Luby's Cafeterias, Inc., 87
Lucille's Catering, 122
Luckett & Associates, Ltd., 119
Lucky Stores, Inc., 73
Ludlow, Roberta, 215
Luke's Almond Acres, 33
Lundberg Family Farm, 58
Lundgren, Bev, 209
Lupton's Fatman's Catering, Inc., 118
Lusco's Sauces, 40
Lutece, 110
Luttrell, David, 202
Lutz, Sue, 252
Lynard Company, Inc., 26
Lyon, Fred, 202
Lyon's Restaurants, Inc., 84

M

Mabry, Michael, Design, 219
McCabe's Gourmet Market, 43
McCarthy, Tom, 202
McChesney, Tricia, 256
McClure Bean Soup Festival, 291
McCluskey, Ellen L., Associates, Inc., 96
MacCombie, Turi, 215
McCormick, Margaret, 250
McCormick, Ned, 202
McCormick & Company, Inc., 71
McCoy, Ellin, 259
McCullar, Owen, 56
MacDonald Design Group, 96
McDonald's, 89
McDuffie, Ann, 252
McFadden Farm, 33
McFarland, Nancy, 202
McGee, Cosette, 209
McGinnis, Reoma, 250
McGinnis Sisters, 42
McGowan, Dan, 215
Macias, Sandra, 256
Mack, Patricia, 250
McKenna, Ann, 205
McKimmy & Elliot Kitchen Design Plus, 161
Mackle, Elliott, 259
McLain, Julia, 215
McLaughlin, Michael, 259
McMahan, John, 60
McMahon, Mark, 215
MacNeil, Karen, 259
McNulty's Specialty Coffee & Tea Company, 29
McNulty's Tea and Coffee Company, 49
Macon State Farmers' Market, 20
Macon Telegraph and News, 252
McPherson, Heather, 252
Macrobiotics Center of Texas, 149
Macuch Studio, 202
Macy, John Wm., CheeseSticks, 24
Madelaine Chocolate Novelties, Inc., 26
Madison, Ltd. (Davis Brothers Wholesalers, Inc.), 173
Magdich, Dennis, 215
Maggie's, 41
Maggio, Marlene, 206
Magic Pan, 84
Magnagrip Division, 173

Magnolia Kitchen Shoppe & Cooking School, Inc., 151
Mahoney, Louis, 254
Maihofer, Karen, Creative Cuisine, 149
Mail Order Muffins, 51
Maine Coast Sea Vegetables, 54
Maine Coast Smokehouse, 61
Maine Department of Marine Resources, 187
Maine Lobster Festival, 290
Maine Organic Farmers' and Gardeners' Association, 53
Maine Potato Board, 186
Maison Glass, 51
Malone, Jann, 254
Ma Maison, 110
Mama Leone's. *See Restaurant Associates Industries, Inc.*
Mama's Old-Fashioned Food Products (Gill/G'Dam Kosher Cheese Company), 62
Manchester Union-Leader, 249
Mandarin Soy Sauce, Inc., 32
Mandel, Abby, 259
Manganaro Foods, 52
Manney, Grace, 205
Manning, Michele, 215
Manning, Selvage & Lee, Inc., 190
Manor Care, Inc., 81, 90
Manor HealthCare. *See Manor Care, Inc.*
The Mansion on Turtle Creek, 103
Mansour's Food Market Company, 45
Manz Specialty Foods, Inc., 46
Maple Grove Farms of Vermont, Inc., 37
Maple Sugaring Days, 289
Marcel et Henri Charcuterie Francaise, 38
Marcella's Taste of Nature, 150
March of Dimes Birth Defects Foundation, 292
Margareten Enterprises, 64
Mariani, John, 259
Marich Confectionery Company, 26
Marie, Rita, & Friends, 203
Marie's Catering Service, Inc., 119
Marion County Ham Days, 289
The Mariner Hotel Corporation, 81
Market Basket, 75
Marketing Agents for the Food Service Industry, 181
The Marketplace, 109
Marriott Corporation, 78, 79, 81, 88
Marriott In-Flite Services, 91
Marshall, Gail, 257
Martucci, Stanley, 214
Mary, Wendy, 208
Mary Ann's Place, 44
Maryland Wholesale Produce Market, 21
Mary of Puddin Hill, Inc., 46, 51
Masa's, 110
Mascitti, Al, 251
Masco, A., Company, 163
The Master Caterers, 118
Master Host Inns. *See Hospitality International, Inc.*
Masters, Charles, 202
Matheis, Shelley, 215

Matheney, Patti, 207
Mather, Robin, 255
Matsuhisa, 106
Mattison & Company Caterers, 117
The Maui Chip, Inc., 39
Mauk, Cathy, 255
Mauna Kea Coffee Company, 49
Maverick Industries, Inc., 165
Maverick Ranch Beef, 59
Maxim Company, 165
Maxime's, 108
Maxim's, 107
Mayacamas Fine Foods, Inc., 40
May Department Stores, 78
Mayfair Kitchen Center, Inc., 159
Mayle, Mary, 252
The Maytag Company, 163
Maytag Dairy Farms, 48
Mazzio's Corporation, 89
M-B Hard Candies, Inc., 26
M B R Industries, Inc., 173
MCL Cafeterias, Inc., 87
Meadowbrook Catering, 124
Meadowbrook Herb Gardens, 55
Meal Mart/Schreiber, 64
Meat Industry Suppliers' Association, 279
Medical College of Georgia, Georgia Institute of Human Nutrition, 266
Megaware, Inc. of California, 173
Meier, John C., Grape Juice Company, 22
Meisel Associates, Ltd., 97
Meisels Photography, Ltd., 202
Meitus, Marty, 257
Melba Food Specialties, Inc., 32
Melitta USA, Inc., 173
Memphis Culinary Academy, 145
Menda, George, Inc., 202
Mendel's Haymish Brand, 64
Mendix Corporation, 173
Menendez, Mary Ann, 254
Menuchah Farms Smokehouse, 38
Menzie, Karol, 253
Merchant of Vino, 45
Meshejian, Zabel, 206
The Metal Ware Corporation, 173
Metro, 102
Metromedia Company, Inc., 89
Metropolitan Chicago Healthcare Council, 90
Metsch, Steve, 254
Metz Baking Company, 73
Mexican-American Grocers' Association, 181
Meyer, Fred, Inc., 75
Meyer, Gordon, 202
Meyer, Jeanne, 255
Meyer, Pucci, 250
Meyer Corporation, U.S., 165
The Miami Herald, 252
The Miami Produce Center, 20
Michael's, 104
Michael's Catering, 125
Michael's Fine Cheese & Gourmet Foods, 42
Michael's Mountain Honey, 56
Michael's Waterside, 105
Michael's Waterside Inn, 116
Michela's, 103
Michelle's Bakery & Cafe. *See Vie de France Restaurant Corporation*
Michels, Joyce, 257
Michel's Magnifique of

NYC, Ltd., 38
Michigan Asparagus Advisory Board, 188
Michigan Bean Commission, 186
Michigan Blueberry Growers' Association, 185
Michigan Cherry Committee, 185
Michigan Plum Advisory Board, 185
Michigan State University Beef Cattle Research Center, 264
Michigan State University Dairy Research and Teaching Center, 264
Michigan State University Pesticide Research Center, 263
Micromeals, Inc., 173
Microwise Cookware USA, 173
Mid-America Dairymen, Inc., 71
Miguel's, 32
Mill City Sourdough Bakery, 60
Mille Lacs MP Company, 33
Miller, Bryan, 259
Miller, Frank, 215
Miller, Wendy, 258
Miller Kitchens, 161
The Mill Falls Restaurant, 111
Millstream Natural Health Supplies, 57
The Milwaukee Journal, 256
Milwaukee Sentinel, 256
Milza, Jane, 250
Mimi's, 147
Minneapolis Star & Tribune, 255
Minnesota Wild Rice Festival, 290
Mintcheff, Deborah, 205
Minyard Food Stores, Inc., 47
Miraglia Catering, 116
Miraglia Contract International, 96
Mirro/Foley Company (The Newell Group), 173
Miss Grace Lemon Cake Company, 51
Mississippi Farmers' Central Market, 21
Mississippi State University, Human Nutrition Option, 266
Mississippi State University Department of Food Science and Human Nutrition, 263
Mississippi State University Meat Laboratory, 264
Miss Ruby's Cafe, 101
Miss Scarlett, Division of Rhett, Inc., 25
Mister Donut of America, 89
Mitchell, Carlson & Associates, Inc., 98
Mitchell, Celia, 215
Mitchell, Cynthia, 255
Mitchell's Catering, 124
Miyamoto, Linda Y., 215
M & M Distributing, 57
The Mobile Press-Register, 251
Modern Maid, 163
The Modesto Bee, 258
Moeller, Walter L., 207
Moine, Tobe Le, 208
Mon Cheri Cooking School & Caterers, 116, 150
Monfort, Inc., 70
Montana Mercantile, 150
Monterey Bay Canners. *See Trans/ Pacific Restaurants, Inc.*
Monterey House, Inc. *See Integra Hotel and Restaurant Company*

Montgomery Advertiser, 251
Montgomery State Farmers' Market, 20
Montrachet, 107
Moran, Rita, 258
Morash, Marian, 259
Moreau, Inc., 26
Moreland's Restaurant, 110
Morello, Joe, 202
Morgan, Donna Lou, 257
Morgan, Jacqui, 215
Morgan, Jinx and Jefferson, 259
Morgan, Pat, 256
Morin's, Inc., 120
Morning Advocate, 253
The Morning Call, 250
Morningland Dairy, 60
The Morning News Tribune, 259
MorningStar Foods, 71
Morren Design, 219
Morris, Pat, 256
Morris, Philip, Companies, Inc., 69
Morris Erde, Inc., 64
Morrison, Ruth, Associates, Inc., 191
Morrison's, Inc., 84
Morrison's Custom Management, 79, 90
Morrison's Family Dining, Inc., 87
Morris Stuhl, Inc., 166
Moses, David, 215
Mother Myrick's Confectionery, 43
Motooka, Jacqueline, and Associates, 208
Moultrie State Farmers' Market, 20
Mount, Charles Morris, 96
Mountain Star Honey Company, 58
Mount & Company, 96
Moye, Elizabeth, 253
Moyer Packing Company, 73
Mozzarella Company, 27
Mr. Coffee, Inc., 166
Mr. Gatti's, Inc., 89
Mr. Steak, 83
Mr. Zablotsky's, 61
Mrs. Adler's Food, Inc., 64
Mrs. Fields Cookies, Inc., 51, 78
Mrs. P.J.'s Catering Company, 115
Mrs. Weinberg's Food Products, 64
Ms. Desserts, Inc., 24
M2=Mitchell x Mitchell, Inc., 97
Muer, C.A., Corporation, 78
Mullen, Holly, 255
The Multiflex Company, 26
Mundth, Michele, 251
Munsey Products, Inc., 166
Murcott, John H., Inc., 52
Murphy's Catering, 118
Murray Bakery Products, 65
Mushroom Mardi Gras, 288
Mustards Grill, 107
M.Y. Quality Trading, 64

N

Nabisco, RJR, Inc., 69
Nagel, Pat, 208
Nahas, Margo Z., 215
Najaka, Marlies Merk, 215
Narsai's Market, 52
Narsai's Specialty Foods, 37
Nashville Banner, 253
Nathan, Amy, 210
Nathan's Detroit. *See Lifestyle Restaurants, Inc.*

Nathanson, Morris, Design, Inc., 96
National Alliance of Supermarket Shoppers, 277
National-American Wholesale Grocers' Association (NAWGA), 181, 279
National Anorexic Aid Society, 266
National Anti-Hunger Coalition, 280
National Asparagus Festival, 290
National Association to Advance Fat Acceptance (NAAFA), 266
National Association of Anorexia Nervosa and Associated Disorders (ANAD), 266
National Association of Catering Executives (NACE), 181
National Association of College and University Food Services, 182
National Association of Concessionaires, 182
National Association of Food Equipment Manufacturers, 182
National Association of Fruits, Flavors & Syrups, 187
National Association of Margarine Manufacturers, 280
National Association of Meat Purveyors, 182, 280
National Association of Specialty Foods & Confection Brokers, 187
National Association for the Specialty Food Trade, Inc. (NASFT), 182
National Automatic Merchandising Association, 182
National Basque Festival, 290
National Beef Cook-Off, 292
National Broiler Council, 186, 280
National Candy Brokers' Association, 187
National Candy Wholesalers' Association, 182, 187, 280
National Caterers' Association, 182
National Cheese Institute, 280
National Cherry Festival, 290
National Cherry Foundation, 185
National Coalition Against the Misuse of Pesticides, 277
National Coalition to Stop Food Irradiation, 277
National Coffee Association of the USA, 184
National Coffee Service Association, 280
National Confectioners' Association, 187, 280
National Dairy Council, 184
National Date Festival, 288-289
National Fisheries Institute, Inc., 187, 280
National Food Brokers' Association (NFBA), 182
National Food Distributors' Association (NFDA), 182
National Food Processors' Association, 280
 Political Action Committee, 280
National Frozen Food Association, 280
National Frozen Pizza Institute, 280

National Grocers' Association, 182, 280
National Hard Crab Derby, 290
National Honey Board, 187
National Housewares, Inc., 173
National Housewares Manufacturers Association, 182
National Institute for Off-Premise Catering, 182
National Kitchen & Bath Association, 159
National Livestock & Meat Board, 186
National Mushroom Hunting Championship, 290
National Nutritional Foods Association, 266
National Nutritional Foods Association (NNFA), 182
National Obesity Research Foundation, 266
National Onion Association, 188
National Orange Show, 292
National Pasta Association, 186, 280
National Peanut Council, 280
National Peanut Festival, 288
National Pizza Company, 89
National Pork Board, 280
National Pork Producers Council, 186, 280, 292
National Presto Industries, Inc., 166
National Red Cherry Institute, 185
National Restaurant Association, 182
National Retail Merchants' Association (NRMA), 182
National Shrimp Festival, 288
National Soft Drink Association, 184
National Sunflower Association, 185
National Supermarkets, 75
National Turkey Federation, 186
National Yogurt Association, 184
Natural Beef Farms Food Distribution Company, 59
Natural Food Associates, 277
Natural Food Distributors, Inc., 49
The Natural Gourmet Cookery School, 145
Naturally Good Foods, 64
Natural Organic Farmers' Association, 54
Natural Organic Farmers' Association of Massachusetts, 54
Natural Resources Defense Council, 277
Natural Way Mills, Inc., 62
Nature Food Centres, 49
Nayphe's International Foods, 46
Nebraska Custom Kitchens, 161
Needham, Steven Mark, 202
Neely, Jamie, 259
Negev Caterers, 122
Nejaime's of the Berkshires, Inc., 29
Nell's Harbour Shop, 44
Nelson, Will, 215
Nelson Crab, 49
Nestle Enterprises, Inc., 78, 84, 86
Nestle Foods Corporation, 69
Neuhaus (USA), Inc., 26
Neuman & Bogdonoff, Inc., 123

Nevco Housewares, Inc., 173
Newark Farmers' Market, 19
Newark Star-Ledger, 249
New Braunfels Smokehouse, 50
Newcomer, Robin, 259
The Newell Group, 171, 173
New England Cheesemaking Supply Company, 48
New England Country Fare, 52
New England Culinary Institute, 143
New England Dairy-Deli Association, 184
New England Fisheries Development Foundation, Inc., 187
New England Food Company, Inc., 62
New England Produce Center, Inc., 19
The New French Cafe, 100
New Haven Food Terminal, Inc., 19
New Haven Register, 249
New Jersey Department of Agriculture, Fisheries Development Advisory Council, 292
New Leaf Farm, 54
New Mexican Tex-Mex Cookery School, 146
New Mexico Organic Growers' Association, 57
The New Orleans School of Cooking, 147
The News (Greenville, S.C.), 253
The New School, Culinary Arts at, 145
The News and Courier, 253
Newsday, 250
The News-Gazette, 254
The News-Journal (New Castle, Del.), 251
News-Journal (Pensacola, Fla.), 252
The News & Observer, 253
Newspaper Food Editors' and Writers' Association, 182
News-Press, 252
News-Register, 254
The News-Sentinel, 254
News and Sun-Sentinel, 252
News Tribune, 250
Newton, Richard, 216
New York Association of Cooking Teachers, 182
New York Cherry Growers' Association, Inc., 185
New York Daily News, 250
New York Food and Hotel Management School, 144
New York Post, 250
New York Restaurant School, 144
The New York Times, 250
New York Women's Culinary Alliance, 182
Niagara Frontier Food Terminal, 19
Niagara Frontier Growers' Cooperative Market, 19
Nicholas Gold, Inc., 39
Nicho's. See Investors' Management Corporation
Niefield, Terry, Studio, 202
Nikko, 105
94th Aero Squadron Restaurants. See Specialty Restaurants Corporation
Nishinaka, Jeff, 216

Noam Gourmet, 64
Noble/Sysco, 98
Noble Tennant, 191
Nodine's Smokehouse, 50
Nonesuch, Ltd., 150
Nordic Ware, Inc. (Northland Aluminum Products), 173
Norelco Consumer Products Company (North American Philips Corporation), 166
Normandy Distributors (National Housewares, Inc.), 173
Norpro, Inc., 173
Norris, Jan, 252
North American Blueberry Council, 185
North American Philips Corporation, 166
North Atlantic Seafood Association, 187
North Carolina Yam Commission, Inc., 188
North Central Food Systems, Inc., 78
Northcutt, James, Associates, 99
North Dakota State University Food & Nutrition Research Laboratory, 267
North Dakota Wheat Commission, 292
Northern Natural Foods, 49
Northern Ohio Food Terminal, Inc., 21
Northland Aluminum Products, 173
Northwest Airlines, Inc., 91
Northwest Culinary Alliance, 182
Northwest Specialty Bakers, Ltd., 24
Norton, H.G., Company, Inc., 32
Norton National Marketers' Group, The H.G. Norton Company, Inc., 32
Nowco International, Inc., 34
Nozicka, Steve, Photography, Ltd., 202
Nueske Hillcrest Farm Meats, 38
Nunes Farms Almonds, 39
Nurse, Anna Amendolara, Cooking Classes, 146
Nutritional Effects Foundation, 267
Nutrition Information Center, 267

O
The Oakland Tribune, 258
Oberholtzer, Sharon, 254
Obesity Foundation, 267
O'Brien, Kathy, 216
Occidental, 102
Ocean Club. See Entertainment One
Ocean Spray Cranberries, Inc., 71
Ochagavia, Carlos, 216
O'Connell, Jean, 249
Odeon, Bistrot a Vin, 100
O'Donnell, Gail, 208
O'Donnell, Wicklund & Pigozzi, 97
Oehme Pie Company/Rewco, 62
Ofentoski, Rick, 202
Ogden Allied Services Corporation, Air La Carte, 91
Ogilvy & Mather Public Relations (Ogilvy Public Relations Group), 191

Oh! Brian. *See Investors' Management Corporation*
O'Hara, Jo Ellen, 251
Ohio State University Dairy Center, 264
Ohio State University Food Industries Center (FIC), 263
Ohio State University Human Nutrition Research Laboratory, 267
Ohio State University Meat Laboratory-Animal Science, 264
Ohio State University Ohio Agricultural Research and Development Center, 263
The Oklahoman, 256
Oklahoma State University Human Nutrition Center, 267
Okra Strut, 291
Okun, Janice, 250
Old Covered Bridge Farm Gift Shop, 52
Olde Tyme Delicatessen, 44
The Old-Fashioned Kitchen, Inc., 62
Old Man's Creek Organics, 56
Old Town Gourmet, 46
Old Tyme Soft Drinks, Inc., 23
Old Wisconsin Sausage Company, 38
Olis, Ruth, 249
The Olive Garden. *See General Mills Restaurant Group, Inc.*
Oliver's. See daka
Olive's, 103
Olsen, Cheryl, 249
Olsen Catering, 115
Olson, Richard A., 216
Olson, Susan, 209
Omaha Steaks International, 50
Omaha World-Herald, 255
Omni Hotels Corporation, 81
One Design Center, Inc., 97
150 Wooster, 100
O'Neill, Molly, 259
Oquendo, William, 202
Orange Blossom Catering, 118
Orange Blossom Groves, 49
Orange County Register, 258
Orba, Josephine, 208
Oregon Cherry Growers, 185
The Oregonian, 258
Oregon Potato Commission, 186
Oregon State University Hatfield Marine Science Center, 264
Oregon State University Nutrition Research Institute, 267
Oregon State University Seafoods Laboratory, 265
Oregon-Washington-California Pear Bureau, 185
Organic Crop Improvement Association, 55, 57
Organic Food Production Association of North America, 54
Organic Foods Express, 56
Organic Growers' and Buyers' Association, 57
Organic Growers of Michigan, 57
Organicly Yours, 54
Oriental Food Market and Cooking School, 52, 148
Original Great American Chocolate Chip Cookie Company, 78

Original Hamburger Stands. *See Galardi Group*
The Original Trenton Cracker Company, 29
The Orlando Sentinel, 252
O'Rourke, Randy, 202
Orsini Design Associates, Inc., 96
Oscar's Hickory House, Inc., 50
Oster/Sunbeam Appliance Company, 166
Ostman, Eleanor, 259
Ostmann, Barbara G., 255
O'Toole's, Dooley, Catering, 119
Ovations Catering & Special Events, 124
Overeaters Anonymous, 267
Oxnard Strawberry Festival, 289
Ozark Mountain Smoke House, 50

P

Pace Foods, Inc./La Martinique, 39
Pacific Coast Canned Pear Service, Inc., 185
Pacific Gold, 33
Padys, Diane, Studio, 202
Page, Dian, 256
Palate Pleasers, 115
Paleta Frozfruit International Corporation, 64
The Palm Beach Post, 252
Palmer, Jane, 255
Palmer Manufacturing, Inc., 166
Palm Restaurants, 84
Panache, 104
Panasonic, 166
Pango's. *See Shoney's, Inc.*
The Pantagraph, 254
Pantera's Corporation, 89
Papa Gino's of America, Inc., 84
Papa Leone Food Enterprises, Inc., 40
Papaya Administrative Committee, 185
Pappas, Lou, 258
Paprikas Weiss Importer, 52
Paradise Bakery. *See CHE, Inc.*
Paradise International Trading, Ltd., 64
Paragon Restaurant Group, Inc., 84
Parco Foods, Inc., 24
Parik, Carol, 209
Park Bistro, 103
Parker, Earl, 216
Parker, Edward, 216
Parker, Robert M., Jr., 259
Parkers' Lighthouse. *See Stouffer Restaurant Company*
Parker's Restaurant, 101
Parsons, John, 216
Parties Plus, Inc., 115
Party Fare, Inc., 118
The Party Specialist, 120
Parve Frozen Delights, Inc., 64
Pasadena Star-News, 258
Paskesz Candy Company, Inc., 64
Patchwork Organic Gardens, 53
The Patriot-News, 250
Patti, Joyce, 216
Paul's Grains, 56, 60
Paulship International, Inc., 173
Paulson, Fran, Picture Foods, 208
Paulware (Paulship International, Inc.), 173
Peacemeal Farm, 53
Peachey's Catering, Inc., 119

Peanut Advisory Board, 185
Peanut Butter and Nut Processors' Association, 280
Peckolick & Partners, 219
Pecos Valley Spice Company, 32
Pedrini USA, Inc., 173
Pelican Bay, Ltd., 36
Pelikan, Judy, 216
Peloponnese, 32
Pendleton, Roy, 216
Peninsula Times-Tribune, 258
Pentagram Design, 219
Pepera, Fred, 216
Pepin, Jacques, 259
Peppercorn's Catering, Ltd., 119
Pepper House International, 61
Pepperidge Farm Mail Order Company, 52
Pepper Patch, Inc., 52
PepsiCo, Inc., 69
PepsiCo Foodservice Division, 78, 88, 89, 90
Perfect Host Catering, 121
Perfect Parties, 123
Perfect Touch Caterers, 123
Perkins, Ray, Photography, 202
Perkins, Sue, 249
Perkins Family Restaurants L.P., 85
Perko's Koffee Kup. *See The Happy Steak, Inc.*
Perrin, Gail, 249
Perry, Richard, Caterers, Inc., 121
Persimmon Festival, 289
Perugina Chocolates & Confections, Inc., 26
Perugina of Italy, 48
Peter Kump's New York Cooking School, 145
Peters, Michael, Group, 219
Peterson, Dorothy, 208
Peterson, M.A., Inc., 159
Petrossian, 100
Petrucelli Associates, 202
Petty's Fine Foods, 46
Pfaelzer Brothers, 50
P F F/Contract, 99
Pfister, Charles, Associates, 99
Phelon, R.E., Company, Inc. (Magnagrip Division), 173
PHH Environments, 96
Philadelphia Daily News, 251
Philadelphia Fresh Food Terminal Authority, 20
Philadelphia Women's Culinary Guild, 182
Philbrick, Andrea R., 249
Phillips, Bernard, Photography, 202
Phillips, Laura, 216
Phillips Seafood Restaurants, 85
The Phoenix Gazette, 256
Phoenixware, 173
Piane Caterers, 117
Piccadilly Cafeterias, Inc., 87
Piccuito, Paul E., 205
The Pickle Barrel, 44
The Picnic People, 116
Pike Street Restaurant, 107
The Pillsbury Company, 70, 293
   Restaurant Group, 78, 85, 88, 89
Pilossof, Judd, 202
Pineapple Growers' Association of Hawaii, 185
Pine Meadow Farm, 59
Pinkney, Deborah, 216

Pink Tomato Festival, 288
Pinneys USA, Inc., 32
Pittsburgh Post-Gazette, 251
Pittsburgh Press, 251
Pizza Hut, Inc. (PepsiCo Foodservice Division), 89. *See also Restaurant Management Company*
Pizza Industry Manufacturers' Association, 183
Pizza Inn. *See Pantera's Corporation*
Pizza Inn Franchise. *See Atlanta Family Restaurants, Inc.*
Pizza Management, Inc., 89
Pizzeria Uno. *See Uno Restaurants Corporation*
P.J. Enterprises International, Inc., 173
A Place for Cooks, 43
The Plain Dealer, 255
Plain and Fancy Caterers, 123
Plantations Caterer, 125
Plant City, State Farmers' Market, 20
Planters LifeSavers Company, 293
Plaza Club. *See daka*
Plaza Sweets Bakery, 24
Pleasant Valley Farm, 53, 59
The Plummer Group, 191
The Plum Street Market, 21
Podoll, David, 57
Po Folks, Inc., 89
Pointe Resorts, 81
Poll, William, Gourmet Shop, 52
Poll, William, Inc., 42
Pollio Dairy Products, 28
Polly Jean's, 23
The Polo, 101
Polvay, Marina, 207
Pompano State Farmers' Market, 20
Ponderosa, Inc. (Metromedia Company, Inc.), 89. *See also U.S. Restaurants, Inc.*
Poole, Marcia, 255
Popcorn Institute, 187, 280
Popeyes Chicken & Biscuits. *See A. Copeland Enterprises, Inc.*
Poplis, Paul, Photography, 202
Pork, Peanut and Pine Festival, 291
Pork Industry Group, 186
Port-A-Pit BBQ, Inc., 118
Port Chatham Packing Company, 32
Portland Press Herald, 249
Post, Alice, 249
Post Cereals (General Foods), 64
The Postilion School of Culinary Art, 145
Postrio, 104
The Post-Standard, 250
The Post-Tribune, 254
The Potato Board, 186
Pot au Feu, 102
The Pot Shop, 173
The Poughkeepsie Journal, 250
Poultry Science Association, 186
Powell, Mary Alice, 256
Prairie, 106
Prairie Farms Dairy, Inc., 73
Prairie Path Catering, 118
Prana Foods, 55
Predroza, Richard, Associates, Inc., 99
Premier Food Services, Inc., 116

The Press-Democrat, 258
The Press-Gazette, 256
Press & Sun-Bulletin, 250
Price, Maret, 205
Price Chopper, 76
Primavera PR, 191
Prime Marketing, 169
Prime Motor Inns, 81
Primex International Trading
    Corporation, 173
Primi, 110
Princess Hotels International, 81
Prindle, Judy Peck, 210
Printer's Row, 104
Pritchard, Russell, 206
Private Label Manufacturers'
    Association (PLMA), 183
The Procter & Gamble
    Company, 70
Proctor-Silex/Wear-Ever, 166
Produce Marketing Association,
    Inc., 183
Producer Realty Corporation, 21
Products-From-Sweden, Inc., 32
Prodyne Enterprises, Inc., 173
Professional Foodservice
    Management, Inc., 79
Professional Interiors, Ltd., 98
Profit Targets, Inc., 173
Progressive International
    Corporation, 174
Progressus Company, 174
Project Associates, Inc., 99
Prospect Store & Catering, 119
The Prospect of Westport, 121
Prost, Andre, Inc., 25
Providence Bulletin, 251
Providence Produce Market, 20
Prufrock. See Unigate Restaurants,
    Inc.
Pruzan, Michael, 203
Public Voice for Food and Health
    Policy, 278
Publix Super Markets, 74
Puckett, Susan, 252
Puett, Beth Kent, 208
Pulcrano, Shari, Interior
    Design, 99
Pullo, Barbara, 206
Pulver, Louis, 55
Purdue University, Food Sciences
    Department, 266
Purdue University Agricultural
    Experiment Station, 263
Purdue University Calvert-Purdue
    Beef Research and Teaching
    Center, 264
Purdue University Food Sciences
    Institute, 263
Purepak Foods, Inc., 32
The Pushpin Group, 219
Putney Pasta Company, Inc., 35

Q
Q5, Inc., 95
The Quaker Oats Company, 69
Quality Inns, Inc. See Manor
    Care, Inc.
Quality International Inns. See
    Manor Care, Inc.
Quik Wok, Inc. (The Pillsbury
    Company Restaurant Group), 89
The Quilted Giraffe, 111
Quincy's Family Steakhouse. See
    TW Services, Inc.

R
Raadvad American, Ltd., 174
Rabert, Bonnie, Food
    Consultant, 208
Radisson Hotel Corporation, 81
Ragu Foods, Inc., 72
Rahn, Peggy, 259
Rainbow Grocery, 56
The Rainbow Room, 108
Rakel Restaurant, 105
Raley's, 75
Rally's. See Restaurant Management
    Company
Ralph's Grocery Company, 74
Ralston Purina Company, 70
Ramada Inns, Inc., 81
Ram Island Farm Herbs, 50
Randall's, 44
Randall's Food Market, 76
Range Kleen Manufacturing,
    Inc., 174
Rania's To Go, 147
Raphael, Davie, 205
Rare Fruit Council
    International, 185
The Rattlesnake Club, 109
Rax Restaurants, Inc., 89
Raygal Design, 98
Reading Eagle, 251
Reco International
    Corporation, 174
The Record, 249
Red Carpet Inns. See Hospitality
    International, Inc.
Red Food Stores, 76
Red Gate Farm, 59
Red Lion, 85
Red Lobster USA. See General Mills
    Restaurant Group, Inc.
Red Maple Farm, 53
Red Robin International, 85
Red Rose Catering Company, 116
Reed, Herb, 216
Reese Finer Foods, Inc., 32
Regal Ware, Inc., 166
Regan, Mardee Haidin, 259
Regent-Sheffield, Ltd. (Wiltshire
    International), 174
The Register-Guard, 258
The Registry Hotel
    Corporation, 81
Reichl, Ruth, 259
Reis, Gerald, & Company, 219
Rema Bakeware, Inc., 174
Remember Basil, Ltd., 122
Remi, 100
Reno Gazette-Journal, 256
Renoir, Bonnie, Cordon Bleu
    Cooking School, 150
Renovation & Design, Inc., 97
Residence Inns. See Marriott
    Corporation
Resorts International, Inc., 81
Restaura Dining Services, 79.
    See also Greyhound Food Manage-
    ment, Inc.
Restaurant Associates
    Caterers, 123
Restaurant Associates Industries,
    Inc., 82, 85
Restaurant Enterprises Group, Inc.,
    85
Restaurant Jean-Louis, 104
Restaurant Lafayette, 110
Restaurant Management
    Company, 85

Restaurant Osteria Romana, 103
The Restaurant at the
    Phoenix, 110
The Restaurant School, 144
Restaurant at Smith Ranch
    Homes, 105
Restaurants Unlimited, Inc., 85
Restivo, Jean, 216
Reston Lloyd, Ltd., 174
Reuben's. See Restaurant Enterprises
    Group, Inc.
Revere Ware Corporation, 174
Rex Il Ristorante, 110
Rezny, Aaron, Inc., 203
Rhett, Inc., 25
Rhode Island School of Design,
    Culinary Arts Apprentice-
    ship, 144
Rhode Island Seafood Council, 187
Rhode Island Sea Grant Marine
    Advisory Service, 265
Ribby's. See USA Cafes
Rib-It. See U.S. Restaurants, Inc.
Rice, William, 259
Rice Council of America, 186
Rice Growers' Association of
    California, 186
Riceland Foods, Inc., 72
Richard, Jackie, 258
Richard B. Russell Agricultural
    Research Center (RRC), 263
The Richard Group, 174
Richard Perry Restaurant, 107
Richards, Brock, Miller, Mitchell &
    Associates, 220
Richards Natural Food
    Farm, 57, 60
Richardson/Smith, Inc., 220
Richardson or Richardson, 220
Rich Lynn Forest Farm, 55
Richman, Phyllis, 259
Richmond, Jack, 203
Richmond News Leader, 254
Richmond Times-Dispatch, 254
Rich Products Corporation, 72
Riedy, Mark, 216
The Riese Organization, 78
Riser Foods, 75
Rising Sun Distributors, 55
Rival Manufacturing
    Company, 166
The River Cafe, 102
The River Club, 110
Riviana Foods, Inc., 73
Rixford, Ellen, 216
Roanoke Times & World
    News, 254
Robbins Bianco Catering, 123
Robert Charles Caterers, Inc., 120
Roberts, Bill, 257
Roberts, Ray, 216
Robertson's Catering Sevice,
    Inc., 126
Robinette & Doyle Caterers, 126
Robinson, William, 250
Rocco's, 111
Rochester Public Market, 19
The Rochester Times-Union, 250
Rocky Hills Farm, 54
Rocky Mountain News, 257
Rocky Rococo, 89
Rodeway Inns International,
    Inc., 81
Rodriguez, Robert, 216
Rogers, Lilla, 216
Rogers, Lue, 253

Roller, Becky, 209
Rolling Acres Farm, 56, 60
Roma Corporation, 78
Romanoff Foods, Inc., 33
Ron-Matic Systems, Inc., 163
Ronniger, David, 58
Rosalie's, 107
Rosa Mexicano, 105
Rosco, Delro, 216
Rose Catering, Inc., 116
Roseland Farms, 60
Rosella's, Inc., 43
Rosenberg, Lynn, Design, 97
Rosenblatt, Ricki, 206
Rosencrans, Joyce, 255
Roshco, Inc., 174
Ross Culbert Holland & Lavery,
    Inc., 220
Rosson, John, 251
Rosti (USA), Inc., 174
Rothschild Berry Farm, 40
Rothchild's Incorporated
    Catering, 126
Round Table Franchise
    Corporation, 89
Routh Street Cafe, 108
Rowenta, Inc., 166
Rowes Wharf Restaurant, 101
Rowoco, Homecraft Consumer
    Products Group (Dynacast), 174
Royal Household Products,
    Inc., 174
Royal Oak Kitchens, 161
Roy Rogers. See Marriott
    Corporation
RPM Pizza, Inc., 89
R&R. See Entertainment One
RSVP, 115
R.S.V.P. International, 174
RTM, Inc., 78
Rubin, Hank, 259
Rubin, Marilyn McDevitt, 251
Rubschlager Baking
    Corporation, 24, 61
Ruby Tuesday. See Morrison's, Inc.
Ruden, Mary, 207
Ruder-Finn, Inc., 191
Ruggless, Ron, 257
Rus Organic Farm, 55
Russell, Kathryn,
    Photography, 203
Russell Hobbs, Inc., 166
Rusty Pelican Restaurants, Inc. See
    Paragon Restaurant Group, Inc.
Rusty Scupper. See Stouffer
    Restaurant Company
Rutgers University Agricultural
    Experiment Station, 263
Rutgers University Center for
    Advanced Food Technology,
    263
Rutgers University Shellfish
    Research Laboratory, 265
Rutherford, Michael W., 203
Ryan's Family Steak Houses,
    Inc., 85
Rykoff, S.E., & Company, 52
Design Division, 99

S
Sabra Food Products
    Corporation, 64
The Sacramento Bee, 258
The Sacramento Union, 258
Safeway Stores, 74
The Saginaw News, 255

Sagon, Candy, 257
Sailmaker. *See Shoney's, Inc.*
St. Charles Kitchens of
    Boston, 159
St. Charles Kitchens by
    Deane, 159
St. Clair, Rita & Associates, 97
Saint Estephe, 109
St. John, Lynn, 203
St. Louis Culinary Society, 183
St. Louis Post-Dispatch, 255
St. Louis Produce Market, Inc., 21
St. Mary's County Oyster
    Festival, 290
St. Paul Pioneer Press
    Dispatch, 255
St. Petersburg Times, 252
Saintz Farm, 57
Saito, Masao, 216
Salentine, Katherine, 216
Sally's Marketbasket
    International, 47
Salomon, Debbie, 251
Salsman, Robert T.,
    Caterers, Inc., 121
Salt Institute, 280
Salt Lake City Tribune, 257
Salton, Lewis L., Company, 168
Salton Housewares, Inc., 166
Sammy's, 124
Sammy's Restaurant, 103
Sampson, Linda, 206, 207
San Antonio Light, 257
San Antonio Produce Terminal
    Market, 22
The San Bernardino County
    Sun, 258
Sanders, Kathy, Studios, Inc., 203
Sand Hill Farm, 53, 59
San Diego County Times-
    Advocate, 257
The San Diego Tribune, 258
The San Diego Union, Union-
    Tribune Publishing
    Company, 258
Sandison, Teri, 203
San Domenico, 106
Sandro's, 104
Sands & Company, Inc., 79
Sandy's Kitchen (Clearview
    Baking), 62
Sanford State Farmers' Market, 20
The San Francisco Chocolate
    Company, 26
San Francisco Chronicle, 258
San Francisco Examiner, 258
San Francisco Herb Company, 50
The San Francisco International
    Cheese Imports, 28
San Francisco Produce
    Terminal, 22
San Francisco Professional Food
    Society, 183
The San Francisco School of
    Cooking, 150
San Jose Mercury/News, 258
Santa Cruz Orchards, 58
Santa Fe Cookie Company, 51
Santini's Italian Cafe. *See Consoli-
    dated Specialty Restaurants, Inc.*
Sanyei America Corporation,
    Household Division, 174
Sanyo Fisher (USA)
    Corporation, 166
Sarabeth's Kitchen, Inc., 37
Sara Lee Corporation, 69

Sarasota Herald Tribune, 252
Sara's Ravioli, 64
S&A Restaurant Corporation (The
    Pillsbury Company Restaurant
    Group), 85
Sato, Susumu, Photography,
    Inc., 203
Saucy Sisters, 114
Sauvion, Mariann, 206
Savannah Foods & Industries,
    Inc., 71
Savannah News, 252
Savannnah State Farmers'
    Market, 20
Savories, 126
Sax, Irene, 259
Sax, Richard, 259
Sayles, Elizabeth, 216
Sbarro Licensing Corporation, 85
Scanpan USA, Inc., 174
Scarlatti, 100
Schaefer, Dennis W., 60
Schaefer's Catering, 124
Schaller and Weber, Inc., 38, 50
Schapira Coffee Company, 49
Schapira's Coffee & Tea
    Company, 29
The Schechter Group, Inc., 220
Schenectady Gazette, 250
Scherman, Joan, 206
Schiller & Asmus, Inc., 174
Schmitt, Heimo, 203
Schneider, Elizabeth, 259
Schneider, Sallie, 259
School for American Chefs, 144
Schrambling, Regina, 259
Schreiber, Dana, 216
Schreiber/Meal Mart, 64
Schumaker, Ward, 216
Schur, Sylvia, 259
Schwalbach, Paul, 256
Schwartz, Arthur, 250
SCI Scandicrafts, Inc., 174
Scott, Sarah, Catering, 115
Scottish Inns. *See Hospitality
    International, Inc.*
Scottsdale Culinary Institute, 144
Scotty's Grocery, 43
Seafood, Inc., 33
Seafood Broiler Restaurants, 85
Sea Galley Stores, Inc., 89
Seagram, Joseph E., & Sons,
    Inc., 70
Sea Grill. *See Restaurant Associates
    Industries, Inc.*
Seasoned To Taste, Inc., 120
Seasons, 107
Seattle Post-Intelligencer, 258
Seattle Times, 259
Sebastopol Apple Blossom
    Festival, 289
The Seckinger-Lee Company,
    Inc., 29
Segal, Donna Salle, 254
Seidman, Barry, 203
The Seiler Corporation, 79
Seitz, L.E., Associates, Inc., 97
Sekine, Hisashi, 217
Select Origins, Inc., 36
A Sense of Taste, 122
Senter & Chess, 117
Service America Corporation, 79
Servico, 97
Servico Management
    Corporation, 78
Sesser, Stan, 259

Setton International Foods, 64
Seward Silver Salmon Derby, 288
Shaker Kitchen Festival, 290
Shakey's, Inc., 89
Shammo's Fancy Foods, 42
Shapiro, Laura, 259
Shaw's Crab House, 109
Shaw's Supermarkets, Inc., 75
Shega, Marla, 217
Shelby County Growers'
    Association, Inc., 21
Sheraton, Mimi, 259
The Sheraton Corporation, 81
Sheraton Harbor Island Hotel, 101
Sherman, Chris, 252
Sherwood, Mary, 256
Shetland Corporation, 166
Shimabukuro, Betty, 259
Shmulka Bernstein Kosher
    Meats, 62
Shofar Kosher Foods, 63
Shoney's, Inc., 85
Shoney's Franchise. *See Atlanta
    Family Restaurants, Inc.*
Shoney's Restaurants. *See
    Shoney's, Inc.*
Shotwell, Charles,
    Photography, 203
Showbiz Pizza Time, Inc. *See
    Integra Hotel & Restaurant
    Company*
Showcase Kitchens, 162
Shreveport Times, 253
Shufelt, Gail, 250
Shully's Catering, 127
Sidell and Sasse, 120
Sidjakov, Berman & Gomez
    Partners, 220
Sierra's Catering, 118
Sietsema, Tom, 256
Sievers, Linda, 259
Signature Kitchen and Bath/M.A.
    Peterson, Inc., 159
The Sign of the Dove, 103
The Silo, Inc., 146
Silverman, Ellen, 203
The Silver Palate, Inc., 37
The Silver Palate Kitchens, 52
Silver Spoon. *See Morrison's, Inc.*
Simmons, Dianne, 207
Simmons, Marie, 259
Simply Elegant Catering, Inc., 120
Simpson, Jerry, 203
Simpson, Joan, 258
SinBad Sweets, Inc., 61
Singer, Niki, Inc., 191
Sioux City Journal, 255
Siskin, Charles, Catering, 125
Sitram USA, Inc., 174
Six Flags Corporation, 81
16th Street Bar and Grill, 107
S.J. International Corporation, 172
Skaar, Al, 217
Skardinski, Stan, 217
Skipper's, Inc., 89
Skott, Michael, 203
Sky Chefs, Inc., 91
Slack, Chuck, 217
Slavin, Sara, 210
SLC Design, 98
Sleepy Hollow Custom Kitchens,
    Inc., 159
Slight Indulgence, 114

Smith, Ralph, Photography, 203
Smith, Vicki, 217
Smithfield Collection, 50
Smithfield Foods, Inc., 71
Smithfield Packing Company, 50
Smith & Hemingway
    Associates, 191
Smith/Osburn Design, 160
Smith's Management, 74
Smith and Sons Foods, Inc., 87
Smitty's Super Valu, 76
Smoler, Carol, 208
Smucker, J.M., Company, 73
Snack Factory, Inc., 39
Snack Food Association, 280
Snak's Park Avenue. *See Consolidated
    Specialty Restaurants, Inc.*
Snow, Jane, 255
Snuffin, Sharon, Catering, 126
Snyder, Carolyn, 258
Society for the Advancement of
    Foodservice Research, 183
Society for Cuisine in America, 183
Society for Foodservice Manage-
    ment, 183
Society for Nutrition
    Education, 267
Soderland, Kirsten, 217
Soiree, Ltd., 117
Solomon, Rosiland, 217
Soloski, Tommy, 217
Sonic Industries, Inc., 89
Sonny's Real Pit Bar-B-Q, Inc., 90
Sonoma Cheese Factory, 48
Sonoma Mission Inn, 109
Sophie Serves, Inc., 120
Sorghum Sopping Days, 288
Source, Inc., 220
South Carolina Peach Board, 185
Southern California Culinary
    Guild, 183
Southern Foodservice Management,
    Inc., 79
Southern Living Cooking
    School, 147
A Southern Season, 44
The Southland Corporation, 79
South Tex Organics, 58
South Water Market, 21
Space Design International, 98
Spago, 108
Spanek Enterprises, 174
Spangler, Blair, Interior & Graphic
    Design, Inc., 99
Sparrer Sausage Company, Inc., 38
Spartan Food Systems (TW
    Services, Inc.), 86
A Special Event, 127
A Special Occasion, 116
Special Occasions, 117
Specialty Coffee Association of
    America, 184
Specialty Restaurants
    Corporation, 86
Spectrum Ascona, Inc., 34
Spectrum Foods. *See American
    Restaurant Group, Inc.*
Spencer, Marilyn, 253
Spencer's, 103
Spener Restaurant Design, Inc., 98
SPGA Group, Inc., 95
Spiaggia, 106. *See also Levy
    Restaurants, Inc.*
The Spice Hunter, Inc., 36
Spice of Life Caterers, 117
The Spice Market, Inc., 36, 50

Spitler, Sue, Incredible
    Edibles, 209
Spitzer & Associates Architects, 96
The Spokesman-Review, 259
Sprenger Catering, 124
Springfield Union-News, 249
Springston, Dan, 203
Square One Restaurant, 104
S&S Cafeterias. See Smith and Sons
    Foods, Inc.
Staley, A.E., Manufacturing
    Company, 70
Stallard, Peter, 217
Stanard, Michael, Inc., 220
Stanco Metal Products, Inc., 174
Standal, Barb, 209
The Standard-Times, 249
Starr Organic Produce, Inc., 55
Stars, 104, 110
Stash Tea Company, 29
The State, 253
State Farmers' Market, 21
State Journal, 255
State Journal-Register, 254
State of Maine Blueberry
    Festival, 290
The Staten Island Advance, 250
Stater Brothers Markets, 75
The Statesman-Journal, 258
Stauffer Cheese, Inc., 28
Steak and Ale. See S&A Restaurant
    Corporation
Steak House. See Paragon
    Restaurant Group, Inc.
Steak'n Shake. See Consolidated
    Products, Inc.
Steamers, 115
Stearns Organic Farm, 54
Steele, C., & Company, 46
Stefano's Gourmet Products, 24
Steindler, Mary-Helen, 208
Steiner Foods, Inc., 32
Steingarten, Jeffrey, 259
Stem, Linda Hanks, 252
Stendahl (Bill Bernal), 259
Sterling Inn Catering, 121
Stern, Cynthia, 203
Stern, Jane and Michael, 259
Sternberg Pecan Company, 49
Stevens, Harry M., Inc., 79
Stevens, Muriel, 256
Stewart, Martha, Entertaining
    Seminars with, 146
Stewart, Norman, 210
Stewart, Pat, 217
Stewart, Walter, Market, 41
Stichler Products, Inc., 26
Stiger, Susan, 256
Stinnett, Taryn, Photography, 203
The Stocked Pot & Company, 148
Stockman, Judith, & Associates, 96
Stockmeyer (North America),
    Inc., 38
The Stockton Record, 258
Stoetzer, Nancy, 255
Stone, Marraccini and
    Patterson, 99
Stoneback, Diane, 250
Stop & Shop Companies, 74
Stouffer Hotel Company, 81
Stouffer Restaurant Company
    (Nestle Enterprises, Inc.), 86
Stovill, Waltrina, 259
Strange Seafood Exhibition, 290
Strings, 103
Stroster, Maria, 217

Stuart Anderson's. See American
    Restaurant Group, Inc.
Stuart Kitchens, Inc., 160
Stubbins Associates, 95
Studebaker's. See Entertainment One
Studio 400, 203, 220
Stuhmer, Robert, 217
Stump's Catering, 119
Sugar Association, Inc., 187
Sugarman, Carol, 259
Sugar's Kitchen, 52
Sullivan/Perkins, 220
Sumichrast, Jozef, 217
Summerfield Farm, 59
The Sun, 253
Sunbeam Appliance Company, 166
Sun Diamond Growers, 72, 185
The Sun Herald, 253
Sunkist Growers, Inc., 71, 185
Sun Mountain Medicine Ways, 58
Sunshower, 57
Superior Coffee & Foods
    Company, 29
Supermarkets General, 74
Susanna Foo, 104
Sutter's Catering Service, 115
Sutton, Judy, 217
Sutton, Yvonne, and
    Associates, 208
Sutton Place Gourmet, 43
Swamp Cabbage Festival, 289
Swan Caterers, 117
Swanke Hayden Connell, 96
Swedesboro Auction, Inc., 19
Sweetener Users' Association, 280
Sweet Wind Gardens, 59
Swensen's Ice Cream Company, 86
Swenson, Joan, 257
Swerz, Charles, Interior Design, 96
Swing-A-Way Manufacturing
    Company, 167
The Swiss Colony, 52
Swissmar Imports
    (Gra-Mic, Inc.), 175
Swissrose International, Inc., 28
Switzer Group, 96
Syracuse Herald-Journal, 250

T

Taam Tov Foods, Inc., 65
Tabatchnick Soups, 63
Taco Bell, Inc. (PepsiCo
    Foodservice Division), 90
Taco Bueno. See Unigate Restaurants,
    Inc.
Taco John's International, 90
Taco Time International, Inc., 90
Taim Salad, 65
Tait, Elaine, 259
Take Pleasure in Cooking, 149
Talbott, Polly, 205
Taleporos, Plato, 217
Tamarind, Inc., 99
Tami Great Food Corporation, 65
The Tampa Tribune, 252
Tampa Wholesale Produce Market,
    Inc., 20
Tanasychuck, John, 255
Tankersley, Paul, 217
Tanner, Jack, 254
Tante Marie's Cooking School, 145
Tapawingo, 107
Tappan/WCI Appliance Group
    (WCI), 167
Tappan Appliances, WCI Major
    Appliances Group, 163

Taquet Restaurant, 110
Tarlow, Phyllis, 217
Tartan-Sparks, Beth, 253
Taste 1, Inc., 65, 210
Taste Caterers, 123
Tastee Freez International, Inc. See
    DeNovo Corporation
Tastefully Yours, Inc., 125
A Taste of Kentucky, 43-44
A Taste of the Mountains, 146
Taste Unlimited, 45
The Tasting Spoon, 149
Tatoris, Dalia, 208
Taylor & Ng, 175
TCBY Enterprises, Inc., 90
Tea Association of the USA,
    Inc., 184
Tefal Appliance Company, 167
Temple, Karen, 206
The Tennessean, 253
Tentation, 123
Terczak's Restaurant, 110
Terrell, Angie, 251
Terrell, Judy, School of
    Cooking, 149
T-Fal Corporation, 175
TFI, 125
TGI Friday's, Inc., 86
Tharp Did It, 220
Thermador/Waste King, A. Masco
    Company, 163
Theurich Catering Service, 127
Things Are Cooking!, 147
Tholstrup Cheese USA, Inc., 28
Thomas, Barbara, 254
Thomas, Dian, 209
    Company, 191
Thomas, Kathy, 208
Thomas, Mark, 203
Thomasville State Farmer's
    Market, 20
Thompson, Sharon, 252
The Thompson Candy
    Company, 26
Thomson Berry Farms, 37
Thorn Apple Valley, Inc., 72
3D/International, 98
Thrice Cooking School, 149
Thurston, Inc., 161
A Thyme to Cook, Inc., 117
Tihany, Adam, International, 96
Tila's Restaurant, 103
Tillamook County Creamery
    Association, 48
Tillamook Swiss Festival, 291
Timber Crest Farms, 52, 58
Times (Scranton, Pa.), 251
Times Herald-Record, 250
The Times-Picayune, 253
Tinmouth Channel Farm, 55
Tivall, USA, 61
Toastmaster, Inc., 167
Todaro Brothers, 42, 52
Toelke, Cathleen, 217
Toelke, Ron, 217
Tofutti, 63
The Toledo Blade, 256
Top Bananas, Inc., 118
Top Restaurants. See Stouffer
    Restaurant Company
The Topeka Capital-Journal, 255
Tops Manufacturing Company,
    Inc., 175
Tops Markets, 76
Torburg, Kathy, 254
Torn Ranch Wholesale, 33

Torp, Cynthia, 217
Toscani & Sons, 42
Total Foodservice Direction,
    Inc., 79
Tout de Suite a la Microwave,
    Inc., 147
Tracey Shiffman Roland Young
    Design Group, 220
Track Marketing, 65
Tracy, Janis, Photography, 204
Trade Marcs Group, Inc., 29
Trans/Pacific Restaurants, Inc., 86
Trans World Airlines, Inc., 91
Trapani, Carol, 250
Trappey's Fine Foods, Inc., 65
Trappist Preserves, 37
Traulsen & Company, Inc., 163
The Trellis, 103
Trendex International, Inc.,
    167, 175
Trend Products Company, 175
The Trentonian, 250
The Trenton Times, 250
Tri/Valley Growers, Inc., 72
Triangle Design Kitchens,
    Inc., 160
Trident Cutlery Company, 175
Trillin, Calvin, 259
TrimB's Restaurant &
    Catering, 127
Trio's Original Italian Pasta
    Products Company, Inc., 35
Tripp, Marian, Communications,
    Inc., 191
Tropical Blossom Honey
    Company, Inc., 37
Trotta, Geri, 259
Truffles, 106
Truffles, Inc., 47
Truffles Catering, 126
Trumps, 109
Trusthouse Forte Hotels, Inc., 81
Tucson Citizen, 256
Tughan, James, 217
Tull, Jeff, 217
The Tulsa Tribune, 256
The Tulsa World, 256
Turf Cheescake Corporation, 24
Turner, Clay, 217
Tuscany, 101
Twenty-One Federal, 105
Twin City Catering, 121
TW Services, Inc., 79, 82, 86
Tyson Foods, Inc., 70

U

UCLA Extension, Culinary Arts
    Program Department, 144
Uher, John, Photography, 204
Ultimate Kitchens, 162
Unangst, Andrew, 204
Unicare Health Facilities, Inc., 90
Unigate Restaurants, Inc., 86
Union Square Cafe, 109
Unique Delicatessen, 46
United Airlines, 91
United Brands Company, 70
United Dairy Industry
    Association, 184
United Egg Producers, 280
United Fresh Fruit and Vegetable
    Association, 183, 281
    Political Action Committee, 281
United Press International, 251
United States Government
    Printing Office, 269

Universal Foods Corporation, 72
Universal Services, Inc. International, 79
University of Alaska, Fairbanks, Institute of Marine Science, 265
University of Arizona Environmental Research Laboratory, 263
University of California, Davis, Marine Food Science Group, 265
University of California, Davis, Plant Growth Laboratory, 264
University of Connecticut, Storrs, Agricultural Experiment Station, 264
University of Connecticut Marine Sciences Institute, 265
University of Florida, Florida Sea Grant College, 265
University of Hawaii, Manoa, Sea Grant College Program, 265
University of Hawaii Livestock Research Station, 264
University of Oklahoma Aquatic Biology Center, 265
University of Oklahoma Aquatic Ecology and Fisheries Research Center, 265
University of Texas Human Nutrition Center, 267
University of Wisconsin, Madison, Aquaculture & Food Engineering Laboratories, 265
University of Wisconsin, Madison, Center for Dairy Research, 264
Uno Restaurants Corporation, 86
Unterman, Patricia, 259
Upper Crust Caterers & Special Events, 119
Upper Montclair Country Club, 105
Urbani, Paul A., Truffles, 52
Ursula, 172
USACafes, 86
USAir Inc., 91
USA Today, 251
U.S. Box Corporation, 34
Usinger, Fred, Inc., 50
U.S. Restaurants, Inc., 90

V
Vacaville Fruit Company, Inc., 33
Vaccarello, Paul, 217
Valentine, Ann, 257
Vance, Judy, Food Stylist and Consultant, 208
Van Cortlandt Coffee Corporation, 29
Vandel International, Inc., 175
Van Der Boom, Virgil, 57, 60
Van Gorder, Jan, Studios, 204
Vanilla Information Bureau, 187
Vanns Spices, Inc., 36
Van Sant, Clarence, 56
Varah, Monte, 218
Varkonyi, Charlyne, 259
V.C.F. Packaging Films, Inc., 34
Ventura County Star-Free Press, 258
Vermont Country Kitchen, 43
Vermont Maple Festival, 291
VHA, Inc., 98
VICORP Restaurants, Inc., 82, 86
Victorian Pantry, 23
Victoria Packing Corporation, 36

Vie de France Corporation, 24
Vie de France Restaurant Corporation (VICORP Restaurants, Inc.), 86
Village Food Store, 44
Village Inn Family Restaurants. *See VICORP Restaurants, Inc.*
Villas, James, 259
Villaware Manufacturing Company, 175
Vincent's on Camelback, 104
The Vindicator, 256
The Vinegar Institute, 187
V.I.P Foods, 64
VIP Caterers, 121
Virginia Association of Biological Farmers, 56
Virginia Marine Products Board, 187
The Virginian Pilot, 254
Vita Food Products, 61
Vitantonio Manufacturing Company, 175
Vivande, 47
Vollmer Products, Inc., 175
Vons Companies, 74
Voo, Rhonda, 218
Voyageur Trading Company, 35
Vreeland, Tom, 57

W
Waco Tribune-Herald, 257
Wade, Sue, & Associates, Inc., 98
Waffle House, Inc., 90
Wagner, John, & Sons, Inc., 33
Waine, Michael, 204
Waldron, Sarah, 218
Walker, John Frederick, 259
Walker Foods, Inc., 28
Wall, Pam, 218
Wallace, Kurt, 218
Wallach, Lou, 204
Walnut Acres, 49, 55
Walnut Marketing Board, 186
Walter, Carole, 146
Wans Studio, Inc., 204
Ward, Les, Photography, Inc., 204
Waring Products (Dynamics Corporation of America), 167
Warner-Lambert Company, 72
Washington Asparagus Growers, 188
The Washington Post, 251
Washington Rhubarb Growers' Association, 186
Washington State Apple Commission, 186
Washington State Fruits Commission, 186
Washington State Potato Commission, 186-187
Washington Street Cafe, 123
The Washington Times, 251
The Water Club, 107
Watermelon Festival, 288
Water Wheel Sugar House, 54
Watkinson, Brent, 218
Watson, Janet, 255
Watson, Michael, Studio, 204
WCI Appliance Group (WCI), 167
WCI Major Appliances Group, 163
We 3 Catering/We 3 Markets, Inc., 119
Wear-Ever, 166

Weatherbee Company, 175
Weathervane Foods, Inc., 25
Webb, Del E., Corporation, 78
Weber Design, 220
Weber-Stephen Products Company, 163
Weddell, Leslie, 257
Wegman's, 75
Weinberg Caterers, 122
Weinberg and James Foodstyle, 210
Weinrib, Helga, 206
Weis Markets, 75
Weiss' Kiwifruit, 58
Welbilt Appliance Company, 167
Welbilt Corporation, 163
Welch Foods, Inc., 73
Weldons. *See Galardi Group*
Wellborn Henderson Associates, 96
The Well-Bred Loaf, Inc., 24
Weller, Dean, & Company, 191, 220
The Weller Institute for the Cure of Design, Inc., 220
Wells, Ann, 255
Wells, Patricia, 259
Well-Sweep Herb Farm, 50
Wendland Catering/A Thyme to Cook, Inc., 117
Wendy's International, Inc., 90
West, Carolyn, 254
West, Susan, 206
West Bend Company, 167
Westbrae Natural Foods, 49
Western Culinary Institute, 144
Western New York Apple Growers' Association, Inc., 186
Western North Carolina Farmers' Market, 21
Western Research Kitchens, 192
Western Steer-Mom'n'Pop's, Inc., 86
The West Point Market, 46
West Valley Produce Company, 58
West Virginia Black Walnut Festival, 291
Westwood International, 175
Wetzel, Marcia, 218
Whataburger, Inc., 90
What's Cooking, 148
Wheel Works. *See Consolidated Specialty Restaurants, Inc.*
Whibdons, Roger, 252
Whirlpool Corporation, 163, 165
The Whip and Spoon, 146
White, Bill, 204
White Castle System, Inc., 90
White Coffee Corporation, 29
White Oak Farm, 54
Whitman Corporation, 70
Whole Foods Market and Restaurant, 58
Wholesale Produce Market of Pittsburgh, 20
Whyte, Douglas, 204
The Wichita Eagle-Beacon, 255
Wieland, Kitchens by, Inc., 159
Wienerschnitzel. *See Galardi Group*
Wiggin Farms, 58
The Wildflower Inn, 102
Wilds of Idaho, 37
Wilds of Idaho-Gourmet Huckleberry Products, 52
Wilkinson, Diane, Cooking School, 147

Wilkinson Sword, Inc., USA, 175
Willardson and Associates, 218
William Groceries & Meat Fair, 42
Williams-Sonoma, 52
Willow Pond Farm, 54
Wills, Bret, Photography, 204
Wilson, Amanda, 218
Wilson, Dorothy, Caterers, 116
Wilson, Phil, 218
Wilson & Associates, 98
Wilson Foods Corporation, 71
Wilton Enterprises, 170, 175
Wilton Foods, 65
Wilton School of Cake Decorating and Confectionery Art, 145
Wiltse, Kris, 218
Wiltshire International, 174
Winchell's Donut House, 90
Windsor Shad Derby, 289
Wind Spirit, 57
Wine, Thayer, 259
W.I.N.E., The Wine Information & News Exchange, 183
Wine World, Inc., Beringer Vineyards, 144
Wingknife, Inc., 175
Winn-Dixie Stores, 74
Winston-Salem Journal, 253
Winters, Patricia, 206
The Wire Whisk, 147
Wisconsin Aluminum Foundry Company, Inc., 175
Wisconsin Canned Vegetables, 188
The Wisconsin Cheeseman, 52
Wisconsin Cheese Makers' Association, 184
Wisconsin Cheese & Specialty Food Merchants' Association, 183
Wisconsin Dairies Cooperative, 72
Wisconsin Milk Marketing Board, Dairy Farmers of Wisconsin, 184
Wisconsin Potato/Vegetable Growers' Association, 188
Wisconsin State Journal, 256
Wisconsin Wilderness Food Products, Inc., 40
Wise, Jim, 253
Witherell, JoAnn, 208
Witschonke, Alan, 218
Wittstrom, Elaine, 256
Wok on Wheels, 123
Wok and Whisk, Inc., 147
Wolf, Bruce, 204
Wolf, Clark, 259
Wolf, Paul, 218
Wolferman's, 25, 45
Original English Muffin Company, 51
Wolfe's Neck Farm, 59
Wolfsohn, Reeta, Party Designing & Catering, 123
Women's Culinary Guild of New England, 183
Wonder Bar Products, Inc., 33
Wonderful Parties Wonderful Foods, 115
Wooco International Corporation, 175
Wood, Jim, 259
The Wood Company, 79
The Wood Creek Cooking School, 146
Wooden Angel, 108
The Wooden Spoon, 52
Wood Prairie Farm, 53, 59

Woods & Woods, 220
Woodward, Nance, 250
Worcester Telegram and
    Gazette, 249
Work of Art Cakes, 208
World Catfish Festival, 290
World of Cuisine, 148
World Hunger Education
    Service, 267
World of Spices, Inc., 36
The Worm Concern, 58
Wright, John, (Donsco), 175
Wrigley, Wm., Jr. Company, 71
Wu, Ron, 204
Wudke, Don, & Associates, 99
Wusthof/Trident Cutlery
    Company, 175
Wyatt Cafeterias, Inc., 87
Wynn, Dan, 204
Wynn, Joyce K., Inc., 98

X

Xanadu Design, Ltd., 96
Xcell International Corporation
    (Trendex International), 167

Y

Yan Can International Cooking
    School, 150
Yankel & Company Catering, 123
Yates-Silverman, Inc., 99
Yelaska, Bruce, Design, 220
The Yellow Brick Toad, 122
Yohay Baking Company, Inc., 25
Yoni's Kosher Pasta, 65
York Steakhouses. *See General Mills
    Restaurant Group, Inc.*
Yoshiko, 206
Yoshi's Cafe, 105
Young, Fred H., Jr. &
    Associates, 161
Young's Pecan Sales
    Corporation, 49
Your Chef, Inc., 127
Your Land, Our Land, 58
Youssi, John, 218
Yuchi Pines, 55

Z

Zabar's, 42, 52
Zagoren, Judy, Catering, Inc., 117
Zakaspace Corporation, 97
Zambrana's, The Food
    Emporium, 45
Zanetti, Gerald, Associates,
    Inc., 204
The Zanger Company, 175
Zani America, Inc., 176
Zan Productions, 204
Zanzarella, Marianne, 205
Zapp, Carl, 204
Zarela Restaurant, 106
Z Contemporary Cuisine, 102
Zechmann, Susan, 209
Zekauskas, Ann, 206
Zephyr Convection Cooking
    Systems Company, Inc., 167
Zetov, Inc., 65
ZGF Interiors, 99
Zick, Brian, 218
Ziegler Cooper, Inc., 98
Ziemienski, Dennis, 218
Ziff, Lloyd, Design Group, 220
Zim Manufacturing Company, 176
Zimmerman, David, Studio, 204

Zingerman's Delicatessen, 45
Zivi Hercules, Inc., 176
Zojirushi America
    Corporation, 167
Zona Spray Cooking School, 145
Zudeck, Darryl, 218
Zumbo, Matt, 218
Zuni Cafe, 109
Zupan, Fran, 253